Administrative Theory and Practice In Physical Education and Athletics

ADMINISTRATIVE THEORY AND PRACTICE IN PHYSICAL EDUCATION AND ATHLETICS

edited, with selected chapters by

EARLE F. ZEIGLER, *Editor*

The University of Western Ontario

and

MARCIA J. SPAETH, *Associate Editor*

State University of New York
College at Cortland

Prentice-Hall, Inc., *Englewood Cliffs, New Jersey*

Library of Congress Cataloging in Publication Data

Zeigler, Earle F   1919-
   Administrative theory and practice in physical education and athletics.

   Bibliography: p.
   1. Physical education and training—Administration.
I. Spaeth, Marcia J., joint author.   II. Title.
GV343.5.Z43   658'.91'6137   74-2066
ISBN 0-13-008581-2

© 1975 by Prentice-Hall, Inc., Englewood Cliffs, New Jersey. All rights reserved. No part of this book may be reproduced in any form or by any means without permission in writing from the publisher. Printed in the United States of America.

10   9   8   7   6   5   4   3   2   1

Prentice-Hall International, Inc., *London*
Prentice-Hall of Australia, Pty, Ltd., *Sydney*
Prentice-Hall of Canada, Ltd., *Toronto*
Prentice-Hall of India Private Limited, *New Delhi*
Prentice-Hall of Japan, Inc., *Tokyo*

DEDICATION

To all those women and men who regularly help administrators
get the job done somehow,
this book is gratefully and respectfully dedicated and to Lloyd J. McCleary,
formerly of the University of Illinois, now at the University of Utah.

Contents

Preface			xi
Foreword			xvii
Part I	**Development of a New Dimension**		1
Chapter 1	*Theory and Research in the Administration of Physical Education,* Earle F. Zeigler, Marcia J. Spaeth, and Garth Paton		2
Chapter 2	*Theoretical Propositions for the Administration of Physical Education and Athletics,* Earle F. Zeigler		22
Chapter 3	*Administrative Research in Physical Education and Athletics,* Marcia J. Spaeth		35
Chapter 4	*An Analysis of Administrative Theory in Selected Graduate Administration Courses in Physical Education,* Garth A. Paton		49

Chapter 5	*The Meanings Associated with Selected Administrative Concepts: A Need for Understanding*, William J. Penny	66

Part II Studies about the General and Specific Administrative Processes — 79

Chapter 6	*Leader Behavior of Junior College and University Physical Education Administrators*, Gordon A. Olafson	80
Chapter 7	*Leadership Effectiveness Contingency Model: Implications*, Martha Bagley	98
Chapter 8	*Group Cohesion Reconsidered*, A. Mikalachki	113
Chapter 9	*Organizational Climate in Physical Education*, Wayne E. Dannehl	135
Chapter 10	*Faculty Job Satisfaction in Physical Education and Athletics*, Juri V. Daniel	152
Chapter 11	*Economic Factors Influencing Athletics*, Ronald Bole	176
Chapter 12	*Violence in Spectator Sports*, Cyril M. White	189
Chapter 13	*Role Expectations of Teachers and Chairmen*, Shirley J. Wood	214
Chapter 14	*The Communication Structure of a Physical Education Unit*, Robert Lewis Case	228
Chapter 15	*Interpersonal Communication Patterns in Physical Education*, Beatrice V. Yeager	247
Chapter 16	*Environmental Characteristics in a Physical Education Unit*, Thomas E. Flanigan	265

Contents ix

Part III Studies about Technical Administrative Concerns   279

Chapter 17 *Human Relations in the Administration of Intramural Sports and Recreative Services,* Frank Beeman   280

Chapter 18 *The Planning and Construction of Physical Recreation Facilities,* James A. Peterson   294

Chapter 19 *Comparison of Two Central Administrative Agencies in Sport,* Eric F. Broom   316

Chapter 20 *An Analysis of Employment Theory and Practice,* Emory F. Luck   332

Chapter 21 *Assessment of Nonrevenue Sports,* K. Ladd Pash   344

Chapter 22 *Physical Education Budgetary Processes in an Ontario School System,* Terry R. Haggerty   355

Part IV Looking Inward, Outward, and to the Future   373

Chapter 23 *The Employment of Philosophical Analysis to Supplement Administrative Theory and Research,* Earle F. Zeigler   374

Chapter 24 *The Environments of the Administrator,* Earle F. Zeigler   399

Chapter 25 *Looking into the Future: Theoretical Approaches to Administrative Action,* Earle F. Zeigler   419

Appendix

A Selected Bibliography on Completed Research on Administrative Theory and Practice in Physical Education and Athletics, Earle F. Zeigler, Marcia J. Spaeth   436

Index   **454**

Preface

The complexity of educational administration, at *any* level in both public and private schools and universities, is well known even to the layman today. Administrative positions are of such a nature that educators seem to be fleeing from administrative responsibility at what often seems to be an alarming rate. Why is it then that this trend has not yet set in within the field of physical education and athletics?

There is not sufficient evidence to speak authoritatively on this matter, but there may be several reasons why physical educator/coaches are willing to move into positions of administrative responsibility. Initially, such positions do pay relatively higher salaries, and it is true further that the rewards for scholarly work in this field have not been great either in regard to academic prestige or salary. Secondly, it could be argued that physical educators/coaches are better suited constitutionally for administrative roles (i.e., they are of the body type and temperament which are presumably necessary for so-called positive leadership.)

Thirdly, there is a strong likelihood that a steady diet of gymnasium and classroom teaching six or seven hours a day (with little time for one's own exercise), followed by overtime coaching (often for extra salary) in two or three sports during the academic year, finally wears a person out both "physically and mentally." Thus, any one or a combination of these reasons—and perhaps some others not mentioned—could account for the urge to be selected as department chairman or head, athletic director, supervisor of physical education and/or athletics, or even head coach.

The new administrator of physical education and/or athletics is typically not aware of the fact that a managerial revolution has taken place over the past few decades. He has only a vague understanding of the many aspects and ramifications of the position which he is undertaking. Even after he is on the job, he is probably not cognizant of the unbelievable complexity of the post. He works overtime to get control of the new assignment and to meet the seemingly innumerable demands of higher administration, faculty, staff, and students.

Quite soon he gets the feeling that he is "on a treadmill angled so that he must run at a dog trot just to keep from falling off the back end." It's an uneasy feeling because the pressure is there constantly and work tends to pile up in enormous quantities when one is absent from the office for just a few short days. Then, too, all the while one has the feeling that he is merely doing that which is practical and expedient at the moment. The pattern of operation is apt to become one of trial and error, and it seems impossible to take time out for extended future planning. Finally, because of the many, increasing, and persistent demands that are made upon his office, the administrator reasons that he needs more help—both administrative and secretarial. No matter whether budgetary pressures increase, there will continue to be an increase in positions of this type now and in the foreseeable future. It's the simple truth that "assistants need assistants of their own!"

The knowledge explosion which has affected all of mankind has also had its impact on the administrating of organizations, and more specifically on the *individuals* administrating organizations. Administration tends to be a dynamic process with steady, almost constant change as a typical pattern of life. The Industrial Revolution of the mid-eighteenth century was the precursor, the effects of which soon spread to all aspects of life including education. Technological change of necessity has been closely related to administrative change; new methods and techniques of administration became part of the technological development itself. "The administrative revolution has been characterized by more organization, larger-scale organization, more bureaucracy, and more administrators" (Gross, *The Managing of Organizations*, p. 38). With all of this, there is a strong trend toward the dehumanization of man. Individuals are losing their identities as work tasks become increasingly splintered. Individual man is becoming more subordinated to the organization with resultant alienation from his fellow man. Our overorganized society may be developing a "sickness"—a condition that is fostered by our inability to work in relatively closer cooperation with other ideological systems. All around us we see examples of inflexibility as totalitarian patterns of management compete with more democratic models. These models are often subjected to great strain, and the increasing complexity may be bringing the large modern organizations to the point where

Preface

they will face what presumably was the fate of the dinosaur. This is a threat that looms large on the horizon because of failing dynamism and lack of adaptability (Gross, pp. 73-88).

If examination of the literature of a profession means anything, the field of physical education and athletics appears to be almost completely unaware of the development of administrative theory and research in other fields. This new text represents the first substantive effort to remedy this situation, although the Editor did make a case method, human relations approach to the teaching of human relations and administration available in the middle and late 1950s. King J. McCristal, Professor and Dean at the University of Illinois, Champaign-Urbana, and the Editor did promote the area of administrative theory and practice as one of six subject-matter areas in the Big Ten Body-of-Knowledge Project. In the fall of 1972 a symposium on the subject was held as part of this Project at The University of Michigan in Ann Arbor with Paul A. Hunsicker as Conference Chairman.

This book is based on the premise that it is now necessary to prepare people carefully and thoroughly for the "assumption of the administrative risk" in the years immediately ahead. In the near future it is quite possible that selection committees will know enough to ascertain to what extent a candidate for an administrative post actually meets the criteria laid down for that particular position. The trial-and-error management approach in which the leader functions by hunch, habit, and common sense—sometimes called the "seat of the pants approach"—should soon become a thing of the past. A profession such as physical education and sport should truly decide that it is vitally important to prepare men and women professionally as administrators. Presently it is almost a cardinal sin the way prospective scholars and researchers are "drained away" from academic endeavors to often become "inadequate and reluctant paper-shufflers."

A student will soon discover that many conceptual developments relating to the problems of administrators are taking place. Management studies both within and outside of the field of education have emphasized that the basic features of administration in different organizations are more common than unique. These investigations in administrative theory and practice have not been limited to a particular group of individuals in a specific discipline. On the contrary, in addition to the studies described herein that were carried out at the University of Illinois, a vast number of political scientists, psychologists, sociologists, educational administrators, and other theoreticians have all contributed to the growing body of knowledge about human behavior and the decision-making process. And what is most important is that these theoretical and scientific contributions are being applied to organizations of many kinds. At present the field of physical education and sport is not one whose subdivisions have received any significant help from this development.

And yet—strangely enough—there has been a proliferation of administration and/or organization courses in physical education and athletics at both the undergraduate and graduate levels. If new courses are added to a curriculum because of an accumulation of knowledge about various aspects of a subject-matter field, one can't help but wonder where all of the "new knowledge" for these added courses originated. It could be hypothesized that this "knowledge" emanated from master's and doctoral studies that have been carried out over the years in greater number perhaps than in any other aspect of the field. An examination of these investigations soon indicates that such is not the case. Still further, few writers on the subject of the administration of physical education and athletics have gone beyond the listing of prescriptive policies and procedures. Nor have any of these volumes gone beyond the level of the identification and establishment of utilitarian principles—principles which under close scrutiny dissolve into value-laden declarative statements with often dubious application to actual situations in life and little if any "predictive strength." The underlying premise of this volume is that physical education and sport needs to build a social-scientific foundation for its administrative endeavors. A corollary to this would imply that this foundation should be incorporated as soon as possible into the field's professional preparation schematic.

The text is organized in such a way that the student is first introduced to the background and development of this new dimension in the administration of physical education and athletics (Part I). In Part II the reader is introduced to the scope, methodology, summary, findings, conclusions, and implications of eleven studies which investigated what might be called the "broad and specific administrative processes" (*see* Figure 1). Six investigations of so-called technical administrative concerns make up part III of the volume (*see* Figure 1 again). In Part IV the student of administrative theory and practice is urged to "look inward, outward, and to the future" by the Editor. First, philosophical analysis is offered to administrators as a supplement and as an expedient. Next the reader is introduced to the various social forces which impinge on all organizations functioning within social systems. Lastly, the student is exhorted to look to the future and to follow the recommendations for further study and research made by the various contributors.

The Editor is pleased by means of the publication of this volume to recognize the work of some twenty scholars in administrative theory and practice. Sixteen of these chapters are based on doctoral studies carried out at the University of Illinois (one at The University of Michigan) under the supervision of the Editor. James Peterson and Martha Bagley both studied with the Editor, but their studies were carried out under the chairmanship of David O. Matthews and Laura J. Huelster, respectively, at Illinois (both excellent administrators and students of administrative theory. The same situation applies with Terry Haggerty, whose study was completed with Garth A Paton at The University of Western Ontario. The paper on group cohesion was contributed by the Editor's colleague and good friend, Professor Alexander Mikalachki of The University of

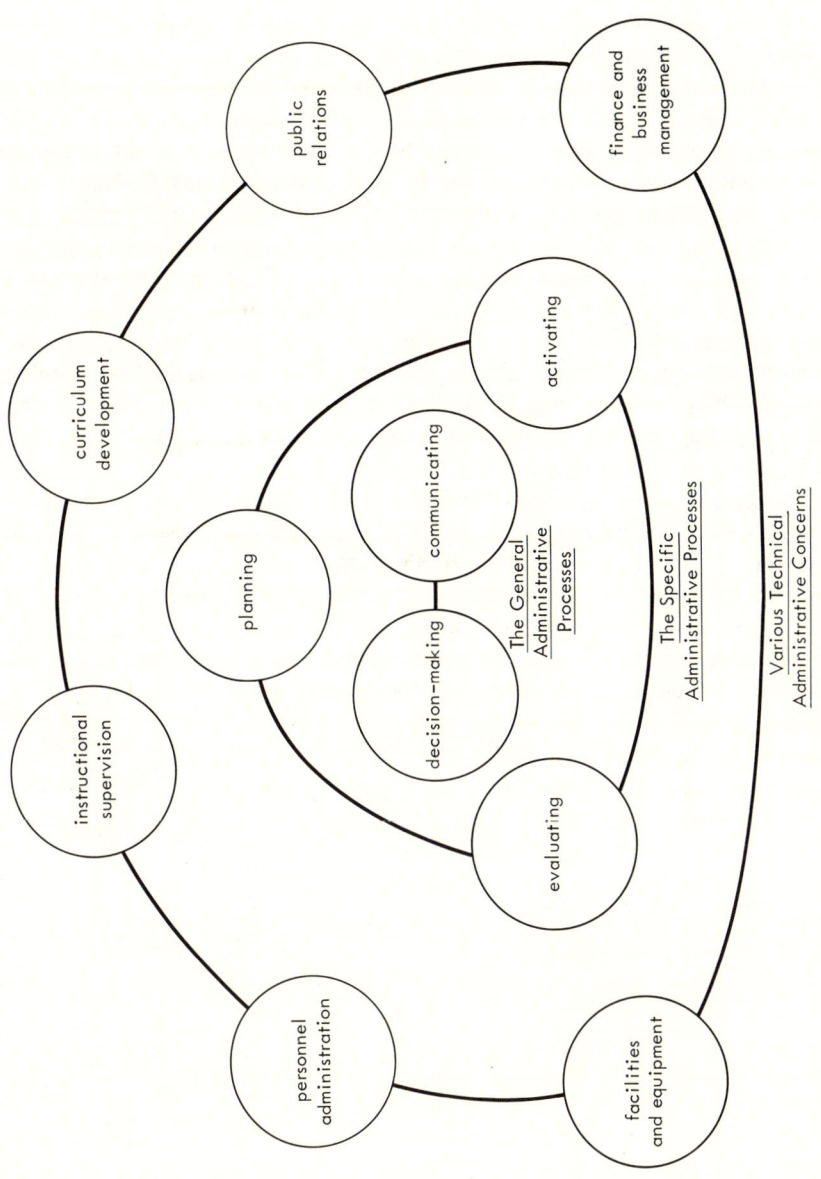

Figure 1. Proposed Areas of Administrative Research in Physical Education*

*Adapted from Gross, *The Managing of Organizations*, Free Press, 1964.

Western Ontario's School of Business Administration. Professor Mikalachki is an Honorary Lecturer in the Faculty of Physical Education. Certain master's studies carried out at Illinois, and a few doctoral studies recently completed or still in process, could not be included because of space limitations.

There is every reason to believe that this text will add a fresh new dimension to professional preparation for administrative leadership in physical education and sport. Instructors are urged to experiment with this administrative theory and practice approach to the teaching of decision-making, human relations, and problem-solving in management. The Editor, the Associate Editor, and the contributors are all presently involved in administration to varying degrees. We are grateful to our colleagues, instructors, and students, many of whom have made most worthwhile suggestions and recommendations. The Editor thanks King McCristal for writing the Foreword, but much more for his continuing support to this area of study. Prentice-Hall, Inc., and specifically Walter Welch, Assistant Vice-President, and Sandra Messik, Production Editor, are to be congratulated for their patience and encouragement over the past few years while this publication was being developed.

In his autobiography Mark Twain expressed disappointment in the human being, because he did not appear to be a considerable improvement over the monkey. If investigators in various disciplines will continue their quest to develop tenable administrative theory, there is yet reason to believe that man will survive and rise significantly higher on the evolutionary scale than the simian. Man may yet solve his organizational problems in such a way that he will be able to live peacefully, profitably, and happily on this earth.

Earle F. Zeigler
London, Ontario

Foreword

All professions and trades had their beginnings at some point in time. The same can be said for the relatively more recent development of areas of inquiry known as disciplines. In this evolutionary process, practice led to the establishment of a definite approach or pattern of operation. Eventually, established practices were enunciated as principles, although quite often the theory underlying such principles may never have been proved in a scientific manner. Theory implies testable hypotheses, and disciplines start to take shape when a substantive body of knowledge accrues.

There has been some skepticism concerning the claim that administration should be considered as a full-fledged profession, and that administrative theory (management science) has a justifiable place among the established disciplines. Presumably such doubts would be expressed by these skeptics when viewing educational administration—and subsequently for administration in physical education and athletics. These critics argue that the subject of administration possesses little academic content and no established theories; therefore, an administrator simply performs his duties and responsibilities as artfully as possible. These people might even be ready to agree with Litchfield who pointed out in the 1950s that "we seem to be saying that there is business administration, hospital administration, public administration, but there is no administration." (Litchfield, Edward H., "Notes on the General Theory of Administration," *Administrative Science Quarterly* 1:7, June, 1956).

Behind the theories upon which established disciplines have been built can be found men of vision, curious men whose minds probe unexplored areas in order to supply logic and order in place of the aimlessness of repetitive trial and error. Administrative theory and practice in physical education and sport is beginning to emerge from the trial and error period—but barely so. Researchers are postulating testable hypotheses based on ad hoc theories that have been partially explored in one or more of the behavioral sciences. Tenable "theories of the middle range" will soon emerge based on the ever-growing inventory of human behavior that is becoming available day by day as the "bricks in the wall" of a more-encompassing theory of management are being "laid."

Although primarily concerned with the philosophy and history of sport and physical education, Dr. Earle F. Zeigler, the Editor of this book, spearheaded research in this area for a period of eight years at the University of Illinois, Champaign-Urbana. He has served as advisor to some twenty-five studies relating to administrative theory and practice at both the doctoral and master's level there, while at the same time working cooperatively with other graduate professors assisting with the development of this area of specialization.

The writer is most pleased to have served as Chairman of the Big Ten Physical Education Body-of-Knowledge Symposium Project, which pioneered in the middle and late 1960s a series of symposia in six different sub-disciplinary areas. Administrative theory and practice was one of the six original areas in the Project. In October, 1972, Dr. Paul A. Hunsicker, of The University of Michigan, chaired the Big Ten Symposium on Administrative Theory and Practice held in Ann Arbor. This writer and Dr. Zeigler were both involved in the planning for these sessions, which resulted in a publication through the cooperation of The Athletic Institute, 805 Merchandise Mart, Chicago, Illinois 60654.

There is obviously a great need for the development of sound administrative theory to guide practice in the world today, and this need may be related to the management of physical education and athletics equally well. There must be a link, of course, between administrative theory and human aspirations as they may possibly be realized through human activities. We now have some of the tools for discovering knowledge that can in turn be applied to practical ends. The correlation of tenable administrative theory with the effort to achieve personal and social values in a world culture will result in policies and procedures that may help mankind realize its aspirations.

As a result of the efforts mentioned above, there are now men and women serving in the administration of physical education and athletics who have contributed significant ideas to the developing theory of administration. Hundreds of millions of dollars have been spent to erect the facilities which house programs of physical education and athletics, as well as to engage the faculties who administer and supervise these programs. In educational institutions at all levels, additional hundreds of millions of dollars are expended annually to keep these programs functional. Many times the administration of such enterprises operates

Foreword

on a "catch-as-catch-can" basis. Far too often, managers, directors, deans, and department heads operate so informally that program successes occur almost in spite of, rather than because of, intelligent, farsighted administrative leadership.

Other things being equal, physical education and athletic programs will be more successful if they are administered by men and women who have thoroughly acquainted themselves with both the theoretical and practical aspects of decision-making and communication; of planning, activating, and evaluating; and also of finance and business management, public relations, personnel administration, and the other technical administrative concerns.

This book provides a solid introduction to administrative theory and practice especially as it relates to physical education and sport. It is not a "how to" handbook that will provide the ready-made answers to common sense problems that arise in day-to-day practice. It can be used profitably by undergraduates who have a sincere interest in an adequate introduction to the subject. It can also be employed, perhaps somewhat differently, by graduate students who are searching for topics upon which to base term papers and research projects. A great number of questions have been raised in these studies which can give rise to hundreds of master's and doctoral theses and dissertations.

This text is a pioneering effort in a truly exciting area, and will prove to be a valuable source of reference to graduate students and other scholars. I am pleased to have had the opportunity to be so closely involved with this new development in physical education and sport, and I commend this book and its many authors for the sound guidance which has been provided to administrative theory and practice in the field.

King J. McCristal
*Professor and Dean-emeritus
University of Illinois
Champaign-Urbana*

I

DEVELOPMENT OF A NEW DIMENSION

1

Theory and Research in the Administration of Physical Education

Earle F. Zeigler / Marcia J. Spaeth / Garth Paton

Few would deny that advances have been made in the world in the last quarter century, although it is undoubtedly true that many "benign achievements also have their malign sides." The many historical events, social influences, scientific discoveries, and inventions of these years hold implications for the field of physical education both inside and outside of the field of education. The knowledge explosion has caught up with us, just as it has with our colleagues in other disciplines, and the geometric increase of knowledge threatens to engulf us all. We are faced with the absolute necessity of retooling and upgrading our research efforts. In the process our graduate programs are being structured so that we may cope with the knowledge that is becoming available to us from our own and other, closely related disciplines.[1]

The potentialities for pure and applied research in physical education are limitless. This is true especially because of the unique nature of this field and its possible relationships with so many of the humanities, social sciences, and natural sciences. Such is the case with the developing social science of

---

Earle F. Zeigler is from the University of Western Ontario; Marcia J. Spaeth is from the State University of New York (Cortland); and Garth Paton is from the University of Western Ontario.

[1] A paper originally presented at the AAHPER Convention in Las Vegas, Nevada, March 11, 1967.

administration. If we don't do something about developing this possible relationship quickly, for example, we are going to miss a fine opportunity to relate to our colleagues in educational administration and the behavioral sciences as they endeavor to learn how men may best manage organizations. In addition, we must always keep in mind that others are not going to do *our* work for us. At the very best it will be done belatedly and in a secondhand manner. A perfect example of this is the work completed in our field relative to physical fitness and the physiology of exercise. People like Cureton and his associates have been laboring for more than a quarter of a century to develop this body of knowledge, while the large body of physiologists and cardiologists have treated it as a "stepchild." Now they are finally realizing that this area is very important, and they will no doubt do many of the same or similar studies over again. Thus, we must recognize that our physiologically oriented "scientific wing" has done much to help us obtain some academic respectability. Similar respectability can be earned by us in eleven other related disciplines, or at least these are the ones that are looming on the horizon at the moment.

Professional Status for Administrators in Our Field

The phenomenon of organized physical education, including competitive athletics, that has taken place in the United States within the past one hundred years has today become a vast enterprise that demands wise and skillful management. The situation is now such that the appointment of a director of physical education or an athletic director or a person with some combined title is a very ordinary and expected occurrence. These men and women have now assumed many of the earmarks of a profession. Having said this, we should keep in mind that a recognized profession needs an organized body of knowledge based on research. A profession that is fully worthy of the name must, of course, meet many other criteria. For now, however, we must keep this particular criterion firmly in mind: The existence of an organized body of knowledge based on research. Thus, the perpetuation of our "species"—the administrator of physical education and athletics—as a profession requires that some organizational structure be developed within educational institutions through which the body of professional knowledge may be transmitted to those who follow.

If we grant the above statements concerning the primary criterion of a true profession, as well as the continuing need to prepare new administrators professionally through some sort of experience in which this background knowledge is transmitted, then let us consider briefly how administrators of physical education and athletics at all educational levels received their preparation for this demanding position in the past. The answer to this question is immediately obvious: Generally speaking, many, if not all, of these men and women worked their way up through the ranks in some sort of an apprenticeship scheme. One basic prerequisite seems to be that they themselves were interested and active in physical education and sport activities. Quite often, as well, they were physical education majors and took certain courses at the undergraduate or graduate levels that were of an administrative nature. In some cases, and especially for men, they were not physical education majors in college, but later decided to cast their lots with our field because of successful competitive athletic experiences. Highly important, furthermore, has been the fact that these people demonstrated many fine personality and leadership traits. They knew how to get along with people, they made fine appearances, they knew how to get things done, they were willing to work very hard, and they believed strongly in the importance of physical education and athletics.

Such a method of "preparing" administrators is not unique to the field of physical education and athletics; Halpin has explained that a similar circumstance is evident when one examines the professional programs in schools of education, business, public administration, hospital administration, and social work. Still further, he stated that the more mature professional schools of medicine, law, and engineering exhibited a similar pattern in earlier stages of their development. This is in contrast, of course, to the recognized academic disciplines, where administrators were picked typically on the basis of scholarly and research endeavor (and perhaps also because they possessed certain desirable personality traits as well). In the latter case, this method of selection is still practiced quite generally today, and the large majority of this group may have never taken a course in administration.

There have been many charges that the above-mentioned professional schools are offering "trade-school" programs. Halpin characterized the situation as follows:

> Professional schools, however much nurtured and protected by the university, are sired by a clientele of practitioners. They are elaborations of an apprenticeship system and are close to the grass roots. Their first faculties are chosen for demonstrated success and reputation in the professional field regardless of the usual trappings of academic qualifications. Despite their popularity with students and practitioners, however, these people are considered by the rest of the university as poor relations. They are forced to defend themselves against charges that they are operating trade schools. Under pressure to attain recognized status as a profession and to achieve academic respectability, they therefore raise the academic standards for faculty members. Gradually this encourages them to think that there are other useful approaches to their subject and reduces their subservience to their immediate clientele. Eventually, at least in the cases of medicine and engineering, the professional school incorporates into its own structure representatives of related basic disciplines and seeks to make fundamental contributions to knowledge (1958, p. 38).

Can we in this field argue that Halpin is not describing us when he writes of the situation in certain professional programs in the late 1950s? If we were realistic, we might even agree that our situation is worse. Yet it is true that we are making every effort to improve the qualifications of our faculty members. Can we say, however, that we are "considering more abstract materials and deemphasizing techniques"? And to what extent are we incorporating into our faculties representatives from the social sciences?

Big Business within Big Education

In the United States we find a situation where everything is getting big, including education. We have Big Business, Big Government, Big Labor, Big Science, Big Agriculture, Big Religion (a much older phenomenon), *and* Big Education. In the case of our gate-receipt competitive sports, the problem seems more specifically that it is a question of Big Business within Big Education. There are a considerable number of people who feel that these two are incompatible; in other words, like oil and water, they don't mix too well. It would certainly appear to be true that they will have to learn to mix better in the future. However this may be, the physical education and athletics administrator is seemingly being placed in a somewhat untenable position. Why is this so? The answer would seem to be quite elementary—there is no *documented* body of research knowledge, there is practically no theory or ongoing research about the administrative task taking place, and the professional preparation of physical education and athletic administrators is being carried out almost universally by physical educators in a haphazard and poorly articulated fashion. All of this leads a rational, concerned individual to ask the question, "What are the prospects that our field will use other than a 'trade-school' approach in the future to prepare fine administrators of physical education and athletics?" The truth of the matter is that marked progress in the form of scientific investigation has been made in the fields of public administration, business administration, educational administration, and the behavioral sciences relative to the management of organizations and human behavior. *In physical education and athletics, however, the sad fact is that we are not even remotely aware of this development.* In the long run such ignorance can only result in still lower status, minor catastrophe, or even disaster.

Practitioners and Scientists Mistrust Administrative Theory

Up to the present therefore there has been little evidence to indicate that administrators of physical education and athletics, either in practice or in administration courses, are concerned with the theoretical aspects of administration.[2] In fact, a paradoxical situation arises in physical education and athletics at the college and university level when one is imprudent enough to discuss such a thing as "administrative theory." The paradox arises because the field seems very definitely to be divided into two groups, neither of which can see the need or importance of such a subject. These two groups might be labeled as the "practitioners" and the "scientists." The practitioners can't see the need for administrative theory, and the scientists would relegate it to limbo for its nonscientific quality.

The practitioners' viewpoint stems from the belief that theory of this nature is of no use in practice. Their belief is that practicing administrators are required to find immediate solutions to day-to-day problems, and that

> The Administrators are the practical, effective, get-the-job-done men who know what will work and what will not work, because they have tried the solutions available, or they know good men who have. Further, through skill and experience and prestige, they make things work, whether or not the same device might work for others (AASA, 1960, p. 101).

The attitude of the scientist within our field in higher education is opposed to the idea of administrative theory, but for a different reason. He tends to see the study of administration as merely practical and vocational in nature; thus, it really cannot be considered as an academic, disciplinary study. Contributing further to this position is the fact that research in administration is essentially social science research—an endeavor that has many inherent difficulties not found in natural science research. Such "difficulties" include the problems of suppressing bias, of obtaining valid and reliable measurements and of the seeming impossibility of controlling all save one variable. All of this adds up to a belief by many that such investigation represents second-class research. As Gross points out, "many great institutions of splendid achievement disdain to enter a field which they regard as vocational instead of theoretical or scientific" (1964, vol. 1, p. 9). The only possible rejoinder from "nonscientists" at this time is that "scientists" are emerging so rapidly nowadays that quite soon there will be two of them available for each man, woman, and child in the country.

Despite these objections, however, courses in the organization and administration of physical education and athletics have been offered since 1890 (Zeigler, 1951, p. 28), and by 1927 they were included typically in professional

---

[2]For the purposes of this paper the delimitation of the term "administration" is based upon the following definition: "Administration may be defined as 'the total of the processes through which appropriate human and material resources are made available and made effective for accomplishing the purposes of an enterprise' " (American Association of School Administrators, 1955, p. 17).

curricula throughout the country (Elliott, 1927, p. 46). Since that time there has been a proliferation of similar courses relating to administration, supervision, and curriculum at both the undergraduate and graduate levels. In addition, literally hundreds of master's theses and doctoral dissertations have been deposited on the shelves of our libraries. Most of these studies involve survey-method research, or some technique thereof, and there is unquestionably a body of knowledge of sorts about practice of an administrative nature. But there has been practically no research in administrative theory. Furthermore, there isn't a person alive who can tell you what all of these studies relating to administrative practice add up to; it is a "monstrous, amorphous blob"! Thus, we have had an endless stream of articles, theses, dissertations, monographs, and texts on the subject of administration, supervision, and curriculum.

The "Administrative Revolution"

Past administrative practice in our field, mostly of a trial and error nature, has sufficed up to the present, but now a most disturbing fact confronts us as we look to the future. An *administrative revolution* has been and is taking place. It is here to stay, and "modern man has no escape from the complexities of organizations and their management" (Gross, 1964, vol. 2, p. 808). There is a dynamism about it that is sweeping aside the traditions of many generations. If you don't agree with this statement, just figure out roughly how many man-hours are spent each week in your programs with duties that are administrative in nature. We think you will find that the results are frightening. Still more frightening is the fact that the rate of change is accelerating.

Developments in Related Fields

While we in our field have been reasonably satisfied with our own professional preparation in administration and with the administrative practice of an ongoing nature, many leaders in public administration, business administration, and educational administration (not to mention the behavioral scientists within the social sciences) have been making significant strides in the area of administrative theory. In educational administration, for example, Halpin introduced a 1958 publication of the Midwest Administration Center by saying that:

> Traditionally, our training programs have stressed the "practical" and have concerned themselves more with techniques than with understanding. During the postwar period, however, administrators have become increasingly aware of the role of theory.... (Halpin, 1958, p. 1).

Similarly, a 1960 publication of the American Association of School Administrators pointed out that "of all the many areas of knowledge in which a school administrator needs to keep up to date the most crucial, at the present time, is knowledge of administrative theory" (AASA, 1960, p. 99). In this same publication, a number of other administrative theorists, such as Moore, Thompson, Litchfield, Halpin, Walton, and Griffiths, indicated their concern for the development of administrative theory.[3]

Interest in theoretical concepts within the field of educational administration began during the 1940s when a "ferment in school administration" developed (Moore, 1964, p. 15), and the American Association of School Administrators became concerned about the state of the profession. This concern developed because of a variety of social influences with the result that a National Conference of Professors of Educational Administration was inaugurated in 1947. This group played a significant role in obtaining grants from the Kellogg Foundation for the study of school administration. As a direct outgrowth of this financial assistance, the Cooperative Program in Educational Administration (CPEA) began in 1950. A few years later the University Council in Educational Administration supplanted this Cooperative Program and extended its work toward the further development of the field of educational administration (Halpin, 1958, p. 2).

Another facet of the "theory movement" in administration is typified in a statement by Litchfield:

> The most serious indictment which must be made of present thought is that it has failed to achieve a level of generalization enabling it to systematize and generalize administrative phenomena which occur in related fields.... We seem to be saying that there is business administration, and hospital administration, and public administration; that there is military administration, hotel administration, and school administration. But there is no administration (1956, p. 105).

This trend toward unity of the various fields concerned with administration has continued to grow in the past ten years since Litchfield's statement was made. Gordon (1966, pp. 6-23) indicated that there have been four approaches to administration in America (traditional, behavioral, decisional, and ecological). He continued by suggesting a conceptual framework which "permits the incorporation and comparison of many approaches as well as the joining of values, substance and process." He believed that it will be possible to develop a "synthesis that transcends the currently competing approaches" (p. 23). But even though this is self-evident, and it obviously does have implications for a great many fields, ideas about the growth of a unified movement don't seem to have caught up with administrators of physical education and athletics. Walton's description of educational administration seems to describe our practices most accurately:

---

[3]"A theory is essentially a set of assumptions from which a set of empirical laws (principles) may be derived. A theory is *not* a law" (Griffiths, 1959, p. 28).

> In addition to the fragments appropriated from other disciplines, the content of the course in school administration has consisted of a description of practices, the cautious recommendation of promising techniques, personal success stories, and lively anecdotes, all surrounded with the aura of common sense, and often purveyed by a more or less successful administrator. . . . It has not done much for the development of the subject (1955, p. 106).

If all of this sounds familiar to you who administer, and to those of you who teach administration, you may perhaps be ready to agree that we should immediately muster a reasonable portion of our resources, human and otherwise, to meet this urgent need. A theoretical basis seems to be absolutely essential if we are to meet the attacks of current educational critics. When James B. Conant, on that "infamous" page 201 of *The Education of American Teachers* (1963) said:

> I am far from impressed by what I have heard and read about graduate work in the field of physical education. If I wished to portray the education of teachers in the worst terms, I should quote from the descriptions of some graduate courses in physical education. To my mind, a university should cancel programs in this area,

he was speaking to us loudly and clearly, and we should be forewarned.

Whether one agrees or disagrees with this statement, the criticism has already had considerable effect on the field of physical education and athletics. Witness to this influence are a number of papers at conventions, special conferences, and many articles in professional publications that attempt to justify the place of physical education in higher education. In addition, a National Conference on Graduate Study, sponsored by the American Association for Health, Physical Education, and Recreation, was held in January of 1967. Still further, the Western Conference Physical Education Meetings (for male directors in the Big Ten) have been devoted since 1964 to the body of knowledge in physical education, and the subject of administrative theory and practice was included among the six avenues of scholarly interest and research in 1966.

The Need for Research in Administrative Theory

There are very obvious implications for the study of administration in physical education and athletics that arise out of the above concerns. The first is the ever-present need for academic respectability. Even though organization and administration have a long history in professional preparation in our field, they have not achieved the recognition that has been accorded to research in the physiology of exercise, in kinesiology, in sport psychology, or in history. The emergence of sound investigation relative to administrative theory, and not only to descriptive analysis of administrative *practice,* could provide "substance" to this type of research endeavor. In this regard Thompson recommends that anyone working in this area might in the long run be contributing to the development of an adequate theory of administration. He makes some interesting predictions about the characteristics that this theory will display when it is formulated. Thus, he suggested the following five characteristics:

1. *The variables and constants for such a theory will be selected for their logical and operational properties rather than for their congruence with common sense.*
    a. By this is meant that terms and concepts must be clear, and that they must be related to systematic theory. Thompson claims, for example, that the line-staff distinction seems to be common sense to many, but that really its use has hampered administrative theory development.
2. *An adequate theory will be generalizable, hence abstract.*
    a. Here he means that a theory becomes more powerful when it clarifies and explains fully a broad range of events. This goes back to the earlier point that people in many areas must examine the process of *administration* and not limit their investigation only to business administration, educational administration, etc.
3. *The values capable of being attached to education and to administration will not be incorporated into the theoretical system itself; instead the system will treat such values as variables.*
    a. This means that administrative theory and research should not be basically value-oriented. Theory and research should be as value-free as possible.
4. *An adequate theory of administration will be rooted in the basic social and behavioral sciences.*
    a. The behavioral processes in *administrative* situations should be considered as basic to the total task. We will have to extend the foundations being laid by the social and, still more specifically, the behavioral sciences.
5. *The focus of an adequate theory will be on processes rather than on correlations* (Thompson, in Halpin, 1958, pp. 29-33).
    a. Thus, a particular administrative pattern may be shown to have a certain correlation with a quality of performance; yet, the entire process is so complex that we mustn't be misled into thinking that a simple cause-and-effect relationship is *the* answer.

This recommended approach would enable *our own* best social and behavioral scientists, of which we have very few at present, to make a contribution to a configuration or synthesis of administrative theory being developed by researchers in many disciplines. As an inventory of administrative theory and research is being developed, we would supplement this by a "body of knowledge" that applies specifically to physical education and athletics (and there is a considerable amount of knowledge of varying quality available already about administrative practice in our field). This is the type of foundation that we will have to make available if future administrative leaders in our field are to have optimum preparation for their profession. Such synthesis and integration of knowledge into concepts will inevitably have considerable practical value in providing the finest kind of operational basis.

The problem of the synthesis and integration of research knowledge faces graduate professors in all disciplines today—it is most certainly not a problem unique to us. The knowledge explosion (as a result of expansion of research in all fields in a society in which the rate of change is accelerating) has, along with a number of social forces, helped to create the "administrative revolution." There is a most crucial need to organize, catalogue, and make readily available the present body of knowledge in all fields. This need is most apparent in our own field when we consider the forlorn, and sometimes irate, cries of our practitioners and teachers of teachers. These are the some 45,000 members of our own Association, and the unreached masses of unaffiliated teachers and coaches, who think that the *Research Quarterly* is written in a foreign language. The profession is making headway, relatively speaking, but there is always the frightening specter of the physical educator possibly "losing ground in the race of the disciplines." In the face of this, can some universities be criticized for placing emphasis on programs of graduate study designed to turn out highly qualified scholars and researchers?

To return more specifically to the subject of administrative theory and research, it is perhaps unfortunate that the interdisciplinary nature of investigation relating to administration increases the difficulty of keeping abreast of change. Other fields have also found this problem to be crucial. Certain of them have already made publications available which *synthesize* research findings and conclusions. One fine example of this type of synthesis is *Human Behavior* by Berelson and Steiner, which offers ordered generalizations gleaned from 1056 studies which were in turn selected from thousands of studies. R. E. Peierls has attempted a similar compilation in *The Laws of Nature.* At the University of Illinois a few master's students, and a number of doctoral students, are engaged in like efforts—but of a much smaller magnitude, of course. Others are engaged in similar projects elsewhere.

Conclusion: Which Direction for Progress?

This, then, is the situation with which we are faced if we hope to place professional preparation for administrative leadership within our field on an academically sound basis. Seemingly, there doesn't appear to be much choice, *if we wish to progress.* If those of us interested in administration within the field continue as we have done in the past, we are doomed to second-class status even within our own field of physical education and athletics. Furthermore, we will always be embarrassed when we are asked to justify our curricula to colleagues in related fields within higher education. There is no doubt but that physical education and athletics has achieved greater recognition within educational circles on this continent than in any other area of the world. This achievement is an accomplished fact. If we wish to continue our steady improvement, especially in relation to the professional preparation of administrative leadership, there are some definite positive steps that we must take in the very near future. Some of the following recommendations are clarified by charts and diagrams. An understanding of them should assist in the establishment of a "shaky consensus" that may well serve as a point of departure for future efforts.

Research in physical education has frequently been classified into content areas, one of which has been designated administration, or organization and administration. The attempt to define and delimit administration as a *content* area is a frustrating one, often producing one of two results: (1) a rigidly limited group of studies that does not represent the broad range of administrative responsibilities; or (2) a broad, catchall category that overlaps considerably with the other content areas designated (aims and objectives, curriculum, etc.).

Figure 1 suggests that administration, seen as a process or a group of processes rather than as an area of content, can be viewed more simply and directly in relation to its scope and nature in regard to practice and research. Almost all of the completed administrative research in physical education was centered in the various technical administrative areas rather than in the more fundamental, broader processes of administration that might be designated as decision-making, communicating, activating, planning, evaluating, etc.

Figure 2 suggests a broadened approach to the teaching of administration courses in physical education and athletics. The area of content specifically related to physical education *(D)* should depend increasingly on a body of knowledge developed through administrative research and theory in *our* field.

Educational institutions provide the setting within which many physical education and athletic programs are administered. Current efforts to develop administrative theory and research on the broad administrative process mentioned above within the educational setting *(C)* are directly relevant to our field. The fact that administration is practiced in a specific setting has tended to obscure the fundamental similarities of the administrative process. The study of administration *as* administration *(B)* will eventually provide a sounder theoretical base for understanding the administrative process.

Underlying all administrative theory and research are the social sciences (and still more specifically, the behavioral sciences). Concepts and theories related to the behavior of people in organizations *(A)* have much to offer to an understanding of effective administration.

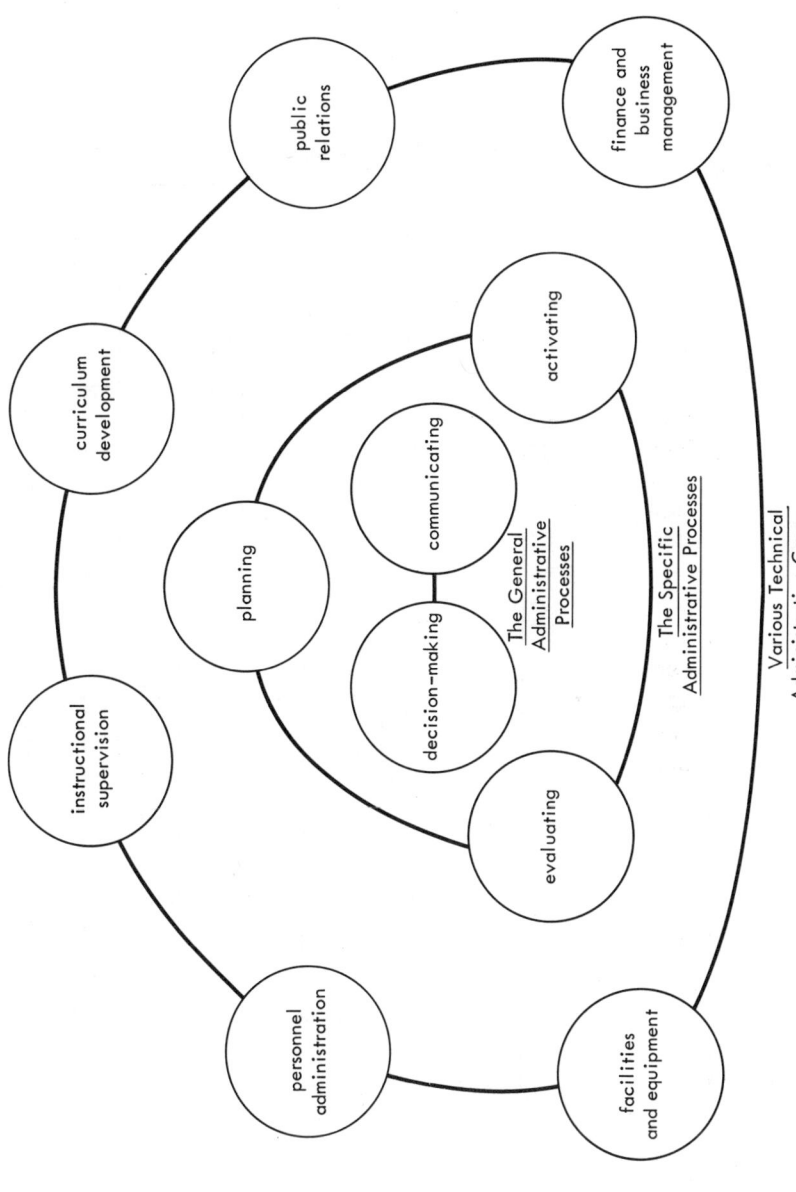

Figure 1. Proposed Areas of Administrative Research in Physical Education[4]
[4] Adapted from Bertram Gross, *The Managing of Organizations* (New York: the Free Press, 1964).

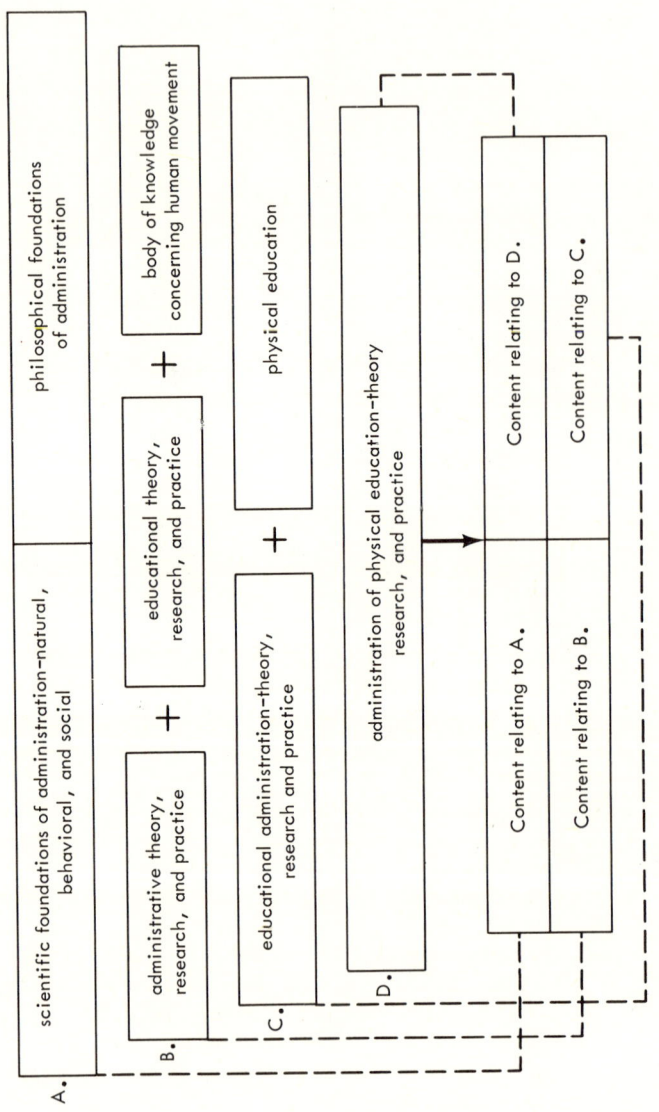

Figure 2. Proposed Content for Physical Education Administration Course

Figure 3 is self-explanatory. Under four headings are listed the names of many of the scholars and researchers who have contributed more or less significantly to the literature of administration.

Figure 4 shows some of the interrelationships possible among theory in administration, research in administration, professional preparation in administration, and the practice of administration.

Having come this far in our discussion, we are now faced with the need to determine a step-by-step plan whereby we may be able to make progress from our present state of seemingly inadequate content and proportions. The following steps, involving what is believed to be a logical progression, are recommended for your consideration:

1. *Establish the best possible criteria as goals* for the professional preparation of physical education and athletic administrators.
   a. These may be determined by the following approaches:
      i. Planning with interested and knowledgeable colleagues.
      ii. Surveying the literature of this and related fields.
      iii. Conducting a job analysis of the requirements of the administrative positions in the field.
      iv. Encouraging sociological analysis of the past, present, and possible future structure of our society (including possible implications for this field).
      v. Employing philosophical investigation of a normative and analytical nature of the present situation with possible predictions for the future and its demands.
      vi. Constructing a logical composite of the seemingly best criteria based on the above approaches.
2. *Survey and describe accurately* what is taking place in management training programs in business administration, educational administration, and public administration (and other related fields).
   a. In doing this, particular attention should be paid to the following:
      i. Course sequences at both the undergraduate and graduate levels.
      ii. The various aims and objectives of the specific courses.
      iii. To what extent emphasis is placed on theory as opposed to practice—what basic knowledge is needed, and what practical skill and competencies are necessary.
      iv. The knowledge and ability of graduates in the various related fields.
3. *Survey and describe accurately* current practices regarding the professional preparation of physical education and athletic administrators.
   a. Follow a similar approach to that described in No. 2 above in regard to course sequences; course aims and objectives;

A. SCIENTIFIC FOUNDATIONS OF ADMINISTRATION	B. ADMINISTRATION– BUSINESS AND PUBLIC	C. EDUCATIONAL ADMINISTRATION	D. ADMINISTRATION OF PHYSICAL EDUCATION AND ATHLETICS
Halpin, Andrew W.	Taylor, Frederick W.	Getzels, Jacob W.	Williams, Jesse F.
Charters, W. W., Jr.	Fayol, Henri	Coladarci, Arthur P.	Brownell, Clifford L.
Gross, Bertram M.	Gulick, Luther H.	Sargent, Cyril G.	Vernier, Elmon L.
Hemphill, John K.	Urwick, Lyndall	Belisle, Eugene L.	Voltmer, Edward F.
Agger, Robert E.	Follett, Mary Parker	Hagman, Harlan L.	Esslinger, Arthur A.
Gouldner, Alvin W.	Mayo, Elton	Schwartz, Alfred	Forsythe, Charles E.
Benne, Kenneth D.	Roethlisberger, Fritz	Griffiths, Daniel E.	Duncan, Ray O.
Bennis, Warren G.	Barnard, Chester I.	Campbell, Roald F.	Nash, Jay B.
Chin, Robert	Simon, Herbert A.	Gregg, Russell T.	Moench, Francis J.
Cartwright, Dorwin	Dill, William R.	Moore, Hollis A.	Saurborn, Jeannette B.
Zander, Alvin	Presthus, Robert V.	Guba, Egon G.	Scott, Harry A.
Lewin, Kurt	Waldo, Dwight	Carlson, Richard O.	Means, Louis E.
Moreno, J. L.	Cyert, Richard M.	Lipham, James M.	Bucher, Charles A.
Etzioni, Amitai	March, James G.	Culbertson, Jack A.	Zeigler, Earle F.
Brim, Orville G., Jr.	Thompson, James D.	Downey, Lawrence W.	Havel, Richard C.
Berelson, Bernard	Likert, Rensis	Enns, Frederick	Seymour, W. Emery
Steiner, Gary A.	Argyris, Chris	Miles, Matthew B.	Hughes, William L.
Lippitt, Ronald	Drucker, Peter F.	Willower, Donald J.	French, Esther
Merton, Robert K.	Pigors, Paul	Lonsdale, Richard S.	Lehsten, Nelson G.
Parsons, Talcott	Mathews, B. Phelps	Miller, Van	Howard, Glenn W.
Greer, Scott A.		Wynn, Richard	Masonbrink, Edward
Hare, A. Paul		Iannaccone, Laurence	Bookwalter, Karl
Weber, Max		McCleary, Lloyd E.	Shepard, George E.
Trow, Martin		Mooney, Ross L.	Jamerson, Richard E.
Homans, George C.		Seeman, Melvin	
Guetzkow, Harold		Harlow, James G.	

Stogdill, Ralph	Hencley, Stephen P.
Shartle, Carroll L.	Millett, John D.
Selznick, Philip	Sachs, Benjamin
Blau, Peter M.	Walton, John
Lazarsfeld, Paul F.	Fisk, Robert S.
Becker, Howard S.	Hall, Roy M.
Caplow, Theodore	Haskew, Laurence D.
	Litchfield, Edward H.

Figure 3. Contributors to Recent Administrative Thought

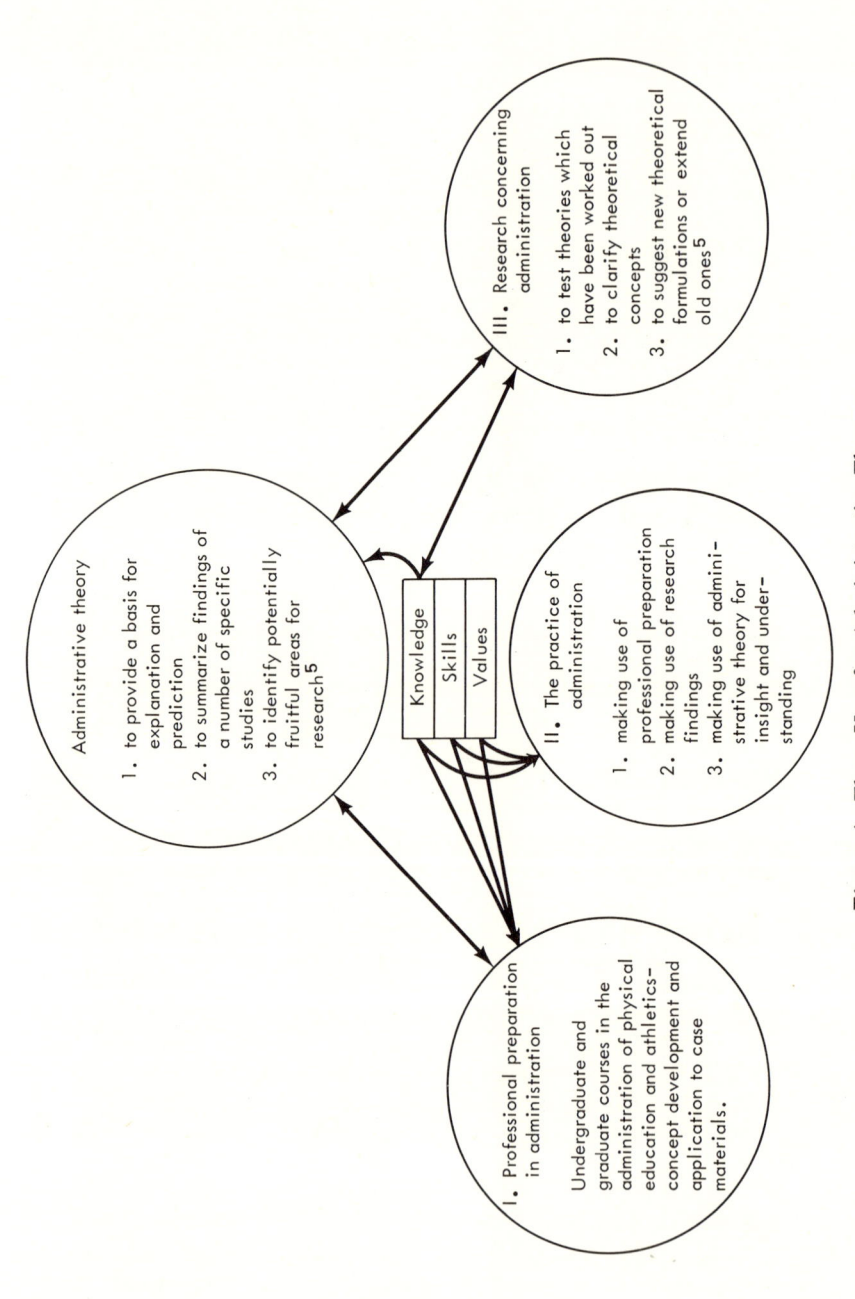

Administrative theory

1. to provide a basis for explanation and prediction
2. to summarize findings of a number of specific studies
3. to identify potentially fruitful areas for research[5]

III. Research concerning administration

1. to test theories which have been worked out
2. to clarify theoretical concepts
3. to suggest new theoretical formulations or extend old ones[5]

| Knowledge |
| Skills |
| Values |

II. The practice of administration

1. making use of professional preparation
2. making use of research findings
3. making use of administrative theory for insight and understanding

I. Professional preparation in administration

Undergraduate and graduate courses in the administration of physical education and athletics—concept development and application to case materials.

Figure 4. Three Uses for Administrative Theory

[5]Selltiz, Clare, et al, *Research Methods in Social Relations* (New York: Holt, Rinehart and Winston, 1966), pp. 498-99.

emphasis placed on theory as opposed to practice; and the evaluation of the knowledge and ability of the B.S., M.S., Ed.D., P.E.D., and Ph.D. graduates.
4. *Make a comparative analysis* between the programs in related fields and the programs in physical education and athletics.
   a. In so doing, note the strengths and weaknesses of each *in relation to established criteria* (see No. 1 above).
      i. Retain the strong points of the best curricula in physical education and athletics.
      ii. Where weaknesses are noted, restructure our curricula to incorporate the stronger points of the curricula in related fields.
      iii. If none of the curricula examined in *any* of the various fields meet certain of the objectives listed in *the ideal set of criteria,* determine what additions and/or changes must be made in order to approximate the ideal.
      Note: This may necessitate some radical changes in present curricular patterns. It may mean that trainees will need involvement in course experiences in the behavioral sciences; increased use of a variety of teaching aids in the programs; and planned internship experiences for the participants. We simply do not know at present what changes will have to be made to produce a "fully qualified product." When we know what needs to be done, we will have to decide to what extent we will be able to approximate the highest standards.
5. *Provide for continuing administrative research relative to theory and practice.*
   a. Such research should employ historical, descriptive, philosophical, and experimental group methods and techniques.
      i. The employment of such a broad spectrum of research methodology will of necessity involve scholars and researchers from many disciplines with a variety of backgrounds.
      Note: Such a comprehensive research program would appear to be absolutely necessary to keep up to date in these rapidly changing times. In this way it may be possible for physical education and athletics personnel to work their way out of the present unfortunate situation.

Whether physical education and athletics will continue to consolidate its position within general education remains to be seen. *It is our task alone!* Times *are* changing all too rapidly. Innovation may be needed in many aspects of our total program. The main conclusion of this paper is that every effort should be made *now* to restructure our efforts so that we may offer sound administrative theory as a basis for practice in physical education and athletics at all levels of our educational system.

General Bibliography

American Association of School Administrators, *Staff Relations in School Administration.* Washington, D.C.: The Association, 1955.

―――, *Professional Administrators for America's Schools,* thirty-eighth yearbook of The Association. Washington, D.C.: The Association, 1960.

Belisle, Eugene, and Cyril G. Sargent, "The Concept of Administration," in Roald Campbell and Russell T. Gregg, *Administrative Behavior in Education.* New York: Harper & Row, Publishers, 1957.

Berelson, Bernard, and Gary A. Steiner, *Human Behavior.* New York: Harcourt Brace Jovanovich, Inc., 1964.

Callahan, Raymond E., and H. Warren Button, "Historical Change of the Role of Man in the Organization: 1865-1950," in *Behavioral Science and Educational Administration,* sixty-third yearbook of the National Society for the Study of Education, part 2. Chicago: The Society, 1964.

Conant, James B., *The Education of American Teachers.* New York: McGraw-Hill Book Company, 1963.

Design Conference of Physical Education as an Area of Scholarly Study and Research, Chicago, Illinois, October 13-16, 1965. Unpublished report of a symposium.

Elliott, Ruth, *The Organization of Professional Training in Physical Education in State Universities.* Contributions to Education, no. 268. New York: Columbia Teachers College, 1927.

Gordon, Paul J., "Transcend the Current Debate on Administrative Theory," *Hospital Administration,* 11, no. 2 (Spring 1966), 6-23.

Griffiths, Daniel E., *Administrative Theory.* New York: Appleton-Century-Crofts, Inc., 1959.

Gross, Bertram M., *The Managing of Organizations,* vol. 1 and 2. New York: Crowell-Collier Publishing Company, 1964.

Halpin, Andrew W., "The Development of Theory in Educational Administration," in *Administrative Theory in Education,* ed. Andrew W. Halpin. Chicago: Midwest Administration Center, The University of Chicago, 1958.

Henry, Jules, *Culture Against Man.* New York: Random House, 1963.

Litchfield, Edward H., "Notes on a General Theory of Administration," *Administrative Science Quarterly* 1, no. 7 (June 1956).

Moore, Hollis A., "The Ferment in School Administration," in *Behavioral Science and Educational Administration,* sixty-third yearbook of the National Society for the Study of Education, part 2. Chicago: The Society, 1964.

Peierls, Rudolf E., *The Laws of Nature.* London: Allen & Unwin Ltd., 1955.

Sapora, Allen V., and Marilynn Guillaume, "Retrieval of Research Literature Related to Recreation." Paper presented at the Convention of the American

Association for Health, Physical Education, and Recreation, Washington, D.C., May 9, 1964.

Sellitz, Clare, et al, Research Methods in Social Relations, New York: Holt, Rinehart, and Winston, 1966, p 498-99

Walton, John, "The Theoretical Study of Educational Administration," *Harvard Educational Review* 25 (Summer 1955) 169-78.

Zeigler, Earle F., *A History of Professional Preparation for Physical Education in the United States,* 1861-1948. Eugene, Oregon: Microcard Publications, University of Oregon, 1951.

2

Theoretical Propositions for the Administration of Physical Education and Athletics

Earle F. Zeigler

Background of the Problem

Evidence at hand points to the offering of a course in the organization and administration of physical education and athletics as far back as 1890 (Zeigler, 1951, p. 28), and by 1927 such courses were typically included in professional curricula throughout the country (Elliott, 1927, p. 46). Today courses are offered at the undergraduate, master's, and doctoral levels in physical education, and the subject matter of organization, administration, supervision, and curriculum—broadly or narrowly defined—is included to such an extent that a distinterested observer would suspect the presence of a vast storehouse of knowledge.[1]

Still further, a vast number of master's theses and doctoral dissertations may be found on the shelves of our libraries, and some of this information is readily available through University Microfilms or Microcard Publications. The large majority of these investigations were carried out using descriptive method research, or a technique thereof, and there exists undoubtedly a body of knowledge about the various aspects of administrative practice. The availability

---

Earle F. Zeigler is from The University of Western Ontario.
[1] A paper presented to the thirty-ninth Annual Meeting of the American Academy of Physical Education, St. Louis, Missouri, March 28, 1968.

of pure or applied research relative to administrative theory is a completely different matter, however, and was the subject of a recent study by Spaeth. She concluded that "there is an almost total lack of theoretical orientation in the design of research and interpretation of findings in the sample of administrative research . . . . reviewed in this investigation" (Spaeth, 1967, p. 145). The conclusion is, therefore, that we have witnessed an endless stream of articles, studies, and texts, but that we don't know what it all adds up to, and where we can or should go from here!

The title of this paper, as recommended to the writer, was not meant to sound too formidable. "Theoretical" means "existing only in theory (hypothetical)," and a proposition is a "statement of a truth to be demonstrated" (*The Random House Dictionary,* 1967). "A theory is essentially a set of assumptions from which a set of empirical laws (principles) may be derived" (Griffiths, 1959, p. 28). Administration may be considered as "the total of the processes through which appropriate human and material resources are made available and made effective for accomplishing the purpose of an enterprise" (American Association of School Administrators, 1955, p. 17). The matter at hand, therefore, is to consider the availability and possibility of some hypothetical statements that may be shown to be true about the most effective means of organizing and administering programs of physical education and athletics.[2]

For the past fifteen years this writer has been aware of the need to make the teaching of administration more effective. To this end an effort was made to introduce the teaching of human relations and administration through employment of a technique known as the Harvard case method of instruction (Zeigler, 1959). Typical student reaction has rated this approach most useful in the achievement of the desired objectives, but it soon became apparent that we were functioning on the basis of largely unproven administrative theory. We felt it was the best approach for an evolving democratic society, but this could well be a value judgment based on inconclusive evidence. First, the question of whether it produces results that can be verified should have been asked. Value judgments can then be made *after* scientific evidence about the efficiency of the approach is known.

Concurrent with an inability to convince large numbers of my colleagues that the case-method approach of teaching human relations and administration should be employed universally, and keeping in mind also that certain social influences were effecting a definite swing toward educational essentialism, an awareness of the administrative revolution taking place grew to the point that it had to be recognized for its urgency. As Gross has indicated, "modern man has no escape from the complexities of organizations and their management" (1964, vol. 2, p. 808). In an effort to keep up with the organizational revolution that was taking place, many leaders in public administration, business administration,

---

[2]No definitions of the terms "physical education" and "athletics" are offered at this point.

the behavioral sciences, and finally educational administration made fairly significant strides in the area of administrative theory. A 1960 publication of the American Association of School Administrators stressed that "of all the many areas of knowledge in which a school administrator needs to keep up-to-date the most crucial, at the present time, is knowledge of administrative theory" (p. 99).

Recent Developments

Despite these developments there was no evidence until the academic year of 1966-67 that administrators of physical education, either in practice or in administration courses, were concerned with the possibility of administrative theory. If such thoughts did ever come to mind, they must have been dismissed for lack of evidence. Practitioners generally seemed to believe that such theory is of no use in practice. The scientists in our midst seemed to be opposed to investigation in this area for another reason: they tended to see it as an area of study that is nonacademic and merely practical or vocational in nature. In fact, it wasn't until the third year of the Big Ten Body of Knowledge Project in Physical Education that administrative theory was included as one of six areas for scholarly study (Zeigler and McCristal, 1967). Some did not see it as basic to, and an integral part of, a possible developing body of knowledge. Others, while granting the premise that its relationship to "man moving purposefully" is tenuous, argued that the efficient management of organizations is so basic to our efforts that it cannot be ignored. Whether any possible investigation of this nature should be "pure" as opposed to "applied" research had not yet been decided.

Thus, three presentations of this nature were made during the 1966-67 year at Chicago, San Diego, and Las Vegas. McCristal and others presented a comprehensive assessment of administrative theory at the Western Conference Physical Education Directors Meeting in Chicago in December 1966. Zeigler and Paton discussed administrative theory as a basis for practice in intercollegiate athletics at the NCPEAM meeting in San Diego (*Proceedings* of the NCPEAM, 1967, pp. 131-39). And Zeigler, Spaeth, and Paton's paper "Theory and Research in the Administration of Physical Education" was presented at the AAHPER Convention in Las Vegas.

Concurrently, Spaeth completed an investigation in which she analyzed "administrative research in physical education and athletics in relation to current approaches to behavioral research in educational administration" (unpublished Ph.D. dissertation, University of Illinois, 1967). A second study now in process is an effort by Paton to determine "the present status of administrative theory in graduate courses in administration within the field of physical education" (unpublished Ph.D. dissertation, University of Illinois, 1970). Supplementing these approaches is a third study by Penny in which he studied "the similarities in the meanings attached to selected concepts in administrative theory by (1) practicing administrators in physical education, (2) graduate faculty teaching administration courses in physical education, and (3) professors of educational administration in the Big Ten universities." A form of the Osgood Semantic Differential Instrument was employed to measure quantitatively the meanings applied to these concepts (unpublished Ph.D. dissertation, University of Illinois, 1968).

There are indications, therefore, that the field of physical education could quite possibly relate to the behavioral approach in educational administration. It would seem appropriate to assess as carefully as possible what results an administrator's behavior has in relation to the task and the organization's objectives in physical education. Such an approach, coupled with more rigorous application of appropriate research techniques, should enable our field to follow a *programmatic* approach to research in the area of administration as it might relate to physical education and athletics.

Characteristics of Theory

If and when tenable administrative theory does become available, it should prove to be quite a boon to those who are struggling with problems of administrative leadership. Prior to consideration of certain theories generally, and some theoretical propositions specifically, it seems advisable to examine a list of characteristics that this theory may display when we have it. Thompson has made the following interesting predictions:

1. *The variables and constants for such a theory will be selected for their logical and operational properties rather than for their congruence with common sense.*
    a. By this is meant that terms and concepts must be clear, and that they must be related to systematic theory. Thompson claims, for example, that the line-staff distinction seems to be common sense to many, but that really its use has hampered administrative theory development.
2. *An adequate theory will be generalizable, hence abstract.*
    a. Here he means that a theory becomes more powerful when it clarifies and explains fully a broad range of events. This goes back to the earlier point that people in many areas must examine the process of administration, and not limit their investigation only to business administration, educational administration, etc.
3. *The values capable of being attached to education and to administration will not be incorporated into the theoretical system itself; instead the system will treat such values as variables.*
    a. The meaning of this is that administrative theory and research should not be basically value-oriented. Theory and research should be as value-free as possible.

4. *An adequate theory of administration will be rooted in the basic social and behavioral sciences.*
    a. The behavioral processes in *administrative* situations should be considered as basic to the total task. We will have to extend the foundations being laid by the social and, still more specifically, the behavioral sciences.
5. *The focus of an adequate theory will be on processes rather than on correlations.*
    a. Thus, a particular administrative pattern may be shown to have a certain correlation with a quality of performance; yet, the entire process is so complex that we mustn't be misled into thinking that a simple cause-and-effect relationship is *the* answer.
    (Thompson, in Halpin, ed., 1958, pp. 29-33).

Sources for Administrative Theory

At present, then, we may find a multitude of administrative and organizational theories emanating from a variety of disciplines, which is very confusing. Thompson has indicated to us further that there seem to be "four primary sources of theory for administration" (in order of appearance historically):

1. The comments and reports made by practicing administrators.
2. The survey research of teachers.
3. The deductive reasoning of teachers.
4. The adaptation of models from other disciplines.
   (Thompson, in Halpin, ed., 1958, p. 24)

Griffiths has reviewed eight different attempts at theorizing in the area of administration. At the same time he has categorized them according to the research methodology which they seem to be employing and recommending (Griffiths, 1959, pp. 47-70). He feels that most of these attempts at theorizing are characterized by a need for more careful development of the concepts or language used. These theories, four taken from educational and four from noneducational administration, seem to be either too narrow or too inclusive. Still further, perhaps because the theory construction could be marked by greater precision, Griffiths indicates that they haven't produced very many testable hypotheses.

Before attempting to list some general and specific theoretical propositions, a brief listing of selected attempts at theorizing outside of physical education will be presented to show the types of approaches that have been suggested, and that the reader may wish to review:

Theoretical Propositions

Name	Type of Research	Date[3]
Argyris-Bakke	Organizational processes derived from assumptions (deductive reasoning)	1953, 1957
Barnard	Administrative theorizing based on comments and reports of practicing administrators	1938
Griffiths	Administration as decision-making (an adaptation of Dewey's problem-solving approach)	1959
Halpin	Study of administrative behavior in a programmatic manner in which a research paradigm is offered, and change in performance is measured statistically	1966
Hemphill	Administrative leadership as group problem-solving (small-group research involving various techniques including experimental group method where possible)	1954
Litchfield	Assumptions based on universals arrived at through deductive reasoning; development of clearer concepts and control of variables	1956
McClelland	Correlation of parental demands for achievement and subsequent achievement drive (statistical analysis)	1953
Midwest Center (Getzels)	Adaptation of model from outside discipline (hypothetico-deductive theory in which administration is viewed as a social process with two dimensions)	1958
Mort and Ross	Cultural sanctions defined and stated as principles to guide action (deductive reasoning)	1957
Sears	Administrative function derives its nature from study of service it is to manage (deductive reasoning)	1950
Shartle (Ohio State Leadership Studies)	Study of human behavior in organizations with variables, concepts, and research methods from several disciplines	1958
Simon	Offers an approach including discussion of underlying concepts and mathematical formulations	1954
Southern States CPEA (Graff)	Competency concept with emphasis on values	1955

[3] See the general bibliography at the end of this chapter for specific references.

General Theoretical Propositions

Now let us consider several general theoretical propositions relative to human behavior according to several categories.[4] From the area of *small-group research (face-to-face relations)*, the following propositions (or assumptions) can be investigated:

1. That the manner in which the administrator leads his department is determined more by the existing regulations of the educational institution itself, and the expectations of his faculty and staff, than by his own personality and character traits.
2. That a department head will find it most difficult to shift the departmental goals away from established norms.
3. That the department head will receive gradually increasing support from staff members to the extent that he makes it possible for them to realize their personal goals.
4. That an administrator who attempts to employ democratic leadership will experience difficulty in reaching his personal goals for the department if there are a significant number of authoritarian personalities in it.

In the area of *organizations (organizational theory)*, a few propositions have been selected as representative:

1. If an organization (e.g., a division of health, physical education [men and women], recreation, and intercollegiate athletics) is geographically decentralized, and if the component units are relatively autonomous, there will be many conflicting points of view and understandings.
    a. Thus, if great differences exist insofar as aims and objectives are concerned, and there is a desire to maintain the various units within one organization, decentralization should be employed.
2. If the administrator is helpful and friendly, the productivity of the department should be greater, the staff members will identify with the unit more strongly, and the staff morale should be very high.
3. A departmental administrator's approach to leadership is influenced by the manner in which he himself is led.

A very small sampling of theoretical propositions that might be pertinent to this specialized field within the area of *educational institutions* could include such statements as the following:

---

[4]Many of these propositions have been adapted from Berelson and Steiner (1964).

1. When colleges and universities are under attack on matters of academic freedom during periods of crisis, those institutions with the highest ratings respond most strongly.
2. The relationship between a teacher's personality (and his method of teaching) and mastery of knowledge on the part of the student is undetermined.
3. The peer group at all levels of the educational ladder exerts a strong influence on individual and group behavior both in and out of school. This influence extends to attainment levels as well.

Theoretical propositions relating to the area of mass communications are significant for the student of administrative theory who needs to know how to inform and influence the many "publics" with which his field comes into contact. Two examples of relevant propositions are:

1. That the effectiveness of the various informational media varies with the educational level of the intended audience.
2. That to make communications more effective, these media should be directed to those people who may be called the "opinion leaders" of the group.

When it comes to the question of *opinions, attitudes,* and *beliefs,* an administrator should keep in mind that all of the groups with whom he comes in contact have opinion leaders—certain individuals to whom the others look for guidance. One example of a theoretical proposition in this area would be:

1. That a person's behavior may often be changed before his underlying beliefs regarding a particular matter have been altered.

Possibility of Applied Research within Physical Education

Having considered a minute number of the general theoretical propositions that might be basic to administrative theory, the reader may well ask how and why this should be related to the field of physical education and athletics. The contention here is that we are vitally concerned with the management of organizations, and that we should at least be conducting applied research in this area. It is almost impossible at times to know whether an investigation can be labeled as "pure" or "applied" anyhow. Still further, a body of sound applied research will in time undoubtedly contribute to the storehouse of knowledge developing in the area of administrative theory.

The way matters stand at present, we can only be regarded as "parasites"—despite the fact that literally hundreds of studies are being undertaken each academic year. Is there any reason why these studies can't be of a programmatic character? At present we are so far off the pace of behavioral scientists and theoreticians that anything we might suggest of a specific nature would sound like repetitions of Parkinson's (First) Law—"Work expands so as to fill the time available for its completion" (Parkinson, 1957).

Some General Propositions for Investigation

Being firmly convinced that value-free investigation of an applied nature is needed in physical education and athletics (and in an effort to get some "laws" named after him!), this writer has postulated a number of theoretical propositions. Although these propositions may seem slightly humorous, it may be agreed that there is enough of a grain of truth in many of them to warrant one or the other of two reactions: (1) a response with sufficient supporting rationale to make the proposition seem ridiculous; (2) further study based on evidence available through related literature to prove or refute many of these propositions as they might apply to physical education and athletics. Some of the following propositions are seemingly more general in nature, but it is quite possible that they can be related to this field:

1. Any administrative theory is better than no theory (and especially so when the field of physical education is under consideration).
2. When the facts do not conform to one's personal administrative theory, it is quite possible that they have been reported incorrectly.
3. Established principles of administration are incontrovertible; thus, the less physical education relates to the established behavioral sciences, the more tenable its administrative theory will be.
4. Enough talk about administrative theory, and the more complex and grandiose the structure, the more most of the people will be fooled into thinking that this area of study has something to offer.
5. The best way to select a departmental administrative head is to search for a personable scholar or researcher with an authoritarian streak in his make-up.
6. The higher a person's administrative position, and the more impressive his title, the more authority he will think that he has.
7. The more essentialist the educational philosophy of the administrator, the more he sees administration as an art practiced by a scholar in his spare time.
8. A discipline in which the administrator takes pride in the efficiency of his managerial efforts is probably not characterized by an advanced body of knowledge.

Theoretical Propositions 31

9. The administrator can get maximum production from his staff members by keeping them rarely happy, usually sullen, but never openly mutinous.
10. Democratic administration should be employed in such a way so that staff members are encouraged to vote on any and all minor matters.
11. If an administrator finds that a staff member is lacking in integrity and is two-faced, the least that he should do is to patiently make every effort to help the fellow keep his stories straight.
12. Administrators who are anxious to improve departmental quality should spread the word surreptitiously that the only way to get a decent raise is to get another offer—any offer—and demand a counter offer within twenty-four hours.
13. A staff member who publishes under duress will leave an indelible impression on the body of knowledge in his specialized area.
14. Staff members who work hard at it can fool some administrators all of the time.

Some Specific Propositions

If by now the reader has gotten into the spirit of these propositions, the addition of several more of a highly specific nature will not seem unduly burdensome at this point:

15. A discipline and/or profession most anxious to gain strength and influence should divide itself according to sex and move in different directions.
16. An effective professional organization is best maintained and developed by alternating elective offices annually according to sex rather than by proven ability and the will of the majority of the members.
17. Under conditions not so carefully controlled, football coaches and athletic directors behave as they damned well please.
18. The power and influence of the director of physical education on campus varies inversely with the success of the football team.
19. Physical educators rarely respond with a strong stand either as individuals or groups when the academic freedom of college and university faculties is challenged.
20. College presidents and deans, if careful not to offend and cautious about maintaining their rightful place, can play games such as golf with athletic directors and football coaches.

21. Because of their understanding of democratic human relations, successful football coaches make the best directors of physical education and athletics.
22. An unsuccessful football coach is uniquely qualified for the post of assistant athletic director.
23. If things seem to be going better, you have probably overlooked something.

Conclusions and Recommendations

At this point the reader is probably so bedazzled by the brilliance of the assembled administrative theory on these pages that he doesn't know which way to turn. If a suggestion may be permitted, it would seem logical to turn to the steadily increasing body of knowledge available through the behavioral sciences. It does now appear that we are on the way to a truly definitive inventory of administrative theory and research. Gradually there will be a synthesis and integration of the knowledge made available by social and behavioral scientists, and then we will have a body of concepts that will provide a vastly improved operational basis for those concerned with the application of administrative theory to educational problems (Gordon, 1966).

The logic of this approach seems evident, and it is most assuredly up to the field of physical education to what extent a relationship with this movement will be established. There is one major point that must be kept in mind as we look forward to the day when value-free, scientific investigation will tell us as administrators how to bring about such-and-such an effect in our managerial efforts. This knowledge *will never tell us whether it is desirable* to function in a certain way in our own educational system. Thus, even after we have truly tenable administrative theory, the ultimate decisions that we make will in all probability be based on the value system of the particular culture concerned. This is a condition from which we shouldn't wish to escape.

General Bibliography

American Association of School Administrators, *Staff Relations in School Administration.* Washington, D.C.: The Association, 1955.

——, *Professional Administrators for America's Schools,* thirty-eighth yearbook of The Association. Washington, D.C.: The Association, 1960.

Argyris, Chris, *Executive Leadership.* New York: Harper & Row, Publishers, 1953.

Barnard, Chester I., *The Functions of the Executive.* Cambridge, Mass.: Harvard University Press, 1938.

Berelson, Bernard, and Gary A. Steiner, *Human Behavior.* New York: Harcourt Brace Jovanovich, Inc., 1964.

Elliott, Ruth, *The Organization of Professional Training in Physical Education in State Universities*. Contributions to Education, no. 268. New York: Columbia Teachers College, 1927.

Getzels, Jacob W., "Administration as a Social Process," in *Administrative Theory in Education*, ed. A. W. Halpin. Chicago: Midwest Administration Center, The University of Chicago, 1958.

Gordon, Paul J., "Transcend the Current Debate on Administrative Theory," *Hospital Administration* 11, no. 2 (Spring 1966), 6-23.

Griffiths, Daniel E., *Administrative Theory*. New York: Appleton-Century-Crofts, Inc., 1959.

Gross, Bertram M., *The Managing of Organizations*, vols. 1 and 2. New York: Crowell-Collier Publishing Company, 1964.

Halpin, Andrew W., "The Development of Theory in Educational Administration," in *Administrative Theory in Education*. Chicago: Midwest Administration Center, The University of Chicago, 1958.

―――, *Theory and Research in Administration*. New York: The Macmillan Company, 1966.

Hemphill, John K., "Administration as Problem-Solving," in *Administrative Theory in Education*, ed. A. W. Halpin. Chicago: University of Chicago Press, 1958, pp. 89-118. (Reprinted by The Macmillan Company in 1967).

Litchfield, Edward H., "Notes on a General Theory of Administration," *Administrative Science Quarterly* 1, no. 7 (June 1956).

McClelland, David C., et al., *The Achievement Motive*. New York: Appleton-Century-Crofts, 1953.

McCristal, King J., R. J. Donnelly, and W. G. Helms, "Administrative Theory," unpublished paper presented at the Big Ten Physical Education Directors' Meeting, Chicago, December 8, 1966.

Mort, Paul R., and Donald H. Ross, *Principles of School Administration*. New York: McGraw-Hill Book Company, 1957.

Parkinson, C. Northcote, *Parkinson's Law*. New York: Ballantine Books, 1964.

Paton, Garth A., "Administrative Theory in North American Graduate Physical Education." Ph.D. diss., University of Illinois, 1970.

Penny, William J., "Similarities in the Meanings Attached to Selected Concepts in Administrative Theory in Big Ten Universities." Ph.D. diss., University of Illinois, 1968.

Sears, Jesse B., *The Nature of the Administrative Process*. New York: McGraw-Hill Book Company, 1950.

Shartle, Carroll L., "A Theoretical Framework for the Study of Behavior in Organizations," in *Administrative Theory in Education*, ed. A. W. Halpin. Chicago: University of Chicago Press, 1958.

Simon, Herbert A., "Some Strategic Considerations in the Construction of Social Science Models," in *Mathematical Thinking in the Social Sciences*, ed. Paul F. Lazarsfeld. Glencoe, Ill.: The Free Press, 1954.

Southern States Cooperative Program in Educational Administration, *Better Teaching in School Administration.* Nashville, Tenn.: George Peabody College, 1955.

Spaeth, Marcia J., "An Analysis of Administrative Research in Physical Education and Athletics in Relation to a Research Paradigm." Ph.D. diss., University of Illinois, 1967.

Thompson, James D., "Modern Approaches to Theory in Administration," in *Administrative Theory in Education,* ed. A. W. Halpin, pp. 29-33. Chicago: Midwest Administration Center, The University of Chicago, 1958. pp. 29-33.

Zeigler, Earle F., *A History of Professional Preparation for Physical Education in the United States, 1861-1948.* Eugene, Oregon: Microcard Publications, University of Oregon, 1951.

_____, *Administration of Physical Education and Athletics: The Case Method Approach.* Englewood Cliffs, N.J.: Prentice-Hall, Inc., 1959.

Zeigler, Earle F. and King J. McCristal, "The Big Ten Body of Knowledge Project in Physical Education," *Quest* 9 (December 1967).

Zeigler, Earle F., and Garth A. Paton, "Administrative Theory as a Basis for Practice in Intercollegiate Athletics," *Proceedings* of the National College Physical Education Association for Men, Seventieth Annual Meeting, San Diego, California, December 29-30, 1967, pp. 131-39.

Zeigler, Earle F., Marcia J. Spaeth, and Garth A. Paton, "Theory and Research in the Administration of Physical Education." Paper presented at the AAHPER Convention, Las Vegas, Nevada, March 11, 1967, 25 pp.

3

Administrative Research in Physical Education and Athletics

Marcia J. Spaeth

Introduction

A new dimension in the administration of physical education and athletics is the gradual development of a body of knowledge derived from research that will provide the basis for a more effective approach to administrative problems. This research effort within our field has evolved from a study of administrative research in education and other types of organizations.

Recent developments in administrative thought make it imperative for any field to look beyond its own experience to the accumulating body of knowledge and theory about administration. These developments are in turn based upon progress in the social sciences toward a better understanding of human behavior in organized groups. In recent years these social science theories, concepts, and research methods have been applied to the study of administration in various organizational contexts.

Administrative research in physical education and athletics has been concerned primarily with programs in schools, colleges, and universities. Dramatic changes in the study of educational administration provide a background for the appraisal of this research. A review of these developments

Marcia J. Spaeth is Associate Dean of Health, Physical Education, and Recreation at State University College, Cortland, New York.

and the related literature that led to this appraisal of administrative research in physical education and athletics is summarized briefly for the reader.

Background and Related Literature

An extensive body of literature on administration has developed during the twentieth century. A review of this literature reveals three major eras of administrative thought.

MAJOR ERAS

In the early years of the twentieth century, administrative thought focused on job performance and the formal organization. The work of Frederick Taylor on efficiency, and of others on the formal structure of organizations, may be summarized as the "scientific management" era of administration (Gross, 1964, p. 38). During this period principles of administration were formulated which were widely adopted in business and in education (Callahan and Button, 1964, pp. 80-89).

Between the years of 1925 and 1933 a series of studies in industry took place which had a profound effect on administrative thought (Gross, 1964, pp. 50-51). These studies at the Hawthorne plant of the Western Electric Company revealed the importance of the social aspects of job performance, and the emphasis in administration gradually shifted from an almost exclusive concern with formal organization to a human relations approach (1964, p. 55). This human relations era was based on the belief that worker satisfaction was the key to greater productivity. The human relations approach gradually appeared in the literature of business and of educational administration.

The third major era of administrative thought could be called the era of administrative science or administrative theory. Beginning with the writings of Barnard and Simon in business and public administration, respectively, this emphasis has resulted in efforts to develop a general theory of administration and a professional practice based on scientific research.

DEVELOPMENTS IN EDUCATIONAL ADMINISTRATION

During the second half of the twentieth century a significant change in the study of educational administration has taken place. Prior to the mid-1940s, a traditional approach to school administration prevailed. This approach gradually was influenced by the human relations movement and later the movement toward administrative theory. An important event in this later movement was the organization of the National Conference of Professors of Educational Administration in 1947. During the next ten years this organization provided the principal means for the exchange of new ideas and for contact with social scientists whose background provided new insights for professors and students of educational administration.

Another important event was the organization of the University Council for Educational Administration in 1956, which provided a new impetus for further development of the new ideas. Much of the recent literature in educational administration has emphasized research findings based on concepts and theories of the social sciences.

ADMINISTRATIVE THOUGHT IN PHYSICAL EDUCATION

These same periods of administrative thought have tended to appear later and persist longer in the administrative literature specific to physical education and athletics. Much of this literature reflects the traditional era of administrative thought, which stressed the teaching of principles of administration and other formal aspects of organization.

The human relations era of administrative thought appeared in the physical education literature of the 1950s and the 1960s. The search for a more effective way to present administrative concepts to students led Zeigler to adopt the Harvard case method of instruction in human relations and administration as an alternative to the traditional approach (Zeigler, 1959). The two related themes of human relations and of democratic administration are characteristic of the reaction against the traditional or classical era of administrative thought. The human relations approach has tended, however, to overemphasize the informal as contrasted with the formal aspects of organization.

The era of administrative theory has had little influence on the administrative literature in physical education and athletics. One of the most explicit descriptions of theory as a basis for practice appeared in *Theory in Physical Education* (Brown and Cassidy, 1963). Of particular interest in relation to administration is "Part 5: The Process" which draws on resources in the social sciences in relation to the process of planned change, an area which has been of considerable theoretical and practical importance in recent administrative thought.

REVIEWS OF ADMINISTRATIVE RESEARCH

Previous reviews of administrative research in educational administration and in physical education are summarized as part of the background and related literature for this study.

Reviews in educational administration. One of the major characteristics of the recent literature in educational administration has been the emphasis placed on empirical research. The *Encyclopedia of Educational Research* provides a comprehensive review of this research which is organized by topics and is brought up to date by an authority in each area at approximately ten year intervals. The *Review of Educational Research* provides a different type of review article on educational administration by concentrating on research completed during the previous three year period. Although not as comprehensive in scope as the *Encyclopedia* articles, the *Review* articles are essential for the more recent research.

Reviews in physical education. Administration has been an area of research in physical education and athletics for more than three-quarters of a century. Most early investigations were by administrators themselves and concerned facilities or departmental organization and staffing. As graduate programs developed in the universities, masters theses and doctoral dissertations became the primary source of administrative research.

Reviews of this research have appeared primarily in one of two forms: (1) in the related-literature chapters of theses and dissertations on administrative topics; and (2) in comprehensive reviews of research which have included administration as a subtopic. Reviews of related literature and research are found in most theses and dissertations and these are important sources of information on specific administrative topics. The more comprehensive reviews of physical education research are described briefly for the reader.

The first summary of physical education research in the *Encyclopedia of Educational Research* appeared in the 1941 edition (Esslinger, 1941, pp. 801-14). Esslinger used seven categories to classify the research; the category most directly related to administration was "Status of Physical Education."

A summary of research for the period 1930 through 1946 appeared in the *Research Quarterly* (Cureton, 1949, pp. 21-59). The article included the complete listing of the 420 doctoral theses in the review.

The second edition of the *Encyclopedia of Educational Research* included a revised and updated article on physical education research (Esslinger, 1950, pp. 820-35). The categories of "Objectives," "Organization and Administration," and "Inter-school Athletics" were added to the one used in the first edition article pertaining to administration.

The most comprehensive review of research was a doctoral dissertation completed by Trethaway in 1953. Trethaway collected the titles of 3,083 research reports in physical education, interschool athletics, and school recreation completed between 1895 and 1940; he then analyzed a sampling of 789 of the abstracts. Trethaway summarized the major developments in the function of administration between 1895 and 1940 as being associated with "the increased number of facilities, the combining of health, physical education and recreation into one department, and the organization and control of interschool athletics and school recreation" (Trethaway, 1953, p. 458).

In the third edition of the *Encyclopedia of Educational Research,* physical education research was again reviewed (Rarick, 1960, pp. 973-95). The space devoted to administration was increased considerably over the previous two editions. The heading of "Administrative Practices" included seven studies pertaining to colleges and universities and nineteen pertaining to the public schools. The reports summarized were primarily concerned with policies, procedures, practices, and regulations—the more formal aspects of administration.

Research Methodology and Techniques

The primary purpose of this study was to analyze administrative research in physical education and athletics in relation to recent approaches to behavioral research in educational administration.

RESEARCH METHODS

Three methods of research were used: description, integration, and evaluation.

Descriptive method. The descriptive method was used to present facts concerning the nature and status of administrative research (Good and Scates, 1954, p. 259). First, the recent literature of educational administration was reviewed to identify developments in administrative thought and major emphases affecting research. This review of related literature showed that what the administrator actually does (i.e., his job performance or behavior as a decision-maker and group leader) was a central concern of recent administrative research. Therefore, a research paradigm involving this central aspect of administration was chosen (Halpin, 1966, pp. 22-77).

Second, data consisting of a selected sample of published research reports in physical education and athletics were described and analyzed in relation to the research paradigm. The primary criterion for selecting a particular research report for review was the relationship of its basic concepts to those of the paradigm for research.

Integrative method. The second method used was the integration or synthesis of published findings (Good and Scates, 1954, pp. 121-25). The need for such efforts has been well documented in the literature. The possibility of an integration or synthesis of findings depends on the quality of the research completed on the problem. One of the basic prerequisites for integrating behavioral research is the appropriate use of the scientific method in the individual research projects.

A theoretical framework for synthesis of research was used. Halpin's paradigm for research on administrator behavior was chosen as the broad organizing framework for the selection and review of research reports in physical education and athletics. Where integration of findings was not possible the descriptive and evaluative methods were used to provide an analysis of the selected research.

Evaluative method. The process of evaluation is not generally regarded in the literature as one of the basic research methods. It is an aspect of the research process, however, which is particularly important to this study. Evaluation involves the judgment of the investigator. The conclusions drawn are more subject to bias than conclusions based entirely on the descriptive and integrative methods. Therefore, the basic assumptions held by the investigator will be stated as accurately as possible:

1. A basic function of administrative research is to develop fundamental knowledge about administrative behavior as well as to solve immediate or localized problems.
2. The behavior of the administrator as a decision-maker and group leader is central to an understanding of administration as an evolving profession.
3. Research in educational administration has potential implications for the administration of physical education and athletics.

Based on these assumptions a research paradigm for educational administration was chosen as a framework for reviewing a sample of research in our field.

THE DATA

The sample of administrative research in physical education and athletics consisted of doctoral dissertations on microfilm or microcards and published abstracts or research reports based on dissertations completed from 1940 through 1966. All of the selected dissertations were sponsored by colleges or universities in the United States and all were concerned with the administration of programs in the United States or Canada. Research reports which were directly related to the paradigm were studied more intensively.

A THEORETICAL FRAMEWORK

Halpin proposed a paradigm for research on administrator behavior to guide the design of administrative research so that the findings would be cumulative and would provide a basis for the development of administrative theory (Halpin, 1966, pp. 22-77). The paradigm serves two major purposes: First, it identifies systematically the major classes of variables which must be taken into account in designing research on administrator behavior; second, it suggests the direction of the relationships between the variables which is most likely to be significant.

A condensed version of the paradigm is presented as *Figure 1*. It identifies the major elements and the relationships between them. The reader is referred to Halpin's article for a detailed explanation of the paradigm. The most significant relationship is the one between the behavior of the administrator (Panel II) and the changes in organization achievement and maintenance (Panel IV, B)(1966, p. 62). If intermediate criteria of the administrator's effectiveness, such as evaluations or ratings by the administrator's superiors are used (Panel IV, A), the relationship between the immediate criteria and the changes represented by Panel IV, B must still be demonstrated (1966, p. 63). A second relationship to be noted is the one between the variables in Panel III and the administrator's behavior in Panel II. Panel III variables should be selected on the basis of theoretical propositions about relationships to significant aspects of administrator behavior (1966, p. 65).

Administrative Research in Physical Education and Athletics 41

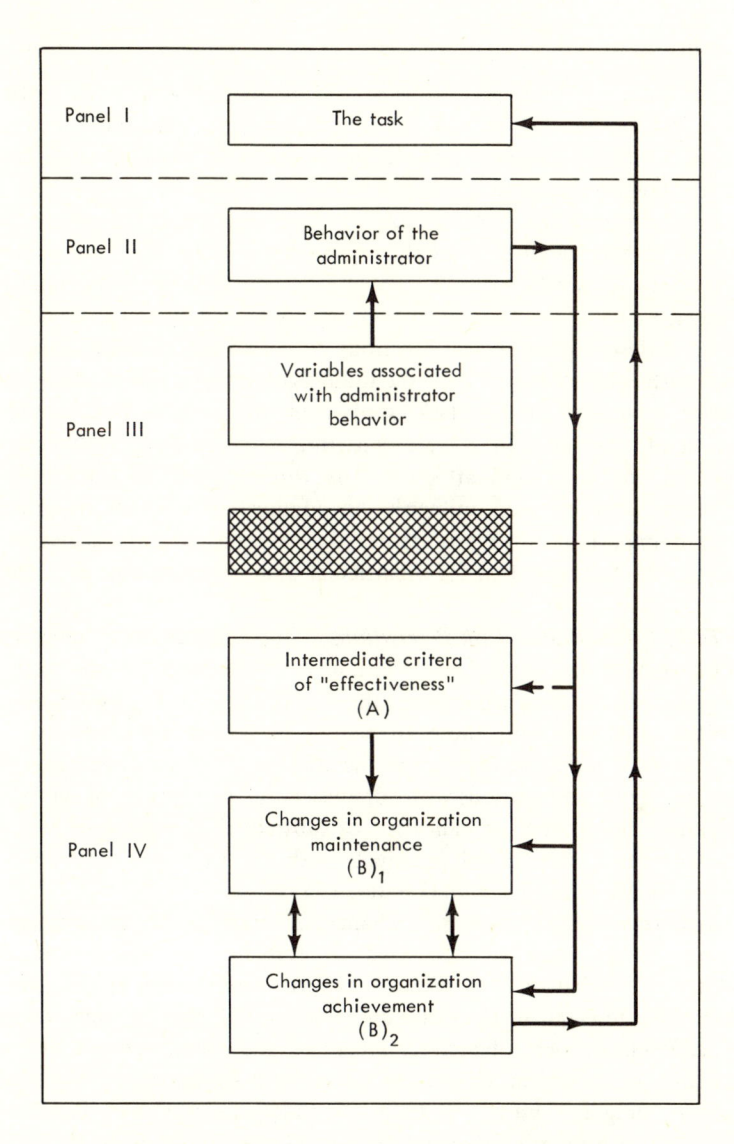

Figure 1. Condensed version of the paradigm.*

*Andrew W. Halpin, *Theory and Research in Administration* (New York: The Macmillan Company, 1966), p. 64.

Findings and Conclusions

A paradigm for research on administrator behavior was used as a guide for the analysis of thirty-five research reports selected from a larger sample as being most relevant to the concepts presented in the paradigm.

FINDINGS

The principal findings of this study are presented by first stating the primary relationships to be studied in research on administrator behavior as identified in the paradigm; the relevant research in physical education and athletics is then summarized in relation to these variables.

Achievement/Task. Achievements of an organization should be studied in relation to the stated tasks of the organization. Three task studies reviewed from the sample of administrative research in physical education and athletics were descriptions of the task or purpose of physical education as viewed by the public in different geographical locations. The findings of these three studies differed with each other and with the findings of a nationwide study of the task of public education. Other task studies in the sample investigated state legislation and the function of state departments of education as they pertained to physical education and athletics. The three studies involving criteria of effectiveness were focused primarily on administrative duties or procedures considered important by a jury rather than on organization achievement in relation to the task specified for a particular administrative unit at a particular time.

Task/Administrator Task Perception. The administrator's perception of the task should be studied in relation to statements of the task. Five investigations in the sample compared the task perceptions of physical education or athletic directors with those of school or college administrators. Three investigations of public perceptions of the purpose of physical education did not provide any direct comparisons with administrators' perceptions of the task. One investigation did provide an indication of substantial agreement of high school department heads and school principals with the California Education Code objectives for physical education (Dexter, 1959).

Achievement/Effectiveness. Changes in organization achievement from one time to the next can be used to evaluate the effectiveness of the administrator's behavior. No research reports were found in the sample of administrative research in physical education and athletics in which changes in group achievement were objectively measured and used as criteria of effective performance by an administrator. The many status studies of physical education and athletic programs are not by themselves adequate criteria of the administrator's performance for the following reasons: (1) by definition status studies do not provide measures of either positive or negative changes taking place over a period of time, and (2) these status studies do not adequately analyze the influence of limiting and facilitating factors other than the administrator's performance. One study provided a description of variables related to maintaining the group as an effective working unit, but this study was not designed to measure changes in organization (group) maintenance as criteria of the administrator's effectiveness (Small, 1955).

Another approach to evaluating the effectiveness of the administrator's behavior is through the use of intermediate criteria such as ratings of performance by colleagues and others. These criteria should be regarded as supplementary to evaluations based on organization achievement. Only one study in the sample provided descriptions of the administrator's behavior which could be interpreted as intermediate criteria of effectiveness, in this case, of department heads in college physical education (1955). This study showed the need for a more adequate definition of the concept of administrative leadership, especially as it is related to the concept of democratic group process. A second study used a nominating technique as an overall judgment of effective performance by athletic directors (Kelliher, 1956). No studies were found in the sample which developed or used rating instruments of known reliability as intermediate criteria of administrator effectiveness.

Variables/Behavior/Effectiveness. Of the many variables associated with the administrator's behavior (e.g., training, experience, personal characteristics), research emphasis should be placed on those which are known to have a significant effect on desired changes in organization achievement. The investigations of administrator variables in physical education and athletics were not designed to produce evidence useful in predicting aspects of administrator performance as related to desired outcomes of organization maintenance and achievement. Situational variables (within and outside the department) have been investigated primarily by the descriptive method using normative survey techniques. Investigations of these variables accounted for most of the administrative research in the thirty-five research reports selected, but these variables were not explicitly related to administrator behavior or performance as required by the paradigm for research. Small's investigation (1955) was one of very few in the sample which used concepts and theories of the social sciences as guides for selecting the variables to be studied.

CONCLUSIONS

The following conclusions are based on an analysis of a sample of administrative research in physical education and athletics in relation to the research paradigm described in the previous section.

1. The behavioral approach to research in educational administration, as reviewed in this investigation, is equally relevant to the administration of physical education and athletics. This approach focuses on the interactions between people rather than on the technical aspects of administration.
2. The paradigm chosen as an organizing framework for the review of research was useful in selecting, classifying, and analyzing the individual research reports. A radical departure from the traditional ways of classifying administrative research was made by focusing on variables influencing administrative performance and

measures of change in group relationships and achievements as criteria of the administrator's effectiveness.
3. It was evident from the study that there is an almost total lack of theoretical orientation in the design of research and interpretation of the findings in the sample of administrative research studied. Concepts of the social sciences were seldom used; when such concepts were used, the investigators in physical education failed to relate their findings to the relevant findings or theoretical interpretation in the social sciences.
4. Due to the lack of theoretical orientation, no scientific hypotheses were stated in this sample of research. The few hypotheses given were generally statements of belief which could neither be proved nor disproved rather than predictions of specific outcomes which were then tested empirically.
5. The administrative research in physical education and athletics reviewed in this study also generally lacked the methodological rigor necessary for contributions to the development of scientific knowledge about administrative performance. Evidences of this were found in inadequate sampling techniques, lack of objective measurement in data collection, inadequate control of variables and statistical treatment of the data for the complexity of the problems, and the general lack of theoretical orientation.

The findings and conclusions of this research have obvious implications for the professors and graduate students in our field who specialize in the study of administration. Of what importance are these findings and conclusions to the person at the focal point of this research—the administrator who is on the job?

Implications for Practicing Administrators

The value of administrative research is ultimately determined by its usefulness to the practicing administrator. What are the possible implications of past, present, and future administrative research in our field?

RESEARCH AND PRACTICE

The findings and conclusions stated above indicate that administrative research in physical education and athletics has tended to focus on technical aspects of administration related to various task areas such as program, personnel, facilities and equipment, and public relations. The research generally was descriptive rather than analytical. It has resulted in information about the content of administration rather than knowledge of the administrative process in which the administrator has a key role. This type of research is useful to the practicing administrator primarily as a source of specific information about a problem or topic being considered. The findings appear in individual theses and dissertations. The most recent investigation on a particular topic should provide references to previous research on the topic.

Sources of information about recent administrative research include the ten-year reviews in the *Encyclopedia of Educational Research* and the three-year reviews in the *Review of Educational Research*. A selected bibliography of completed research on administrative theory and practice in physical education and athletics was published in the proceedings of a symposium on that topic held at the University of Michigan (Zeigler and Spaeth, 1973). This bibliography includes the titles of 248 research studies completed in the four decades preceding the seminar.

Although the task areas provide one means of categorizing the content of administration, a realistic understanding of administration emerges only as we can begin to define a process or a role in relation to these task areas. Thus, administration is increasingly viewed as a social process or a cycle of interaction between people. The administrator's role is to guide this process in such a way that the goals and objectives of a particular organization are achieved. It is evident that a redirection of our research efforts is essential to meet the challenges inherent in administrative positions in our field today.

NEW DIRECTIONS IN RESEARCH

The potentialities for pure and applied research in physical education and athletics are limitless. This is especially true because of the unique nature of this field and its possible relationships with so many of the humanities, social sciences, and natural sciences. Such is the case with the developing social science of administration (Zeigler, Spaeth, and Paton, 1967, p. 1).

In recent years there has been a redirection of administrative research in physical education and athletics based on the understanding that research on the administrative process is essentially social science research and must be approached with the concepts, techniques, and methodologies appropriate to social science research. The chapters in Parts 2 and 3 of this book reflect this search for a body of knowledge for professional practice that is based upon the social and behavioral sciences and is specific to physical education and athletics. Implications for practicing administrators are suggested in each of these chapters. It is recommended that these be studied as a source of propositions about the administrative process that are to be tested in practice by many administrators in as many situations. This interaction of research and practice will eventually lead to theories of administration that will clarify and explain a broad range of events (1967, p. 13). Such theories will be useful in predicting probable outcomes of alternative actions being considered by the administrator on the job.

There is a need for continuing administrative research relative to theory and practice. Such research should employ historical, descriptive, philosophical, and experimental group methods. Employing such a broad spectrum of research methodology will of necessity involve scholars and researchers from many disciplines with a variety of backgrounds. Such a comprehensive research program would appear to be absolutely necessary to keep abreast in these rapidly changing times (Zeigler and Paton, 1966, p. 16).

A LARGER PERSPECTIVE

Developments in administrative thought during the twentieth century include a growing emphasis on empirical research to develop a scientific body of knowledge about administration. Marked progress in the form of scientific investigation has been made in the fields of public administration, business administration, educational administration, and the behavioral sciences relative to the management of organizations and human behavior (Zeigler, Spaeth, and Paton, 1967, p. 6).

The behavioral processes in administrative situations should be considered as basic to the total task. Concepts and theories related to the behavior of persons in organizations are essential for an understanding of effective administration. The concept of professional management implies the use of this knowledge by the practicing administrator. Administrators in our fields can enhance their knowledge of current developments by reading some of the recent books based on extensive research programs and written in an interpretative style for the practicing administrator. (See, for example, Maslow, 1965; Halpin, 1966; Likert, 1967; McGregor, 1967; Ready, 1967; Carver and Sergiovanni, 1969.) Ideally, relevant research will be replicated in the administrative settings of physical education and athletics. Meanwhile, the practicing administrator may use these readings to provide additional background for the chapters which follow and as a source of ideas to be tested in his own professional practice.

General Bibliography

Brown, Camille, and Rosalind Cassidy, *Theory in Physical Education: A Guide to Program Change.* Philadelphia: Lea & Febiger, 1963.

Callahan, Raymond E., and H. Warren Button, "Historical Change of the Role of the Man in the Organization, 1865-1950," *Behavioral Science and Educational Administration,* pp. 73-92. (Sixty-third Yearbook of the National Society for the Study of Education, part 2). Chicago: The University of Chicago Press, 1964.

Carver, Fred D., and Thomas J. Sergiovanni, eds., *Organizations and Human Behavior: Focus on Schools.* New York: McGraw-Hill Book Co., 1969.

Cureton, Thomas K., "Doctorate Theses Reported by Graduate Departments of Health, Physical Education and Recreation, 1930-1946, Inclusively," *Research Quarterly,* 20 (March 1949), 21-59.

Dexter, Genevie, "Physical Education Programs in California Public Junior,

Senior, Junior-Senior High Schools in 1956-57." Ph.D. diss., Stanford University, 1959.

Esslinger, Arthur A., "Physical Education," in *Encyclopedia of Educational Research*, pp. 301-14. New York: The Macmillan Co., 1941.

―――――, "Physical Education," in *Encyclopedia of Educational Research*, 2nd ed., pp. 820-35. New York: The Macmillan Co., 1950.

Good, Carter V., and Douglas E. Scates, *Methods of Research: Educational, Psychological, Sociological.* New York: Appleton-Century-Crofts, 1954.

Gross, Bertram M., "The Scientific Approach to Administration," *Behavioral Science and Educational Administration,* pp. 33-72. Sixty-third yearbook of the National Society for the Study of Education, part 2. Chicago: The University of Chicago Press, 1964.

Halpin, Andrew W., "A Paradigm for Research on Administrator Behavior," in *Theory and Research in Administration.* New York: The Macmillan Co., 1966.

Kelliher, Mayville S., "A Job Analysis of the Duties of Selected Athletic Directors in Colleges and Universities." Ph.D. diss., University of Oregon, 1956.

Likert, Rensis, *The Human Organization.* New York: McGraw-Hill Book Co., 1967.

Maslow, Abraham H., *Eupsychian Management.* Homewood, Ill.: Richard D. Irwin, Inc., 1965.

McGregor, Douglas, *The Professional Manager,* ed. Caroline McGregor and Warren G. Bennis. New York: McGraw-Hill Book Co., 1967.

Rarick, G. Lawrence, "Physical Education," in *Encyclopedia of Educational Research,* 3rd ed., pp. 973-95. New York: The Macmillan Co., 1960.

Ready, R. K., *The Administrator's Job: Issues and Dilemmas.* New York: McGraw-Hill Book Co., 1967.

Small, Ella M., "Staff Relationships in College and University Physical Education Departments." Ph.D. diss., University of California, Los Angeles, 1955.

Spaeth, Marcia J., "An Analysis of Administrative Research in Physical Education and Athletics in Relation to a Research Paradigm." Ph.D. diss., University of Illinois, 1967.

Trethaway, Edwin H., "The Relationship between Research in Physical Education, Interschool Athletics, and School Recreation, and the Major Developments in These Fields (1895 to 1940)." Ph.D. diss., New York University, 1953.

Zeigler, Earle F., *Administration of Physical Education and Athletics: The Case Method Approach.* Englewood Cliffs, N.J.: Prentice-Hall, Inc., 1959.

Zeigler, Earle F., and Garth Paton, "Administrative Theory as a Basis for Practice in Intercollegiate Athletics" Paper presented to the Intercollegiate Athletics Section, National College Physical Education for Men Seventieth Annual Meeting, San Diego, California, December 29-30, 1966.

Zeigler, Earle F., and Marcia J. Spaeth, "A Selected Bibliography of Completed Research on Administrative Theory and Practice in Physical Education and Athletics." *Proceedings* of the Big Ten Symposium on Administrative Theory and Practice, Ann Arbor, Michigan, November 1973, pp. 143-153.

Zeigler, Earle F., Marcia J. Spaeth, and Garth Paton, "Theory and Research in the Administration of Physical Education." Paper presented at the AAHPER Convention, Las Vegas, Nevada, March 11, 1967.

4

An Analysis of Administrative Theory in Selected Graduate Administration Courses in Physical Education

Garth A. Paton

Introduction

The concern of professional organizations, such as the commission established to study professional preparation by the American Association of School Administrators, and various writers in administration in regard to the theory problem is typified by the following quotations:

> It is the contention of this Commission that of all the many areas of knowledge in which a school administrator needs to keep up to date, the most crucial, at the present time, is knowledge of administrative theory (AASA, 1960, p. 99).

> Traditionally, our training programs have stressed the "practical" and have concerned themselves more with techniques than with understanding. During the postwar period, however, administrators have become increasingly aware of the role of theory.... (Halpin, 1958, p. 1).

A similar appeal for reliance upon theory in the professional preparation and practice of administration in physical education has been raised by different

Garth A. Paton is from The University of Western Ontario, London, Canada.

writers in our own field (Zeigler, Paton, and Spaeth, 1969). There has been considerable research within our own field as well that has been labeled "administrative research."

Considering the activity in our own and several administrative fields (for example, education, political science, and business), it seemed appropriate to ask the question, What are the current developments in administrative theory, and to what extent are these theories utilized in professional preparation of physical educators? As a means of coming to terms with this problem the theoretical orientation of graduate administration courses in several United States universities was examined. The examination of the courses was bolstered by a careful analysis of the literature in the administration area of physical education, and selected literature in business administration.

STATEMENT OF THE PROBLEM

The main problem of this study was to examine the current developments in administrative theory, and to determine the extent to which these theories are utilized in the professional graduate preparation of physical educators.

There are several subproblems, stated as questions, that are attendant to the main problem:

1. What related literature is available pertaining to: (a) administrative theory and practice, and (b) administrative theory and professional preparation?
2. What type of professional backgrounds have the professors teaching graduate courses in the administration of physical education?
3. What beliefs and opinions do these professors hold regarding some of the important issues surrounding graduate administration courses?
4. What are the characteristics of the graduate courses in the administration of physical education?
5. What is the present status of knowledge in the related administrative field of business?
6. What is the present status of knowledge in the administrative area of physical education?
7. What ordered generalizations can be developed based on the current knowledge and research in business administration and administration of physical education?
8. What parallels can be drawn between physical education and the field of business administration in regard to the knowledge appropriate for inclusion in the graduate course experience?

Methodology

THE FIELD SURVEY

The field survey sought answers to the following questions: (1) What are the professional backgrounds of the professors teaching graduate courses in the administration of physical education? (2) What beliefs and opinions do these professors hold regarding some of the important issues surrounding graduate administration courses? (3) What are the characteristics of the graduate courses in administration in physical education? Hence, a questionnaire was developed with three major sections: the instructor, the opinionnaire, and the course, corresponding to each of these subproblems.

Questions specific to section one, the instructor, dealt with the position, rank, formal preparation, professional experience, present responsibilities, recent publications, and research of the respondents. Section two, the opinionnaire, used open-ended questions to sample opinions of the respondents toward pertinent issues surrounding graduate administration courses in physical education. Section three, the course, asked the respondents to provide information relative to the objectives, course content, teaching methods and evaluation techniques, utilized in the course by the instructors. The questionnaire was developed and then administered as indicated below:

1. Two institutions were selected as pilot schools; the questionnaire was administered; the results were analyzed; some revisions were then made prior to printing of the final form of the questionnaire.
2. The *Directory of Professional Preparation Institutions* was used to select fifty institutions offering the doctoral degree, the master's degree, and an undergraduate major for both men and women.
3. Current academic catalogues for these fifty institutions were procured and searched for graduate course offerings in the administration of physical education. Eighteen institutions were finally included.
4. A packet including the questionnaire and two letters was mailed to each individual selected to participate in the survey.
5. The respondents were informed that they would be contacted by telephone soon after they received the survey material. At the time of the telephone call, an interview was to be arranged for the date specified in the letter.
6. An interview time was arranged for the specified date, and it was indicated that the interviewer would clear up any questions that arose regarding the questionnaire, and would pick up the completed questionnaire at the time of the interview.

7. During the meeting, the interviewer clarified any questions, but tried not to bias the responses.
8. At the completion of the interview, the questionnaire was picked up, or a self-addressed envelope was given for the mailing of the complete questionnaire to the University of Western Ontario.
9. When there was no alternative, the interview was conducted on the telephone with the stipulation that the questionnaire be returned by mail. Questions and problems were handled in the same manner as in the personal interview.

THE LITERATURE ANALYSIS

The second phase of the project centered upon an examination of theory in the literature of administration in physical education and the literature in business administration. An analysis was conducted making use of an integrating taxonomy borrowed from business administration.

The initial question to be answered in the literature phase of this project was, What is the present status of knowledge in the administrative area of physical education? Spaeth's study, "An Analysis of Administrative Research in Physical Education and Athletics in Relation to a Research Paradigm," was used as the basis for assessing doctoral research. Seven administrative texts were used extensively in the field of physical education and were included as the basis for assessing administrative writings in physical education.

The literature of business administration included six books selected by a jury of eight business administration professors and an extensive review of doctoral dissertations completed in the business administration field. These materials were organized into an integrating taxonomy that was borrowed from Gordon and Howell in their book entitled *Higher Education for Business* (1959). The classifications were:

Management Analysis:
Any technique that helps the decision-maker to discover and evaluate alternatives and to make that choice which seems in the light of given objectives, to be most rational. In this broad sense, management analysis includes all analytic and informational tools that contribute to a scientific approach to any management problem.

Organization Theory:
This category includes areas concerned with (a) how people function in organizations; (b) effecting action within organizational environment. Organization theory is closely aligned with the behavioral sciences and is concerned with the "inter-action between individuals and their organizational environment."

Principles of Management:
... principles of management is *[sic]* concerned with describing and distilling the best current management practice into a set of

generalizations which workers in this area call principles. It differs from organization theory also, in terms of methodology (more pragmatic), level of abstraction (less theoretical), the viewpoint from which problems are considered (more the viewpoint of higher management officials), and emphasis placed on individual attitudes and motivation (less emphasis on the individual as a variable).

Human Relations:
... practical orientation can be found. "Human relations" cuts across subject areas of personnel administration, administrative practices, personnel management, etc. "Human relations" draws upon social psychology, sociology, and industrial psychology, and has an orientation to such problems as employee morale, motivation, satisfaction, or, in brief, the human problems of management.

The objective of reading, analyzing, and categorizing the administrative literature in these two fields was to provide a basic line of a theoretical body of administrative knowledge in physical education and business administration.

Following the survey of the literature and the resulting classification of this material into the four categories of the Gordon and Howell taxonomy, each category was carefully summarized. The information was utilized to develop a set of recommendations regarding the body of theory in administration in physical education.

Findings

FIELD SURVEY

The questionnaire was completed by eighteen respondents; the majority held senior positions (fourteen full professors), and twelve also held administrative positions. Most respondents stressed experience as the means of preparing themselves for teaching and practicing administration. Seventeen respondents held doctorates; however, only two had completed doctoral dissertations in administration and three others in the professional preparation area. The respondents indicated that they had not completed much writing and research of an administrative nature during the last five years.

Opinion was not unanimous, but some respondents (five) felt that administrative theory represented a major development in the administrative area in the last few years. Other respondents (four) pointed to developments in facilities and scheduling as major changes. Major difficulties confronting the administration instruction appeared to be a lack of leadership, internships, theory, and research and writing. Each of these difficulties were cited by four respondents. The preparation of practitioners was the major area of concentration indicated by half of the respondents; however, two-thirds of the instructors felt the courses were not making a significant contribution toward the development of potential administrators. There was complete agreement by all eighteen respondents that the behavioral sciences were disciplines basic to the study of administration.

The returned information indicated a wide variety of course objectives emphasizing the administrative processes.

The questionnaire's focus was upon the use of administrative theory. Fifty percent of the respondents exhibited some familiarity with the concept of administrative theory, although in several cases not an in-depth knowledge; however, only 25 percent of the respondents included a significant amount of theory in their courses.

LITERATURE ANALYSIS

Within the field of physical education there was a lack of theoretical orientation in the doctoral dissertations; similarly, the textbooks in physical education included little material of a theoretical nature. The human relations classification included some mention of personnel administration and morale which appeared in most textbooks but the approach was not theoretical. Only three textbooks discussed material within the management analysis category, and again there was little theory evident. Organization theory was largely ignored in physical education except for some discussion of democratic administration. It was within the principles of management category that the majority of administrative material in physical education textbooks was classified. The principles approach was the most widely utilized in regard to administrative processes; however, the major portions of the textbooks were devoted to program planning in physical education.

The review of doctoral dissertations in business indicated a predominance of descriptive research. Two categories, management analysis and organization theory contained the most theoretical research. Of the six textbooks included in the review, one was classified as human relations, one as principles of management, and the remaining four were classified in the organization theory category. The textbooks all had a theoretical approach to administration.

Some Generalizations Based on the Findings with Implications for Physical Education

The aim was to develop a few generalizations based upon the administrative knowledges as indicated by the doctoral studies and selected textbooks in the field of business administration. With a view then toward what presently exists in the field of physical education in the way of administration textbooks and the content of graduate administration courses in physical education, some implications will be drawn for administrative study in physical education. These generalizations will be presented in subsections arranged in a fashion similar to those in the preceding sections of this chapter; namely, human relations, management analysis, organization theory, and principles of management.

HUMAN RELATIONS

The literature included in this subsection was almost totally descriptive research and definitive statements were difficult to extract. There were, however, certain areas that received considerable attention and the material viewed in its entirety permits some tentative generalizations. Two of these areas appeared to be job satisfaction and the problem of leadership. The three generalizations that follow touch upon these areas and some possible implications for administration programs in physical education.

>   1. Job satisfaction is a very complex phenomenon. Present evidence suggests that there are at least two types of job satisfiers—"motivators" and "hygiene factors."

Herzberg, Mausner, and Snyderman (1967) classified these job satisfiers into two areas—the "motivators," including factors that relate to an individual's need for self-actualization or self-realization, and the "hygiene factors," including supervision, interpersonal relations, physical working conditions, salary, security, and employee benefits. The authors conceptualized these two areas as operating on independent continuums with the hygiene factors serving primarily to *prevent dissatisfaction* and the motivators having the potential to *produce satisfaction.*

The doctoral literature reflects considerable concern for searching out factors that produce job satisfaction; yet, the limitations of most studies prevented a useful conceptualization of the area. Writers in physical education have shown concern for job satisfaction; however, upon review of the literature the emphasis has been restricted to the hygiene factors with little emphasis on the motivating factors.

Implications for Physical Education. The problem of job satisfaction is as significant in the field of physical education as in any other field. The research in physical education has not been of a high caliber in this area and the Herzberg model may offer possibilities for extended research in physical education.

There are certainly strong implications in this area of study for organizational morale. The problem has received much attention in different branches of the field ranging from staff morale to team morale and its effect on athletic team performance.

>   2. Evidence suggests that management often fails to understand, or misinterprets, the things workers view as important in a job situation.

Several writers included in this study commented upon this issue: Herzberg et al. in the present section, as well as Argyris (1957), Likert (1961), and McGregor (1960) in the organization theory section. Several doctoral dissertations also substantiate this generalization. These studies indicate that this misinterpretation exists at different organizational levels and is not simply a "white collar-blue collar" problem.

There appears to be several reasons for the existence of this misinterpretation such as the changing nature of work and society, management's historical view of the worker, or persistent trade union demands for material benefits.

Writers in physical education have not generally considered the problem in this fashion. Typically, the approach to this area of superior-subordinate relationships has placed great credence in "principles of management" and considered the problem from the perspective of management only or employee only, with little thought given to the dynamic relationship of the two points of view.

Implications for Physical Education. Physical education is characterized by many superior-subordinate relationships. Consider such relationships as principal-department head, department head-department member, teacher-pupil, supervisor-teacher, and coach-player. These relationships involve requests, demands, bargaining, and compromise. Frequently the nature of this situation can lead to misinterpretation over issues that may receive greater emphasis in terms of satisfaction to one party or the other.

This generalization also appears to offer the possibility of clearer understanding of subordinate performance as well as many possibilities for research studies in physical education.

> 3. Leadership is a crucial problem in most organizations; yet knowledge of changing leader behavior and discovering potential leaders is lacking.

Leadership has been a continuing area of interest and the doctoral research in this section reflects that interest. Unfortunately most of the studies are purely descriptive, and conclusions that can be generalized are not found. The few studies that included a pretest, a training program, and a post-test failed to indicate behavioral changes attributed to the program.

Various approaches have been taken to study the development of leaders. These have included among others the study of traits and characteristics, the study of various facets of the leaders' background, and the use of predictive techniques to discover potential leaders. There has been little success, particularly with materials that might show cause-and-effect relationships.

Implications for Physical Education. Physical education has faced similar problems in regard to leadership. Few would doubt the need for competent leaders to fill roles in the profession. Leadership and administration are generally considered to be closely related. Indeed, the training for administration normally includes leadership development. By and large the profession has not committed many resources to understanding this phenomenon. The leadership area appears to be one area in which physical educators might well make a contribution of significance to other fields with an interest in leadership studies.

MANAGEMENT ANALYSIS

The literature included in this section was composed of doctoral dissertations only, concentrated primarily in the years 1964-66; there were no textbooks included in the business administration literature. The studies had a decided emphasis on the use of data processing techniques and the implications of automation for administration.

Physical education writers have shown concern with the decision process in administrative literature. The main emphasis of the writings in the field have focused upon democratic and autocratic decision-making, but writers have only been concerned with the morale problems that might arise because of autocratic or democratic styles of leadership. This approach has seriously limited research and theory expansion related to decision-making.

1. Automation and various data processing techniques have had considerable impact upon organizations. The impact will be even more significant in the future and affect the administrative processes of organizations not appreciably affected heretofore.

The doctoral dissertations in business administration dealt with automation in several different ways, including its use in different types of decisions, the effect of increased information on the firm, and its role in simulating human analysis. Based on these studies, automation has changed methods of forming decisions in organization, altered the structure of organizations, reduced numbers of clerical personnel, and shifted the responsibility for decision-making slightly upward in some organizations.

Implications for Physical Education. Administrative preparation in physical education has not included material on automation. There are several areas frequently included in administration courses such as record-keeping, scheduling, and clerical work, that may be affected by automation. Presumably, professional preparation in administration should consider this influence.

If the student is considered as an organization member, and normally this is a fair assumption, automation may have an increasing effect on them at all levels of education. In a positive way automation may provide detailed information about the student, better evaluation procedures for the student, and improved program opportunities, all of which may improve the physical education experience. Automation may also reduce some of the human relations experiences for students and create negative feelings toward physical education.

2. The use of decision-making models is useful in studying and conducting research on administration.

Decision-making models included in the literature have permitted detailed analysis of many administrative phenomena. Analysis of organizational objectives and the relationship of decisions to these objectives are possible. The communications process can be related to the decision process. Decision-making is a useful way to studying administrator behavior. Relationships of concepts such as power, authority and responsibility can be shown and studied as part of the decision process. Styles of leadership, or democratic-autocratic behavior, are put into more significant perspective when considered as part of decision-making.

Implications for Physical Education. The use of models (decision models represent one type) may lead to improved research in physical education. The model, along with the necessary theory, permits the generation of testable hypotheses; administrative studies in physical education have not capitalized on this type of research.

As physical education texts were reviewed, a major shortcoming appeared to be a lack of depth in discussing certain administrative phenomena. In part this shortcoming was due to the absence of a general theory of administration, resulting in a fragmentation of many concepts. Decision theory represents one means of explaining concepts such as human relations, communications, authority and responsibility, power, and democratic administration.

Decision theory also has the potentiality of explaining the "why" rather than the "how." This shift in emphasis may improve professional preparation in administration by increasing the depth of understanding.

ORGANIZATION THEORY

This section contained more literature than any of the other three sections; included were thirty-five doctoral dissertations and four of the six books reviewed. The research and writing covered a broad range of topics, including such diverse areas as organizational decentralization and behavioral constraints. On the other hand, the four textbooks tended to dwell on the human behavior patterns of people functioning in organizations.

In the textbooks of administration in physical education very little material could be classified as organization theory. Two textbooks published most recently did treat democratic and autocratic administration through organizational theory concepts, but this was very limited indeed.

1. There is some evidence that organization theory, based on behavioral science research, can aid in explaining human behavior in many different types of organization.

Several authors have discussed the possibility of a general theory of administration that would reduce or eliminate the adjectival form of administration. In other words, rather than *public* administration, *educational* administration, and *business* administration, the adjective would be dropped. Such a change would mean that the focus would be on generalizable administrative concepts applicable to organizations regardless of the particular field specifically concerned. Regardless of these discussions there has not been a widely accepted general theory of administration.

As the research is reviewed in this section, one is struck by the contributions of studies in the behavioral science fields of psychology, social psychology, cultural anthropology, and economics, as well as business administration. As research crosses the lines of disciplines, the theories developed will explain a broader range of phenomena and become more generally accepted.

Implications for Physical Education. As more disciplines become interested in organizations, greater demands will be placed upon preparation in administration in physical education. The increased knowledge, however, presumably means that more techniques for training administrators will become available and may ultimately affect the practice of administration.

2. Human behavior appears to go further toward explaining organizational dynamics than the study of organization structure.

Several doctoral studies investigated the various aspects of organization structure. Considerable attention was devoted to decentralization; however, conclusions were indefinite and no "ideal" organizational models were proposed.

Physical educators have devoted much discussion to the problem of organization structure. Several textbooks offer models organized in different fashions, but aside from the description of these organizations there has been little significant research conducted in this area.

Implications for Physical Education. Studies of organizations that stress factors other than structure should be considered by investigators in physical education. In order to prepare people capable of conducting and consuming research on organizational behavior, it may be necessary to change the emphasis of present programs and broaden the foundations in behavioral sciences. If administrative research in physical education is to be developed, the study of behavioral dynamics appears to be more fruitful than the descriptions of various methods or organizing departments, schools, or divisions. Because physical education research has focused on the latter approach, a reevaluation of research directions may be required.

3. A knowledge and understanding of the need satisfactions of organization members is very important.

Several doctoral studies and each of the four textbooks classified in this section treated the problem of needs and need satisfactions. The key question,

What do people want from their job? was central to the Herzberg study reviewed earlier. Argyris and McGregor attempted to develop their theories by explaining the needs of individuals, although each author did this in a slightly different fashion.

There is evidence suggesting that when an organization imposes demands that are not compatible with an individual's personality, bad attitudes may result. There is also evidence suggesting that superiors are able to influence employees' satisfaction significantly and evidence suggesting that the "human relations-oriented" supervisor is capable of producing greater employee satisfaction than the "task-oriented" supervisor. It seems fair to conclude that the supervisor who is able to provide an answer to the question, What do people want from their job? and to relate this to the organizational goals may prove to be most effective.

Implications for Physical Education. This issue is important to employees of and participants in physical education programs. Frequently, when student "needs" are considered, the context is, What is *good* for the student? rather than, What is it that the student *wants* in this program? There is an important difference, and this difference may have important implications for physical education clientele.

Similar questions might be asked of team members in athletics. Why does a boy play football, basketball, or hockey? These questions may have important implications for team morale, for the development of training rules, and, most importantly, for the satisfaction a participant may experience.

4. The problem of establishing organizational goals, communicating these goals, and employee acceptance of these goals is a crucial administrative issue.

Once again considerable literature and research in this section deals with the problem of organizational goals or, alternately, individual goals as they relate to the goals of the organization. There are many aspects to this problem: the perception of both subordinate and superordinate is involved; communication may be involved; and the problem of establishing both individual and organizational goals may be a key issue. These and other problems have been investigated, but there have been few conclusions established.

McGregor places considerable stress upon selling organizational goals to employees. Implicit in Likert's position is the establishment of a structure to insure communication between organizational levels; presumably, the suggested structure would allow a free exchange of information on many matters of mutual concern. Argyris works toward satisfying employee needs and goals and developing compatibility with the goals of the firm, after initially pointing out that typically these goals are very different.

Implications for Physical Education. Very little has been written in physical education that touches upon the problem of relating the goals of individuals and organizations. Some emphasis has been placed upon the development of goals but primarily from a philosophical standpoint. This interface between the individual and the organization has not been studied formally in physical education except as a human relations problem, and the human relations approach has dwelt on the phenomena of democratic and autocratic administration. (This problem has been referred to earlier.)

The emphasis by writers in other administrative fields, the apparent success of some research projects investigating the area of objectives, and the theory presented by several writers suggests that professional preparation in the administration of physical education might well include study of this area.

PRINCIPLES OF MANAGEMENT

The research included in this section was all descriptive research, plus the writings of Barnard (1948). The doctoral studies investigated such principles as the scalar principle, span of control, delegation, and unity of command. Problems such as decentralization, leadership development, and the effects of cybernation were also treated. Barnard's book, which contributed to and reinforced many principles of management, was reviewed earlier.

Physical education textbooks fell within the principles of management area; exceptions to this were discussed earlier in this chapter. The "principles approach" has been characteristic of the research and training in the administration of physical education professional courses.

1. Research in administration centering on the "principles of management" has not been an effective approach in terms of explaining and theorizing on the administrative process.

The principles of management developed through the years have tended to describe organization without accounting for human variables in a satisfactory way, or as one writer described it, "organizations with frozen people." Empirical research on principles of management is difficult to conduct due to a lack of control groups and difficulty in gaining cooperation of organizations that exist for reasons other than research.

Aside from the difficulties associated with the research methodology, studies dealing with various principles seem to indicate that many of these principles are either violated or are simply ignored by many business organizations. Establishing cause and effect relationships between particular principles and success criteria have not been accomplished.

Much of the more recent literature and research has focused on behavioral dynamics of people and has led to the formulation of testable theories. This approach is reinforced by writers such as Herzberg, Likert, McGregor, Argyris, Simon and March, and partially by Zeigler in the field of physical education.

Implications for Physical Education. The above generalization has implications for professional preparation courses and for research in physical education. First, it suggests that the administration courses in physical education may require a reorientation of emphasis. Much of the literature and structure of present courses may not be incorporating the most recent concepts exhibited in other administrative areas.

Second, the directions of administrative research in physical education should be carefully considered. There has been very little research published that has adhered closely to accepted research standards.

Third, and closely related to the two preceding points, is the suggestion that professional preparation courses in administration should include more research material and a goal of producing people capable of conducting and consuming administrative research. The success of the research emphasis in other areas of physical education attests to the importance of stressing the research aspect in administration also.

2. The concept of the "informal organization" is a very important concept in the administrative process.

Barnard attributed much importance to the informal organization and in fact suggested that an informal organization was a necessary condition for the development of a formal organization. He also stressed the importance of the informal organization in aiding organizational communication, cooperation and motivating employees.

There is further evidence to substantiate the importance of the informal organization; for example, the need satisfaction of employees is tied closely to informal organization. Evidence suggests that the peer group is very important in influencing individuals in the organization. There is evidence to show that power groupings are very significant influences in decision-making. Other studies indicate how the informal organization can affect production, influence morale, and strongly influence individual performance.

Implications for Physical Education. Physical education textbooks have placed considerable importance on the formal organization and have not stressed the informal organization and researchers in physical education have followed the same process. The formal organization has been widely studied; it is easier to examine, lends itself to statistical analysis, and can be studied on a comparative basis. Perhaps it is factors such as these that have encouraged these studies. However, writers and investigators have suggested that the informal organization is a preliminary condition to the formal organization and exercises strong influences. If this is the case, then physical educators might be well advised to redirect their research efforts.

Many facets of the field provide opportunities for investigating informal organizations. Aside from the wide variety of employees available, there is an infinite number of athletic groups of different types available. There are also many sports organizations that warrant study. From an organizational point of view this research might have both theoretical and practical implications.

Again it is emphasized that the professional administration courses must include this type of material and must direct attention to theoretical concepts and draw implications for practice if the theory-practice dichotomy is to be overcome. This is important, furthermore, in order to upgrade administrative research in the field of physical education.

Conclusions

The major problem of the study was, What are the current developments in administrative theory, and to what extent are these administrative theories utilized in professional preparation of physical educators? Within the limitations of the study the following conclusions are drawn:

1. Based on the investigation, current administrative theory has a behavioral focus and emphasizes the interaction between the organization and the individual within the organization. There appears to be a primary concern with the need satisfaction of individuals, specifically with the need for self-fulfillment and self-realization.
2. The field survey of professional graduate administration courses in physical education indicated that in only a few instances are reasonably significant sections of administrative theory included.
3. It was possible to state broad generalizations related to a body of knowledge in administration. The generalizations were developed by use of an integrating framework and a careful analysis of the literature.
4. There are many possibilities for conducting administrative research in the field of physical education; however, the research emphasis should be redirected from the present focus on principles of management to a focus on organization theory, management analysis, and human relations. A redirection of research efforts will necessitate the use of theory and models developed in related administrative fields, the application of these theories to physical education situations, and a heavier emphasis on research in graduate administration courses in the field of physical education.

General Bibliography

American Association of School Administrators. *Professional Administrators for America's Schools,* thirty-eighth yearbook of The Association. Washington: The Association, 1960.

Argyris, Chris, *Personality and Organization*. New York: Harper & Bros., 1957.

Barnard, Chester I., *The Functions of the Executive*. Cambridge, Mass.: Harvard University Press, 1948.

Berelson, Bernard, *Graduate Education in the United States*. New York: McGraw-Hill Book Co., 1960.

Bucher, Charles A., *Administration of School and College Health and Physical Education Programs*. St. Louis: The C. V. Mosby Co., 1967.

Campbell, Roald, and Russell Gregg, eds., *Administrative Behavior in Education*. New York: Harper & Bros., 1957.

Campbell, Roald, and James Lipham, eds., *Administrative Theory as a Guide to Action*. Chicago: Midwest Administrative Center, The University of Chicago, 1960.

Colardarci, Arthur, and Jacob W. Getzels, *The Use of Theory in Educational Administration*. Stanford, Cal.: Stanford University Press, 1955.

Culbertson, Jack A., and Stephen P. Hencley, eds., *Preparing Administrators*. Columbus, Ohio: University Council for Educational Administration, 1962.

Forsythe, Charles E., and Ray O. Duncan, *Administration of Physical Education*. Englewood Cliffs, N.J.: Prentice-Hall Inc., 1951.

Gordon, Robert A., and James E. Howell, *Higher Education for Business*. New York: Columbia University Press, 1959.

Halpin, Andrew W., ed., *Administrative Theory in Education*. Chicago: Midwest Administration Center, University of Chicago, 1958.

Havel, Richard C., and Emery W. Seymour, *Administration of Health, Physical Education and Recreation*. New York: The Ronald Press, 1961.

Herzberg, Frederick, Bernard Mausner, and Barbara B. Snyderman, *The Motivation to Work*. New York: John Wiley & Sons, 1967.

Howard, Glenn W. and Edward Masonbrink, *Administration of Physical Education*. New York: Harper & Row, 1963.

Hughes, W. L., Esther French, and N. G. Lebsten, *Administration of Physical Education for Schools and Colleges*. New York: The Ronald Press Co., 1962.

Likert, Rensis, *New Patterns of Management*. New York: McGraw-Hill Book Co., 1961.

McGregor, Douglas, *The Human Side of Enterprise*. New York: The McGraw-Hill Book Co., 1960.

March, J. G., and Herbert A. Simon, *Organizations*. New York: John Wiley & Sons, 1958.

Nash, J. B., F. J. Moench, and J. B. Saurborn, *Physical Education: Organization and Administration*. New York: A. S. Barnes and Co., 1951.

Voltmer, E. F., and A. A. Esslinger, *The Organization and Administration of Physical Education*. New York: Appleton-Century-Crofts, 1967.

Williams, J. F., C. L. Brownell, and E. L. Vernier, *The Administration of Health Education and Physical Education*. Philadelphia: W. B. Saunders Co., 1964.

Zeigler, Earle F., *Administration of Physical Education and Athletics.* Englewood Cliffs, N.J.: Prentice-Hall, Inc., 1959.

Zeigler, E. F., and G. A. Paton, "Administrative Theory as a Basis for Practice in Intercollegiate Athletics." *Proceedings,* Seventieth Annual Meeting, National College Physical Education for Men, 1967, pp. 131-39.

Zeigler, E. F., G. A. Paton, and M. J. Spaeth, "A Plan for Preparation of Administrators," *Journal of the Canadian Association for Health, Physical Education and Recreation,* 36, no. 1 (October-November, 1969).

5

The Meanings Associated with Selected Administrative Concepts: A Need for Understanding

William J. Penny

Introduction

Inherent in any undertaking to understand selected aspects of a field of study is the need for the identification of the parameters of that field. It is obvious that administration as a field of study is similar to physical education in that each contains elements from several diverse disciplines which provide insights essential for clarification and understanding. For example, for one to understand the biomechanical aspects of human movement, knowledge of structure and function of the human being from the fields of anatomy and physiology is requisite. There is no suggestion here that anatomy and physiology are part of the field of study of physical education; however, those aspects appropriate for understanding man in movement are part of the physical educator's knowledge base. Similarly, an understanding of the social and behavioral sciences as they relate to the field of study of administration is necessary for the individual dealing with why and how people participate in organizational settings. A casual investigation of both physical education and administration leads one to the conclusion that neither contains a well-defined, highly organized body of knowledge.

William J. Penny is from East Stroudsburg State College, East Stroudsburg, Pennsylvania.

Past efforts in understanding the administrative process have been geared toward the solution of practical problems without serious attention to administrative theory and the development of meaningful concepts and process models. Griffiths supports this notion by indicating that administrative thought in the past has involved "folklore, testimonials of reputedly successful administrators, and the speculations of college professors" (Griffiths, 1959, p. v).

NEED FOR THE STUDY

Three specific concerns prompted the undertaking of this particular study. The first was the finding of Spaeth that suggested the idea that the study of administration historically had focused on providing answers for immediate problems of a topical nature. She concluded that administrative research in physical education and athletics has been directly geared toward the gathering of information for the solution of immediate or localized problems (Spaeth, 1968). The second was a more pervasive feeling that administrators, particularly in physical education, have tended to latch on to "principles of administration" as unchanging and absolute guidelines for application and operation. Leighton states (with reference to the social sciences) that we have used administrative principles "the way a drunk uses a lamppost, for support rather than for illumination" (1949, p. 128).

The third suggests that in an age when the validity of certain physical laws previously accepted as absolute are being questioned, is it possible for those of us interested in administration to adhere to "principles" for operation—particularly when these principles are being applied to situations involving the dynamics of human interaction?

Although it might be possible to argue there are existing principles which can be applied to facilitate the technical functions in administration, it does not seem possible to apply unchanging principles of operation to the human and conceptual functions of administration.

Gross identifies the need for a common language of administration. He points out that really effective communication between people from different organizations is next to impossible, unless they have a "common language which is adequate to deal with the complexities of the problem they face." A maturing language of administration can provide theoreticians and researchers with the basic concepts without which facts cannot be classified and generalizations formed (1964, pp. 14, 15).

I believe that current and developing administrative theories tend to cluster around a definable set of concepts. If this is true then the study of administration could perhaps be conducted on a "body of knowledge" approach.

This investigation was undertaken to determine the similarities in meanings attached to selected concepts in administrative theory by practicing administrators and those teaching graduate level courses in the organization and administration of physical education programs.

As a point of clarification, the term "concept" is being used to identify a term to which a particular meaning has been attached (Griffiths, 1959, p. 38). Concept identification differs from the "principles" idea in that change and continuing interpretation are basic to the understanding of a concept—this is not true of a "principle," which denotes stability and rather specific definition.

The role of concept-development and understanding as it relates to the field of study of administration can be best illustrated by Spaeth's definition of administrative theory:

> It is generally recognized in the current literature that there is at present no well-developed, comprehensive theory of administration. Administrative theory, when developed and empirically tested, will be part of a general theory of social action, and a theory of administrative behavior will be a part of a general theory of human behavior. The lack of administrative theory is partly attributable to the corresponding lack of these more comprehensive theories in the social sciences (Spaeth, 1968, p. 6).

Background and Related Literature

The essence of understanding administrative theory rests in the idea that the field of study is generalizable. There is not hospital administration, school administration, public administration and so on ad infinitum—but administration *qua* administration. As administrative theory develops it is assumed that students of this field will understand and possess administrative tools and insights appropriate for dealing with the administrative process in any organizational setting.

THE "NEW" MOVEMENT IN EDUCATIONAL ADMINISTRATION

Prior to 1950 the field of educational administration was considered well defined, and there was little controversy concerning its content.

> The textbooks in general administration could be exemplified by that of Moehlman, in fact, all others were once compared with it as a type of validating procedure.... The field is no longer neatly defined.... Present-day books are characterized by a search for the substance of administration and for the theory which binds the substance together (Griffiths, 1959, pp. 1, 2).

For the past several years dramatic changes have taken place in the area of administrative thought in educational administration. One of the earliest and most important parts of the "new movement" in educational administration was the inception of the National Conference of Professors of Educational Administration (NCPEA) in 1947. As a result of the early work of the members of the NCPEA, *Administrative Behavior in Education* (Campbell and Gregg, 1957) was published. This text centered around the interpretation and synthesis of concepts and the relationship of the social sciences to research in administrative behavior in education.

Beginning in 1946, the W. K. Kellogg Foundation of Battle Creek, Michigan, became interested in the administration of public schools. From that date to 1959, grants estimated at over $9 million were made mostly to universities for the study of educational administration (Griffiths, 1959, pp. 4, 5).

The American Association of School Administrators secured funds from the W. K. Kellogg Foundation for the creation of eight regional centers in the Cooperative Program in Educational Administration (CPEA). The next step in the "new movement" in administrative thought was the organization of the University Council for Educational Administration in 1956 (UCEA) as an outgrowth of the Cooperative Program in Educational Administration. The founders of the UCEA set the pattern for an emphasis on general rather than specific interests. The period from 1959 to 1962 was instrumental in determining whether or not the initial responses of UCEA could be extended into more substantial programs to improve educational administration (Culbertson, 1968).

The development of and prospects for educational administration reviewed here have taken place primarily at the university level among certain professors, students, and research specialists. It may be safely stated that progress in concept development and empirically researched hypotheses concerning administration within organizations is not yet widespread (Gregg, 1965, pp. 42-49).

Studies of administration both within and without the field of education during the past decades have emphasized that the basic features of educational administration in different organizations are more common than unique.

UNDERSTANDING MEANING

Social scientists would agree that individual behavior is dependent upon what a given situation means to the individual, even though "meaning" might be interpreted as connoting "attitude" or "value." Nevertheless, to define meaning adequately, and then to measure it quantitatively, is a complex problem indeed.

A review of the literature revealed no widely accepted standardized instrument for the measurement of meaning prior to the semantic differential. Although the semantic differential has been widely recognized, several individuals have approached its use with caution. While the semantic differential technique may not be the complete answer to the study of meaning, it has proven validity and reliability in a number of research studies (Stagner and Osgood, 1946, and Tannenbaum, 1953).

Carroll views the semantic differential in the following way:

> What can we say about the semantic differential technique? That it measures *something,* there can be no doubt, for there is evidence of

reasonably high interscale, interconcept, and inter-subject consistency of results (Carroll, 1957, p. 77).

The use of the common-learnings approach in educational administration is a recent effort toward the improvement of training personnel for administrative positions. Such attempts represent tangible evidence of a philosophy that there exists a body of knowledge, understandings, and abilities which are decisive to effective administration, and *common* to the total preparation of administrators at all educational levels.

Research Methodology and Techniques

The major purpose of this chapter is to study the similarities in the meanings attached to selected concepts in administrative theory by practicing administrators in physical education, graduate faculty teaching administration courses in physical education, and professors of educational administration in the Big Ten universities. An attempt will be made to measure qualitatively the meanings attached to these concepts using a form of the Osgood semantic differential (Osgood et al., 1957).

If there is a body of knowledge concerning administrative thought, there should be a limited degree of general consensus relating to the meanings associated with selected significant concepts typically employed in administrative theory and research.

Three groups in the Big Ten universities were asked to respond to a form of the semantic differential as set forth in the *Measurement of Meaning* (Osgood et al., 1957) as follows: (1) the deans and heads of colleges or departments of physical education, (2) graduate professors teaching administration courses in physical education, and (3) professors of educational administration.

The nature of the literature in educational administration is such that the body of material has been realized from several diverse disciplines. In an attempt to narrow the survey of literature relating to administrative theory, a letter was sent to the members of the editorial boards of the leading journals in educational administration. The journals selected were *The Journal of Educational Administration, The Educational Administration Quarterly,* and *The Administrative Science Quarterly.* The individuals contacted represented the areas of sociology, political science, educational administration, business and public administration, industrial and labor relations, and those holding various administrative positions in educational institutions and research centers. Each member of the various editorial boards was asked to recommend five or six sources which represented the most significant contributions to date in the area of administrative theory and practice. Of the forty-nine different sources recommended, six were recommended by five or more individuals. The six sources recommended by five or more individuals were used as the primary sources for the identification of key concepts in administrative theory and practice. They were as follows:

1. Barnard, Chester I., *The Functions of the Executive.* Cambridge: The Harvard University Press, 1937. (Seven recommendations.)
2. Campbell, Roald F., and Russell T. Gregg, *Administrative Behavior in Education.* New York: Harper & Row, Publishers, 1957. (Five recommendations.)
3. Halpin, Andrew W., *Theory and Research in Administration.* New York: The Macmillan Company, 1966. (Five recommendations.)
4. March, James G., and Herbert A. Simon, *Organizations.* New York: John Wiley & Sons, 1965. (Seven recommendations.)
5. Simon, Herbert A., *Administrative Behavior.* New York: The Free Press, 1957. (Six recommendations.)
6. Thompson, James D., *Organizations in Action.* New York: McGraw-Hill Book Company, 1967. (Five recommendations.)

An analysis was made of the six recommended sources in an attempt to identify key concepts in the literature in administration.

The concepts which appeared repeatedly and were treated most significantly were *authority, communication, cooperation, decision-making, formal organization, informal organization,* and *rationality.* The seven concepts identified were randomly arranged and presented to the sample groups.

Each concept was identified at the top of a single response sheet and included ten pairs of words with polar meanings as follows:

1. potent-impotent
2. contemporary-noncontemporary
3. simple-complex
4. scientific-unscientific
5. stable-changeable
6. familiar-strange
7. powerful-weak
8. central-peripheral
9. harmonious-dissonant
10. important-unimportant

The basis for the semantic differential is semantic space. Osgood divides semantic space into a seven-point scale defined by a pair of polar adjectives. A subject judges a concept against a series of scales, e.g.:

The Concept Of Formal Organization

central : ___ : ___ : ___ : ___ : ___ : ✓ : ___ : peripheral

pleasant : ___ : ___ : ___ : ✓ : ___ : ___ : ___ : unpleasant

important : ___ : ___ : ___ : ___ : ___ : ___ : ✓ : unimportant

Two properties, direction and distance from the origin, can be identified with quality and intensity, respectively. For the purposes of this study the author was interested in the differences in scale position for the groups being studied.

Supporting information on each of the respondents was requested to provide additional information for the analysis of data. Besides information concerning their professional role and position each provided their age, sex, year of receipt of the doctoral degree, major field of study, and total number of years in an administrative position.

In order to avoid the parametric "t" test assumptions, one of which is that there is normal distribution, the Mann-Whitney "U" test was chosen for the purposes of this study. In using this nonparametric test the data was changed from scores recorded on the test to ranks or "U" scores. The significance of "U" scores can be determined by transforming them to "z" scores which are based on the normal distribution. The "z" scores which appear in decimal form are then transformed into percent, or probability values (Siegel, 1966, p. 247). The most important scores in terms of this investigation are the probability values, or percent differences between groups. The data for this investigation were keypunched and verified, and computations were completed on the IBM 7094 computer.

Findings and Conclusions

Comparisons were made between five subgroups of physical educators and professors of educational administration as follows:

1. Physical educators currently holding full-time administrative positions in physical education
2. Administrators in physical education teaching a graduate administration or organization course in physical education
3. Administrators in physical education teaching *other than* a graduate administration course in physical education
4. Graduate faculty members in physical education teaching an administration or organization course in physical education
5. Professors of educational administration

With reference to the levels of significance to be discussed the author recognized that relationships in the natural sciences can be expressed at a more sophisticated level than those generally associated with behavioral research. For the purposes of presentation differences at the 10 percent level or above will be noted with the reader making judgments concerning significance.

Full-time administrators in physical education and professors of educational administration differed at the 10 percent level or above on all seven concepts identified for use in this study. In the above comparison differences at the 10 percent level were found for the concepts of formal organization, rationality, informal organization, at the 5 percent level on the concepts of communication and authority, and at the 1 percent level on the concepts of decision-making and cooperation.

Similarly, *significant differences between full-time administrators in physical education teaching a graduate course in administration and professors of educational administration were found for all seven concepts.* In the above groups the concepts of informal organization and authority both yielded differences significant at the 10 percent levels. Differences at the 1 percent level were evident on the concepts of decision-making, rationality, communication, and cooperation.

Each time a sample group in physical education was compared with the group comprised of professors of educational administration, significant differences were found on five or more concepts.

An analysis was made of the responses of these groups to each pair of polar adjectives to determine the direction of responses. In general the sample in physical education tended to view the concepts as impotent, contemporary, simple, unscientific, stable, familiar, weak, peripheral, dissonant, and unimportant.

The entire sample was divided into four age groups: from twenty to thirty years of age; thirty-one to forty, forty-one to fifty; and fifty-one to seventy. Differences significant at the 1 percent level were found on two concepts (authority and cooperation) in a comparison between thirty-one to forty-year-olds and fifty-one to seventy-year-olds.

As indicated previously, somewhat of an "administrative revolution" occurred during the early 1950s. To the extent that it would be possible to reflect the changes in administrative thought which took place during this period, the sample was divided according to the year in which they received the doctoral degree. Those completing the doctoral degree prior to 1955 comprised one group and those completing degree work after 1955 the other. Significant differences at the 10 percent level and above were found between the two groups on the concepts of formal organization, communication, authority, and cooperation.

The entire sample group was then divided into three groups based on their major field of study for the doctoral degree. The first was comprised of those who completed degree requirements in physical education; the second, in educational administration; and the third, individuals who studied in fields other than physical education or educational administration, such as elementary education, higher education, and secondary and continuing education.

A comparison of those who studied in physical education with individuals prepared in educational administration yielded differences significant at the 5 percent level for the concept of informal organization, and at the 1 percent level for the concepts of decision-making, rationality, communication, cooperation, and authority. Significant differences at the 1 percent level were found in a comparison between those who completed doctoral degrees in physical education and individuals who completed their degrees in fields other than physical education and educational administration, on the concepts of decision-making, rationality, communication, cooperation, and authority.

The entire sample group was categorized with respect to years of administrative experience; from zero to ten years, eleven to twenty years, and twenty-one or more years of administrative experience.

A comparison of those reporting up to ten years' experience with individuals reporting eleven to twenty years' experience yielded differences significant at the 5 percent level for the concepts of communication, cooperation, and authority.

CONCLUSIONS

1. Full-time administrators in physical education (who might be considered as those practicing administration) and professors of educational administration (who might be considered as those involved in the study of administration) ascribe different meanings to the concepts typically found in the literature in administrative theory and practice.
2. Administrators in physical education teaching a graduate administration course and professors of educational administration tend to differ in the meanings they associate with the established concepts in administrative theory and practice.
3. Physical educators, both administrators and faculty, differ with professors of educational administration in the meanings they associate with the concepts typically found in the literature in administration and associated behavioral sciences.
4. As determined by the direction of their responses, professors of educational administration view the concepts in administrative theory as being generally more scientifically based, complex, changeable, powerful, central, and important than physical education administrators and faculty.
5. The field of preparation for the doctoral degree is a major predictor of the way in which concepts in administrative theory and practice are viewed. Individuals prepared in physical education attach different meanings to the concepts found in the literature than those prepared in educational administration and other fields of education.

Implications for the Practicing Administrator

If there is a common language of administration then the findings support the need for an increased concern for interdisciplinary study by physical educators who wish to specialize in administration. Because it was possible to conclude that the major field of study was an indicator of the way in which one would view administrative concepts, individuals interested in administrative theory and practice should pursue course experiences in educational administration and related behavioral sciences which are concept oriented. It would be unrealistic to indicate that course experiences or professional preparation alone would provide the final answer for action in administration. Although administrative theory and research may in time be an indicator of how to bring about certain effects, an administrator's value system is inextricably woven into every decision and action within an organization. Zeigler supported this thought when he wrote:

> Value-free, scientific investigation may in time tell us how to bring about such-and-such an effect, but it will never tell us whether it is desirable to function in a certain way in our educational system. It is at this point that individual and group values come into the picture—a condition from which we can't, and shouldn't wish to escape (Zeigler, 1967, p. 1).

If it is possible to agree that certain experiences in educational administration or the associated behavioral sciences courses are indicators of the way in which individuals view certain concepts in administration, what effect would the number of years of administrative experience have in determining how these concepts are perceived? To proceed one step further, some would agree that individuals recently completing their professional training (who may or may not be theoretically oriented) would view concepts in administration differently after spending a number of years in a practical administrative position.

This possibility was evident in a comparison of the sample group divided according to total years of administrative experience. This comparison reflected differences on the concepts most closely related to the human relations aspects of administration, or the relationship between the administrator and his staff (communication, cooperation, and authority). To further support this idea, differences at the 1 percent level on the concepts mentioned above were found in a comparison between young administrators and those having twenty or more years of experience. Whether these differences occurred because of a rather idealistic orientation of young administrators or the fact that practical experiences tend to change the way in which concepts are viewed, the relationship warrants futher inquiry.

Differences between physical education faculty and administrators on the concepts of decision-making, communication, and authority suggest that the sample groups differed most on the concepts associated with the relationship between an administrator and his staff.

It would seem that administrators in educational settings might have to be particularly concerned with the human elements of administration as well as the technical aspects. Most educational institutions are part of a much larger superstructure which controls the financial and physical plant. The job of the administrator might very well be centered around setting the climate for good human relations or, in other words, an administrator might have to be what is termed an expert in human relations. An administrator must rely on the members of the organization for the achievement of the organization's objectives. This concern for setting the climate for beneficial human interaction, consistent with the beliefs of those involved, should be considered a key aspect of the administrative process.

RECOMMENDATIONS

There is an expressed need for administrators in physical education to be concerned with the study of administrative theory and research. It would seem reasonable to assume that physical educators have tended to accept outdated meanings of certain concepts in administration and associated behavioral sciences to the extent that they have been renamed "principles." This assumption is supported by the fact that of the twenty-five or so texts in physical education administration are referred to as "principles of administration" texts. Physical educators have accepted "principles" (or concepts) as being unchanging in nature, rather than a source for continued study and reevaluation.

If there is a need for a common language of administration as an aid to the development of administrative thought it would seem there is an increased concern for interdisciplinary study by physical educators who wish to specialize in administration, focusing particularly on understanding the dynamics of human interaction in an organizational setting.

General Bibliography

Barnard, Chester I., *The Functions of the Executive.* Cambridge, Mass.: Harvard University Press, 1937.

Campbell, Roald F., and Russell T. Gregg, *Administrative Behavior in Education.* New York: Harper & Row, 1957.

Carroll, John, "Reviews," *Language* 35 (1957).

Culbertson, Jack., ed., *Toward the Development of a 1969-74 Plan for Advancing Educational Administration.* Columbus, Ohio: University Council for Educational Administration, 1968.

Gregg, Russell T., "Essay Review: Behavioral Sciences and Educational Administration," in *The Educational Administration Quarterly,* 1 (Winter 1965).

Griffiths, Daniel E., *Administrative Theory.* New York: Appleton-Century-Crofts, Inc., 1959.

Gross, Bertram M., *The Managing of Organizations.* New York: The Free Press, 1964.

Halpin, Andrew W., *Theory and Research in Administration.* New York: The Macmillan Co., 1966.

Leighton, Alexander H., *Human Relations in a Changing World.*, New York: E. P. Dutton and Co., 1959.

March, James G., and Herbert A. Simon, *Organizations.* New York: John Wiley & Sons, 1965.

Osgood, Charles E., George J. Suci, and Percy H. Tannenbaum, *The Measurement of Meaning.* Champaign: University of Illinois Press, 1957.

Siegel, Sidney, *Nonparametric Statistics for the Behavioral Sciences.* New York: McGraw-Hill Book Co., 1956.

Simon, Herbert A., *Administrative Behavior.* New York: The Free Press, 1957.

Spaeth, Marcia J., "An Analysis of Administrative Research in Physical Education and Athletics in Relation to a Research Paradigm." Ph.D. diss., The University of Illinois, 1967.

Stagner, R., and Charles E. Osgood, "Impact of War on Nationalistic Frame of Reference: 1. Changes in General Approval and Qualitative Patterning of Certain Stereotypes," *The Journal of Social Psychology,* 29 (1946).

Tannenbaum, P. H., "Attitudes toward Sources and Concept as Factors in Attitude Change through Communication." Ph.D. diss., University of Illinois, 1953.

Thompson, James D., *Organizations in Action.* New York: McGraw-Hill Book Co., 1967.

Zeigler, Earle F., "What to Do in the Absence of Tenable Administrative Theory and Research." Mimeographed. Champaign, Illinois, 1967.

II

STUDIES ABOUT
THE GENERAL AND SPECIFIC
ADMINISTRATIVE PROCESSES

6

Leader Behavior of Junior College and University Physical Education Administrators

Gordon A. Olafson

Introduction

The role of an administrator within an institution of higher education demands "a greater range of skills and includes a greater diversity of tasks than any business or military organization" (Caplow and McGee, 1965, p. 2). The integration of the multiplicity of responsibilities with which the department chairman must be involved requires that a balance be established between the organizational nature of the institution and the faculty members of that enterprise. Thus, the chairman is required to make decisions, choices, and judgments based upon a clarified, well thought out theory in order to have "a frame of reference that will create some order of what otherwise might appear to be a disorganized situation that invites something of the order of trial and error behavior" (Coladarci and Getzels, 1956, p. 8).

Campbell, Charters, and Gregg, in writing about the need for collaboration between the researcher and the practitioner, contrast the nature of the worlds of the administrator and the scientist as follows: "The administrator's world is . . . the complex, baffling world of the here and now. It is the unique concrete situation" (1960, p. 177).

Zeigler, in advocating the need for the teaching of human relations and

Gordon A. Olafson is from the University of Windsor, Windsor, Ontario, Canada.

administration in physical education, states that "the administrator must possess a certain store of facts about the nature of his work" (1958, p. 77). Commenting further on this point, he notes that

> the important qualities are the ability to work cooperatively with others; the ability to think and act responsibly; and the ability to provide an "atmosphere" where co-workers will have the opportunities to work effectively and with true satisfaction as members of the group (1958, p. 77).

The department chairman, then, must provide for this by means of sound management practice in order to direct and control the internal social pressures which arise in the course of his tenure as an administrator (Selznick, 1957, p. 8).

Although considerable research in this area has been completed in the past, the motivation has been related "more to the solution of immediate or localized problems" (Spaeth, 1967, p. 151) than toward the systematic evolution of a body of knowledge "rooted in academic theory and research" (Gross, 1964, p. 838). The work of Spaeth previously noted, and a more recent investigation by Olafson, concluded that there was an apparent lack of theoretical orientation in the research design and in the interpretation of the findings of many of these studies. Both investigations supported the need for more empirically oriented studies in the administration of physical education and athletics.

An important aspect of the broad field of administration is the study of leadership behavior. Early research conducted almost exclusively by psychologists and social psychologists dealt with nonschool environments and therefore has questionable application to the field of administration in physical education.

The study of leadership has historically passed through two phases—the trait approach and, more recently, the situational approach. Following the impetus generated by the Ohio State leadership studies, several investigators have concentrated upon the observable leader behavior rather than on the innate-capacity approach. In order to systematically direct the study of leader behavior, Halpin devised a paradigm that "centers upon the behavior of the officially designated administrators of formal organizations" (Halpin, 1966, p. 27). The paradigm is predicated upon two strategic assumptions, one of which is most relevant to this study, namely "that greater strides will be made . . . if research efforts are focused upon the behavior of administrators rather than upon either administrative behavior or the totality referred to as 'administration' " (Halpin, 1966, p. 26).

Employing Halpin's suggestion, the study focusing upon the situational determinants of administrative behavior at two different levels of higher education was one of a series attempting to add to a body of knowledge in the administrative theory of physical education.

Background and Related Literature

BACKGROUND

Institutions of higher education historically have been bypassed as laboratories for investigation in the field of administration. McConnell noted the absence of this type of research in the following statement: "So little research has been done on how colleges and universities are organized and administered, it is fair to say in fact that the field has not been touched" (McConnell, 1963, p. 113). Corson supported this claim by noting that all phases of university governance need to be investigated (1960, p. 185). Paralleling this point of view, Doi suggested that "college and university administrators still remain untouchable as objects for systematic research ... (1965, p. 352), and further that "the organization and administration of colleges and universities are virgin territories for research" (1965, p. 357).

Thus, the department chairman was selected for investigation because he is a key administrative officer who holds an intermediary position between the dean and his own faculty. Further directing the focus of this investigation, Quick has noted that "... more research is needed in the area of leadership and university administration, especially concerning the role of the department chairman" (1966, p. 131). He also concluded that "it is not known what kind of men are being attracted to positions of leadership in higher education" (1966, p. 131).

If this is the case, how then can administrators be prepared to work in institutions of higher education when so little is known about the nature of the position to be filled? As the need for qualified administrators becomes more apparent, universities and colleges charged with the preparation of administrators should become more "aware of the type of leadership situations into which the individual should be successively guided..." (Fiedler, 1967, p. 250). Although "leadership is not currently predictable, the recruitment and selection of future administrators can be effective only when we can also specify the relevant components of the situation for which the leader is being recruited" (Fiedler, 1967, p. 250).

It is the contention of this author, therefore, that because of the unique role that the two-year college has in higher education, the administrator who is being prepared to work at that level should have some special educational preparation to improve his understanding of the situation in which he will be operating. In support of the necessity to study specific situations, Campbell asks, "How do the variables in one situation compare with the variables in another?" (1957, p. 267). That a basic theory of administration should underly this application to specific situations is emphasized by Thompson:

The administrator uses theory as a basis for deriving answers or approaches to specific situations; he seeks principles capable of guiding the application of general notions to specific situations (1957, p. 21).

The complicated nature of a department need not deter the investigator from selecting a specific aspect to be studied. As Gross noted, "knowing everything about a department would be self-defeating" (1964, p. 853). To minimize the possibility of error variance, the department chairman was selected for investigation, rather than attempting to study the department in its entirety. His behavior is a function of the organizational situation in which he is placed and thus can be analyzed based upon the perceptions of the persons with whom he interacts. Pierce and Merrill suggest that "the process of leadership can be analyzed and understood only when consideration is given to the ... situation in which it arises" (1957, p. 333). Simon, one of the pioneers of the human relations era, supports the need to study the situational leadership role by stating, "The first task of administrative theory is to develop a set of concepts that will permit the description, in terms relevant to the theory, of administrative situations" (1957, p. 37). In supporting the situational and behavorial nature of leadership, Petrullo and Bass point out that "leadership is a function of the situation and its requirements and the followers and their expectations as well as the qualities of the leader" (1961, p. xxii).

How then does the department chairman's leader behavior at two levels of higher education vary when viewed by those with whom he interacts? Are both levels of education similar with respect to a set of perceived department dimensions? The extent to which an administrator's behavior "in different situations (i.e., in different school systems ...) varies is an empirical question that still remains to be answered" (Halpin, 1959, p. 11).

Throughout the literature in administration, a common theme persists that indicates a need to formulate a theoretical basis for the study of administration. Studies of the leadership aspect of administration have thus far had little specific application to either physical education or related educational situations. As a means of ordering future administrative research, Campbell proposed that "it seems highly desirable that further research on situational variables be related to some overall conceptualization ... a more definitive conceptual model may be the one presented in Chapter V" (1957, p. 261). The model to which Campbell referred is Halpin's paradigm for research on administrator behavior. Employing the paradigm, Spaeth conducted an exhaustive review of doctoral dissertations completed between 1940 and 1966. Using the paradigm as a means of classification, Spaeth recommended that

> the behavioral approach to administrative research be used ... to study the administration of physical education and athletics (e.g., through the replication of studies involving leader behavior, organizational climates, and role expectations) in order to develop a more

scientific basis for professional preparation and practice (1967, p. 153).

As a follow-up study to her own work, she suggested that

> perhaps the approach with the greatest immediate potential for physical education and athletics would be the replication of studies in educational administration using standardized data-gathering instruments such as the *Leader Behavior Description Questionnaire*.... This approach would provide data specific to physical education and athletics but having a sound empirical basis (1967, p. 152).

This study incorporated the suggestion of Spaeth that

> any plan for behavior research must also take into consideration its potential subjects—the administrators and staff members of departments of physical education and athletics

by using the department chairman, his superior, and his subordinates to comment on the leader behavior of the physical education administrator (1967, p. 153).

Assuming that the results of the investigation indicate agreement concerning the perceived leadership behavior within and/or between each level of higher education, further insight would be obtained which may contribute to the developing body of knowledge in physical education administration, and which may contribute to the formation of a sound empirical basis for the structuring of curricula in this area.

RELATED LITERATURE

Throughout man's history, noted philosophers and scholars from Confucius to Bertrand Russell have at some time attempted to analyze the differential exercise of power of individuals over individuals. Since the turn of the century, the field of administration, as a means of organization and influence, has gradually begun to evolve a body of knowledge based upon empirically verified research. Lipham, in writing about the emergence of administration, noted that "paralleling if not antedating the recent development of administrative theory has been the unprecedented concern with the study of leadership" (1964, p. 119). Andrews suggests that the terms "leadership" and "administration" very closely parallel each other in meaning and, as further support for this contention, states:

> No matter what other abilities an administrator may have, it is widely recognized that if he does not show leadership he cannot be

an effective administrator. Thus it is apparent that skill in leadership is considered to be one of the most important ingredients of administrative success (1958, p. 15).

Thompson has suggested that the development of an empirically based body of knowledge in the science of administration should be predicated upon an understanding of the behavior of the administrator. Thus, the remainder of this section will focus upon brief overviews of (1) the trait and situational approaches to the study of leadership, (2) the theoretical bases of leader behavior, and (3) research which has employed the *Leader Behavior Description Questionnaire.*

Prior to the early 1950s, the personal attributes of the leader were the central focus of leadership research. The trait approach to leadership, as it is known, concentrated upon the identification of the innate potentialities of the leader as contrasted to those of the nonleader. Stogdill, in an extensive review of over one hundred studies, concluded that the person who occupies a leadership position will generally exceed those comprising his member group in terms of intelligence, scholarship, dependability in exercising responsibilities, activity, social participation, and socioeconomic status. As another general conclusion, Stogdill noted a uniformly positive trend toward the possession of the following characteristics: sociability, initiative, persistence, self-confidence, alertness to and insight to situations, cooperativeness, popularity, adaptability, and verbal facility (1948, p. 63). An awareness of the immediate environment has received considerable attention in the literature as a leadership trait. As a general finding, the studies suggested that "alertness to the surrounding environment and understanding of situations are intimately associated with leadership ability...." (Stogdill, 1948, p. 48).

Gibb completed a survey of leadership in which he briefly elaborated upon the earlier work of Stogdill. Using the categories of traits which Stogdill ascribed to the leader, Gibb concluded that there were indications that leaders possessed certain traits such as intelligence, surgency (talkativeness, alertness), dominance, self-confidence, and social participation (1954, p. 889).

The trait approach to the study of leadership eventually led researchers to attempt to relate the traits found in the leader to the group or situational context within which the leader functioned. In recent years, the direction of research in leadership has followed Stogdill's observation that "an adequate analysis of leadership involves not only the study of leaders but also of situations" (1948, p. 65).

A subsequent pattern of leadership research, particularly in administration, has, as Gibb suggested, focused attention on the nature and distribution of behavior by which the administrator functions within the context of his group (1969, p. 205). Thus the possession of a set of traits will not, as claimed by previous research findings, guarantee that a leader will be successful in a particular position.

The necessary and sufficient traits for a particular leadership position will thus be related to the context within which the leader must operate. The trait approach is predicated upon the fact that "leadership is a function of the physical, intellectual, or personality traits of the leader" (Andrews, 1958, p. 15). The situational approach evolved as researchers who were searching for universal leadership traits discovered instances when the characteristics of leaders varied from one situation to another. Thus, this approach has now taken precedence and will be briefly reviewed in the following section.

The situational approach to leadership, which is predicated upon the notion that leadership is a product of the environment in which it is exhibited, has been postulated by a number of researchers (Campbell, 1957, pp. 228-68). Hemphill, in analyzing the situational determinants of leader behavior, made two assumptions relevant to the situational nature of leadership, namely that

> leadership is the behavior of an individual directing group activities and that adequacy of leadership is an evaluation of the correspondence between the individual's behavior and the behavior demanded by the situation (1949, pp. 5-6).

Stogdill supports this contention when he states, "Leadership must be conceived in terms of the interaction of variables which are in a constant state of flux" (1948, p. 64).

Halpin in his study of school superintendents noted that "the behavior of leaders varies widely from one leadership situation to another" (1956, p. 10). In outlining the nature of the problem under study, he noted:

> On the whole, current research appears to support the "situational" in contrast to the "trait" approach in the study of leader behavior. Nothing in the findings of the research with the Leader Behavior Description Questionnaire thus far contradicts this "situational" position (1956, p. 10).

The situational approach parallels the behavioral approach to administration as outlined by Gordon. Recognizing the human nature of administration, the behavioral approach emphasis is on people and how they behave in organizations. The nature of this approach is summed up when Gordon states:

> One of the essential characteristics of the behavioral approach is the insistence on observable and verifiable phenomena that may serve, at least in part, as evidence for anything to be recognized as knowledge, principle, or finding. For example, instead of asking about a man's traits, ... the behavioralist is more likely to ask—what does he do?—what does he say?—what does he not say? (1966, p. 12).

The application of the situational approach and the behavioral approach to the study of leader behavior is based upon the structure of the interpersonal relations within a group. The social interaction inherent in both approaches is reflected in the interdependence of the administrator's behavior and the behavior demanded by the situation, the followers, and their expectations. The goals set by the administrator and his method of achievement of the goals are predicated upon the pattern of interrelationships among the group members and administrator. Thus, leader behavior can then be measured in terms of the number of influence acts which an individual exerts or the number of leadership actions in which he engages.

The focus of research on the behavior of the executive or administrator grew out of the notion that "we will greatly increase our understanding of leadership phenomena if we abandon the notion of leadership as a trait, and concentrate instead upon an analysis of 'the behavior of leaders' " (Halpin, 1966, p. 81). As previously noted, the behavior of the administrator is in part dependent upon the situation within which it is exhibited. Halpin succinctly outlined the behavioral approach when he stated:

> First of all, it focuses upon observed behavior rather than upon a posited capacity inferred from this behavior. No presuppositions are made about a one-to-one relationship between leader behavior and an underlying capacity or potentiality presumably determinative of this behavior. By the same token, no a priori assumptions are made that the leader behavior which a leader exhibits in one group situation will be manifested in other group situations.... Nor does the ... term suggest that this behavior is determined either innately or situationally. Either determinant is possible, as is any combination of the two, but the concept of leader behavior does not itself predispose us to accept one in opposition to the other (1956, p. 12).

The focus of the behavioral approach is upon the officially designated leader of the organization and does not deal with the distribution of leadership within the informal nature of the organization under investigation. The leader's behavior is generally measured only in relation to the specified formal organization of the institution.

Thus far, the development of the study of leader behavior has relied upon the use of several theoretical models. The interrelationship of meanings attached to each paradigm rests with the researcher as he attempts to relate an empirical investigation to a particular theoretical framework. Two of the most frequently used models include Halpin's paradigm for research on administrator behavior (1966) and Morris and Seeman's paradigm for the study of leadership (1950, pp. 149-55). The whole design of both of these paradigms poses, as the major problem, the discovery of the relation of group and individual factors to differentials in leader behavior.

As a consequence of this paradigm, numerous monographs and publications on leadership behavior have been produced by the Ohio State Bureau of Business Research, some of which will be reviewed in the next section. Instruments such as the *Organizational Climate Description Questionnaire (OCDQ)*, the *Principal Behavior Description Questionnaire (PBDQ)*, the *Responsibility, Authority,* and *Delegation Scales (RAD Scales),* and the *Leader Behavior Description Questionnaire (LBDQ),* have been designed to observe and analyze the behavior of leaders in highly organized groups such as the navy, industry, and education. One direction the research has taken has been to focus upon various types of groups and individual factors which relate to leader behavior. The combinations which exist in the model will become more evident if the reader consults the original article by Morris and Seeman.

Shartle revised the Morris and Seeman paradigm in 1957 by developing a model for predicting organizational behavior. Based upon the premise that individuals display differences in behavior in organizations, Shartle suggested "we assume that part of individual behavior can be accounted for by the more stable or more repetitious events that occur in the organization" (1958, p. 79). Because of the constant fluctuation within organizations, the following model is a means of ordering the research to serve as a basis for future study:

Independent antecedent variables

1. Value patterns
2. Situational patterns
3. Measures of aptitude, knowledge, and skill
4. Measures of personality and interest
5. Measures of physical energy and capacity
6. Past individual and organizational performance

Dependent variables

Performance in the organization, including:

1. Decisions made
2. Ratings of performance
3. Measures of attitude change
4. Objective measures of performance
5. Tenure and mobility
6. Work patterns
7. Leader behavior dimensions
8. Sociometric ratings
9. Learning behavior

Illustrative Variables in a Model for
Predicting Organizational Behavior (1958, p. 81)

The ability to predict leader behavior is the central theme of the model as proposed. Symbolically the model can be represented by the summation of each of the independent and the dependent variables, taken separately or in combination.

As a result of the paradigm developed by Morris and Seeman, and its revision by Shartle, numerous areas of opportunity for the study of leadership were suggested which have led to widespread use of the *Leader Behavior Description Questionnaire (LBDQ)*. (A review of the research which has employed this instrument can be found in the author's dissertation.)

The *LBDQ* as a research instrument has been used almost exclusively in education and in the military. No comparable research in either physical education or athletics was reported in the *LBDQ* literature reviewed.

Research Methodology and Techniques

The primary objective was to measure the leader behavior of the physical education chairman at two levels of higher education—the university and the junior college. A second objective of the study was to relate the significant leader behavior subscales to a set of departmental dimensions.

The method used to gather information for the achievement of these objectives was the descriptive survey method, which provides a means of identifying present conditons and, as a research tool, "is more realistic than the experiment in that it investigates phenomena in their natural setting" (Mouly, 1963, p. 234).

In order to describe the leader behavior of the department chairman, the *LBDQ* XII was employed as a means of assembling data which would "include present facts or current conditions concerning the nature of a group of persons" (Good, 1963, p. 192). In addition to the *LBDQ*, descriptive instruments were also used to identify the dimensions of the physical education department and to classify the background of the respondents.

SELECTION OF INSTITUTIONS

A letter and a prospectus of the study were sent to physical education department chairmen at all Big Ten universities, requesting permission to include their departments in the study. The junior colleges were selected on the basis of having met each of the following criteria:

1. A member of the National Junior College Athletic Association
2. An accredited member of the North Central Association of Colleges and Secondary Schools
3. An enrollment of at least 1,000 students
4. A location within the states served by the universities included in the study—Illinois, Indiana, Iowa, Michigan, Minnesota, Ohio, and Wisconsin.

From a possible total of ninety-eight junior colleges listed in The *Blue Book of Junior College Athletics,* thirty-two institutions met all four of the above criteria. The physical education department chairmen at these thirty-two junior colleges were sent a prospectus advising them of the research project and a letter requesting permission to include their department in the study. The department chairman was also asked to designate his immediate superior and to supply a list of his faculty. A follow-up procedure resulted in a total of nine universities and thirteen junior colleges granting permission to include their institutions in the study.

SELECTION OF RESPONDENTS

The manual for administering the *LBDQ* XII suggests that a "minimum of four respondents per leader is desirable, and additional respondents beyond ten do not increase significantly the stability of the index scores. Six or seven respondents per leader would be a good standard" (Halpin, 1963, p. 12). In addition to the department chairman, two additional groups were employed, a group of immediate superiors and a group of subordinates.

SELECTION OF MEASURING INSTRUMENTS

The *LBDQ* XII was chosen because it was designed to

> describe the behavior of the leader, or leaders, in any type of group or organization, provided the followers have had an opportunity to observe the leader in action as a leader of their group (Stogdill, 1963, p. 1).

In addition to this survey instrument, the *Departmental Dimensions Questionnaire,* developed by the author, was used, based upon the identification of paired key-word concepts from *The Academic Marketplace* and *The Organization Man.*

SURVEY PROCEDURE

Each institution and respondent was given a four-character identification number by an anonymous recorder. The coding system was used by the anonymous recorder to identify each respondent, to ensure anonymity, and to facilitate the follow-up procedure. This was followed by a second reminder two weeks later. Because of the importance to the design of the study of responses from the superiors and administrators, it was necessary to send a second folder and a third follow-up letter to a number of superiors and administrators who had not replied to the earlier requests.

DATA TRANSPOSITION

As the returns were received, the raw score data from the *Departmental Dimensions Questionnaire (DDQ)* and the *Substantive Information on Respon-*

dent were transferred onto the Digitek Optical Scanning Utility Form 4203. At the same time, the *LBDQ* responses on the Digitek score sheets were also checked for completeness.

SCORING THE LEADER BEHAVIOR DESCRIPTION QUESTIONNAIRE—FORM XII AND THE DEPARTMENTAL DIMENSIONS QUESTIONNAIRE

The *LBDQ* is composed of twelve subscales, each of which is summed independently. In completing the *LBDQ* XII, the respondent recorded his selected choice on the Digitek answer sheet, rather than on the test booklet, by responding to five columns: 5 = Always; 4 = Often; 3 = Occasionally; 2 = Seldom; 1 = Never. The instrument was scored according to the above format with the exception of twenty starred items which were scored in the reverse direction. The responses were then transferred to an IBM card.

The scoring system for the *DDQ* is based upon a seven-point scale (one through seven). The direction of the respondent's choice on each paired item indicates his interpretation of the significance (or lack of significance) of each concept within his physical education department. Each respondent's dimensions scores were transferred to the same IBM card that was used for the *LBDQ* subscales.

The Digitek score sheets containing the raw score data for the *LBDQ* and the *DDQ* were also scored by means of the optical scanner at the instructional resources office, University of Illinois, Champaign-Urbana campus.

SUBSTANTIVE INFORMATION ON RESPONDENTS

The transposed information derived from the *Substantive Information on Respondents* was also scanned at the instructional resources office. The data gathered by this form was used only to classify the characteristics of the respondents.

STATISTICAL ANALYSIS

For the comparison of leader behavior between the universities and junior colleges, a 2 X 3 (X12) factorial design was used. The design employs two levels of higher education (the universities and the junior colleges); three levels of respondents within each level of higher education (the immediate superior, the department chairman, and the faculty); and the twelve subscales of the *LBDQ*. A 2 X 3 (X9) factorial design was used to test the significance of the nine departmental dimensions.

The major statistical procedure employed in this study was multivariate analysis (MANOVA) which was modified by Wardrop at the University of Illinois, Champaign-Urbana campus. Using the summed raw scores for each of the twelve subscales and the nine paired dimensions, and taking into account the unequal number of respondents in each category, the means for each respondent group within each level of higher education were tested for the significance of their differences by using MANOVA. With the levels of higher education as independent variables, and the *LBDQ* XII subscales and the departmental dimensions as the dependent variables, the main purpose of MANOVA was "to determine how and to what extent the independent variables explain or predict the responses of the subject represented in the dependent variables" (Bock and Haggard 1968, p. 102).

By treating all the dependent variables as a unit, a single probability statement can be designed to serve all variables which is not the case in univariate statistical tests. A univariate analysis which was a subroutine of the MANOVA program was also computed, however, to test the significance of each leader behavior subscale and each pair of departmental dimensions. A basic premise of multivariate tests is that the sample statistics "take into account the correlations between variables and have a known exact sampling distribution from which the required probabilities can be obtained" (Bock and Haggard, 1968, p. 102).

Discriminate function analysis, a specific MANOVA test, was also employed, "to determine the coefficients of the linear combination of variables which best discriminates between groups of subjects, in the sense that the between groups sum of squares is a maximum with respect to the within groups sum of squares" (Bock and Haggard, 1968, p. 117). Based upon this analysis, subjects were selected or classified according to their educational level via-à-vis leader behavior. By including discriminate analysis in MANOVA, it can be used as an aid to characterize the differences between groups (i.e., the superior, the department chairman, and the faculty), rather than as a device for classifying subjects. Discriminate function analysis determines the linear combination of variables most sensitive to the departure from the proposed null hypothesis. Bartlett's Chi Square Test of the significance of successive canonical variates was computed for each discriminant function comparison.

To measure the relationship between the dimensions of leader behavior and the dimensions of the department, a 9 × 12 matrix using the Pearson Product Moment coefficient of correlation was computed.

All statistical analyses were completed on the IBM 360/75 computer at the University of Illinois, Champaign-Urbana, Statistical Service Unit. For the purpose of the investigation, differences from the 10 percent level to the 1 percent level will be considered significant.

Findings and Conclusions

Administrative research, in fields other than physical education, has increasingly emphasized the empirical method whereby testable hypotheses represent the basis for study. Similar research in physical education administration is essential to the development of a body of knowledge in this area. Such empirical studies must further be integrated so that each contributes sequentially to this overall development. The central figure providing the theme for these investigations should, in this investigator's opinion, be the department chairman, as he represents the link between his superiors and subordinates. It is often through him that interaction between the other two groups occurs. No prior assumptions can be made, however, concerning the administrator's behavior in one situation as compared to another. Thus this determination must be made scientifically and a deductive approach applied to the results. The researcher's primary task is then to describe the behavior of the leader in various situations in empirically verified dimensions using the following null hypotheses as direction:

1. There will be no significant difference between the perceived leader behavior, as measured by the *LBDQ XII*, of the university and junior college physical education department chairmen.
2. There will be no significant difference in the description of leader behavior as measured by the *LBDQ XII* and as perceived by each of the three groups of respondents.
3. There will be no significant difference between the two levels of education in the perception of the dimensions of the department as measured by the *DDQ*.
4. There will be no significant difference in the description of the departmental dimensions by each of the three groups of respondents.
5. There will be no significant relationship between the perceived departmental dimensions and the leader behavior subscales.
6. There will be no significant interaction between each of the three respondent groups for the *LBDQ XII*.
7. There will be no significant interaction between each of the three respondent groups for the *DDQ*.

FINDINGS

Departmental Dimensions. The overall comparison of the university and junior responses to the *DDQ* yielded a significant MANOVA statistical difference at less than the 1 percent level between the overall university and overall junior college returns. The dimensions of teaching-research, student-content orientation, theoretical-practical orientation, coaching-teaching, broad-specialized curriculum, community-professional service, and competition-cooperation were all significant at less than the 1 percent level. Results of the discriminant analysis indicated that the university physical education department emphasized research, a specialized curriculum, and service to professional organizations, whereas the junior college physical education department emphasized both teaching and coaching. Based upon the significant multivariate F, hypothesis number 3 (above) can be rejected because the university and junior college physical education departments were shown to exhibit different departmental dimensions.

The superiors, faculty, and department chairmen did not differ significantly within each of their respective groups when contrasted with each other and thus hypothesis number 4 is accepted. Only two paired dimensions, coaching-teaching and administrative decisions, yielded differences significant at less than 10 percent. The multivariate test for the interactive effect of the three respondent groups was not statistically significant, and thus hypothesis number 6 is accepted.

Leader Behavior. The leader behavior of the department chairman was perceived to be significantly different for the university level and for the junior college level which supports the rejection of hypothesis number 1 and acceptance of its alternative. Five subscales—initiating structure, role assumption, integration, and superior orientation—were significant at less than the 5 percent level and one subscale, representation, approached significance at the 10 percent level. Based upon the discriminant function analysis, the university respondents tended to emphasize demand reconciliation, persuasiveness, tolerance of freedom, and production emphasis, whereas the junior college respondents perceived the department chairman as emphasizing those subscales which were mentioned above as being statistically significant.

A multivariate comparison of the three groups of respondents yielded a significant difference at less than the 5 percent level with the greatest difference occurring between the superior-faculty groups, and thus hypothesis number 2 must be rejected. Superiors perceived the department chairmen as being associated with consideration, productive emphasis, and role assumption, whereas the faculty emphasized the subscales of demand reconciliation and persuasiveness. No significant difference was found between the department chairmen and the faculty.

The multivariate test of the interactive effect of the three respondent groups was not statistically significant. Hypothesis number 7 is therefore accepted.

In testing the possible relationship between the *DDQ* and the *LBDQ* subscales, thirty-two correlations were statistically significant. Thus hypothesis number 5 can be partially rejected.

CONCLUSIONS

The results of the study appear to support a situational and behavioral approach to research in administrative behavior. The perceived leader behavior and the perceived departmental dimensions in the two situations studied—the university and the junior college—were shown to be significantly different.

Several university superiors and faculty members indicated a desire not to participate in the study. Of the thirty-two junior colleges invited to participate, only thirteen department chairmen gave permission for their institutions to be included in the study. Thus one may conclude that a degree of sensitivity to this type of investigation is present within these two levels of higher education.

The leader behavior of the physical education administrators has been shown to be somewhat different at the junior college and university levels of higher education. Within each level of higher education, there was considerable agreement among the three groups of respondents as to the nature of the physical education department. The relationship between the leader behavior and departmental dimensions is inconclusive in that less than one-third of the correlations were found to be statistically significant.

In relation to the null hypotheses posed for this investigation, and based upon the subsequent statistical treatments, the following conclusions seem plausible:

1. The junior college and university departments of physical education have different departmental dimensions.
2. The superiors, faculty, and department chairmen at the junior college level and at the university level each perceived their respective department's dimensions in a consistent pattern.
3. The overall leader behavior of the department chairmen at both levels of higher education was perceived to follow a consistent pattern.
4. The superiors as a group perceived the leader behavior of the department chairmen differently than did the faculty as a group.

Implications for the Practicing Administrator

In general, the findings of this investigation support the situational and behavioral approaches to the study of administration. Assuming that this factor can be considered to approach the level of a generalization, the practicing administrator, who elects to work at either level of higher education, should prepare himself for that role by studying the complexity of the junior college or university physical education environment of a harmonious and efficient administrative unit. However, with the expanding body of knowledge in the area of administration, and with specialization so prevalent in large organizations, it is becoming increasingly more important for the practicing administrator to better understand the theoretical complexities of modern management techniques.

The selection of the administrator will in the future demand an expanded knowledge of the situation in which he or she is to function. An awareness of the unique departmental characteristics, of desired administrator behavior, and of the components of micro- and macroorganizations will result in a more efficient and satisfying administrative setting.

General Bibliography

Andrews J. H. M., "Recent Research in Leadership," *Canadian Education and Research Digest*, 13 (September 1958), 15-24.

Blue Book of Junior College Athletics, The. Cleveland: Akron Engraving Company, 1969.

Bock, R. Darrell, and Ernest A. Haggard, "The Use of Multivariate Analysis in Behavioral Research," in *Handbook of Measurement and Assessment in Behavioral Sciences,* ed. Dean K. Whitlaw, pp. 100-142. Reading, Mass.: Addison-Wesley Publishing Co, 1968.

Campbell, Roald F., "Situational Factors in Educational Administration," in *Administrative Behavior in Education,* ed. Roald F. Campbell and Russell T. Gregg, pp. 228-68. New York: Harper & Row, 1957.

Campbell Roald, W. W. Charters, and William T. Gregg, "Improving Administrative Theory and Practice: Three Essential Roles," in *Administrative Theory as a Guide to Action,* ed. Roald F. Campbell and James M. Lipham, pp. 171-90. Danville, Ill.: The Interstate Printers and Publishers, 1960.

Caplow, Theodore, and Reece J. McGee, *The Academic Marketplace.* New York: Anchor Books, 1965.

Coladarci, Arthur P., and Jacob W. Getzels, *The Use of Theory in Educational Administration.* Monograph no. 5. Stanford, Cal.: Stanford University Press, 1955.

Corson, J. J., *Governance of Colleges and Universities.* New York: McGraw-Hill Book Co., 1960.

Doi, James I., "Organization, Administration, Finance, Facilities," *Review of Educational Research,* 35 (October 1965), 347-60.

Fayol, Henri, *General and Industrial Management.* Cited in Bertram M. Gross, *The Managing of Organizations.* New York: The Free Press, 1964.

Fiedler, Fred E., *A Theory of Leadership Effectiveness.* New York: McGraw-Hill Book Co., 1967.

Gibb, Cecil A., "Leadership," in *Handbook of Social Psychology,* vol. 2, part 4, ed. G. Lindzey. Reading Mass.: Addison-Wesley Publishing Co. Inc., 1954.

Gordon, Paul J., "Transcend the Current Debate on Administrative Theory," *Hospital Administration,* 11 (Spring 1966), 6-23.

Gross, Bertram M., *The Managing of Organizations.* New York: The Free Press, 1964.

Halpin, Andrew W., *The Leadership Behavior of School Superintendents.* Chicago: Midwest Administration Center, The University of Chicago, 1956.

―――――, *Theory and Research in Administration.* New York: The Macmillan Co., 1966.

Hemphill, J. K., *Situational Factors in Leadership.* Monograph no. 32. Columbus, Ohio: The Bureau of Educational Research, The Ohio State University, 1949.

Lipham, James M., "Leadership and Administration," *Behavioral Science and Educational Administration,* sixty-third yearbook of the National Society for the Study of Education, pp. 119-41. Chicago: The University of Chicago Press, 1964.

McConnell, T. R., "Needed Research in College and University Organization and Administration," in *The Study of Academic Administration,* pp. 113-32. Boulder, Colorado: Western Interstate Commission for Higher Education, 1963.

Morris, R. T., and M. Seeman, "The Problem of Leadership: An Interdisciplinary Approach," *American Journal of Sociology,* 56 (1950), 149-55.

Petrullo, Luigi, and Bernard M. Bass, ed., *Leadership and Interpersonal Behavior.* New York: Holt, Rinehart and Winston, 1961.

Pierce, Truman M., and E. C. Merrill, Jr., "The Individual and Administrative Behavior in Education," in *Administrative Behavior in Education,* ed. Roald F. Campbell and Russell T. Gregg, pp. 318-53. New York: Harper & Row, 1957.

Quick, Wendle Randolph, "The University Departmental Chairman: His Role in Patterns of Faculty Selection, Promotion, and Termination." Ph.D. diss., Indiana University, 1966.

Selznick, Phillip P., *Leadership in Administration – A Sociological Interpretation.* Evanston, Ill.: Row, Peterson, and Company, 1957.

Shartle, Carroll L., "A Theoretical Framework for the Study of Behavior in Organizations, in *Administrative Theory in Education,* ed. Andrew Halpin, pp. 73-88. New York: The Macmillan Co., 1958.

Simon, Herbert A., *Administrative Behavior,* 2nd ed. New York: The Macmillan Co., 1957.

Spaeth, Marcia J., "An Analysis of Administrative Research in Physical Education and Athletics in Relation to a Research Paradigm." Ph.D. diss., The University of Illinois, 1967.

Stogdill, Ralph M., *Manual for the Leader Behavior Description Questionnaire Form XII.* Columbus, Ohio: Bureau of Business Research, The Ohio State University, 1963.

Thompson, James D., "Modern Approaches to Theory in Administration," in *Administrative Theory in Education,* ed. Andrew W. Halpin, pp. 20-39. New York: The Macmillan Co., 1967.

Zeigler, Earle F., "Case Method Teaching of Human Relations and Administration in Physical Education and Athletics," in *Sixty-Second Proceedings* of the National College Physical Education Association for Men, pp. 76-80. New York: December 28-30, 1958.

7

Leadership Effectiveness Contingency Model: Implications

Martha Bagley

Introduction

There are many concepts related to the social sciences but none has received more attention in the past several years than that of leadership.[1] "The behavioral sciences are devoting greater time, effort and money to the problems revolving around leadership as a significant phenomenon wherever people are found in organized relationships with each other" (Browne, 1958, p. 417).

There have been a number of studies done concerning leadership but our knowledge in this area is still limited. Of the completed investigations, only a limited number have been concerned with leadership in complex organizational settings. The methods used and conclusions drawn from leadership studies concerned with small, unstructured, randomly selected groups are likely to be of only limited value when transplanted indiscriminately to large, complex, hierarchical organizations (Lipham, 1964, p. 125).

The selection and retention of effective leaders in educational institutions is a continuing problem the goal of which is to be able to predict the consequences of leader-worker behavior in given structured educational situations.

A leadership effectiveness model was developed by Fiedler (1967) that

---

Martha Bagley is from the University of Wisconsin, Milwaukee.
[1] Unpublished doctoral dissertation, University of Illinois, Urbana, Ill., 1972.

incorporated the leader and group in various situational settings. Fiedler's contingency model states that the effectiveness of the group will be contingent upon the matching of leadership style and the degree of favorableness of the group situation for the leader to influence the group members. The favorableness of the group situation is measured by three dimensions: leader-member relations, task structure, and position power. Fiedler assumed that leadership was an influence process and that each of the three dimensions measures one aspect of the situation that determines how much influence the leader would have. Another assumption was that the leader-member relationship is the most important dimension in determining the favorableness of the situation, and that the degree of task structure is the second most important dimension. Based on these assumptions, Fiedler ordered the three dimensions: first, according to whether the leader-member relations were good or poor; second, according to high versus low task structure; and finally, according to relatively strong versus weak position power. The resulting order is reflected in the numbering of cells or octants, with octant I being most favorable and octant VIII being least favorable in this classification system (Fiedler, 1967, pp. 133-51). (See *Figure 1*)

	Leader-Member Relations	Task Structure	Position Power
Octant I	Good	Structured	Strong
Octant II	Good	Structured	Weak
Octant III	Good	Unstructured	Strong
Octant IV	Good	Unstructured	Weak
Octant V	Moderately Poor	Structured	Strong
Octant VI	Moderately Poor	Structured	Weak
Octant VII	Moderately Poor	Unstructured	Strong
Octant VIII	Moderately Poor	Unstructured	Weak

Figure 1. Fiedler's Contingency Model for Interacting Groups

Research studies have tested this model in business organizations, military organizations, small laboratory groups, and industrial organizations (Fiedler, 1967; Hunt, 1966). A small amount of work has been done using Fiedler's model in educational settings (McKague, 1970; Lanaghan, 1972; Wyrick, 1972), none of which applied the model to departments of physical education.

This study used the university educational setting of graduate departments in the United States which offer doctoral degrees in physical education, to test Fiedler's Contingency Model.

DEFINITION OF TERMS

The following definitions are taken from Fiedler (1967).
The Group. A set of individuals who share a common fate, that is, who

are interdependent in the sense that an event which affects one member is likely to affect all. This kind of group is termed "interacting." *Coacting* groups also work together on a common task but each group member does his job relatively independently of other team members. *Task* groups, which are the major concern in the model, are usually a part of a larger social organization. The larger organization has much to do with assigning members to the group, appointing a leader and specifying the task.

The Leader. The member of the group given the task of directing and coordinating task-relevant group activities. He carries the primary responsibility for the work of the group. *Leadership* is an interpersonal situation in which one individual has influence over the other members of the group for the purpose of performing an assigned task. *Leader's effectiveness* is defined in terms of his group's performance on its assigned task. *Leadership style* is the underlying need structure of the leader which motivates his behavior in various leadership situations. Leadership style thus refers to the consistency of goals or needs over different situations.

Background and Related Literature

Approaches to the study of leadership have tended to progress from simple to complex, from examining leadership in terms of a few variables to looking at it with respect to many variables. Early leadership study began with a primary focus on the personality characteristics which make a person a leader. But the yield from this approach was fairly meager and often confused, as Stogdill (1948) and Mann (1959) documented in their surveys of this literature.

Dissatisfaction with the trait approach gave rise to a view of leadership which stressed the characteristics of the group and the situation in which it exists. The main focus of this approach was the study of leaders in different settings, defined especially in terms of different group tasks and group structure. In studying groups, Hemphill (1949) identified fifteen group dimensions with viscidity and hedonic tone correlating more highly with leadership adequacy than did the other dimensions.

It seemed clear from an examination of these studies that only a few of the variables had been tested which should be included in a comprehensive theory of leadership. Sanford advocated an approach based on the assumption that leadership was a function of three interacting yet delineable factors: "(1) the leader and his psychological attributes; (2) the follower with his problems, attitudes, and needs; and (3) the group situation" (Burke, 1964, p. 62).

THE DEVELOPMENT OF FIEDLER'S CONTINGENCY MODEL

In 1951, a series of programmatic studies were started at the University of Illinois Group Effectiveness Research Laboratory by Fred Fiedler and his associates. During many years of research concerning groups, Fiedler sought to clarify the relationships between leadership style, group effectiveness in task performance, and other group properties. The major implication of Fiedler's extensive research was that "leadership is a function of leader-follower relations, the relative power of the leader to enforce sanctions, and the structure of the task—as well as the leader's style" (Sherif and Sherif, 1956, p. 180).

The research in leader behavior was built around a personality or attitude measure that was administered to group leaders. It was called the least-preferred coworker (LPC) score. The LPC score was obtained by asking the leader to think of all the individuals with whom he has ever worked. He then described the person whom he considered to be his least-preferred coworker on several personality attributes. This description was made on an eight-point bipolar adjective checklist, including such items as pleasant-unpleasant, cooperative-uncooperative, helpful-frustrating. The LPC score was obtained by summing the item scores on the scale (Hunt, 1966, pp. 52-54).

The leader who had a high LPC score was considered to be person-oriented and a leader who had a low LPC score was considered to be task-oriented. High LPC leaders tended to be more concerned with establishing good interpersonal relations (consideration), while low LPC leaders tended to be more concerned with the task (initiating structure) (Fiedler, 1967, p. 45).

The use of LPC as an index of leader behavior was consistent with the tradition of viewing leadership in terms of polarized behaviors. Previous research into leader behavior found that leaders tended to be either task-oriented or person-oriented, self-centered or group-centered, in their relations with others (McKague, 1970, pp. 1-14).

Having developed a measure of leader behavior, Fiedler next related types of behavior to measures of group performance. He investigated the effectiveness of leaders who were either high or low on the LPC scale. The various groups studied by Fiedler and his associates differed widely: high school basketball teams, rifle teams, military units in different countries, and work teams in business management, research or production (Fiedler, 1967, and Hunt, 1966).

The results of these studies were indefinite and ambiguous. Most of the studies were interpreted as showing that the direction of the relationship between leader LPC and performance was contingent upon his relations with the members of his group. Also, the relationship between LPC and performance was contingent upon the nature of the group-task situation with which the leader had to deal (Hunt, 1966, p. 60).

A critical evaluation of his research led Fiedler to the following conclusions:

1. A meaningful system for categorizing group task situations would have to be developed.
2. An underlying theoretical model which would integrate the seemingly inconsistent results in his studies would have to be induced.

3. The validity of the model would have to be tested by extensive research (Fiedler, 1965, p. 540).

Fiedler's resulting contingency model stated that the effectiveness of the group would be contingent upon the matching of leadership style and the degree of favorableness of the group situation for the leader to influence the group members. The favorableness of the group situation was measured by three dimensions: leader-member relations (group atmosphere), task structure, and position power. These three dimensions were ordered along a continuum of favorableness to form the eight octants of the model with octant I being the most favorable situation and octant VIII being the least favorable situation. (See *Figure 1.*)

Fiedler next examined the relationship between LPC and performance under each of the octants. By reanalyzing his previous research, he was able to find empirical data showing the relationship between LPC and group performance for all of the octants but one. Based on sixty-three group-task situations representing more than 800 groups which were tested over a fourteen-year period, under very favorable or very unfavorable conditions, there was a negative correlation between leader LPC and group performance. In conditions intermediate in favorableness there was a positive correlation between LPC and performance (Hunt, 1966, pp. 61-65).

Thus, Fiedler's contingency model predicted that the task-oriented type of leadership style would be more effective in group situations which were either very favorable for the leader or which were very unfavorable for the leader. The relationship-oriented leadership style would be more effective in situations which were intermediate in favorableness (Fiedler, 1967).

In 1966, McNamara and McKague used Fiedler's model to study the behavior of elementary and secondary school principals. They were concerned with describing the behavior of principals who scored high or low on the LPC scale. The results of their studies indicated that principals who scored high or low on the LPC scale possessed distinctive behavioral characteristics. The low LPC principals, whether of elementary or secondary schools, tended to be system-oriented in their behavior and were directed to the attainment of a high level of output. They did not, however, ignore the personal factors which affect productivity (McKague, 1970).

McKague (1970) also tested the power of group atmosphere (GA) as an intervening variable between LPC scores and certain behaviors and attitudes of teachers. In the schools where the behavior of the principal was directive and managing, the morale of teachers tended to be high and their degree of disengagement low, provided that the leadership of the principal was considered acceptable to the teachers. McKague concluded that the degree to which the staff of a school accepted the behavior of the principal had a significant effect on the relationship between the principal's leadership style and teacher behaviors and attitudes. He also found that low LPC principals were associated with the most desirable behaviors and attitudes on the part of teachers. McKague did not take into consideration the variables of task structure and position power.

Wyrick (1972) used forty-four graduate departments in the University of Illinois to test the contingency model. He combined situational factors of leadership (group atmosphere, formalization, and position power) with LPC. The effectiveness measures were departmental output, satisfaction, and faculty perceptions. The results did not give consistent endorsement to the model, but partial support was given to the thesis that leader influence was related to the leadership favorability continuum.

Lanaghan (1972) investigated the applicability to the elementary school situation of Fiedler's contingency model in sixty-five elementary schools. This was the first study to test the model in its entirety in an educational setting. The situational variables (group atmosphere, position power, and task structure) were used to place the schools in the various octants of the model. Leaders' LPC scores were correlated with effectiveness measures. The effectiveness measures were Likert and Likert's *Profile of a School* and three global measures of teacher's perception. No evidence was found to indicate that the model was applicable to the elementary school. Lanaghan concluded that the relations-oriented principal was more likely to be effective in the elementary school.

Research Methodology and Techniques

The basic design of this study involved the application of Fiedler's leadership effectiveness contingency model to university graduate departments of physical education in the United States offering doctoral degrees in physical education. It was necessary to obtain data concerning the variables outlined by the contingency model. They were (1) least-preferred coworker score (LPC), (2) leader-member relations (group atmosphere), (3) task structure, (4) position power of the leader, and (5) effectiveness measures.

Five effectiveness measures were utilized and correlated with the least-preferred coworker (LPC) measure in the favorableness situation, intermediate favorableness situation, and unfavorableness situation of the model.

The departments that were asked to participate in the study were those in the United States which offered a doctorate in physical education as listed in the latest *Directory of Professional Preparation Institutions* published by the American Association for Health, Physical Education, and Recreation (1966). Twenty-four departments (70.5 percent of those known to be offering specific doctoral degrees in physical education) participated in the study. A total of 293 questionnaires was sent to the graduate faculty members of the participating departments. Two hundred questionnaires (68 percent) were returned.

LEAST-PREFERRED COWORKER MEASURE (LPC)

The LPC measure is a semantic differential form using a series of bipolar adjective scales in describing the person with whom one can work least well. Leaders who score high on the LPC index (perceive their least-preferred coworker in a relatively favorable manner) are more permissive, considerate and interested in developing good interpersonal relations. Leaders who score low on the LPC index (describe their least-preferred coworker in very unfavorable terms) are more controlling, managing, and task oriented in their relations with others (Fiedler, 1967, p. 45).

In terms of group effectiveness, Fiedler's data indicated that the task-oriented (low LPC) leadership style was more effective in group situations that were very favorable or very unfavorable for the leader. The relations-oriented (high LPC) leadership style was more effective in situations which were intermediate in favorableness (Fiedler, 1967, p. 45).

The department chairman's esteem for his least-preferred coworker was measured using Fiedler's LPC questionnaire.

GROUP ATMOSPHERE MEASURE (LEADER-MEMBER RELATIONS)

The leader-member relations score can be obtained by asking the leader to rate the group atmosphere. This score indicates the degree to which the leader feels accepted by the group and relaxed in his role. The department chairman's rating of group atmosphere was measured using Fiedler's bipolar adjective scales with ten eight-point items. The contingency model requires the group atmosphere scores to be divided into "good" and "moderately poor" scores. The median score of the participating departments was used as the dividing point. Above the median was considered as "good" leader-member relations and at the median or below was considered as "moderately poor" leader-member relations. This was consistent with Fiedler's method of dividing the GA scores.

TASK STRUCTURE MEASURE

Task structure is the degree to which the task requirements are known and understood by the group, the degree to which the task can be solved by a variety of procedures. In measuring task structure, four scales or dimensions of Shaw's system for classification of tasks were used. They are decision verifiability, goal clarity, goal-path multiplicity, and solution specificity. Each of these four dimensions was rated by the faculty members on an eight-point scale. A mean score was derived for each department. The contingency model requires the task-structure scores to be divided into "structured" and "unstructured" tasks. The mid-point of the possible range was used as the dividing point which was consistent with Fiedler's method of dividing the scores. For supplementary analyses, the task structure scores were also divided into "structured" and "unstructured" tasks by using the median score of the departments, which was consistent with the method of dividing the group atmosphere scores.

POSITION-POWER MEASURE

Position power is the degree to which the position itself enables the leader to get his group members to accept his direction and leadership. Each faculty member's rating of the position power of the department chairman was measured using Fiedler's position-power index instrument consisting of seventeen true-false statements. A mean score was derived for each department. The contingency model requires the position-power scores to be divided into "strong" and "weak" position power. This was done using the mid-point of the possible range which was consistent with Fiedler's method of dividing the scores. For supplementary analyses, the position-power scores were also divided into strong and weak by using the median of the group as the dividing point which was consistent with the division of group-atmosphere scores and task-structure scores.

EFFECTIVENESS MEASURES

Most of Fiedler's research concerned groups that provided easily acceptable production or success records which were used as criteria for group effectiveness. The outcomes, benefits, or effects of education are seldom specified in terms which can be evaluated.

The quality of a university or a department is difficult to appraise. In lieu of definite, tangible evidence of quality, there exists a tendency to equate quantity with quality. Number of faculty publications, volumes in the library, salary levels, degrees granted, etc., are used and accepted as indications of quality. The departments that are regarded as really good are those that demonstrate an active and recent output of research publications, graduate students, receipt of federal monies, and receipt of fellowships from national organizations (Dressel, Johnson, and Marcus, 1970). "In an operational sense, quality is someone's subjective assessment, for there is no way of objectively measuring what is in essence an attribute of value." Lacking agreed-upon units for precise measurement, we can at present only approximate an elusive entity (Cartter, 1966, p. 4).

The effectiveness of the participating departments was determined by the following criteria:

First-Job Index. The first-job index, as proposed by Fiedler and Biglan (1969), is an index to be used to evaluate the performance of academic departments granting doctoral degrees. The index is based on the rated quality of the job a student obtains after receiving his doctorate. "We assume that by and large an institution will offer a position to the most qualified man it can find and that a job candidate will accept the most desirable position which he is offered" (Fiedler and Biglan, 1969, p. 2). Accepting this assumption it is possible to estimate the department's quality by the type of jobs it is able to get for its students.

A list of each department's last fifteen doctoral graduates (or the graduates of the last five years) in physical education and the first job they obtained after receiving the doctorate was obtained from the department chairmen. These jobs were then listed on first-job-index forms to be returned to the department chairmen for ratings. The forms contained a list of approximately thirteen jobs (total number of jobs, 311, divided by number of participating departments, 24) that were to be rated on an eight-point scale. The jobs for each list were randomly selected with the exception that no chairman's list contained first jobs of that department's graduates. The first-job-index scores were summed for each department and a mean score was derived.

Meetings Index. The members of each department and the department chairmen were asked to indicate on the questionnaires the number of professional meetings they had attended in their field in the last four years. The number of meetings were summed and a mean score derived for each department.

Publications Index. The members of each department and the department chairmen were asked to indicate on the questionnaires the number of publications they had published since the awarding of their highest degree. These publications were summed according to weighted values and a mean score was derived for each department.

American Council on Education Ratings. The ACE rating form was taken from Cartter's (1966) study, "An Assessment of Quality in Graduate Education," published by the American Council on Education.

The members of each department and the department chairmen were asked to complete an effectiveness form containing a list of schools to be rated on the quality of graduate faculty and the effectiveness of doctoral program in their field. The scores were summed for each participating school and a mean score derived for each department for quality of graduate faculty and effectiveness of doctoral program.

Each of the five effectiveness measures was compared with the leaders' LPC scores in the favorable-leader situation, intermediate-favorable situation and unfavorable situation as determined by the situation variables (group atmosphere, task structure, and position power) using Spearman's Rho as the index of correlation. For the hypotheses' testing, Fiedler's method of dividing the situational variables was used to place the departments in the octants of the model. For supplementary analyses, the hypotheses were also tested by using the median of the group method for dividing the situational variables and placing the departments in the octants of the model.

Findings and Conclusions

Fiedler's contingency model predicted that the task-oriented (low LPC) type of leadership style would be more effective in group situations which are either very favorable for the leader or which are very unfavorable for the leader. Therefore, hypothesis I stated that in those situations that have favorable leader conditions (octants I, II, and III) there will be a significant negative correlation between the least-preferred-coworker scores (LPC) and each of the five effectiveness measures. This hypothesis was not supported by the data. No significant correlations were found using Fiedler's method of dividing the situational variables (median of the group for group atmosphere, mid-point of the possible range for task structure and position power). (See *Table 1.*)

Table 1. Spearman's Rho Correlations Between Department Leaders' LPC Scores and Effectiveness Measures in the Favorable Leadership Situation (Hypothesis I) and Intermediate Favorableness Situation (Hypothesis II)

Effectiveness Measures	Hypothesis I $n = 11$	Hypothesis II $n = 13$
Quality of Graduate Faculty	.26	.20
Effectiveness of Doctoral Program	.36	.27
Meetings Index	.25	.27
Publications Index	.51	.13
First-Job Index	−.10	.04
Direction of Correlation Predicted by Fiedler's Contingency Model	Negative for all of above	Positive for all of above
Significance needed at .05 level (one-tailed test)	.52	.48

When median of the group was used to divide the situational variables into high and low for placement in the octants of the model, three of the possible five correlations were significant. However, they were in the direction opposite from that predicted by the model. They were a significant positive correlation between LPC and quality of graduate faculty and effectiveness of doctoral program and publications index. The data indicated that in the favorable-leadership situation the relations-oriented leader tended to be more effective when the five measures of effectiveness as used in the study were the determinants of effectiveness. (See *Table 2.*)

Fiedler's contingency model predicted that the human-relations oriented (high LPC) type of leadership style would be more effective in group situations that have intermediate favorableness for the leader. Therefore, hypothesis II

Table 2. Spearman's Rho Correlations Between Department Leaders' LPC Scores and Effectiveness Measures in the Favorable Leadership Situation (Hypothesis I) and Intermediate Favorableness Situation (Hypothesis II), Using "Median of the Group" Method of Dividing the Variables

Effectiveness Measures	Hypothesis I $n = 8$	Hypothesis II $n = 13$
Quality of Graduate Faculty	.83*	−.02
Effectiveness of Doctoral Program	.88*	.17
Meetings Index	.41	.18
Publications Index	.64*	.07
First-Job Index	−.12	.05
Direction of Correlation Predicted by Fiedler's Contingency Model	Negative for all of above	Positive for all of above

*Significance at <.05 level
(one-tailed test)   .64   .48

stated that in those situations that have intermediate favorableness leadership conditions (octants IV, V, VI, and VII), there will be a significant positive correlation between the leader's least-preferred-coworker scores (LPC) and each of the five effectiveness measures. The data did not support any of the five possible significant relationships for hypothesis II. Using Fiedler's method of dividing the situational variables, all five relationships were in the direction predicted by the contingency model but were not significant. (See *Table 1.*)

When median of the group was used to divide situational variables for placement in the octants of the model, four of the five correlations were in the predicted direction but were not significant. (See *Table 2.*)

Hypothesis III stated that in those situations that have unfavorable leadership conditions (octant VIII), there will be a significant negative correlation between the leaders' least-preferred-coworker scores and each of the five measures of effectiveness. There were not sufficient data to test this hypothesis. According to Fiedler's division of situational variables, none of the twenty-four departments of physical education was determined as having unfavorable leadership conditions.

When median of the group was used to determine the division of the situational variables, only three departments were determined as having unfavorable leadership conditions.

Supplemental Analyses. For supplemental analyses the variables of Fiedler's model (LPC, group atmosphere, task structure, and position power) were examined as to their relationship with each other, to the five effectiveness measures used in the study, and to the leader's biographical data. The relationship between group atmosphere and age of the leader approached significance that indicated that the older leaders tended to view their department members as more congenial and pleasant. The correlation between group atmosphere and position power also approached significance which indicated that the leaders who were rated by their staff as having high position power tended to view the staff as being pleasant and harmonious.

There was a significant positive relationship between position power and first-job index. The departments whose first jobs of their graduates were rated high tended to have leaders with high position power. There was a significant negative relationship between position power and years as leader and size of department. The leaders who had been in their leadership position fewer years tended to have higher position power. The smaller departments tended to have leaders with higher position power.

These findings are consistent with the findings of Lanaghan's study involving elementary principals. His findings indicated that the human relations-oriented leader was more effective in both the favorable and intermediate favorableness situation.

Implications for the Practicing Administrator

It is hoped that these findings will be of interest to leaders and those appointing leaders in educational programs by providing some insight into effective recruitment, selection, and leader behavior of graduate program leaders. Apparently, graduate departments of physical education require leaders who can establish good interpersonal relationships with the persons with whom they work. This does not mean that the task is ignored but that the major concern is developing good relationships with the group.

Education, in the past decade, has emphasized "democratic action." The trend seems to be for faculty to become involved in the decision-making processes and to participate in the direction of group action. If this is the goal, then the human-relations oriented leader would be more effective by obtaining the willing cooperation of his group to participate in the leadership of the group. As the situation becomes more favorable for the leader, more time and effort can be devoted to obtaining this goal and more relations-oriented leadership is practiced.

One of the reasons why such a small number of significant relationships was found in this study could be because of the small number of participating departments. Many of the findings in this study that approached significance were consistent with Lanaghan's (1972) significant findings. Lanaghan's study involved sixty-five schools, whereas this study included twenty-four departments. Another reason may be due to the lack of precise criteria for determining departmental effectiveness. More research is necessary to develop more precise measures of effectiveness for educational departments.

Most of Fiedler's work with the contingency model was done with small groups in which there was an opportunity for a great deal of interaction between the group leader and members of the group. Graduate departments of physical education very often do not provide the opportunity for much interaction between the department leader and the faculty members. The leader and the faculty members may not see each other for days at a time. There is not the close supervision in the educational departmental situation that there was in most of the group situations studied by Fiedler and his associates. Educational faculty members are considered to be professional, educated persons and do not require the day-by-day supervision and directive type of leadership that was necessary in the groups used by Fiedler. Perhaps future research with Fiedler's model in a school situation should involve smaller, more interacting groups that require closer supervision by the leader, such as committees chaired by the department leader, program directors and their group and advisory groups.

Lanaghan (1972) suggested that the school situation may be an intermediate favorableness leadership situation and if this is so, the findings from his study and from this study would support the contingency model. Further research should entail refinement of the model, particularly concerning the intermediate favorableness situation to enable the model to predict leadership effectiveness in the school situation.

There is some question as to whether the three situational variables (group atmosphere, task structure, and position power) used by Fiedler in the model are the crucial variables in determining the leadership favorableness of the school situation. This study found that the three situational variables did not seem to be important variables in determining the effectiveness of the department leader. Lanaghan (1972) found group atmosphere to be the only variable that was closely related to school principal effectiveness.

There is also the question of whether school groups are interacting groups or coacting groups. "Fiedler has suggested in a personal communication to McNamara that he sees school staffs as coacting groups" (Lanaghan, 1972, p. 7). McNamara, however, does not believe that this is necessarily true. Future research should try to resolve this question before definite conclusions concerning Fiedler's models are reached.

This study found that when the situational variables were divided at the median of the group, significant relationships occurred, and that when the variables were divided according to Fiedler's method (median of the group for group atmosphere, mid-point of the possible range for task structure, and position power) no significant relationships occurred. Further study is needed to determine the best method of defining good and poor group atmosphere, structured and unstructured tasks, and strong and weak position power for the school situation.

The results of this study and of Lanaghan's (1972) and Wyrick's (1972) studies indicate that Fiedler's leadership-effectiveness contingency model is not applicable to the educational setting and should not be used for selecting, retention, evaluation, or prediction of educational leadership. Further research using the present model in educational settings seems inappropriate. The next research effort must study the variables that determine the favorableness of educational settings and determine the best method for dividing these situational variables.

General Bibliography

American Association for Health, Physical Education and Recreation, "Directory of Professional Preparation Institutions." Washington, D.C.: 1966.

Blau, Peter, and Richard Scott, *Formal Organizations*. San Francisco: Chandler Publishing Co., 1962

Browne, C. G., and Thomas Cohn, eds., *The Study of Leadership*. Danville, Ill.: Interstate Printers and Publications, Inc., 1958.

Burke, Warner, "Leadership Behavior as a Function of the Leader, the Follower and the Situation," *Journal of Personality,* 33, no. 1 (1964), 60-81.

Campbell, Roald, and Russell Gregg, eds., *Administrative Behavior in Education.* New York: Harper & Row, 1957.

Cartter, Allan, "An Assessment of Quality in Graduate Education." Washington, D.C.: American Council on Education, 1966

Dressel, Paul, Craig Johnson, and Philip Marcus. *The Confidence Crisis.* San Francisco: Jossey-Bass, Inc., 1970.

Fiedler, Fred, "The Contingency Model: A Theory of Leadership Effectiveness," in *Basic Studies in Social Psychology,* ed. H. Proshanksy and B. Seidenberg, New York: Holt, Rinehart and Winston, 1965.

_____, *A Theory of Leaderhip Effectiveness.* New York: McGraw-Hill Book Co., 1967.

Fiedler, Fred, and Anthony Biglan, "The First Job After Graduation as a Means of Departmental Effectiveness." Technical Report no. 74, Urbana, Ill.: Group Effectiveness Research Laboratory, Department of Psychology, University of Illinois, April, 1969.

Fiedler, Fred, and W. A. T. Meuwese, "The Leader's Contribution to Task Performance in Cohesive and Uncohesive Groups," *Journal of Abnormal and Social Psychology,* 67 (1963) 83-87.

Gibb, Cecil, "Leadership," in *Handbook of Social Psychology,* Vol. 2, ed. Gardner Lindzey, Chap. 24. Cambridge, Mass.: Addison-Wesley Publishing Co, Inc., 1954.

Gouldner, A. W., *Studies in Leadership.* New York: Harper & Row, 1950.

Griffiths, Daniel, *Administrative Theory.* New York: Appleton-Century-Crofts, 1959.

Hemphill, John, *Situational Factors in Leadership.* Columbus: Ohio State University, 1949.

Hunt, J. G., "A Test of Fiedler's Leadership Contingency Model." Ph.D. diss., University of Illinois, Urbana, Illinois, 1966.

Kerr, Clark, *The Uses of the University.* Cambridge, Mass.: Harvard University Press, 1964.

Lanaghan, Richard, "Leadership Effectiveness in Selected Elementary Schools." Ph.D. diss., University of Illinois, 1972.

Lipham, James, "Leadership and Administration." In *Behavioral Science and Educational Administration*, ed. Daniel Griffiths. NSSE Yearbook. Chicago: University of Chicago Press, 1964.

McKague, Terrence, "A Study of the Relationship between School Organizational Behavior and the Variables of Bureaucratization and Leader Attitudes." Ph.D. diss., University of Alberta, Edmonton, 1968.

_____, "LPC–New Perspective on Leadership," *Educational Administration Quarterly,* 6 (Autumn 1970).

McNamara, Vincent D., "The Principal's Personal Leadership Style, the School Staff Leadership Situation and School Effectiveness." Ph.D. diss., University of Alberta, Edmonton, 1968.

Mann, Richard, "A Review of the Relationships Between Personality and Performance in Small Groups," *Psychological Bulletin,* 56, no. 4 (1959); 241-70.

Sherif, Muzafer, and Carolyn Sherif, *Social Psychology.* New York: Harper & Row, 1956.

Shaw, M. E., and J. M. Blum. "Effects of Leadership Style Upon Group Performance as a Function of Task Structure," *Journal of Personality and Social Psychology,* 3 (1966), 238-42.

Stogdill, Ralph, "Personal Factors Associated with Leadership: A Survey of the Literature," *Journal of Psychology,* 25 (1948).

Wyrick, Floyd, "The Effect of Departmental Leadership on Faculty Satisfaction and Departmental Effectiveness." Ph.D. diss., University of Illinois, 1972.

8

Group Cohesion Reconsidered

A. Mikalachki

The study (Mikalachki, 1969) reported in these pages was concerned with group cohesion. However, because it took place in an industrial setting, it may be more accurate to say that the study was concerned with work-group cohesion. The study dealt primarily with a statement of the behaviors and feelings of group members that differentiated high-cohesive groups from low-cohesive groups. A secondary concern was the investigation of the conditions that facilitated group cohesion and an examination of the relationship between the degree of cohesion and certain consequences, such as the level of productivity, the degree of tension, and the rate of absenteeism manifested by group members. Essentially, we considered the concept of group cohesion by endeavoring to denote what it is, what conditions facilitate its development, and what effects it has on such variables as tension, absenteeism, and level of productivity.

Literature Review and Statement of Research Aims

WHAT IS GROUP COHESION?

Just as there are many definitions of group cohesion, there are also many different labels for group cohesion itself. Group cohesion can be defined as the

A. Mikalachki is from the School of Business Administration, The University of Western Ontario, London, Ontario.

degree of member attraction to the group or the "stick-togetherness" of the group; this general description has also been used to define solidarity (Durkheim, 1933), the primary group (Cooley, 1909), internal group development (Zaleznick, 1958), cooperation (Mayo, 1945), morale (Zeleny, 1939), cohesiveness-morale (Fessenden, 1953), peer-group loyalty (Likert, 1961), pride in the work group (Katz, 1950), hedonic tone and viscidity (Hemphill, 1956), and concerted activity (Sayles, 1958).

Different operational devices have been used to measure the phenomena defined by each of the above labels for group cohesion.[1] In fact, two or three measuring devices have been used for some of the labels. Consequently, it is difficult to define succinctly the specific phenomenon to which group cohesion refers. In retrospect, however, it appears that cohesion was referred to differently during each of two rather distinct periods of time. We have arbitrarily labeled the first period, from 1900 to 1945, as the Durkheim-Cooley-Mayo period and the second period, from 1945 onward, the survey research period.

During the Durkheim-Cooley-Mayo period, we discern two major types of cohesion. Three labels, organic solidarity, primary groups, and cooperation, all refer to the first type; that is, cohesion characterized by the attraction of members to each other, by the cooperation of members in interdependent activities, and by a well-developed system of rights and duties shared by group members. The second type of cohesion, mechanical solidarity, is characterized by the attraction of members to each other, by the cooperation of members in limiting the range of behaviors in which the members can participate, and by a well-developed system of punitive sanctions. Punitive sanctions hold a group together by limiting the range of behavior instead of encouraging an interdependent diversity of behavior on the part of its members. Mainly through the writings and research of Mayo, the study of cohesion moved from a focus on society to a focus on industrial work groups.

During the survey research period that prevailed in the decade following the Second World War, researchers developed and employed a number of labels and measures of group cohesion, although they seldom thought of cohesion as being divided into types. Much of the research done during this period was of the survey type that measured cohesion either through sociometric or Likert-type questionnaires.[2] The sociometric questionnaires were generally one-item scales that ignored the situation or condition in which the choice was made. The Likert-type scale generally included five or more items that yielded internal-consistency reliability measures.

The definitions of cohesion during the survey research period, although

---

[1] We shall use the label "cohesion" to embrace all the labels that refer to the degree of member attraction to the group or the "stick-togetherness" of the group.

[2] For example, see Seashore, 1954; Katz et al., 1950; Goodacre 1951 and 1953; Festinger et al., 1950; French and Zander 1949; Van Zelst, 1952; Zeleny, 1939; Fessenden, 1953; Martin et al., 1952.

difficult to summarize precisely, clustered around three kinds of phenomena: (1) the degree of affection existing between group members, such as the group members' liking for each other; (2) the degree to which the members functioned as a unit, such as helping each other out, engaging in nonwork activities, choosing to spend more of their free time with group members rather than nongroup members, and acting in concert in the face of adversity; and (3) the degree to which the members evaluated their group positively in comparison to other groups, such as making statements like "We are a better group," "I prefer working in this group," and "We get along much better than group X."

The survey researchers' definitions differed from the earlier definitions of cohesion essentially in two ways: First, they were measured through such survey techniques as questionnaires and structured interviews; secondly, the operational definitions were stated with greater precision.

The main criticisms made of group cohesion as a concept were published during the survey period and specifically aimed at the concept as it was being defined and operationalized during this period. Many of these criticisms dealt with the preoccupation of the researchers with establishing the determinants and consequences of group cohesion without concentrating on the conceptual development of group cohesion itself.

Gross and Martin (1953) leveled the first comprehensive criticism of group cohesion as a concept. They felt that the survey methods of measuring cohesion did not measure the significant dimensions of the concept as it was being generally defined. For example, they contended that the ratio of ingroup to total possible sociometric choices of friendship did not measure the significant dimensions of cohesion which were defined as "the total field of forces which act on members to remain in the group." Friendship choices, they felt, were not exhaustive of this total field of forces.

Another of their criticisms was that the various operational definitions of group cohesion used by survey researchers were not positively and highly correlated. They presented data which showed low and negative correlations between different measures of cohesion. This criticism was reinforced by Eisman (1959), who measured each of fourteen natural student groups on five different measures of cohesion. The rank correlation coefficients obtained among the five measures revealed no significant relationship.

Albert concluded that it was time to sharpen the operational definition of group cohesion:

> Perhaps what is most needed at present is the determination conceptually of the concept, the nature of the group to which it refers (surely not all one-person-plus relationships) and the time perspective of this group's function and organization, as well as the particular kind of relationship called for within such a grouping of persons. (1953, p. 234).

Gross and Martin, Eisman, and Albert have aptly noted that it is time to reconsider group cohesion in terms of delineating the phenomena to which it refers.

Our brief review of the definitions of group cohesion and the criticisms leveled at it reveal the confusion and complexity that surround the concept. First, there are numerous operational definitions of group cohesion. Second, the studies aimed at exploring the relation between the various operational definitions generally come up with negative results. Third, there are no studies aimed at exploring the constituent parts of group cohesion. To summarize, the situation is one in which the relationship between group cohesion and other variables is being investigated while the constituent parts of the concept are not agreed upon or even sufficiently explored. To persist in exploring the relationship of group cohesion to other variables without investigating the constituent parts of the concept is to generate confusion and complexity unnecessarily. We decided, therefore, that the primary aim of the study reported here was to describe the behaviors and feelings of group members that differentiate high from low cohesive groups.

WHAT ARE THE CONDITIONS THAT FACILITATE GROUP COHESION?

A secondary question pursued in this study dealt with the conditions that facilitate group cohesion. Some alleged determinants have been stated by researchers in the form of hypotheses; however, there have been few systematic studies of the determinants of group cohesion which would test out these hypotheses.

A cogent criticism regarding the present knowledge of the conditions that facilitate group cohesion is presented by Cartwright and Zander, who say:

> There is very little systematic knowledge about the conditions which heighten cohesiveness, since only a few studies have been aimed directly at this problem. It is possible, nevertheless, to draw certain inferences about these conditions from investigations in which cohesiveness was an incidental part of the research problem (1953, p. 79).

Actually a review of the existing literature on group cohesion reveals only one study that systematically investigated the determinants of group cohesion—Seashore (1954). Generally, writers discussing the conditions that facilitate group cohesion either state them as research findings without giving references, as did Costello and Zalkind (1963, p. 445); present them as refinements of clinical studies, as did Whyte (1961, p. 540) and Deutscher and Deutscher (1955, p. 340); or deduce them from personal theories, as did Argyle (1957, p. 124).

The paucity of knowledge regarding the conditions that facilitate group

Group Cohesion Reconsidered 117

cohesion precipitated our second research aim, which was to denote the conditions that facilitate the development of group cohesion by:

1. A comparative clinical investigation of work groups, some of which are high and some of which are low on the dimension of group cohesion.
2. The use of survey methods to test the veracity of certain alleged determinants of group cohesion, specifically the homogeneity of the group members' social characteristics, the degree of group prestige, and the opportunity for interaction.

Five predictions derived from three hypotheses were tested by survey methods.[3]

Hypothesis i		The cohesion of a group varies positively with the homogeneity of the group members' social characteristics (Keedy [1956], Seashore [1954], Whyte [1961]).
Prediction a		The cohesion of a group varies positively with the homogeneity of the group members' age.
	b	The cohesion of a group varies positively with the homogeneity of the group members' education.
	c	The cohesion of a group varies positively with the homogeneity of the group members' pay.
Hypothesis ii		The cohesion of a group varies positively with the degree of prestige the group possesses (Seashore, 1954).
Prediction a		The cohesion of a group varies positively with the group's average job grade.[4]
Hypothesis iii		The cohesion of a group varies positively with the opportunity the members have for interaction (Argyle, 1957; Costello and Zalkind, 1963; Deutscher and Deutscher, 1955; Seashore, 1954; Strauss and Sayles, 1960; Whyte, 1961).
Prediction a		The cohesion of a group varies negatively with the size (number of members) of the group.

[3]The three hypotheses stated here are inferred from general statements made by the indicated authors.
[4]Job grades for female blue-collar workers in this organization range from 21 to 24 and are reflective of the job's worth to the company.

WHAT ARE THE CONSEQUENCES OF GROUP COHESION?

The final aim we pursued dealt with some consequences of group cohesion. The small-groups literature contains a number of studies dealing with group cohesion and its consequences. We dealt specifically with three consequences of group cohesion: absenteeism, tension, level of productivity.

The relationship between group cohesion and employee absenteeism has been investigated by a number of researchers. Fox and Scott (1943), in a comparative case study of three metal shops; Mayo and Lombard (1944), investigating absenteeism and turnover in the southern California aircraft industry; Roethlisberger and Dickson (1939), studying the work group behavior of a "test room"; Mann and Baumgartel (1952), in an attitude study of workers in an electric power company; and Trist and Bramford (1951), studying the long-wall method of obtaining coal, have all reported a negative relationship between group cohesion and absenteeism by group members. These authors suggest that the identification or membership in a highly cohesive work group acts as a force that attracts the members to come to work and conversely dissuades them from staying away.

Tension generated on the job has also been related to the degree of cohesion in a group possesses. Seashore (1954), in his study of industrial work groups, reported a negative relationship between group cohesion and tension on the job. The tension referred to by Seashore is the "jumpiness" or nervousness that results from the work performed by the group members. Likert (1961), in an appraisal of Seashore's results, concurred with the latter and concluded that the greater support and security derived from membership in a highly cohesive group resulted in the group members experiencing little tension from their work.

The level of group productivity has also been related to the degree of cohesion a group possesses; however, the relationship is a contentious one. On the one hand, Katz et al. (1951), studying groups of railroad maintenance workers, and Seashore (1954), investigating industrial work groups, reported no significant relationship between group cohesion and the level of productivity. On the other hand, Van Zelst (1952), dealing with groups of bricklayers and carpenters, Katz et al. (1950), studying clerical office workers, Mayo and Lombard (1944), in their aircraft study, and Goodacre (1953), investigating the effectiveness of combat groups, reported significant positive relationships between group cohesion and the level of productivity. In addition, two experiments on college students conducted by Schacter et al. (1951) and Berkowitz (1954) yield evidence that shows that group cohesion and productivity are positively related when the group members have high production as a group norm. These studies are just a sample of the contradictory findings regarding the relationship of group cohesion and the level of productivity.

We have noted above the relationship of group cohesion to three consequences; namely, absenteeism, tension, and level of group productivity. In the past, these relationships have been investigated primarily through the use of survey methods. Generally, survey methods relate two or more variables, which, if they result in a significant correlation, stimulate the researcher to make or reiterate a theoretical statement regarding the relation of these variables to each other. Such is the case with the relationship of group cohesion to the three above-mentioned consequences.

We pursued these three relationships through an intensive clinical investigation. Some of the questions we wished to answer were, Do high-cohesion groups influence their members to come to work when they might have stayed home, or do low-cohesion groups influence their members to stay away from work? Is tension on the job work-related, or is it related to the social relationships among members? For that matter, can one discriminate the source of tension on the job? Can the contradictory results between group cohesion and level of productivity be reconciled?

These questions can be summarized in our third research aim, which was to examine the relationship between group cohesion and certain consequences which have been related to it in the past, specifically the degree of tension, rate of absenteeism, and level of productivity manifested by group members.

Methodology

The means of selecting work groups for the study resulted in an implicit definition of work groups. Generally, the work group was defined as being made up of members whose supervisors felt they had something in common that differentiated them as a group, for example, similar tasks, like buffing telephones, or common task goals, like the progressive assembly of a product. The essential feature of this definition of a group is that the supervisor sees the members as having something in common and believes that what they have in common makes a difference.[5]

Table 1 summarizes the groups selected in terms of their size,[6] sex, and the department from which they came.

The research design employed in this study was organized into two phases, which we labeled the survey phase and the clinical phase. In the survey phase, we used two established and frequently used measures of group cohesion[7] to rank

---

[5]Olmstead (1959, pp. 21-22) defines a group as having the essential feature, except he takes it from the point of view of the members rather than the supervisor.

[6]Only groups possessing four or more members were considered within the research population. If the membership were less than four, question 6 in appendix B could not be handled in a comparable fashion for all groups, since the groups with less than four members could not make three within-the-group choices.

[7]See appendix A. The Seashore measure (Seashore, 1954) included questions 1 to 5 which showed an internal-consistency reliability of .97 (item-test correlation, Guilford, 1950). The Festinger measure (Festinger, 1950) was made up of question 6 which yielded a ratio reflecting the within-group choices made to the total possible choices a member could make. The intercorrelation of the Seashore and Festinger measures yielded a product moment correlation coefficient of .354 which was significant at the .05 level of confidence.

Table 1. Size, Sex, and Department Source of Group

Size of Group	Number of Groups	Department	Total Number of Groups	Number of Groups Female	Number of Groups Male
4	12	A	13	12	1
5	7	B	15	15	0
6	3	C	6	0	6
7	1	D	3	0	3
8	2		37	27	10
9	4				
10	2				
11	2				
12	2				
13	1				
18	1				
	37				

thirty-seven work groups on the dimension of cohesion. We then tested the association between these rankings and some possible determinants of group cohesion.

In the clinical phase, we selected four of the thirty-seven groups used in the survey phase. Two of the groups, one with four members and one with five members, ranked high on the Festinger and Seashore measures of group cohesion; the other two, with eight members in one and ten in the other, ranked low on both of these measures. All four groups were made up of female members,[8] who reported to the same supervisor and performed a similar type of repetitive, semiskilled work. We investigated these groups intensively by observing them during their daily work routines and during several critical incidents which occurred. We also conducted spontaneous and semistructured interviews (appendix B). In addition to this, we obtained, from record cards, data regarding the group members' productivity and absenteeism. We used the data obtained in the clinical phase to describe the behaviors and feelings that differentiate high- from low-cohesion groups, to denote some conditions that facilitate group cohesion, and to examine the relationship between group cohesion and the degree of tension, rate of absenteeism, and level of opportunity manifested by group members. A summary and discussion of the findings of both phases of our study are presented below.

Summary of Findings

In the introductory portion of this paper, we specified the three research aims of our study and the questions and literature from which these aims were

[8] Using the thirty-seven groups as a sample, we found no significant interdependence between sex and group cohesion.

derived. In this summary of findings, we shall state concisely the extent to which these aims were achieved. Essentially, this study delineates the behaviors and feelings that differentiate high- from low-cohesion groups, explicates four types of group cohesion, denotes the conditions that facilitate the various types of cohesion, and contributes to the clarification of the relation between group cohesion and two consequences, tension and level of productivity.

GROUP COHESION

We distinguished three dimensions of the group members, behaviors and feelings which differentiated the high- from the low-cohesive groups. These were (1) integrated-nonintegrated group behavior, (2) egalitarian-stratified behavior, and (3) feelings of attraction to the group-feelings of indifference or antagonism to the group. The high-cohesion groups manifested integrated group behavior, egalitarian behavior, and feelings of attraction to the group.

The integrated behavior of the high-cohesion group members was reflected by the presence of numerous joint activities, cooperative behavior between members, the lack of interactional subgroupings, and the stability of interaction patterns when newcomers were introduced into the group. The nonintegrated behavior of the low-cohesion groups, conversely, was reflected in the fragmentation of the groups in various activities, the presence of uncooperative behavior, the presence of interactional subgroupings, and the instability of the interaction patterns when newcomers were introduced into the group.

The high-cohesion group members' egalitarian behavior was reflected in the sharing of the drink-getting task, the balance between each member's initiation and receipt of interactions, the even distribution of frequency of interactions, and the absence of a popularity structure. Conversely, the low-cohesion group members' stratified behavior was reflected in the nonsharing of the drink-getting task, the imbalance in the initiation and receipt of interactions for each member, the unequal distribution of interactions, and the numerous popularity structures declared by the group members.

The high-cohesion group members manifested sentiments of attraction to the group and behaviors that were in accord with these sentiments, such as being friendly toward one another, helping one another, and refusing transfers out of the group. The low-cohesion group members manifested sentiments of indifference or antagonism toward the group and such congruent behaviors as accepting transfers, asking for transfers, quitting their jobs, and quarrelling among themselves.

We concluded that three patterns of behaviors and feelings represent the constituent parts of high group cohesion. The patterns and their empirical indicators are

1. Integrated group behavior
   —numerous joint activities
   —cooperative behavior among members

—absence of interactional subgroupings
   —stability of interaction patterns when newcomers are introduced to the group
2. Egalitarian behavior
   —the sharing of service tasks equally
   —the equality between a member's initiation and her receipt of interactions
   —relatively even distribution of interactions frequencies
   —absence of popularity structures
3. Feelings of attraction to the group
   —members' identification with their group
   —members' positive evaluation of their group compared to other groups
   —high within-group friendship choices
   —few expressions of antagonism or open conflict between members
   —many refusals of transfers to another group

We should also like to note briefly the relation of the above three characteristics of group cohesion to previous descriptions of group cohesion. In our introduction, we generally described group cohesion as referring to the degree of attraction to the group or the "stick-togetherness" that members manifested. Of the three characteristics of group cohesion denoted in our clinical study, two can easily be subsumed under this general description. The members' feelings of attraction to their group are obviously related to the general description and are also consistent with the survey researcher's view of group cohesion. The integrated group behavior noted in our study is a more explicit statement of the "stick-togetherness" element that cohesion is popularly believed to possess.

The egalitarian characteristic of the high-cohesion groups in this study is both consistent and inconsistent with findings and data presented by other researchers. Benne and Sheats (1948) present data that could be interpreted to suggest that it is not the stratified or hierarchical organization of group members that would distinguish a high-cohesion group from a low-cohesion one, but rather the egalitarian fulfillment of functional group roles. For Benne and Sheats, a cohesive group would be one in which the members possess and perform the roles necessary for optimum group growth and productivity. This view is supported by our study.

Sherif et al. (1961) investigating two boys' camp groups; Whyte (1943), studying a street corner gang; and Theodorson (1957), studying natural and laboratory groups, all present data that would indicate that the groups they were studying were highly cohesive on the basis of integrated group behavior and feelings of attraction to the group. They also present data indicating that these groups were marked by stratification; that is, the members were ranked ordinally in terms of popularity (liking) and in some cases leadership (initiation of activities).[9]

In a personal discussion with Professor Stanley Seashore on the subject, he suggested that group cohesion could have a curvilinear relation to the egalitarian-stratified behavior dimension. That is, both marked egalitarianism and marked stratification could be characteristic of high group cohesion. This interpretation, which reconciles the conflicting findings, of course, can best be evaluated through further research.

In addition to the above-noted similarities between the two high-cohesion groups studied, there was also a notable difference between these groups. The difference was the focus of integration for the two cohesive groups: One group integrated around a task-productive focus and the other around a social-discussion focus. The observed difference, augmented by the negative results we obtained and what other researchers have reported regarding group cohesion and various facilitative conditions and consequences, prompted us to develop a typology of group cohesion. The result of this effort was four types of group cohesion: task groups, social groups, protective task groups, and protective social groups. These types of cohesion were defined through the use of two dimensions: the focus of group integration and the means of group social control.

The task group's focus of integration is the task the group is ostensibly organized to perform; the means of social control the group members employ is a well-developed system of rights and duties. Frequently observed examples of task groups are some work groups, bomber crews, infantry units, football teams, teams of surgeons, and some families.

The social group's focus of integration is not the goal for which the group is formally organized, but rather a social goal which develops spontaneously. Some examples of social groups are work groups that focus heavily on socioemotional activities and hobby groups that spend most of their time in social activities unrelated to the hobby which ostensibly brought the group members together.

The protective task group's focus of integration is some facet of the group's productive task, which protects the group from undue influence by other groups. Its means of social control are punitive sanctions. The most prevalent example of protective task groups in industry is work groups that control output in order to withstand the potentially dislocating influence of management. Another common example would be professional associations or societies, which through the control of membership may be viewed as limiting or protecting the group from an oversupply of members or conversely an undersupply of work opportunities.

The protective social group also employs punitive sanctions as a means of social control. However, its focus of integration is a social, nonwork goal that

---

[9]Our data on the ranking of members in terms of leadership showed that none of the four groups could rank their members in this way.

develops spontaneously in the group and protects the group's position or stature vis-à-vis other groups. Some university fraternities are examples of protective social groups in which the members engage in joint activities which differentiate them on a prestige basis from other groups.

The notion that there is more than one type of cohesion is an old but infrequently used one. At the turn of the twentieth century, Durkheim (1933) noted two types of cohesion, organic solidarity and mechanical solidarity, which he differentiated in terms of the means of social control employed by group members. In the 1950s, Martin, Darley, and Gross (1952) noted that it was important to differentiate various types of cohesion in terms of the situation (focus) around which the group coheres. We have been influenced by the views of Durkheim and Martin, Darley, and Gross and have extrapolated their views to the extent of the above-mentioned four types of group cohesion. Although these four types emphasize the differences among cohesive groups, we should like to reiterate that the groups have a certain pattern in common; that is, integrated group behavior, egalitarian behavior, and feelings of attraction to the group.

THE CONDITIONS THAT FACILITATE GROUP COHESION

Using survey research methods, we tested five predictions derived from three general hypotheses regarding the association between group cohesion and certain facilitative conditions by correlational methods on a sample of thirty-seven work groups. These conditions were tested against the Seashore and Festinger measures of group cohesion *(Table 2)*. Except for the association between prestige (job grade) and Festinger's measure of cohesion, which was significant but not in the predicted direction, the predicted associations were not significant at the .05 level of confidence. As stated earlier, these negative findings, in part, stimulated us to consider that there was more than one type of group cohesion.

Table 2. Correlational Coefficients Relating Cohesion to Various Conditions

	Homogeneity of			*Prestige (Job Grade)*	*Group Size*
	Age	*Education*	*Pay*		
Seashore	.05	.09	.06	.005	.18
Festinger	.04	.06	.15	.29	.15

Considering the four types of cohesive groups, we have concluded that the conditions that facilitate cohesion in task and social groups are different from those that facilitate cohesion in protective task and protective social groups. In task and social groups, there is a coherence around a goal that is superordinate to each member's peculiar wishes and is always beyond the ability of any one member to attain without the help of the other members. Three conditions facilitate cohesion in task and social groups: (1) the opportunity for member interaction, (2) the members' role interdependence, and (3) the members' high degree of concern for each other. These conditions for the development of group cohesion were borne out in our intensive study of two high-cohesive groups, one of which was a task group and the other of which was a social group. Two other conditions differentiated the task from the social group: the members' identification with the group's formal task and the success of the group in achieving its formal task goals. That is, groups whose members strongly identify with the formal goals of the group and which have a high degree of success in attaining the formal goals will tend to be cohesive task groups. The absence of identification with formal group goals and the frequent failure in attaining formal group goals will tend to disintegrate a cohesive task group. The following is a summary of the conditions that facilitate task and social groups respectively.

1. Task Groups
    - the opportunity for member interaction
    - the members' role interdependence
    - the members' high degree of concern for each other
    - the members' high degree of identification with formal group goals
    - the high degree of success in attaining formal group goals
2. Social Groups
    - the opportunity for member interaction
    - the members' role interdependence
    - the members' high degree of concern for each other
    - the members' low degree of identification with formal group goals

Protective task and protective social groups, of which there were none in our study, cohere around a goal that is peculiar to each member's wishes and that generally requires each member to work individually but in agreement with the other members to attain. The protective group members have little common identification with a superordinate task that requires a diversity of interdependent behavior if it is to be achieved. Three conditions facilitate cohesion in protective task and protective social groups: (1) the opportunity for member interaction, (2) the member's possession of similar social characteristics which lead to similar values, and (3) the members' manifestation of a need for protection from some threat. These conditions for the development of protective task and protective social groups were adduced from the writings of Durkheim (1933) and Roethlisberger and Dickson's (1939) description of the bank-wiring group.

SOME CONSEQUENCES OF GROUP COHESION

Our investigation has shed some light on the relationship between group cohesion and two consequences, tension and level of productivity. As for the relationship between group cohesion and absenteeism, which we also examined, we have little to contribute in the way of added understanding.

High-cohesion groups had as good as or better attendance records than low-cohesion groups. Four main factors resulted in low unnecessary absenteeism: the worker's desire not to lose wages, membership in a high cohesive group, more complex and interesting jobs, and a fearless relationship with the supervisor. These factors and the reasons why they are related to absenteeism have been noted by other researchers. We have presented supportive evidence to these previous studies and have not added anything of interpretive or explanatory significance.

In our study we found that the high-cohesion groups experienced relatively no tension on the job, whereas the low-cohesion groups experienced a great deal of tension on the job. The source of tension in the low-cohesion groups was not the work performed, as some researchers have suggested, but rather the disconcerting interpersonal relations that characterized the low-cohesion groups. It was the members' anticipation of overt conflicts and the strain of working through these conflicts that made the members tense.

As to the relationship of the level of group production and group cohesion, we found that low-cohesion groups do not necessarily produce at a low level of production, nor do high-cohesion groups produce at a high level. The level of group productivity in the high-cohesion groups observed appeared to be a function of the group's focus of integration: Where the focus was a task-production one, the level was high, (140 percent of standard), and where it was a social-discussion one, the level was low (96 percent of standard). This observation stimulated us, in part, to develop the typology of group cohesion which differentiated the four types of cohesive groups discussed earlier. We related these four types to the level of group productivity and specifically concluded that:

1. Task groups will produce at a higher than standard[10] level of productivity.
2. Social groups will produce at a standard or slightly lower level of productivity.
3. Protective task groups, which are generally integrated around the goal of controlling output, will produce at an agreed-upon, generally lower than standard, level of productivity.
4. The cohesive element of the protective social groups will not be related in any systematic way to the group's level of productivity.

---

[10] A standard level of productivity is defined in terms of the production expectations management has of an average group.

The consideration of more than one type of group cohesion has permitted us to present a potential reconciliation of the frequently reported contradictory findings regarding the relation of group cohesion and level of group productivity. Some cohesive groups, such as the social and protective task groups, produce low. The social groups produce at a low level because of the time they spend on socioemotional activities, which does not leave them sufficient time to produce at a higher level. The protective task groups produce at a low level to ward off the undue influence of other groups. The activities of the protective social groups, on the other hand, are so divorced from the productive pursuits of their members that the structure of these groups is not related to the level of group productivity. Finally, the high level of productivity of task groups, whose primary goal is the achievement of the task, is facilitated by the cohesive relations among the members. In reviewing a number of studies on group cohesion and level of group productivity, two attributes, task orientation and control through internalized rights and duties, appeared to be present in all of the studies which reported a positive relationship between group cohesion and the level of group productivity. *Table 3* summarizes the studies showing this relationship.

Table 3. Studies Reporting a Positive Relationship between Group Cohesion and Level of Group Productivity

Author	Group Membership	Task	Measure of Productivity
Bos (1937)	12-to 15-year-old school children	Picture identification	No. of correct identifications
Goodacre (1951)	Army personnel	Combat unit maneuvers	Unit effectiveness rating
Goodacre (1953)	Army personnel	Combat unit maneuvers	Unit effectiveness
Marrow (1957)	Industrial work groups	Production of a unit	Number produced
Cohen (1957)	Army personnel	Maneuvers	Unit effectiveness
Deutsch (1959)	University students	Problem solving	Grading of solution
Hemphill (1956)	University students	Problem solving	Grading of solution
Sherif et al. (1961)	Teenagers	Pulling a truck	Moving the truck

Jones and Vroom (1964)	University students	Problem solving	Grading of solution
Trist (1951)	Coal miners	Mining coal	Amount mined
Berkowitz (1956)	Air Force personnel	Operating a B-29	Crew effectiveness rating
Stogdill (1964)	Football teams	Playing games	Yards gained and lost

The question of the relationship between group cohesion and productivity may be answered by differentiating various types of cohesion. As the studies noted in *Table 3* attest, what we have called task group cohesion appears to be related positively to productivity. What we have called social group cohesion may in fact mitigate against high productivity. By ignoring the differences in group cohesion in the past, we suggest that researchers have contributed to the confounding of the relationship between group cohesion and productivity.

Implications for the Administrator

In our study, we have implied that cohesive task groups will display such group consequences as a low degree of tension, a low rate of absenteeism, and a high level of productivity. It is axiomatic to state that these consequences are desired by most administrators. If these are the administrator's goals, we would suggest that he manipulate the structural and personnel conditions so as to have small-sized groups whose members identify with the formal goals of the group, perform interdependent task roles, manifest a high degree of concern for one another, and have an opportunity to achieve their goal successfully.

In most middle-sized organizations, such as the one in which the study was conducted, there are a number of factors mitigating against the above combination of conditions being manipulated solely by the work group supervisor:

1. For the most part, the size of a work group is indirectly determined by the industrial engineers who design the work flow and define the job requirements of the various tasks performed by workers. We would surmise that the engineers are more cognizant of and concerned with the technological aspect of the layout than they are with the interpersonal relations of the workers. Consequently, little thought is given in these designs to the optimal size of a group for such ends as low absenteeism, low tension, and a high level of productivity.

2. Job specialization in many organizations has reached such a stage of development that there are few remaining tasks that specify interdependent task roles to be carried out by a number of workers. Most industrial tasks are either assembly-line tasks or individual tasks that require the individual effort of one man. The definition of job specifications is also within the responsibility of the industrial engineer.
3. Finally, work group administrators seldom influence completely the selection of the personnel who will work for them. Generally, a centralized personnel department, through its members, selects a number of candidates who can fill a particular vacancy. The work group administrator then accepts one of these candidates.

Given these factors, we would conclude that the type of work group prevalent in most middle-sized organizations is the result of conditions which have been established through the efforts and decisions of three groups of people: the industrial engineers, the personnel officers, and the work group administrators. In effect, we are saying that an organization which is committed to such group consequences as high productivity, low tension, and low absenteeism rates must place the responsibility for these goals not solely with the work group administrator, but rather with a management team made up of work group administrators, industrial engineers, and personnel officers. The actions and decisions of each of these management groups has a significant effect on the development of the work group and the consequences of that group. None of the three management groups can absolve themselves from nor take sole credit for the consequences of work group efforts. Consequently, we would suggest that they themselves form a management task group around the goal of establishing the conditions that would nurture cohesive task work groups. The conditions that facilitate such a management task group are the same as those that facilitate work task groups.

We would also like to discuss some implications for a specific group of administrators—coaches. Group cohesion has significant implications for sports that demand coordinated action by team members—football, hockey, basketball, soccer, and the like. In these sports the coaches' selection of team members should be made on the basis of technical skill *and* capacity of the player to act in concert with his teammates. It has been frequently demonstrated that the coordinated (task cohesive) play of a team is more efficacious than a collectivity of individuals, somewhat superior in skill, who are seeking their own ends. Coaches would also do well to understand the differences between social and task cohesive groups. Both types of cohesion manifest togetherness; however, the latter has a more positive effect on performance. To this end, a coach should select members who show a high degree of identification with the group's formal goals. Coaches should also endeavor to set attainable standards for the team, because success in attaining formal group goals significantly affects task cohesion.

Appendix A
The University of Western Ontario
School of Business Administration

WORK GROUP QUESTIONNAIRE

Name: (Please print) _____

1. Do you feel that you are really a part of your work group?
   - _____ Really a part of my work group.
   - _____ Included in most ways.
   - _____ Included in some ways, but not in others.
   - _____ Don't feel I really belong.
   - _____ Don't work with any one group of people.

2. If you had a chance to do the same kind of work for the same pay, in another work group, how would you feel about moving?
   - _____ Would want very much to move.
   - _____ Would rather move than stay where I am.
   - _____ Would make no difference to me.
   - _____ Would rather stay where I am than move.
   - _____ Would want very much to stay where I am.

3. How does your work group compare with other work groups at the Northern Electric Company in the way the people get along?
   - _____ Better than most.
   - _____ About the same as most.
   - _____ Not as good as most.

4. How does your work group compare with other work groups at the Northern Electric Company when it comes to sticking together to get what the group wants?
   - _____ Better than most.
   - _____ About the same as most.
   - _____ Not as good as most.

5. How does your work group compare with other work groups at the Northern Electric Company in the way the people help each other on the job?
   - _____ Better than most.
   - _____ About the same as most.
   - _____ Not as good as most.

6. Which three people in the Northern Electric Company do you see most of socially (both during and after working hours)?
   1. _____
   2. _____
   3. _____

Appendix B
The Semistructured Interview Questions

1. What are some of the things you like or dislike about the group in which you work?
2. Would you say that there is little or a great deal of tension in your work group?

   Where does the tension come from?
3. Who are the most popular (best-liked) members in your group?

   (a) Could you rank the members of your group in terms of popularity?

   (b) Where do you think you fit in this ranking?
4. Who are the members in your group who decide on different things, such as the topic of conversation or who should go for the coffee?

   (a) Could you rank the members in terms of this question?

   (b) Where do you think you fit in this ranking?
5. How do you feel about your supervisor?

   (a) What are the things you like about him?

   (b) What are the things you dislike about him?
6. Are the production records for your group accurate? (We only asked certain people this question.)

Note: The asking of the subquestions to each major question was contingent on the response to the previous question.

General Bibliography

Albert, Robert S., "Comments on the Scientific Function of the Concept of Cohesiveness," *American Journal of Sociology,* 59 (1953), 231-34.

Argyle, Michael, *The Scientific Study of Social Behavior.* London: Methuen and Co., Ltd., 1957.

Benne, Kenneth D., and Paul Sheats, "Functional Roles of Group Members," *Journal of Social Issues,* 4, no 2 (Spring 1948), 41-49.

Berkowitz, Leonard, "Group Standards, Cohesiveness, and Productivity," *Human Relations,* 7 (1954), 509-19.

──────── "Group Norms Among Bomber Crews: Patterns of Perceived Crew Attitudes, 'Actual' Crew Attitudes, and Crew Liking Related to Aircrew Effectiveness in Far Eastern Combat," *Sociometry,* 19 (1956), 141-53.

Bos, Maria C., "Experimental Study of Productive Collaboration," *Psychologica,* 3 (1937), 315-426.

Cartwright, Dorwin, and Alvin Zander, *Group Dynamics: Research and Theory.* Evanston, Ill.: Row Peterson, 1953.

Cohen, Edwin, "The Effect of Members' Use of a Formal Group as a Reference Group, upon Group Effectiveness," *Journal of Social Psychology,* 46 (1957), 307-9.

Cooley, Charles H., *Social Organization.* New York: Scribner's, 1909.

Costello, Timothy W., and Sheldon S. Zalkind, *Psychology in Administration.* Englewood Cliffs, N.J.: Prentice-Hall, Inc., 1963.

Deutsch, Morton, "An Experimental Study of the Effects of Cooperation and Competition upon Group Process," *Human Relations,* 12 (1959), 81-95.

Deutscher, Vera, and Irwin Deutscher, "Cohesion in a Small Group," *Social Forces,* 33 (1955), 336-41.

Durkheim, Emile, *On the Division of Labor in Society,* trans. G. Simpson. Glencoe, Ill.: The Free Press, 1933.

Eisman, Bernice, "Some Operational Measures of Cohesiveness and Their Interrelations," *Human Relations,* 12 (1959), 183-89.

Fessenden, Seth A., "An Index of Cohesiveness-Morale Based on the Analysis of Sociometric Choice Distribution," *Sociometry,* 16 (1953), 321-26.

Festinger, Leon, Stanley Schacter, and Kurt Back, *Social Pressures in Informal Groups.* New York: Harper, 1950.

Fox, John B., and Jerome F. Scott, *Absenteeism: Management's Problem.* Boston: Graduate School of Business Administration, Harvard University, 1943.

French, John R. O., and Alvin Zander, "The Group Dynamics Approach," in *Psychology of Labor-Management Relations,* New York: American Book-Stratford Press, Inc., 1949. ed. A. Kornhauser, pp. 71-80.

Goodacre, Daniel M., "The Use of a Sociometric Test as a Predictor of Combat Unit Effectiveness," *Sociometry,* 14 (1951), 148-52.

─────── "Group Characteristics of Good and Poor Performing Combat Units," *Sociometry,* 16 (1953), 168-78.

Gross, Neal, and William E. Martin, "On Group Cohesiveness," *American Journal of Sociology,* 58 (1953), 554-62.

Guilford, Jay P., *Fundamental Statistics in Psychology and Education.* New York: McGraw-Hill Book Co., 1950.

Hemphill, John K., *Group Dimensions: A Manual for Their Measurement.* Ohio State University Bureau of Business Research Monograph no. 87, 1956.

Jones, Stephen C., and Victor H. Vroom, "Division of Labor and Performance under Cooperative and Competitive Conditions," *Journal of Abnormal and Social Psychology,* 68, no. 3 (1964), 313-20.

Katz, Daniel, Nathan Maccoby, G. Gurin, and L. G. Floor, *Productivity, Supervision and Morale among Railroad Workers.* Ann Arbor, Mich.: Survey Research Center, 1951.

Katz, Daniel, Nathan Maccoby, and Nancy C. Morse, *Productivity, Supervision, and Morale in an Office Situation.* Ann Arbor, Mich.: Survey Research Center, 1950.

Keedy, T. C., Jr., "Factors in the Cohesiveness of Small Groups," *Sociological Social Research,* (1956), 329-32.

Likert, Rensis, *New Patterns of Management.* New York: McGraw-Hill Book Co., 1961.

Mann, Floyd, and Howard Baumgartel, *Absences and Employee Attitudes in an Electric Power Company.* Ann Arbor, Mich.: Institute for Social Research, 1952.

Marrow, Alfred J., *Making Management Human.* New York: McGraw-Hill Book Co., 1957.

Martin, William E., John G. Darley, and Neal Gross, "Studies of Group Behaviour: II Methodological Problems in the Study of Interrelationships of Group Members," *Educational Psychology Measurement,* 12 (1952), 533-53.

Mayo, Elton, *The Social Problems of an Industrial Civilization.* Boston: Graduate School of Business Administration, Harvard University, 1945.

Mayo, Elton, and George F. F. Lombard, *Teamwork and Labor Turnover in the Aircraft Industry of Southern California.* Boston: Harvard Business School, 1944.

Mikalachki, Alexander, *Group Cohesion Reconsidered.* London, Ontario: School of Business Administration, University of Western Ontario, 1969.

Olmstead, Michael S., *The Small Group.* New York: Random House, 1959.

Roethlisberger, Fritz J., and William J. Dickson, *Management and the Workers.* Cambridge, Mass.: Harvard University Press, 1939.

Sayles, Leonard, *Behavior of Industrial Work Groups.* New York: John Wiley & Sons, Inc., 1958.

Schacter, Stanley, Norris Ellerston, Dorothy McBride, and Doris Gregory, "An Experimental Study of Cohesiveness and Productivity, *Human Relations,* 4: (1951), 229-38.

Seashore, Stanley E., *Group Cohesiveness in the Industrial Work Group.* Ann Arbor, Mich.: Survey Research Center, Institute for Social Research, University of Michigan, 1954.

Sherif, Muzafer, et al., *Intergroup Conflict and Cooperation: The Robbers Cave Experiment.* Norman, Oklahoma: The University Book Exchange, 1961.

Stogdill, Ralph M., *Team Achievement under High Motivation.* Ohio State Bureau of Business Research Monograph no. 113. Ohio State University, 1964.

Strauss, George, and Leonard R. Sayles, *Personnel: The Human Problems of Management.* Englewood Cliffs, N.J.: Prentice-Hall, Inc., 1960.

Theodorson, George A., "The Relationship Between Leadership and Popularity Roles in Small Groups," *American Sociological Review,* 22: (1957), 58-67.

Trist, Eric L., and K. Bramford, "Some Social and Psychological Consequences of the Long-wall Method of Coal-getting," *Human Relations*, 4, no. 1 (1951).

Van Zelst, R. H., "Sociometrically Selected Work Teams Increase Productivity," *Personnel Psychology*, 5, no. 3 (1952).

Whyte, William F., *Street Corner Society: The Social Structure of an Italian Slum*. Chicago: University of Chicago Press, 1943.

―――, *Men at Work*. Homewood, Ill.: Dorsey Press, 1961.

Zeleny, Leslie D., "Sociometry of Morale," *American Sociological Review*, 4 (1939), 799-808.

Zalenznik, Abraham, Christopher R. Christensen, and Fritz J. Roethlisberger, *The Motivation, Productivity and Satisfaction of Workers*. Harvard University, Division of Research, Graduate School of Business Administration, 1958.

9

Organizational Climate in Physical Education

Wayne E. Dannehl

Introduction

In recent years, there has been a shift in emphasis in the study of educational administration. "Prior to 1950, the field was considered well defined and there was little controversy concerning its content" (Griffiths, 1959, p. 1). Moreover, educational administration is no longer considered as separate from administration of business, hospitals, or the military. "Whether one looks at administration from the standpoint of its purpose, its task, its situational milieu, or its process, he will find much that is common in management of business, government, education and other organizations" (Griffiths, 1959, p. 2). Because physical education is a part of the educational community, the study of educational administration is applicable to administration of physical education and athletics.

Studies in the area of physical education and athletic administration have been designed to find a "solution of immediate or localized problems" (Spaeth, 1967, p. 151). This implies that compared to educational administration, physical education is still in the pre-1950 era insofar as studies in the behavioral and decision-making aspects of physical education administration are concerned. Very few physical educators or athletic administrators are even faintly aware of

Wayne E. Dannehl is from the University of Wisconsin-Parkside.

the scientific investigations that are occurring in the area of administration. "In the long run, such ignorance can only result in lowered status, minor catastrophe, or even disaster" (Zeigler and Paton, 1966, pp. 131-39).

The purpose of this study of organizational climate was to attempt to further the body of knowledge of administration of physical education and athletics. With the development of the *Organizational Climate Description Questionnaire (OCDQ)* by Halpin and Crofts (1962), six organizational climates have been identified which help explain what is "out there." The "climates" range from those which are "open" to those which are "closed." The impetus for development of the *OCDQ* came from the fact that the authors sensed differences in schools when they entered them. Some schools seemed to provide a happy experience for all the persons involved, while others were characterized by a mood of despair. Still other schools seemed efficient but hollow, as though the persons involved were performing a ritual. The *OCDQ* was designed with the intent of measuring the "personality" of the school. "Personality is to the individual what organizational climate is to the organization" (Halpin, 1966, p. 131).

The instrument has eight subtests which are divided into two groups, characteristics of the group and behavior of the leader. The four subtests of the group are (1) disengagement, (2) hindrance, (3) esprit, and (4) intimacy. The four subtests of the leader behavior are (1) aloofness, (2) production emphasis, (3) thrust, and (4) consideration (Halpin, 1966, pp. 133-34).

Several studies using the *OCDQ* have been completed. Studies dealing with organizational climate and administrative structure have been limited. One study at the junior college level found no significant relationship between structure and climate. However, certain demographic variables (age, sex, orientation) were found to be significantly related to perception of climate. Additionally, certain climate dimensions were found to be related to individual structure (Smith, 1964, 184 pp.).

The administrative structure of units of physical education varies. Some units are located within their own school or college, others under a college of education, and still others under a college such as fine and applied arts. The focus of this study was on the relationship of the administrative structure and the organizational climate of units of physical education.

Statement of Problem

The main problem of this study was to examine the organizational climate in departments and other administrative units of physical education in twenty midwestern universities to determine if significant differences (p. 01) in climate occur in units with different organizational structures. This study was an attempt to measure organizational climate and the perceived behavior of the group and the leader of the organization.

SUBPROBLEMS

1. To determine if faculty members who hold joint appointments in the athletic and physical education programs perceive the organizational climate significantly differently than those faculty members who hold appointments only in the department of physical education.
2. To determine if there is any significant difference in organizational climate as perceived by the chief administrator in departments of physical education and as viewed by faculty members in these departments.
3. To determine if there is any significant difference in organizational climate as perceived by faculty members who hold different professorial rank (e.g., instructor, assistant professor, associate professor, and full professor).
4. To determine if organizational climate has any significant relationship to the following factors:
   a. Number of years of service on the faculty (i.e., the average number of years of service of the full-time faculty).
   b. Staff turnover (i.e., the number of faculty members who left the department or unit at the end of the last school year).
   c. Staff publications (i.e., the number of books, articles, pamphlets, and monographs published while on the staff).
   d. Number of full-time faculty members on the staff.
   e. Number of full-time undergraduate majors.
   f. Number of full-time graduate majors.

In each of the subproblems, the investigator predicted there would be no significant differences in perception by any of the groups studied and no significant relationships between climate and other demographic measures taken.

DEFINITION OF TERMS:

Administration is the "process (cycle of events) engaged in by members of a social organization in order to control and direct the activities of the members within the organization" (Griffiths, 1959, p. 73).

Administrators are "those members who are officially charged with the function of administration" (Griffiths, 1964, p. 427).

Administrative Theory is a term used to describe scientific theory or theories of administration.

It is generally recognized in the current literature that there is at present no well-developed, comprehensive theory of administration. Administrative theory, when developed and empirically tested, will be a part of a general theory of social action, and a theory of administrative behavior will be a part of a general theory of human behavior. The lack of administrative theory is partly attributable to the corresponding lack of these more comprehensive theories in the social sciences (Spaeth, 1967, p. 6).

Organizational climate is the personality of an organization. "Personality is to the individual what organizational climate is to the organization" (Halpin, 1966, p. 131).

The eight dimensions of the organizational climate of the *OCDQ* are defined as follows:

DIMENSIONS OF TEACHER BEHAVIOR:

1. *Disengagement* refers to the teacher's tendency to be "not with it." This characterizes a faculty which is merely "going through the motions." It is a group which is "not in gear."
2. *Hindrance* refers to the teacher's feeling that the principal burdens him with routine duties, committee demands, and other requirements which interfere with his primary responsibility to teach. Teachers perceive the principal as hindering rather than facilitating their work.
3. *Esprit* is morale. The teachers feel that their social needs are being satisfied, and they are, at the same time, enjoying a sense of accomplishment in their teaching.
4. *Intimacy* refers to the teachers' enjoyment of friendly social relations with each other. This dimension describes a social-need satisfaction which is not necessarily associated with task accomplishment.

DIMENSIONS OF LEADER BEHAVIOR:

5. *Aloofness* refers to behavior of a principal which is formal and impersonal. Such an individual "goes by the book" and prefers to be guided by rules and policies rather than to work face-to-face with teachers.
6. *Production emphasis* is the behavior of a principal which is characterized by close supervision of the staff. He is highly directive and plays the role of a "straw boss." His communication tends to go in one direction only and he is insensitive to feedback from his faculty.
7. *Thrust* refers to behavior of a principal which is typically an effort to "move the organization." Such behavior is not marked by close supervision. The principal motivates by setting a personal example of industry. He asks of teachers only that which he willingly does himself.

8. *Consideration* is that behavior of a principal which is characterized by an inclination to treat teachers "humanly," to try to do a little something extra for them in human terms. Such behavior is apart from rules and stated policies.

The six climates as identified by the *OCDQ* are as follows:

1. The *open* climate describes an energetic, lively organization which is moving toward its goals, and which provides a satisfaction for the group members' social needs. Leadership acts emerge easily and appropriately from both the group and the leader. The members are preoccupied disproportionately with neither task achievement nor social-needs satisfaction; satisfaction on both counts seems to be obtained easily and almost effortlessly. The main characteristic of this climate is the "authenticity" of the behavior that occurs among all members.
2. The *autonomous* climate is described as one in which leadership acts emerge primarily from the group. The leader exerts little control over the group members: High esprit results primarily from the social-needs satisfaction. Satisfaction from a task achievement is also present, but to a lesser degree.
3. The *controlled* climate is characterized best as impersonal and highly task-oriented. The group's behavior is directed primarily toward task accomplishment, while relatively little attention is given to behavior-oriented social-needs satisfaction. Esprit is fairly high, but it reflects achievement at some expense to social-needs satisfaction. This climate lacks openness, or "authenticity" of behavior, because the group is disproportionately preoccupied with task achievement.
4. The *familiar* climate is highly personal, but undercontrolled. The members of this organization satisfy their social needs but pay relatively little attention to social control in respect to task accomplishment. Accordingly, esprit is not extremely high simply because the group members secure little satisfaction from task achievement. Hence, much of the behavior within this climate can be construed as "inauthentic."
5. The *paternal* climate is characterized best as one in which the principal constrains the emergence of leadership acts from the group and attempts to initiate most of these acts himself. The leadership skills within the group are not used to supplement the principal's own ability to initiate leadership acts. Accordingly, some leadership acts are not even attempted. In short, little satisfaction is obtained in respect to either achievement or social needs; hence, esprit among members is low.
6. The *closed* climate is characterized by a high degree of apathy on the part of all members of the organization. The organization is not "moving"; esprit is low because the group members secure

neither social-needs satisfaction nor the satisfaction that comes from task achievement. The members' behavior can be construed as "inauthentic"; indeed, the organization seems to be stagnant (Halpin, 1966, pp. 150-81).

Background and Related Literature

Gross stated that "administrative thought—in the sense of specialized, concentrated, continuous, and recorded observation and speculation—is distinctly a modern development" (1964, p. 32). The work of Mary Parker Follett, Elton Mayo, Fritz Roethlisberger, Chester Barnard, and Herbert Simon can be considered a "new beginning" in administrative thought.

Mary Parker Follett pointed out clearly that in studying administration, "the technical side could not be divorced from the human side" (Gross, p. 47). Mayo and Roethlisberger were involved in the famous "Hawthorne studies," and a simplified conclusion of their work was that people work more efficiently if they are treated like human beings (Gross, pp. 51-55). Barnard authored the book *Functions of the Executive* and pointed out that scientists often did not recognize formal organization "as a most important characteristic of social life, and as being the principal structural aspect of society itself" (Gross, pp. 56-57). Simon freely criticized the work of earlier writers. His central goal was to develop a "value-free science of administrative behavior, if not indeed a 'science of man' " (Gross, p. 64).

After World War II the interest in a more "theoretical approach to administration" mounted. Halpin felt that there were three significant developments in the movement to develop theory in educational administration. The first was the establishment of the National Conference for Professors of Educational Administration (NCPEA) 1947. The second came about through the Kellogg Foundation's support of the Cooperative Program in Educational Administration (CPEA). And the third major development was establishment of the University Council for Educational Administration (UCEA) in 1956 (Halpin, 1964).

The overall result of the creation of these groups appears to be a fusing of the various disciplines studying human behavior in order to better understand and study the administrative process.

METHODS OF STUDYING ORGANIZATIONAL CLIMATE

Etzioni stated that we are born in organizations, educated in organizations, and generally spend much of our lives working for organizations (1964, p. 1). The critical problem in studying organizational climate is to consider both organizational variables and individual variables in describing behavior that occurs in the organizational setting. One of the main problems in conceptualizing integrated synthesis of organizational characteristics has been what to call the characteristics. The term "organizational climate" has been chosen by some to describe these characteristics; climate and morale have often been used synonomously but climate is now considered a more global concept, and morale but one part of the climate.

The problem of using morale as a basic concept was clearly stated by Haire:

> Morale. There is probably no other field in the area of social psychological problems in industry in which there are so many publications as there are under the general heading of morale. The number of independent measurements of the state of morale in different situations and with different instruments is legion, and it has become necessary to fall back on a biennial bibliography simply to keep abreast of those reported in the professional journals. . . . In spite of all this material, it is still difficult to say what is meant by morale, what its springs are in the human organization or a factory, or what its results are. . . . There is no question but what morale—however the concept should be defined—is a real phenomenon. Indeed, there is little question that it is an important variable. However, this field, representing a triangular meeting of difficult grounds in motivational theory, the theory of social organizations, and these techniques of interviewing, is still largely unrewarding. It remains as a technical problem both from the point of view of the industrial executive or consultant social scientist, who does not know quite how to handle it, but who feels that it is there and that it must be important (1954, p. 118).

Halpin concurred when he said "the difficulty, of course, is that this approach rests upon the a priori assumption that a single dimension—that is morale—can usefully summarize the essence of the variations that occur in organizational climates." He maintained that all research to date about morale yielded one clear finding: "Morale, whatever it may or may not be, is not unidimensional in its structure" (1964, pp. 141-42).

Early attempts at describing organizational climate used the morale approach. Another method, that of producing long lists of adjectives which describe organizational characteristics, was introduced after the morale approach. This method is faulty also, in that the terms chosen are not derived by theoretical formulation, but by armchair speculations. Halpin felt that a major weakness in these two methods of studying organizational climate "lies in the faulty and rather silly assumption that the *word* for whatever we may seek to study is somewhere in the catalog; all we need to do is find the event or the phenomenon which corresponds to the word." Halpin continued by stating that in studying organizational climates and . . . to name these climates only *after* we had analyzed the specific behaviors" (1964, pp. 140-45).

Forehand and Gilmer stated that there have been four basic methods used for making systematic observations of behavior in organizations: (1) field studies, (2) objective indices, (3) climate manipulation, and (4) perception of members (1966, p. 612).

Two basic methods of observing climate variation in ongoing organizations have been (1) examining behavior in contrasting organizations (comparative studies), and (2) studying the effects of changing conditions in a single organization (longitudinal studies).

One of the most common approaches to the study of organizational properties has been to use objective indices. Almost every company has a large file of records which can be analyzed to see what various relationships exist between variables. The advantage of this type of research in studying organizations is obvious; the records are there, waiting to be analyzed. This approach, like the field method, has been most popular in business and industry. The results of many studies using this method are congruent with a model which Argyris has formulated concerning individual adaption to organizational conflict. The basic assumption of this model is that organizational behavior develops from interaction of the individual and formal organization. Because of the basic properties of individuals and organizations, interaction causes incongruency between the self-actualization of the two. The individual adapts to the conflict by (1) climbing the organizational ladder; (2) by becoming apathetic, disinterested, and noninvolved; (3) by creating informal groups; and (4) by accepting dissatisfaction as inevitable and increasing desire for material rewards such as money. One of the ways of becoming apathetic and noninvolved is to identify "minimum levels of acceptable work and/or plaguing the company with practices that are annoying" (1957, pp. 175-76).

In using field studies and/or objective indices, there is an underlying assumption that there is some "climate" out there and the intent of the research is to discover whatever that climate may be. The experimental manipulation of climate attempts to create relevant dimensions of climate and vary them systematically.

The vast majority of research in this area has been concerned with small groups. "Extrapolations from small groups [to large organizations] have been free and easy" (Leavitt and Bass, 1961, p. 371). In other words, much of what is known about climate manipulation variables has been taken from research concerning small groups.

The study of climate in groups has developed along two different patterns. The first of these is communication networks. Many studies have looked at patterns of communication and individual position in the pattern. By manipulation of organizational arrangement, variations in communications can be studied.

The second approach to group manipulation has occurred since the "Hawthorne study" and the resulting concern for "human relations" in management. Most of these studies have been concerned with the effects of democratic versus authoritarian, employee-centered versus job-centered, or participative versus nonparticipative types of climates.

The fourth method of investigating organizational climate is through the perceptions of the participants in the organization. A major argument for use of perceptions is that the perceptions are based on experience which is more extensive and involved than that of any outside observer.

Several instruments used to record the perception of participants have been developed and used extensively. Pace and Stern were coauthors of the *College Characteristics Index (CCI)*, which was designed to identify the climate of a college as perceived by the students (Pace, 1962, p. 47). The "interaction-influence" model constructed by Likert assigns central importance to perceptions of organizational characteristics by organization members (Likert, 1961, pp. 195-303).

Business and industry have also used perceptions of members to study the organizational climate. The *Organizational Analysis Audit* is an eighty-two-item questionnaire which seeks to measure nine variables of an organization (Seashore, 1964, pp. 43-44). Hemphill reported the designing of a *Group Dimensions Description Questionnaire* in 1956. The questionnaire yielded scores on thirteen group dimensions and has been administered to such diverse groups as sororities, departments of a liberal arts college, and elementary and high school faculties. Assessment of an individual group member's particular orientation toward a group in which he is a member and description of major dimensions of a group as seen by its members can be made with this instrument (Hemphill, 1956, 66 pp.).

Null stated that "a major breakthrough resulting from investigations in the area of organizational climate was not achieved until the year 1963" (1967, p. 2). This breakthrough was the development of the *Organizational Climate Description Questionnaire (OCDQ)* by Halpin and Croft (1962, 187 pp.). Since its inception, the *OCDQ* has been used over two hundred times in elementary schools, junior high schools, senior high schools, junior colleges, and one study reported in a high school in India. Although these studies vary in their approach and methods, they fall into five basic groups: (1) validity studies, (2) variables of teachers, administrators, and communities, (3) organizational structure and social group structure, (4) innovations in education, and (5) student achievement.

Methodology

In order to identify institutions for the study, a letter was sent to the chairman of the department of physical education in over one hundred universities in the Midwest. The intent of the letter was to classify the various departments of physical education according to their administrative structure. Four basic types of administrative structure were described in the questionnaire.

Structure one has a department of physical education which is located within a college of education. The highest administrative position in this department or unit is the department chairman or head, and he is responsible directly to the dean of the college of education.

Structure two is much the same as number one, except that this department is located within a college other than education (fine and applied arts, liberal arts and sciences, etc.).

Structure three is also located in a college of education, but has a division of various areas of physical education, health, and recreation. The highest administrative position is a director's position, and the director is responsible to the dean of the college of education. The head of the physical education department is one of several heads responsible to the director.

Structure four consists of a department of physical education which is found in a college of physical education. The department of physical education is but one of several departments within the college of physical education. The highest administrative position in this structure is the dean of the college of physical education.

Twenty schools (five in each structure) were selected according to the following criteria: (1) an accredited member of the North Central Association of College and Secondary Schools; (2) a department of physical education unit which as an administrative structure falls into one of the types described in the questionnaire; (3) an enrollment of 5,000 or over; (4) a department or unit of physical education faculty with ten or more members.

SURVEY PROCEDURE

All institutions and respondents were assigned a code number by an anonymous recorder. The coding system was used in order to ensure anonymity, and to aid the follow-up procedure. Four hundred and eleven questionnaries were sent out in the first mailing. A second questionnaire was sent by the anonymous recorder after two weeks and a third after four weeks. Of the 411 questionnaires sent, 368, or 89.5 percent, were returned.

The completed instruments were scored at New Mexico State University. Raw scores, double standardized scores, and climate scores for both individuals and groups were returned on IBM sheets.

ANALYSIS AND INTERPRETATION OF THE DATA

The main method of statistical analysis used in this study was multivariate analysis of variance. The summed scores of the eight subtests of the *OCDQ* were derived through the scoring services provided by the New Mexico State University Testing Services, Inc. The four subtests pertaining to the leader (aloofness, production emphasis, thrust, and consideration) and the four subtests pertaining to the faculty (disengagement, hindrance, esprit, and intimacy) were each analyzed in separate designs. Significant differences ($p < .01$) between (a) four administrative structures; (b) type of appointment (joint or single); (c) professorial rank (instructor, assistant professor, associate professor, and full professor); and (d) position of responsibility (faculty versus department chairman) on faculty as well as leader variables were analyzed by means of a one-way multivariate analysis of variance (MANOVA). In addition, a univariate analysis of variance was computed using the "openness"[1] of the climate score for each of the four independent variables previously cited.

Findings and Conclusions

The major purpose of this investigation was to study the organizational climate in units of physical education which were organized under different administrative structures. In conjunction with this, an attempt was made to study the relationship of certain department and demographic variables with the organizational climate.

The following hypothesis was tested statistically: *There will be no significant variation in the perception of climate in units with different organizational structure.* (Rejected.) The multivariate F-ratio for both leader and faculty subtests were found to be significant at less than the .01 level. On the leader dimensions, the discriminate function coefficients indicated that the subtests aloofness, thrust, and consideration were responsible for a major part of the variance. The univariate F-ratio showed the subtests aloofness and thrust significant at the .01 level. Additionally, the univariate F-ratio between "openness" and structure was significant at less than the .01 level. The leaders in structure two were perceived with the highest degree of aloofness, while the structure one leaders were scored as being less aloof than the other three structures. Faculty in structures three and four both perceived the leader as displaying more thrust and consideration than did the faculty of structures one and two. The results show that structures one and two tended to have similar results, while scores for structures three and four also seemed to cluster.

On faculty dimensions, the multivariate F-ratio and three of the four univariate tests were significant at less than the .01 level. Disengagement, esprit, and intimacy were all found to be significant. Discriminant function coefficients for the multivariate test showed the subtests disengagement and intimacy as showing major variation. The scores for the four structures clustered in much the same way as they did on the leader subtests. Structures three and four tended to view all group subscales in a more favorable manner than did structures one and two.

For types of appointments, the following hypothesis was tested:*There will be no significant difference between the perceptions of faculty members who hold joint appointments (physical education and athletics) and those faculty members who are employed only in the department of physical education.* (Partially rejected.) The multivariate F-ratio for the four leader subtests was

---

[1]"Openness" scores are computed by adding the subtests esprit and thrust and subtracting the subtest disengagement.

significant at less than the .01 level. The computed discriminant function coefficients showed the subtests aloofness and consideration were the major areas of variance. The univariate F-ratios found aloofness significant at the .01 level and consideration at less than the .05 level.

The analysis of the four group dimensions found no significant difference on the multivariate test. Additionally, the univariate tests on the four dimensions were not significant at the .01 level. The computed discriminant function coefficients did show that disengagement accounted for most of the variance on the multivariate test. The univariate F-ratio for the subtest disengagement was found to be significant at the .05 level. The last analysis comparing appointment to "openness" was found to be not significant.

On the basis of these analyses, this hypothesis is only partially rejected. There was a significant difference on the multivariate leader subtests, but not on the group subtests. Coaches perceived the leader as more aloof and less considerate than did the faculty members who were not coaching any sport. Moreover, the coaches perceived higher degrees of disengagement than did the teaching faculty members. Although the difference on the disengagement univariate test was at the .05 level, it should probably be considered in looking at the overall climate picture.

The third major hypothesis tested was: *There will be no significant differences between the organizational climate as perceived by the chief administrators (chairman or department head) of the administrative units and by the faculty members of those units.* (Rejected.) The multivariate F-ratios for both the leader subtests and the faculty subtests were significant at less than the .01 level. The discriminant function coefficients showed aloofness to account for a major part of the variance. In addition, the univariate F-ratio for aloofness was significant at less than the .01 level while the subtests consideration and thrust were significant at less than the .05 level.

Three univariate F-ratios, disengagement, esprit, and intimacy, were significant at less than the .01 level on the faculty subtests. The univariate tests between position of responsibility and "openness" scores were also significant at less than the .01 level. The unit chairmen perceived the majority of the subtests as well as the overall climate in a significantly more favorable way than did the faculty.

The fourth major hypothesis to be tested was: *There will be no significant difference between the organizational climate as perceived by the faculty who hold different professorial rank (instructor, assistant professor, associate professor, and full professor).* (Accepted.) The results of the multivariate tests for leader and faculty dimensions found neither test significant at the .01 level. The results of all eight univariate F-ratios were also found to be not significant at the .01 level. The univariate test between professorial rank and "openness" scores was not significant at the .01 level.

Although the results of these analyses showed no significant difference at the .01 level, they do warrant some discussion. The multivariate test for leader dimensions was significant at the .02 level. The univariate F-ratio for disengagement was also significant at the .02 level. An analysis of discriminant function coefficients, univariate F-ratios, and mean subscale scores shows that the assistant professors saw higher levels of disengagement and lower esprit and intimacy than did the other three ranks. In addition, the assistant professors perceived the leader as less considerate and as providing less thrust than did the other three ranks.

The final hypothesis investigated was as follows: *Organizational climate, as viewed by the faculty, will have no significant relationship to the following factors: (1) number of years service on the faculty, (2) staff publications, (3) staff turnover, (4) number of full-time faculty, (5) number of full-time undergraduate majors, and (6) number of full-time graduate majors.* (Accepted.) The results of the six product-moment correlations between the "openness" scores and two individual and four group factors showed no correlations which were significant.

CONCLUSIONS

The results of this study confirm the investigator's belief that more research needs to be carried out in physical education and athletics employing the behavioral approach. The perception of organizational climate by members of four different administrative structures was shown to be significantly different. The analyses used in this study assessed not only the overall climate, but also the perceived leader and faculty behavior.

Based on the result of the statistical analyses completed in this study, the following conclusions are submitted:

1. The organizational structure of an academic unit of physical education evidently has a more significant influence on perception of climate by faculty members than is generally recognized.
2. Individuals who teach *and* coach tend to perceive the climate and its dimensions in significantly different ways than individuals who teach *only*.
3. The leaders of units of physical education perceive the climate and its dimensions in significantly different ways than the faculty of these units.

Implications for the Administrator

The four administrative structures of units of physical education were found to be significantly different in overall organizational climate and its various dimensions. Structures one and two tended to cluster in perception of climate, while structures three and four were also found to be very similar to each other. Exactly what factors in the structures are responsible for the significant differences is not clear. The discussion to follow will be an attempt to put forth plausible explanations for the differences.

The fact that the structures tended to cluster into two groups is particularly noteworthy. Structures one and two are similar in that the highest administrative position in the unit is that of department chairman or head. Physical education and related areas such as health, safety, and recreation are located under one departmental structure. In structures three and four, there is more autonomy than in the first two structures. The latter two structures are physical education units within schools or colleges of physical education, respectively. The most important factor here is that in structures three and four, the physical education unit is separate from other areas generally associated with physical education. In structures one and two, persons who may be more interested in health, safety, or recreation are located *within* the department of physical education. This is not true in the latter two groups. Related areas are located in their own units within the overall school or college of physical education.

If persons in related areas are working under the same administrative unit, there is the possibility that the group will be divided by persons with different professional interests and goals. In addition, the perceived goals of the leader, either overt or covert, could be in considerable conflict with those of one or more subgroups.

On the group dimensions of the *OCDQ,* structures one and two showed higher levels of disengagement and lower levels of esprit and intimacy. The leader was also viewed as having less thrust and consideration in structures one and two.

The fact that structures one and two perceived the climate and its dimensions in less-favorable ways than did structures three and four may be related to the first component of Halpin's paradigm—the task. If organizational members perceived the task differently, the organization may have difficulty functioning. As Halpin stated: "many dilemmas in administration arise simply because the organization's task has been formulated too loosely to permit efficient operation" (1966, p. 22).

There are indications that more departments of physical education would like to become, or are moving toward becoming, a school or college structure. A study by Nixon in 1949 showed only seven institutions with either schools or colleges of physical education. By 1967, this number had grown to twenty-three. Furthermore, thirty-one other institutions were planning to move in this direction (McCristal, 1968).

The findings of this study support the general concept of a more autonomous administrative structure for units of physical education. The mixing of persons with different professional goals and interests can create organizational conflict and make the task of the organization unclear. The fact that persons in areas of health, safety, and recreation have ever-widening task perceptions with physical education is exemplified by the fact that several schools and/or colleges of physical education are considering changing the college or school name to something more comprehensive than physical education.

The findings of this investigation show significant differences also between the perceptions of faculty members who coach and those who teach only. The overall relationship of physical education and athletics in modern universities is certainly an area which deserves considerable research in the immediate future.

The coaches saw the group as having higher levels of disengagement and the leader as more aloof and less considerate than did the teachers. The problem of task perception may be a partial answer to the perceived differences in the two groups. Coaches may be more interested in the goals of athletics than those of physical education. Coaches may also tend to associate more often with other coaches than with teachers, and hence perceive higher levels of group disengagement. In addition, the leader may have been deemed less considerate by the coaches because of behavior which would indicate the leader was primarily interested in the so-called physical education task.

These findings appear to support the concept of separate units for physical education and for athletics. In a comprehensive study of the relationship of physical education and athletics, Marshall found that there was a general movement in American universities to separate physical education and athletics:

> There appears to be considerable desire to foster and maintain separate administrative units for physical education and intercollegiate athletics among physical education and athletic administrators in American colleges and universities. This attitude seems especially prevalent among directors of athletics. Directors of physical education and athletics and directors of physical education, while more favorable toward the combined administrative unit for both programs, also indicated apprehension about organizing intercollegiate athletics as a function of the physical education department (Marshall, 1969).

The perceptions of the leaders and the faculty were found to be significantly different. The chairmen saw the climate much more favorably than did the faculty. These results seem to point out that the leaders are not completely aware of the behavior within the organization; or they are not willing to describe it. It is not too surprising that the leader would rate himself higher on the leader dimensions than the faculty rated him. The results showed also, however, that the leader perceived the group as more functional than did the staff. The exact reasons for these differences are not easy to describe. The leader may naturally assume that the organization is functioning more successfully than do members of the staff. It does seem apparent that physical education administrators need to be more aware of the behavioral aspects of administration. The fact that there was a very significant difference on the subtest aloofness is particularly interesting. Because the universities are so large and complex, it may be that the leader needs to make special efforts to make himself available to the faculty.

The area of physical education holds great potential for further research in the area of administration. The number of studies using the situational and behavioral approach have, up to this point, been limited. One of the main problems to be overcome in this area of research is the development of unobtrusive measures with which to study leader and group behavior. Many persons are sensitive to questions concerning behavior of themselves and others. Also, it is difficult to describe and not to evaluate at the same time. In the case of this study, a department with a closed climate is not necessarily a "bad" one. Instead, it is one in which behavior is such that the organization may be hindered in its ability to attain its goals. All physical educators, and especially physical education administrators, must become more aware of the forces which cause persons to behave as they do. Educational administrators have forsaken the "principles" approach to administration in favor of a situational and/or behavioral approach. Physical education might do well to adopt this same approach.

General Bibliography

Argyris, Chris, *Personality and Organization*. New York: Harper & Brothers, 1957.

Etzioni, Amitai, *Modern Organizations*. Englewood Cliffs, N.J.: Prentice-Hall, Inc., 1964.

Forehand, Garlie, and B. von Haller Gilmer, "Environmental Variation in Studies of Organizational Behavior," in *Readings in Organizational Theory: A Behavioral Approach*, ed. Walter Hill and Douglas Egan. Boston: Allyn and Bacon, 1966.

Griffiths, Daniel, *Administrative Theory*. New York: Appleton-Century-Crofts, 1959.

Gross, Bertram M., *The Managing of Organizations*. New York: The Free Press, 1964.

―――――, "The Scientific Approach to Administration," in *Behavioral Science and Educational Administration*, ed. Daniel Griffiths. Chicago: The University of Chicago Press, 1964.

Haire, Mason, "Industrial Social Psychology," in *Handbook of Social Psychology*, ed. Gardner Lindzey. Cambridge, Mass.: Addison-Wesley Publishing Co., Inc., 1954.

Halpin, Andrew, ed., *Administrative Theory in Education*. New York: The Macmillan Co., 1967.

Halpin, Andrew, and Donald Croft, *The Organizational Climate of Schools.* Washington, D.C.: The United States Office of Education, 1962.

Hemphill, John K., *Group Dimensions: A Manual for Their Measurement.* Columbus, Ohio: Bureau of Business Research, 1956.

Leavitt, H. J., and B. M. Bass, "Organizational Psychology," *Annual Review of Psychology,* 10 (1948), 271-99.

Marshall, Stanley J., "The Organizational Relationship between Physical Education and Intercollegiate Athletics in American Colleges and Universities." Ph.D. diss., Springfield College, 1969.

Null, Eldon J., *Organizational Climate of Elementary Schools.* Danville, Ill.: The Interstate Printers and Publishers, Inc., 1967.

Pace, C. R., "Implication of Differences in Campus Atmosphere for Evaluation and Planning of College Programs," in *Personality Factors on the College Campus,* ed. R. L. Sutherland, W. H. Holtzman, E. A. Doile, and B. K. Smith. Austin, Texas: Hogg Foundation for Mental Health, 1962.

Seashore, Stanley E., ed., *Assessing Organizational Performance with Behavioral Measurements.* Ann Arbor, Mich.: The Foundation for Research on Human Behavior, 1964.

Smith, David S., "Relationships between External Variables and the Organizational Climate Description Questionnaire." Ph.D. diss., Northwestern University, 1966.

Spaeth, Marcia, "An Analysis of Administrative Research in Physical Education and Athletics in Relation to a Research Paradigm." Ph.D. diss., University of Illinois, 1967.

Zeigler, Earle F., and Garth Paton, "Administrative Theory as a Basis for Practice in Intercollegiate Athletics," National College Physical Education Association for Men, *Proceedings of Seventieth Annual Meeting.* San Diego, California, 1966, pp. 131-39.

10

Faculty Job Satisfaction in Physical Education and Athletics

Juri V. Daniel

Introduction

GENERAL

Administration of physical education and athletics, although unique in respect to certain characteristics, can possibly be best understood as a social process and as an integral part of organizational, group, and individual behavior. Knowledge that would contribute to organizational and administrative theory can best be advanced by research that attempts to deal concurrently with data at different levels of organizational behavior—that of the individual, the group, and the organization. Attempts toward a better understanding of administration and organizational theory have yielded a number of theories, models, and paradigms, all contributing to an interdisciplinary approach.

Literature in the administration of physical education and athletics suggests that the prevailing trend of "solutions of immediate or localized problems" (Spaeth, 1967, p. 151) based on the point of view that administration is a technology—that is, a matter of applying appropriate techniques to the solutions of relevant practical problems—is changing toward a search for sound

Juri V. Daniel is from The University of Toronto, Canada.

theoretical bases in understanding the administrative process in physical education and athletics. Evidence is cumulating to show a "reaching out" by investigators in physical education toward other disciplines for the purpose of an interdisciplinary approach to research in administration grounded in the social and behavioral sciences.

For the purpose of this study, the concept of administration as a social process was selected (Getzels et al., 1968). Getzels and his associates see administration as a social process taking place in a social system that is structurally a hierarchy of superordinate-subordinate relationships. Functionally, it is a hierarchy of relationships in which roles and facilities are allocated and integrated for the purpose of best achieving the goals of the system. Operationally, it takes place in person-to-person situations.

Administration, then, is a social process of directing organizational resources toward established goals.

One of the more important problems in this process and in the life of formal organizations, and the one to which this study relates, is the basic incongruency often found between the goals of the organization and the needs of the individuals within it. Investigators representing a variety of approaches and points of view have provided considerable insight into this phenomenon and, though findings and theoretical interpretations do not agree on the solution of the problem, considerable agreement exists on its causes.

Somewhat oversimplified, the problem can be reduced to the satisfaction of what Maslow has called "hierarchical needs" of the individual through the achievement of organizational goals (Maslow, 1943, pp. 379-96).

As part of a formal organization, the individual meets a variety of situations, relationships, tasks, pressures, interactions, and expectations which tap his potential and affect his need dispositions. The characteristics of these social processes may range from relative incongruency with certain of his needs (and, therefore, frustration, and dissatisfaction) to relative congruency with most of his needs (and, therefore, satisfaction, high morale, and self-actualization).

The "Operational Model of Major Dimensions of Social Behavior" of Getzels et al. and its dynamic nature as the basis of the administrative process is appropriate in illustrating the congruency-incongruency phenomenon in the interaction of the nomothetic (institutional) and idiographic (individual) dimensions (1968, p. 106). The model also lends itself to derivations and applications relevant to issues in the study and practice of administration. Among these issues are (1) the source of conflict in a social system; (2) the problems of adaptation and adjustment; (3) the meaning of effectiveness, efficiency, satisfaction, and morale in the administrative setting; (4) the nature of authority and leadership-followership styles; and (5) the problem of organizational change. The first and third issues are of particular interest to this study. Simplified diagrams from the original model are offered as illustrations in *Figures 1* and *2*.

Nomothetic Dimension

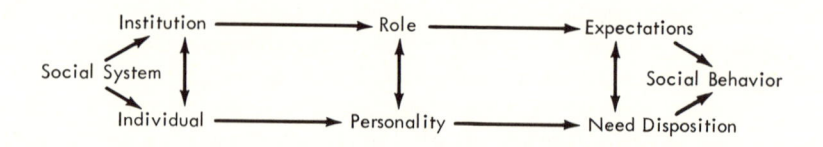

```
                Institution ─────────► Role ─────────► Expectations
              ↗            ↕            ↕               ↕          ↘
Social System                                                        Social Behavior
              ↘            ↕            ↕               ↕          ↗
                Individual ─────────► Personality ──► Need Disposition
```

Idiographic Dimension

Figure 1. Adapted from the "Operational Model of Major Dimensions of Social Behavior" in J. W. Getzels, J. M. Lipham, R. F. Campbell, *Educational Administration as a Social Process: Theory, Research, Practice*, New York: Harper and Row Publ., 1968, p. 106.*

The relationship of satisfaction of the individual in the social system can be derived from the model as follows:

```
Role ─────────► Expectations ╲
                     ↕          ╲ Effectiveness
                                   ╲
                 Satisfaction        ► Behavior
                     ↕             ╱
                                 ╱ Efficiency
Personality ──► Need Disposition ╱
```

Figure 2. Adapted from the "Relation of Role Expectations and Need-Dispositions to Effectiveness, Efficiency, and Satisfaction" in J. W. Getzels, J. M. Lipham, R. F. Campbell, *Educational Administration as a Social Process: Theory, Research, Practice.* New York: Harper and Row Publ, 1968, p. 128.**

Behavior can be viewed as a function of role expectations and need dispositions and, because these in turn are influenced by the institution and the interaction of the institutional and individual dimensions, the importance of the study and understanding of the incongruency phenomenon becomes evident.

A multitude of studies with various approaches have attempted to assess either directly or indirectly this incongruency between the individual and the organization and its possible effects upon such organizational factors as productivity, turnover, absenteeism, group cohesion, morale, and job satisfaction, to name some.

*This figure originally appeared in *Readings in the Social Psychology of Education*, W. W. Charters, Jr., and N. L. Gage, eds. Boston, Mass.: Allyn and Bacon, Inc., 1963, p. 312.

**This figure appeared earlier in "Social Behavior and the Administrative Process," by Getzels et al., *School Review* 65, 433 (1957). Courtesy the University of Chicago Press.

Job satisfaction, for example, chosen as the dependent variable in this study, has been intensively researched in industrial psychology and educational administration. The findings are not conclusive. In part, this is because of difficulties in definition and differences in methodology. Nevertheless, the concept of job satisfaction is directly related to the incongruency or conflict between the normative and individual dimensions of organizational life and administration.

For the purpose of the present study, job satisfaction was defined as referring to the affective orientation on the part of the individual toward his/her job situation. It refers to the feelings the individual has toward the job he/she is involved in at the time (Smith et al., 1969, p. 6).

Determinants of job satisfaction and the concept itself will be discussed later in this report.

PURPOSE OF THE STUDY

Within the broad goal of better understanding of administration of physical education and athletics, the purpose of the study was to search for the possible existence of consistent relationships between organizational differentiation, thus role differentiation, and the job satisfaction of respective faculty members in departments of physical education and athletics in selected Ontario universities. More specifically, the influence of organizational and program specialization stemming from serving varying goals, which range from essentially academic to essentially service, on the satisfaction with work of faculty members in the specific roles, was studied. The influence of selected organizational and personal variables (other than roles) on job satisfaction of faculty members was also investigated.

SPECIFIC FOCUS

Divisions of Ontario universities dealing with athletics and physical education offer a variety of programs to presumably meet the expressed goals of the respective institutions. These goals vary from being essentially congruent with the general academic goals of the institution (undergraduate degree program, graduate education, research) to being complementary and of a service nature (intercollegiate athletics, intramurals, recreational programs for students, staff, and faculty, etc.).

This differentiation of function has gradually produced a variety of organizational structures and faculty roles. This variety ranges from integrated departments in which all aspects of the program are within the jurisdiction of one administrative unit, with many of the faculty being involved in a cross-section of responsibilities and a concomitant diffusion of clear division between what is academic and what is nonacademic, to a specialization of separate departments with their own hierarchical lines of responsibility and communication and consequent faculty specialization in particular program aspects.

A number of questions seem to be pertinent to this situation. What particular structure (and goals) contribute best to job satisfaction and why? Are faculty members who deal with essentially academic matters more satisfied than those dealing with matters such as administration, teaching noncredit courses, supervising recreational programs, etc.? Does separation into men's and women's divisions of programs that could be offered coeducationally affect the job satisfaction of respective faculty members? What is the general level of job satisfaction of physical education faculty, which often finds itself on the fringe of the university community? Are physical education professors more satisfied than coaches or those faculty members who wear several "hats" in an integrated system?

These and other questions need to be answered to provide a better theoretical frame of reference for the appropriate administration of physical education and athletics at the university level. The report that follows will attempt to answer some of these questions.

The author feels that this study was urgently needed for a better understanding of the effects of widely varying organizational structures and administrative functions relative to the job satisfaction of professional physical educators working in departments of physical education and athletics in Ontario universities. This urgency was accentuated by developments in Ontario which have brought about reorganization of these departments, often on an a priori basis rather than on well-founded empirical evidence of organizational effectiveness and efficiency.[1]

Furthermore, because most of us spend a considerable part of our life at work, and before that in preparation for it, the study of job satisfaction in general is important in order to provide better understanding about one of man's most important involvements. On humanistic and materialistic bases, the congruency of organizational effectiveness and behavior efficiency of individuals within the organization is an implicit goal of a democratic society. Studying job satisfaction should add to the "know-how" of tapping human potential more efficiently with greater realization of higher human needs for a larger number of people.

The specific focus will shed light upon the job satisfaction of professional physical educators who because of talent, interest, and organizational structure are involved in physical education and athletics in Ontario universities.

Finally, understanding the influence of differentiation of professional involvement upon such needs as self-esteem and self-actualization is becoming

---

[1] Effectiveness refers to accomplishment of the cooperative purpose and is essentially nonpersonal in nature. Efficiency refers to the satisfaction of individual needs, which is personal in character (Barnard, 1964, p. 60).

increasingly more important in the development of better administrative and personnel practices.

Background and Related Literature

THE INCONGRUENCY PHENOMENON

Organizations are usually created and maintained to achieve objectives that can best be met collectively. This means that the activities necessary to achieve the objectives are too much for the individual, and thus must be divided into manageable units. At the individual level the units are roles; at the group level the units are departments. These units are integrated or organized in a particular pattern designed to achieve the objectives. The resulting pattern constitutes the organizational structure.

Organizations have many sources of energy. One such source involves the psychological state of individuals; any energy input is hypothesized to increase as the individual's experiences of psychological success increase and to decrease with psychological failure.

The organization, through administrative control systems typically used in complex formal organizations, requires the individuals to experience dependence and submissiveness and utilize few of their relatively peripheral abilities. The degree of dependency, submissiveness, etc., tends, according to Argyris, to increase as one goes down the chain of command and as the job requirements and managerial controls increasingly direct the individual; and to decrease as one goes up the chain of command and as the individual is more and more able to control his job requirements (1964, p. 58). McGregor's Theory X and Theory Y give an explicit account of the different ways of using human resources under the traditional view of "direction and control" and the more recent view of "integration of individual and organizational goals" (1960, pp. 33-57). The degree of incongruency and conflict seems to vary directly with the emphasis on the "mechanistic" versus the "humanistic" approach to the use of human resources, particularly psychological energy.

The incongruency or conflict is also illustrated in the model by Getzels et al., referred to earlier. The main sources of conflict are the discrepancies between cultural and institutional expectations, between role expectations and personality dispositions, between and within roles, and are also derived from personality disorders and unclear perception of role expectations (Getzels et al., 1968, p. 105).

Numerous other writers have referred to this basic conflict. Absolute congruency between expectations and needs, among expectations in a role-set, and among needs of an individual is not found in reality. There exist only various degrees of incongruency with consequent greater or lesser degree of conflict for the individual and strain in the organization.

Administration must cope with the resultant organizational conflicts and the potential dysfunctional modes of reaction to them by the individual in the system. From this point of view, the reduction of the incongruency between the normative and personal aspects of organizational life is a fundamental task of administration.

THE CONCEPT OF JOB SATISFACTION

The terms "job satisfaction" and "job attitudes" are typically used interchangeably, and both refer to the affective orientation of the individual toward the work roles he is occupying at the time (Vroom, 1964, p. 99). Similarily, Smith, Kendall, and Hulin have defined job satisfaction as the feelings an individual has about his job: "Job satisfactions are feelings or affective responses to facets of the situation" (1969, p. 6). They have hypothesized that these feelings are associated with a perceived difference between what is expected as a fair and reasonable return; or, when the evaluation of future prospects is involved, what is aspired to and what is actually experienced in relation to possible alternatives available. The relation of job satisfaction to behavior depends upon how the individual conceives that form of behavior to be of help to him in achieving the goals he has accepted. Smith and her associates substantiate their position by suggesting that

> basically our general model subsumes what is common to those posed by many others (e.g., Brown, 1959; England, Korman, and Stein, 1961; England and Stein, 1961; Geogopoulus, Mahoney, and Jones, 1957; Guion, 1958; Harding and Bottenberg, 1961; Jaques, 1961; Kahn and Morse, 1951; Katzell, Barrett, and Parker, 1961; Lawler and Porter, 1967; Mann, 1953; Morse, 1953; Patchen, 1960, 1961; Porter, 1962; Rotter, 1960; Thomsen, 1943; Vroom, 1964; Zaleznik, Christenson, and Roethlisberger, 1958) (1969, p. 7).

Thus, job satisfaction is viewed as a result or consequence of the individual's experience on the job in relation to his own values—i.e., to what he wants or expects from it.

The term "morale" has been given a variety of meanings, some of which correspond closely to the concept of satisfaction. Guion has proposed that morale depends upon the extent to which the individual's needs are satisfied and the extent to which the individual perceives that satisfaction from his total job situation (Guion, 1958, pp. 59-61).

The definitions of job satisfaction and morale have a common denominator in that both deal with the complex system of need satisfaction. Although both have conceptually been found to be basically similar by most investigators, some have proposed differences, theorizing that job satisfaction is part of job morale and that morale is a more hypothetical construct (Stagner, 1958, pp. 64-70).

Because greater agreement exists on the definition of job satisfaction, and because its measurement lends itself to greater validity and reliability (Smith et al., 1969), the concept of job satisfaction was central to this study, and the concept of morale entered it only by implication.

FACTORS AFFECTING JOB SATISFACTION

The factors as studied in industrial psychology and other disciplines that might have an effect on the job satisfaction of individuals in organizations are far too numerous to be reported here. However, those most intensively studied underlie consistently the specific dimensions that have emerged within the general concept of job satisfaction. These are (1) a pay and material rewards factor, (2) a factor dealing with work itself, (3) a supervision factor, and (4) a factor related to other people on the job. These areas relate very closely to those suggested by Smith et al. (1969) in their review of the relevant literature, and in their design of a measuring instrument for work satisfaction. The reader is thus referred for more detailed information to that source. In general, the findings have supported the hypothesis that factors which affect the individual's job satisfaction are those which relate to his need satisfaction either directly or indirectly.

No investigation of job satisfaction can overlook the motivation-hygiene theory of job attitudes. Herzberg and his associates (1959) proposed a theory of *motivation* versus *hygiene.* They identified those factors dealing with the conditions surrounding the job as "hygiene factors" and those factors dealing with the satisfaction of the individual's need for self-actualization in work as "motivators." They further proposed that a duality existed—the lack of hygiene factors could produce dissatisfaction, but when optimal would not produce significant satisfaction; the motivators would lead to positive attitudes and satisfaction, but the lack of motivators would not produce dissatisfaction (Herzberg et al., 1959, pp. 113-19; see also Herzberg, 1969, pp. 103-104; Herzberg, 1965, pp. 393-410).

This issue of the possible discontinuity of satisfaction and dissatisfaction and the related issue of satisfiers or motivators and dissatisfiers or hygiene factors is not conclusive and has not inhibited the development of the uniscalar approach to the research, measurement, and understanding of job satisfaction. An example is the work of Smith et al. (1969), which theorized that a particular job condition can be a satisfier, a dissatisfier, or an "irrelevant," depending on (1) conditions in comparable jobs; (2) conditions of other people; (3) the qualifications and past experience of the individual; and (4) the alternatives available to him, as well as on numerous situational variables of the present job. Each facet was seen as a simple continuum capable of producing satisfaction and dissatisfaction. Again the reader is referred to the work of Herzberg et al. (1959) and Smith et al. for very elaborate research and discussion on the concept and determinants of job satisfaction.

ROLE DIFFERENTIATION AND JOB SATISFACTION

Using the model of major dimensions of social behavior of Getzels et al., satisfaction may be conceived as being directly related to the congruence between individual needs and institutional expectations. With increasing congruence, greater satisfaction, identification, and feelings of belongingness can be anticipated.

Hypothesizing that the need for the satisfaction of hierarchical wants is fairly universal and that the variability of personality characteristics is randomly distributed, role expectation could be considered as the variable that tends to change with organizational and cultural factors. The various theories and research findings in the organization-individual dilemma support the existence of this basic organizational influence upon the individual as an organism seeking self-realization.

Extensive studies in relating organizational structure to employee attitudes bear this out (Worthy, 1950, pp. 169-79). Organizational specialization, vertical structure, role differentiation and specialization, specialization to meet varying goals within an organization, repetitive task specialization, and other organizational and cultural factors which impose greater and greater rigidity on role expectations may increase the conflict between role expectations and need dispositions of the individuals involved. In brief, roles are often determined for purposes of the effectiveness of the organization in meeting its goals without concomitant attention to meeting the needs of the individuals who will enact these roles. This, it was postulated, will be reflected in job satisfaction.

MEASUREMENT OF JOB SATISFACTION

The measurement of job satisfaction falls within the broad spectrum of measuring attitudes. An attitude can be defined as "a relatively enduring system of affective, evaluative reactions based upon and reflecting the evaluative concepts or beliefs which have been learned about the characteristics of a social object or class of social objects" (Shaw and Wright, 1967, p. 10). The reader is also referred to Thurstone (1931), Likert (1932), and Guttman (1944) for further information on measurement of attitudes.

The techniques and approaches used in the measurement of job satisfaction have been too numerous to be reviewed here. Most have been rather specific to a particular subjective interest of the researcher involved. Very few have found broad acceptance and even fewer have evoked generalizations.

Perhaps the most widely used instrument has been the SRA Employee Inventory. According to Smith et al. (1969, p. 27), it is one of the most thoroughly analyzed of the currently available summary measures of job satisfaction, rewards and attitudes. These researchers, however, have presented a convincing argument that multiple rather than summary measures of job satisfaction are needed. They have presented the rationale and supporting evidence from numerous studies which point to the different dimensions of job satisfaction, to their relative independence, and to the need for an instrument which would provide information on the satisfaction with the various aspects of jobs as well as information on job satisfaction in total. They developed over a period of years, with painstaking validation, scales that would measure five dimensions of job satisfaction (work, pay, promotion, supervision, coworkers). The reader is reminded that these dimensions had emerged either implicitly or explicitly in numerous studies. The *Job Descriptive Index* by Smith et al. (1969) has found wide acclaim and the five scales, in the judgment of this writer, are the best available in the measurement of job satisfaction as a multidimensional concept.

This short review of literature offers the basis of some of the rationale for the study of the organizational differentiation and, therefore, role differentiation found in departments of physical education and athletics; (as well as showing how the different role expectations, in their integration with need dispositions of role incumbents, might be reflected in job satisfaction).

The general hypothesis emerging, and in need of testing, was that certain organizational and administrative factors in certain combinations provide jobs (role expectations) in physical education divisions of Ontario universities which vary in their intrinsic and extrinsic characteristics sufficiently to reflect in levels of job satisfaction.

Methodology

To meet the objectives of the study and test the hypotheses set, the causal comparative technique of research was used. Causal comparative studies try to discover not only what a phenomenon is like, but if possible, how and why it occurs. Causal comparative studies compare the likenesses and differences among phenomena to find out what factors or circumstances seem to accompany certain events, conditions, processes, or practices. Although the experimental method is preferred in the study of causality, the causal comparative technique of the descriptive method, sometimes referred to as the *ex post facto* design, lends itself to the study of many problems in behavioral and social sciences where the experimental method cannot be used.

SELECTION OF INSTITUTIONS AND SUBJECTS

Institutions of university status which offered a variety of programs in physical education and athletics, including an undergraduate degree program, were chosen. This was a logico-deductive choice based on the purpose of the study. Thus, ten universities in Ontario were included.

All full-time members of faculties of physical education, and/or health education, and/or recreation, and/or athletics from the selected universities, who held at least the rank of an instructor (September 1969), were chosen to be the subjects making up the population of the study.

Based on these criteria, a population of 208 subjects was established.

SELECTION OF INSTRUMENTS

Based on a selective review of psychometric instruments used in the measurement of job satisfaction, the *Job Descriptive Index* (appendix A) developed by Smith et al. was selected as being the most suitable and valid set of scales available for the purpose of measuring job satisfaction of subjects in this study. For a summary of the development, extensive work on validation, and the reliability of the *Job Descriptive Index (JDI)*, the reader is referred to the original source (Smith et al., 1969).

The significance of the development of the *JDI* is perhaps best expressed by Lyman Porter, himself a known researcher in work satisfaction (e.g., Porter, 1961, 1962), who in the foreword to the book by Smith et al. (1969) summarized its contribution to the study of satisfaction as follows:

> The focus of the book can be summed up in its sub-title: *A Strategy for the Study of Attitudes.* This strategy is developed by devoting considerable attention to the nature of the concept of satisfaction, and particularily, to the requirements for scientifically adequate measures of satisfaction. In fact, it is the emphasis on a comprehensive set of requirements for sound measurement, rather than just one or two elements of it, which is the quality that sets this book apart from any previous report in the area of job satisfaction.
>
> ... the book provides ... rewards. First, it contains the finished form of the JDI—an instrument that can be used with widely varying groups of individuals working under quite different kinds of employment situations. Here is a tangible, tested instrument that can be taken into the field and applied tomorrow.

A *Personal Data and Information Form* was developed by the writer to obtain (1) information on personal and job variables, and (2) information to allow classification of subjects according to emerging differentiated roles. (See appendix B.)

COLLECTION AND ANALYSIS OF DATA

The researcher attempted to use the best methodology in the survey method of collecting data and the most appropriate statistical techniques available in the treatment and analysis of the data.

The received coded data from the respondents, (94 percent of original population responded) was subjected to procedural techniques yielding numerical scores (ranging from 0 to 54) on each of the five dimensions of job satisfaction for each respondent. The five scores were added for each respondent to obtain a *JDI* total score. The received data also provided needed information for the classification of subjects into differentiated roles based on an *a priori* decision of time spent in certain roles to be classified for particular role characteristics. Finally, the data gave selected organizational and personal information on each respondent (age, sex, marital status, etc.).

Before subjecting the data to statistical analyses to test hypotheses set, the satisfaction scores from the *Job Descriptive Index* were checked for distribution characteristics and, although two scales (coworkers, supervision) showed skewness in distribution, the variability and distribution in general supported the use of parametric statistics as originally planned.

Analysis of variance, the Pearson product-moment correlation coefficient, and descriptive statistics were used where appropriate to analyze the data. In addition, where necessary, Kramer's extension of Duncan's new multiple range test was used (Kramer, 1956, pp. 307-310).

Findings and Conclusions

FINDINGS

The reader will remember that job satisfaction was defined as the feelings a person has about his/her job. This definition also implied that different feelings exist toward differentiable aspects of the job. Research dealing with job satisfaction has consistently pointed to these differentiable aspects of the job as a pay and material rewards factor, a factor dealing with work itself, a supervision factor, a factor related to others on the job, and a general factor. The investigator in this study chose, therefore, the instrument that would measure the feelings a person had about the different dimensions of the job, and that would at the same time provide an indication of the individual's feelings toward the job as a whole. As pointed out earlier, the *Job Descriptive Index,* consisting of five scales (work, pay, promotion, supervision, and coworker) with the total score expressing total satisfaction (total *JDI*), designed and validated by Smith et al. (1969), was chosen as the most suitable instrument for the study.

The findings of this investigation suggest that physical educators in Ontario universities are not all equally satisfied with their jobs; differences, however, do not appear uniformly in all dimensions of job satisfaction. Thus, feelings toward the nature of work itself seem to differentiate very little between the subjects, whereas feelings toward promotional opportunities differ greatly and are dependent on job roles and certain personal and organizational variables. The discussion that follows will examine the findings in the light of each dimension and the job in total.

The nature of work itself. The findings suggest that professional physical educators (in this study) do not differ significantly in their feelings toward the kind of work they do. Basically, they like what they do, be it coaching, teaching in service programs, doing research, or doing a combination of things.

Characteristics of remuneration. In respect to this dimension, the feelings of the subjects differed significantly. Female subjects whose roles were essentially academic showed a higher level of satisfaction with financial returns than female subjects whose roles were essentially nonacademic. The underlying conditions for these feelings probably include the fact that the salaries for women were low in general and adequate only for those whose jobs were essentially academic, and who had therefore received a reasonable amount of recognition from the respective institutions.

The more specific the role, the clearer were the findings in suggesting that academic roles and senior administrative positions created conditions that produced relatively high satisfaction with remuneration. Roles that dealt essentially with coaching or teaching nonacademic courses brought little financial recognition from the institutions and thus dissatisfaction with this dimension of job satisfaction. Tenure and senior rank provided conditions that reflected high satisfaction with this dimension. Considering that tenure is often related to senior rank, and that both are related to seniority and appropriate remuneration, this trend favoring subjects with tenure and senior rank should be expected.

Promotional opportunities. The findings suggest that this dimension (institutional recognition) was the aspect of job satisfaction where the most marked differences were observed. Subjects whose roles were essentially academic were significantly more satisfied with promotional opportunities. More specifically, senior academic administrators, teachers in academic programs, and subjects whose roles included a predominant proportion of academic work exhibited significantly higher levels of satisfaction than their colleagues. Tenured subjects felt significantly more satisfied with this dimension, as did subjects with three degrees or senior rank. Finally, subjects in certain institutions were comparatively more satisfied.

The major condition underlying these findings seems to be the general pattern of promotional opportunities in universities. Promotion is granted essentially on the basis of scholarly work; the importance of one's contribution to the department, the institution, and the community at large; and one's seniority and appropriate experience. In physical education and athletics, a number of the respondents fulfilled roles in universities which were somewhat incongruent with the accepted roles that fit established patterns of promotional policies and practices. Thus, the coach, for example, whose essential role is coaching, might be very happy with the work he is doing and might even be happy with his financial returns, but he tends to be relatively dissatisfied with the lack of recognition he is receiving from the institution in regard to academic promotion.

The institutions that stand out in the satisfaction exhibited by their faculty members with promotional opportunities tend to show that their subjects possess higher-than-average academic qualifications, higher-than-average ranks, command higher-than-average salaries, and fulfill predominantly academic roles.

Characteristics of supervision. The findings suggest that, in general, professional physical educators in Ontario universities, regardless of their specific roles or selected personal and organizational variables, do not differ significantly in their feelings about supervisory techniques and supervisory personnel. When grouped according to institutions, significant differences appeared. The underlying conditions may be organizational climate or leadership style, both of which were beyond the scope of this study. Possibly being satisfied with several other dimensions and with the job in general had a carry-over "halo" effect on this dimension.

Relations with coworkers. The findings reveal that the subjects have relatively positive feelings about their coworkers and that they do not differ significantly in these feelings (based on differentiated roles). However, subjects, if grouped by institutions, differ in their feelings toward their colleagues. Again, subjects in institutions with the combination of above average salaries and ranks, and where they fulfilled academic roles essentially, showed the highest satisfaction in their relationship with their colleagues.

Total satisfaction. Total satisfaction was based on summing the scores of the five scales for each subject. The findings show that subjects in academic roles, compared to those in service-oriented roles, were more highly satisfied with their jobs in total. Institutional conditions and personal satisfaction seems to favor those who are in roles that are congruent with the main function of the university. Total satisfaction differed with specific roles (senior academic administrator, teacher in academic programs, and those whose main responsibilities were in academic work), with tenure, with senior rank, and with academic qualifications. All of these factors related to significantly higher satisfaction with the job.

Finally, subjects differed in levels of satisfaction with the job in total according to their institutions. The conditions underlying these differences were the same as the conditions that seemed to underlie the differences on certain dimensions of job satisfaction; namely, higher-than-average salary, higher-than-average rank, higher-than-average academic qualifications, and predominantly academic roles for most subjects in that institution.

In summary, faculty members from divisions of physical and health education and athletics in ten selected Ontario universities tend to differ little in their feelings about work itself, or the nature of their particular daily tasks; about supervision; and about their colleagues; and, in fact, show relatively high satisfaction in these aspects of their jobs. The only departure from these trends appeared in the comparison of institutions.

Distinct differences were observed, however, in the subjects' feelings about financial returns, or tangible recognition by the institution; promotional opportunities, or status recognition; and the job in total which reflected the sum total of feelings about the different aspects of the job.

CONCLUSIONS

The results of this study appear to support the existence of certain consistent trends in the relationship between job satisfaction and job characteristics, between job satisfaction and certain personal variables, and between job satisfaction and certain organizational variables of faculty members in departments of physical education and athletics in ten Ontario universities as measured by the five scales of the *Job Descriptive Index*. Certain statistically significant differences emerged between groups of subjects classified according to selected characteristics dealing with job roles, and dealing with personal and/or organizational variables.

The data that were collected and analyzed have provided partial answers to some of the questions posed in the introduction. Levels of job satisfaction were not the same for all physical educators in Ontario universities. The variance seemed to be related to the incongruency, or conflict, between the individual's expectations and organizational "givens." This variance was often large enough to suggest consistent relationships rather than random individual differences or mere chance occurrence.

In summary and within the limitations of this study, the findings made the following conclusions plausible:

1. Differentiated roles were found to be related to job satisfaction. Respondents whose roles tended to be more congruent with the expected roles of the academic community and whose institutional recognition, therefore, tended to be more congruent with accepted and established institutional patterns, exhibited higher levels of job satisfaction.

2. Consistent relationships also emerged between certain personal and organizational variables and job satisfaction. Variables that related to institutional requisites and recognition of accepted roles (rank, tenure, academic qualifications, years of service, salary) tended to relate to higher levels of job satisfaction.

3. Differences in levels of job satisfaction manifested themselves in *some*, but not all, dimensions of job satisfaction. Thus, the respondents tended to differ in satisfaction with financial returns, with promotional opportunities, and with the job in total. However, regardless of role or other variables (except the institution the respondent worked in), the respondents tended not to differ significantly in their satisfaction with the nature of their work, with the characteristics of supervision, and with their relationship with their colleagues.

4. The respondents' institution of employment was also found to be related to their level of job satisfaction. The combination of certain factors (rank, salary, academic qualifications, tenure, academic role) at a favorable level in a particular institution tended to manifest itself in higher levels of job satisfaction of respondents in that institution.
5. Finally, the sex of the respondents was found to be related to job satisfaction. Female respondents tended to be less satisfied with promotional opportunities than were their male colleagues. Whether this trend was based on a cultural sex-linked bias or on a combination of roles and related factors was not determined.

Implications for the Administrator

SPECIFIC RECOMMENDATIONS

Satisfaction can be regarded as an evaluation of equity of treatment on conditions. The reported study has contributed to the understanding of treatment and conditions underlying the job satisfaction of physical education personnel in selected Ontario universities. Administration deals directly or indirectly with these conditions and situations. The study has supported the necessity for using separate and discriminable measures in a multidimensional domain involving feelings about work. Identification of feelings about discriminable aspects of the individual's job provides not only a truer picture of the feelings involved, but gives important information about specific conditions and situations existing in the administrative process. The specific recommendations that may be justified on the basis of this study are of two kinds: (1) practical administrative ones, and (2) those dealing with further research.

Recommendations about administration of physical education and athletics. The investigator feels justified in recommending:

1. Integration of structures and roles to minimize the occurrence of roles dealing exclusively with so-called service or nonacademic programs;
2. Selection of all faculty with qualifications appropriate to academic work;
3. Leadership and supervision of the service or nonacademic programs by fully qualified academic personnel to enhance the educational ingredients of such programs;
4. Equity of personnel practices within the total physical education and athletics administrative unit in an institution;
5. Integration of women's and men's programs to enhance better use of faculty resources and to increase the probability of appropriate faculty experiences.

In summary, it seems that administrative structures and functions that could serve the various objectives of physical education and athletics, ranging from goals that are essentially academic to goals that are essentially of a service nature, need to be designed in such a manner as to give the human element a place to function congruently with general objectives of the institution. It would seem necessary, therefore, to develop structures and functions with programs and staffs that can demonstrate their contribution to objectives of higher education on par with other divisions of the academic community.

Recommendations for further study. In respect to furthering knowledge in administrative theory in physical education and athletics, the following recommendations seem warranted:

1. Comparative studies on the job satisfaction of physical educators in variant professional roles (i.e., high school teaching, recreation, administration, etc.);
2. Comparative studies of job satisfaction between members of physical education departments and other disciplines at university level;
3. Studies of university disciplines which have a similar variety of roles as physical education (i.e., library science and library service, medical education and health service, etc.);
4. Case studies of "successful" administrative settings as found by the present study and "not successful" ones in relation to job satisfaction and underlying conditions;
5. Further study of the "nonequity theory of physical education roles" which emerged from the present study and the role of administration in reducing this nonequity.

Finally, an effective and efficient administrator must exhibit "initiation action" to move the organization toward its goals and he should exhibit "consideration" to win faculty support (Halpin, 1959, p. 4). He must, also in the pursuit of organizational goals, satisfy the needs of the individuals within the organization to such an extent as to provide for psychological growth for each individual. This is probably particularily important in university settings because individuals working in universities expect personal growth as one important return for their efforts. It is, therefore, the administrator's task to address himself to the question of facilitating the growth of the potential of human resources through responsibilities and tasks of "higher" order. This is by way of asking: Can the people in the organization, the department, the team, the class become psychologically taller than they are? Can they grow? What must I, as an administrator, do to maximize this growth?

For psychological growth to take place, the provision for the opportunity of the following growth factors are important: knowing more, seeing relationships in what we know, being creative, being effective in ambiguous situations, maintaining individuality (Herzberg, 1969, p. 70).

The above factors relate to the fulfillment of higher needs, and an administrator who maximizes job satisfaction (thus need satisfaction), will concurrently facilitate psychological growth. The reader is reminded that in university physical education and athletics, psychological growth will tend to be facilitated with jobs that tend toward increased academic involvement. And to put it differently, academic roles and concomitant institutional recognition will tend to reflect in higher satisfaction with the job.

Provision of opportunities for psychological growth and for higher levels of job satisfaction means reducing the incongruency between the organization and the individual—that is, between role expectations and need dispositions. This means reduction in organizational dysfunction. Although the relationship of "satisfied subjects" to the effectiveness and productivity of an industrial organization is anything but a clear-cut cause-and-effect relationship, the writer hypothesizes that provision for psychological growth and greater job satisfaction will be reflected in both higher unit morale and organizational climate and higher "productivity" and achievements by faculty members.

General Bibliography

Argyris, Chris, *Integrating the Individual and the Organization.* New York: John Wiley & Sons, Inc., 1964.

Barnard, Chester I., *The Functions of the Executive.* Cambridge: Harvard University Press, 1964.

Carver, Fred D., and Thomas J. Sergiovanni, *Organizations and Human Behavior: Focus on Schools.* New York: McGraw-Hill Book Co., 1969.

Getzels, Jacob W., J. M. Lipham, and R. F. Campbell, *Educational Administration as a Social Process: Theory, Research, Practice.* New York: Harper and Row, 1968.

Guion, R. M., "Industrial Morale: The Problem of Terminology," *Personnel Psychology,* 11 (Spring 1958), 59-61.

Guttman, L., "A Basis for Scaling Qualitative Data," *American Sociological Review,* 9 (April 1944), 139-50.

Halpin, Andrew W., *The Leadership Behavior of School Superintendents.* Chicago: Midwest Administration Center, University of Chicago, reprinted 1959.

―――, *Theory and Research in Administration.* Chicago: The Macmillan Co., 1966.

Herzberg, Frederick, "The Motivation to Work among Finnish Supervisors," *Personnel Psychology,* 18 (Winter 1965), 393-410.

———, *Work and the Nature of Man.* New York: World Publishing Co., 1969.

Herzberg, Frederick, B. Mausner, and Barbara B. Snyderman, *The Motivation to Work.* New York: John Wiley & Sons, Inc., 1959.

Kramer, C. Y., "Extension of Multiple Range Tests to Test Group Means with Unequal Numbers of Replications," *Biometrics,* 12 (September 1956), 307-10.

Likert, Rensis A., "A Technique for the Measurement of Attitudes," *Arch. Psychol.,* 140 (1932), 1-55.

Maslow, A. H., "A Theory of Human Motivation," *Psychological Review,* 50 (1943), 370-96.

McGregor, Douglas, *The Human Side of Enterprise.* New York: McGraw-Hill Book Co., 1960.

Porter, Lyman W., "A Study of Perceived Need Satisfactions in Bottom and Middle Management Jobs," *Journal of Applied Psychology,* 45 (February 1961), 1-9.

———, "Job Attitudes in Management: I. Perceived Differences in Need Fulfillment as a Function of Job Level," *Journal of Applied Psychology,* 47 (December 1962), 375-84.

Shaw, Marvin E., and Jack M. Wright, *Scales for the Measurement of Attitudes.* New York: McGraw-Hill Book Co., 1967.

Smith, P. C., Kendall, L. M., and Hulin, C. L. *The Measurement of Satisfaction In Work and Retirement: A Strategy for the Study of Attitudes.* Chicago: Rand McNally and Co., 1969.

Spaeth, Marcia, "An Analysis of Administrative Research in Physical Education and Athletics in Relation to a Research Paradigm." Ph.D. diss., University of Illinois, 1967.

Stagner, Ross, "Motivational Aspects of Industrial Morale," *Personnel Psychology,* 11 (Spring 1958), 64-70.

Sutermeister, Robert A., *People and Productivity,* 2nd ed. New York: McGraw-Hill Book Co., 1969.

Thurstone, L. L., "The Measurement of Social Attitudes," *Journal of Abnormal Social Psychology,* 26 (October-December 1931), 249-69.

Vroom, Victor H., *Work and Motivation.* New York: Wiley & Sons, Inc., 1964.

Worthy, James C., "Organizational Structure and Employee Morale," *American Sociological Review,* 15 (April 1950), 169-70.

Appendix A
Job Descriptive Index*

CODE NUMBER ‾‾‾‾‾‾‾

Think of your present work. What is it like most of the time? In the blank beside each word given below, write

‾‾y‾‾ for "Yes" if it describes your work
‾‾n‾‾ for "No" if it does NOT describe it
‾‾?‾‾ if you cannot decide

WORK ON PRESENT JOB

‾‾‾‾‾‾‾ Fascinating

‾‾‾‾‾‾‾ Routine

‾‾‾‾‾‾‾ Satisfying

‾‾‾‾‾‾‾ Boring

‾‾‾‾‾‾‾ Good

‾‾‾‾‾‾‾ Creative

‾‾‾‾‾‾‾ Respected

CONFIDENTIAL

‾‾‾‾‾‾‾ Hot

‾‾‾‾‾‾‾ Pleasant

‾‾‾‾‾‾‾ Useful

‾‾‾‾‾‾‾ Tiresome

‾‾‾‾‾‾‾ Healthful

‾‾‾‾‾‾‾ Challenging

‾‾‾‾‾‾‾ On your feet

‾‾‾‾‾‾‾ Frustrating

‾‾‾‾‾‾‾ Simple

‾‾‾‾‾‾‾ Endless

‾‾‾‾‾‾‾ Gives sense of accomplishment

*Researchers wishing to use these scales in their own work are asked to inform the senior author of their intentions and to request permission for use. In this way we hope to be able to cumulate further statistics on the JDI.

Smith, P. C., Kendall, L. M., & Hulin, C. L. The measurement of satisfaction in work and retirement. Chicago: Rand McNally, 1969.

Turn page . . . . . .   Go on to the next page. . . . .

Think of the pay you get now. How well does each of the following words describe your present pay? In the blank beside each word, put

__y__ if it describes your pay
__n__ if it does NOT describe it
__?__ if you cannot decide

Think of the opportunities for promotion that you have now. How well does each of the following words describe these? In the blank beside each word put

__y__ for "Yes" if it describes your opportunities for promotion
__n__ for "No" if it does NOT describe them
__?__ if you cannot decide

PRESENT PAY		OPPORTUNITIES FOR PROMOTION	
Income adequate for normal expenses	_____	_____ Good opportunities for promotion	
Satisfactory profit sharing	_____	_____ Opportunity somewhat limited	
Barely live on income	_____	_____ Promotion on ability	
Bad	_____	_____ Dead-end job	
Income provides luxuries	_____	_____ Good chance for promotion	
Less than I deserve	_____	_____ Unfair promotion policy	
Highly paid	_____	_____ Infrequent promotions	
Underpaid	_____	_____ Regular promotions	
		_____ Fairly good chance for promotion	

Now please turn to the next page . . . .   Go on to the next page . . . .

Think of the kind of supervision that you get on your job. How well does each of the following words describe this supervision? In the blank beside each word below, put

- __y__ if it describes the supervision you get on your job
- __n__ if it does NOT describe it
- __?__ if you cannot decide

Think of the majority of the people that you work with now or the people you meet in connection with your work. How well does each of the following words describe these people? In the blank beside each work below put

- __y__ if it describes the people you work with
- __n__ if it does NOT describe them
- __?__ if you cannot decide

SUPERVISION ON PRESENT JOB

Asks my advice _____
Hard to please _____
Impolite _____
Praises good work _____
Tactful _____
Influential _____
Up-to-date _____
Doesn't supervise enough _____
Quick tempered _____
Tells me where I stand _____
Annoying _____
Stubborn _____
Knows job well _____
Bad _____
Intelligent _____
Leaves me on my own _____
Around when needed _____
Lazy _____

PEOPLE ON YOUR PRESENT JOB

_____ Stimulating
_____ Boring
_____ Slow
_____ Ambitious
_____ Stupid
_____ Responsible
_____ Fast
_____ Intelligent
_____ Easy to make enemies
_____ Talk too much
_____ Smart
_____ Lazy
_____ Unpleasant
_____ No privacy
_____ Active
_____ Narrow interests
_____ Loyal
_____ Hard to meet

Please go on to the next page . . . .

Appendix B

Code Number: _____

Personal Data and Information Form

The information requested will be considered strictly *confidential*. Do not sign the form or put your name on it. The data is required for the purpose of a dissertation study. Some of the data will be used for continual revision of norms of the attached *Job Descriptive Index* by Professor Patricia Smith at Cornell University.

Please use check marks, figures, and comments as called for by the form below. Answer *all* parts to ensure completeness of the information.

Male	_____	Married	_____	Canadian Citizenship:	
Female	_____	Single	_____	Native	_____
Age in years	_____	Divorced	_____	Naturalized	_____

Name of City of Residence _____

Not a Canadian Citizen _____

Size of University (student population) _____

University Rank:

Instructor _____

Total Years of Service in P. E. and Athletics _____

Lecturer _____

Assistant Prof. _____

Years of Service at Present University _____

Associate Prof. _____

Professor _____

Number of Degrees _____

University Tenure:

College of Education:

Yes _____

    Yes _____

No _____

    No _____

Annual Salary:
(from all University sources to nearest $500.00) _____

Highest Degree _____
When did you receive your last degree? _____

Are you at this time proceeding to a degree? _____

Code Number: _____

Please estimate as closely as possible the % of time your job can *best* be defined by involvement in one or more of the following divisions of university physical education and athletics. The total should add to 100%.

Women's Required and/or Service Program	_____ %
Men's Required and/or Service Program	_____ %
Women's Intercollegiate Athletics	_____ %
Men's Intercollegiate Athletics	_____ %
Women's Intramurals	_____ %
Men's Intramurals	_____ %
Co-educational Required and/or Service Program	_____ %
Co-education Intercollegiate Athletics	_____ %
Co-education Intramurals	_____ %
Degree Program—men and women	_____ %
Degree Program—men	_____ %
Degree Program—women	_____ %
Graduate Program	_____ %
Research	_____ %

Administration

(as part of an administrative *position* and *not* administration due to teaching and/or coaching responsibilities) _____ %

Specify administrative position by checking one or more:

    professional _____

    service physical education _____

    athletics _____

                                  Total _____ %

Additional comments:

11

Economic Factors Influencing Athletics

Ronald Bole

Introduction

Is winning all you need to solve your financial problems in intercollegiate athletics? When one listens to the typical athletic director or football coach or popular press, one gets the impression that winning is all it takes. Produce a winner and the turnstiles will really click. Recent evidence in two schools in the Big Ten Athletic Conference suggests that the problem of financing athletics and attracting paying customers is a complex one.

University of Minnesota. Minnesota set an all-time record attendance at 1972-73 basketball games but didn't come close to maximizing its revenue potential. The football team at Minnesota played to record low crowds in 1973, despite a new public relations effort, new coach, and respectable win-loss record. An editorial cartoon in the *Minnesota Daily* painted the economic picture when it depicted the sports promotion billboard, which sits in a prominent campus location, as advertising, "Basketball '73-'74, more money, less students" (*Minnesota Daily*, 1973, p.1). All athletic ticket prices are being raised for 1973-74 in the hopes of generating more revenue. The ironic aspect of the situation at Minnesota is that raising ticket prices on the one hand is seen as cutting down the number of students and staff who buy basketball tickets, but on the other

Ronald Bole is from the University of Minnesota, Minneapolis.

hand it is hoped that somehow it will help the total revenue situation. Basketball at Minnesota is a unique situation. The University of Minnesota athletic attendance problem is somewhat unique compared to other Big Ten schools.

University of Illinois. The major thrust of this chapter deals with economic factors as they relate to football attendance at the University of Illinois (Bole, 1970, p. 2). The analysis tries to assess the relative weight of economic factors such as ticket price and disposable income. The Illinois situation was characterized by its relative remoteness from a major metropolitan area and by a lack of any long-term dynasty in one of the major revenue-producing sports. Regardless of the uniqueness of a particular situation, the following economic principles are basic.

ECONOMIC CONSIDERATIONS

The football consumer. Economics deals with the most fundamental of human relationships. It is in the marketplace where fundamental properties of goods and services can be well understood. A commodity in high demand has a correspondingly high price. Goods of which there is a surplus are bid lower and lower in price. The basic principles of supply and demand, pricing, substitution of products, consumption, investment, inflation, and business cycles apply equally as well to football as to automobiles.

Football developed in much the way that economic theory was developed. Initially the problem was one of underproduction in economics. There were not enough goods to go around; therefore, the economist concentrated on production, costs of production, and supply. Eventually certain goods became readily available and their worth was determined in the marketplace. It was the consumer who then determined the worth of a good—not the cost of production with a reasonable profit added.

During the first thirty years of the twentieth century, football as a commodity was in great demand. Not only were the schools able to meet the costs of producing football, but the surplus was building stadiums, physical education buildings, recreation facilities, and financing the rest of the intercollegiate athletic program. Some schools were netting over $500,000 per year, which meant that roughly 75 percent of football income was profit (Wallace, 1929, p. 10).

During the period 1900 to 1930, the hypothetical football consumer looked different. The types of exposure to football were fewer in 1925; the football consumer then had few real alternatives if his desire was to witness the violence of the semimodern game.

Today the football consumer has real alternatives. He can watch the NCAA regional game of the week; he can go to the city and watch the local professional team; he can mow the lawn on Saturday afternoon and sit back in his easy chair and identify with Tarkenton or Griese on Sunday afternoon; or he can go to the local college game.

The consumer who turns up at the gate for a college football game is no random animal. He is most likely a college graduate. His income is well above average. He is more likely to own a color television set and probably was one of the first with a black and white television set. He is not terribly sensitive to small fluctuations in ticket price. His present demand for tickets in relation to price is represented in *Figure 1*.

Elasticity of demand. Assuming in *Figure 1* that all of the 30,000 tickets available are equally desirable, a ticket manager could theoretically dispose of as many tickets as could be printed at a price of $2. The tickets are not equally desirable, and this leads one to speculate that if the fan pays $5 for

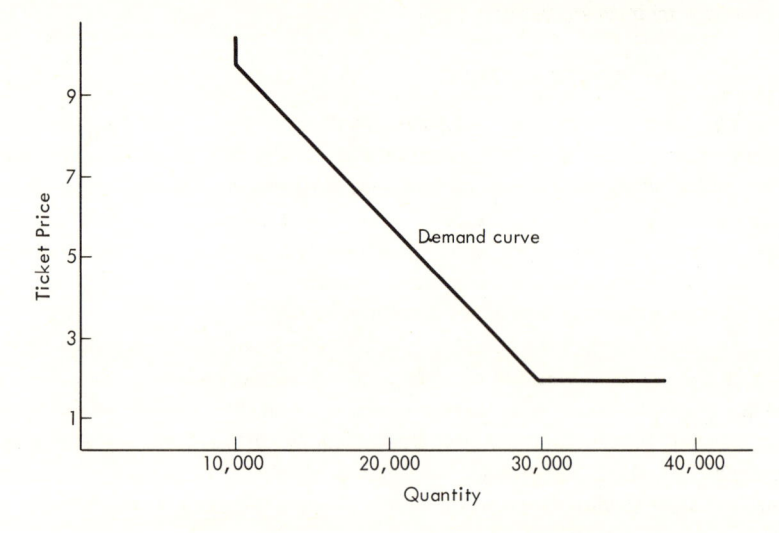

Figure 1. Hypothetical Demand Elasticity for Football Tickets

a seat in the corner of the end zone, what might he pay for a seat between the 40-yard lines? Ten thousand loyal, well-to-do alumni would probably come to the game at a price of $10 or perhaps even $15 or $20. In actual practice the economist is not concerned with what happens at prices above $10 or below $2; because as one looks at *Figure 2*, it is apparent that maximum revenue occurs at a ticket price of $7. This could well be the rationale that Notre Dame used in upping its individual game price to $7 for the 1968 season. *Figure 2* simply shows the price of tickets multiplied by the number demanded at that price with the resultant revenue figures for each price.

The average football consumer of today, when faced with a $7 ticket price, will consider substituting professional football, television football, or simply no football at all. This concept of substitution arises when the consumer works at the margin of the use that he has for the competing products.

Substitution effect and the marginal fan. Substitution occurs first with

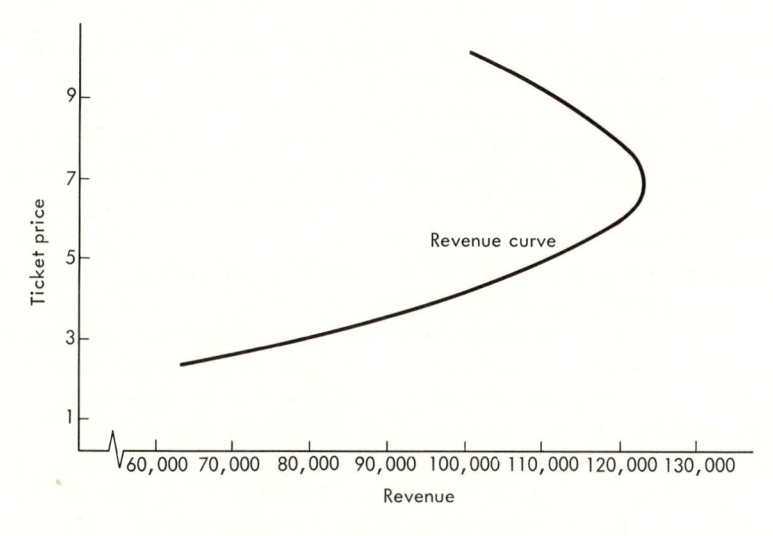

Figure 2. Hypothetical Revenue Curve Based on Demand Curve for Football Tickets

the marginal sporting events. Thus, high school football, small college football, and minor league baseball are marginal sport events that might evidence the effects of substitution before major college football. The problems of minor league baseball are an example of substitution for marginal sporting events. "The period 1924-1934 saw an increase in college and professional football attendance, a decrease in minor league baseball attendance, and major league baseball attendance stationary" (Wallace, 1929, p. 10).

This leads naturally to a discussion of the business of football. The literature on the business of football falls into periods marked by economic cycles and technological innovation. The following section discusses football as a business. The first period was prosperous for football.

Background and Related Literature

Because the main topic of this chapter is the relationship between economic factors and football attendance, this section relates mainly to a review of the growth of football as a big business.

Beginning football. From football's beginning in 1869, Harvard and Yale had advanced to the point where in 1875 the price of admission was raised from 25¢ to 50¢, and the Harvard-Yale game drew 2,000 spectators. Harvard's share of the receipts was $70. (These and following figures are from Lewis, 1965, pp. 25-111.) By 1878, Harvard's receipts for the year were $1,398.87. Attendance at football games in the East ranged from 200 to 3,000 in 1882. Only the championship games were well attended by the public.

Pennsylvania paid out $15,000 in 1885 for a playing field and stands. The financial ramifications of football were beginning to be felt. The promoters saw this as they moved the championship games off the campus and into the city. The city in this period was New York, where in 1887 the Yale-Harvard championship game drew 17,000 spectators. During the period 1883 to 1893, the number of spectators at the championship game in New York rose from 10,000 to 50,000. The demand for tickets rose faster than the colleges could build stands. Ticket prices soared as the Yale-Princeton game in 1893 cost $15 for a reserved seat and $150 for a box.

"Yale's ability to finance football with gate receipts took a dramatic turn in the mid-eighties. In 1885, receipts of $2,674.49 matched expenses but revenues in 1892 nearly doubled the expenses" (Ibid., p. 30). From four games in 1893, the gate receipts total $36,065.54. The growing affluence brought charges of extravagance. Camp defended the revenue-gathering as democratic and proper. Demand, according to Camp, should determine ticket prices, and Yale football should profit from the attraction (Ibid., p. 68).

The progress of football in the Midwest was less dramatic. In 1894, Illinois cleared $60 for the Northwestern game (Pullen, 1957, p. 13). Admission to the early games was 25¢. Many students climbed the fence, and women just walked in without paying. The Athletic Association realized just $7 on one game. Students raised money for the bleachers to seat 300 in 1901 (Ibid., p. 19).

The Chicago area offered a sizable market for football. The Michigan-Chicago game in 1896, played indoors because of bad weather, had receipts of $10,812 for a new mark (Voltmer, 1935, p. 13).

Big Business era. Even if football did arrive belatedly to the Midwest, the economic possibilities of the game were soon realized. By 1905, Chicago beat Michigan 2-0 before a crowd of 26,000 that had paid $35,000 to watch (Ibid., p. 15).

At Illinois 9,500 attended the Illinois-Chicago game in 1910. In 1914, Illinois beat Chicago 21-7 before 17,000 spectators (Ibid., p. 32). Illinois' field could seat only 4,000 in 1914 and 12,000 in 1918 which could be expanded to only 20,000 by using temporary bleachers (Pullen, pp. 28, 32, 83).

The obvious popularity of the game was not without criticism. Academicians felt too much emphasis was placed on the game, and that students and players might forget the purpose of the university. Early games were rougher, and protective equipment was poor; so, many injuries and deaths occurred. The sizable game receipts came under scrutiny, and occasional charges of professionalism were heard. Solberg echoes the traditional administrative and faculty concern over athletics: "Modern intercollegiate athletics benefitted Illinois profoundly. They put Illinois on the map and improved faculty-student relations. . . . At the same time athletics diverted the University from its central mission as a place of scholarship and athletics created cultural conditions which made it harder for Illinois to fulfill its proper role" (1968, pp. 383, 384).

This concern was primary in the establishment of the Intercollegiate

Conference of Faculty Representatives. The faculty were not content to let something as culturally and economically potent as football be run without their participation and consent.

In the era of Big Business the graduate system of coaching gave way to the hiring of professionals to coach the teams. At Illinois Robert C. Zuppke was hired in 1913 for $2700 (Pullen, 1957, p. 31).

By 1920, a wave of football enthusiasm swept the country. Illinois sold 20,000 tickets for the Ohio game, and George Huff commented that 40,000 to 50,000 could have been sold. The most money that Illinois could guarantee opponents at Illinois Field was $15,000. Some schools were already demanding $45,000 guarantees; so Illinois was faced with a scheduling problem (Wilson, 1948, p. 25). The need for a stadium was becoming apparent.

Elsewhere the football business was also big business. Baylor football receipts were handled by a business firm which owned the grandstand (Savage, 1929, p. 87). Football was becoming "the bird that lays the golden egg that pays for most of the other sports in the colleges" (*The New York Times,* 1928, sec. 5, p. 12). Football contributed 95 percent of athletic revenue at California and eight-ninths of athletic income at Southern California (Savage, 1929, p. 87). Football gate receipts provided the major source of income and financing for high school sports. Concern that high school athletics were being saturated with commercialism was evidenced (Wagenhorst, 1926, p. 102).

Certain factors such as the shortening of the work week, labor-saving devices, improved transportation, rule changes, and better accommodations for the spectator were contributing to the boom in attendance (Laughter, 1963, p. 111-16). One writer suggested that the "elemental joy of combat holds football crowds" (Marvin, 1923, p. 186).

In 1925, college football games were attended by 12,000,000 fans. Red Grange was the leading attraction as he played before 371,000 people in his final season (*The New York Times,* 1925, p. 13).

In 1926, Danzig commented on the demand for tickets: "Some of the colleges have raised the price of admission in order to keep out the general public and make the game solidly for the undergraduates and the alumni, who, apparently will pay any price to get in" (Danzig, 1926, p. 3). Tickets were $5 for most Eastern games and $10 for the Army-Navy game (Ibid., p. 3).

In 1928, Yale football revenue amounted to $1,119,000 (Savage, 1929, p. 87). This prompted the statement that in 1929 college football had reached a stage of development where it was classed with Big Business. Drawing power was $50 million per year. Some schools netted profits of $500,000 in a year, and as much as 75 percent of football income was profit. Suggested reasons for the high return were that football charged for intangibles such as academic and social prestige, spirit, and tradition and, furthermore, it got its raw material at slight cost (Wallace, 1929, p. 11).

Depression, War, Inflation. The period following the Big Business era of football was marked by unusual economic and international developments. A severe economic depression was felt by all segments of the economy, including football. A three-year decline, 1930 to 1933, was followed by a gradual increase in football attendance until 1941. There was decreased attendance for four years and then in 1945 a gradual increase accelerated to boom proportions in the early 1950s.

The modern era, 1953 to 1973. In 1959, college football was up 1.74 percent with a drawing power of 19,600,000. That marked the sixth straight year that attendance was up, and the total fell just short of the record 19,651,000 of 1949 when fifty-nine more teams participated (*The New York Times*, 1959, p. 53).

It is ironic to note that after a 5.4 percent increase in attendance in 1958, the Big Ten Conference complained about its limited television appearances to the NCAA. This represented a complete reversal of their position in 1950 (*The New York Times*, 1959, p. 20).

College football crowds passed the 20,000,000 mark in 1960. This was a 4 percent increase over 1959, and a school like Ohio State averaged 82,000 per game (*The New York Times*, 1960, p. 48).

The year 1961 resulted in the eighth consecutive rise in attendance (*The New York Times*, 1961, p. 66). Attendance continued at a record pace in the sixties, and yet as many as 26,000,000 fans watched college football in their homes each Saturday (*The New York Times*, 1963, p. 15).

Even though attendance was at record proportions, it was apparent that college football was getting less and less of a percentage of the entertainment dollar. Personal disposable income was up from $200 billion in 1950 to $589 billion in 1968. The population was up, and especially so in the under-thirty age range which constitutes the bulk of the football crowd. Ticket prices were up, but some were still below the price of the 1920s. The economics of college football were becoming progressively less entertaining to such spectators as university regents and trustees.

Summary. Football developed rapidly as a strong spectator attraction from its inception in 1869. In the early days only championship games were popular. The game developed in the East but rapidly spread to the Midwest. The 1900s saw continued steady and sometimes spectacular growth to the point where Yale receipts for football topped $1 million in 1928.

Football attendance lagged a year behind the economic recession, but eventually attendance fell off for a short period. This caused some concern, because many stadiums had been built in the 1920s, and there were heavy fixed charges associated with the stadiums. Football attendances climbed during the late 1930s and into the war year 1941. A brief retreat during the years 1942 and 1943 was quickly recovered, and a postwar boom continued until 1949. Attendance then leveled off. A controversy developed around the use of television and its effect on attendance.

Attendance has climbed slowly since 1953, but the growth rate has not kept pace with consumer income or comparable growth rates in other popular sports. Ticket prices have not kept pace with the consumer price index, and this has resulted in considerable financial pressure on overburdened football gate receipts.

Research Methodology and Techniques

Prediction is the forecasting from measures (knowledge of results and causes) of the future results of an established criterion. The more knowledge we have concerning the characteristics of a result, the more accurate we may be in determining causes and in framing statements of a predictive nature (AAHPER, 1952, p. 71).

It is desirable to be systematic in the tracing of the theoretical relationships. The fluctuations in quantitative variables may be the results of many causes. Only through some systematic analysis of the possible variables that are related to the variable one wishes to predict can greater insight be gained into possible causes. Causal analysis proceeds backwards from the observed effect to the cause. Only through carefully controlled scientific experiments can exact causes be determined. In many phenomena worthy of investigation, it is not possible to adequately control all of the variables. To isolate all of the economic and psychological variables that condition an individual's propensity to consume a product is beyond the scope of controlled experimentation. It is possible, however, to assess the more important relationships among phenomena subjectively and combine them into a regression model to predict future results. Although it can be demonstrated that causality does not necessarily exist between highly correlated variables, the converse is not automatically true. Until someone can point out that a high degree of relationship may be due to a third, possibly undiscovered variable, then the prediction equation may well be the best evidence available for causality. Many times the prediction equation provides the impetus for further analysis of the competing variables.

The technique used in this study was the development of an economic model to predict attendance at the University of Illinois football games. A survey of related literature and interviews provided the rationale for inclusion of variables. Documentary analysis provided the basic data. The techniques of correlation and multiple regression provided the statistical analysis. The application of logic and reason interpreted the results.

Variables. Data was collected for the years 1926 through 1968 for the following variables on a game by game basis: name of opponent; date of game; score of game; temperature; precipitation; total attendance; cheap ticket attendance; complimentary tickets issued; band, ushers, gatemen, etc; homecoming designation; and ticket prices in various categories. An attempt was made to get a breakdown of advance ticket sales and the gate sale of tickets, but it was not humanly possible to get accurate data for more than a few recent years.

Yearly data from 1926 through 1968 was collected for the following variables: enrollment at the Champaign-Urbana campus, University of Illinois;

national personal disposable income, unadjusted for price level; number of families (households) with television sets; number of home football games; and Big Ten win-loss record for the University of Illinois football team.

Certain data were computed from the above data. Average home attendance was computed by dividing the total attendance for the year by the number of home games. Average premium tickets were computed by dividing the total premium tickets per year by the number of games. Complimentary tickets, cheap tickets, and student tickets were also divided by the number of games to yield a per-game average figure for each year. The temperature and precipitation figures for each game were added and divided by the number of games each year to yield early average temperature and precipitation figures.

The win-loss record was computed by dividing the games played by the games won to yield a figure between zero and one. The win-loss record was lagged one year to provide a previous year win-loss record.

Eight of the above variables were transformed from yearly absolute average value to a change from one year to the next year's value. This was done by subtracting the 1927 score from the 1926 score, the 1928 from the 1927, etc., to get a value that represented the change in magnitude from the previous year. This change was computed on the following variables: average home attendance, average premium tickets, average cheap tickets, enrollment, personal disposable income, and families with television sets.

Sources of data. All of the data used in this study was collected in the summer of 1969. The data was collected from the following locations: Illinois Water Survey, Climatological Data Section; Communications Library; Reference Section, University of Illinois Main Library; Ticket Office, Assembly Hall; Publicity Office, Assembly Hall; Business Office, Assembly Hall; and storage room under West Main Stand, Memorial Stadium.

Analysis of data. The data was analyzed by computer using a stepwise multiple correlation program. This output was further analyzed by a linear regression program used in economics to test for serial correlation effects and for nonrandom residual variation.

Findings and Conclusions

Independent variables that were thought to affect football attendance were subjectively selected for this analysis. Data for eight dependent and seventeen independent variables was collected. In addition to the game-by-game and average-per-year breakdown, the data is further partitioned into three time periods. The total time period (1926 to 1968), the early period (1926 to 1941), and the later period (1946 to 1968) comprise the method of division.

The dependent variables were the various categories of tickets. The premium ticket (the $6-per-seat ticket) has the most impact on total revenue so this category is presented in detail.

Premium tickets. The prediction equation based on the later time period for predicting average premium tickets takes the following form:

$$X_2 = 75665 - 10075X_8 - 11019X_9 + 42.3X_{11} - 3415X_{13} + 2339X_{14} + 5841X_{15} + 13020X_{20} + 132X_{22} - 1581$$

where:
X_2 = Average premium tickets (per game)
X_8 = P price (premium ticket price)
X_9 = C price (cheap ticket price)
X_{11} = PDI (personal disposable income)
X_{13} = # games (number of home games)
X_{14} = WL_t (current year)
X_{15} = WL_{t-1} (previous year)
X_{20} = Δ C price (change in price)
X_{22} = Δ PDI (change in income)

The standard error of the estimate for the above equation is 2769.81. To predict the average number of $6 tickets sold per game in 1969 requires estimating what future variables might be. Variables X_8, X_9, X_{13}, X_{15}, and X_{20} are known. It is possible to estimate X_{11}, X_{22}, and X_{14}. Personal disposable income has been going up about $40 billion per year; so, it can be estimated at 630. A personal disposable income of 630 makes X_{22} equal to 40. Assume that Illinois loses all of its games in 1969. The estimate of X_2 then becomes

$$X_2 = 75665 - 10075(6) - 11019(1) + 42.3(630) = 3415(6) + 2339(0) + 5841(.143) + 13020(0) + 1581 = 18,051$$

Because the adjusted standard error of the estimate for this equation is 2770, it is reasonable to expect that 68 percent of the time the estimate of 18,051 will be within 2770 of the real value.

Income and price play a significant role in explaining this variable. *Table 1* shows the relative contribution of each variable to the explained variance.

TABLE 1. Percentage Contributions of Variables to R^2 in Different Time Periods for X_2 (Average Premium Tickets)

1926-1968			1926-1952			1946-1968		
X_8	P Price	36.6%	X_{11}	PDI	84.7%	X_8	P Price	54.1%
X_{23}	Δ TV	36.2%	X_{14}	WL_t	12.3%	X_{11}	PDI	28.7%
X_{11}	PDI	13.9%				X_{13}	# games	5.5%
X_{21}	Δ Enroll	9.8%				X_9	C Price	5.2%

It can be seen from *Table 1* that income and win-lost explain 97 percent of the explained variance in the early time period. The premium price variable is the most important variable in the later time period. The importance of the price variable can be further shown by referring again to the prediction equation. A $1 price increase would be reflected by a decline of 10,075 premium price tickets per game if all other factors remained the same. In actual practice, price increases have not had such a severe effect because the other variables have also been changing periodically.

Game-by-Game Results. Two additional variables came into play when the data was analyzed on a game-by-game basis. The homecoming variable was a dummy variable for which the number one was used to designate a homecoming game and zero was used to designate all other games. The quality of opponents variable was also a dummy variable with quality ratings inserted on the following basis:

1—Schools currently designated as small colleges
2—Nonconference big college opponents
3—Big Ten conference opponents
4—Notre Dame and Army

The other difference in the game-by-game analysis is that variables X_1 through X_7 are changing on a game-by-game basis.

The multiple Rs obtained on a game-by-game basis were relatively low (<.85) and the dummy variables obscured the interrelationships of the other variables. When two variables account for 80 percent or more of the variance in the criterion, it is difficult to analyze meaningfully relationships between the other variables.

The quality of opponents variable and the homecoming variable accounted for 75 percent or more of the variance when data was analyzed on a game-by-game basis.

Conclusions. It was possible to explain 85 percent of the variance in football attendance at the University of Illinois. The later-period model used a different combination of factors to explain attendance than the early-period model. The yearly average data prediction equations had lower standard errors and thus were more useful for predicting attendance than the game-by-game equations. The economic variables of price of tickets and personal disposable income were more important than win-loss records.

Implications for the Practicing Administrator

The win-loss, personal disposable income, and price variables have the most implications. The reason that the data partially supports the win-loss hypothesis is that there appears to be a shift taking place that puts more weight on the win-loss varialbe in the later time period for total attendance. It is strange that the shift is just the opposite, although less pronounced, when the criterion is premium tickets sold. It should be noted that the win-loss variable that is heavily weighted in the later time period is the previous year's win-loss record. This is appropriate because many tickets are bought in advance of the actual games. It may be that as more alternatives to college football are presented, the win-loss record becomes more important.

The most obvious difference in the data in different time periods is the shift from an emphasis on income (*PDI*) in the early period to price (*P* price or ΔP price) in the later period. This may be because economic cycles were more pronounced during the early period, and there were more marginal consumers of football. In 1968, the football consumer had the money to go to the game, but he apparently based his decision on the ticket price and the alternate uses of the money and the time.

The importance of ticket price can be shown many ways. It contributed 38 percent of X_1 (total attendance) variance in the later period using average data. It contributes 59 percent of X_2 (premium ticket attendance) variance in the later period using average data. It contributes 13 percent of X_2 variance in the later period using per-game data. If all other variables were held constant, an increase of $1 in the premium ticket price would result in 10,000 fewer tickets sold per game. It appears that the other variables cancelled each other out in 1968 when attendance fell 10,000 per game coupled with a price increase of $1. The premium ticket price should not be increased unless other factors are operating to offset the expected decrease in attendance.

Administrators of big-time football might consider the following questions: How would a sliding scale of ticket prices for seat locations and different calibre of opponents affect the drawing power of your football team? How might monies be spent more constructively for publicity? How would a round-robin conference schedule of nine games affect the drawing power of your football team? Have alternative methods of financing athletics been explored now, *before* a financial crisis develops?

RECOMMENDATIONS FOR FURTHER STUDY

1. Time series studies should be conducted using smaller schools, or a large school located in a large urban population center.
2. A similar analysis of a group of big-time football schools should be done using cross-section data for a recent year.

The period when football was the "goose that laid the golden egg" is over. The harsh financial facts point to inflationary price increases which have put big-time football out of reach for many smaller schools, and make those involved in it unable to meet expenses. A multiplicity of factors are keeping spectators away from college stadiums. Big-time football at colleges as we know it today will not quickly lose cultural approval, but financing based on gate receipts will undergo a severe test.

General Bibliography

Bole, Ronald E., "An Economic Analysis of the Factors Influencing Football Attendance at the University of Illinois, 1926-1968." Ph.D. diss., University of Illinois, 1970.

Danzig, Allison, "Football as a Big Business," *The New York Times*, sec. 9, p. 3, October 17, 1926.

Laughter, Robert James, "Socio-Psychological Aspects of the Development of Athletic Practices and Sport Ethics." Ph.D. diss., Ohio State University, 1963.

Lewis, Guy Maxton, "The American Intercollegiate Football Spectacle, 1869-1917," Ph.D. diss., University of Maryland, 1965.

Marvin, George, "Big Business of Football," *Outlook*, 135: (October 3, 1923), 183-87.

Minnesota Daily, editorial Cartoon, p. 1, March 14, 1973.

The New York Times, "Twelve Million Persons Saw Games This Year," p. 13, November 30, 1925.

_____, "And Now the Big Games Are with Us," sec. 5, p. 12, November 11, 1928.

_____, "9.9% Attendance Drop in East," p. 20, June 9, 1959.

_____, "AP Attendance Report Up Slightly," p. 53, December 17, 1959.

_____, "Record Football Attendance," p. 15, January 9, 1963.

Pullen, Carol Francis, "A History of Intercollegiate Football at the University of Illinois." Master's thesis, University of Illinois, 1957.

Research Methods Applied to Health, Physical Education and Recreation, American Association for Health, Physical Education, and Recreation, Washington, D.C., 1952.

Savage, Howard J., *Bulletin #23, The Carnegie Foundation for the Advancement of Teaching*, New York, 1929.

Solberg, Winton U., *The University of Illinois 1867-1894: An Intellectual and Cultural History*. Urbana, Ill., University of Illinois Press, 1968.

Voltmer, Carl D., *A Brief History of the Intercollegiate Conference of Faculty Representatives with Special Consideration of Athletic Problems*. New York: George Banta Publishing Co., 1935.

Wagenhorst, H. H., *The Administration and Cost of High School Inter-Scholastic Athletics*. New York: Bureau of Publication, Teachers College, 1926.

Wallace, F., "This Football Business," *Saturday Evening Post*, 202 (May 28, 1929), 10-11.

Wilson, R. A., "A History of the Administration of Intercollegiate Athletics at the University of Illinois." Master's thesis, University of Illinois, 1948.

12

Violence in Spectator Sports

Cyril M. White

Introduction

Sport, and in particular various types of football, appears to be almost the only activity serving as a social institution in society, where controlled violence witnessed by an audience is offered as an integral part of a contest. Thus, violence in varying degrees as exhibited on the field of play is accepted, understood, and controlled by established rules. However, the fact that both spectators and players erupt into outbursts of uncontrolled violence from time to time is not understood theoretically, is not accepted socially, and is often not adequately covered by the regulations in force. This is well illustrated by the loss of life, and/or injury to persons and property resulting from riots and/or other social disturbances at recent football games. Although players, through participation, have had many opportunities to internalize the restraints and sanctions that active participation involves, many spectators have not had these or similar opportunities. Spectators' reactions to any given incident, therefore, may differ from those of the players, and on occasions may be violent and uncontrolled.

Violence on the part of spectators, or uncontrolled violence on the part of the players, is distinctive, unconventional and noninstitutionalized. This kind of

Cyril White is Senior Lecturer in Sociology at University College, Dublin, Ireland.

outburst is classified as collective behavior, for it is the outcome not of defined or structured social situations, but rather of undefined and unstructured situations.

Social disturbances involving violence at sporting events are examples of one aspect of collective behavior—the hostile outburst—and an approach to an understanding of these episodes is the use of a sociological model to describe, analyze, and interpret the reported observed happenings. Such models (Lang and Lang, 1961, 1968; Smelser, 1963; Turner, 1964; Brown, 1965; Milgram and Toch, 1969; Evans, 1969; Turner and Killian, 1972) are available, and the purpose of this study was to use one of these models to describe, analyze, compare, and explain the observed happenings at selected amateur football games in which hostile outbursts have occurred.

There appears to be sufficient reason for studying hostile outbursts in football if the published literature and serious social consequences are any guide. In Britain, for example, there have recently been three official government inquiries to investigate hostile outbursts in soccer (Harrington, 1968; Department of Education and Science Report (Chester), 1968; Lang, 1969). In addition, the specific need for an investigation of this kind can be seen to be indicated by the fact of 318 deaths as a result of an amateur game during the preliminary rounds of the 1964 Olympic Soccer Championship in Lima, Peru; the fact of 42 deaths at an obscure second division soccer game in Turkey in 1967; the fact of 485 personal injuries, many requiring hospitalization, at a high school football championship game in Washington, D.C. in 1962; and the fact of increasing disturbances at football games in many parts of the world.

Furthermore, because of its vast public interest, major football games are extensively and intensively reported by teams of professional and experienced observers. An episode of collective behavior, particularly a hostile outburst, is a dramatic affair and is, therefore, most likely to be reported in considerable detail.

Outside of sports settings, other instances of collective behavior cannot be as assured of such an extensive and intensive coverage and by as many professional observer-reporters. Two distinguished writers on collective behavior clearly acknowledge this. "The nature of the subject matter makes observation difficult. . . . Often only a lucky accident puts an observer in a position to make significant observations" (Lang and Lang, 1961, pp. 133-35). Another writer on the same topic goes even further:

> The paucity of investigation is seen easily by surveying the literature on forms of collective behavior. . . . Most investigations are in the nature of reporting either by persons fortuitously on the scene or by historians who describe, after their occurrence, certain collective events (Strauss, 1947, p. 352).

Sports, therefore, offer a unique and rich resource of documentary data of research value.

In addition, little is known as to why hostile outbursts occur where they do, when they do, and in the ways they do. Because of this lack of knowledge, the availability of data in sports settings, and the potential magnitude of the social consequences if an episode of collective behavior in a sports setting occurs, the need for a systematic study of hostile outbursts in sports is clearly indicated.

Finally, because the social consequences of disturbances involving violence at football games range from disturbances involving actual or potential legal intervention to outright social catastrophes, it is incumbent upon those occupying leadership roles to recognize and gain some understanding of the social forces that underlie these outbursts.

Background and Related Literature

Although the literature in regard to the analysis of collective behavior in sports, and in particular to hostile outbursts in sports, is limited, a number of studies are reported which show a growing concern vis-à-vis the social implications of violent crowd behavior in a sports setting. In addition, a number of investigations in which football was studied are relevant to greater or lesser degree.

Kleinman, in his study of crowd behavior at basketball games, used questionnaires and interviews to gather data. After a comprehensive review of the literature on collective behavior up to 1960, he identified sports crowds as a focused, factional, expressive, and active collectivity which are characterized as selected and primed audiences. Using the rationale of Turner and Killian to study the characteristics of groups, he gathered data from four general areas considered to be important. Analysis of the data indicated that the factors causing variance in the crowd behavior of the high schools studied were related specifically to the coach and the administration. The coach's background and behavior during the course of a game had a significant influence upon the resultant behavior of the crowd. In addition, the administration set the climate of opinion in which the coach's behavior was found to be significant. The crucial factor of leadership was clearly identified, but no systematic theory was used as a means of analysis and interpretation.

Lang and Lang, in their work on "collective dynamics" (their term for collective behavior), use a riot that occurred at an ice hockey game in Montreal as one case study among four instances of riotous crowds. Their intention was to illustrate the range of conditions out of which unrest may develop. In each case the behavior of the crowd developed as a defense against the widespread anxieties and diffuse fears characterizing the specific times and milieux. Description of the hockey riot was drawn from press stories and informal interview. Their explanation for the riotous behavior of crowds is a function of (1) feelings whose expression normally produces anxiety and (2) the absence, or at least the breakdown, of routine defenses against anxiety in the form of conventions, techniques, and reliance on authorities (1961, pp. 133-35).

Shellow and Roemer reported a social situation in which a riot was expected at a national motorcycle race at Marlboro, Maryland. Because of adequate social control and the "nonappearance" of a group expected to cause trouble, no disturbance occurred. Data was gathered through observation and interview, and reference made to Killian and Turner's work.

Schul reported a riot that occurred at a national sports-car race at Garnett, Kansas. The investigation and report was conducted by the office of the attorney general of Kansas and gives a detailed report of the hour-by-hour unfolding of the riot. The data were gathered through observation and interview. No explanations, except some general views, were offered, but strong recommendations were made regarding the training of local law-enforcement officers in crowd control, riot prevention, and riot control.

Gluckman, in his study of crowd behavior, used participant observation and personal experience to identify the interaction of crowd and team. He studied two professional soccer teams in the same city (Manchester, England) and attempted to identify the different crowd behaviors of the followers of each team and their effects on each team. He presents some views about what happens in crowds, and how they affect the success and failure of team play, and also the play of individual team members. A marked difference was noticed between the supporters of one team as compared to the supporters of the other team. The playing record of one team produced a crowd of supporters who are always hoping for victory, but who never really expect to get it. The supporters of the other team were always sure of winning, but this "sureness" produced doubt and, as a consequence, anxiety grew which on occasion destroyed the cohesion of a fast-moving team. Gluckman's conclusion is that supporters of such a team may well become unwitting "enemies" of it—i.e., when a team keeps winning, supporters are led to expect too much, and this high level of expectation may have an effect on the team's efficiency.

Hasdorf and Cantril, in their study of spectators' reactions to a Dartmouth-Princeton football game, demonstrated clearly that football crowds, like other sports crowds, are generally factional (that is, they are composed of two groups with different and opposing viewpoints and objectives). As a consequence of this "factionality" or readiness to take opposing sides and express partisanship, individual members of the crowd will tend to see and experience entirely different versions of the same game. Through questionnaires and a showing of the game film to a sample of students at each school, data was gathered on what the respondents thought "happened" during the game. Those people comprising the samples were asked to note the violations they saw during the film. The "Dartmouth sample" saw their team make only half of the infractions the "Princeton sample" saw the Dartmouth team make. The Princeton sample saw fewer infractions made by their team, as compared to the infractions made by the Dartmouth team. The ratio of "flagrant" to "mild" infractions was about one to one when the Dartmouth sample judged its own team, but it was about one to two when it judged the Princeton team. As the study reports, "People experience those occurrences that reactivated significances they brought to the occasion; they failed to experience those occurrences which did not reactivate past experiences."

Again dealing with soccer football crowds, a report on crowd disturbances at soccer games in Britain is reported. This investigation, conducted by a multidisciplinary research team headed by a psychiatrist, was commissioned by the then British Minister for Sport, Dennis Howell, and was published in 1968. Questionnaires, interviews, observation using ethological techniques, documentary analysis, and psychiatric examination of those convicted of hooliganism were the research techniques used in the study. Data on collective behavior were gathered from all parts of Britain in the hope that as comprehensive a survey as possible would result. The results show trends in regard to this kind of collective behavior as follows: (1) the majority of people rated the problem of hooliganism in sport as a serious matter; (2) the people responsible for this kind of behavior are male, mostly between the ages of 15 to 19 years, and of low socioeconomic status; and (3) the problem is associated with supporters of the more prominent teams situated in large industrial cities. The ethological study indicates that the behavior patterns fall into a number of well-defined groups of responses, and this response pattern is directly related to what is happening on the field of play. In addition, the consequences of officiating were considered, and the vast majority of informants had no doubt but that the standard of officiating influences crowd behavior. Various suggestions regarding crowd control were suggested, but the most significant approach to greater understanding was through further ethological studies of crowd behavior ("Harrington Report," 1968).

The second British report issued by the government's Department of Education and Science, presents the findings of its committee on football. The purpose of this government committee was to inquire into the state of soccer football at all levels, including the organization, management, finance, and the means by which the game may be developed for the public good—and then to make recommendations. The report has two chapters relevant to the present investigation, one dealing with the machinery of discipline, and specifically with discipline as it relates to players. The other chapter deals with crowd behavior. Regarding the latter, the report does not agree with all the suggestions in the Harrington Report on crowd behavior, or even with the use of the term "hooliganism" to describe the kinds of behavior the Harrington Report treats. However, three findings link the two investigations and their views about the game of football in Britain in general. The three findings are: (1) the need for firm and clear refereeing, (2) the need for better facilities at many grounds—in this regard from the viewpoint of crowd safety and behavior, and (3) the need for club management to take wider responsibility than just for team success ("Chester Report," 1968).

The third British report, this time issued by the government's Ministry of

Housing and Local Government, presents the findings of its working party on crowd behavior at football matches. The purpose of this working party was to examine the problems associated with football crowd behavior in the hope that it would be possible to offer advice and guidance to football clubs and other interested parties which might lead to some improvement in crowd behavior at football games in Britain. The working party was unable to find a simple solution to the problem, which they found is often due to a combination of factors liable to arise on any occasion when large crowds assemble, especially if the circumstances are exciting. However, three major recommendations are suggested as focal points for alleviating the difficulties experienced: (1) maximum cooperation between a football club and the police, (2) absolute acceptance of the decision of the referee by everybody, and (3) the provision of seats in place of standing accommodation for spectators. In addition, a large number of other recommendations were also made with a view to keeping the inevitable excitement of a football game within reasonable limits and so minimizing the likelihood of it leading to misbehavior among the crowd ("Lang Report," 1968).

A study by Leach on spectator control at interscholastic basketball games in the New Jersey State Interscholastic Athletic Association found that most of the schools having problems at their games could locate the problem to a specific area—inside the gymnasia. Using questionnaires, Leash gathered data from 149 out of 202 schools contacted, a response rate of 73.8 percent. Seven factors in the following order were found to be responsible for problems in crowd behavior: (1) reaction to officiating, (2) overcrowded condition, (3) inflamed rivalry, (4) closeness of score, (5) alcohol, (6) players' poor sportsmanship, and (7) conduct of the coach. No explanation or interpretation was offered, but a comprehensive series of recommendations were made.

As an outcome of the serious incidents and disorders that occurred at a high school football championship game in Washington, D.C., a detailed and comprehensive report was submitted to the superintendent of public schools by a special committee on group activities. The report sought to identify the factors responsible for the riot that resulted in the stadium at the conclusion of the game. The data was gathered by the committee through personal interviews before the committee, the submission of written evidence, inspection trips to the stadium and schools involved in the disorders, police reports, and observation of the television and game films. Although no theoretical framework was used to interpret the data, various suggestions were made which went far beyond the context of football games. This report is perhaps the most comprehensive published on a football disturbance, and has resulted in guidelines for subsequent school games in Washington, D.C., and elsewhere in America (MacCarthy, 1963).

As an outcome of the above report and based upon the report's findings, two distinguished American political journalists, Ben A. Franklin and Alvin Shuster, who were at the game, wrote a case study for a national magazine. This study is a detailed panoramic view of the incident reconstructed through analysis of the investigating committee's report and the personal experience of the journalists (Schuster and Franklin, 1963).

As a result of the disorderly conduct of spectators at recent high school sports contests, the American Association for Health, Physical Education, and Recreation set up two programs devoted to a search for solutions to this problem. The programs were scheduled at two national meetings, the Conference of City and County Directors of AAHPER, and the Second National Conference on Secondary School Athletic Administration. Some of the papers have been published in the AAHPER Journal, and the complete proceedings are now available ("Crowd Control," 1970). Motivation for these programs is the feeling that "an increase in disorders at high school games can threaten the continuation of traditional interscholastic athletic programs" ("Crowd Control," 1969).

Another case study similar to the Schuster and Franklin study, but this time on a disturbance at a soccer game in Lima, Peru has been reported as well. This case study was written from newspaper and eye-witness reports of the game, as well as television and game films. It also presents a detailed panoramic view of the incident reconstructed through the analysis of documentary material (Blank, 1965).

Finally, a study conducted by a sociologist on the causes of football disturbances in Britain is available. The study investigates soccer violence and suggests that it is another symptom of increasing working-class alienation from their old institutions which, under the impact of the commercialization of modern sport, now fails to represent this group. This form of behavior is a response to the loss of control exercised by a football subculture of working-class origin over its public representatives (the players). A frustration-aggression approach is postulated as the causative factor, and the phenomenon is linked to the political protest movement of youth and the politically underprivileged. This study *implies* that the violence in British football is "reactionary," and that it is evoked in retaliation for rights once enjoyed but now threatened. No systematic theory was used, but various speculations based on a variety of sociological and psychological approaches were mentioned. Personal experience was the method used in gathering the data (Taylor, 1969).

Research Methodology and Techniques

SELECTING THE DISTURBANCES

The present investigation was limited to four selected episodes of hostile outbursts which occurred at two amateur American football games, one amateur soccer game, and one amateur rugby football game.

Although the episodes selected may appear arbitrary, there is an underlying logic to the sequence and the selection. This logic is based on a twofold rationale. The first reason for selection is the range of social consequences—from a social disturbance in which a number of participants engage in offensive behavior toward other participants to a full-scale outburst resulting in the death of hundreds of participants. The second reason is the vast amount of documentation available on these particular episodes. In three of the episodes there was the added advantage of participants or eyewitnesses being available for interview.

However, because the data were at hand and the interpretations subsequently applied to them rather than being collected through the empirical testing of a predesigned hypothesis, the interpretations of the data were, therefore, post factum. Such interpretations are at the level of plausibility, not proof, and this limitation should be kept in mind when interpreting the results.

RESEARCH DESIGN

Various research strategies, tactics, and methods were investigated in an attempt to decide how the data could best be collected. Finally, a strategy based on the use of documentary analysis and to a lesser extent on interviews was adopted as the most appropriate research technique for this particular investigation. This strategy is similar to that used by Brinton in his work on revolution and by Smelser in his work on collective behavior and which he calls "systematic comparative illustration" (Smelser, 1963, p. 386).

Because of the elaborate record-keeping and documentation in our society, particularly in connection with sports competitions, data are available in great quantity and cover a wide range of aspects of the subjects. The great variety of data available, therefore, constitutes a most significant resource for the researcher. As Festinger and Katz observe, "They provide unique access to historical social situations and to some current social situations which are otherwise difficult or expensive to observe. Moreover, these are data in a 'natural' social setting" (1966, pp. 322-23). Riley describes the present situation regarding the use of this kind of data: "If anything, the sociologist has not made enough use of them and has given too little attention to the possible methods for their use." She goes further by recommending that

> Through creative analysis of well-chosen materials from existing stores the researcher should be able to widen the scope of the problems investigated, formulate new study objectives more clearly, and interpret new materials within a broader framework of scientific understanding (1963, p. 254).

The researcher in the field of collective behavior should, therefore, be

> Something of a detective-reporter, forever keeping his eyes open and ears to the ground, while at the same time he constantly keeps in mind the over-all pattern which has to be constructed out of the many small items of information (Lang and Lang, 1961, p. 552).

To enable the investigator to function in this way, a flexible research design was necessary and was consequently adopted.

TECHNIQUES OF DATA COLLECTION

The data was collected through the use of three research techniques: (1) case method, (2) documentary analysis, and (3) interviews. Though the limitations of such a strategy were well recognized, the usefulness of data collected this way is nevertheless important and capable of being used in a systematic investigation.

The *case study* method was chosen because it preserves a full view of the episodes in their natural settings, thereby adding to their qualitative richness. Case studies have been used to provide detailed information about individuals, institutions, situations, or episodes. They are concerned primarily with determining the unique characteristics of the exceptional rather than the characteristics which are typical of the many. However, an accumulation of data from several similar episodes frequently furnishes significant data for comparative studies and for examining attributes or characteristics associated with specific problems. In the fields of social inquiry, where precise methods are not available for establishing cause-and-effect relationships, the case method has provided evidence for establishing well-defined hypotheses concerning the interaction of associated variables. The case method, therefore, is an effective research technique in resolving a particular difficulty and frequently provides valuable data for formulating tentative generalizations concerning episodes that are highly similar in some significant aspects (Rarick, 1959, p. 260).

Documentary analysis in this investigation was used as a research technique to study the available facts concerning the episodes from written or printed material or radio, television, and film tapes. The first requirement in this analysis was to decide the kind of information needed. A comparison chart based on Smelser's determinants with fifty-one empirical indicators was developed. This chart enabled the data to be grouped into categories so uniformities, similarities, differences, and functional relationships could be established between and within the episodes.

Interviews were used in addition but supplementary to the preceding methods. A number of persons who were either participants or spectators at the episodes were interviewed by the investigator. Other people who could supply additional information on the various backgrounds of the places where the episodes have occurred were also interviewed. The empirical indicators of the comparison chart were used as the basis for questioning in the interviews, because it was felt that a focused interview would yield the most pertinent data (Merton et al., 1956, p. 3).

In summary, the data were collected primarily through the analysis of documents dealing with the episodes under investigation and, in addition but supplementary to the above, through interviews.

RATIONALE FOR SELECTING CASES

Because of the recognized limitations and controversies over single cases as the focus of analysis, four episodes of hostile outbursts at amateur football games were selected. These episodes are discrete in terms of their social consequences. The social consequences ranged from (1) people being pushed about or otherwise socially disturbed, but not injured in any way that required medical or paramedical attention; (2) people being injured needing attention but not hospitalization; (3) people being injured and requiring hospitalization; and finally (4) people being killed. Examples from these four categories were selected for analysis as follows:

1. The hostile outburst that occurred at the Big Ten Championship game between the University of Illinois and Northwestern University on November 18, 1967, at Dyche Stadium, Evanston, Illinois, U.S.A.
2. The hostile outburst that occurred at the International Rugby Football Championship game between Ireland and Wales on March 9, 1968, at the headquarters of the Irish Rugby Football Union, Lansdowne Road, Dublin, Ireland.
3. The hostile outburst that occurred at the final game of the Washington, D.C. football champoinship between Eastern High School and St. John's High School on Thanksgiving Day, November 22, 1962, at the Robert F. Kennedy Stadium, Washington, D.C., U.S.A. (formerly the District Stadium, Washington, D.C.).
4. The hostile outburst that occurred at a preliminary round of the XVIII Olympiad Soccer Championship game between Peru and Argentina on Sunday, May 24, 1964, at the National Stadium, Lima, Peru.

ANALYZING THE DATA

The data were analyzed, categorized, compared, and outlined in a temporal sequential pattern through the use of a model specifically adapted for the purpose, and based upon a theory of collective behavior postulated by Smelser. Brinton makes the case for a model or conceptual framework by stating that a scientist cannot work without one. To support his thesis he uses L. J. Henderson's classic definition of "fact" as "an empirically verifiable statement about phenomena in terms of a conceptual scheme." Because theory constitutes the most important research tool available to the scientist and in addition makes the investigator sensitive, in a general way, to the facts he should be looking for, a conceptual framework or model was clearly indicated (Phillips, 1966, p. vii).

Although hostile outbursts are by definition unstructured, noninstitutionalized, and unconventional behavior, they are not exactly chaotic or random. In fact, the assumption of some kind of pattern is indispensable. The determinants that account for this pattern are perspectives, and the researcher using a flexible research design "has to reconstruct underlying patterns out of the partial and divergent perspectives of a multiplicity of observers" (Lang and Lang, 1961, p. 553).

Because the data do not have "sense built into them—that is, they were not collected to test specific hypotheses nor with any firm presumptions of relevance—the analysis is an attempt to make sense of them after the fact" (Liebow, 1966, p. 12).

To do this, two approaches are used in analysing the data: (1) the case study method, which presents the episodes in full view and in their natural settings, and (2) the use of a comparative chart of empirical indicators which enables the researcher to reconstruct the underlying pattern and correlate the documentary or interview data with the model. These analytic approaches enabled the following goals to be achieved:

1. Describing and sociologically locating and identifying the episodes;
2. Categorizing the episodes, i.e., classification and systematization;
3. Comparing the episodes to determine if uniformities and similarities can be identified;
4. Tracing the pattern of the episodes over a time sequence to ascertain if the "value-added" logic exists in any or all of the episodes;
5. Comparing the findings with the model selected to determine whether the findings seem to fit the model in a reasonably accurate way.

Finally, to analyze the differences existing among the episodes, the uniformities, similarities, dissimilarities, and nonuniformities were treated statistically through the use of the chi-square test. The .05 level of significance was chosen as the level at which the differences would be accepted as rejecting the null hypothesis.

IDENTIFYING THE EPISODES IN TERMS OF THE MODEL

The phenomena described in the selected episodes that this study investigated are clearly identified under the type of collective behavior that Smelser calls "the hostile outburst" and defines as "action mobilized on the basis of a generalized belief assigning responsibility for an undesirable state of affairs to some agent." Furthermore, Smelser writes, "to fit our definition the participants in an outburst must be bent on attacking someone considered responsible for a disturbing state of affairs" (1961, p. 226).

From the preceding discussion we can clearly identify and establish in terms of the model the character of the phenomena under study as "hostile outbursts." In order to develop some precision in the identification and correlation of the raw data with the model, empirical indicators were developed. The logic of empirical indicators is based on the work of Trow (1968, p. 7).

Fifty-one indicators were developed based upon the general characteristics of the determinants as postulated by Smelser. These indicators were then sought in the documentary analysis or interview data, and their occurrence was recorded in appropriate cells in the chart. From this, uniformities and similarities were identified. The comparison chart, therefore, indicated the presence or absence of the empirical indicators. In this way patterns of association were revealed showing uniformities and similarities so that comparisons could be make among the episodes. Conversely, nonuniformities and nonsimilarities were also identified by the same method. Finally, a statistical analysis was possible based upon the magnitude of the empirical indicators appearing under each episode.

Findings and Conclusions

To illustrate how the research methods and the documentary materials were meshed, one of the episodes will be presented in its case study form. The background and broader sociological milieu is first presented as a means of placing the specific disturbance into its social and historic context.

THE BACKGROUND

This hostile outburst occurred in the District Stadium (now renamed the Robert F. Kennedy Stadium) in Washington, D.C. on Thanksgiving Day, November 22, 1962 during a high school football championship game. This contest would determine the high school football champions of the capital of the United States. The two school involved, Eastern High School, the defending champions, and St. John's High School, the challengers, were sharply divided along both racial and socioeconomic lines. Eastern was regarded as a Negro public school, whereas St. John's is a private school where the majority of students are white and from well-to-do middle-class families. As a result the partisanship and loyalty of the spectators was almost entirely on a racial and class basis. In addition, the population of Washington, D.C. in 1962 was 54 percent Negro, with 84 percent Negro attendance in the public school (Meyer, 1966, p. 209). In 1968, the former figure had risen to 66.7 percent, and the latter to 93.2 percent (*News Gazette*, p. 1).

Though the public schools in Washington, D.C. are desegregated, a constantly growing Negro population and a constantly diminishing white population means that the District schools are becoming more segregated (as the quoted statistics clearly show). Furthermore, the mass of the Negro population at that time were unskilled, uneducated, and impoverished. They lived in overcrowded conditions, suffered from extensive unemployment, and were subjected to interracial tension and strife (Meyer, p. 207). The percentage of illegitimacy in Washington was one of the highest in the country, and the venereal disease rate was not only the highest in the United States, but 3.5 percent of the total cases were in that city (Ibid., p. 211).

The crime rate had increased by 17 percent in 1962 over the previous year and the police chief, Robert V. Murray, stated that 85 percent of the District's crimes were committed by Negroes (Ibid., p. 208). Many of the offenses were committed by unemployed young Negroes who, for the previous fifteen years, had been crowding into the city from the urban and rural slums of the South. They had hopes of a better life in Washington, but instead they encountered overcrowded living conditions, no opportunity for work, and no social contact except with other Negroes suffering the same frustrations. The result was racial tension and a smouldering hatred of the white population which prompted Columbia University's Eli Ginzberg to comment in 1961, "Washington represents as backward a community as any that I know in the northern part of the United States" (Ibid., p. 208).

Predominantly Negro Washington has enormous racial problems which have been largely ignored. These problems are well described, however, by Elliott Liebow in *Tally's Corner*. The hostile outburst at this game had its roots in socio-racial problems which extend far beyond high school rowdyism.

THE BROADER CONTEST

The civil rights movement of the 1960s was just about getting started at this time. The condition of the Negro in America, and particularly in the cities, had reached explosive levels in the early 1960s due to poor housing, poor education, unemployment, and poverty. "For the great mass of urban Negroes poverty or near poverty seems as much a part of their condition as the color of their skin.... The urban Negro is in a fundamental sense *the* urban problem" ("Cities," in *Time*, 1967, p. 11).

Two out of every three Negroes live in towns and cities, most of them in big cities, and fewer than 5 percent live in suburbs. In 1964 the median family income of Negroes was approximately $3,800 and of whites $6,800. About 40 percent of Negro families have incomes below the poverty level of $3,000 and live in substandard housing, whereas only 15 percent of whites do (*Chicago Tribune Magazine*). The pattern of this urban Negro "culture of poverty" seems to be as follows: a low-paying job or none at all, leading to housing in a slum, leading to a segregated, second-rate school, and leading back to an inferior and low-paying job ("Cities," *Time*, p. 12).

The social outcome of all this is published in the United States Department of Labor's report, *The Negro Family: A Case for National Action,* written by the former Assistant Secretary of Labor, and former Presidential Advisor on Urban Affairs, Daniel P. Moynihan. This report shows that fewer than half of all Negroes reached the age of 18 having lived all of their lives with both parents;

21 percent of all Negro families were fatherless; at least 25 percent and maybe as many as 40 percent of Negro children were illegitimate.

Said the report: "The evidence—not final—but powerfully persuasive—is that the Negro family in the urban ghettos is crumbling. For vast numbers, the fabric of conventional social relationship has all but disintegrated."

This then was the background of the game which is now reported.

THE GAME

The following account of this hostile outburst is taken from an article in the *Saturday Evening Post,* May 4, 1963, entitled "How a Race Riot Happened," by Alvin Shuster and Ben A. Franklin, pp. 15-19.*

>Nobody is quite certain when the first ugly little acts of violence began to erupt. Afterward a few spectators said they sensed trouble almost from the start. They were offended because so many young people remained seated with hats on when the national anthem was played, and they watched the game uneasily as groups of rowdy teenagers swigged secretively from bottles of wine and gin. But the vast majority of spectators who made up the record-breaking crowd that jammed the massive new District of Columbia Stadium last November 22 were in no mood to pay attention to such things. They were there to watch the city's annual high school championship football classic. From the way they surged through the turnstiles and raced for the unreserved seats, it was clear they were filled with a holiday spirit and suffering from the pleasant, exuberant madness that seizes football fans everywhere. The cheerleaders were pert and energetic, the bands blared competitively, and here and there whole families sat together, waved school colors and shouted themselves hoarse.
>
>The crowd was orderly at first. Except that the majestically familiar dome of the Capitol was clearly visible in the distance, anyone who stood at the top of the stadium and judged the crowd solely by its noise and outward behavior would have noted nothing to distinguish it from any typical high school football crowd at a Thanksgiving game in any typical big United States city. In one significant respect, however, the crowd was untypical. Of the 50,033 spectators packed into the stadium about 42,000, roughly 80 percent, were Negroes, but nobody was overwhelmingly surprised. Everybody was aware that a great deal of race pride was involved in the game. Eastern High, defending its title as public school champion, was considered a Negro school; it had only five whites among its 2,400 students. St. John's High, the challenging school whose team was champion of the Catholic League, was for boys mostly from well-to-do families and was predominantly white.

*Reprinted by permission from *The Saturday Evening Post.* © 1963 The Curtis Publishing Company.

St. John's, which had two Negro players on its squad, had a sprinkling of Negro supporters in the stands, and a handful of whites were rooting for Eastern. It was perfectly clear, however, that the loyalties of the crowd were split almost entirely along race lines. There was a mighty resounding roar when the Eastern Ramblers trotted on the field; St. John's Cadets were greeted with a thunderous roll of boos.

Eastern fans began to taste an easy victory when St. John's fumbled on an early play and Eastern recovered and drove to a touchdown only eight minutes after the game started. Neither team scored again in the first quarter, but in the second period, St. John's pushed over two touchdowns and took a 13-7 lead. Most white spectators were not conscious of it, but a sullen resentment was spreading like a blight among some Negroes. Simeon S. Booker, Jr., a Negro magazine correspondent, reported later, "As St. John's amassed their winning margin, a moody dejection set in among certain elements, clearly a small but uninhibited minority. Behind me I could hear shouts of 'Kill him,' on tackle plays. Then I heard such comments as 'Let's get out before the fighting starts.' "

The first really frightening signs of mass misbehavior began at half time. When adults left their seats in the lower levels to go to refreshment stands or rest rooms, many youngsters in the upper levels, mostly Negroes, ran down and took their seats. Some adults who protested were taunted, cursed or threatened. Several white girls who visited ladies' rooms were pummelled or bullied; eight Negro youths gang-whipped a white boy in a men's room; a Negro at a refreshment stand was struck by two white boys. Numerous groups of Negro youths, who obviously had been drinking, began swaggering through the aisles, shouting boisterously, jostling spectators and occasionally shouting obscenities at people they passed. Fights broke out in various parts of the stadium. Not everybody in the huge crowd saw these unpleasant incidents. But a mood of apprehension began to spread.

When play was resumed in the second half, most spectators hoped the unruly behavior in the stand would stop. But on the opening kick-off Eastern fumbled, and St. John's recovered the ball and promptly drove 22 yards for a touchdown and what was to be the final score of the game: 20-7. Almost immediately the fabric of order began to rip.

As violence spread it also assumed a pattern. One father related that he and his family watched in awe as a band of Negro boys ... ran down the St. John's side of the stadium swinging their open hands and fists at boys, girls and parents sitting in the front row.

A mother who attended the game with her husband and children recounted their experience: "I had been watching the field intently when suddenly I realized that a Negro man was beating my husband, who was sitting to my left. Before I could move, a tall, light-skinned

Negro struck me a blow on the right temple with his knuckles and knocked my glasses to the ground. There were about ten Negroes. Each . . . turned and attacked his neighbor. I screamed for the police, but the cheering at the play on the field masked my screams; then several of the Negroes turned and began hitting my husband again, for he too was yelling, 'Police.' The Negroes then turned and disappeared down the walk. My husband went for a policeman. Several Negroes—not the ones who attacked us—crowded the policeman, and he was powerless to do anything."

Both of these families left the game. As rowdyism and violence spread, there was a steady trickle of offended or anxious spectators, white and Negro family groups leaving the stadium. As the game neared an end the trickle through the exits became a widening stream, particularly after the violence in the stands, like an uncontrolled brush fire, suddenly jumped to the playing field.

The clash on the field came as a surprise to most people. Actually, though, officials and sportswriters alike considered it an exceptionally clean game. Eastern's players and coaches had been seething since the half because they felt St. John's was playing an unnecessarily tough brand of football, using elbows and hands on offense. An Eastern player complained, "St. John's backs looked as though they hated us."

Trouble exploded with only six minutes left in the game. On an incomplete pass, husky Eastern tackle Calvin Harris tried to take St. John's fullback Jay Calabresse out of the play with a body block. Calabresse said he warded Harris off by thrusting out his forearm—a routine and legal defensive tactic. But somehow Calabresse's elbow caught Harris on the right side of the face. Harris was convinced he had been struck after the referee's whistle ended the play. Infuriated, he squared off to punch Calabresse. Referee Ray Wrenn, a detective on the Police Department's juvenile squad, spotted Harris, penalized Eastern 15 yards and ordered Harris out of the game.

At this point Eastern head coach Richard Mentzer, who is white and a highly regarded veteran of high school athletics, stormed onto the field. He angrily protested the penalty and shouted that he would use official motion pictures of the game to prove that St. John's had been fouling repeatedly. He also reenacted in broad pantomine all of St. John's alleged transgressions, gesturing frequently toward the Eastern stands as well as his players. An investigating committee later decided that Mentzer's actions seemed inflammatory. Perhaps Mentzer's performance had some effect on Calvin Harris, who was brooding about being thrown out of the game. "I went the the sideline," he said later, "and felt blood coming down my face and lost the sight of my right eye. Before I know it I was back on the field."

Harris charged directly for Calabresse and started swinging. The reserve players on Eastern's bench also surged onto the field. For a few brief minutes there was a wild, milling free-for-all. Finally Harris was subdued by three teammates and order was restored. Harris was strapped to a stretcher and taken off to a hospital. Police rushed up reinforcements to hold back a crowd of Negro youths who had spilled from the stands and gathered menacingly on the sidelines. In the suddenly hushed stadium, it had become clear that ugly trouble was in the offing.

As play resumed a thin line of policemen was strung out in front of the Eastern stands. Then, as the stadium clock began to tick off the final seconds in the game, the crowd, as fans often do at football games, counted them down with a full-throated roar: "Five! Four! Three! Two! One!" The gun sounded, there were cries of "Let's get them, let's show them"—and terror was unleashed.

A mob of some 2,000 yelling, jostling young Negroes burst from the stands and rushed across the field toward the St. John's section.

"I was just terrified," a Catholic teaching brother said. "It was like a moving tarpaulin about 30 or 40 yards long," said another spectator. "They overwhelmed the people still in the stands. I myself saw young boys knocked down and stamped. I saw them struck. I tried to help an old lady coming up the aisle ... My hat was knocked off. Streams of teen-agers went by on both sides, and I was struck about 15 times. I had a black eye, and my ears still hurt from it. I had lumps all over my head. The woman was struck—the lady I was trying to help. They saw she was an old woman. Her hat was knocked off. She had two little kids with her."

"We were pushed back to the wall," the wife of a St. John's alumnus said. "There must have been 15 Negro boys, face to face with us, with all kinds of things in their hands, but mostly knives."

Most victims agreed the mob was made up chiefly of teen-agers, with a sprinkling of 11 and 12 year old boys and some men in their early 20's. Some carried knives, but used them mostly to cow victims while they struck or kicked them. Others ruthlessly swung sticks or hurled rocks and bottles. One person saw a chain; there was one report of a tree branch being used. Only a few agreed with a St. John's teaching brother that it was a "preplanned, mob-rule scene." There was evidence that some of the youths had come to the game prepared for trouble, but the random, clumsy savagery indicated that the rioters had no real leaders. More than 3,000 persons were engaged in the rioting at Gate E alone. In a swarming frenzy, they cursed, slapped, punched and kicked their victims, paying no attention to age or sex. Most spectators caught only brief, terrifying close glimpses of the rioting. A panoramic view can be reconstructed only through eye-witness reports gathered by the police and an investigating committee.

SUMMARY

Having described all the episodes in the form of case studies the second stage in the analysis of the data was then undertaken. This analysis sought to categorize, compare, and establish a temporal sequential pattern in the episodes. This was accomplished through the utilization of a comparative chart based upon the general characteristics of the determinants of collective behavior as postulated by Smelser. Empirical indicators were developed from these general characteristics and the indicators sought in the documentary or interview data. The chart enabled the empirical indicators to be adapted to meet the specific needs of the research situation. In this way patterns of association were revealed showing uniformities, similarities, and dissimilarities so comparisons could be made among and within the episodes. In addition, the similarities and uniformities were quantified and the results subjected to statistical analysis.

The statistical results showed that the kind of social consequence resulting is not a chance one and in addition the direction of the outcome is related to the number of empirical indicators appearing. This means that the more empirical indicators that appear, the more serious the outcome of the episode. Conversely, the fewer the empirical indicators, the less serious the outcome. Finally, chance can be eliminated as a cause of this difference.

For the more statistically inclined here are the basic figures.

Number of Empirical Indicators

Indicators	Episode A	Episode B	Episode C	Episode D
Possible	51	51	51	51
Observed	22	25	39	44
Expected	32.5	32.5	32.5	32.5

Computed $X^2 = 10.491$. Tabled X^2 at .01 level of significance for one-tailed test = 9.837.
Decision: reject null hypothesis.
Conclusion: a significant difference exists among the episodes and direction is indicated (Runyon & Haber, p. 252).

Although the .05 level of significance was chosen as the level at which the null hypothesis would be accepted or rejected, the computed figure was significant at the .01 level and is consequently reported at this level.

RESULTS

The investigation produced the following pertinent findings:

1. The phenomena of social disturbances involving violence at the selected amateur football games can be established and identified in terms of the model derived from Smelser's theory of collective behavior.

This finding is significant because other studies using empirical data and seeking to identify episodes of collective behavior in terms of Smelser's theory have not been able to achieve this degree of precision.

2. The phenomena can be classified in terms of the determinants established by Smelser as the necessary conditions for the appearance of an episode of collective behavior.

This finding shows that the theory is capable of being used as a taxonomy or systematic classification system. This is a significant finding because it helps to establish the theory as a means of systematic interpretation.

3. The comparative chart of empirical indicators developed from the model enabled the episodes to be compared and contrasted for similarities, uniformities, dissimilarities, and nonuniformities.

This chart reduced the vast amount of data to a manageable and significant set of indicators for subsequent analysis.

4. The comparative chart of empirical indicators enabled the episodes to be analyzed in such a way that statistical treatment of the results was possible.
5. Patterns of association were revealed through vertical and cross tabulation of the empirical indicators.
   The vertical tabulations revealed a pattern of association between the magnitude of the appearance of the indicators and the severity of the social consequences of the episodes.

A statistical treatment of this finding shows that a significant difference exists among the episodes at the .01 level.

6. The magnitude of the need for success in sports is related to the degree of insecurity of the social structure of the community in which the game is played.

A secure social structure tends to produce and sustain a concept of sportsmanship that the insecure social structure lacks. Success, therefore, is vital to an insecure community because it fulfills a sociological need; i.e., a public assurance that the community or group as represented by its team is not inferior.

DISCUSSION

In comparing the findings of this investigation with others using Smelser's theory in the study of collective behavior, one is immediately struck by the relative ease of application in this study. This may well be due to a lower level of social complexity obtaining in sports settings than elsewhere in the social structure. Sports take place in a defined and confined geographic area with a clear-cut focus, relatively simple regulations, and an agreed and clearly defined definition of success or failure. In addition, polarization of attention and crowd homogeneity would appear to be greater here than elsewhere in the culture. The natural laboratory of a sports setting affords an unusual kind of social setting where many kinds of social elements, usually controlled or not readily observable, come into the open and are observable in "naked" or "pure" form. Sports, therefore, offer an unusual kind of natural laboratory or social setting in which the direct study of certain components of human behavior (which usually lie dormant) is possible.

Also sports, and in particular success in sports, represents one of the few channels available to the socially underprivileged to gain some measure of success—thereby being reassured that they are not inferior. Sports may, in addition, be a means of expressing the hostility and tensions of the socially underprivileged in a controlled and defined context. However, this has its dangers as well as its advantage and if the social structure in which the contest takes place is unstable or insecure, as it was in Lima and in Washington, D.C., the results could be disastrous, as they unfortunately proved to be in these two episodes. The magnitude of the social consequences of the reported episodes clearly shows a relationship between an insecure social structure, a lack of or the absence of a concept of sportsmanship, and the severity of the hostile outburst. In addition, an insecure social structure may well be the major reason for the lack of a concept of sportsmanship, a concept that would appear necessary in the development of the preventive component of social control. This component minimizes conduciveness and strain and operates before the outburst materializes. From the data it was seen that this component was totally absent or lacking in the Lima and Washington, D.C. episodes, thereby contributing to the breakdown of the final and sufficient determinant of collective behavior, social control. In the other two episodes its effects were certainly present to a degree not seen in the two former cases.

Finally, a reevaluation of the model indicates that greater formulation and an increase in the number of empirical indicators, resulting in greater clarity and precision, would produce a more useful model. However, the basic model has proved extremely useful because it has been based on a theory which manages to encompass a wide range of historical, sociological, and economic factors and express them within a single explanatory system. No theorist prior to Neil Smelser has managed to do this. This is Smelser's significant and influential contribution to the field of collective behavior and its implications for hostile outbursts in spectator sports.

Implications for the Practicing Administrator

The practicing, and usually harried, administrator might well ask what all this sociological theory, statistical analysis, empirical indicators, comparative international studies, and all the rest has to do with the job in hand (which might well be the organization and running of a Little League basketball tournament next Friday night in the school gym). Well, the short answer might be that every sporting assembly today could result in a hostile outburst of unknown magnitude with a result of very adverse publicity for all concerned— and this would be the least that could be expected! A more serious outburst might well produce injury to persons or damage to property or both. This would certainly involve legal intervention. The prudent administrator would therefore seek to anticipate such a situation and take precautionary action. However, unless one has some rationale for one's decisions, the decisions are no better than hunches, guesses, short-term panaceas, or stop-gap solutions. In other words, if meaningful solutions or even answers to problems are to be of value they must be based on some kind of systematic model, conceptual frame of reference, or theory. Facts may well lead to information, but facts gathered under the guidance of some theoretical frame of reference lead to explanation and understanding. This is how modern scientists operate whether they be physical, biological, behavioral, or social scientists. If we want to benefit from the results of modern science, then our thinking, behavior, and decision making must be congruent with theirs.

If one accepts this argument then the following suggestions and conclusions could be deduced from the study.

1. The model of collective behavior as developed by N. J. Smelser is a most useful frame of reference for analyzing hostile outbursts at sporting events. It is built upon two constructs, the *components of social action* and the *"value-added"* process. The former is a means of describing the components of social action. The latter is an analytic framework of six determinants for explaining collective behavior. These determinants are not a mere listing but are related in a *systematic* way and organized in a *patterned sequence* so that the outcome is an episode of collective behavior and only collective behavior. The determinants are (1) *structural conduciveness* (a social situation where collective behavior *could* result), (2) *structural strain* (a social situation in which people feel that something is wrong with their social environment), (3) growth and spread of a generalized belief (a belief that some agent or group is responsible for the strain, that something should be quickly done and that the solution suggested will work immediately), (4) precipitating factors (a dramatic action or event publicly performed which confirms the generalized belief), (5) mobilization of participants for action (a getting together of those who hold the generalized belief) and finally (6) the breakdown of social control. The model requires that all these determinants combine according to the patterned sequence; i.e., one after the other and within the conditions set by the earlier determinants. These determinants can be seen and the pattern identified in the outburst in Washington, D.C. and reported earlier.

2. The model enables hostile outbursts occurring at sporting events to be classified, compared, analyzed, and interpreted. Although the episodes were restricted to football games it would appear that the model could be used in other team sports—for example, basketball and baseball.
3. The forms of violence identified in the four episodes as examples of "modern" violence are in accordance with Tilly's analysis of modern collective violence as coming into being under the impetus of industrialization, urbanization, population growth, rapid migration from rural to urban areas, and enduring economic and political associations. The view, therefore, of human aggression as a sometime response to intolerable social frustrations and as a symptom of stress in human societies would tend to be supported. This view of human aggression is termed the *conditional* view and is based upon the assumption that nature provides man only with the capacity for violence; it is social circumstance that determines whether and how that capacity is exercised.
4. Sport is a social institution of society, and consequently is interrelated to and influenced by the other social institutions of the culture. This study seems to demonstrate that the social structure influences sports and sports followers, and is in turn influenced by them. To expect sports and the behavior of its followers not to be influenced, little influenced, or marginally influenced by the social structure of the society in which it occurs is untenable. The behavior of sports crowds, therefore, does not exist, or can it be adequately analyzed, in a social vacuum. For an adequate analysis the social structure, as well as the social history of the area in which the episodes occurred, must be given adequate attention.

(It is suggested that sports offer an unusual kind of natural laboratory in which the direct study of certain components of collective behavior is possible. Modern competitive sports could well be utilized as a social situation more amenable to direct empirical study of collective behavior than other social situations used in the past.)

5. This study would tend to suggest that anticipation and control of hostile outbursts at sports events is now a possibility.

(It is suggested that the same schematic model—with perhaps greater elaboration—can be utilized in formulating means for systematic anticipation and precautionary control of hostile outbursts of a sports nature.)

RECOMMENDATIONS FOR FURTHER INVESTIGATION

As an outcome of this investigation the following recommendations for further study are made:

1. The relative and apparent homogeneity of sports crowds could

well be investigated, identified, and established through the use of trained observers. If this homogeneity could be established, the sports crowd and the collective behavior exhibited there would be an excellent natural laboratory setting for the testing of pre-designed hypotheses.

2. A systematic study on the lines similar to this one could be carried out in other sports, notably basketball and baseball, with a view to establishing similarities and uniformities between these sports. This would make the results of this study more applicable in a broader sports context.

3. The various uniformities and similarities identified in this study, though not commonplace, are sufficiently recurrent to enable predesigned hypotheses based on this study to be put to the empirical test.

4. It is finally suggested that more research be conducted into episodes similar to the outbursts reported here with a view to identifying the negative case. Through the use of the negative case, Smelser's theory might then be either confirmed or refuted. This would take subsequent studies from the realm of the "context of discovery," as it is in this study, to the "context of justification." This is necessary if the theory is finally to be verified (Kaplan, 1963, pp. 13-18).

General Bibliography

Blank, J., "Sport's Worst Tragedy", *The Kiwanis,* 50, no. 3 (March 1965).

Brinton, C., *The Anatomy of Revolution,* rev. and expanded ed. New York: Vintage Books, 1965.

Brown, R., *Social Psychology.* New York: The Free Press, 1965.

Chicago Tribune Magazine, October 15, 1967.

"Cities, Light in the Frightening Corners," *Time,* July 28, 1967.

"Crowd Control at Athletic Events," *Journal of the American Association for Health, Physical Education & Recreation,* 40 (April 1969).

Crowd Control for High School Athletics. Washington, D.C.: AAHPER, 1970.

Department of Education and Science, *Report of the Committee on Football.* London: H.M.S.O., 1968. "The Chester Report."

Evans, R., "Theoretical Viewpoints in Collective Behavior," *Readings in Collective Behavior,* ed. R. E. Evans. Chicago: Rand McNally & Co., 1969.

Festinger, L., and D. Katz, *Research Methods in Behavior Sciences.* New York: Holt, Rinehart and Winston, 1966.

Gluckman, M., "Football Players and the Crowd," *The Listener,* 9. London: The British Broadcasting Corporation, February 19, 1959.

Harrington, J., *Soccer Hooliganism.* Bristol, England: John Wright and Sons Ltd., 1968. "The Harrington Report."

Hasdorf, A., and H. Cantril, "They Saw a Game: A Case Study" *Journal of Abnormal and Social Psychology,* 44, no. 2 (1954).

Inkeles, A., *What is Sociology?,* p. 28. Englewood Cliffs, N.J.: Prentice-Hall, Inc., 1964.

Kaplan, A., *The Conduct of Inquiry.* San Francisco: Chandler Publishing Co., 1964.

Kleinman, S., "A Study to Determine the Factors that Influence the Behavior of Sports Crowds." Ph.D. diss., Ohio State University, 1960.

Lang, K., and G. Lang, *Collective Dynamics,* pp. 133-35. New York: Thomas Y. Crowell Co., 1961.

―――――, "Collective Behavior," *International Encyclopedia of the Social Science,* vol. 2. New York: The Macmillan Co., 1968.

Leach, G., *Spectator Control at Interscholastic Basketball Games.* Trenton, N.J.: Athletic Dept., Rider College, 1959.

Liebow, E., *Tally's Corner.* Boston: Little, Brown and Co., 1966.

McCarthy, S., *Report to the Superintendent of Schools* from *Special Committee on Group Activities.* Washington, D.C.: Public Schools of the District of Columbia, 1963.

Merton, R. K., M. Fiske, and P. Kendall, *The Focused Interview.* Glencoe, Ill.: The Free Press, 1956.

Meyer, A., "The Nation's Worst Slum: Washington, D.C.," *Current Perspectives on Social Problems,* ed. Judson R. Landis. Belmont, Calif.: Wadsworth Publishing Co., 1966.

Milgram, S., and H. Toch, "Collective Behavior," *The Handbook of Social Psychology,* ed. Gardner Linzey and Elliot Aronson, vol. 4, 2nd ed. Reading, Mass.: Addison-Wesley Publishing Co., 1969.

Ministry of Housing and Local Government, *Crowd Behavior at Football Matches.* London: H.M.S.O., 1969.

News Gazette, Champaign-Urbana, Ill., October 28, 1968, 556-650.

Phillips, B., *Social Research: Strategy and Tactics* (New York: The Macmillan Co., 1966),

Rarick, L., "The Case Study," *Research Methods in Health, Physical Education and Recreation,* 2nd ed. Washington, D.C.: AAHPER, 1959.

Riley, M. W., *Sociological Research.* New York: Harcourt, Brace and World, Inc., 1963.

Runyon, R., and A. Haber, *Fundamentals of Behavioral Statistics.* Reading, Mass.: Addison-Wesley Publishing Co., 1967.

Schul, B., *A Study of the Garnet Riot.* Mimiographed. Topeka, Kansas: Office of the Attorney General, 1963.

Shellow, R., and D. Roemer, "The Riot that Didn't Happen," *Social Problems,* 14, no. 2 (Fall 1966).

Shuster, A., and B. Franklin, "How a Race Riot Happened," *Saturday Evening Post,* May 4, 1963.

Smelser, N. J., *Theory of Collective Behavior.* New York: The Free Press of Glencoe, 1963.

Strauss, A., "Collective Behavior: Neglect and Need," *American Sociological Review,* 12 (June 1947).

Taylor, I., "Soccer Hooligans," *New Society,* 14, no. 358. London: New Science Publications, August 9, 1969.

The Negro Family: A Case for National Action, U.S. Dept. of Labor. Washington, D.C.: Government Printing Office, 1965.

Tilly, C., "Collective Violence in European Perspective," *Violence in America,* ed. H. D. Graham and T. R. Gurr, p. 5. New York: Bantam Books, 1969.

Trow, M., "Notes on Sociological Research," *Sociology,* 4th ed., ed. L. Broom and P. Selznick. New York: Harper and Row Publishers, 1968.

Turner, R., "Collective Behavior," *Handbook of Modern Sociology,* ed. R. E. L. Faris, pp. 382-425. Chicago: Rand McNally & Co., 1964.

Turner, R., and L. Killian, *Collective Behavior,* 2nd ed. Englewood Cliffs, N.J.: Prentice-Hall, Inc., 1972.

13

Role Expectations of Teachers and Chairmen

Shirley J. Wood

Introduction

The general purpose of the study reported here was to investigate (1) the level of agreement that existed among and between women physical education teachers and their respective department chairmen in relation to particular expectations for those two positions, and (2) the relationship that existed between consensus on expectations and the teachers' satisfaction with their chairmen's professional leadership. Concepts of role theory provided the theoretical bases for the investigation.

Very little is known about the role expectations actually held by physical educators. Though the literature abounds with statements concerning how teachers and chairmen should act, research concerning the acceptance or rejection of such behavioral expectations has been meager. If, as the current literature on the subject seems to indicate, role expectations are factors that affect organizational operation, it would appear that information concerning such factors would be of some value to physical education administrators.

Congruity of expectations between teachers and administrators appears to be a factor of some importance. An administrator must meet the expectations of the faculty or run the risk of having his or her authority severely undermined.

Shirley Wood is from the Iowa State University, Ames, Iowa.

On the other hand, a teacher must meet the chairman's expectations or be subject to sanction in relation to salary and tenure recommendations. Incongruencies of expectations or inaccurate perceptions of the role prescriptions of others may complicate the problem of satisfactory role performance and may have consequences in job satisfaction. The study reported here was undertaken with the hope that additional information concerning role expectations and role conflict would contribute a better understanding of conditions that influence the behavior of chairmen and teachers, and that the findings would be of relevance to administrators. The questions asked in the study were mainly concerned with three problems of role analysis: expectation agreement, expectation perception, and the consequences of role expectation discrepancies.

EXPECTATION AGREEMENT

Broadly conceived, role theory holds that the behavior of a position incumbent is a product of both his own concept of his role and relevant social interaction. Individuals learn that certain expected types of behavior are appropriate to the society in which they live. The patterns of appropriate behavior may differ slightly from one social subsystem to another, but, despite these variations, nearly all human beings learn that certain patterns of behavior are expected in various situations. These expected patterns of behavior are considered the norms for particular situations, and much of a person's behavior is defined by such cultural norms. The recognition of the social-cultural influence on an individual's performance is essential to an understanding of role behavior. Expectations are not independently derived, but are the products of social interactions. Thus, the family group, the community, colleagues, administrative superiors, and professional bodies are but a few of the many sources from which an individual gains information concerning role expectations.

A distinction is generally made between the expectation-prescription aspect and the behavioral-enactment aspect of the role concept. Though these aspects are referred to by varying labels, role expectations and role behavior are two major elements of role theory. Role expectations represent the prescriptive, or the "ought to" factor; and role behavior represents the actual behavior. That there is not always congruence between the "oughts" and the "does" factors is clearly evident. As a result, problems in human relationship may result.

Why actual behavior does not always fit the pattern of expectations is of more than academic interest. Social prescriptions, or role expectations, are not always clearly defined. Nor are they, even when clearly defined, always agreed upon by interacting individuals. The existence of some expectations which are generally recognized in a given society is evident, but, when examining smaller groups, there may often be considerable disagreement among the members of a group on the matter of expectations for any given role. That students, teachers, and deans do not always hold the same expectations for a university department chairman seems patently evident.

EXPECTATION PERCEPTION

In addition to the problems of vaguely defined expectations and differing role definitions, the possibility that individuals may not accurately perceive expectations held by others is a factor of some importance. Just as role expectations and role behaviors may be considered as two separate aspects of social role, so may role perception be factored. One factor, which may be termed own- or self-expectations, relates to an individual's perception of appropriate behavior for a position which he occupies. A second factor refers to expectations which any individual perceives that others hold for him. That the expectations attributed to another may not coincide with those actually held by that individual should be as evident as the possibility of expectation-behavior contradictions.

It is entirely possible that an administrator may define a subordinate's role in a manner very similar to the subordinate's own definition of the role, but the subordinate may perceive the administrator's expectations entirely differently. The problem of perception appears to be a crucial one when viewing role incongruencies. Scott has established certain generalizations concerning perception which appear to be pertinent.

1. That which an individual perceives when confronted with a stimulus situation may not correspond to "objective reality."
2. Several individuals confronted with the same stimulus situation may perceive the same situation quite differently.
3. The manner in which an individual perceives a stimulus situation is affected by biological, psychological, social, and cultural factors.
4. The individual responds to his environment in terms of his perception of that environment (1956, p. 122).

CONSEQUENCES OF ROLE EXPECTATION DISPARITIES

The extent to which there is a consensus on role definitions may be an important factor in determining affective relationships within a small social system. It would appear that if pairs of members of various groups, or groups as a whole, differ on role expectations, some discernible consequences ought to be apparent. One such consequence of role expectation disparities appears to be related to the broad area of morale or job satisfaction. Several studies have indicated that a low level of agreement on expectations is negatively related to various aspects of satisfaction expressed by individuals (Ferneau, 1954; Moser, 1957). Such findings have broad implications for administrators.

Background

Role theory involves the conceptualization of human behavior at a relatively complex level, and there is not yet widespread agreement regarding the terms used to clarify the concept of role. Biddle and Thomas (1966, p. 15) maintain that there is not one accepted theory of role, and that "role field" would be a more appropriate term. Although there is yet confusion regarding the terms and concepts used to clarify the idea of role, role theory has assumed a key position in the social sciences. The concept has been frequently used as a central term in conceptual schemes for the analysis of the structure and functioning of social systems and for the explanation of individual behavior (Gross et al., 1958, p. 3).

Biddle and Thomas aptly described the role study approach in the following statement. "The role perspective consists of a particular viewpoint regarding those factors presumed to be influential in governing human behavior. . . ." (1966, p. 4). The particular viewpoint to which Biddle and Thomas referred is one of a limited social determinism. That is, it focuses attention on the normative structure that guides behavior. An assumption of the role perspective is that behavior is shaped by the social prescriptions, behaviors, and sanctions of others, and by the individual's own understanding and conceptions of what his behavior should be.

A major problem in utilizing the role concept has been the fact that many varying definitions have been proposed. Even a cursory review of the literature reveals that the concept of role is being viewed from many different vantage points. Some writers appear to be viewing role in terms of normative cultural patterns; some think that role is best explained by what actors actually do in their occupancy of positions; and yet another group view role as being influenced by cultural, situational, and personal determinants. Regardless of the vantage point from which the writer starts, there are three common elements in the various definitions: social location, behavior, and expectations (Gross et al., 1958, p. 17).

Because there is not widespread agreement with respect to terms associated with role, it is extremely important that the concepts upon which an investigation is based are clearly defined. The role terminology is used in this study is based upon the work of Gross, Mason, and McEachern (1958).

In their expository work on role constructs, Gross, Mason, and McEachern question the validity of the postulate of role consensus assumed by many role theorists. These authors viewed the degree of consensus on any expectation as empirically problematic, and they proceeded under the following assumptions:

> that the extent to which there is consensus on role definition may be an important dimension affecting the functioning of social systems whether they are total societies or subsystems within them. In addition, significant role definers as perceived by an actor may be an important variable affecting his behavior (1958, p. 5).

In their sophisticated and complex work, Gross and his associates presented a body of concepts and a set of terms which are precisely defined. The concepts are presented under four main headings: position; expectations; role, role behavior, and role attributes; and sanctions.

POSITION

The term "position" is defined as "the location of an actor or class of actors in a system of social relationships" (Gross et al., 1958, p. 48). A position is a unit or an element in a network of positions, and it must be considered in relation to other positions to which it is joined. Because it would be extremely difficult for an investigator to deal empirically with all of the relationships associated with a single position, it becomes necessary to deal with partial systems of relationships.

A further complicating factor in examining a position is that a focal position may be involved in different sets of systems. Thus, a simple social system, such as a university department, is also related to larger social systems such as the division of which it is a part, the total university, and a profession. Though a simple dyad model of position analysis can be the subject of investigation, a precise specification of positional sectors must be given. Besides a clear positional specification, a situational specification is required. This refers to the scope of the social system in which the position is to be studied.

EXPECTATION

An expectation is defined as "an evaluative standard applied to an incumbent of a position" (Gross et al., 1958, p. 58). Whereas a position is a social location, an expectation deals with how the incumbents of a position should behave. Because the term "expectation" has been used by some role theorists in a predictive sense, it is important to clearly delineate the terms as used by Gross and associates. To them, expectation is used in a normative sense to denote what should happen as opposed to a probability statement as to what will happen. Second, the applicability of an expectation to an actor is dependent upon how the position has been specified. The authors also note that expectations for a particular position incumbent are affected by such factors as the perceptions that one actor holds for the position specifications, the incumbent's personal characteristics, and the number of other positions occupied by the incumbent.

One final point concerning expectations is that a single expectation may be considered in two dimensions: intensity and direction. Direction refers to proscription or prescription of behavior, and intensity refers to a continuum running from the completely permissive through the preferential to the mandatory.

ROLE, ROLE BEHAVIOR, AND ROLE ATTRIBUTES

The definition of role set forth by Gross, Mason, and McEachern is deceptively simple. A role is defined as "a set of evaluative standards applied to an incumbent of a particular position" (Ibid., p. 60). Though this definition allows the term to be used at all levels of relational and situational specificity, it becomes necessary to further delineate the term before it may be used in empirical inquiries. The assumption of internal organization is basic to a further examination. That is, the writers assume that expectations for a position are organized and are more than a simple random collection. Thus, expectations can be classified into groups or sets. The three categorizations of expectations are: role sectors, rights and obligations, and expectations for behaviors and attributes. A role sector is "a set of expectations applied to the relationship of a focal position to a single counter position" (Ibid., p. 62).

The distinction between rights and obligations is made with respect to whether the expectation is made of the focal or the counter position. "Rights of the incumbent of a focal position are defined as expectations which are applied to an incumbent position" (Ibid., p. 62). On the other hand, "Obligations of the incumbent of a focal position are defined as expectations which are applied to the incumbent of the focal position" (Ibid., p. 62). Role expectations may also be examined in terms of behaviors and attributes: what an actor "should do" and what an actor "should be."

SANCTIONS

"A sanction is a role behavior the primary significance of which is gratificational-deprivational" (Ibid., p. 65). This concept is related to social control and conformity to expectation, and can be viewed in terms of a reward-punishment dimension. That is, a sanction is behavior which is intended to cause change in some other behavior.

Research Methodology and Technique

THE SUBJECTS

The subjects of the study were 102 women physical education teachers and 10 chairmen from 10 universities in Indiana and Illinois. Modified random sampling procedures were used to select the sample of teachers. The subjects were described on the basis of age, teaching experience, academic rank, and marital status.

THE INSTRUMENTS

Data relative to expectations of the teachers and chairmen were secured through an instrument constructed specifically for the study. Items were drawn from expectation statements found in pertinent literature and from interviews with physical education personnel. The final selection of items was made after a panel of five judges, ten pilot subjects, and two research consultants had evaluated the items. The same procedures were used in the construction of the satisfaction instrument.

The role expectation instrument consisted of twenty-four items pertaining to expectations for teachers and twenty-eight items pertaining to expectations for chairmen. The teacher items were grouped under the broad categories of: (1) departmental rights and obligations, (2) professional behavior, and (3) behavior toward students. The chairman expectations were also grouped into three categories: (1) promoting effective interpersonal relationships; (2) organizing, planning, and coordinating group work; and (3) staff personnel matters.

On the teacher expectation items, the teachers were asked to indicate whether and to what extent they felt obligated to perform each of the behaviors specified and to indicate what they believed their chairmen expected of them. Chairmen were asked to indicate their expectations for teachers. On the chairman items, the chairmen reported their own self-expectations, and teachers responded in terms of their belief as to how a chairman should act in relation to each statement. Response categories were: *definitely should, preferably should, may or may not, preferably should not,* and *definitely should not.*

The instrument used to measure satisfaction with the chairman's professional leadership consisted of thirteen items which focused on administrative functions and relationships. Response categories were: *very well satisfied, fairly well satisfied, somewhat satisfied, somewhat dissatisfied, fairly dissatisfied,* and *very dissatisfied.*

To secure information about the subjects, a personal information sheet was devised. Information regarding such factors as age, academic rank, years of teaching experience, and marital status was requested.

THE ANALYSIS OF THE DATA

Consensus on the expectation items among the groups of role definers was determined by use of a measure of ordinal consensus (Leik, 1966) which reflected the degree to which choices were spread over the set of available options. To examine levels of agreement in relation to categories of expectations, mean agreement scores were computed for each category of the role instrument. To indicate the average responses of the groups on the expectation items, prevailing response (mean) scores were determined for each item. The prevailing response (PR) scores of the teachers and chairmen were compared so that similarities and differences between the two groups could be described.

Dyadic consensus was examined by correlating (1) a teacher's own response with the response she attributed to her chairman, (2) the response a teacher attributed to her chairman with her chairman's response, and (3) a teacher's own response with her chairman's response. Item correlation coefficients were thus obtained which reflected how well the relative position of one group followed that of another group.

To study the relationship between the satisfaction teachers expressed with their chairmen and congruence on expectations, the satisfaction scores were compared with the dyadic consensus scores. Dyadic consensus scores were obtained by finding the difference between responses on two sets of descriptions. The four consensus scores represented a convergence of expectations of (1) a teacher and her chairman, as perceived by the teacher; (2) a teacher and her chairman on the teacher expectation items; (3) a teacher and chairman on the chairman expectation items; and (4) a chairman's expectations as perceived by the teacher and the chairman's real expectations.

Two separate methods were used to examine the relationship between satisfaction and consensus. First, Pearson product-moment correlation techniques were used to determine the relationship between each of the consensus scores and the satisfaction a teacher expressed with her chairman. Second, the Mann-Whitney U test was used to determine whether the satisfaction scores of the high and low scorers on the consensus measures differed significantly.

Certain demographic characteristics of the teachers were examined to determine if any of the characteristics were related to any of the consensus measures. Comparison groups were formed for each of the following variables: age, academic rank, total years of teaching experience, marital status, and faculty size of the department. The consensus scores of each of the comparison groups, with the exception of the marital status groups, were then examined by means of the Kruskal-Wallis one-way analysis of variance. The marital status comparison groups were examined by means of the Mann-Whitney U test.

A test-retest procedure was used to estimate the reliability of the role and satisfaction instruments. An attempt was made to present evidence of content validity for both the role and satisfaction instruments.

Findings and Conclusions

The questions asked in the study were mainly concerned with three areas of role analysis. Because the investigation produced a large number of specific findings which cannot be readily summarized, the results are reported in general terms.

INTRAGROUP CONSENSUS AND PREVAILING RESPONSES

Varying degrees of consensus were found within both samples of role definers on the different role items. The expectations studied were found to be characterized by a wide range of agreement levels rather than by high or low consensus over all items. The overall level of agreement of both groups was lower on the chairman expectation items than on the teacher expectation items.

When role items were grouped according to type, some slight category differences were apparent. Inspection of the levels of agreement within each category of expectations revealed that both the teachers and the chairmen were in least agreement on the items concerning a teacher's behavior toward students. The teachers were in highest agreement among themselves on items concerning departmental rights and obligations, and the chairmen were in highest agreement among themselves with respect to expectations concerning the professional behavior of teachers.

On the chairman expectation categories, the chairmen were in lowest agreement on items pertaining to the promotion of effective interpersonal relationships, and the teachers were in lowest agreement on staff personnel matters. The chairmen and teachers were in highest agreement on the items concerning organizing, planning, and coordinating group work.

The mean agreement scores differed between categories, but not to any great extent. The total agreement scores for the two positions, however, differed considerably. The evidence suggests that there is considerably less agreement on the chairman position than on the teacher position.

The analysis of the teachers' and chairmen's responses in terms of whether they viewed the specified behaviors as mandatory, preferred, or permitted revealed that the role definers viewed the majority of items as being either mandatory or preferred ones. That is, both samples of role definers tended to view both the teacher and chairman expectation items as ones which either *definitely should* or *preferably should* be performed. However, both groups identified more of the teacher expectations as ones that should be viewed with absolute insistence than they did with respect to the chairman items. Neither the teachers nor the chairmen used the response category of *may or may not* extensively. Few of the items for either position were viewed as representing optional behavior.

INTERPOSITION CONSENSUS OF DYADS

The item correlation coefficients obtained from the comparison of the teachers' responses with the responses of their chairmen were low. The r's ranged from $-.24$ to $.36$. On the teacher expectation items, only three correlation coefficients were significant at the .05 level, and on the chairman expectation items, seven coefficients were significant at the .05 level. Measured in correlational terms, it appears that the teachers and chairmen were not in high agreement on the majority of expectation items. A much higher relationship was seen, however, when the teacher's self-expectations and the expectations which they perceived their chairmen to hold for them were compared. The r's obtained between the teachers' own expectations and those they attributed to their chairmen ranged from .09 to .85. On twenty of the twenty-four items, the r's were significant at the .01 level. Measured in correlational terms, it appears that the teachers perceived their chairmen's expectations for teachers as being reasonably similar to their own.

Though the teachers perceived their chairmen's expectations as being reasonably similar to their own, the evidence suggests that the teachers were not extremely accurate in predicting their chairmen's expectations. The r's obtained between the responses of the teachers when attributing expectations to their chairmen and the chairmen's responses ranged from $-.21$ to $.25$. Only four of the correlation coefficients were significant at the .05 level.

The findings must be viewed with caution for two reasons. First, examination of only the correlation coefficients indicates a much greater degree of disagreement than is evidenced by inspection of the raw data. Inspection of the raw data clearly indicates that differences in expectations were, for the most part, differences of intensity and not direction. Second, the effect of the small variances on items responses must be considered when attempting to interpret the correlation coefficients obtained.

INTERPOSITION CONSENSUS AND SATISFACTION WITH THE CHAIRMAN'S LEADERSHIP

The data was examined to determine what relationships existed between the satisfaction that teachers expressed with their chairmen and (1) teacher-chairman congruence on expectations, (2) the accuracy with which teachers perceived their chairmen's expectations, and (3) teacher-chairman congruence on expectations as perceived by the teachers. An r of $-.68$ between satisfaction with the chairman's leadership and a similarity of expectations as perceived by the teacher was obtained. An r of $-.47$ between satisfaction with the chairman and the accuracy with which a teacher perceived her chairman's expectations was obtained. No significant relationship existed between satisfaction with the chairman and the actual level of agreement between a teacher and chairman.

When the differences between the satisfaction scores of the high and low scorers on the consensus measures were tested for significance by use of the Mann-Whitney U test, the results were:

1. The satisfaction scores of those teachers who perceived high similarity and those who perceived low similarity between their own and their chairmen's expectations were demonstrated to differ at the $p < .001$ level.
2. The satisfaction scores of those teachers who were most accurate and those who were least accurate in predicting their chairmen's expectations were demonstrated to differ at the $p < .001$ level.
3. The satisfaction scores of those teachers whose expectations were most similar and those whose were least similar to their chairmen's expectations did not differ significantly.

CONCLUSIONS

On the basis of the data obtained, and within the limits of the study, the following conclusions seem appropriate:

1. *Expectations for both teachers and chairmen appear to be characterized by a wide range of agreement levels.*

The evidence suggests that consensus on role expectations varies from very high to very low, depending upon the substance of the expectation statement.

The evidence also suggests that in many instances neither teachers nor chairmen have clearly defined expectations relative to appropriate behavior for teachers or chairmen.

> 2. *Expectations for the position of chairman are less agreed upon than are expectations for the position of teacher.*

Expectations for the position of chairman do not appear to be well-defined. If the findings of this study may be generalized at all, then it might be concluded that awareness of the role expectations which others hold for the chairman role should be of major concern to an administrator. It seems important that chairmen be alert to individual differences in expectations among their teachers. Unless such differences are recognized, they cannot be dealt with intelligently.

> 3. *The demonstrated relationship between the accuracy with which teachers perceive their chairmen's expectations and the satisfaction which teachers express with their chairmen indicates that administrators might find it advantageous to try to communicate to their staffs their own perceptions of both the chairman and the teacher roles.*

When a teacher misperceives a chairman's expectations, and the misperception is in a direction which leads the teacher to believe that the chairman's expectations are similar to the teacher's own, satisfaction with the chairman's leadership does not appear to be adversely affected. However, there appears to be an inverse relationship between misperception and satisfaction when the misperception is in a direction which leads the teacher to perceive little similarity between the chairman's and the teacher's own expectations. This study did not investigate how inaccuracies in the perception of expectations are created, but it can be concluded that inaccuracies do exist and that they are related, in some manner, to teacher-chairman associations. If an administrator recognizes that expectations are not always perceived accurately, then an intelligent effort may be made to correct such misperceptions.

Implications for the Practicing Administrator

In general, the results of this study indicate that the degree of consensus on role expectations varies from very high to very low, depending upon the substance of the expectation statement. It is not readily discernible why there is a high level of agreement on some items and so little agreement on others, but that agreement levels range from near zero to high consensus is clear.

Many of the items upon which both teachers and chairmen were in low agreement concerned the teachers' participation in the determination of policies and in the governance of departmental affairs. One might contend that values and concepts concerning the governance of the internal affairs of most educational systems have been, and still are, changing. As an example, more and more teachers and students are demanding the right to participate in the determination of policies that affect them. Such a period of transition must result in changing expectations, or at the very least, less stable role definitions. Though it is merely supposition, the low level of agreement seen on many of the expectation items may be an indication of the uncertainty of the respondents about both the teacher and the chairman roles because of changing cultural values.

Regardless of why there is ambiguity, examination of the responses of the teachers and chairmen participating in this study revealed that expectations, especially for the position of chairman, are not always clearly defined. The consequences of such ambiguity were not investigated, but cautious speculation might center about the difficulties such ambiguity might cause a chairman in the performance of her duties. Given a situation in which there is a wide variation in expectation among the teacher group, the chairman's role performance cannot fulfill the expectations of all the group members. Although no administrator can reasonably be expected to fulfill all of the expectations of all teachers, a chairman cannot afford to be naively unaware of the actual and potential conflicts which may be generated by incompatible expectations or perceptions of expectations.

In general, the teachers were not extremely accurate in perceiving the expectations of their chairmen. In the majority of cases, the teachers assumed there were fewer and smaller differences than actually existed. However, approximately one out of every four teachers perceived a greater disparity of expectations than actually existed. The evidence suggests that the teachers believed the chairmen were less restrictive in their expectations than the chairmen actually were. It seems that the chairmen's expectations for teachers were more rigid than the teachers perceived them to be. The consequences of misperceptions of this type may only be surmised. However, the possibility may be entertained that an individual's choice of action may be the result of not recognizing that a specific behavior is demanded rather than just preferred or permitted.

Though this study did not investigate the teachers' perceptions of the chairmen's expectations for the chairman role, it might be anticipated that the teachers would be no more accurate in those perceptions than they were in perceiving the chairmen's expectations for the teacher role. If this were found to be true, the problems facing a chairman are exceedingly complex. Incompatibility of expectations may be perceived when it does not, in fact, exist. Recognized differences in expectations may result in serious problems, but incompatibilities which are the result of inaccurate perceptions may be equally serious. As this study has indicated, it is the individual's perception of conflict that is significant.

A considerable disparity was found between what the chairmen said were their expectations for the teachers and what the teachers perceived those expectations to be. The reasons why the teachers were not more accurate in their perceptions are undoubtedly not simple. It may be that a chairman's actions are not consonant with what she says are her expectations. That is, it may be that expectations a chairman professes differ significantly from the expectations, as demonstrated by the chairman's behavior, perceived by the staff. Because others' role expections may be inferred by their role performance, the overt acts of individuals are the most significant indicators of their role perceptions. For example, staff members of an administrator who speaks of the desirability of decision-sharing, but who makes all decisions in an authoritative manner, will be more likely to infer the chairman's expectations for the role from overt behavior than from verbal statements.

On the other hand, the teachers' difficulty in perceiving their chairmen's expectations may be the result of a variety of social and psychological factors. Selective perception of expectations may be the result of personal factors which enter into the chairman-teacher relationship. Emotional considerations are undoubtedly important ones and it may well be that the perception of similar or dissimilar expectations is determined on the basis of personal factors.

Chairmen and teachers participate in a system of reciprocal role expectations. If either teachers or chairmen perceive that the others' expectations do not coincide with their own, then a possible source of disturbance to the system may be in evidence. It matters little whether the administrator is projecting a different set of expectations than is professed, whether the teacher is inaccurate in perception, or whether the identified differences are genuine. The significant factor is that incompatible expectations are perceived.

All of the consequences of incompatibilities in role expectations are not known. As this and other investigations have indicated, perceived similarity of expectations is related to improved satisfaction with the leadership. Perhaps an even more important consequence is the effect of disagreement or consensus on the achievement of group goals. Research that will answer that question is yet to be completed. Though knowledge concerning the results of misperceptions and incongruence of expectations is limited, it would seem that a clear understanding of the expectations of both teachers and chairmen would contribute to better staff relations and, perhaps, to more effective functioning of a staff.

It might be suggested that chairmen should devote some attention to the individual nature of expectations. Once the problem of the heterogeneity of expectations is identified, the general issue of how to resolve these conflicting expectations may be faced. An awareness of conflicting expectations will not eliminate conflict, but it will perhaps produce a greater understanding of a potential source of tension. If all interacting members of a group were made aware of the contradictory demands placed on an administrator, efforts might then be directed toward the development of a realistic view of what could properly be expected of the administrator. Improved communication could perhaps help teachers and chairmen to develop a clearer understanding of each other's expectations and perceptions. Open discussion of value differences might well provide the framework for better understanding and compromise.

General Bibliography

Biddle, Bruce J., *The Present Status of Role Theory.* Columbia, Missouri: University of Missouri Press (mimeographed), 1961.

Biddle, Bruce J., and Edwin J. Thomas, eds. *Role Theory: Concepts and Research.* New York: John Wiley & Sons, Inc., 1966.

Ferneau, Elmer F., "Role-expectations in Consultations." Ph.D. diss., University of Chicago, 1954.

Foskett, John M., *The Normative World of the Elementary School Teacher.* Eugene, Oregon: University of Oregon Press, 1967.

Getzels, J. W., "Conflict and Role Behavior in the Educational Setting," *Readings in the Social Psychology of Education,* ed. W. W. Charters, Jr., and N. L. Gage. Boston: Allyn and Bacon, Inc., 1963.

Gross, Neal, Ward Mason, and Alexander McEachern, *Explorations in Role Analysis: Studies of the School Superintendency Role.* New York: John Wiley & Sons, Inc., 1958.

Leik, Robert K., "A Measure of Ordinal Consensus," *Pacific Sociological Review,* 9 (1966), 85-90.

Moser, Robert P., "The Leadership Patterns of School Superintendents and School Principals," *Administrator's Notebook,* 6, no. 1 (1957), 1-4.

Scott, Ellis, *Leadership and Perceptions of Organization.* Ohio Studies in Personnel, Research Monograph No. 82. Columbus: The Ohio State University, 1956.

14

The Communication Structure of a Physical Education Unit

Robert Lewis Case

Introduction

A multitude of material has been published describing specific types of administration (i.e., hospital, business, educational, and physical education administration). Many of the earlier writings have decreed prescribed principles or rules to follow in dealing with a specific type of organizational climate. Currently, however, there appears to be a trend toward viewing administration in a more general and theoretical manner. Individuals catering to this school of thought have proposed various conceptual models which will inevitably lay the foundation for future organizational theory. The clarification of concepts and the evolution of sound administrative theory will be invaluable in the overall administration of social organizations. Penny explains the relevance and usefulness of concepts to physical education in this way:

> The task of working effectively with concepts is as important to administrators in physical education as the traditionally accepted "human" and "technical" factors in administration. Concepts provide the framework for gaining knowledge, and for the transmission

Robert Case is from Georgetown College, Georgetown, Kentucky.

of knowledge from one member of a professional group to another (1968, p. 6).

"Much has been learned, and much has been written, about the work which administrators perform, but all too little has been learned to date about administration as a process" (Gregg, 1957, p. 269). Although administrator behavior is an important factor in effective administration, it is the contention of many that a thorough understanding of the administrative process is also essential in order to effectively serve the organizational goals and the personal needs of its employees (Gregg, 1957, p. 113). Administration has recently been conceptualized as "the total of the processes through which appropriate human and material resources are made available and made effective for accomplishing the purpose of an enterprise" (AASA., 1955, p. 17). Seven components can be identified within the scope of the administrative process.

1. Decision-making
2. Planning
3. Organizing
4. Communicating
5. Influencing
6. Coordinating
7. Evaluating (Gregg, 1957, p. 113)

Although the seven components are highly interrelated, the writer elected to investigate "communication." Essentially our environment is controlled by and composed of human beings. Most of our actions toward others and their responses are communicative acts whether or not they are of a verbal nature. Considering the establishment and continuous development of an organization, it becomes readily apparent that the exchange of information and the transmission of meaning is the very essence of such a social unit (Katz and Kahn, 1966).

Prior to the 1940s few articles and studies had been devoted to the exploration of communication; however, since that period a proliferation of material has appeared. It is interesting to note that, although much research has been compiled, few studies have addressed themselves to communication in "natural" organizational climates. The investigation presented here is one that attempted to involve itself in this realm.

This study was an attempt to apply an organizational theory concept, that which treats organizations as a social structure, to the College of Physical Education at the University of Illinois. The term organization:

> labels the condition of cooperation of two or more individuals engaged in some regular activity over a period of time—acts of one

individual coordinated with the acts of others to accomplish some purpose. Organizations exist only when individuals who are *willing to cooperate* with each other and who can communicate work to accomplish a common *purpose*. The three conditions of communication, cooperation, and purpose are the necessary and sufficient conditions of organizations (McCleary, 1957, p. 2).

Relationships develop among personnel within an organization which inevitably become the "communication structure" of that unit. Jacobson and Seashore view the communication structure as the composite pattern of the actual contacts of individuals and the patterns of contacts among subgroups due to interindividual contacts (1951, pp. 28-40). The relationships between individuals, as reflected in such characteristic communication events, are appropriate and useful units for data gathering and analysis in connection with the study of the organizational structure and communication patterns in an organization.

There is ample evidence that communication among the members is indispensable to the effectiveness of a complex formal organization at any level. Barnard states:

> Historically and functionally all complex organizations are built up from units of organization, and consist of many units of "working" or "basic" organizations, overlaid with units of executive organizations, and that the essential structural characteristics of complex organizations are determined by the effort of the necessity for communication upon the size of a unit organization (1964, p. 113).

Cook has formulated three propositions concerning communication:

1. All communication involves interaction of two organizations (people or groups).
2. Communication takes place through a medium of symbolic behaviour.
3. Communication therefore is a social process (1964, p. 516).

Organizations, out of necessity, develop formal networks of communication. These networks represent the "official" lines of communication. They are designated on organization charts and specified in descriptions of positions. These relationships are normally specified between line and staff, between superiors and subordinates, between departments and divisions, etc. In addition to the formal channels, organizations develop informal means of communication. "The term *informal* has usually been used to describe those relationships or channels diverging from the official ones and arising from human reactions spontaneously generated between and within groups" (Redding, 1964, p. 46).

Subsequently, it becomes apparent that formal and informal are merely artificial terms denoting the totality of the process of communication within an organization. In this study the investigator was primarily concerned with analyzing the informal communication structure of an organization.

PURPOSE

The purpose of this study was to describe the prevailing communication patterns within a university administrative and instructional unit, the treatise being that such description and analysis may offer possibilities for improving administrative practice based upon scientific evidence. Furthermore, it is anticipated this effort may add to the existing knowledge with regard to the operation of communication structures.

The body of knowledge concerning communication theory indicates that groups (1) tend to make an effort to reach agreement; (2) alter attitudes and their resultant behaviors; and (3) create a stable structure which produces influence of that structure on interpersonal communication between its members. Subsequent evidence reveals that proximity—centralization versus decentralization—is a determining factor in interpersonal communication. Thus, there is ample evidence to substantiate the theory that each formal organization will be supplemented by an informal structure. It was the writer's premise that it is possible to describe the communication pattern within an organization and reflect against it certain elements of communication such as the key communicators,* liaisons,* isolates,* cliques, departmental and divisional intra- and interaction, and selected determinants of the contact communication structure.*

An Overview of Communication

"Communication is so indigenous to organized activity that its crucial importance seems to be recognized only when we suffer from its failure" (McCleary, 1965, p. 5). Whether man is concerned with the organization of a sports club, a literary group, or an institution of higher education, nothing can be accomplished in a coordinated manner without communication.

An organization out of its very nature creates various communication channels or directions of "message-flow." Hagman and Schwartz state, "com-

---

Key Communicator—An individual who has established regular contacts with a minimum of eight colleagues.

Liaison—An individual who communicates with at least one person in each of three or more subgroups.

Isolate—An individual who is without any regular contacts.

Contact Communication Structure—These are contacts that are established by reciprocal faculty preferences. The bonds determine the informal network of the communication network. The total number of bonds represent the contact communication structure.

munication is the catalytic means by which organizations are created, the means by which they are coordinated, and the means by which their purposes are translated into action" (1955, p. 182). Effective communication is of greatest importance in keeping people informed, promoting a healthy morale, facilitating the decision-making process, and providing the means by which constructive action can be taken in a variety of circumstances and generally establishing a coordinated endeavor. "Communication is a means of informing, a means of educating, a means of directing; it is the energizing substance that flows through the structure" (Ibid., p. 200).

FORMAL COMMUNICATION STRUCTURE

"The first function of the executive is to develop and maintain a system of communication" (Berelson and Steiner, 1964, p. 226). This system may be referred to as the formal structure, and it consists of those networks and media of communication which are consciously and deliberately established in the organizational system. The formal communication structure must be carefully organized in order to permit accurate and efficient transmission of all messages. It should be so established as to promote a free flow of information and ideas in all directions: upward, downward, and horizontally.

Initially, the chief administrator should provide some mass media communication by the use of handbooks, memoranda, and orientation materials for new employees (Redding, 1964, pp. 29-58). Even these, however, must be directed along proper channels if they are to be received and understood by the appropriate recipients. Barnard suggests several controlling factors in the character of formal communication structure (1964, pp. 175-77). First, the appropriate channels must be clearly understood by all personnel. This may require a general announcement of official liaison appointments, or the printing of organizational charts made available to all employees. Second, objective authority requires definite channels of communication to every organizational member. Employees need accessible avenues of horizontal and vertical communication. Effective communication dictates that networks be as direct and as short as possible; as the number of individuals involved is reduced, the degree of accuracy is increased. Nevertheless, information should generally filter down through the entire line authority. In the final analysis, however, the responsible administrator must select competent liaison assistants carefully in order to provide an effective communication structure.

McCleary asserts that control of communication is critical to authority and discipline.

> The agency which controls communication patterns is in a position to control decision, impose its definitions and values on the whole, and advance its status above others. It is in a position to resist change or challenge. The converse of these principles is critical to a

democratic social system which prizes flexibility and a capacity to change (1957, p. 39).

Communication is one of the chief concerns of any administrator. Barlo notes that

> A basic principle of communication in administration is that role-behavior prescriptions, descriptions, and expectations should be closely related to each other. People should (a) be told what they are to do, (b) be given an accurate prescription, and (c) be led to expect what will happen before it happens. When prescriptions, descriptions and expectations differ significantly communication breaks down (1960, p. 155).

Ultimately, successful communication is determined by the executive as he perceives his role in the organization. The democratic style of administration can promote the utilization of the formal structure. The organization will survive only if opportunity exists for the development and exchange of ideas. The formal system is the means for insuring the existence of these opportunities (Hagman and Schwartz, 1955, p. 200).

McCleary (1968, p. 55) provides us with several questions upon which the conscientious administrator should reflect:

1. Are checks made to see that communications are received and understood?
2. Are routes of appeal defined in event of disagreement or conflict between staff members and superiors?
3. Is the staff surveyed in a systematic way for opinions and suggestions relative to problems and issues?
4. Are communication channels specified in written materials?
5. Do staff members complain of the volume of communication?
6. Do staff members voluntarily report breakdowns in communication?

The communication system cannot be expected to function well unless the prevailing climate offers abundant opportunity for employees to express their ideas and ideals freely. Although the "open-door" policy is to be commended, it must be supplemented by other types of formal communication feedbacks. Advisory, ad hoc, and standing committees have proved an effective means of facilitating the formal communication structure. Interestingly enough, however, although these forms of media are capable of dispensing vast amounts of information and propaganda, they are relatively ineffective as agents of influence. Opinions may be reinforced via formal communication, but rarely altered.

The vast majority of changes in attitudes and behaviors is determined by interpersonal communications. Subsequently, it is most fortunate that despite a conscientious administrative effort to create and promote the utilization of a formal structure, it will ultimately be supplemented by an informal network (Gregg, 1957, p. 299).

INFORMAL COMMUNICATION STRUCTURE

In the same way that the formal system represents the authority and position of the organization, the informal structure may be recognized as meeting the personal and social needs of the group. At times the structures may be inconsistent with one another. This will depend greatly upon the extent to which the organizational goals are in harmony with the personal goals and attitudes of the group. The informal structure is created as a result of informal contact and relationships which develop among organizational members (Gregg, 1957, p. 300). This structure provides various channels of human relationships through which messages may be transmitted. Larson and Hill (1958, p. 497) inform us that as these groups develop stabilized structures, the channels or networks become increasingly predictable in terms of reciprocal relationships of the members.

McCleary, based upon his own investigation and that of W. W. Charters, Jr., provides certain theoretical assumptions which have been substantiated by research:

1. Person-to-person relationships established in the process of accomplishing organizational tasks constitute the real structure of the organization.
2. These relationships take on a regularity (in time) and a consistency (resistance to changes of patterns) which provide stability to the organization and are the basis of members' ability to predict the behavior of other members.
3. These relationships represent the major work-oriented relationships, but, in addition, they are the channels of communication through which attitudes, opinions, and norms are developed relating to the organization, to individual members, to outsiders, to the other organizations, and the like (1962, p. 1).

The interpersonal relationships form the actual work-oriented organization and represent the functioning communication structure of the school. It is within these channels that the formal communications are received and interpreted; subsequently, this determines both individual and group behavior (McCleary, (1962, p. 4).

COMPARISON OF FORMAL AND INFORMAL COMMUNICATION STRUCTURES

Formal and informal structures should not be viewed as separate entities, but as integrated structures created and developed in order to promote optimal gains for both the organization and organizational employee. "The formal aspect of organization contributes stability, certainty, routine efficiency. The informal provides exploration, appraisal, and change" (Miller, 1952, p. 5). Miller provides a useful comparison depicting the variables of each structure:

Informal Systems

1. Individuals view one another in interaction as persons in the *full* sense;

2. Activities are ends in themselves;

3. Expression of reason and emotion is relatively free and spontaneous;

4. Cooperation is implicit and activity is for the most part spontaneously coordinated;

5. Cooperation restricts the individual's liberty relatively little;

6. Systems are covert and private;

Formal Systems

1. Individuals view one another in interaction as performers of function;

2. Activities are means to ends;

3. Reason and emotion are channeled in the interest of achieving calculated or pre-determined joint purposes;

4. Cooperation is explicit and activity is always consciously coordinated;

5. Cooperation restricts the individual's liberty to a high degree;

6. Systems are public and overt (1952, p. 6).

Methodology

RESEARCH METHOD

This study employed the behavioral approach to administration emphasizing the way people live and behave in organizations. The research being reported was conducted in the College of Physical Education at the University of Illinois. The endeavor attempted to describe the prevailing contact communication structure within the college which encompassed four academic departments and two nonacademic divisions. The approach employed analyzes the organizational structure as a communication system, views the dynamic communication bonds, develops communication flow charts, and attempts to discuss relationships within and between the formal and informal organization, and how they are affected by selected independent variables and personality factors.

The writer hypothesized that the communication structure within the college may be impeded as a result of apparent decentralized departments and divisions and the relatively infrequent need for interdepartmental/divisional meetings. As a result the researcher further hypothesized that interdepartmental/divisional breakdowns may be witnessed that could ultimately lead to misunderstandings and redundancies within the organizational structure.

In order to analyze the contact communication structure of the college the writer attempted to reslove the following subproblems: (1) Who are the "key communicators," "liaisons," and "isolates" within the communication structure? (2) What are the ratios of the communication potentials used within the various subunits of the college (possible versus actual bonds)? (3) Do "key communicators" possess more contact personality tendencies than do "isolates"? (4) To what extent do the factors of age, sex, academic rank, years of employment at the University of Illinois, nationality, occupational specialty, departmental affiliation, and proximity affect the contact communication structure? (5) With what frequency do the subunits interact via the communication bonds?

THE POPULATION: COLLEGE OF PHYSICAL EDUCATION UNIVERSITY OF ILLINOIS

The college employed 205 academic personnel in the four departments and two divisions including Health and Safety Education, Physical Education for Men, Physical Education for Women, Recreation and Park Administration and the Divisions of Intramural Activities and Rehabilitation Education Services. They occupied office space and/or teaching facilities in no less than nine buildings on the Champaign-Urbana Campus.

The faculty members ranged in rank from graduate teaching assistant to full professor with intermediate ranks of teaching associate, instructor, assistant professor, and associate professor. Several staff members have been at the University for more than thirty-five years, while others can claim Illinois for only a year. The composition of the faculty was representative of all races and many nationalities with ages ranging from twenty-two through sixty-eight. The majority, 69 percent, of the staff function in teaching capacities with many individuals also claiming administrative, research, coaching and/or field service responsibilities in varying degrees.

RESEARCH TECHNIQUES

Three research techniques were used in gathering the data for the study: (1) a communication structure questionnaire; (2) a personal data check list, and (3) the Sixteen Personality Factor Questionnaire (Cattell and Eber, 1957).

COMMUNICATION STRUCTURE QUESTIONNAIRE

Initially each subject received a "communication structure questionnaire,"* a faculty directory, and a letter explaining the purpose of the questionnaire. All results were coded to preserve anonymity of subjects. The questionnaire was modeled in part from McCleary's (1957) efforts but originally based on the procedures outlined by Moreno in *Who Shall Survive?* (1934). The original test designed by Moreno consisted of asking individuals to select associates from within their specific work group on the basis of positive or negative choices to simple social preference type questions. The results were presented in a graphic illustration termed a sociogram. Since Moreno's early exploits other investigators have found that if the questions pertain to this choice-rejection pattern, the responses can elicit information relative to communication, coordination, and influence within specific groups or total organization (Blocker, McCabe, and Prendergast, 1964).

In 1957 McCleary examined communications in a school and found that "evidence from this investigation indicated that the method identified the person-to-person communication networks with a high degree of accuracy" (p. 95). Hovland et al. following extensive communication study, stated that if

> careful attention has been given to question wording, ... subjects are informed that differences of opinions are to be expected, and usual assurances are given that answers will remain anonymous. Under these conditions, it seems fairly safe to assume that the individual's overt verbal responses will correspond fairly well to his implicit verbal responses (1953, p. 9).

PERSONAL DATA CHECK LIST

A "personal data check list" was designed to gather information pertaining to eight specific categories: age, sex, rank, years of employment at Illinois, nationality, position specialty, departmental affiliation, and office location. The departmental secretaries were most cooperative in obtaining the necessary information and recording it on the appropriate form.

Communication Structure Questionnaire. This study is an attempt to identify the contact communication structure in the College of Physical Education as part of a general communications study. Enclosed please find a list of the college faculty. Consider your discussions, telephone conversations, news, and other communications during the past week or so and list the name of each colleague with whom you discuss college or university affairs. List as few or as many individuals as you wish, so long as they represent *actual regular* contacts.

PERSONALITY INVENTORY

The Sixteen Personality Factor Questionnaire, designed by Cattell and Eber (1957), was distributed to all individuals previously classified as "isolates" or "key communicators" in order to resolve subproblem three.

ANALYSIS OF DATA

Several methods were used to analyze the data including matrix analysis, clique analysis (Blocker, McCabe, and Prendergast, 1964), Sixteen Personality Factor analysis (Cattell and Eber, 1957), and content analysis. The data were initially subjected to sociomatrix analyses. The matrix is a set of elements arranged in a rectangular array. Thus the sociomatrix analysis depicted the reciprocal choices and rejections of each person to every other person within the group. The first-order matrix produced the reciprocal contact communication bonds—those individuals who communicated with each other on at least a weekly basis (i.e., $a \leftrightarrow b$). The data were utilized in assessing the effect of certain variables upon the communication patterns; depicting the "liaisons" (individuals who communicate with at least one person in each of three or more departments/divisions); key communicators and isolates; and the numbers of actual to possible contacts within respective departments and divisions and between the departments and divisions.

The second-order matrix produced the two-step channels of communication (i.e., $a \leftrightarrow b \leftrightarrow c$). The third-order matrix evidence the potential of any individual reaching any other individual via a three-step procedure (i.e., $a \leftrightarrow b \leftrightarrow c \leftrightarrow d$). Thus a has the potential of contacting d through channels (persons) b and c and visa versa. Both the second- and the third-order data were utilized to determine the potential of the dean of the college and the department heads and division leaders relative to contacting personnel within the college.

The clique analysis is a process designed to enumerate all third-order or higher interrelationships (communication chains) that exist in a matrix. In other words, each person in a clique has established direct communication bonds with every other person in that clique. The cliques are then examined to ascertain if any commonalities exist that might be determinants in the clique compositions.

The Sixteen Personality Factor Questionnaire was employed to determine whether key communicators would rate significantly higher than isolates in terms of exhibiting extroversion tendencies as measured by this questionnaire. This trait indicates a contact, as opposed to noncontact, personality tendency which may be paramount to the entire communication structure.

Finally a content analysis of the informal structure was reflected against the formal organization, depicted by the college organizational charts, to determine whether the key communicators and liaisons were in fact the individuals in supervisory and administrative positions of authority and responsibility.

Findings and Conclusions

The purpose of this study was to describe the prevailing communication patterns within the College of Physical Education at the University of Illinois. There is ample evidence to substantiate the theory that each formal organization will be supplemented by an informal structure. The writer surmised that it was possible to describe the communication patterns and to reflect against it certain elements of communication such as the key communicators, liaisons, isolates, cliques, departmental and divisional intra- and interaction, and selected determinants of the contact communication structure. Several research instruments were employed to assist the researcher in his task. Among these were (1) a communication structure questionnaire, (2) a personal data check list, and (3) the Sixteen Personality Factor Questionnaire. These instruments were utilized to analyze the contact communication structure in view of the findings related to the five specific subproblems.

FINDINGS

In attempting to answer the various subproblems, the researcher used the information requested in the communication structure questionnaire. The data was analyzed by the computer, subsequently resulting in first-, second-, and third-order matrices. The first-order matrix provided the necessary data to resolve the first subproblem, *Who are the key communicators, liaisons, and isolates within the communication structure?*

1. Key communicators, thirty-six in all, were observed in each of the six major units.
2. Liaisons, twenty-seven in total, many of whom were also key communicators, were observed in each department and division.
3. Isolates, twenty-six in all, were essentially first-year graduate teaching assistants under the age of thirty. However, in fairness to this group, it should be noted that, although they were not in "regular" contact with division or departmental leaders or even fellow colleagues, they could still be reached through the formal structure. (It is the writer's opinion that several of the "isolates" *may* have been so labeled due to acts of omission rather than commission.)

Subproblem two deals with the question, *What are the ratios of the communication potentials used within the various subunits of the College (possible versus actual bonds)?* This question was also answerable by studying the data analyzed in the first-order matrix. The findings reveal that the units utilize from 5 to 50 percent of their total possible contacts. The smaller units (divisions) used a far greater number of their potential bonds than did the larger departmental units.

Once the investigator had established which individuals were key communicators and which were isolates, the Sixteen Personality Factor Questionnaires were distributed to members of each group. The comparison of a specific second-order factor provided the answer to subproblem number three: *Do key communicators possess more contact personality tendencies than do isolates?* Based on the results of the questionnaire, the key communicators exhibited, at the .05 level, a significantly higher contact tendency than the isolate group.

The personal data check list information was utilized to resolve subproblem number four: *To what extent do the factors of age, sex, academic rank, years of service at Illinois, nationality, position specialty, departmental affiliation, and office location affect the contact communication structure?* The information was made available via the departmental/divisional offices. Of the characteristics studied, only sex, departmental affiliation, position specialty, and office location were found to be highly relevant in the determination of communication contact bonds.

Subproblem five was examined in two ways. Initially, the researcher attempted to determine *the actual to possible communication saturation between personnel of one unit and the total college faculty.* Second, the cliques were analyzed to determine *the interaction within and between various units.* The former effort revealed that each department and division utilized less than 1 percent of its total possible communication channels within the college. The latter analysis exhibited only twenty-four of the ninety-five cliques as being interdepartmental/divisional in composition. Thus, the majority of contacts are established *within* rather than *between* units.

The last piece of descriptive research was an attempt to determine *which of the key communicators and liaisons held executive positions within* the formal structure. Twenty-five of the thirty-four persons in formal supervisory positions were classified as key communicators and/or liaison people in the informal structure. (This is indicative of a closely knit and well-organized communication structure.)

CONCLUSIONS

The purpose of this study was to describe the prevailing communication patterns within the College of Physical Education at the University of Illinois. In order to more fully explain the contact communication structure, several subproblems were investigated. Based upon the findings revealed by the analysis of the communication structure questionnaire, the personal data check list, and the Sixteen Personality Factor Questionnaire, relative to the subproblems, the writer has reached the following conclusions:

1. Key communicators and liaison personnel were found in each department and division based on the findings revealed in the matrix.
    a. The dean of the college and the two assisting deans each achieved the rating of key communicator and liaison.
    b. The department heads and division directors, save one, were classified as key communicators and liaisons.
    c. The dean of the college and his assisting deans had established interpersonal communication contacts with each of the six major college units.
    d. Based upon the findings, the key communicators and/or liaisons were witnessed in most of the vital roles (twenty-five of thirty-four) in the formal structure. Therefore, the departments and divisions have established regular contact communication bonds with each other and the administrative unit of the college.
2. The ratios and percentages exhibited in resolving subproblems two and five were the basis for the conclusion that departments and divisions communicate more within their respective units than between them. The findings in the first-order matrix analysis revealed that each of the four departments and two divisions displayed a greater number of contact communication bonds within their respective units than between them.
3. Employing a one-tailed T-test at the .05 level of significance, the key communicator group, as evaluated on the 16 PF second-order factor extraversion-intraversion, possessed more contact personality tendencies than did the isolate group.
    a. Using a two-tailed T-test at the 0.5 level of significance the thirty-six key communicators were characterized by such traits as "warm," "sociable," "conscientious," "persistent," "thick-skinned," "controlled," and displaying "exacting willpower."
    b. The isolates, twenty-six in all, most of whom (twenty-one of twenty-six) were first-year graduate teaching assistants, rated significantly higher, at the .05 level, than the key communicators on factor 0 ("timid," "insecure").
4. The independent variables studied in this research provided some interesting insight into the determination of various contact communication bonds and cliques. Sex, departmental affiliation, and office location are highly significant factors in the formation of communication channels. Position specialty appeared to be an important factor in the composition of contact bonds, but showed little effect in the determination of the clique formations.

Implications for the Practicing Administrator

Currently a strong thrust in administration is to establish useful generalizations, based on empirical social science research, and to use these as a framework to develop tenable theory which in turn might provide the impetus for further investigation. The administrative process is possibly composed of seven components: decision-making, planning, organizing, communicating, influencing, coordinating, and evaluating. The belief is that these components may be studied independently or in conjunction with one another relative to the entire administrative process.

This writer, based on his own personal involvement in the college and his interest in the study of the communicative process, has attempted to describe the prevailing contact communication structure in the College of Physical Education at Illinois. The venture will hopefully serve to provide specific generalizations that may be made relative to the development of tenable communication theory for the practicing administrator.

If specific conclusions, such as those previously presented, are to be of real value in the development of administrative theory, they must be replicated and substantiated by similar types of investigation—not in physical education alone, but in a variety of intra- and interdisciplinary research. Sellitz expresses the point in this way:

> Theory increases the fruitfulness of research by providing significant leads for inquiry, by relating seemingly discreet findings by means of similar underlying processes and by providing an explanation of observed relationships. The more research is directed by systematic theory, the more likely are its results to contribute directly, to the development of further organization of knowledge (1960, p. 16).

With this in mind, the researcher will attempt to assimilate and synthesize the past efforts of communication research with the present findings of this work.

USEFUL GENERALIZATIONS AND THEORETICAL ASSUMPTIONS

The following are generalizations and theoretical assumptions that have been substantiated previously by communication research:

1. Each formal organization will be supplemented by an informal structure which adds vitality to that organization. These informal units develop into stable structures (Barnard, 1964).
2. The person-to-person relationships established in the process of accomplishing organizational tasks constitute the real structure of the organization (McCleary, 1962, p. 1).
3. These relationships represent the major work-oriented relation-

ships, but, in addition, they are the channels of communication through which attitudes, opinions, and norms are developed relating to the organization and its individual members (McCleary, 1962, p. 4).
4. If the chief executive is perceptive enough to identify the key communicators, he will be able to transmit information rapidly (Gregg, 1957, p. 229).
5. Traditionally, the speed of informational transmission by the grapevine (informal structure) exceeds that of the formal structure (Rollins and Charters, Jr., 1965).
6. The informal structure appears to be highly selective and discriminating in its transmission of information (Davis, 1964).
7. The chief executive needs to create a fully functioning communications system that provides continuous and accurate feedback (McCleary, 1968, p. 61).

GENERALIZATIONS BASED ON THIS RESEARCH

Relative to the present study, the following generalizations have been reached:

1. Most communication bonds and cliques are exhibited within rather than between work units in a social organization.
2. Academic rank, age, nationality, and years of employment at the institution studied had little effect, if any, upon the communication structure of the organization.
3. The communication structure will be efficient and effective if the unit leaders provide an atmosphere conducive to social interaction.
4. Certain individuals, by their very personality make-up, become better communicators than others.
5. Individuals in positions of authority, almost without exception, are the key communicators and liaisons in the communication structure as well.
6. Communication is an integral part of administration. Without it nothing can be organized or accomplished in a coordinated fashion.

If administrators truly wish to communicate effectively with their personnel, they need to be aware of and become involved in the informal structure. It is a permanent and stable component of organizations, and can be utilized to create a pleasant and functional working climate for both employee and employer.

Supplementary studies are badly needed to verify or reject the findings of the communication efforts thus far. Subsequently, if the results and theory generated are to be a valuable tool, they must be reported in journals and pamphlets which are available to the practicing administrator. Efforts such as this are of little value if they cannot provide useful generalizations for the practitioner.

RECOMMENDATIONS FOR FURTHER INVESTIGATION

Several individuals have been cited for their contributions in communication research. In fact, their endeavors have provided a conceptual or theoretical framework for this effort. These studies, including the one just reported, can be utilized as models for future investigation relative to the nature of communication and the patterns of relationships developing as a result of informal communication networks.

As a result of this study, the author has arrived at two recommendations relative to further communication investigation:

1. Additional studies are needed in "natural" organizational situations, both small and large, which are aimed at describing the effects of communication upon such components of the administrative process as coordination, evaluation, planning, decision-making, and influence.
2. Although morale is an issue which is often discussed, rarely has anyone attempted to study it from a specific perspective. In this writer's opinion the effects of communication upon staff morale is fertile ground for such investigation.

Studies which at one time were not feasible because of their very magnitude can now become realities with the aid of elaborate technical equipment. For the truly interested researcher, theoretical models and computers are available to scan the virgin territories of administrative research.

General Bibliography

Books

Barlo, David K., *The Process of Communication: An Introduction to Theory and Practice.* New York: Rinehart and Winston, 1960.

Barnard, Chester, *The Functions of the Executive.* Cambridge, Mass.: Harvard University Press, 1964.

Berelson, B., and Gary Steiner, *Human Behavior—An Inventory of Scientific Findings.* New York: Harcourt, Brace and World, Inc., 1964.

Blocker, Clyde, Robert McCabe, and Albert Prendergast, *A Method for the Sociometric Analysis of the Informal Organization Within Large Work Groups.* Austin, Texas: University of Texas Press, 1964.

Cattell, Raymond B., and Herbert W. Eber, *Handbook for the Sixteen Personality Factor Questionnaire.* Champaign, Ill.: Institute for Personality and Ability Testing, 1957.

Cook, P. K., "An Examination of the Nation of Communication in Industry," in *Business and Industrial Communications,* ed. Charles Redding and George A. Sanborn. New York: Harper and Row, Pub., 1964.

Davis, Keith, "Management Communications and the Grapevine," in *Business and Industrial Communications,* ed. Charles Redding and George A. Sanborn. New York: Harper and Row, Pub., 1964.

Gregg, Russell T., "The Administrative Process," *Administrative Behavior in Education,* ed. Ronald F. Campbell, and Russell T. Gregg. New York: NCPEAM, Harper and Bros. Pub., 1957.

Hagman, Harlan L., and Alfred Schwartz, *Administration in Profile for School Executives.* New York: Harper and Bros. Pub., 1955.

Hovland, Carl I., Irving L. Janis, and Harold H. Kelley, *Communication and Persuasion.* New Haven: Yale University Press, 1953.

Katz, Daniel, and Robert Kahn, *The Social Psychology of Organizations.* New York: John Wiley & Sons, Inc., 1966.

McCleary, Roland H., *Policy Change in Prison Management.* East Lansing, Mich.: Governmental Research Bureau, Michigan State University Press, 1957.

Moreno, J. L., *Who Shall Survive?* New York: Beacon House, 1934.

Redding, Charles W., "The Organizational Communicator," in *Business and Industrial Communications,* ed. Charles Redding and George A. Sanborn. New York: Harper and Row, Pub., 1964.

Selltiz, C. et al, *Research Methods in Social Relations.* New York: Henry Holt and Co., 1960.

Periodical Articles

American Association of School Administrators, "Staff Relations in School Administration," Washington, D.C.: The Association, 1955.

Jacobson, Eugene, and Stanley Seashore, "Communication Practices in Complex Organizations," *The Journal of Sociology Issues,* 73, no. 3 (1951).

Larson, Otto, and Richard Hill, "Social Structure and Interpersonal Communication," *American Journal of Sociology,* 63 (March 1958).

McCleary, Lloyd E., "Communications in Large Secondary Schools, A Nationwide Study of Practices and Problems," *The Bulletin-NAASP,* no. 325 (February 1968).

Rollins, Sidney P., and W. Charters, Jr., "The Diffusion of Information within Secondary School Staffs," *Journal of Social Psychology,* 65 (1965).

Unpublished Materials

McCleary, Lloyd E., "An Approach to the Study of Organization," presented at NCPEA, August 1962.

———, "A Study of Interpersonal Influence within a School Staff: The Development and Trial of a Method of Analyzing Influence within Established Networks of Communication." Ph.D. diss., University of Illinois, 1957.

———, "Communications and Educational Organization," Department of Education Administration, University of Illinois, Urbana, Ill.

Miller, Van, "Formal and Informal Human Interaction," adapted from *Autonomous Groups Bulletin,* Summer-Autumn 1952.

Penny, William, "An Analysis of the Meanings Attached to Selected Concepts in Administrative Theory." Ph.D. diss., University of Illinois, 1968.

15

Interpersonal Communication Patterns in Physical Education

Beatrice V. Yeager

Introduction and Statement of Problem

Communication plays an extremely important role in the functioning of organizations and is of vital concern to administrators. Whether communication is conceived as "the essence of organizational behavior" (Rubenstein and Haberstroh, 1966, p. 368), or as one of the "seven components . . . identified within the scope of the administrative process" (Case, 1969, p. 2), the fact remains that no organization can exist without it.

Paradoxically, there appear to be two main problems that confront the would-be investigator of communication. The first of these relates to the idea that this is an area that everyone knows and takes for granted. We have been talking, writing, utilizing various gestures, etc., practically all of our lives and for thousands of years. Consequently, to some, it seems superfluous to do any extensive investigations in this area. However, in everyday life, we are constantly confronted with evidence of miscommunication. The following poem, from an unknown source, exemplifies a communicative experience, which I am sure we have all had at some time or another.

Beatrice V. Yeager is from Western Illinois University, Macomb, Illinois.

Communication

I know that you believe
you understand what you
think I said . . .

but I am not sure you
realize that what you
heard is not what I meant.

The second problem area resides with those who do believe there is a need to gain understandings and knowledge relevant to communication and do realize a need for study in this area. This problem stems from the fact that there is no accepted definition of the term "communication." John B. Newman, in his article entitled "A Rationale for a Definition of Communication" (1966), helps to clarify this mysterious lack of definition. He lists three problems that are present when one attempts to define communication. I have included one of these which is relevant to this discussion. "Communication is so diverse and discursive, that the attempt to create a generally accepted definition becomes so profoundly involved, that it hinders rather than helps further thought on the subject" (in Smith, 1966, p. 56). Barnlund, in his discussion of the problem in defining communication, states that "part of the difficulty lies in the widespread use of the word—there are few disciplines that cannot claim the term as their own" (1968, p. 4). However, Barnlund does believe it is necessary to have a starting point and recommends the following by S. S. Stevens:

> Communication is the discriminatory response of an organism to a stimulus. This definition says that communication occurs when some environmental disturbance (the stimulus) impinges on an organism and the organism does something about it (makes a discriminatory response). If the stimulus is ignored, there has been no communication. The test is a differential reaction of some sort. The message that gets no response is not communication (in Barnlund, 1968, p. 4).

The major criticism of this definition is that communication is not the response itself but the relationship that emerges from the presentation of the stimuli and the evocation of responses. Cherry clarifies the preceding thought with the following definition of communication:

> It is that which links any organism together. Here "organism" may mean two friends in conversation, newspapers and their reading public, a country and its postal service and telephone system. At another level it may refer to the nervous system of an animal, while at another it may relate to a civilization and its culture. When

communication ceases, the organism breaks up (in Smith, 1966, p. 36).

At this point, I am sure the reader (interactor) is wondering where we go from here. Though apparently there is no or very little agreement concerning a definition of the term "communication," it appears that just the opposite is true concerning the elements that go together to make up a communicative act or relationship. In order for any communication to occur through any medium, whether it be verbal, written, or nonverbal, there must be a sender, a receiver, and a message.

At this point, it might be beneficial to present the reader with a frame of reference for the term "communication" as it is used in this chapter. The following does not attempt to define the process of communication, but presents the reader with the characteristics an act must have in order for it to be communication. A communicative act is that act which involves a sender, a receiver, and a message.

"Communication," as used in the study referred to frequently throughout this chapter, is limited to verbal relationships recorded by the subjects. These verbal relationships were subdivided into three types depicting various levels of potential or actual communicative acts.

1. *Contact acts* refer to all verbal relationships expressed by the subject. This was the type of relationship investigated by Case and reviewed in the preceding chapter by him. The study I am presenting also identifies the contact structure but does not go on the assumption that communication, which assumes a sender, a receiver, and a message, is present in every contact or even every repeatedly expressed contact. The potential for communication is there, but whether it occurs or not is another question. Just because subject A frequently sends messages to subject B does not necessarily mean subject B has assumed a receiver role. An example of this would be an argument in which you and another person are sending messages to each other, but neither of you is receiving.

2. *Link acts* refer to verbal relationships expressed by the subject which include mutually acknowledged complementary sender-receiver roles. These are contacts which express the ability of the subjects to play complementary sender-receiver roles, but which for some reason do not entail a mutual topic. An example of this would be if you and your friend both recorded a conversation that you had. Your friend records it in a receiver role with the topic being last night's football game; whereas you record it in a sender role with the topic being the chemistry test scheduled for Monday morning. Though the topic was not the same, mutually acknowledged roles were recorded. I believe that these contacts may represent communication, but because of the perception of the subjects as to what conversations should be recorded, do not necessarily have a mutually acknowledged topic. Because it is apparent that they do relate to each other in

compatible roles, the possibility of communication is greater than in a contact in which the roles have not been ascertained.

3. *Bond acts* refer to verbal relationships expressed by the subjects which include mutually acknowledged complementary roles and mutually acknowledged topics of conversation. This represents mutually perceived communicative acts.

Two other terms that will be used and might need clarification are "desired" setting and "actual" setting. The "desired" setting or contacts refer to those expressed by the subject in a wishful manner. ("I would like to tallk to _____ about _____ ") These conversations do not actually occur; whereas in the "actual" setting the subject does talk with the other person.

The study presented in this chapter identifies the organizational communication networks, as does Case, but actually focuses upon the interpersonal communication within the organization. "Interpersonal communication," according to Barnlund, "usually refers to interaction among two to four persons" (1968, p. 10); however, for the purpose of this study it refers to interaction between two persons.

The general hypothesis is that an analysis of organizational and interpersonal communication patterns within a formal organization will reveal information indicating that contact between persons does not necessarily involve communication. The basic assumption is that in order for communication to occur, mutually acknowledged sender-receiver roles must be perceived by the subjects between whom "contact" has occurred.

In addition to the general hypothesis proposed for investigation, the following subproblems phrased as questions were considered:

1. Were the desired communication contacts the same as the actual communication contacts?
2. Were the communication contacts perceived by the sender the same as those perceived by the receiver?
3. Did the sender and the receiver acknowledge the same topic of communication in the actual setting?
4. Did the sender and the receiver acknowledge the same topic of communication in the desired setting, and what reasons did they give for not communicating?
5. Were the characteristics the "key" communicator related to himself the same characteristics that were ascribed to him by "others"?
6. Were the characteristics the "isolate" or "near-isolate" related to himself the same characteristics that were ascribed to him by "others"?
7. Were the characteristics the "liaison" person related to himself the same characteristics that were ascribed to him by "others"?

Interpersonal Communication Patterns in Physical Education 251

8. Did contacts between persons necessarily involve communication?

It should be noted that in the following review of the literature and in the preceding review presented by Case, no study related directly to communication as a process involving an interaction which included identified sender-receiver roles and identification of the topics involved in the exchange.

Background and Related Literature

Because the preceding is in the same general area and a review of the literature would be repetitive in nature, this section will entail a mini-presentation of historical aspects in relationship to communication and the research studies which have been done concerning communication in a school setting. The literature review relating to theoretical models depicting the communicative act will be dealt with in greater detail.

HISTORICAL REVIEW

From reviewing a variety of sources, one might conclude that the first means of communicating was that of gesture. When or how this began is unknown, and whether or not in its infancy it entailed verbal sounds for clarification and emphasis is also unknown. Thus, the verbal aspect probably played a minor role, if any role at all, in the communicative acts of early primitive man. Eventually the vocal aspect became dominant and gestures were and are used to accompany the spoken language. From the spoken language evolved a graphic and pictorial means of communicating which marked the beginning of the written word.

Evidently in primitive societies there was also a need to convey messages over long distances. This was originally done by using a means that could be either seen or heard over what then *was* a great distance. Some natives used drums; others used smoke by day and fire by night to communicate. This of course included prearranged signals.

Whatever the medium for communication, man presently deals primarily with the spoken and/or written word.

> But what about words? For the purpose of communicating ideas, our clumsy languages of alphabets and words are far from perfect. The "lower animal" purrs, howls, hisses, or snarls, and his mate instantly understands what he is saying. The moron and the "horny-handed son of toil" who never learned to read or write can communicate their desires or their ideas, such as they are, with ease and celerity. But just as soon as people acquire a smattering of philosophy and become local orators or politicians, the vocal noises

they make have less meaning; their audience becomes restless and inattentive, and even their closest friends are frequently at a loss to understand either what they are talking about or why they are talking about it.

With a further advance in knowledge and sophistication, we come slap up against the intellectual elite—the scholars, professors, lawyers, philosophers, and literary critics. These people all know how to spell, how to string together a number of meaningless characters called letters to produce words which correspond more or less to a particular sound when spoken and conjure up a more or less well-defined mental image when written. These words are then pushed around until they fall into certain patterns called "phrases"; the phrases are grouped together to make sentences, and the sentences occasionally make sense. As previously stated, and generally admitted, words and also groups of words are merely verbal symbols. If we try to define them, we must of necessity use other words—more words, more symbols; and from this nightmare there is no awakening (Still, 1946, p. 9).

COMMUNICATION RESEARCH

Research material that relates to the communicative acts of persons within the social system of school is scanty. The first study of this nature was done by McCleary in 1957. This study, carried out in a school setting, was based upon the underlying assumption that the expressed, self-perceived, regular contacts of the subjects were indicative of communication. McCleary employed a questionnaire method of data gathering and identified the communication structure within the organization by using sociometric procedures. The communication questionnaire used in the study asked the subjects to list the names of all staff members "who represented his regular contacts in school," and in a second section they were asked to respond to "specific issues in the school which were likely to arise during the course of the study" by listing persons with whom they would most likely discuss these issues (1957, p. 32). By combining the results from the two sections, McCleary identified the communication contact structure within the organization. Additional studies done by Anderson, Berner, Blocker, Ross, Piper, and Case utilized questionnaires similar to that used by McCleary.

In the analysis of the data, the more recent studies all used matrix analysis, and by manipulation of the matrices were able to ascertain the subgroups, isolates, liaison persons, and stars (key communicators) within the organizational setting.

The study referred to in this chapter also uses matrix analysis and sociometric procedures. However, instead of using a "communication structure questionnaire," a "diary of personal conversations" was used. The diary was patterned after an instrument designed by Emerson in his study entitled "Mount Everest: A Case Study of Communication Feedback and Sustained Group Goal

Striving." The questions in the diary were designed to elicit responses that "plug in" to a model of the social act constructed by Hulett (Emerson, 1966, pp. 15-16).

MODELS OF COMMUNICATIVE ACTS

In reviewing the literature relevant to communication, one area that has not been tapped as much as it should perhaps have been is that of theoretical frameworks or models designed to explain the component parts of the phenomenon and give the researcher direction. These models offer to the researcher a means of examining concepts and techniques that might be employed to gain additional information about the act. Because space is limited, I have included *brief* verbal explanations of selected models of a communicative act.

The Thompson model (Thompson, 1969, p. 14) includes: (1) a sender who is "the source of the messages and the initiator of the communication cycle" (p.6); (2) a receiver who is defined as "the interpreter of messages" (p.7); (3) a message which is defined "as an ordered set of symbols the meaning of which is clear only from the *behavior of each receiver*" (p. 10); (4) a medium which is defined as "the channel or network of channels connecting sender and receiver" (p. 12); and (5) "a feedback system or a return network from receiver to sender" (p. 13).

Berlo (1960, p. 72) presents a source-message-channel-receiver model with the source being the sender and the channel being the medium of Thompson's model, but he also presents a more detailed explanation of the elements within each structure. For example, the source includes communication skills, attitudes, knowledge, social system, and culture. Each one of his major elements is subdivided into several aspects.

Fabun utilizes the sender-message-receiver cycle with the necessity of a closed "loop" or "circuit" in some situations (1968, p. 33).

Shannon's model (in Smith, 1966, p. 17), although not designed originally for interpersonal communication, is "sufficiently flexible and suggestive to permit application to a broad range of human communication problems through slight changes in terminology." This model includes an information source, transmitter, channel, receiver, and destination. "When I talk to you, my brain is the information source, yours the destination; my vocal system is the transmitter, and your ear ... is the receiver" (ibid., p. 17).

The complexity of the models varies, the terminology varies, and the number of the elements included varies, but they all contain at least the three elements mentioned in the introduction: a sender, a receiver, and a message.

Research Methods and Techniques

The study reviewed in this chapter dealt with interaction within a group of persons in an organizational setting; consequently, a social psychological theory of communication was appropriate and therefore used.

"One shortcoming of many current communication models ... is inadequacy to deal with the dynamics of message generation" (Auer, 1967, p. 27). The Hulett model, presented in the following illustration (Hulett, 1966, p. 13), overcomes this inadequacy. The versatility of this model based upon symbolic interactionism is apparent in that it can relate to three levels of analysis in the area of communication—i.e., interpersonal, intrapersonal, and organizational. Because this study dealt with both interpersonal and organizational communication, it was necessary to find a model that could be related to both levels. Another important reason for the selection of this particular model is that it does not have to be used in total. It is possible to focus on certain aspects. The "motivating stimulus" and the "covert rehearsal" phases were of particular importance to this study.

The symbolic interactionist sees each individual's share of communication transaction as requiring five phases which are depicted in the Hulett model and briefly defined here:

1. "Motivating stimulus" refers to any form of stimulus which activates an arousal motive or need.
2. "Covert rehearsal" refers to the phase where "the individual interprets the motivating stimulus input pattern and organizes his forth-coming response, his instrumental act" (Hulett, 1966, p. 15).
3. "Instrumental act" refers to the response of the individual; the action he decides to take or more clearly perhaps the act he performs.
4. "Environmental event" refers to the change that must occur in order for the individual to obtain his goal. In other words, does Beta's "instrumental act produce the environmental change required by Alpha to attain his goal?" (Hulett, 1966, p. 16).
5. "Goal response" refers to the attainment of the goal.

In order for one to better understand the covert rehearsal stage, it is suggested that the reader consult general references on symbolic interactionism or see the original study done by Yeager (1971, pp. 47-50).

The study reviewed was conducted in a women's physical education department which employed twenty-two staff and administrative personnel. The subjects were given questionnaires and asked to fill them out every day for ten days. The questionnaire, based upon the Hulett model, was designed by this writer. The instructions given indicated to the subject that there was *no* restriction on topics of conversations, but that the conversation should be *deliberately initiated with a purpose*. The questionnaires were coded by an outside source before being returned to the investigator. The following is an

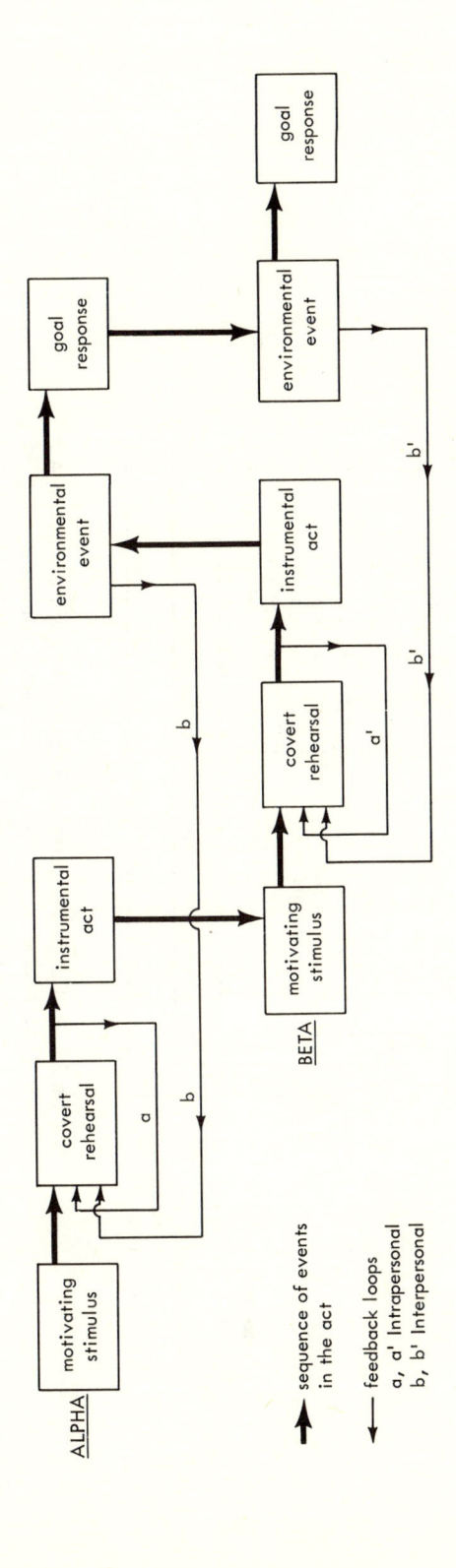

Figure 1. Block Diagram of a Social Act Between Two Interacting Individuals, According to Symbolic Interactionist Principles

(Figures 1 and 2 from J. Edward Hulett, Jr., "A Symbolic Interactionist Model of Communication, Part I," *AV Communication Review* 14: 5-33 (Spring 1966). Reprinted by permission of the author.

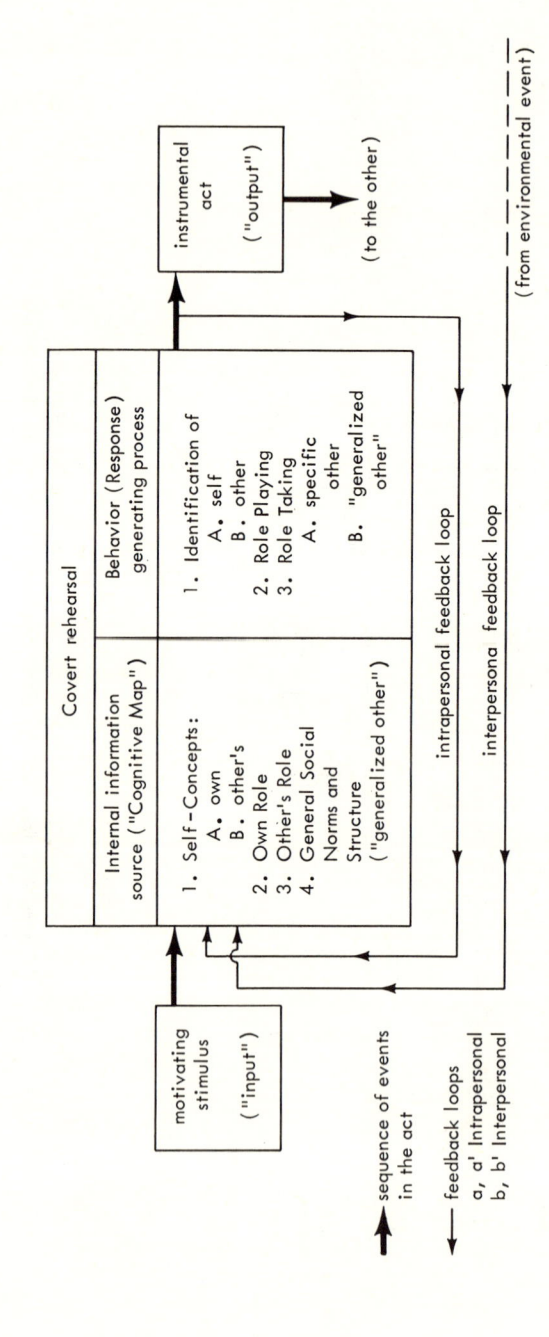

Figure 2. The Covert Rehearsal of Either Participant in a Social Act, According to Symbolic Interactionist Principles (From J. Edward Hulett, Jr., A Symbolic Interactionist Model of Communication, Urbana, Illinois, 1965)

example of the questionnaire with the type of response the writer wished to gain via the various statements in the diary:

A. I talked to *[indicates actual communication links as perceived by the sender]* today, because I wanted to tell or discuss *[motivating stimulus determined by the sender]*. Before approaching him/her, I decided to *[identification of self by sender]* instead of *[identification of another aspect of self, also an example of intrapersonal feedback]*. I thought his/her reaction would be *[identification of other]*. He/she actually reacted *[identification of other and indication of interpersonal feedback]* so I *[may or may not change approach]*.

B. *[Indicates actual communication link as perceived by the receiver]* talked to me today because he/she wanted to tell or discuss *[motivating stimulus of sender as perceived by the receiver]*. His/her approach was *[identification of other]*, so I reacted *[identification of self]*.

C. I really would like to talk to *[desired communication link determined by the sender]* about *[motivating stimulus]*, but I won't because *[self-concept, role of other, generalized or perhaps a combination of these]*.

D. I wish *[desired communication link as determined by the receiver]* would talk to me about *[motivating stimulus ascribed to the sender by the receiver]*. If he/she would, then I could tell him/her *[motivating stimulus of the receiver]*. If his/her reaction were *[identification of other]*, then I would be *[identification of self]* (Yeager, 1971, pp. 56-57).

The data was analyzed via matrix analysis and reported through the use of matrices, sociograms, and charts with accompanying narrative. From the analysis it was possible to determine:

1. Actual and desired communication as perceived by:
   a. the individual in a sender role
   b. the individual in a receiver role
   c. "others" and ascribed to the individual in a receiver role
   d. "others" and ascribed to the individual in a sender role
   (This included an investigation of both contacts and messages)
2. Identification of reciprocated communication and/or contacts with:
   a. mutual topic and complementary roles
   b. mutual topic but without complementary roles
   c. complementary roles but nonmutually perceived topics
3. Identification of "significant others"

4. The "motivating stimuli" for the communication subjectively classified as "self"-oriented, "other"-oriented, or "generalized other"-oriented
5. Clarification statements concerning reciprocated and nonreciprocated communicative relationships
6. Identification of "self" as perceived by:
   a. the individual
   b. the "other(s)" and ascribed to the individual
   c. the "significant others(s)" and ascribed to the individual

After this information was obtained, a more extensive examination of the data was made. In order to make this examination, use was made of the previously identified sender and receiver roles, and attention was given to: (1) the topics of conversations; (2) the roles played by the subjects—i.e., sender and/or receiver; (3) the reciprocated contacts and what they entailed; (4) "self"-descriptions as reflected in the recorded conversations by subject; and (5) in the recorded conversations by "other(s)" and ascribed to the subject.

A matrix analysis was primarily used to identify "contacts" and to look at the organizational level of analysis. Sociograms indicating sender and receiver roles and general charts of "communication links" and types of contacts established were developed to analyze interpersonal communication. After these were completed, composites were made on persons previously identified in the various positions of "key communicator, liaison persons, and isolates or near-isolates." These included:

1. Percentage of "self" perceived contact with total staff
2. Percentage of "other" perceived contact with total staff
3. Which contacts were reciprocated and which were not
4. Percentage of "self"-perceived sender roles out of total contacts
5. Percentage of "other"-perceived sender roles out of total contacts
6. Percentage of "self"-perceived receiver roles out of total contacts
7. Percentage of "other"-perceived receiver roles out of total contacts
8. Which roles were mutually perceived
9. Which topics were mutually perceived
10. "Significant others" as perceived by "self" and also as perceived by "others"
11. "Motivating stimuli" as predominantly "self"-, "other"- or "generalized other"-oriented as perceived by "self" and as perceived by "others" and ascribed to the subject

After these points were reported for both the desired and actual setting, a composite of "self"-perceived and "other"-ascribed words and phrases used in relationship to the various subjects were presented in chart form. An example of the chart follows (Yeager, 1971, p. 111):

Self as perceived by the individual:

1. a. informative

   b. explains—gives reasons for decisions

2. agreeable

3. congenial

4. considerate

5. interested

6. inquiring

Self as perceived by significant others and others:

1. a. not informative
   b. takes too much time to discuss matters
   c. explains—gives reasons for decisions

2. a. agreeable
   b. negative
   c. have to produce threat in order to get things done

3. a. friendly
   b. unfriendly
   c. hostile
   d. defensive

4. inconsiderate

5. none expressed

6. none expressed

Summary and Conclusions

The preceding pages include a discussion of the concept of communication, some problems that confront one when attempting to conduct research in this area, and a brief review of the literature relative to the study of communication with special emphasis placed upon studies that have been conducted within a school setting. The remainder of the chapter includes a description of a study I conducted in 1971 which applied a symbolic interaction model of the social act to communicative acts within a school setting. The main difference between this study and others is that no other study has attempted to identify sender-receiver roles or mutually perceived topics of conversation. In essence, the study was designed to look at contact structure to determine whether or not contact actually includes communication. Based upon the findings revealed by the analysis of the data, the following conclusions were reached:

1. There are actually two communicative settings within a formal organization. Each of these can be described from the view of the subject and that of the other who has a contact relationship with the subject. These settings may be referred to as the desired setting and the actual setting. They appear to be separate but overlapping entities.
2. Interrelationships within a formal organization may be studied from three separate but overlapping approaches. A reciprocated contact study indicates that each subject perceives some sort of relationship with the other; a communicative link study indicates which subjects have mutually perceived sender and receiver roles; and a communicative bond study includes which subjects have mutually perceived sender and receiver roles, and which subjects have related to mutually perceived topics. The three approaches will yield different results.
3. Liaison persons will generally be key communicators; however, key communicators will not necessarily be liaison persons.
4. A key communicator may function as a dominant receiver, or a dominant sender-receiver.
5. There are two types of isolates; those that are self-determined and those that are other-ascribed.
6. Those persons with whom an individual has repeated acknowledged interaction will generally ascribe to that individual a self-image similar to that perceived by him.
7. The overall conclusion of this research is that contacts do not necessarily involve the elements necessary for a communicative act; consequently, a contact investigation does not necessarily yield communicative patterns within an organization, even if those contacts are reciprocated.

Recommendations for Administrators

Administrators too often are totally unaware of the dynamics of their organizations. They are aware and rightly so of the formal structure their organizations assume, their goals and objectives, chain of command, positional authority, and the "fact" that people talk to people. In the past, administrators have been identified as the key communicators within their respective formal organizations, but are they? If one assumes that communication is directly related to the answer to the question "Whom do you *send* messages to?" then I agree that the administrator is probably not only a key communicator within a formal organization but in essence is *the* key communicator. However, if you ask the second part of the question—"Whom do you receive messages from?"—the picture may change. Adding the third ingredient of mutually perceived topics further complicates the situation. In the studies I have conducted, it is evident that to say an administrator is a key communicator is not enough. Are they dominant senders, dominant receivers, dominant sender-receivers? Is their self-concept, as far as communication is concerned, the same as that ascribed by others? In a dental office, the key communicators were dominant senders as perceived by others and dominant sender-receivers as perceived by self. In the physical education department, they were sender-receivers and dominant receivers as perceived by self and others. Are these structurally determined? Does one type of organization demand a specific communicative role whereas another does not? Which is most effective for educational organizations, for physical education organizations, colleges, and/or departments? Does it differ for athletics and intramurals? Men's and women's departments?

When hiring an administrator, does it make a difference whether your department is composed of mostly senders or mostly receivers? Is this a basic pattern that is an integrated part of an individual's personality or does it change frequently? Are senders and receivers situationally determined or can we identify a dominant pattern of communicative behavior?

Communication is a vital process in living together; it is the essence of any organization and is the least understood ingredient therein.

It is difficult to set down a "how-to-do-it" formula for administrators in the area of communication. It is impossible, in my opinion, to write a list of recommendations for one to follow. Consequently, this section is somewhat inappropriately titled, for I have lots of questions, but only one recommendation. The recommendation is that you take an active part in researching your organization. It is essential that the administrator knows who talks to whom, who listens to whom, and what the topics of exchange are.

In this age of committees it could be useful for the administrator to be able to identify not only the actual communicative acts occurring within the organization but also the desired communicative acts. The results of information gleaned from the desired setting might be extremely useful in the formulation of ad hoc committees or work groups. A committee is more likely to succeed if there is concern about a mutual topic and its members are capable of playing reciprocated sender-receiver roles. Have you ever been on a committee where every one is talking and no one is listening? This seems to be the general format followed by most committees.

How do isolates fit into a formal organization? Is it enough to say an isolate is an isolate is an isolate? Studies in the past have identified self-perceived isolates not necessarily other-ascribed. Is the role outcome the same? How does this relate to position turnover? What part does nonverbal communication play and what about the most developed form of communication with a formal organization—that of rumor?

Interest in communication has existed for centuries.

> The Greeks accounted for the phenomenon in the following manner...: Their wingfooted god Mercury would pluck the appropriate idea from the speaker's brain and plunge it on the end of his spear into the brain of the listener (Thayer, 1968, p. 3).

At the present, even though practically every science concerns itself directly with communication, we do not have a much better explanation. It has been speculated that the main problem in studying communication is that everyone assumes they understand it.

> If someone talks about a communication problem, we usually nod our heads. It's all too easy to assume that we know what he is talking about. It's even easier to assume that he knows what he is talking about. Scientifically, we know much less about human communication than we do about animal husbandry—this in spite of the fact that our lives are infinitely more affected by communication than the genetics of a particular breed of hogs (Ibid., p. 5).

It is the intent of the paper presented here to encourage you to gather information concerning the process of communication which may lead to a greater understanding of the phenomenon; however, I leave you with the following quotation as a word of caution:

> The venturer into the maze of human communication had best gird himself with humility and with humor. The humility will protect him from thinking he has found the secret. And in case he ever does think so, the humor will help for laughing at himself when he gets lost (Lerbinger and Sullivan, 1965, p. 5).

General Bibliography

Auer, Emma, "Two Communication Models Heuristic for Advertising Study," *Occasional Papers in Advertising,* I (September 1967).

Anderson, Norma Brandon, "A Clique Analysis of the Effects of Proximity upon Communication Structure and Interpersonal Relationships for Permanent and Non-permanent College Staff Members." Ph.D. diss., University of Illinois, 1957.

Barnlund, Dean C., ed., *Interpersonal Communication: Survey and Studies.* New York: Holt, Rinehart and Winston, 1960.

Berlo, David K., *The Process of Communication: An Introduction to Theory and Practice.* New York: Holt, Rinehart and Winston, 1960.

Berner, Marshall Keith, "Development of Procedures and Techniques for the Analysis of the Relationships Between the Formal Organization of High School Systems and the Informal Communication Structures Within These Systems." Ph.D. diss., University of Illinois, 1957.

Blocker, Clyde, Robert McCabe, and Albert Prendergast, *A Method for the Sociometric Analysis of the Informal Organization Within Large Work Groups.* Austin, Texas: University of Texas Press, 1964.

Case, Robert Lewis, "An Analysis of the Communication Structure of a University Administrative and Instructional Unit." Ph.D. diss., University of Illinois, 1969.

Cherry, Colin C., "The Communication of Information," in *Communication and Culture,* ed. Alfred G. Smith. New York: Holt, Rinehart and Winston, Inc., 1966.

Emerson, Richard, "Mount Everest: A Case Study of Communication Feedback and Group Goal Strivings," *Sociometry,* XXIX (1966).

Fabun, Don, *Communications: The Transfer of Meaning.* New York: The Free Press, 1968.

Hulett, J. Edward, Jr., " A Symbolic Interactionist Model of Human Communication," part I: "The General Model of Social Behavior; The Message-Generating Process," *A V Communication Review,* 14 (Spring 1966).

———, "A Symbolic Interactionist Model of Human Communication," part II: "The Receiver's Function; Pathology of Communication; Noncommunication," *A V Communication Review,* 14 (Summer 1966).

———, "Communication and Social Order: The Search for a Theory," *A V Communication Review,* 12 (Winter 1964).

Lerbinger, Otto, and Albert J. Sullivan, *Information, Influence, and Communication.* New York: Basic Books, Inc., 1965.

Manis, Jerome G., and Bernard N. Meltzer, eds., *Symbolic Interaction: A Reader in Social Psychology.* Boston: Allyn and Bacon, 1967.

McCleary, Lloyd E., "A Study of Interpersonal Influence within a School Staff: The Development and Trial of a Method of Analyzing Influence Within Established Networks of Communication." Ph.D. diss. University of Illinois, 1957.

Moreno, J. L., *Who Shall Survive?* New York: Beacon House, Inc., 1953.

Newman, John B., "A Rationale for a Definition of Communication," in *Communication and Culture,* ed. Alfred G. Smith. New York: Holt, Rinehart and Winston, Inc., 1966.

Piper, Donald Lee, "Generation of Organization Climate Dimensions with Organization Communication Structures." Ph.D. diss., University of Illinois, 1968.

Ross, George Edwin, "A Study of Informal Communication Patterns in Two Elementary Schools." Ph.D. diss., University of Illinois, 1960.

Rubenstein, Albert H., and Chadwick J. Haberstroh, *Some Theories of Organization.* Homewood, Ill.: Richard D. Irwin, Inc., and the Dorsey Press, 1966.

Smith, Alfred G., *Communication and Culture.* New York: Holt, Rinehart and Winston, 1966.

Still, Alfred. *Communication Through The Ages.* New York: Murray Hill Books, Inc., 1946.

Thayer, Lee, *Communication and Communication Systems.* Homewood, Ill.: Richard D. Irwin, Inc., 1968.

Thompson, James J., *Instructional Communication*. New York: American Book Co., 1969.

Yeager, Beatrice Virginia, *An Analysis of Interpersonal Communication Patterns Utilized by A Selected Small Group*. Eugene, Ore.: Microform Publications, School of Health, Physical Education, and Recreation, University of Oregon, 1973.

16

Environmental Characteristics in a Physical Education Unit

Thomas E. Flanigan

Introduction

Recent emphasis on administrative theory in physical education has resulted in increasing interest in institutional climate as it relates to the achievement of organizational goals. The central theme is the concept that the goals of the unit can be successfully realized more easily if the administrators have useful knowledge about the climate or "personality" of the organization.

In the case of institutions of higher education, there has been an increased emphasis on investigations which will provide methods of predicting, with some amount of reliability, probable attainment of educational goals by students. These "predictors" are commonly associated with high school rank in class and scores on standardized tests.

Little, if any, consideration has been given to the study of the "intellectual environment" of the institution and its effect on the success of college students. The common thought is that the "inferior" student is "weeded out," with little information available to indicate how many potentially successful scholars are grouped with the "inferior," "nor do we know to what extent remaining in college is a matter of gamesmanship or capacity to adapt oneself to conventional pressures" (Sanford, 1962, p. 15).

Thomas E. Flanigan is at St. Ambrose College, Davenport, Iowa.

There is some evidence to support the notion that not all of the failure by students to complete degree requirements can be blamed on poor scholarship, but may be, rather, the lack of compatibility between student needs and the environmental pressures of the institution. It has been suggested by Learned and Wood that the "intellectual environment" of the institution may influence the achievement of the students; their studies indicated that performance by students on comprehensive tests was significantly higher at some institutions than were the scores of students with the same initial ability who attended colleges where the average student ability was lower (1938, p. 216).

The central theme of this discussion centers around the notion that students react to stimuli in the institutional environment which are outside the classroom itself. The students perceive pressures with which they must successfully cope, or they will fail regardless of their ability to operate effectively in the classroom. Such pressures are described by Murray as *presses* and defined as "a temporal gestalt of stimuli which usually appear in the guise of a *threat of harm* or a *promise of benefit* to the organism" (1938, p. 40).

An additional element of this concept is that the personality needs of the students in a particular institution or unit of the institution must be satisfied by the environmental press under which the students are operating. Stern, Stein, and Bloom reported that the prediction of performance was related to the identification of the psychological demands of the environment (1956).

The suggestion is that students who can react effectively to the perceived pressures of the particular institution in which they are enrolled will be more able to attain their objectives. Because this is the goal of the institution—that students achieve their educational objectives—administrators are by necessity obligated to consider the means by which they can more effectively identify the elements of the environment that contribute to the satisfactory attainment of goals by the students.

Pace describes the college environment as that which is:

perceived by the students and organized into their consciousness with some unanimity of impression is the effective environment of any school, no matter what is printed in college catalogues, written into objectives, or claimed by faculty members and administrators (1964, p. 4).

Herrscher feels that peer group pressures play an important part in success patterns of students. This point of view is reinforced by his statement that "the importance of the campus environment as an influence on the student is an accepted fact" (1968, p. 2).

Pace recognized the importance of environment in the total structure of progress toward goals by the students. In an attempt to identify relationships between environmental press and student needs, Pace and Stern developed the

College Classification Index (CCI) (Pace, 1963), and, in a later version, the *College Characteristics Analysis (CCA)* (1964, p. 8).

In responding to items on the CCA, the student was reacting to a wide range of topics relative to such factors as rules and regulations, facilities, student-faculty relationships, classroom methods, extracurricular activities, etc. The student was, in effect, describing the educational press under which he was operating in the major program of study. He was expressing an awareness of the college environment which was exerting a directive influence on his behavior (CUES, Pace, 1963, p. 78).

From the earlier work with the CCI and CCA, Pace was able to develop the *College and University Environment Scales, 2nd ed (CUES* II) as a means of identifying the dominant characteristics of the institution or a subculture within the institution (Pace, 1963, p. 7).

The environment is identified along the dimension of five scales, *practicality, community, awareness, propriety,* and *scholarship* and two subscales, *campus morale* and *quality of teaching and faculty-student relationships* (Ibid., p. 9).

It was felt that the *CUES* II would serve as a useful instrument for the purpose of identifying specified environmental characteristics of a college unit within a large university, as perceived by students and faculty members in that college. The unit selected for this study was the College of Physical Education at the University of Illinois, Urbana-Champaign, which was established on the Urbana campus in 1957 after beginning as the School of Physical Education in 1932 (*Undergraduate Study, 1970-1971,* 1970, p. 417).

The college was comprised of four academic departments: Department of Health and Safety Education, Department of Physical Education for Men, Department of Physical Education for Women, and Department of Recreation and Park Administration. (Since the study has been completed, the Departments of Physical Education for Men and Women have been reorganized into a single administrative unit. The Division of Intramural Activities and the Division of Rehabilitation Education Services are non-degree-granting units in the college.)

Related Literature

The collection of facts related to the climate of the institution is important in the administrative process as it relates to theory building. Such theory building should begin "with observations of some sort or other" (Griffiths, 1959, p. 36). It seems quite appropriate then, especially in light of current trends toward more student involvement in the university programs, to place more emphasis on students' perceptions of their undergraduate environment.

It would appear that a much better understanding of the climate of the institution and its subcultures can be obtained by giving serious consideration to the perception of the students who operate in the system. Effective changes in the environment can only be accomplished when the administrators are aware of the climate that is to be changed to attain goals. Good describes the need as follows:

> It should be rather obvious that the administrator who is charged with the responsibility for the work under his supervision is constantly in need of information as to the conditions in his school or school system. Much of this information comes by word of mouth or by personal visitation and observations; but a moment's reflection will suggest that a great deal of the information needed cannot be obtained this way (1966, pp. 256-57).

Clark and Trow speak of the need for more knowledge of the climate of the institution when they call for "detailed knowledge of the actual forms of student cultures in American colleges and their consequences for education" (1966, p. 19). The detailed knowledge can be provided by descriptive studies which "are of large value in providing facts on which professional judgments may be based" (Good, 1966, p. 258).

The attention being given to the study of institutional climate as a factor in the administration of physical education and sport received early support from Zeigler, who wrote that research "may ultimately provide the knowledge whereby administrative leaders in education can function most effectively" (1968, p. 132). Spaeth supported this contention by suggesting that data-gathering instruments which had been used in educational administration could be used in physical education units in order to gather "data specific to physical education and athletics, but having a sound empirical base" (1967, p. 152).

Dannehl studied the organizational climate in physical education departments and administrative units in twenty Midwestern universities in an "attempt to measure the organizational climate and the perceived behavior of the group and the leader of the organization" (1970, p. 6). He found that the perceptions of the leaders and faculty were significantly different and concluded that the leaders "are not completely aware of the behavior within the organization; or they are not willing to describe it" (Ibid., p. 137).

Olafson's study involved an attempt to describe and analyze behavior of physical education department chairmen in universities and junior colleges (1969, p. 8). He concluded that the leader behavior of department chairmen varied significantly between the junior college group and university group, with significantly different perceptions of roles being reported by faculties in each group (ibid., p. 131).

Case took a different approach in the investigation of organizational climate by attempting to study the communications structure of a university administrative and instructional unit in an attempt to identify patterns within the College of Physical Education at the University of Illinois (1969, p. 122). As a partial description of the organizational climate he concluded that "the formal structure is supplemented by a well-developed informal structure which adds vitality to the organization" (Ibid., p. 122).

The related literature cited above deals basically with perceptions of the organizational climate as reported by faculty members and administrators. The findings are useful in that they provide basic information relative to the environment. However, it appears that little attention has been given to the important element of student perceptions of the climate of the organization. The students' perceptions of the climate are based on their close identification with the environment. For example, the work of Carson and Schultz is mentioned in relation to their investigation of the junior college setting—a study of the leadership behavior of deans of colleges. In addition to responses obtained from presidents and department heads in junior colleges, student leaders were also surveyed. They concluded that there was evidence that role conflict existed on the part of the deans because:

> Student leaders and department heads taken together from school to school do not agree in their perceptions of nor their expectations of the leadership behavior of the dean on either dimension of leadership behavior (1964, p. 360).

Schlegel used student input to analyze factors that influence students to major in physical education. The expected love of sports, interest in children, and "coaching desire" were given as reasons for enrolling in the program, but Schlegel added:

> The reputation of the University of Illinois and the increasing influence of its graduates from physical education were prominent factors influencing the students to select the College of Physical Education at Illinois as their first choice (1967, p. 93).

It might be argued that the students recognize a desirable climate within the college insofar as the opportunity for career-oriented academic success is concerned.

The importance of a knowledge of the climate or "personality" of the organization is recognized in the overall scheme of administrative theory:

> An administrator today must rely on the members of his organization for the achievement of the organization's objectives. This concern for setting the climate for beneficial human interaction, consistent with the beliefs of the constituents, should be considered a key aspect of the administrative process (Penny, 1968, p. 125).

The desired outcomes in higher education include the successful attainment of academic goals by students. Students perceive specific institutions as possessing the climate which they feel will best afford them the opportunity to realize educational goals. Schlegel was able to identify factors that influenced students to major in physical education but also indicated a need to investigate the factors that influenced the men to withdraw from the physical education major program (1967, p. 93). Is such withdrawal the result of grades, disinterest, lack of funds, or job prospects? Or is it possible that the climate or "personality" of the department is such that the students succumbed to the decision to leave. Are there presses, for example, from peer groups and faculty which made continuation in a program seem contraindicated?

Pedersen concluded in his study that "dissatisfied students apparently reflect mainly negative attitudes toward both self and environment" (1968, p. 3). Demaree and Aukes investigated the degree of satisfaction on the part of students and hypothesized that students who express dissatisfaction with large numbers of aspects of the environment are the students who will probably be the dropouts from the institution (n.d., p. 1).

Wertheimer, in describing the development of the clinical school concept, emphasized, "close student-teacher relationships were also considered an essential characteristic of the climate we want to create." (1971, p. 527).

Lindgren points out that students learn both in and out of the classroom. In recognizing that instructors are indeed part of the college environment "and to a large extent *are* the college environment," he suggests that conflicts between student goals and instructor goals must be alleviated in working toward the common educational objectives (1969, p. 105).

Research Methodology

The survey method was used to administer the *College and University Environment Scales, 2nd ed.* to students and faculty members in the four academic departments in the College of Physical Education, University of Illinois. The instrument consists of 100 basic items which are statements about college life—aspects of the institution which help to define the environmental climate as the respondent perceives it. Each item falls along the dimension of one of the five scales: *practicality, community, awareness, propriety,* or *scholarship*. Some items also fall along the dimensions of the two subscales: *campus morale* and *quality of teaching and faculty-student relationships*.

Completed questionnaires were returned by 359 of the 580 students in the college for a 61.9 percent return. Sixty-three of 81 faculty members in the college participated for a 77.8 percent return.

SCORING THE COLLEGE AND UNIVERSITY ENVIRONMENT SCALES

The major objective of the study was to attempt to identify the characteristics of the environment and to analyze the differences in these characteristics of the environment as perceived by groups of students and faculty members. Therefore, the primary method of statistical analysis used here involved techniques which would permit the researcher to identify responses that are dominant in each of the scales and subscales.

> Does this item describe a condition or event or practice characteristic of the institution, in the sense that the vast majority of reporters who live in the environment recognize it as true of the environment? If it does, then the item is a potential stimulus for some sort of adaptive response. The number of such characteristics, or potential stimuli, all falling along a single dimension such as Scholarship indicates the degree to which the institution exerts a press of stimulus in the direction of Scholarship. The result is a count of dominant collective perceptions, not an average of individual perceptions. An institutional score, therefore, is quite different in meaning and in educational significance from an average of individual scores (Pace, 1969, p. 45).

In order to obtain the scores for the scales and subscales, it was necessary to identify those items on which there was a consensus in either a positive or negative direction. Therefore, Pace's method of scoring was used. All items in a particular scale to which 66 percent or more of the respondents agreed in the keyed direction were computed and added to a basic score of 20 (20 was used because this eliminates any net negative score). Essentially the complete scoring procedure is:

1. Add the number of items answered by 66 percent or more . . . in the keyed direction.
2. Subtract the number of items answered by 33 percent or fewer . . . in the keyed direction.
3. Add 20 points to the difference so as to eliminate any possibility of obtaining a negative score (Ibid., p. 13).

The reason for including the negative perceptions is the rationale that all items which indicate consensus are useful in describing the environment. If respondents

> agree two-to-one or better that a statement *is not true,* that fact identifies a characteristic of the environment just as clearly as when students agree by an equally high level of consensus that a particular statement *is true* of the environment (Ibid., p. 12).

Scores for the subscales were computed in the same manner, with the only variation occurring in the addition of points to insure positive scores. Twenty-two points are used on the *campus morale* subscale and 11 points are added on to the score of the *quality of teaching and faculty-student relationships* subscale.

The respondents set down their answers to the *CUES* II items on answer sheets which permitted the use of optical scanning techniques to transfer the responses to IBM cards for analysis. The data was analyzed using the *QUEST* program, a questionnaire analysis package, as described by Costa (1971).

The *QUEST* program of analysis permitted the computation of the mean and standard deviation for each item as well as similar analyses for each scale and subscale. However, by the very nature of the data and scoring method to be used for data of this type, such analysis was not appropriate. The computation recommended by Pace for scoring the results was given priority.

Through the use of *QUEST* programming, the percent of responses to each item in the keyed direction was made available. This information was used to compute the raw scores for each scale and subscale for the students and faculty and for subgroups comprised of all students in each department and all faculty members in each department.

The raw scores for each group and subgroup were converted to percentile scores because percentile scores are more meaningful in the interpretation of the data.

Findings and Conclusions

Figure 1 shows the profile of the perceptions held by students as compared to faculty members in the college. The total student sample in the college produced scores that revealed rather close agreement with the total faculty on the perception of the environment insofar as the *practicality* and

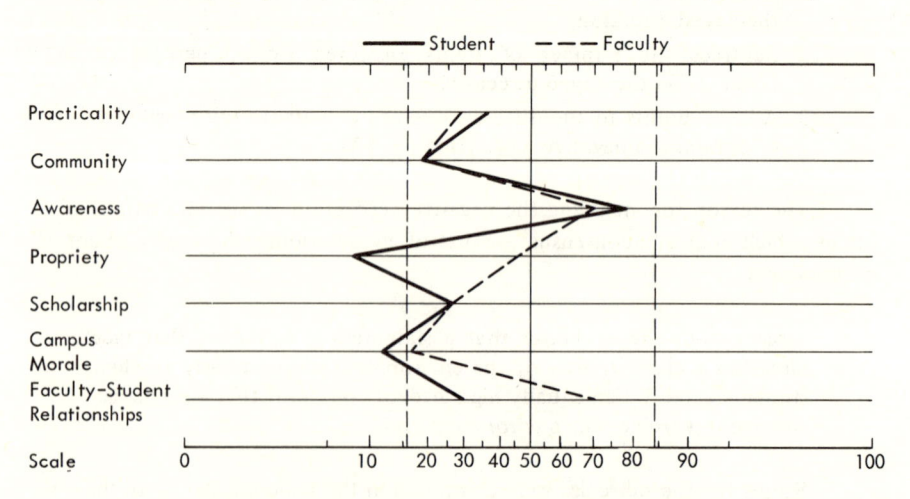

Figure 1. College of Physical Education Students and Faculty *CUES* II Percentile Scores.

awareness scales and *campus morale* subscale are concerned. Additionally, there was complete score agreement on two other scales— *community* and *scholarship*.

The faculty score on the *propriety* scale would indicate a strong feeling of a conventional, proper atmosphere characterized by group adherence to standards of decorum. The students disagree with this perception, as evidenced by a much lower score on the scale.

The faculty members view the atmosphere as one that is scholarly and has high standards of performance and is flexible. Again, the students take the opposite view, as evidenced by the comparatively low score on the *quality of teaching and faculty-student relationships* subscale.

The Atmosphere of the College. Insofar as the students in the college are concerned, the climate can be characterized as one in which there is little reliance on or recognition of student leaders. The students as well as faculty members perceive little emphasis on student elections and perhaps because of this, it is not considered important to be a member of the "right club." There appears to be little concern for personal appearance, and new fads and sayings continually arise on the campus.

There is a recognition of a need to know the right people to insure success, and people who are admired seem to find emulation from the students.

The students feel that the structure of the classroom is such that informality is present. Instructors do not emphasize checking on students to see if assignments are carried out or completed. The students are expected to be self-reliant. For the most part, seats are not assigned and written excuses are not required for missing class. Faculty members agree with the students on the perception of informality in the classroom as part of the *practicality* scale.

The students and faculty do not view the campus as being friendly, cohesive, and group-oriented. This may be a reflection of the size of the institution, which gives students a feeling of lack of consideration for individuals. Both students and faculty agree that there is little done to help everyone get acquainted, especially on the part of upperclassmen helping new students. Although there is a feeling that it is easy to get a group together for social activities (cards, a movie, etc.) the study indicates that the institution does not have a reputation for being friendly.

Students for the most part do not feel close to the faculty, at least in relationships such as performing errands or other personal services for the instructors. However, there is a pronounced recognition of the practice of faculty calling students by their first names on a friendly basis.

Students feel that they learn quickly "what is done" and "not done" on the campus, but do not feel pressured to follow the code of conduct too closely.

There is little feeling that the history and traditions of the institution are given any special emphasis. An example of this is the recognition that such practices as graduation are carried out in a rather unemotional manner.

Although personal relationships mentioned above would indicate that there is little opportunity to "get to know" people, it appears to be evident that when friendships are formed they seem to be lasting associations.

The high score registered by both students and faculty on the *awareness* scale indicates agreement on the perception of a noticeable concern for personal, poetic, and political meaning in the environment.

Although public debates are not perceived to be too common on the campus, there is a recognition that many famous people are brought in for concerts, lectures, and student discussions. Furthermore, there is a feeling that these speakers, if controversial, stir a lot of student discussion. The students and faculty feel that there are many colorful and controversial faculty members on campus.

There appears to be much student concern about national and international affairs, with these students developing a strong sense of responsibility regarding their role in contemporary life, both social and political. This reaction from the respondents might be expected, at least in part, because the students are in professional degree programs related to social service.

Students and faculty members recognize that art and music get much attention in the environment being assessed. There is a knowledge of special museums and collections that are accessible on the campus. Facilities and opportunities for creative activity are available. Strong personal beliefs are apparent in the environment.

The perception of the students relative to the characteristics associated with the *propriety* scale revealed very little recognition of agreement with members of the faculty. Although there was agreement at a high level of significance by both groups—students and faculty—on some items, the distinct difference in total scores indicates that this characteristic of the environment is perceived quite differently by the two groups.

The explanation for the difference in perception between the two groups on this scale may lie in the notion that the faculty members are not familiar enough with the nonclassroom, social elements of the environment to perceive them accurately. In any case, the faculty views the environment as polite and considerate with emphasis on the importance of decorum. Additionally, they perceive the atmosphere to be mannerly, proper, and conventional.

On the other hand, the students perceive the environment to be one in which parties are lively and colorful. The parties may be loud and somewhat disorderly.

There is a feeling that permission is not required for deviating from school policies and practices, and there is no expectation to report violations of rules and regulations. Such practices are tolerated despite regulations.

Activities are undertaken on the spur of the moment, with students occasionally plotting various escapades or "rebellions," such as dorm raids, water fights, or other student pranks.

Students do not feel that others should adapt to them. Dress is casual and no one seems to mind. There seems to be little concern for taking care of property. There is no hesitation by student publications to lampoon dignified institutions and people.

Scholarship characteristics are given equal emphasis by both students and faculty members. It is felt that the professors do not push the students' capacities to the limit. Class discussions are not especially vigorous and intense, and students do not put a lot of energy into everything they do relative to academic activity. Although the scholastic work is not considered to be extremely intense, personality, "pull," and bluff are not actions that are considered to get students through many courses.

The perception of *campus morale* by both students and faculty is in fairly close agreement, with neither group giving much emphasis to this dimension. Strong beliefs and convictions are considered to be recognizable in student groups.

There is an indication that supportive and spirited personal and social relationships are not too prevalent. There is a lack of group cohesiveness.

There is a marked difference in the emphasis on the *quality of teaching and faculty-student relationships* dimension. Faculty members perceive themselves as professors who go out of their way to help students and as people who are interested in the problems of the students. In the students' view, this was not the situation. Similarly, the students did not conclusively express the opinion that faculty members made frequent changes in courses, exams, and readings. Faculty members felt that they did.

Implications for the Administrator

Administrative behavior required to successfully achieve desired outcomes of a particular organization is dependent upon an understanding of the current status of the organization. Constant attention must be given to ways of determining the best method of promoting the successful attainment of the goals of the institution or unit within the institution.

In higher education the goals must be dependent on the needs of the students who are operating in the environment. Students can find more success in environments that meet their own needs—needs which they bring into the organization, chosen on the basis of their impression of the "personality" of the institution, often gained by perusing information supplied by administrators— information that may or may not accurately describe the climate. Consideration of the organizational structure as described in official documents is important, to be sure. However, it is equally important to have information about the informal structure of the organization and how such informal structure may affect the outcomes either positively or negatively.

The administrator, in order to make valid and useful decisions, needs to have available all useful information relative to the organization. Information about the organizational climate can supplement the usual demographic data available to the practicing administrator.

Additional consideration for the use of environmental studies comes in the area of attrition of students and faculty. For example, we usually attribute withdrawal from college to be the result of poor grades; the students who can't "hack it" fall by the wayside. More information is needed to learn the extent to which institutional presses are responsible for the withdrawal from college by some students who apparently should be able to succeed. Perhaps some of the process of attrition is the result of failure of some students to find attainment of objectives possible in a particular type of institution.

Furthermore, it should be pointed out that a student's perception of a particular instituion or unit within the institution may not be realistic, but rather based on official documents which give a description of climate which the student perceives to be agreeable (only to learn differently once he has matriculated).

It would be useful to replicate the study reported here by attempting to investigate any changes that may have occurred recently in the perception of the students relative to the climate of the college. Additionally, it is suggested that an investigation should be made to determine *when* changes in perception might occur. Perhaps when students have been part of the environment for a longer period of time, their perceptions might more closely agree with faculty perceptions. The author has found little evidence of such a phenomenon occurring, but additional studies may produce more clearly defined answers (Flanigan, 1973, pp. 96, 105).

An important aspect of the study of college environment centers around the relationship between the perception of the climate of the institution and success in college. It would, therefore, seem advisable to recommend that studies of this nature be initiated for the purpose of determining the relationships in this area.

Finally, it would seem appropriate to suggest that consideration be given to developing studies of the perception of the climate of institutions with attention to differences in perception as reported by sex. There is some evidence that sex of the student does make a difference in the way the climate is viewed (Spencer and Feldman, 1969, p. 27).

General Bibliography

Carson, J. O., Jr., and Raymond E. Schultz, "A Comparative Analysis of the Union College Deans' Leadership Behavior," *The Journal of Experimental Education*, 32 (Summer 1964), 360.

Case, Robert L., "An Analysis of the Communication Structure of a University Administrative and Instructional Unit." Ph.D. diss., University of Illinois, 1969.

Clark, Burton R., and Martin Trow, "The Organizational Context," in *College Peer Groups,* ed. Theodore M. Newcomb and Everett K. Wilson. Chicago: Aldine Publishing Co., 1966.

Costa, Irene A., *Mermac Manual Test and Questionnaire Analysis Programs Written for the IBM System/360.* Urbana, Ill.: The University of Illinois Press, 1971.

Dannehl, Wayne E., "The Organizational Climate in Physical Education Administration Units in Selected Mid-Western Universities." Ph.D. diss., University of Illinois, 1970.

Demaree, Robert G., and Lewis E. Aukes, "Students' Evaluations of Various Aspects of the University," report no. 104, Office of Instructional Research, University of Illinois, n.d.

Flanigan, Thomas E., "A Comparative Assessment of Specified Environmental Characteristics of the College of Physical Education, University of Illinois, Urbana-Champaign." Ph.D. diss., University of Illinois, 1973.

Good, C. V., *Essentials of Educational Research.* New York: Appleton-Century-Crofts, Inc., 1966.

Griffiths, Daniel E., *Administrative Theory.* New York: Appleton-Century-Crofts, Inc., 1959.

Herrscher, Barton R., "Patterns of Attainment and the Environmental Press of UCLA Student Groups." Ed.D. dissertation, University of California at Los Angeles, 1967.

Learned, W. S., and B. D. Wood, *The Student and His Knowledge.* New York: The Carnegie Foundation for the Advancement of Teaching, 1938.

Lindgren, Henry C., *The Psychology of College Success: A Dynamic Approach.* New York: John Wiley & Sons, Inc., 1969.

Murray, Henry A., *Explorations in Personality.* New York: Oxford University Press, 1938.

Olafson, Gordon A. A., "Leader Behavior of Junior College and University Physical Education Administrators." Ph.D. diss., University of Illinois, 1969.

Pace, C. Robert, *The College and University Environment Scales,* 2nd ed., Technical Manual. Princeton, N.J.: Educational Testing Service, 1963.

―――――, "Differences in Campus Atmosphere," in *Readings in the Social Psychology of Education,* ed. W. W. Charters, Jr. and N. L. Gage. Boston: Allyn and Bacon, Inc. 1963.

―――――, *The Influence of Academic and Student Subcultures in College and University Environments,* Cooperative Research Project no. 1083. Los Angeles: University of California at Los Angeles, 1964.

Pace, C. Robert, and Leonard Baird, "Attainment Patterns in the Environmental Press of College Subcultures," in *College Peer Groups,* ed. Theodore M. Newcomb and Everett K. Wilson. Chicago: Aldine Publishing Co., 1966.

Pedersen, James O., "An Exploratory Study of Nonintellective Variables and

Related Deviation from Predictive Academic Performance." Ph.D. diss., Purdue University, 1968.

Penny, William J., "An Analysis of the Meanings Attached to Selected Concepts in Administrative Theory." Ph.D. diss., University of Illinois, 1968.

Sanford, Nevitt, "Implications of Personality Studies," in *Personality Factors on the College Campus,* ed. Robert L. Sutherland, Wayne H. Holtzman, Earl A. Koile, and Bert K. Smith. Austin: The Hogg Foundation for Mental Health, University of Texas, 1962.

Schlegel, Ronald P., "Factors Influencing the Decision to Major in Physical Education." Master's thesis, University of Illinois, 1967.

Spaeth, Marcia J., "An Analysis of Administrative Research in Physical Education and Athletics in Relation to a Research Paradigm." Ph.D. diss., University of Illinois, 1967.

Spencer, Richard E., and Susan Feldman, "A Pilot Study of Students' Judgment of the Campus Environment at the University of Illinois, Urbana," research report no. 296, Measurement and Research Division, Office of Instructional Resources, University of Illinois, Urbana, 1969.

Stern, George, M. I. Stein, and B. S. Bloom, *Methods in Personality Assessment.* Glencoe, Ill.: The Free Press, 1956.

Undergraduate Study 1970-1971, vol. 67. Urbana, Ill.: University of Illinois, 1970.

Wertheimer, Patricia A., "School Climate and Student Learning," *Phi Delta Kappan* 52, no. 9 (May 1971), 527.

Zeigler, Earle F., "The Employment of Philosophical Analysis to Supplement Administrative Theory and Research," *The Journal of Educational Administration,* 6, no. 2 (1968), 132.

III

STUDIES ABOUT TECHNICAL ADMINISTRATIVE CONCERNS

17

Human Relations in the Administration of Intramural Sports and Recreative Services

Frank Beeman

Introduction

The awareness of the importance of comprehensive and judicious intramural administration was born in this writer in October, 1955. It became clear, as Co-Chairman of the first National Conference on Intramural Sports for College Men and Women held in Washington, D.C., that direction must be provided for those responsible for the administration of the tremendously expanding sports programs. One hundred and ten men and women, representing seventy-nine institutions from thirty-nine states and Canada, gathered to formulate guides useful to the preparation of intramural administrators.

Because of the concern to prepare people for intramural administration rather than to continue to accept the "old coach" or the "lame duck" teacher or supervisor as intramural directors, a study exploring the most crucial element, human relations, was completed in 1960.

Administrative skills are universal. Because the common element with which all administrators must work is people, administrative skills, techniques, and concerns cross all boundaries between education, industry, armed services, or government. With this in mind two techniques were borrowed from business and industry. The Harvard University Business School had successfully used the

Frank Beeman is from the Michigan State University, East Lansing, Michigan.

case study method in the administration of business and industry (McNair and Hersum, 1954). Adaptation of this method was made by Bauer (1955, p. 35) in developing the *case problem technique*. This technique was the primary tool used.

A case problem is defined by Bauer as that type of case that contains two elements, the facts crucial to the problem and the problem itself. "The problem is one easily identified and contains only the facts that have direct and immediate bearing on the problem" (1955, p. 36).

The secondary tool used was the *critical incident technique*. This was developed by John C. Flanagan (1954), Director of the American Institute for Research. Flanagan describes a critical incident as

> any observable human activity that is sufficiently complete in itself to permit inferences and predictions to be made about the person performing the act. To be critical, an incident must occur in a situation where the purpose or intent of the act seems fairly clear to the observer and where its consequences are sufficiently definite to leave little doubt concerning its effect. (Ibid., p. 327).

Because the universities of the Western Conference involved more than 50,000 students in their intramural programs and because of the similarities among Conference institutions, these ten schools were the subjects of the investigation. To provide potential and practicing administrators with some tangible guidelines to foresee problems and to help solve administrative problems that occur, even with conscious foresight, it was necessary to

1. Determine administrative problems areas;
2. Gather data from the administrative problem areas that could be developed into case problems;
3. Offer alternate solutions to those situations involving human relations;
4. List the "critical incidents" in the cases that led to satisfactory or unsatisfactory solutions;
5. Suggest currently useful generalizations based upon the cases as guideposts for the Western Conference Intramural Directors.

Intramural programs have progressed beyond the stage of small "extras," offered by athletic departments to mollify critics of varsity athletics. The President's Council on Youth Fitness, the AAHPER Youth Fitness Project, the changing emphasis toward do-it-yourself sport activity among all segments of the population, but particularly among girls and women, have created intramural buildings and facilities worth millions of dollars on hundreds of college and university campuses throughout the country. The administrators of these facilities must deal effectively with the student desires and demands for organized and informal participation.

Because many of their administrative problems will be in the area of human relations, it is imperative that some "life experience" be made available to them for professional preparation and in-service training purposes. The establishment of some uniformities or useful generalizations through analysis of research case problems gives the students a clearer insight or understanding of their responsibilities.

Each director employs, trains, and directs hundreds of students each year. Supplies and equipment must be purchased to successfully coordinate participants' use of facilities and areas. Plans for expansion of physical facilities as well as program content must be continually plotted. These responsibilities bring the administration of an intramural program on this level ever closer to the administering of a business or industry.

Directors have had to learn about the responsibilities and intricacies involved in administration largely by trial and error. The responsibilities for thousands of participants and hundreds of thousands of dollars in budgets requires that efficient methods of administration be insured to safeguard the privileges of all individuals as well as to insure the proper use of public funds.

There has been no accumulation of solutions, decisions, methods, or techniques for solving the administrative problems of the Western Conference Intramural Directors. Duties and responsibilities are listed in most intramural texts. No real insight, however, into some of the solutions or methods that are effective in working with people drawn from true life has been available. As Bauer states,

> There is a great need for material that throws light on the effect of formal and informal organization, interpersonal relations, subgroup behavior, and pressures from the environment surrounding the administrative situation. Finally, there is practically no material available that concentrates on, and contributes to an understanding of, the process of decision-making in the college or university setting. These are the areas in which the development and study of cases may be expected to make a significant contribution (1955, p. 44).

As early as 1955 the College Physical Education Association, AAHPER, and the National Association for Physical Education of College Women recognized the potential of intramural programs to contribute to the students' overall development. To aid in the development of intramural directors and administrators, these groups sponsored the National Conference on Intramurals. The Conference was reminded by Ruth Abernathy, president of AAHPER, to "fit the intramural sports program into the administrative pattern of the colleges" (1955, p. 35).

Review of Related Literature

BRIEF HISTORICAL BACKGROUND OF THE CASE METHOD

The use of the case method to analyze and investigate human relations and problems has been prevalent for many years. As early as 1871 the technique was used in the Harvard Law School to bring more reality to the study of law. Various fields have made extensive use of this method of investigation where the laboratory or experimental methods were not appropriate. Public administration, social services, youth delinquency groups, school counseling departments and, more recently, personnel in educational administration are using the case method to teach, to prepare, and to gain insight into the problems of people.

The use of case histories by the social services and school counselors differs in its objectives from the use of case studies made by colleges of business administration and educational administrators. In the first instance, the purpose is to determine factors that cause problems for the individual. Having found the causes, the worker attempts to reduce or remove them and, at the same time, tries to rehabilitate the individual. In the field of business administration and in educational administration, the case study is used to prepare leaders in the respective fields. In these fields this technique is also used extensively to resolve problems that appear to be reducing the efficiency of a particular staff or department.

In 1920, a significant event occurred in the development of social research studies. The personal document, which may well be considered as the forerunner of the case study, advanced from the uncritical stage to the critical status required of clinical work.

> If any line can be drawn between the era of uncritical and the era of the critical use of personal documents, the research of Thomas and Znaniecke, *The Polish Peasant,* in 1920 marks the date (Allport, 1942, p. 29).

Since 1920 the case method has undergone considerable refinement. Improvements have been made in the collection of data and in the interpretation of the information drawn from the data. Educational administrators are exploring this technique thoroughly in attempting to prepare school administrators.

The use of the *critical incident technique* is also relatively new, particularly in the field of education and especially in the area of intramural administration.

This technique had its origin in the studies of Sir Francis Galton seventy-odd years ago. Interim developments were time sampling studies, controlled observation tests, and anecdotal records. According to John C. Flanagan (1954, p. 325), the critical incident technique grew out of studies in the Aviation Psychology Program of the United States Air Force of World War II. This program was initiated to improve the instruction of pilots, navigators, and other crew members.

Harvard President Conant's enthusiasm for the case method of study in the business school was the result of many years of hard work by the Harvard faculty in both the law school and the business school. C. C. Langdell initiated the use of the method in 1871 for the study of law. The method, which was resisted at first, proved its practical value and by 1915 all the better law schools in the country were using it (Bauer, 1955, p. 29).

In 1920, Melvin T. Copeland, the instructor at the Harvard Business School who had been given the approval to use the case method, completed a book entitled *Marketing Problems*. Cases in the book were drawn from the Bureau of Business Research from newspaper items, from business publications such as the Federal Trade Commission Report, and from personal business acquaintances.

In 1932, the Harvard Business School decided to concentrate on collecting cases concerned with a particular administrative problem and to attempt to develop a better understanding of that problem, rather than to try to draw guides from a diversified group of cases about varied problems.

As the refining of cases developed, this business school noted that there were two parts of a research case:

1. Description of a situation observed accurately;
2. Diagnosis of situation—specific suggestions for action. (Suggestion for action is that order of statement which would be useful to a person who has to administer the situation being described.) It should make sense to those who live in the situation—it is to clarify for them things which they have intuitively acted upon, but which they have not previously put into words.

In summary, the case method has been developed and accepted predominantly in the study of law and business. Educational administrators are expanding this technique as more texts and more courses utilizing the method are created. Physical education, intramurals, and athletics, three phases of the educational program particularly concerned with administrative problems, have begun to explore the use of the case method. The technique has developed in the various fields because of the concern of administrators who are searching for ways to resolve human relations "bottlenecks" and inefficient administrative practices.

Very little research has been done in the field of education and particularly in the field of physical education using the critical incident technique. The technique itself needs further refining, as do all techniques used in determining human relations factors. Rather than collecting opinions, estimates, and hunches, it obtains a record of specific behaviors from those people in the best position to make the most accurate observations and evaluations.

Methodology

SELECTION OF PROBLEM AREAS

The problems and problem areas were drawn from three sources. The first was from the Western Conference intramural directors themselves, and their predecessors. The minutes of the annual meetings of the conference directors from 1948 to 1958, inclusive, were collected and studied. Those problems that appeared more than once in the minutes and those that gave evidence of difficulty were recorded.

The second source was from those areas in which problems occurred that were recorded in the report of the National Intramural Conference for College Men and Women sponsored by the AAHPER, NAPECW, and CPEA in Washington in 1955.

The third source was from those problem areas which the writer has become aware of in twenty-five years as a university intramural director; four years as Chairman of the Intramural Section of the AAHPER; Co-Chairman of first National Intramural Conference noted above; and co-author of the text, *Intramural Sports,* for professional physical education students.

The problem areas and outline for the study were presented to the 1959 meeting of the Western Conference intramural directors. Each problem was to be checked as "most difficult to solve" or "most frequently encountered," or in both categories. Space was made available for additional comments adjacent to each response.

Each director and school was assigned a code number to mask the identity of the institutions and the source of any case information. This was necessary to reduce the "halo effect" that might occur when the directors studied the decisions and solutions of their fellow directors.

The directors were supplied with the problem areas they, as a group, had selected as important in their administrative duties. At the same time, the directors were furnished with a case reporting form. The form helped the directors in recording the pertinent facts about the case problems they encountered and also aided in standardizing the recorded interviews.

The writer made arrangements to visit each director personally at his particular school for a tape-recorded interview. Each director collected a number of cases to be prepared for the interview. The reporting form was used as a guide during the interviews to form a basis for questions and to guide each interview along similar channels. The cases were told to the writer in story form. The writer broke into the report only to clarify points or to identify an individual's statements or actions. In some instances original letters and papers were submitted by directors to substantiate the case problems.

TREATMENT OF REFINED CASE PROBLEMS

The writer then refined the thirty-two taped interviews and wrote them in narrative form with all the facts retained. Twenty-three of these case problems were determined to contain sufficient facts and to be in areas of common interest to the directors. With the exception of two case problems, the actions of the directors were not disclosed, because this would have revealed the actual steps and decisions made by them. In these two long cases involving a number of people and considerable time, the complete information was recorded for each director's reaction.

The writer devised alternate solutions for each case problem and listed these solutions, with the actual solution at the end of each case. Provision was made for the directors to rank the alternatives from best to worst.

The cases with the alternate solutions and critical elements were then returned to all the directors. The actual solutions were included in the list of alternate solutions so that no director (except the person at the school involved) knew what decisions were actually made. The directors were given the opportunity to offer additional solutions in the event they agreed with none of those listed.

In addition to ranking the solutions in order of best to worst, the directors also indicated the incidents they determined to be critical in each case.

Intramural directors, as with all persons in administrative positions, react humanly and thus with some variance, even to very similar situations. The intramural director must act and solve, in one fashion or another, the multitudinous situations he encounters in an efficient and yet individually creative manner many times a week. He does not possess the time, staff, or, in many cases, the desire to collect a case history or even a case report.

The case history requires much background research and additional information not easily accessible to the director. For these reasons, the case problem is more suited to his needs. He is interested predominantly and usually has access only to the "facts that have direct and immediate bearing on the problem" as described on the last page of Bauer's book (1955, p. 213).

This present study is an attempt to examine one segment of the physical education field using this technique. In other words, the plan was to collect cases from those individuals concerned with the administration of intramural programs and to cumulate the evaluations of the administrative procedures and decisions reached by these directors. From the analysis of these cases, currently useful generalizations were prepared, or as stated by Lombard (in Andrews, 1953, p. 228),

> that order of statement which would be useful to a person who has to administer the situation being described.

Findings and Conclusions

Intramural programs are conducted for the benefit of the students at the various institutions. The better programs are service programs concerned with the development of the individual as well as with the provision of various activities. In the majority of the cases the directors involved the student participants in the decision-making process. The directors recognized that the students would have additional opportunity for development if they were allowed to contribute to the decisions controlling their actions.

The directors are concerned with those problem areas in which they experience difficulty in determining fair solutions and those which they encounter frequently. The following three tables indicate the areas in which the Western Conference intramural directors find their greatest concern.

Table 1. The Problem Areas Determined by the Western Conference Intramural Directors as "Most Difficult to Resolve."

*1. Enforcement of eligibility rules
2. Publicity in school paper
3. Building management
4. Office management
5. Preparation of fields and facilities
6. Health clinic cooperation
7. Relations with superiors
8. Relations with other departments and faculty
9. Allotment of intramural budgets

*Random order

Table 2. The Problem Areas Determined by the Western Conference Intramural Directors as "Most Frequently Encountered."

*1. Enforcement of eligibility rules
2. Publicity in school paper
3. Building management
4. Office management
5. Preparation of fields, facilities
6. Relations with other departments and faculty
7. Relations with coaches and physical education staff in the use of activity areas
8. Selection of supervisors and officials
9. Control of contestants by student officials

*Random order

Table 3. The Problem Areas Determined by the Western Conference Intramural Directors to Fall in Both Categories of "Most Difficult to Resolve" and "Most Frequently Encountered."

*1. Enforcement of eligibility rules
2. Publicity in school paper
3. Office management
4. Building management
5. Relations with other departments and faculty

*Random order

There appear to be acts or omissions of acts that affect the development of administrative problems. An arbitrary number of three repetitions was selected to depict an incident as consistently critical. When an incident occurred in three or more cases, that incident was deemed to be significant and important for a director to consider when conducting an activity. There were a total of sixty-nine critical incidents drawn from the sixteen cases.

Critical incidents initiated by Western Conference Intramural Directors indicate the following points:

1. Inadequately written sport rules and participation regulations create a significant number of the administration problems;
2. Permitting abusive participants or spectators to remain in an activity area will help intensify existing situations;
3. All-year point systems tend to create pressure that builds tension and induces problem situations.

CURRENTLY USEFUL GENERALIZATIONS

There were a total of seventy-two generalizations drawn from the sixteen case problems. Those generalizations repeated as pertinent guides for successful administrative action in three or more cases were summarized into statements useful to individuals administering similar situations. In some instances information found in the incidents determined to be critical by the directors was also found in the generalizations.

The nine generalizations which meet the required three or more repetitions are ranked below according to the number of case problems in which they appear.

Currently Useful Generalizations Concerning Western Conference Intramural Administration

1. Directors recognize and seriously consider recommendations from student organizations.

2. Intramural game rules and participation regulations often prove to be incomplete and are not infallible.
3. An equitable all-year point system is difficult to devise, and a point system tends to create tensions among units.
4. Errors caused by supervisory mistakes and inadequate regulations do not cause units or individuals to be penalized.
5. Strict disciplinary action is invoked for direct intentional violations of rules and such problems as the exhibition of personal disrespect of the director.
6. Rulings pertaining to individuals and units are discussed by all concerned before the rulings are invoked.
7. Direct lines of communication are to be maintained between the director, students, and officials concerned with student affairs.
8. Game rules or regulations proven unworkable should be modified immediately.
9. Consideration is given to the replay of contests under protest because of rule misinterpretation rather than determining the winner by rule alone.

USEFULNESS OF CASE PROBLEM METHOD

The usefulness or value of the case problem method in gaining valid knowledge about human relations in the administration of Western Conference Intramural Programs is demonstrated in the findings following. Questionnaires and statistical studies would not have indicated how the directors might change their decisions after further study of an actual problem (*Table 4,* item 4). This item indicates that in seven out of the fifteen cases directors changed their original decisions because of the opportunity for a more thorough and objective study of the problem. In each case the new decision was the one supported by a majority of the other directors. The tensions created by point systems, which may be the basis for innumerable other problems, are clearly brought out by this method of investigation. The modification of rules determined to be inadequate (Table 4, item 2) was best brought out by the directors' investigation of actual life situations. The directors were willing to waive or modify rules in favor of individual fairness and justice. Their responses indicated involvement of students in determination of rules and penalties concerning their participation. These two statements above are well demonstrated (Table 4, item 5) by the case problems.

Implications for the Administrator

Individuals who are responsible for the actions and performance of others are unfortunately often acting only on intuition. This intuition is too often based only upon their own narrow experiences which are limited to the policies of the previous administrator. In many instances there is no chance for the

Table 4. Indication of Cases from which Significant Information about Western Conference Intramural Administration Was Drawn.

Information Drawn from Directors' Responses	Percent	1	2	3	4	5	6	7	8	9	10	11	12 A	12 B	13	14	15
1. Human relations are clearly involved in Western Conference intramural administration because fourteen cases out of sixteen were concerned with team or individual conflict.	87	X	X	X	X	X	X		X			X	X	X	X	X	X
2. *Inadequate regulations caused eight out of eleven of the administrative problems involving intramural rules and regulations.	73				X	X	X	X	X	X		X			X		
3. The student protest is a definite part of the intramural regulation system. There were ten case problems that involved team or individual violations. Seven of these were reported to the director by means of a protest.	70				X		X	X	X	X	X	X	X		X		
4. **The original decision by the director involved was not supported in eleven of the sixteen case problems.	68		X	X		X	X	X	X	X		X		X	X	X	X
5. The Western Conference Intramural Directors recommend and encourage student participation in the determination of decisions and regulations concerning eligibility and conduct violations. In ten cases out of sixteen, student participation was required by the directors.	62	X		X	X	X	X	X	X	X	X	X				X	

290

Table 4 - Continued

Information Drawn from Directors' Responses	Percent	1	2	3	4	5	6	7	8	9	10	11	12 A	12 B	13	14	15
6. Pressures created by point systems are a significant source of problem to the directors. Seven out of thirteen case problems reported that involved team protests, or individuals' problems arose from the all-around point system.	54				X		X		X	X			X	X	X		
7. The directors indicated they were reluctant to award a contest to a team by rule alone. In three of the six games protested, rather than determine the game by rule, the directors rescheduled the game in part, or completely.	50				X			X				X					
8. Student supervisors and officials are a significant source of administrative problems. In seven of the sixteen cases, these student employees were involved.	44	X		X	X			X				X				X	X
9. Problems involving the control of participants, such as ineligibility, make up the most difficult single problem area for the directors. Seven of the sixteen cases concerned eligibility.	44		X			X	X				X		X		X	X	

*In each of the eight cases concerning inadequate regulations, the directors modified the regulations. By this action they indicated they considered the individual more important than the rules.

**In seven instances directors who had made an original decision to solve a problem changed their decisions after a more thorough study of the problem in a objectively written form. This supports the use of the case problem method as a dynamic means for gaining insight to Western Conference intramural administrative action.

291

departing executive or director to pass on even what he has learned to the new director.

If each director could record cases concerning various problems he encounters, including those incidents that appear to be crucial to a successful solution of the problems, a tremendous backlog of actual experience would be available. Even the directors gathering the cases would benefit by being able to review their actions and decisions in previous problems of a similar nature.

All scientific investigators keep records of performances of various agents, materials, and conditions. The justice courts and the practice of law give considerable weight to precedence. Is it not even more important that the practice of governing individuals be given the benefit of past methods and results? Is it impossible to envision a case book available to every intramural director? Obviously, no set rules would be prescribed for each problem the director might encounter. Cases similar to those the director must deal with plus guides or generalizations pertaining to these cases would certainly aid in the formulation of intelligent, comprehensive decisions.

The methods and techniques available for other purposes such as experimental, statistical, and questionnaire are more concerned with the end results of certain situations or sets of questions. The recording of life experiences in case form provides more information about the actual process of human action and decision-making. In human relations it is often more important to know why and how the participants reacted than to know what the end result was.

From a growing log of cases intramural administrators may well find that the one common and crucial element in all situations is the relationship between people. Any collection of cases will show the ever-widening relations touching the director and staff, director and student employees, director and participants, director and other colleagues, and all these individuals with their circle of relationships with the director and each other.

Administrators may discover: (1) that efficient and successful human relationships call for attacking the problem a person has—not the person with the problem; (2) that an administrator or director directs best by serving, and serving a staff means, first not to be the bottleneck at which all fresh, new ideas are blocked; (3) that removing obstacles and making decisions, rather than procrastinating, enables a staff to perform unhindered; and (4) that, through a continual study of the human relations involved in every situation, and by the awareness of those critical incidents pinpointing problems, the director may come to the realization that people are more important than things.

Finally, additional work should be initiated to further explore this area so crucial to effective (in terms of people) administration. Some suggestions for further investigation follow.

1. Only one small segment of the administrative areas concerned with Western Conference intramural administration was investi-

gated in this study—a phase of the "controlling" area. The other phases of planning, organizing, directing, and coordinating need to be studied in a similar manner before a comprehensive scheme of the position of intramural director may be recorded.
2. More intensive study should be made over a number of years in order that numerous cases may accumulate additional administrative actions appropriate to similar situations.
3. One school and one director, determined to be competent, efficient, and successful in terms of student participation, growth, and development, might be studied intensively in the same manner.
4. Further study should be made to investigate the development of a system to enable directors to recognize and record immediately critical incidents occurring in their daily administrative duties.

General Bibliography

Abernathy, Ruth, "President's Address," AAHPER, NAPECW, CPEA, Intramural Sports for College Men and Women: Report on First National Conference on Intramurals. Washington, D.C., 1955.

Allport, Gordon, "The Use of Personal Documents in Psychological Science," *Social Science Research Council,* Bull. 49 (New York, 1942), 19.

Andrews, Kenneth, et al., *Human Relations and Administration.* Cambridge, Mass.: Harvard University Press, 1953.

Bauer, Ronald D., *Cases in College Administration.* New York: Teachers College, Columbia University, 1955.

Beeman, H. F., and J. H. Humphrey, *Intramural Sports.* Dubuque, Iowa: W. C. Brown Publishing Co., 1954.

Flanagan, John C., "Critical Incidents in Individuals," Educational Conference, *Modern Educational Problems,* 1952.

McNair, Malcolm and Anita Hersum, *The Case Method at the Harvard Business School.* New York: McGraw-Hill Book Co., Inc., 1954.

18

The Planning and Construction of Physical Recreation Facilities

James A. Peterson

Introduction

Planning educational facilities involves more than designing and constructing a facility with "X" number of square feet to accommodate "Y" number of students. Rather, the process of creating educational facilities can be viewed as a continuous series of closely related but separate events or actions, some of which are prerequisite to others. Unfortunately, there is a wide variety of interpretations regarding either the identification of these events or the conceptualization of a coherent theory of facility development.

A perusal of the literature suggests that the numerous efforts to define the parameters of the process for planning facilities can be categorized into two divergent approaches. On one hand, a number of educators advocate that the proper administrative approach to facility planning is adherence to a semisequential order of steps. The primary tenet of this approach holds that the planning process can be viewed as a specific number of administrative activities which must be undertaken before an optimal level of planning is achieved. In contrast to that approach, other educators postulate that the process for planning facilities should instead be conceptualized in terms of broad planning considera-

James A. Peterson is from the United States Military Academy, West Point, New York.

tions. This viewpoint suggests that, depending on the level of competent leadership and effective communication between the individuals involved with the development of the facility, the essence of the task of the facility planner is the selection, coordination, scheduling, and timing of the diverse planning activities (Council of Educational Facility Planners, 1969, pp. 17-18).

Despite the relative disparity between the two interpretations of the basic elements of the process for planning facilities, one prominent commonality between the two exists: both emphasize that the cornerstone of a well-planned facility is an administrative commitment to careful planning. The need for careful planning in the search for and the subsequent expenditure of capital construction monies has never been more acute. With the cost of constructing educational facilities increasing to almost crisis proportions, there appears to be an immutable realization on the part of most administrators that the extant funds for capital construction must be efficiently employed. Accordingly, building programs must be geared toward the development of functional facilities.

Unfortunately, when the available funds are insufficient to meet all of the building needs of higher education, higher priorities are frequently placed on the construction of "academic" buildings. This preemptive judgment subsequently results in a lower priority for the development of student-service-type facilities, such as physical recreation buildings. As a consequence, if physical educators hope to be reasonably competitive in the quest for a share of the available capital construction monies, it is essential that they commit themselves to an administrative approach which insures that their facility planning efforts are thoroughgoing, efficient, and appropriate. This commitment should begin with the efforts to justify the need for a particular facility and should be sustained throughout the life of the facility.

The usefulness of the instructional material which has been published to aid the physical educator in his attempts to achieve a maximum degree of efficient planning is, unfortunately, subject to question. In many cases, the composition of the material on facility planning can best be described as being quite superficial. As a result, despite the voluminous amount of literature on the subject of planning facilities, the physical educator has very little information at his disposal regarding the inner workings of the process for planning and constructing a physical recreation facility. For the physical educator, the question remains, What is the proper administrative approach for developing a well-planned physical recreation building?

In order to gain a clearer insight into the dynamics of the process for planning a physical recreation facility, the study undertaken by the author examined the facility planning efforts at several universities, each selected for having a substantially large intramural-physical recreation building (Peterson, 1971). Using the case study approach, the individuals who were involved in the planning of each facility were identified, and the extent of their participation in the planning process was determined. Insight into this latter aspect was gained by presenting an overview of the interrelationship between the facility planning efforts and the existing administrative structure of each school.

Historical Background and Related Literature

The efficient planning of physical recreation facilities has long been an administrative concern for physical educators. One of the first references to the fact that the development of facilities was of interest to physical educators appeared as early as the late nineteenth century (*American Physical Education Review,* 1896-99). The literature suggests that since those initial efforts, there has been a substantial increase in the demand and need for information regarding the planning of physical recreation facilities. In response to this demand, many of the aspects attendant to planning educational facilities have been accorded extensive treatment in the literature.

The physical educator seeking assistance in the task of facility planning is confronted, however, with a contradictory dilemma. On one hand, as Boles suggests, "there is hardly a topic in education which has been written about so energetically and voluminously as school buildings" (1965, p.v). On the other hand, despite the proliferation of information on facility planning, little agreement exists among educators regarding the proper approach to planning them. One plausible avenue of assistance for the physical educator who is seeking guidance in his facility planning efforts is to survey the literature on selected aspects of the process for planning educational facilities. The remainder of this section is devoted to a review of the literature concerning the specific aspects of the planning process that were investigated in the present study.

ADMINISTRATIVE APPROVAL FOR THE FACILITY

A primary element of the process for planning facilities is the action that must be undertaken to achieve administrative approval for a proposed building project. On some campuses, this task involves nothing more than submitting a simplified request to an individual or agency with the authority to make the decision to proceed with plans to build the facility. This approach requires minimal preplanning or action on the part of the applicant. At other schools, the process is more complex. These schools require that a more sophisticated, quantitative approach to the evaluation of the relative merits of their proposed projects be adopted. In varying combinations, this approach consists of surveys to assess needs; normative indexes to provide a comparison between the existing facilities and reasonable standards, and projections based on existing requirements, activity trends, etc. of how much activity space will be needed when the facility is completed. Although these various quantitative tools do not represent the complete answer, they do contribute substantially to efforts to make the approach to planning both comprehensive and objective.

A number of inclusive guides have been compiled which offer detailed instruction in how to conduct a space survey and inventory (Bareither and Schillinger, 1968; Dahnke et al., 1970). Within certain situational limitations, a utilization-of-space survey is developed to accomplish the following objectives: (1) to determine the present utilization of existing facilities; (2) to determine how utilization might be improved; (3) to pinpoint institutional strengths and weaknesses in building utilization; (4) to provide information relative to space allocation standards; (5) to provide background data for future plant expansion based on need; (6) to use the findings as a guide in the development of an integrated building priority list; and (7) to keep abreast of the rapidly changing educational scene (Schwehr, 1962, p. 140).

Sumption and Landes suggest that appraising existing plant facilities should include an evaluation of qualitative aspects, as well as a compilation of quantitative data (1957, p. 81). The literature reveals that the usual approach to evaluating the qualitative aspects of a facility has been to develop a check list of specific items and to assign an arbitrary value (score) to each item. A facility is appraised by being evaluated on those items, thus arriving at a total score which, for assessment purposes, is then compared to normative standards.

The use of "evaluation" forms, however, introduces a measure of subjectivity into the process for planning facilities, because the use of any qualitative appraisal is closely related to the selection of the standards which provide the comparative basis. For physical recreation facilities, the most well-known and widely acclaimed source of normative standards has been the guide prepared by Sapora and Kenny (1960). From an extensive inventory of the existing facilities at all of the campuses of the Western Athletic Conference,[1] they developed a list of standards based on what they considered to be the minimum desirable number of square feet per student required to conduct an adequate program in various physical activities. Relative to situational factors, the indices developed by Sapora and Kenny serve not only as an aid in evaluating existing facility needs but also as a normative tool in the projection of future space requirements. For planning purposes, their standards are employed after an assessment of enrollment and activity trends has been undertaken.

THE DESIGN OF THE FACILITY

In this crucial phase of the planning process, the collective efforts of the planning participants are channeled into transforming the ideas for a facility into a tangible form which can guide the construction contractor. Among the more important matters the facility planner must consider during this phase are: the development of a program statement (educational specifications); the selection of the architect; the use of design consultants; the selection of the site; the establishment of aesthetic parameters for the design; and the formulation of landscaping guidelines for the project.

[1] Most commonly referred to as the "Big 10" Athletic Conference.

The literature suggests that there is widespread agreement that the planning efforts for a facility should utilize all persons who can contribute to the planning process. Students, as well as faculty/staff, should be involved. The most viable opportunity for channeling such involvement is to encourage maximum input into the development of the program statement. Simply stated, educational specifications (collectively referred to as the program statement) are the guide the architect follows to design a new facility. They are the means by which an educator describes to the architect the activities to be housed, persons to be accommodated, space requirements, spatial relationships, equipment to be housed, and the special environmental treatment that should be accorded each space in the facility (Council of Educational Facility Planners, 1969, p. 49). Despite the wide variety of educational specifications that are developed, one basic guideline is appropriate: the greater the detail, the greater the likelihood that the architect will be able to design a facility to meet specific needs (Leu, 1965, p. 34).

Another of the critical aspects in the design phase of the planning process is the selection of an architect. This task confronts the facility planner with four basic problems: when to retain the architect for a project, what criteria to base the selection on, what selection method to use, and what services to require from the architect. Although, in many cases, specific legal regulations and guidelines govern the approach to these problems, in other situations such decisions are left to the discretion of the appropriate administrator.

The literature suggests that a prudent approach to the question of when to select the architect is to select him as soon as it can be determined that his services will be required. One of the primary advantages of selecting the architect very early in the planning process is securing his immediate assistance in the overall coordination of the planning efforts (Priest and Oglesby, 1967, p. 26).

Three general methods of selecting an architect are commonly employed: direct appointment, competitive selection, and design competition (American Institute of Architects, 1963, chap. 5, p. 4). The particular method used is usually determined by the type of client and the type of project. The first two methods listed are the most commonly followed procedures for selecting an architect for an educational facility. The direct appointment method bases the selection of the architect on the client's knowledge of the architect's reputation, ability, and experience. In the comparative selection method, the architect is selected from a list of architects who have been asked to submit information and materials concerning their qualifications to the client.[2]

The question of what services to require from the architect is based to a great extent on the type of project involved and when, during the planning process, he is hired. In most cases, the services of the architect usually begin

---

[2]The subject of what constitutes a competent architect is accorded extensive treatment in the AIA's *Handbook of Architectural Practice.* This text examines in detail the appropriate areas of exploration concerning the proper qualifications for an architect.

before the actual design is started and normally continue until the facility has been completed and accepted by the client. In these cases, the architect has extensive involvement in several areas of service: predesign planning, schematic design, design development, construction documents, bidding, and construction.

Consultants and specialists sometimes join the architect on the "design team." Some facilities—physical recreation facilities, for example—frequently necessitate that the architect possess expertise in the design of a number of different types of activity areas. When a client feels that its architectural firm does not have the expertise or breadth of knowledge to design a particular type of activity space, arrangements are made to employ consulting services to assist the architect. For example, the use of pool consultants in the design of physical recreation facilities appears to be a frequent practice.

Another integral element of the design phase of the planning procession is the selection of the site. Although the literature suggests that a wide variety of factors should be considered, several criteria are particularly appropriate, including accessibility to those who will use the facility (e.g., proximity to greater density of residence halls), availability of utility services, proximity to related outdoor recreational areas (e.g., tennis courts and play fields), location to traffic hazards, proximity to safety and health facilities, cost, aesthetic appeal, environment, and suitability of soil for a building foundation. Responsibility for site selection varies from campus to campus. In varying degrees of collaboration, the design architect or someone from the school's planning department or physical plant may undertake this task. In some instances, a landscape architect or an outside consultant may be used to select the site.

Regarding aesthetic considerations in the planning process, facility planners, unfortunately, traditionally follow an approach which holds that anything not essential to the immediate curriculum or the efficient operation of the facility should be labeled as a frill or an extravagance and omitted (AASA, 1960, p. 76). The literature implores facility planners to place a greater emphasis on aesthetic parameters in the design of their facilities. Accordingly, administators should insist that architects not forget one of the most important elements in the design of new buildings—beauty.

THE METHOD OF FINANCING THE FACILITY

Faced with limited monies for capital construction, most administrative officials view this phase as the most critical step in the process for planning facilities. Quite obviously, if the necessary financing is not secured, the project cannot be consummated. Because the capital needs and resources of universities vary from campus to campus, the approach to financial planning also varies from school to school. Despite these differences, the literature indicates that there are several fundamental aspects which the facility planner must usually consider: estimating preliminary costs (translating planning proposals into dollar requirements), determining the sources of funding for a project (including an evaluation of the legal and program stipulations relative to each source), and developing a feasible and effective financial plan that will sustain the building project.

In most cases, the initial step in the financial planning for a project is to calculate preliminary cost estimates. Following the development of preliminary plans and design specifications, these projections of costs are normally made by either the project architect or a financial officer of the university. Preliminary or rough estimates of costs are based on unit costs obtained from past experience. Although this approach does not yield a precise projection of the costs, it does enable the facility planner to proceed with the development of a feasible financial plan for the project.

Later, as more detailed plans are developed, the preliminary cost estimates are reviewed to bring them into line with a more realistic projection of the building's cost (Foreman, 1958, p. 41). The closer the specifications are to the final plans, the more precise the estimate of the project costs. A detailed cost projection usually involves (1) a determination of the time required for each item of work, (2) a calculation of the labor requirements, (3) a computation of equipment requirements, and (4) a determination of the materials required (De La Torre, 1958, p. 1).

Once the cost estimates for a project have been determined, the facility planner must then formulate a plan to finance the project.[3] In general, the financial plan outlines what the sources of funding will be, how these sources are to be tapped, when they are to be utilized, to what part each is to be applied, and how the indebtedness is to be liquidated.

Though the procedures for determining the financial plan for a building project are strictly regulated on many campuses by state statutes and university policies, more often than not, it is frequently simply a process of procuring the funds from whatever source(s) is available. The literature suggests that the traditional sources of funding for university facilities are state appropriations, federal grants and loan assistance, debt services (bonds), private grants and gifts, and use-generated revenues.

The applicability of the various revenue sources for financing physical recreation facilities varies from state to state and from project to project. Most states appear to be reluctant to provide state funding assistance for any but "academic" buildings. These states usually stipulate that the financing of student-service-type facilities (e.g., a student union building) must come from the students themselves. Physical recreation facilities are normally considered to be "service" facilities. In the same token, however, because most physical recreation facilities accommodate some part of the physical education instructional program, several states participate in the financing of these facilities to the percentage extent that they might be construed as serving the "academic" program.

---

[3]On some campuses, these steps are reversed. The financial plan is developed first; and then the project (by necessity) is designed to accommodate the financial plan.

Resulting from both pragmatic and philosophical factors, one of the most prevalent methods of financing physical recreation facilities is through the use of student-fee revenues. In a sense, many educators consider the student-fee assessment to be the charge for services rendered over and above the pursuit of "academic enlightenment." The essence of this position is that students should bear the financial burden for student-service-type facilities. Among the critical questions which the use of student-fee revenues raises for the facility planner are (1) when to initiate the student-fee assessment for a project, (2) when to sell the revenue bonds (before the project begins or when the best interest rates are available), and (3) when to schedule the maturation of the bond issue(s). In addition, the literature suggests that facility planners should develop a "strategy" to minimize any student displeasure over the use of student-fee funding for a particular project.

In some instances, a major source of the funding of collegiate physical recreation facilities has been the assistance of the federal government. Federal assistance in this area is administered under Public Law 88-204, which is also known as the "Higher Education Facilities Act of 1963".[4] Contingent on the percentage of the time that a physical recreation facility is projected for use for instructional purposes, this law contains two provisions for providing assistance for recreational-type facilities. The Title I program provides for the appropriation of grants (up to one-third of a project's costs) for the construction of undergraduate academic facilities. The Title III program provides for loans for the construction of academic facilities. These loans produce long-term (up to fifty years) low interest rate assistance for up to 75 percent of the development costs for a project.

Two additional sources of funds for the construction of facilities for higher education are gifts from private sources and use-generated revenues. The literature emphasizes that though monies from these two sources are certainly welcome, such funds are normally not available in sufficient amounts to be considered a significant source of revenue for the development of physical recreation facilities.

PLANNING INPUT DURING THE CONSTRUCTION PHASE

The construction phase of the planning process involves the final steps in which the preceding planning efforts are expressed in terms of concrete, brick, and steel. The literature suggests that during this stage, facility planning includes a number of integral considerations: awarding the construction contract, the bidding process, the final contract, supervisory procedures during construction, arbitration of disputes concerning the construction documents, change-order procedures, and the final inspection and acceptance of the facility.

Two basic methods of awarding construction contracts are used: competi-

---

[4]Public Law 88-204, 88th Congress, H.R. 6143, December 16, 1963.

tive bidding and direct appointment. Under the direct selection method, the AIA suggests that the contract is awarded on the basis "of the abilities of the contractor in those areas which are particularly important to the project at hand" (1953, p. 2). Under the competitive bidding system, each bidder submits a sealed proposal to execute the work for a specific sum. By law, all public works must be contracted for by competitive bidding.

For public works, the law prescribes awarding the construction contract to the lowest responsible bidder. The task of determining this is by no means a simple step, however. The exact parameters of this tenet are somewhat ambiguous. The Supreme Court of Pennsylvania, for example, defines the "lowest responsible bidder" principle as requiring facility planners to exercise sound discretion. "They should call to their assistance the means of information at hand to form an intelligent judgment" (Foreman, 1958, p. 26). The bidding documents usually provide, however, that the owner has the right to reject any or all bids, or to accept the bid which, in his judgment, will be to his own best interests. If he rejects all bids, the client normally has three alternatives: to resubmit the project as is for new bids, ask the architect to make changes in the specifications which (hopefully) will induce more bid proposals when the project is rebid, or drop the project altogether.[5] If he accepts a bid, the bid deposits of the unsuccessful bidders are returned and the contract awarded.

For the great bulk of construction, bid proposals generally lead to one of four types of agreements: lump-sum, guaranteed upset price, cost plus fixed fee, or management contract (McLean, 1958, Chapter 27, p. 1).[6] For the great majority of schools, the choice of a contractual agreement is closely regulated by both state statutes and university policies.

The agreement between a client and a contractor is usually stipulated on the standard contract form provided by the AIA with modifications to fit the particular project. The construction contract normally includes the contract documents; a description of the scope of the contractor's work; the name of the contract architect; a commencement and tentative completion date for the work; stipulations (if any) regarding liquidated damages, penalty, and bonus clauses; the total contract procedures for progress payments; and references to the final inspection, certification of completion and acceptance of work, and issuance of a final certificate for payment (American Institute of Architects, 1963, chap. 17, pp. 2-4). In addition, the contract also includes provisions regarding the responsibility for clean-up after construction; the procedures for handling disputes over interpretation of the contract documents; the procedures

---

[5]The choice of resubmitting a project for bid as is or of dropping the project altogether is normally rejected as being either unrealistic or undesirable. The process of changing the specifications is referred to as developing a list of deductive alternates. Either less expensive materials are substituted into the specifications for a facility or items are dropped altogether in order to bring the project within feasible (money-wise) boundaries.

[6]An inclusive examination of the relative merits of each type of construction agreement is also offered by Robert McLean (1958, pp. 1-8).

for handling disputes over interpretation of the contract documents; the procedures for change orders; the client's ideas on the specific working relationship between the architect, the contractor, and himself; and the guarantees provided by the contractor.

Once construction actually begins, the responsibilities of the various major participants (architect, contractor, and client) vary somewhat from project to project depending upon the contractual arrangements. An understanding of the scope and intent of all the contract documents is the primary cornerstone of all activity in the construction phase.

When a project nears completion, several procedures are followed. The contractor sends the architect and/or the client a statement claiming substantial completion of the project.[7] Subsequently, the architect and/or a representative of the client conducts a semifinal inspection to determine the status of completion. If the project is found to be substantially complete, a certificate of substantial completion is prepared. Attached to this certificate is a list (referred to as a "punch list") of the items to be completed or corrected by the contractor. This certificate also provides for agreement as to the time allowed for completion or correction of the items, the date upon which the owner will occupy the project or specified areas of the project, and a description of the responsibilities for heat, utilities, and insurance (American Institute of Architects, 1963, chap. 18, p. 10).

If for some reason the inspecting team does not concur in the contractor's claim of substantial completion, another semifinal inspection is scheduled after the contractor submits a new statement. On the average, the typical project does not require more than two such semifinal inspections. Once substantial completion is achieved, a final inspection is then conducted by the representatives of the owner and the architect. If everything is acceptable, a written certificate of completion is prepared. The contractor then submits an affidavit which states that all of his bills have been paid. He then prepares his final application for payment.

Research Methodology and Techniques

The major purpose of the study was to examine, through case analyses, the process involved in the planning and construction of physical recreation buildings which were financed primarily by student-fee revenues. A second objective of the study was to determine which individuals were involved in the planning of these facilities and to investigate the extent of their participation in the planning process. The following subproblems, stated in question form, were posed to direct the investigation:

---

[7]Substantial completion is defined by the AIA as the date when the construction is sufficiently completed in accordance with the construction documents, as modified by any change orders agreed to by the contractual parties, so that the owner can occupy the project or specified area of the project for the use for which it was intended.

1. How did each school gain administrative approval for its building?
2. How did each school arrive at the design of its facility?
3. How was the method of financing determined for each facility?
4. Who had planning input into the construction phase for the facility?

PRELIMINARY PROCEDURES

The initial step was to identify those universities which had a large physical recreation facility that had been financed primarily by student-fee revenues. Based in part upon geographical, time, and cost considerations, five schools were selected: University of Illinois (Urbana), Michigan State University, Oklahoma State University, Purdue University, and the University of Washington. The next step was to contact an individual at each school who had been an active participant in the planning of his institution's physical recreation facility and to request his assistance in the compilation of data pertinent to the planning of his school's facility. At four of the universities, the director of intramurals was the individual contacted; at Oklahoma State University, initial assistance was provided by the chairman of the department of physical education.

The means used to gather information on the dynamics of the planning process was the descriptive survey method. The specific descriptive survey techniques employed were the structured interview and content analysis and appraisal. A questionnaire was developed in order to standardize the data solicited from the interview survey and to achieve a sense of continuity in reporting the data collected at each university.

SURVEY PROCEDURES

Each of the individuals at the five institutions who had agreed to serve as an intermediary contact for the study was sent a copy of both the questionnaire instrument and the horizontal analysis for the study. Requested to conceptualize the parameters of the information sought for this study, these individuals were asked to schedule appointments for this investigator to meet with people who could supply the desired information.[8] Based upon prior arrangements, the author then visited each school for approximately one week.

In cooperation with the intermediary contacts, interviews were held with those individuals who were involved in the planning of their school's physical recreation facility. The approach to the interviews was based, in part, on the check list of recommendations for conducting an effective interview that has been proposed by Good (1966, pp. 235-36). In order to achieve an accurate chronicle of each question-and-answer session, all interviews were tape-recorded.

[8]During those interviews, a number of individuals were identified who had provided input into the planning process for their school's facility and who had not previously been scheduled for an interview. Appointments were subsequently made to see these individuals.

The tapes were subsequently transcribed. Among the numerous individuals who were interviewed at each university were the dean or director of the school or department of physical education; the dean or manager of facilities for the physical education administrative unit (or any other individual who had been assigned this responsibility); the director of intramurals and members of his staff; the director of the campus planning committee; the design architect and members of the university architects staff; the design consultants who were used; the university comptroller or the chief financial officer involved in developing the financial plan for the facility; and the construction contractor. In short, an attempt was made to interview anyone who provided input into the planning of the five facilities. The minutes of meetings of the various planning committees and agencies furnished a second primary source of information for the study. In addition, at a few of the schools, several individuals made their personal archives and other pertinent planning correspondence available to the author.

REPORTING OF THE DATA

The information concerning each school's planning efforts was synopsized into a descriptive narration. Each narration was organized by topical headings corresponding to the study's main subproblems. Subsequent to the five synopses, a content and comparative analysis was completed which pointed out the similarities and differences between the approaches of the five universities to the main aspects of planning.

Findings and Conclusions

The approach of each university to planning its physical recreation facility was dependent on a number of factors: the administrative structure of the school; the extant university policies and procedures for planning facilities; federal, state, and local statutes and regulations; the existing state of technology; the personalities of the individuals involved in the planning efforts for each facility; the influence of cultural and political constraints; and other chronological considerations. Because the situational factors attendant to each university varied considerably, each school's approach to planning its physical recreation facility also varied. The next part of this section is devoted to a succinct (thus somewhat limited) presentation of the findings concerning the approach of each school to the major elements of the process for planning facilities.

ADMINISTRATIVE APPROVAL FOR THE FACILITY

The approaches that the five universities followed to gain administrative approval for their physical recreation facilities can be categorized into two distinguishable groupings. At Purdue, Michigan State, and the University of Washington, the decision to proceed with plans for a new recreational facility was reached by an administrative decree. A strong-willed administrator who possessed the necessary authority simply arbitrarily decided that his university would construct such a facility.

In contrast, officials at the University of Illinois and Oklahoma State were directed by the extant regulations to pursue approval for their physical recreation facility through the proper administrative "channels." At Oklahoma State, these channels consisted, primarily, of directing all capital construction requests to the University's executive committee—an administrative body which included in its many functions the assignment of priorities to building projects. Subsequent to an evaluation of the university's board of regents, the state legislature appropriated a lump sum (as opposed to specific allocations) of state funds to Oklahoma State University for whatever capital projects the school officials deemed worthy.

The procedure that was followed to gain administrative approval for the University of Illinois' physical recreation facility necessitated that the project be reviewed by both a campus and a university system-wide screening committee for capital development. After it had been analyzed and approved by both advisory groups and had received an appropriately favorable priority, the project was included in the university's biennium capital budget request. Unlike the other schools, both the Universities of Oklahoma State and Illinois compiled a detailed listing and assessment of their space needs.

The activity programs that generated space needs for each university also varied. Although all of the schools faced a critical lack of adequate indoor physical activity space, none of these universities, at the time of their efforts to obtain a new building, had constructed an indoor recreational facility in over twenty-five years. Designed solely to meet the recreational needs of the student body, Purdue's "co-rec" gym houses the free-time and competitive programs of the intramural department. It does not service either the intercollegiate athletics program or the instructional program offerings of its department of physical education. In contrast, Michigan State's men's intramural building accommodates an extensive program of varsity sports. In addition, this facility provides space for the instructional program of its department of physical education and both the leisure-time and the organized activity offerings of its intramural department.

Though the University of Washington's intramural activities building was designed primarily to meet the needs of the intramural activities program, it does house some basic instruction classes. A policy was instituted, however, to limit the amount of instructional space allocated for classes. At all times, part of every type of activity space included in the building (e.g., swimming pool or handball courts) is available for free-time recreational use by members of the university community. Varsity athletics are totally excluded from use of the facility. Oklahoma State's Colvin Physical Education Center, similar to the space needs of the University of Illinois' IM-PE building, was developed to accommodate the professional preparation and instructional programs in physical education, the free-time and competitive activities of the intramural program, and the varsity swim team as the only intercollegiate users. The Colvin Center was designed to service the academic-related (e.g., laboratories) and instructional users of the facility, while the IM-PE building stresses the recreational aspects.

THE DESIGN OF THE FACILITY

Each school employed a somewhat different arrangement for the architectural services for its facility. Purdue had members of its physical plant department develop the schematics and the preliminary plans for the co-rec gym. After the basic parameters of the building had been established, the university employed an outside architectural firm to do the working drawings for the project. The selection of the design architect was arbitrarily made by a university vice-president. The architect chosen was an individual who had done practically all of the architecture on the Purdue campus since the early 1920s.[9] After the working drawings were finished, the bids had been taken, and the construction contract awarded, Purdue bought the drawings from the outside architect and turned the project over to its construction department, which supervised the facility to completion.

At the time of the men's intramural building project, Michigan State did not have its own staff of architects. A design architect was arbitrarily selected by the president of the university. This individual was expected to follow the project all the way through—from the development of the schematics for the project to the completion of the construction phase.

The University of Washington used its own university architect's office to direct and coordinate the development of the plans for the intramural activities building. An outside architect was hired to do the design work on the project. The selection of the design architect was made by the university's architectural commission, a group of independent architects who serve as an advisory committee to the board of regents. Their decision was based on a recommendation of three possible architects for the project who had been submitted (in rank-order priority) by the university architect's office. The University of Illinois employed similar procedures to develop the architectural plans for the IM-PE building. Illinois' university architect's office monitored the plans for the project, and an outside architect; appointed by the university's board of trustees, did the design work.

Oklahoma State University employs a unique arrangement for architectural services. Its university architect's office is independent to the extent that it

---

[9]Similar to the Universities of Washington and Illinois, Purdue's design architect had extensive experience with athletic facilities. Michigan State University and Oklahoma State University used design architects whose experience span with athletic facilities encompassed only secondary school gymnasia.

is not salaried. Receiving no budget, it is allotted a percentage of the costs for each project. For the Colvin Physical Education Center, it developed the schematics, did the preliminary plans, wrote the contract, and supervised the construction. The university hired an outside architect to develop the working drawings and detailed specifications for the facility.[10] Together, the outside architect and the university architect's office shared 6 percent of the construction costs for the project. The contract architect for the facility was appointed by the board of regents from a list submitted (in rank-order priority) by the university architect's office.

Two basic approaches to developing the specifications for their facilities were employed by the universities whose planning efforts were investigated in the study. At both Purdue and M.S.U., the director of intramurals was assigned (via the chairman of the department of physical education) the responsibility for developing a listing of the activity areas which should be included in his school's proposed multipurpose physical recreation facility. Neither university devised a program statement per se. In both instances, these individuals were not given detailed instructions or guidelines on how to proceed with the task of determining the specifications for their project. In each case, their primary source of information was input provided by the faculty of each school's department of physical education.

In contrast, the Universities of Washington, Oklahoma State, and Illinois appointed a committee to develop the specifications for their projects. The approach of each committee to its task was characterized by a strong commitment to maximize input attendant to the various elements of the project. Information was solicited from several sources: the physical education faculty, pertinent university personnel, equipment and material representatives from independent companies, and several trips to survey and evaluate the facilities at other schools. All committee decisions were made by consensus.

At four of the universities, the design architect worked closely with representatives of the various campus agencies and departments that had input into the project. Oklahoma State was the only school whose outside architect did not meet regularly with someone from the using department (its contract architect worked directly with the university architect's office). Relative to the specific arrangement for architectural services, the scope and type of input provided by the design architects into each project was generally the same for each of the five universities.[11]

The procedures for selecting the site for each project were somewhat

---

[10] The outside architect employed an aquatics consultant to assist in the design of the pools. Of the other schools, only Illinois employed a design consultant (also an aquatics specialist).

[11] The work of each of the design architects was influenced to a certain extent by either formal policies or implicit understandings regarding "aesthetic considerations" on facility design.

similar for each of the schools. Either a high-echelon administrator, a university department, or a university governing body (e.g., board of regents), acting upon the recommendations of the appropriate university personnel, made the decision on where the facility was to be built. The criteria for site selection varied considerably, however. Among the site criteria employed, in varying combinations, at these schools were proximity to student residence halls, adherence to the university's master plan, accessibility to the various segments of the university community, proximity to outdoor playfields, availability of bus service, proximity to other physical recreation facilities, and accessibility to parking facilities.

THE METHOD OF FINANCING THE FACILITY

Each university used a somewhat different approach for developing the preliminary budget for its facility. Based on a "ballpark" projection of a reasonable scope for the co-rec gym project, the Purdue University treasurer calculated that $2,500,000 of student fees could be allotted to the building. At Michigan State, the design architect developed the initial estimate of the cost of the men's intramural building project. He devised his cost projection by multiplying the cubic footage area of the facility by a per cubic foot cost which he had calculated by averaging the cubic footage costs of five large physical activity-type facilities. Unfortunately, the assumptions on which he based his cost projections were invalid. As a result, he grossly underestimated the cost of the project. In consultation with the comptroller, the business manager of the University of Washington developed a "ballpark" projection of the amount of funds needed to build the intramural activities building. Based upon cost estimates furnished by the university architect's office, Oklahoma State's vice-president of development prepared a preliminary budget for the Colvin Physical Education Center, which included a five-year escalation factor. The University of Illinois' university architect's office developed the preliminary projection of the cost of the IM-PE building. This estimate was based on the space requirements which were generated by the program statement for that project.

The approach to developing the financial plan and the rationale behind that plan were very similar for both Purdue's co-rec gym and the University of Washington's intramural activities building.[12] In both instances, each school had a substantial student-fee revenue bond issue that was being retired within a few months of the time that each university decided to proceed with the planning and constructing of a new multipurpose recreational facility. As a result, both schools had the bonding capability that would generate the necessary funds for

[12] The total project costs for the co-rec gym (143,000 sq. ft. gross area) and the intramural activities building (153,165 sq. ft. gross area) were $2,739,723 and $4,681,096, respectively.

such a facility. It was a relatively simple administrative procedure to arbitrarily reallocate the existing student-fee revenues to a new project once the old bond issue had been retired. Officials at both universities did not attempt to look for alternate sources of funding for two reasons: (1) both felt that this was a legitimate student expense because the building would be used primarily by students; and (2) neither wanted to secure money that would have "strings" attached which might lessen the recreational emphasis of the facility.

With the concurrence of Michigan State University's executive committee, Michigan State's vice-president for business and finance developed the financial plan for the men's intramural building. With the exception of $345,000 of private monies, the entire project was funded by student-fee revenues.[13] At that time, Michigan State had no other source of funding for the project. Neither the state of Michigan nor the federal government provided assistance for this type of capital development.

Oklahoma State's business manager devised the financial plan for the Colvin Physical Education Center. His primary approach to this task was to "look under every rock." In conjunction with assistance from the university's office of development and research, funds from four sources were obtained: a state appropriation, a Title I grant, a Title III loan, and the sale of private bonds.[14] Both the Title III loan and the private bond issue are being retired entirely by student-fee revenues. In the largest student referendum in the school's history, the Oklahoma State student body voted to assess themselves a fee for the Colvin Physical Education Center.

Subject to the agreement of the president, the university's comptroller developed the financial plan for the University of Illinois IM-PE building.[15] Initially, some administrative support existed for funding the project entirely through student fees. Because of a dramatic rise in costs which resulted from a lengthy delay in awarding the construction contract, the university was forced to look elsewhere for funds. Based upon the proposed recreational-instructional usage mix of the facility (75 percent to 25 percent), the university subsequently asked the state for an appropriation for the "academic" portion of the building. In addition, because the state-appropriated funds for the project were at a level below that included in the university biennium capital budget request, the university also applied for federal assistance in financing the building. As a result, the IM-PE building was financed from three sources: a general revenue appropriation from the state, a Title I grant, and a private bond issue. Debt

---

[13]Total project costs for the men's intramural building (198,600 sq ft gross area) were $3,957,133.

[14]The total project costs for the Colvin Physical Education Center (153,000 sq ft gross area) were $3,272,481: state appropriation $683,394; Title I grant $873,087; Title III loan $1,155,000; and student-fee revenue bonds $500,000.

[15]The total project costs for the IM-PE Building (262,484 sq ft gross area) were $11,100,000: state appropriation $909,200; Title I grant $1,082,615; and student-fee revenue bonds $9,100,000.

service for the bond issue is being provided entirely through student-fee revenues.

PLANNING INPUT DURING THE CONSTRUCTION PHASE

As public institutions, each of the schools included in the present study had to award the construction contract for its facility on the basis of open competitive bidding. The bidding system of each university was governed by the public works statutes of its state. These statutes stipulate that if a construction contract is awarded, it must be granted to the lowest responsible bidder.

The type of bids that were taken on these projects differed among the schools. Purdue University, the University of Washington, and the University of Illinois requested a single bid on the entire project. Michigan State University, however, took separate bids on each of the five major components of the men's intramural building project. Michigan State used this component-bidding procedure for two reasons: to develop strong competition in the various trades and (hopefully) to have the bid shopping result in a cost savings to the university. After the bids were taken, a single contract was written with subcontractors being assigned to the general contractor. Oklahoma State took both types of bids—components and a lump sum for the Colvin Physical Education Center.

None of the universities included penalty, liquidated damages, and/or bonus clauses in their contractural agreements with the construction contractors. Each of the five contracts included a provision which suggested a tentative completion date. None of the contractors met this deadline.

The schools varied somewhat in the procedures they followed to handle problems and/or disputes during the construction phase. The three universities (Michigan State University, the University of Washington, and the University of Illinois) which hired outside architects to do all of the design work on the project gave final-decision authority to that architect and/or his appointed representative. These design architects were required to interpret the contract specifications and to arbitrate any disagreements over the contract documents. On the other hand, the two schools (Purdue and Oklahoma State) which employed an outside architect only to do the working drawings had a different arrangement for mitigating problems and/or disagreements. During the construction phase, the only responsibility of these outside architects was to answer all questions regarding an interpretation of their drawings. At Purdue all other matters were handled by the superintendent for construction. The university architect's office managed all other questions concerning the Colvin Physical Education Center.

Except for the University of Illinois, all of the schools employed a similar arrangement for monitoring the construction of their facilities. Each university appointed an individual as the overall "director" (also referred to as a manager, supervisor, and/or superintendent) of the project during the construction phase.

In addition, a full-time on-the-site supervisor was hired to represent the university's interests. Together with inspectors from the physical plant department and/or the university architect's office, these supervisors had the responsibility for quality control on materials and work.

In contrast to this arrangement, the University of Illinois required that the design architect maintain a full-time field representative at the site of the project. This representative was responsible for monitoring the progress of the contractor and maintaining quality control on all materials and work. In addition, the university employed field inspectors to provide cursory supervision of the progress of the contractor.

On all of the construction projects, someone from the using college/school provided almost daily on-the-site inspection of the progress of the work. The extensive efforts of these individuals served as a valuable source of input and quality control on the project.

The procedures for change-order requests were fairly standardized among the schools. All of the schools required that any change in the contract specifications be written up and submitted to the appropriate representative of the university. And finally, although the individuals involved varied, the approach to conducting the semifinal and final inspections was basically similar among the schools.

CONCLUSIONS

Within the limitations of the study, the following conclusions may be drawn:

1. Relative to chronological considerations, there appeared to be an increasing sophistication of the techniques and tools used for planning physical recreation facilities.
2. Relative to chronological considerations, there seemed to be a growing tendency toward the decentralization of the administrative approach to planning multipurpose recreational facilities.
3. Each of the facilities investigated in the present study appeared to be a product of more than the "formal" parameters of planning, such as statutes, regulations, policies, and guidelines. The design of each facility was also affected, to a large extent, by the personalities of the people involved in the planning efforts.
4. Although limited somewhat by the policies of each university, the practice of having someone from the using college/department of physical education involved in the daily inspection during the construction phase served as a valuable source of quality control over work and materials.
5. In the 1960s, the use of student-fee funding for multipurpose recreational facilities necessitated an increasing administrative

commitment to involve students in the decision-making processes of the planning aspects.
6. With the exception of Michigan State, which has a separate intramural building for its women students, the planning efforts at each school emphasized the development of a totally corecreational facility.

Implications for the Practicing Administrator

The findings of this study suggest that although a number of factors influence the approach that a college employs to develop its facilities, effective facility planning results from the cooperative efforts of many individuals and groups. Stated another way, effective facility planning is the product of many individuals working together to devise an "inclusive plan" for guiding the development of a well-planned building. Accordingly, one of the primary tasks of the administrator is to identify and enlist the cooperation of *anyone* who can contribute to the planning of a proposed facility.

The administrative commitment to achieve a well-planned facility, however, requires more than just securing the services of interested and qualified people. It is essential that competent leadership be appointed to coordinate the efforts of the individuals who participate in the planning process. The most critical element required for such leadership is a thorough understanding of the dynamics of the process for planning facilities. This understanding provides the foundation for organizing the collective planning efforts into a unified, objective-oriented approach. The facility planner faces two tasks in this regard. The working relationships between the planning participants must be determined. In addition, guidelines for facilitating communication and coordination between all participants should be formulated.

The actions of the facility planners who were investigated in this study suggest that there are several steps which an administrator should pursue to enhance his planning efforts. He should keep abreast of the extant techniques and tools for planning and developing facilities. Manufacturers' representatives for materials and equipment that are appropriate to the facility should be encouraged to present a documented case for the use of their products to the committee (or a designated committee member) developing the program statement. The design architect should be hired early in the process for developing the project so that he can lend his expertise and experience to the collective planning efforts. In addition, if feasible, it is desirable to employ a design architect with extensive experience in the design of athletic facilities.

Equally as important, the administrator must involve the students in the process for planning facilities. If for no other than feasibility considerations, university officials cannot continue to plan buildings, create schools, and attend to all the other "traditional" college matters without consulting with and involving those young men and women who are most affected by what is done and how it is done. The relatively demure acceptance of the dramatic increase (more than doubling) in the amount of student-fee revenues required to fund the IM-PE building by the University of Illinois' student body stands in sharp contrast to situations where little or no effort was made to induce student input into the planning process. The violent confrontations at Columbia University over the location and construction of a gymnasium and the tumultuous conflicts concerning the People's Park athletic field controversy at U.C. Berkeley offer two dramatic illustrations of the negative potential of the latter approach. Illinois' planners, on the other hand, made numerous attempts to involve students in their planning efforts and to inform the student body (as a whole) of the progress of the IM-PE building project at every stage.

The study's findings also raise several significant considerations regarding the financing of college physical recreation facilities. Opinion is divided over the usefulness of student-fee monies as a source of funding for higher education facilities. Several high-level administrators forecast a diminishing reliance on student-fee revenues as a funding source for university facilities. These officials submit that the administrative headaches, which accrue when students are extensively involved in decision-making processes (operation-wise) for the buildings they finance, are simply not worth the trouble. (Unfortunately, these officials do not speculate on tenable, alternative funding sources.) In contrast, other administrators see an expanded role for student-fee revenues in the financing of facilities. They surmise that in light of the financial difficulties facing higher education, state officials (e.g., at Indiana) will become increasingly willing to finance "academic," as well as student-type facilities, with student-fee revenues. If this procedure is actually adopted, administrators will face even more difficulties in their attempts to obtain adequate financing for physical recreation facilities, because there will be more applicants for the student-fee dollar.

Another aspect of the financial phase of planning is a growing realization on the part of administrators that students are becoming increasingly reluctant to provide funding assistance for space which services intercollegiate programs. Perhaps this is because of a lessening of interest in traditional college activities of all forms. On the other hand, organized and free-time physical recreation programs appear to be growing at an unprecedented pace. Accordingly, the need for indoor physical recreation space has never been more critical. Administrators who wish to fulfill that need, however, must commit themselves to developing a facility that will provide opportunities for all rather than competitive arenas for the "gifted few."

General Bibliography

AASA School Building Commission, *Planning America's School Buildings.* Washington, D.C.: American Association of School Administrators, 1960.

American Institute of Architects, *AIA School Plant Studies: A Selection 1952-1962.* Washington, D.C.: AIA, 1962.

―――――, *Architect's Handbook of Professional Practice.* Washington, D.C.: AIA, 1963.

American Physical Education Review, vols. 1-4, 1896-1899.

Bareither, Harlan D., and Jerry L. Schillinger, *University Space Planning.* Urbana, Ill.: University of Illinois Press, 1968.

Boles, Harold W., *Step by Step to Better School Facilities.* New York: Holt, Rinehart, and Winston, Inc., 1965.

Council of Educational Facility Planners, *Guide for Planning Educational Facilities.* Columbus, Ohio: Council of Educational Facility Planners, 1969.

Dahnke, Harold, Dennis Jones, Thomas Mason, and Leonard Romney. *Higher Education Facilities Planning and Management Manuals,* Preliminary Field Review, (Boulder, Colorado: Planning and Management Systems Division, Western Interstate Commission for Higher Education, November, 1970).

De La Torre, M., "Estimating Building Construction Costs," *Building Construction Handbook,* ed. Frederick S. Merritt. New York: McGraw-Hill Book Co., 1958.

Foreman, Charles M., *A Procedure Guide for School Plant Construction for the State of Wyoming.* Laramie, Wyoming: The Curriculum and Research Center, College of Education, University of Wyoming, 1958.

Good, Carter V., *Essentials of Educational Research.* New York: Appleton-Century-Crofts, Inc., 1966.

Leu, Donald J., *Planning Educational Facilities.* New York: Center for Applied Research in Education, Inc., 1965.

McLean, Robert, "Construction Management," in *Building Construction Handbook,* ed. Frederick S. Merritt. New York: McGraw-Hill Book Co., 1958.

Peterson, James A., "A Case Analysis of the Process Involved in the Planning and Construction of Intramural-Physical Education Buildings Which Were Financed Primarily Through Student-Fee Revenues." Ph.D. diss., University of Illinois (Urbana), 1971.

Priest, B. J., and E. O. Oglesby, "Selecting the Design Team," *Junior College Journal,* 38 (September 1967), 26-30.

Sapora, Allen Y., and H. E. Kenney, *A Study of the Present Status, Future Needs and Recommended Standards Regarding Space Used for Health, Physical Education, Physical Recreation and Athletics at the University of Illinois.* Champaign, Ill.: Stipes Publishing Co., 1960.

Schneider, Raymond C., "Factors Affecting School Site." Ph.D. diss., Stanford University, 1955.

Schwehr, F. E., "Planning Educational Facilities," *Journal of Experimental Education,* 10 (February 1965), 101-103.

Sumption, Merle R., and Jack L. Landes, *Planning Functional School Buildings.* New York: Harper and Brothers, 1957.

19

Comparison of Two Central Administrative Agencies in Sport

Eric F. Broom

Introduction

The tremendous growth of international sport and the leisure explosion that now engulfs modern industrial societies have had a dramatic effect on the administrative structure of amateur sport and physical recreation. A predominant life style which demands decreasing physical effort and provides increasing discretionary time and income has resulted in a rapid rise in participation in a wide range of sports and physical recreation activities.

As a corollary, the functions of governing bodies of sport have extended far beyond their original role of controlling and organizing competition. Inevitably, the additional administrative demands of coaching and promotional activities has rapidly outgrown the capacity of voluntary officers. Kitchen-table administration no longer suffices. New structures are required to coordinate and service the activities of both the governing bodies and the growing government involvement in sport.

The modern central administrative agencies are primarily a post-1945 phenomenon, although their precursors appeared before the turn of the century. In 1969 the major recommendation in the *Report of the Task Force on Sport for Canadians* (Sports Council, p. 75) was for the establishment of a central

Eric F. Broom is from the University of British Columbia, Vancouver.

administrative agency for all nationally organized sports, to be known as Sport Canada. Further, the task force suggested that advantage should be taken of the experience of other countries by studying their organization.

With these recommendations in mind, and the belief that a structure similar to that envisioned by the task force had existed in England partially since 1935, and in entirety since 1965, a comparison of the central sports administration in the two countries was recently completed (Broom, 1971).

Background and Related Literature

Modern sport, as we know it, began to evolve in England in the mid-nineteenth century. Unlike her continental neighbors, whose power had been eroded by two centuries of intermittent wars on their soil, England was protected by her island position and powerful navy. The contrasting stability of life in England allowed the Industrial Revolution and the concomitant transportation revolution and increase in urbanization to occur much earlier there than elsewhere. For the first seventy years of the century, Britain virtually controlled world markets, and all levels of society prospered. Industrialization resulted in great social changes: the ancient rural-based social order gave way to an urban-oriented society; and, perhaps more significantly, a new class society was born with the middle class rising to power socially, politically, and economically. "There was a rise in the scale of human organizations, not only in industry, transport and commerce, but in almost every other social activity from religion to government" (Perkin, 1969, p. 134). Sport was no exception.

To attain their major aspiration of emulating the gentility of the aristocracy, the middle class turned to education. By mid-century they were firmly established in the ancient public schools, previously denied to them, and in these schools they refined, adapted, and organized sport and employed it as an important part of education. "Socially, the cult of athleticism was closely bound up with the rise of a new middle class to educational privilege and political power" (McIntosh, 1968, p. 16).

Sport in the second half of the century spread far beyond the schools and universities. The middle class welcomed the lower class to their sports with missionary zeal, provided they conformed to gentlemanly conduct. It was this insistence on fair play, as differences of rule interpretations and the initial problems of professionalism occurred, that initiated the drawing up of more formal rules and the institution of controlling bodies—a task which gave full rein to the organizing talents of the middle class. Governing bodies in many sports were first developed in England between 1860 and the end of the century (McIntosh, 1963, pp. 73-87).

Thus it was that the transition from sport as an occasional amusement to a system with rules, controlling bodies, organized clubs, and matches occurred in nineteenth-century England. A gamut of factors—constitutional government;

prolonged economic growth; the world lead in industrialization, transportation, urbanization and commerce; an absence of obligatory military training; and a terrain and climate which proffered ideal grass playing fields—made England the womb in which modern organized sport developed (Brailsford, 1969, p. 253; Huizinga, 1950, p. 197). A zealous, social, taste-dictating middle class which, as part of education, adapted, refined, organized, controlled, and disseminated sport, nurtured it to maturity.

In the last third of the century games and sports that had been refined and organized in England were taken abroad by colonial administrators, missionaries, soldiers, sailors, merchants, settlers, and visitors (McIntosh, 1963, pp. 80-85). The paramount influence in the early development of sport in Canada was provided by British army garrisons. Under their guidance, clubs and governing bodies were established in the image of those in the old country. The subsequent patterns of sports development in the two countries, while retaining much of their common foundation, have had their unique characteristics molded by the influence of a number of factors: climate, geography, demography, education, culture, and politics, among others.

National governing bodies of sport in Canada, like their English predecessors, became necessary because of differing rule interpretations and the incursion of professionalism. In England, burgeoning commercialism was checked and firmly controlled only because of the great power of a middle class imbued with the amateur ideal. However, as McIntosh states, "the public schools which were closely associated with athleticism in Britain were copied only spasmodically and imperfectly elsewhere" (1963, pp. 85-86). In consequence, Canada, like other countries, lacked a large influential middle class whose education had inculcated the values of sports participation, who had the desire to organize, control, and disseminate sports for the benefit of the mass of the population, and who were dedicated to amateurism.

The great battle between amateurism and professionalism, which began in Canada in the latter half of the nineteenth century, has been repercussive ever since. All sports were to see the effect of this creeping professionalism—ice hockey, rowing, track and field, lacrosse, cycling, and swimming in particular, and against such a background amateur sports bodies endeavored to solve status problems (Howell and Howell, 1969, pp. 150-52). In 1884 a number of sports bodies formed an association, later to be known as the Canadian Amateur Athletic Union, whose prime purpose was to combat professionalism. The Amateur Athletic Union (USA), the Dansk Idraets-Forbund (Danish Sports Federation), and the Sveriges Riksidrottsförbund (Swedish Sports Federation) were established in 1879, 1896, and 1903 for precisely the same reasons. These organizations, specifically designed to protect the amateur code, were the first manifestations of central administrative agencies. It is of significance that no such organization was established in England.

In England in the 1930s, mass unemployment stimulated the formation and activation of sports bodies to provide recreative physical activity, and in 1935 the Central Council of Physical Recreation (CCPR), a voluntary association of sports bodies, was established to coordinate and service the program. The Canadian Sports Advisory Council, later to become the Sports Federation of Canada, was formed in 1951. Unlike its English counterpart, it did not offer technical and administrative services; its role was confined to acting as the voice of sport. These two organizations are examples of modern central administrative agencies.

Government involvement in sport in England started with the Physical Training and Recreation Act in 1937, and in Canada with the National Physical Fitness Act in 1943, although some funds were made available through earlier Acts for physical training programs to maintain health and morale. From 1945 on, sports bodies and the CCPR in England were the recipients of government grants. In Canada the government became similarly involved with the passing of the Fitness and Amateur Sport Act in 1961. Under this Act the National Advisory Council was formed to advise the government, and the Fitness and Amateur Sport Directorate was established within the Department of National Health and Welfare to administer the program.

At opposite extremes of the 1960s, reports on amateur sport were published in England and Canada. Both investigations were prompted by the general and growing feeling that some new initiative was required in sport to enable it to expand and develop in the light of present-day needs and standards. It is significant that the study in England was commissioned by a voluntary association, the Central Council of Physical Recreation; that in Canada by the federal government. This difference of origin had far-reaching effects in the implementation of the recommendations. Long-delayed action occurred in England, in contrast to rapid implementation in Canada.

The Report of the Wolfenden Committee, *Sport and the Community,* was issued in 1960; that of the *Task Force on Sport for Canadians* in 1969. In both reports the central and major recommendations expressed the need for the establishment of a national organization which would be at the very heart of the central administrative structure of amateur sport and physical recreation. The Sports Council was established in England to advise the government on matters relating to sports development in January 1965. In Canada, the Fitness and Amateur Sport Directorate became Sport Canada and Recreation Canada in 1971. The structure and functions of these and associated central administrative agencies of amateur sport and physical recreation are outlined herein.

Research Methodology and Techniques

In this study the National Advisory Council, the Fitness and Amateur Sport Directorate (now subdivided into Sport Canada and Recreation Canada), and the Sports Federation of Canada at national level, and one selected provincial agency, the British Columbia Sports Federation in Canada, were examined in relation to the corresponding organizations, the Sports Council and the Central Council of Physical Recreation, at national and one selected regional level, in England.

The data required for the study were obtained from personal interviews of senior officers of the agencies under review; documentary analysis of official reports and records; and structured, mailed questionnaires which were sent to national and selected county/provincial governing bodies of sport in both countries. A majority of questionnaire items were designed to elicit evaluative responses on a five-point scale. Completed questionnaires were returned by 75 percent of 113 national and county associations in England and 72 percent of 86 corresponding bodies in Canada.

The organization of the data was made within a sociological theoretical framework developed by Talcott Parsons (1965, pp. 16-96). The model defined three organizational systems and delineated a series of categories under which the structural and functional characteristics of the agencies were examined at national, regional, and local levels. The four stages of Bereday's method—description, interpretation, juxtaposition, and comparison—were employed in the comparative analysis (Bereday, 1964, pp. 11-27).

Findings and Conclusions

STRUCTURE

Terms of Reference. 1. Both the National Advisory Council (NAC) in Canada and the Sports Council in England were established to advise their respective governments on the policy of sports development. The NAC has remained an advisory body and its sphere of influence was severely curtailed in 1970 when its role of advising on grant aid was transferred to the Fitness and Amateur Sport Directorate (FASD). In contrast, the Sports Council became an independent body with its own royal charter in 1971 and assumed complete responsibility for the dispensation of grants to sport.

2. The clearly defined terms of reference of the Sports Council and the Central Council of Physical Recreation (CCPR) in England and the partnership between them contrasts strongly with the vague terms of reference—and the resultant persistent role conflict and illusory relationship—of the NAC and the FASD in Canada.

Organizational Structure. 1. A comparison of the organizational structures of the individual agencies in the two countries reveals that the Sports Council corresponds closely to the NAC (although the latter has no infrastructure to compare with the regional and local sports councils); the CCPR headquarters committee structure corresponds to the Sports Federation of Canada (SF of C); the CCPR headquarters office structure corresponds very closely to the FASD; and an individual region of the CCPR corresponds to the British Columbia Sports Federation (BCSF). (Not all provinces in Canada had sports federations when this study was completed in August 1971, and there is no Canadian structure to correspond to the National Sports Centers in England.)

2. The nine regional sports councils in England (autonomous councils exist in Wales and Scotland) are, in essence, extensions of the Facilities Planning Committee, one of the four committees of the Sports Council. These advisory councils are designed to promote cooperation and coordination in the provision of sports facilities within and between regions and, through the Sports Council, to advise the government.

In England and Canada alike, the main responsibility for development of facilities for sport and physical recreation rests at local level, and in view of this a large majority of members of regional sports councils represent local authorities. The day-to-day work of each council is carried out by an executive committee and a technical panel, the latter comprising the planning officers of each local authority supported by technical experts in sport and physical education.

Sports body representation varies with the size of each council, but in general it includes three members from each of outdoor sports, indoor sports, outdoor activities, and women's sports, and one each from the regional CCPR and the National Playing Fields Association. All sports representatives are elected by regional standing conferences of sports bodies, which were formed specifically for this purpose. The meetings of these bodies provide opportunities for diverse sports interests to understand one another's requirements and to express a combined view on regional provision of facilities. This cooperation between sports associations has made an invaluable contribution toward the integration of sports development. The isolationism in British sport, which has existed since the national associations were formed one hundred-odd years ago, and which similarly exists in Canada, is finally being broken down.

At local level in England, local sports advisory councils bring together the providers and users of sports facilities with the object of promoting more effective relations between sports bodies and local authorities in the provision and optimum use of all types of facility. Each of the more than 500 local councils that already exist cooperates with its umbrella regional sports council.

3. The second pillar of the structure in England is formed by what was formerly known as the Central Council of Physical Recreation. From its inception in 1935 the CCPR operated as a voluntary organization, but in 1972 it transferred its staff and facilities to the Sports Council, while retaining its role as the voice of its member bodies. This development formalized a coalescence which began with the establishment of the Sports Council in 1965 when a number of key personnel were given dual appointments in both organizations.

In composition the CCPR headquarters staff over the last twenty years—some twenty-odd full-time administrative and technical officers with additional secretarial personnel—contrasts markedly with the first salaried executive director of the SF of C, appointed in 1971, but corresponds closely to the staff of the FASD. There are fundamental differences between the bodies in the two countries. The CCPR is both the combined voice of sport and the executive arm of the Sports Council. In Canada the SF of C performs the former, and the FASD the latter role. Second, both the CCPR and the SF of C are national voluntary organizations, while the FASD is a federal government agency.

4. In addition to its headquarters office, the CCPR operates through nine regional offices in areas whose boundaries were adopted by the regional sports councils, branch offices in Wales and Northern Ireland, and eight residential national sports centers. Each regional office is staffed by six to eight full-time male and female technical representatives. In Canada, the provincial sports federations, which have developed as microcosms of the SF of C since 1967, correspond to the CCPR regional offices, but they are very understaffed by comparison, and their autonomy and the tenuous relationship with the SF of C precludes the concerted policy that characterizes the CCPR. There are no national sports centers in Canada.

5. The nationwide, integrated structure of the Sports Council and the CCPR in England is in strong contrast to the fragmentation of the corresponding bodies in Canada. In England there is a strong link between the Sports Council and the regional and local sports councils, and at each of the three levels there is horizontal articulation with the CCPR which services all three councils. At each level the governing bodies of sport are closely involved; nationally through membership of the CCPR; regionally through the standing conferences of sport; and locally through the local sports advisory councils. In Canada the NAC is isolated from the provinces, and the national governing bodies and agencies, and its link with the FASD is tenuous. The SF of C has no regional organization and its relationship with the provincial sports federations is weak. Further, the FASD was confined until 1970 to the federal sphere, although it now has single representatives in Montreal, Winnipeg, and Vancouver. These differences that are illustrated in *Figure 1* are reflected in the functional aspects of the organizations for, in sport, no less than in other facets of modern society, structure determines function.

FUNCTIONS: SPORTS COUNCIL
NATIONAL ADVISORY COUNCIL

Advisory 1. a. The Sports Council, up to 1971, and the NAC until 1969, advised their governments on the policy of awarding grants. Direct comparisons are not always possible, but in the five-year period 1965-66 to 1970-71 some expenditures are noteworthy.

b. In England $7.4 million was allocated to national bodies for administra-

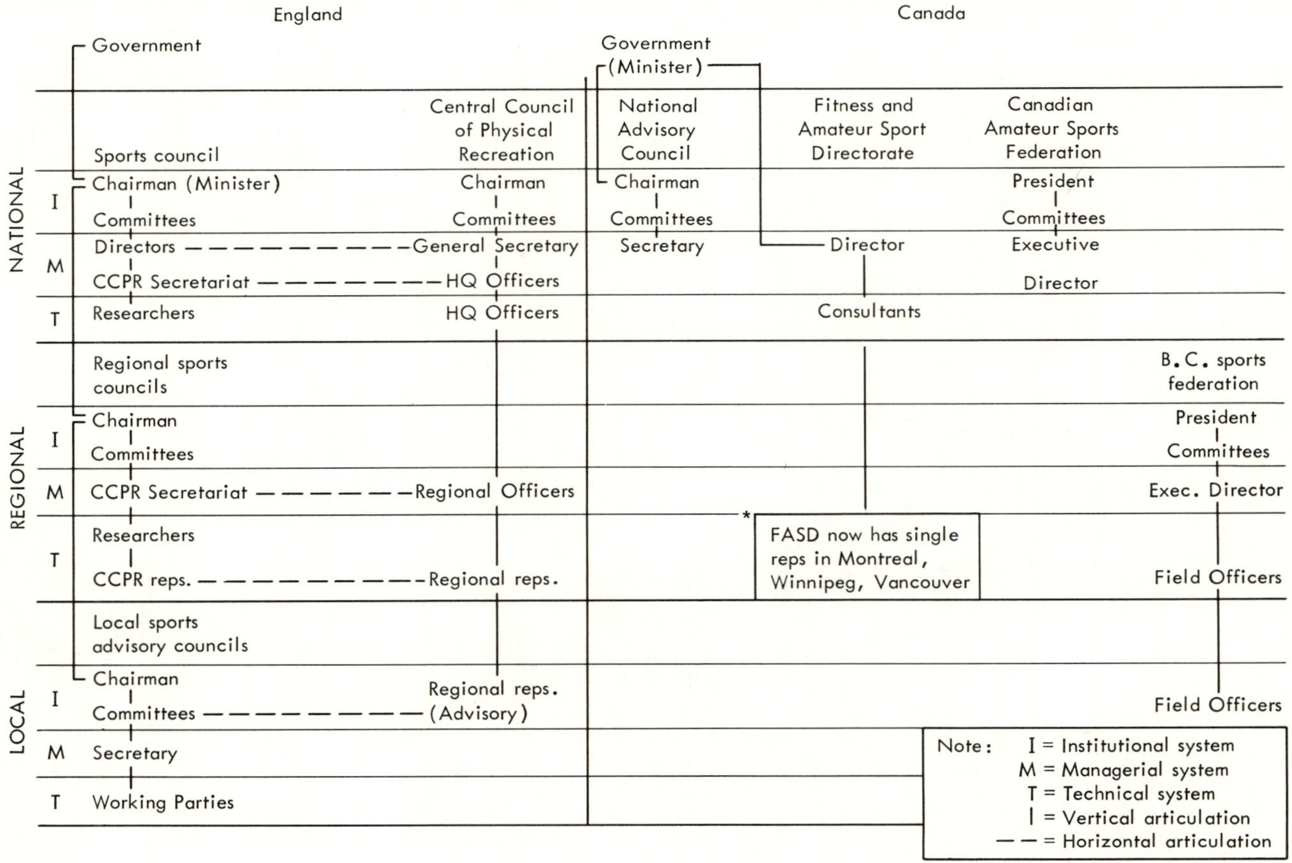

Figure 1. Organizational Systems of the Central Administrative Agencies of Amateur Sport and Physical Recreation in England and Canada, January 1971.

tion and coaching. Of that sum $2.1 million was granted to 57 national bodies and 17 national schools associations, and $5.3 million to the CCPR. During the same period in Canada $3.3 million was awarded to 44 national agencies for similar purposes. (An additional sum of approximately $1.9 million was appropriated for the operational expenses of the FASD, and a further $7.1 million was provided by a federal/provincial agreement on a 60-40 basis.) In 1967-68, 46 bodies in England employed professional administrative personnel, whereas in Canada only 4 did so. Additionally, some 50 full-time professional national coaches were employed in England as compared to 4 bodies with professional coaches in Canada. Further, the CCPR in 1969 employed 124 administrative personnel as well as complementary secretarial staffs.

It should be noted that the period under study was prior to the establishment of the Administrative Center for Sport and Recreation in Ottawa, where the executive officers, support staff, and office expenses of 33 national associations are covered by a government grant.

c. The total grants awarded in England for competition was $628,375; the corresponding figure in Canada was $8.2 million. Canada, unlike England, gives grants to national championships, and in this period hosted the Pan American Games.

d. In England the total research budget was $206,919; while in Canada it was $1.7 million. The major research emphasis in England has been on sociological factors of supply and demand of facilities, patterns of participation—both individual and family, and a fuller understanding of their implications for the design, planning, and management of facilities. In marked contrast, research in Canada has been predominantly concerned with physiology and more than 80 percent of the 120 research grants awarded by the NAC between 1962 and 1970 were in this area.

e. Scholarship grants in England accounted for $10,615; in Canada the sum of $1.8 million was awarded, primarily for undergraduate and graduate study. In England education grants are not normally awarded by the Sports Council. The period under review does not include the $100,000 awarded in 1970-71 and the $1.0 million in 1971-72 for student-athlete grants-in-aid in Canada.

f. Expenditure on facilities by the Sports Council was $9.3 million (not taking into account $104.8 million allocated for facilities in England and Wales through loan sanctions to local authorities). In Canada $1.2 million was expended from federal sources during the same period. This figure does not include the $600,000 jointly contributed by Nova Scotia, Halifax, and Dartmouth toward the capital costs of the first Canada Summer Games, or other provincial and local expenditure on facilities.

2. On behalf of the Sports Council, the regional sports councils advise local authorities and voluntary organizations on the scale of provision and priorities for facilities in their area. The local sports advisory councils keep the local authorities attuned to the sporting needs of their citizens.

3. The Sports Council was instrumental in the establishment of the

Technical Unit for Sport in 1968, whose purpose is to collate information, design sports facilities, publish on such matters, and to advise local government and other interested bodies. A similar agency was suggested by the Task Force on Sport for Canadians, but no action has been taken.

Coordination. 1. The coordination of central government departments, statutory bodies, and local authorities, among whom is dispersed the responsibility for the provision and improvement of facilities, is a primary function of the Facilities Planning Committee of the Sports Council. It is recognized that adequate provision is too large a task to be undertaken in isolation. The circular *Provision of Facilities for Sport* in 1964 drew attention to the possibility of obtaining better value for money by combining educational with other local authority or voluntary resources to provide sports facilities for use by both students and the general public. A second circular in 1970, *The Chance to Share: Cooperation in the Provision of Facilities for Educational Establishments and the Community,* provided procedural guidelines and examples of dual provision. *Planning for Sport,* a guide to local authorities for their provision of facilities, was published in 1968.

In Canada the FASD rather than the NAC is the federal agency that cooperates with provincial and local governments to provide facilities, primarily through the biannual Canada Games. This arrangement has the severe limitation of a very slow rate of provision.

2. Between 1965 and 1970 the regional sports councils conducted comprehensive surveys and follow-up appraisals of existing facilities and future needs covering the whole country. From the series of publications containing these results, and further research which emanated from them, has emerged a national picture of the supply and demand of facilities. In Canada nationwide surveys of facilities were carried out in the summers of 1971 and 1972, but very little data has been published.

3. Based on the aggregation of studies, the Sports Council in 1972 published *Provision for Sport,* an objective assessment of the country's needs in sports and recreational facilities that is projected to 1981. This initial report, which deals only with indoor swimming pools, indoor sports centers, and golf courses, estimates that the total expenditure required for the three types of facilities is $634 million at present prices. It is estimated that other types of facilities will necessitate an expenditure of $200 million. In Canada the task force recommended that a comprehensive development plan, which incorporated shared costs and financial incentives to encourage upgrading of existing facilities, be developed in consultation with all levels of government. However, this recommendation has not been acted upon.

Functions: Central Council of Physical Recreation
Fitness and Amateur Sport Directorate
Sports Federation of Canada
British Columbia Sports Federation

Coordination. 1. Amateur sport in both countries has developed during the past one hundred years in a fragmentary manner. In England the CCPR has had considerable success in a coordinating role through its executive committee structure, which brings together various interest groups; through the organization of conferences which foster cooperation between different agencies; and by acting as a forum for members' views. Neither the FASD or the SF of C have been active in this area, except the latter body acting as a forum for members' views. The formation of regional standing conferences of sports bodies, local advisory sports councils, and the organization of numerous conferences further exemplify the CCPR's coordinating role. In British Columbia the Sports Federation's coordinating function is discharged by its acting as the voice of sport and guiding the multifarious activities of the annual Sports Festival. The CCPR was rated as considerably more effective in its coordinating role than its Canadian counterparts.

2. The availability of grants to provincial governing bodies—initially through the federal-provincial agreement, and more recently in British Columbia from the provincial government—has been a major contributing factor in the rapid development of the organization of these agencies. Financial restrictions have prohibited similar developments in England.

Advisory. 1. The advisory service in both countries is mainly in the technical, administrative, financial, and legislative spheres. Prior to the mid-1960s the service in England was primarily utilized by the governing bodies and included advice on establishing coaching schemes and certification standards, and employing and utilizing professional coaches. Since 1965 there has been a great increase in the number of public and private agencies seeking advice on the provision and management of facilities, both on land and water, and the CCPR has accumulated a vast fund of expertise. CCPR officers also serve in an advisory capacity on regional and local sports councils and on the coaching committees of many sports bodies.

In comparison, the FASD advisory role has been predominantly concerned with the Fitness and Amateur Sport Program which, because of constitutional rights, restricts its sphere of influence to the national level of governing bodies, and has relatively little contact with provincial and local government. The development of integrated coaching schemes, coaches' certification, professional technical directors, and advice on facilities has occupied a minor place in the program. The wider advisory role of the CCPR was rated by the governing bodies as considerably more valuable than that offered by the two Canadian bodies.

Administrative Services. 1. The CCPR acts as the secretariat and executive arm of the Sports Council, regional sports councils, and the regional standing conferences of sport, whereas the FASD performs the same functions for the NAC. The close relationship that exists between the bodies in England is not apparent in Canada.

2. Thirteen of the smaller national governing bodies rent office accommo-

dations in the CCPR headquarters complex, but the concept of an administrative center for all bodies has never proved attractive to the larger, well-established bodies with their own traditional headquarters. The accommodation and services offered by the CCPR do not compare with those available, since 1970, to thirty-three national agencies in the Administrative Center for Sport and Recreation in Ottawa. This study was conducted too soon after the establishment of the administrative center to be able to yield a valid assessment of its value to sports associations.

3. The CCPR offers extensive administrative and technical assistance, mainly at the regional level, to governing bodies in connection with their coaching schemes. These services are primarily concerned with the administration of the work of national coaches and with training courses for amateur coaches. There are few of the close to thirty national coaching schemes with whose operation the CCPR is not, or has not been, closely connected. The CCPR policy of assisting organizations to assume more administrative responsibility is illustrated by examining coaches' training courses in the three-year period 1964-65 to 1966-67. Although the total number of courses increased from 616 to 654, courses administered by the CCPR decreased from 485 to 389. The services to coaching schemes were considered to be valuable by a large majority of both national and county bodies. In Canada similar services by the FASD and the BCSF are in a very early stage of development, but a large majority of both national and provincial bodies expressed the view that such a service would be valuable to them.

Promotion. 1. The organization and administration of instructional courses for beginners and more advanced performers has been an important part of the CCPR work since it began in 1935. Regional courses in more than fifty activities extend either over a weekend or eight to ten evening sessions. They are held in schools, colleges, parks, sports clubs, and industrial and military facilities, and are staffed, under CCPR supervision, by amateur coaches who hold the coaching award of a governing body. The CCPR policy encourages many different agencies, such as further education departments, parks departments, local sports councils, and sports clubs to assume administrative responsibility when courses are firmly established. Approximately 50,000 men and women of all ages attend the close to 2,000 CCPR regional courses each year, and many times that number attend similar courses arranged by other agencies. During the summer months the CCPR leases eight to ten colleges, hotels, and sailing clubs at which are organized a series of one-week instructional holiday courses in a wide range of activities and levels of performance. The courses attract close to 1,500 persons each year, and the introduction of programs that cater to the whole family are leading to a rapid increase in numbers. At both national and regional levels the promotional aspects of the CCPR are much more extensive than those arranged in Canada. The FASD has organized a series of Cross-Canada demonstration clinics and other demonstrations, and the BCSF coordinates an annual provincewide sports festival. The value of these services in England was warmly acknowledged by governing bodies at both levels, and a large proportion of Canadian provincial and national bodies expressed a need for similar assistance.

Publicity/Communications. 1. Details of all CCPR activities are disseminated through an Information Service to 7,000 members. For an annual fee of $2.50, subscribers receive full details of all national events, all courses in the members' area, and four issues of the CCPR journal, *Sport and Recreation.*

2. On behalf of the Sports Council the CCPR publishes the quarterly *Sports Development Bulletin,* which contains details of legislation and government policy on sport, reports on design and costs of new facilities, dual provision developments, and research reports on participation patterns and supply and demand of facilities. Some 30,000 copies of the bulletin are distributed free of charge to the members of regional and local sports councils; local planning officers, town clerks, parks departments, and physical education organizers; and governing bodies of sport officers at all levels, thus keeping a large segment of the population well-informed on matters relating to the development of sport. The publicity/communications functions of the CCPR were assessed by the governing bodies to be of considerably more value than those of either the FASD or the BCSF and 95 percent of Canadian respondents indicated that the type of information contained in the *Sports Development Bulletin* would be valuable to their association.

Sports Centers. 1. The predominant use of the national sports centers in England is for coaches' training courses, training at all levels from beginner to international, and conferences. In 1969-70 the five centers then operating accommodated 905 courses which provided 90,303 days training for 23,752 people in residence. During the same year, Crystal Palace in London was used on a nonresidential basis for periods of up to one day by 451,269 persons.

A large number of English governing bodies reported that the National Sports Centers had made a valuable contribution to the development of their sport. By way of contrast, only ten bodies in Canada indicated that a training center was available to them, but 86 percent expressed the need for such centers.

2. The outstanding success of the English national sports centers has been tempered somewhat by the problem of maximizing use of facilities, including residence, during midweek, both daytime and evening. It is clear that centers are best at sites close to large urban populations, although this is not always possible for specialist centers in such activities as mountaineering. Urban centers may be used by nonresident school children during the day and adults in the evenings, but this is only a partial solution to the problem. In both countries the almost unanimous view of governing bodies was that the need for sports centers could best be met by the development of a planned pattern comprising local centers, one multisports center in each province/region, and a series of specialist centers.

CONCLUSIONS

On the basis of the findings of this study the following conclusions would appear to have merit:

1. On the whole, the findings of this study supported the hypothesis that the development of the structure and functions of the central administrative agencies of amateur sport and physical recreation in Canada in recent years has, fundamentally, been parallel to that of the corresponding agencies in England one or two decades earlier.

2. The nationwide integrated structure of the Sports Council and the CCPR in England, which in 1972 fused into one body under the former name,* is in strong contrast to the fragmentation of the corresponding bodies in Canada, and in consequence the functions of the latter have severe inherent limitations.

3. It is clear that in both countries the costs of providing opportunities for all members of society to participate in amateur sport and physical recreation is far beyond the present means of the governing bodies of sport. National, regional, and local government assistance is a necessity. There appear to be four factors which the central administrative agencies must provide in order for the sound development of amateur sport and physical recreation to occur: (1) grants-in-aid, (2) administrative services, (3) technical services, and (4) facilities. Based on the findings of this study it is concluded that:

　　a. In the five-year period 1965-66 to 1969-70, considerable differences were apparent in grant expenditure in the two countries, most noticeably in the emphasis in England on facilities and in Canada on competition. Further, in comparison with Canada, England obtained considerably better value for money in the areas of administration, coaching, and development.

　　b. The establishment of the Administrative Center for Sport and Recreation in Ottawa, thus separating the executive directors from the honorary officers of sports associations, is a bold experiment.

　　c. The technical services offered by the CCPR in England to governing bodies and other agencies at national, regional, and local levels has been a key factor in the development of amateur sport and physical recreation. A similar service is notably lacking in Canada.

　　d. The lack of a nationwide assessment of facilities needs and a cost-sharing agreement for the provision of facilities has provided a major obstacle to the further development of amateur sport and physical recreation in Canada.

　　e. The location of the early English national sports centers some distance from large conurbations precludes maximum use. Further, although midweek, daytime use of urban-sited centers may be increased by transporting school children, optimum use of all facilities is only possible when the centers have access to on-the-spot user populations.

*The new CCPR retains its role as the voice of its member associations, and advises the Sports Council.

Implications for the Practicing Administrator

The findings and conclusions of this study suggest the following implications have merit for the practicing administrator:

1. If the parts of an organization are to complement the whole, the terms of reference of each part must be clearly delineated and mutually understood. The partnership of the English central administrative agencies and the contrasting role conflict of their Canadian counterparts illustrate this principle.

2. If a single or series of associated organizations is to achieve optimum efficiency, the parts must form an integrated whole. Such a structure facilitates a two-way flow of ideas and information, and involves concerned personnel at all levels. The coordination of the English central administrative agencies exemplify such an integrated structure, in contrast to the fragmentation of the Canadian organizations.

3. When a central agency is responsible for assisting a large number of organizations to attain a widespread objective, it can be most effective by adopting a catalytic role. In the case of the further development of amateur sport and physical recreation, as described herein, the wide range of services—advisory, coordinating, administrative, promotional, publicity, and communications—offered by the CCPR, and the smaller range provided by the FASD and SF of C, are examples of this role.

4. When a deficiency or problem occurs it is best remedied by adherence to the planning principles of identification, evaluation, and the formulation and execution of a sound policy. The lack of facilities in England was identified and evaluated by comprehensive surveys, and from further supply and demand studies have emerged an objective assessment of the country's needs and a policy for meeting them.

5. In the decision-making process every effort must be made to involve a maximum number of concerned persons, particularly those at an operational level. This principle is illustrated by the involvement of sports clubs, governing bodies, and local government at local and regional sports council levels in England in the location, design, and recommendation of sports facilities to the national Sports Council.

6. If the procedure described above is to consistently produce wise decisions, it is imperative that those making the decisions be kept well-informed in all pertinent areas. This is achieved by ensuring that every member of each level of sports council, and a much wider public, receives regular input on such matters as details of policy, reports on the design and costs of new facilities, dual provision developments, multiple use of facilities, and research reports on participation patterns and supply and demand of facilities through the *Sports Development Bulletin*, a quarterly publication of the CCPR.

General Bibliography

Bereday, George Z. F., *Comparative Method in Education.* New York: Holt, Rinehart and Winston, Inc., 1964.

Brailsford, Dennis, *Sport and Society.* London: Routledge & Kegan Paul, 1969.

Broom, Eric F., "A Comparative Analysis of the Central Administrative Agencies of Amateur Sport and Physical Recreation in England and Canada." Ph.D. diss., University of Illinois, 1971. (Available through Microform Publications, HPER, University of Oregon, 1973.)

Department of Education and Science, *Provision of Facilities for Sport.* London: August 27, 1964.

———, *The Chance to Share.* London: February 2, 1970.

Department of National Health and Welfare, *A Proposed Sports Policy for Canadians.* Ottawa: March 20, 1970.

———, *Sport Canada: Recreation Canada.* Ottawa: May 7, 1971.

Fitness and Amateur Sport Act. Ottawa: The Queen's Printer, 1961.

Howell, Nancy, and Maxwell L. Howell, *Sports and Games in Canadian Life: 1700 to the Present.* Toronto: Macmillan of Canada, 1969.

Huizinga, Johan, *Homo Ludens—A Study of the Play Element in Culture.* Boston: Beacon Press, 1950.

McIntosh, P. C., *Sport in Society.* London: C. A. Watts & Co. Ltd., 1963.

———, *Physical Education in England Since 1800.* London: G. Bell and Sons, Ltd., 1968.

Parsons, Talcott, *Structure and Process in Modern Societies,* 4th ed. New York: Free Press, 1965.

Perkin, Harold, *The Origins of Modern English Society.* London: Routledge and Kegan Paul, 1969.

Semotiuk, Darwin Michael, "The Development of a Theoretical Framework for Analyzing the Role of National Government Involvement in Sport and Physical Education and its Application to Canada." Ph.D. diss., Ohio State University, 1970.

Sport and the Community, the Report of the Wolfenden Committee on Sport. London, England: CCPR, 1960.

Sports Council, *Planning for Sport,* report of a Working Party on Scale of Provisions. London, England: CCPR, 1968.

———, *Provision for Sport.* London, England: HMSO, 1972.

———, *Sports Development Bulletin* (Quarterly publication). London, England, 1967-71.

———, *The Sports Council: A Report, November 1966.* London, England, 1966.

———, *The Sports Council: A Review, 1966-69.* London, England, 1969.

Task Force on Sport for Canadians. Ottawa: The Queen's Printer, 1969.

20

An Analysis of Employment Theory and Practice

Emory F. Luck

Introduction

The American educational picture is characteristically a very dynamic one. It is the largest single business in this country. Institutions of higher learning in the United States are expected to double their facilities by the year 1980 in order to accommodate the numbers of students who will be seeking advanced educational opportunities. The great American experiment in education is to get a high percentage of its population involved in higher education, a significantly higher number than perhaps any other country. The expansion of the junior colleges and community colleges certainly speaks of change in the higher education picture.

Increasing enrollments are causing acute demands for faculty. Therefore, the professional preparation and recruiting of a larger number of qualified instructors to serve these masses is imperative. This in effect means that there should be an upward mobility of college faculty members as a result of this challenge to higher education, and there is a sense of urgency as colleges and universities strive to build staffs of size and quality.

It has long been recognized by college physical educators that there is great mobility among coaches and a great amount of mobility among professors.

Emory F. Luck is from Northern Illinois University, DeKalb, Illinois.

Efforts have been made to study certain phases of employment practices in "academia," but no serious attention has been given to meaningful investigation concerning the hiring practices in physical education and coaching on the college level. It is becoming increasingly difficult for administrators of physical education to maintain any large degree of professional competence without a body of knowledge about administrative theory and its application to education and physical education as well.

Education administrators have recognized that the hiring processes *should* be based upon some valid preconceived guidelines. In the past these guidelines have been fairly consistent, but not too scientific. In a study by Samuel Stauffer and associates (1954, pp. 197-209), it was found that Harvard evaluates candidates by naming an ad hoc committee for each vacancy. Ralph Epstein in his study "The Technique of Making University Appointments" (1949) concluded that in nearly all cases in which poor choices are made for faculty and administrative posts, inadequate selection procedures were the reason.

There are quite a few publications in the area of educational administration which treat the hiring of teaching personnel. Henry Herge attacks the problem from the standpoint of the intellectual and personal factors which make the candidate attractive to an administrator (1965). Robert Williams in his text speaks in terms of hiring as dependent upon the educational tone and quality of the institution in years to come. He states that authority to initiate appointments rests with the faculty; consequently, the faculty that recommends the appointment must live with its mistakes. He discusses the policies that departments follow in making appointments, and also explains the qualifications of tentative staff members (1966).

Howard Marshall, an economist, has provided an excellent point of departure from which one can initiate an exploration of the hiring processes. Motivation for this article was provided when he was faced with the need for recruiting three people to fill vacancies at Vassar. He attempted to find out how economists, seeking academic positions, and their employers found each other (1964).

Diekhoff has conducted extensive research on the subject of faculty men and women in education departments throughout the East. His concern deals with conditions of faculty employment. He concludes that the morale and effectiveness of college faculties depend upon their belief in their work and on other more basic conditions of employment (1965).

Administrative decisions should be based upon concrete evidence resulting from sound research and investigation. Physical education has begun to move toward investigation related to administrative theory, as evidenced by two recent dissertations by Marcia Spaeth (1967) and William Penny (1968). These efforts indicate the beginning of a trend toward building an effective line of communication among administrators that will allow for the acceptance of basic concepts that all administrators could possibly use as operative guidelines.

Background and Related Literature

Review of the literature would seem to indicate that higher education, including physical education, is just emerging from the early stages of the process of developing a definitive body of knowledge and technique. In general, the group of studies that is directly related to higher education reflects the growing concern for a greater degree of standardization in the area of definition of teacher qualifications, both for selection and promotion; a need for development of employment practices that will encourage more efficient allocation of professional talent; and a need for development of more sophisticated and sensitive techniques of education administration, in order to guarantee greater job satisfaction, less waste of human resources, and increased stability in the overall employment picture in institutions of higher learning.

Later studies do point toward both a significant recognition of the need for a theoretical framework for use on a practical level and an effort to develop such a process, but they also indicate that educational institutions have some distance to go to achieve this goal.

Material reviewed would seem to indicate that development of a definitive theory of employment practice has reached a considerably higher level in the business world. Techniques available for use in the total employment process, from job analysis through forecasting of needs, establishment of performance standards and qualifications, and selection and retention of personnel, have reached a fairly high degree of complexity and sophistication. Definitive findings have been made to determine the best methods for predicting and measuring leadership capabilities and overall job performance, and objective techniques have been developed and standardized for use in such measurement. Moreover, research in business has found certain factors that are reliable in the analysis of job satisfaction and dissatisfaction, and procedures have been determined that prove successful in the management of such areas as promotion, contract agreements, retirement, etc. In short, a quantitative and qualitative body of knowledge appears to be available for use both by the candidate for employment in business and the agency seeking personnel.

Only one study was found that related specifically to college and university physical education, a study which, while valuable, was concerned only with qualifications for the chief administrative officer of physical education in institutions of higher education.

Given the above set of circumstances—i.e., the embryonic state of employment theory and practice in higher education in general and physical education in particular—the need for further study seems evident. Because the writer's particular field of interest is physical education, the primary concern here will be to determine the practices used in the Big Ten universities in the employment of teaching personnel in physical education. The assumption is that the stated operational procedures, presumably important and relevant, will represent an underlying "employment theory." What actually occurs in practice, however, may well be another matter. (If there is indeed considerable discrepancy between theory and practice it would be well to discover this fact.)

Research Methodology and Techniques

Status studies involving determination of certain aspects of our educational system have become increasingly popular. In fact, large foundations have often encouraged such efforts through grants. In this way a firm basis for comparison and future evaluation is being laid. Although the theory and practice of sample surveys was developed in other fields, education has come to make extensive use of this approach to research.

The purpose of the present investigation was to examine the employment theory and practice within the field of physical education in the Big Ten (Western Conference) universities. We were concerned with (1) the occurrence of vacancies; (2) the search for replacements; and (3) the hiring procedures followed. This information was obtained through the application of certain research techniques (documentary analysis, interview questionnaire, and mailed questionnaire) to the five subproblem areas as follows:

1. Policy of the American Association of University Professors (as approved);
2. University policy (as explained in statutes and operational manuals);
3. Departmental policy (as stated by administrators);
4. How the interviewees (recently engaged faculty) see the above-stated policies in operation;
5. How the total faculty in physical education see these policies operating (as expressed in return of mailed questionnaires).

An effort was made to examine available data that related to the matter of employment within the Big Ten institutions. This included the statutes, job descriptions as they were circulated on notices of vacancies, and operational manuals used by administrators of physical education departments. The *AAUP Bulletin,* a publication of the American Association of University Professors, was also investigated to search out AAUP policy as it relates to employment. A systematic examination of the above documents of the AAUP was undertaken using as a focal point the 1940 specific bulletin which set forth the statement of principles from which the present policies have evolved.

INTERVIEW TECHNIQUE

A letter was written to department heads or chairmen of divisions of physical education for men in the Big Ten (Western Conference) universities requesting permission to conduct interviews with each of them and with the three most recently hired full-time faculty members.

CONSTRUCTION OF THE QUESTIONNAIRE

As a means of developing an instrument which could be employed in this investigation, the writer held a series of discussion with the University of Illinois Survey Research Laboratory.

The questionnaire, developed by the author, was an adaptation of one used in *The Mobile Professors* (Brown, 1967). The instrument was administered to two former heads of departments (education and physical education). Based upon the results of conversations with these two professors, the instrument was altered slightly. The altered product was then returned to the Survey Research Laboratory and, after more discussions, certain other changes were made in order to develop an instrument which it was felt would serve the purposes intended.

SURVEY PROCEDURE

All academic personnel who held full-time teaching positions (including those who coach) in the physical education colleges or departments in the Big Ten universities were sent copies of the specially prepared instrument. A packet which included a letter of explanation, a direction sheet, the questionnaire, and a self-addressed, stamped return envelope was coded by letter and number and mailed to every person who qualified in accordance with the criteria mentioned above. The code was used to insure anonymity and to facilitate follow-up procedure. A total of 227 questionnaires were mailed, and three weeks later a follow-up letter was sent as a reminder to those who had overlooked, or who had not received or returned, the questionnaire.

ANALYSIS OF DATA

Because this investigation was concerned with (1) the occurrence of vacancies, (2) the search for replacements, and (3) the hiring procedures followed, the analyses will categorize the findings of the *research literature, the AAUP, the Big Ten,* and *the administrators* in terms of the three concerns, using a theoretical framework. Each category was also analyzed in terms of the findings of the series of interviews personally conducted by the writer and questionnaires distributed to the remainder of the faculties (as described above), using the actual stated practices as a framework. There was also a comparison made of all the findings in terms of agreement, partial agreement, and no agreement. Finally, by using the areas of *agreement, partial agreement,* and *no agreement,* there was a comparison of theory as espoused in the literature, by the AAUP, by the Big Ten universities, and by the administrators of physical education in the Big Ten colleges or divisions as opposed to actual practices as stated by a cross-section of the most recently hired, full-time faculty members by means of the interviews, and as viewed by the remainder of the faculty from the responses to the mailed questionnaire.

Findings and Conclusions

FINDINGS

The two schedules that were used by both chairmen and peers consisted of three parts each: (1) the vacancy—why, how, and when it occurred; (2) the search—the type of canvassing effort, the type of position, and with what success; and (3) hiring procedures—how the candidate was found, evaluated, and appointed.

The major findings in this study may be summarized by the following statements:

1. The American Association of University Professors has prepared certain statements over the years that are regarded as "acceptable practice" in the search, recruitment, and retention of college and university personnel.
2. The AAUP has developed a means of blacklisting an institution in which administrative personnel ignore these generally accepted employment rules and regulations.
3. Nine of the ten institutions surveyed operate under specific statutes and bylaws that comprise the rules of importance as far as general university organization and policies in regard to faculty employment are concerned.
4. In the area of employment, there is a general philosophical agreement between the AAUP and Big Ten university statutes and bylaws.
5. Mobility of faculty members among colleges and universities is recognized as desirable in American higher education, and is encouraged by department heads when there is opportunity for professional advancement (even if it means a significant loss to a department).
6. Choice of a faculty member in higher education is based generally on the assessment of his credentials, how much he has published, what others say about him in letters of recommendation, his teaching experience, his membership in professional organizations, and, in a few cases, his relationships with his peers.
7. In the search for academic personnel, the Big Ten schools and colleges of physical education will look to other university faculties for the best possible candidate to fill a particular vacancy.

8. There are clear standards of practice in the appointment and termination of employment of members of existing faculties.
9. Administrators attempt to look elsewhere for candidates, rather than hire their own students, in an attempt to avoid inbreeding.
10. When staff members become dissatisfied with their present positions, they begin searching for ways to reenter the job market.
11. Professional and career-minded persons tend to move for reasons that are germane to the advancement of their careers.
12. The "informal method" is still most frequently used and accepted by college physical educators in the search for employment.
13. The majority of the respondents learned of their present jobs as a result of a variety of sources of contact (e.g., at the institution where they did their graduate work, either through graduate professors, colleagues, or professional friends), but a significant percentage of the faculty members stated that they did nothing and were recruited.
14. Candidates learn about *some* of the vacancies, but often do not hear of the prestigious ones.
15. When respondents are established in a position, salary does not seem to be of great concern. But when they are approached to make a move, salary does become an issue.
16. In the filling of a particular vacancy, the first step taken by the administrators was a job analysis, usually made through discussion with their own faculty members.
17. The two major factors that seemed to attract faculty to the Big Ten departments of physical education were prestige and the challenge of responsibilities assigned to the individual.
18. Educational background and experience seemed to be weighted more heavily than other factors in the selection of candidates.
19. Candidates for employment were required to submit placement papers from the degree-granting institution which included letters of recommendation and vitae.
20. The chairman or head of the department is the person most often dealt with by a candidate during the hiring procedures and at the time a formal offer is made.
21. There is very little bidding that occurs during the final stages of the hiring process, although there may have been considerable inducement at an earlier stage, especially if the candidate would bring added prestige to the department.
22. Some faculty members do not sign contracts.

CONCLUSIONS

1. A comparison between employment theory and practice in higher education, generally, and specifically in Big Ten physical

education units, reveals that there is general agreement in regard to adherence to definitive standards, both by the hiring institution and by personnel who are leaving and being appointed to new positions elsewhere.
2. Although vacancies occur for many reasons, the opportunity for professional advancement is by far the most important one. Although administrators may make a serious effort to retain a valued employee, in the final analysis they do not wish to jeopardize what he might feel to be an advantageous move.
3. Institutions must look to each other as resources in finding personnel to fill vacancies, and certain definitive guidelines are followed in the negotiating process.
4. Although the search for replacements followed certain generally accepted practices, there was a surprising amount of informality in the process of seeking new positions on the part of faculty and administrators seeking candidates. Still further, there was great concern about "opportunities for professional advancement," as opposed to such factors as a higher salary and other rewards.
5. Among those searching for new positions, there was widespread agreement as to the qualifications necessary for a particular opening, but only rare communication between the successful or unsuccessful candidate and the administrator concerned as to the rationale underlying the final decision. It can therefore be concluded that some sort of a written statement concerning the final evaluation of credentials should be added as a necessary step in the negotiating procedure.

Implications for the Practicing Administrator

All subjects involved in this study—administrators, most recently employed faculty members, and their colleagues—gave strong evidence that the majority of faculty openings, both those considered prestigious and those in the lower-ranked categories, are filled by informal practices. In the case of prestigious appointments, data revealed that such openings are rarely advertised in the general academic marketplace, but rather are filled through a process that is handled almost entirely on the level of personal contact between administrators and prestigious faculty members in the various universities. In fact, the manner in which such vacancies are filled involves a high degree of decision based on friendship and professional association, a kind of closed-shop situation which works to the advantage of personnel with established "names" in university physical education—but which also appears to limit the ranks of membership.

The same kind of situation appears to exist in regard to filling openings on the lowest-ranked level in this study (assistant professor), with the difference in intensity of the recruitment effort on the part of the administrators and search by faculty members being related to the fact that such positions are more easily filled, and that the demand for, and the mobility of, university personnel make such positions more often available. Nevertheless, lower-rank positions are quite often filled through personal professional contacts, even though recruiters and those seeking positions may also use more formal means such as placement bureaus, professional associations, and other resources when it seems advantageous. It is also interesting to note that, in several instances, respondents stated that they were unaware of those attributes which might guarantee their selection over other candidates for the same position. Although there is no definitive evidence to support such a conclusion, there was supposition that, other things being equal, preference was given to the candidate who already had a friend at court, so to speak.

The findings indicate that, in general, employment practices in physical education do not differ from those in other areas of higher education—except for the usual intercollegiate athletic influence. Data reveals that departments of physical education in the Big Ten universities follow standards set both by the American Association of University Professors and specific university statutes and bylaws, as do the other schools and colleges throughout the university. This maintains some degree of uniformity in the overall employment picture within the entire institution. Moreover, there was agreement in this regard between both administrators surveyed and faculty members who had been recruited, giving added weight to the affirmation of this factor of our hypothesis.

The only apparent failure to conform to at least the "letter of the law" concerned was in the signing of written contractual agreements. In several instances there were reports that no such formal arrangment had been made, a situation that bears further investigation.

More specific discussion of that particular hypothesis which refers to whether or not physical education administrators hire their own graduates as faculty has presented some difficulty. In general, our data indicates that most administrators make a deliberate effort to avoid inbreeding, preferring to fill vacancies from outside their own departments. This is not a universal practice, however, and several persons surveyed reported moving either to a higher rank in the same department or to a full-time, ranked position after completion of graduate study in the department. Again, however, this practice is usually discouraged, but the writer feels that administrators are convinced that departmental harmony, expertise, and receptivity to new ideas might often be enhanced by such a procedure.

In general, the part of this study devoted to consideration of the vacancy as it occurs in departments of physical education in the Big Ten universities has indicated that faculty openings become available for a multiplicity of reasons. There does tend to be a fairly frequent turnover, especially in the lower professional ranks. Although administrators usually accept the decision of a faculty member to change positions with what appears to be genuine interest in encouraging subordinates to seek and accept opportunities for professional advancement, their own self-interest leads to understandable attempts to retain faculty whose loss would seriously disrupt the functioning of an existing program, or whose replacement would present more than the usual problems. Our overall findings indicate also that a large percentage of vacancies require immediate replacement and involve already existing positions. Only rarely were vacancies related to newly created staff positions, although without exception administrators referred to a pressing need for expansion of their departments and, in many cases, the same concern was expressed by faculty members who were surveyed in this study.

In general, the search procedure on the administrative level was a matter of team effort, with most departments handling the matter through establishment of a faculty screening committee, of which the departmental chairman was always an ex-officio member. The position to be filled was usually analyzed in terms of the type of job performance required and the type of credentials that should be demanded of a candidate. Some decision had to be made as to how candidates should be sought. Formal procedures were usually considered, but as mentioned often in the material above, informal contacts were encouraged and were, in fact, the most often successful. Communication occurred between department chairman and the search committees throughout the procedure. The most striking finding in regard to the entire search procedure was that only one administrator interviewed indicated that he did not rely heavily on the assistance of his colleagues. The one "dissenter" assumed complete responsibility himself for decision-making.

It is interesting to note that the data revealed that many faculty members at the higher level were not actively seeking positions at the time they were recruited. This group expressed no real dissatisfaction in their former positions, but apparently possessed qualifications that recruiters were seeking at the time and were sufficiently swayed by inducements offered to make changing jobs worthwhile. This kind of situation is not unusual in a period of educational growth and development such as has existed for the past decade, but the current overproduction of highly trained generalists and specialists, and the beginning of a retrenchment based on financial problems in overall university expansion, is already affecting this trend.

Those faculty members who were either dissatisfied in the former position or were seeking change for various other reasons also found a seller's market. Using a variety of techniques but concentrating on contact available to them on a personal basis, most reported finding positions that were compatible with their training, experience, and desires. Again, however, the changing economic climate is beginning to cause a noticeable decline in general faculty mobility.

Overall uniformity existed in hiring procedures at each university included in this study. Generally speaking, candidates who were contacted, either formally or informally, were in almost continuous communication with administrators of the university at which the vacancy existed. On-campus interviews at university expense were the rule, at which time the candidate was introduced to members of the screening committees and other departmental staff, as well as to the head of the department, dean, and occasionally other university administrative officers.

The usual procedure involved formal offering of an appointment after the candidate's visit, although it appeared almost routine that the decision to appoint or reject was understood at the time of the personal interview. In most cases, tendering of the formal offer was essentially a rubber-stamp procedure.

As a general rule, precise contract negotiations were discussed at the time of the personal interview and spelled out formally in the written contract agreement. We might mention again that very little bidding occurred during the hiring process. Teaching loads, research opportunities, and fringe benefits such as assumption of moving expenses by the university and other fairly standard inducements were most often mutually agreed upon with a surprising degree of consent. Salary levels were reported competitive from university to university. One accepted practice designed to increase monetary reward was that of offering high-ranked faculty contracts involving summer school commitment, whereas it was common to offer nine-month contracts to those of lower rank.

There were few reported exceptions to this above hiring procedure, and data seem to indicate a high degree of standardization in hiring practices at all Big Ten universities.

Administrative theory, when developed and empirically tested, will be part of a general theory of social action, and a theory of administrative behavior will be part of a general theory of human behavior. The first task of administrative theory is to develop a set of concepts to the theory of administrative situations. These concepts, to be scientifically useful, must be operational—that is, their meanings should correspond to empirically observable facts or situations (Penny, 1968).

The following recommendations are based on the results of the preceding investigation:

1. More intensive investigation is needed on the matter of written contractual agreements to determine whether there are frequent instances of failure to provide a formal written agreement to the appointee.
2. A study should be conducted as to the hiring practices relative to the appointment of coaches and other personnel in athletics.
3. A comparative study of hiring procedures should be carried out in regard to practices in the women's departments of physical education (as opposed to those in men's).

General Bibliography

Brown, David G., *The Mobile Professors*. Washington, D.C.: American Council on Education, 1967.

Diekhoff, John S., *The Domain of the Faculty*. New York: Harper Brothers, Pub., 1965.

Epstein, Ralph C., "The Technique of Making University Appointments," *AAUP Bulletin*, 35, no. 2 (Summer 1949), 349-56.

Herge, Henry G., *The College Teacher*. New York: The Center for Applied Research in Education, Inc., 1965.

Marshall, Howard D., *The Mobility of College Faculties*. New York: Pageant Press, Inc., 1964.

Penny, William, "An Analysis of the Meaning Attached to Selected Concepts in Administrative Theory," pp. 8-9. Ph.D. Diss., Department of Physical Education, University of Illinois, 1968.

Spaeth, Marcia, "Analysis of Administrative Research in Physical Education and Athletics in Relation to a Research Paradigm," p. 4. Ph.D. diss., Department of Physical Education, University of Illinois, 1967.

Stauffer, Samuel, et al., *The Behavioral Sciences at Harvard,* Report by a Faculty Committee, pp. 197-209, June 1954.

Williams, Robert L., *The Administration of Academic Affairs in Higher Education*. Ann Arbor, Mich.: The University of Michigan Press, 1966.

21

Assessment of Nonrevenue Sports

K. Ladd Pash

Introduction

Intercollegiate athletic programs throughout the country occupy an important position in our colleges and universities—not only as an advanced form of participation for the athlete, but ideally as a phase of general education for all concerned. Others have geared their athletic programs to a few sports, mainly those which produce or have the potential to produce revenue through gate receipts.

General education should ideally allow any student to pursue activities that will reflect his interests and allow him to develop his potential through any or all channels of education available to him. All too often, athletic programs are extremely limited in scope and do not reflect the stated benefits and values which students can accrue if given the opportunity; so the intent of these programs is thwarted.

If, in fact, varsity athletic programs do contribute to general education, the nation's colleges and universities should provide the very best programs that can be developed—and *equal emphasis* should be placed on each activity in the program.

In the past, different sports have been designated as "major" or "minor"

K. Ladd Pash is from the University of Illinois, Urbana-Champaign, Illinois.

sports according to their appeal within a particular college or university. In 1929 Savage stated, "The implication of rating contained in the terms 'major sports' and 'minor sports' is to the effect that some branches of athletics are more important to a college or university public than others" (Krout, 1929, p. 9). The "major" and "minor" designations are no longer openly or publicly stated, but a few sports are afforded greater attention and prestige because of their public appeal, which, in effect, makes them revenue-producers.

Largely because of this appeal, many intercollegiate athletic programs have often evolved into huge financial enterprises with seeming emphasis not on educational gain but on profit and loss. Most of the revenue produced in past years has come through football and basketball gate receipts, with most of the other sports contributing little in the way of funds to support the programs.

Naturally, if an entire athletic program must depend on one or two sports to carry the financial load without supplemental institutional funds, the revenue-producing sports might tend to push the nonrevenue producers into positions of secondary consideration. Equating athletic programs with financial solvency has tended to split certain sports into "revenue" and "nonrevenue" sport categories, and the resulting practices in the treatment of some sports have made the university and college athletic situation subject to close scrutiny by athletic administrators.

The administration of intercollegiate athletics has become an undertaking of immense proportions, especially in our larger institutions where annual budgets sometimes approach $2.5 million. There are many phases of athletic administration, and two of the most important are developing sufficient funds to operate programs and allotting the funds to the separate activities included in the program.

In the Big Ten Conference the methods of financing have been limited essentially to gate receipts, alumni support, concessions, and, more recently, television. This has necessitated to a great extent the operation of athletic programs strictly as a business without regard for educational objectives. Revenue, then, has quite evidently been the deciding factor in athletic program maintenance in recent years. This is understandable to some degree when one considers the fact that at any given time there is only so much money with which to work. The fact that this does, in many cases, dictate the inclusion or exclusion of certain athletic activities in an intercollegiate program seems to be inconsistent with the stated aims and objectives of college and university athletics.

If the nonrevenue sports are thought to be important in a program, their existence should not have to depend only on the financial health of athletic departments. This study was conceived as a result of strong interest in intercollegiate athletics in general, nonrevenue sports specifically, and dealt primarily with how different groups felt about this particular segment of collegiate activities.

PURPOSE

The purpose of this study was to analyze and assess nonrevenue sports in the Intercollegiate Conference of Faculty Representatives (the Big Ten Conference). Only certain sports within this group were selected for inspection, but they were considered to be representative of all nonrevenue-producing sports in the conference.

As a result of the development of the study, several subproblems, phrased as questions, were investigated as well:

1. What problems have been faced historically by Big Ten athletic administrators?
2. What is the current status of these problems within selected Big Ten intercollegiate sports?
3. What trends seem to be developing in regard to these problems in the Big Ten?
4. Regardless of trends, what recommendations can be made for the ideal development of nonrevenue sports in the Big Ten?

Background and Related Literature

TWENTIETH-CENTURY ATHLETIC PROBLEMS

Much has been written about the development of athletics in the United States, and no report can be complete without some mention of the accompanying problems within sports programs in our colleges and universities. It seems to this writer that, in looking at athletic problems historically, it can readily be seen that problems have always existed.

Even during the twenties, when sport was riding its highest, costs were mounting and sports programs were growing beyond the incomes of particular spectator sports. Thus, in spite of alumni gifts, finances were still a major consideration. One writer indicated that

> The financial end of football should be of primary interest to the head-line colleges as well as smaller ones. Without football, athletic associations at many colleges would be hopelessly involved in debts accumulated by steady money losers like crew, fencing, tennis, squash, and others ("Pigskin Finance," 1936, pp. 41-43).

It can be seen that by this time a great deal of thought concerning athletics was directed toward finances. However, a new aspect of sports programs became increasingly noticeable—the concept of "major" and "minor" sports. The two terms can probably be translated to spectator and nonspectator sports, or even revenue and nonrevenue sports. In referring to the two terms, the spectator would probably base a definition upon his interest in a sport, while an athletic administrator would probably look to see whether or not a sport made money. Thus, it developed that "the implication of rating contained in the terms 'major sports' and 'minor sports' is to the effect that some branches of athletics are more important to a college or university public than others" (Savage, 1929, p. 110).

Two meanings could be attached to the word "important" here. One meaning would refer to the question of institutional prestige, and the other would probably refer to the importance of the "major" sports in terms of financial support of athletic programs.

Support of different sports within athletic programs has varied a great deal, but in most cases, it has been the nonrevenue or "minor" sports which have suffered the most.

The practice of funding programs entirely through gate receipts is less than desirable too for those sports which do not produce revenues. Dave Williams, probably the best-known collegiate golf coach in the United States, felt the nonrevenue sport pinch when he said

> Since golf is not considered a revenue-producing sport, most athletic departments feel they are financially unable to subsidize golf very strongly. This is something we have to live with until the day when high school and college team golf becomes more of a spectator sport (1962, p. 197).

No doubt coaches of other nonrevenue sports have felt this pinch, but it is even more serious when we consider that one sport is considered more important than another *in an educational setting*—with that importance being based on its ability to produce revenue.

Other educators supported the institutional funding concept. In the 1962 National College Physical Education Association for Men (NCPEAM) Convention, the following statement was made:

> If intercollegiate sports are to exert a healthy and influential force on campus, it is necessary that they be given adequate financial support. Fiscal operations which differ radically from established institutional matters pose implications which warrant serious study and review. In most instances activities are not self-supporting and must be underwritten, as are other programs which are valued in the institution (Havel, 1962, pp. 91-98).

In the past ten years, costs have obviously risen so rapidly that many institutions' athletic programs have been endangered. Many solutions, some legitimate and some not, have been proposed. Mason surveyed 983 college and university presidents throughout the country and from the responses determined that intercollegiate athletics should be budgeted, controlled, and given attention equally with any other program conducted by the institution. Recommendations were made that special attention be given to the recruiting of athletes and that, instead of eliminating the intercollegiate athletic program or making drastic changes, administrators, coaches, and faculty should work together to eliminate areas of criticism in the programs (Mason, 1969, p. 569-A).

A more drastic type of change has been recommended as well, such as "abolishing athletic scholarships except for the income-producing sports and even returning to the days of one-platoon football with smaller coaching staffs, bleaker athletic dorms and fewer steaks on the training table" (Cohn and Bull, 1969, pp. 20-25). Several steps the larger conferences could take to cut costs and bring athletics back within the scope of educational objectives were listed. Among the items listed were (1) prohibiting off-campus recruiting, (2) gradually eliminating athletic scholarships, (3) eliminating athletic dorms and training tables, (4) eliminating expense payments to athletes, and (5) turning gate receipts over to the college or university and having the athletic programs financed by institutional funds (Butler, 1970, pp. 8-9, 19). In 1970 the entire National Collegiate Athletic Association Convention was devoted to a consideration of cost reduction in athletics (NCAA, 1970).

It can be seen that many groups and individuals are examining intercollegiate athletics very closely, mainly because financial problems have become so acute that drastic measures are required to retain athletic programs on the level to which they have typically developed. Stopgap measures will do no real good, and concerned administrators must effect realistic change very soon.

In the 1968 Annual Report of the National Collegiate Athletic Association, The Big Ten Intercollegiate Conference reported that

> The conference is holding special meetings to discuss cost reduction measures, but still retain the broad intercollegiate programs that have been conducted in the past.
>
> Many schools reported again this year their concern over rising costs of equipment and general operation. It seems to be a universal problem, but more serious with some institutions than with others. One school had its budget reduced by 10 percent and another expressed the fear that several of its proposed athletic expansions are doomed (NCAA, 1970, p. 29).

It has been apparent for the past several years that most intercollegiate athletic departments cannot continue to support a full program of athletics using only such revenues as the sports can generate themselves. At Minnesota, according to one writer, the athletic program lost $101,931 in 1969 *(Champaign News-Gazette,* 1970, p. 14), and University of Minnesota President Malcolm Moos recently said:

> We don't like the idea that the athletic department is about $100,000 in the red. If the intercollegiate athletic program can't

support itself, we will have to cut down the number of sports to make adjustments in the expenditures *(Champaign News-Gazette,* 1971, p. 19).

The major problems in the twentieth century have been mostly of a financial nature in that most programs have been supported primarily by those revenues produced by spectator gate receipts. Out of a need to generate more revenue, other problems have arisen such as control of athletics, recruiting and subsidization of athletes, and the discriminatory practices directed at certain sports. And now institutions are faced with rapidly rising costs and relatively fixed incomes, making full athletic programs difficult, if not impossible, to support.

Much has been said about the problems in intercollegiate athletics, and in most cases primary emphasis has been on the "major" or revenue-producing sports. On the other hand, the "minor" or nonrevenue producing sports have typically received secondary consideration, and have not really been considered in the light of their problems or their ideal place in a sound educational program.

Research Methodology and Techniques

COLLECTION OF DATA

In order to analyze and assess the problems of selected sports in intercollegiate athletics, the descriptive method of research was used to accomplish this purpose.

Four subproblems grew out of the main problem, and data was collected concerning them through the use of documentary analysis of many sources of material from the University of Illinois archives. In addition to documentary analysis, a questionnaire was used to gather further data concerning the four subproblems mentioned previously. The questions in the survey were developed as a result of careful examination of the literature available, and because of the extensive nature of this problem, the questionnaire was closed-ended.

Prior to sending out the questionnaire, it was given to several individuals for critical comment and was next sent through the Survey Research Center at the University of Illinois for refinement.

The final step was to conduct a pilot study at a nearby university. The questionnaire was administered as it was to be done in the study and then was checked once more for adherence to criteria for questionnaire construction selected previously.

SURVEY PROCEDURE

Several different groups were sent the questionnaire and accompanying materials. These groups were: (1) presidents of all Big Ten institutions, (2) chancellors, (3) deans of selected colleges within the institutions of the conference, (4) intramural directors, (5) directors of physical education, (6) athletic directors, (7) faculty representatives, (8) athletic board chairmen, and (9) coaches of selected sports. The nine categories were then split into two groups. The first group of presidents, chancellors, deans, intramural and physical education directors comprised the "nonathletic" group of respondents, and the second group, consisting of athletic directors, faculty representatives, athletic board chairmen and coaches, was considered to be the "athletic" group of respondents.

When responses were in, analysis of the data was accomplished by comparing the responses of the "nonathletic" group with the "athletic" group selected for the study. A second analysis was made between athletic directors and coaches (athletic subgroup I) and faculty representatives and athletic board chairmen (athletic subgroup II).

The comparative analysis was carried out by showing intergroup and intragroup responses (means and standard deviations) in terms of agreement, partial agreement, and disagreement. The original questionnaire responses ranged from 1 to 5 with values from *strongly agree* (1) to *strongly disagree* (5). The step intervals for each number were set up as follows: (1) (1-1.80); 2 (1.81-2.60); 3 (2.61-3.40); 4 (3.41-4.20); 5 (4.21-5.0). This was done to facilitate placing the mean responses of groups within specified limits and to provide a basis for comparison.

In order to determine consensus, limited consensus, or no consensus, the following procedures were used: (1) if the mean responses of groups fell within the same interval, consensus was assumed regardless of the size of standard deviations; (2) if the mean responses of groups fell in adjacent step intervals, limited consensus was assumed unless the standard deviations clearly showed no overlap in the groups' responses; (3) if the mean responses of groups were separated by one or more step intervals, the groups were said to show no consensus regardless of the size of the standard deviations.

REPORTING OF DATA

All data generated by use of the research techniques were presented in the order in which they appeared in the survey forms. The responses are presented as tables comparing the intergroup and intragroup responses. In addition, the tables were constructed to show the groups' responses to each statement in the survey forms.

Reporting was carried out by dividing the presentations into two sections. The first presentation was made by showing comparisons of the "nonathletic" group with the "athletic" group. This included questions 1 through 10 (part A). The second presentation compared responses of athletic subgroup I (athletic directors and coaches) with the responses of athletic subgroup II (faculty representatives and athletic board chairmen) and covered both part A and part B of the survey forms.

FINDINGS AND CONCLUSIONS

Intercollegiate athletic programs in the United States are currently in the midst of an extremely critical period. These programs have, in the recent past at least, enjoyed considerable prosperity, and extensive programs have been developed in most large institutions of higher learning. However, during times of financial stress, certain portions of programs have typically suffered from cutbacks in budgets, and in some cases even elimination from varsity programs.

And now, when our country exists in a very strong inflationary economy, financial problems in intercollegiate athletics are threatening to force change, particularly in those sports which do not contribute revenue for program maintenance.

Athletic programs have occupied a strong position, albeit an extracurricular one, in our institutions of higher learning. Seemingly they will continue to do so, even if somewhat modified. The writer felt that a study of certain aspects of athletic programs might focus the thinking of athletic administrators more directly on these areas than has been done in the past. Thus, an investigation of this type could provide a basis for possible improvement of all or part of the total athletic program.

Data for the investigation were generated by analyzing the responses of different groups of administrators and faculty concerning the problems identified earlier; it is interesting to note that even though the respondents were not a homogeneous group, their feelings about the problems were remarkably similar.

Most of the problems identified historically remain as current problems today. Some of these problems include differences in treatment and use of coaching personnel, poor or inefficient scheduling practices, "major" and "minor" emphasis on sports, and financial stress, which seems to be the problem of greatest magnitude.

Respondents agreed that there was a need for coaches to have strong academic qualifications and interest in teaching and that pressure to win should be reduced in all coaches. This is not consistent with practices of past years, and clearly the pressure to win is an ever-present entity in big-time coaching.

The different groups also agreed that scheduling practices should be changed to upgrade athletic programs, but that problems in scheduling are mainly those of finances and time, so the much-needed upgrading would be next to impossible to accomplish without the expenditure of more money. This would do little to curb the cost, which nearly all administrators feel is too expensive.

Another problem, possibly one of semantics but very real in the administrative treatment of different sports, is the "major" and "minor" designations given to the sports in athletic programs. Most respondents felt that revenue or "major" sports deserve more emphasis than the nonrevenue or "minor" sports. Many of the nonathletic administrators indicated that all sports should be deemphasized to some extent, and this was at variance, to a degree, with the athletic administrators, who felt that present emphasis is proper or possibly that all sports should be emphasized to a greater extent.

All problems identified through the study hinge a great deal on finances. There was little disagreement in that regard, and though financial stress is currently affecting recruiting and grant-in-aid subsidies for athletes, the predominant feeling among most administrators was that lack of money is the prime deterrent in the development of the nonrevenue sports.

The overall trend with regard to nonrevenue sports is not optimistic in terms of comparison with athletic programs as we know them now. Programs will change, that is certain. Support will probably be reduced or withdrawn from sports with little or no revenue-producing potential. In some programs, these sports will probably revert to club sports, and it is inevitable that the disparities that exist between the revenue and nonrevenue sports will increase in all but the most educationally sound programs.

The study revealed little if any concerted effort to alleviate the acknowledged problems except to cut back on the nonrevenue producers. Most of the administrators expressed a desire to continue programs as they are now run, which may indicate some sort of "administrative conscience"; however, consensus showed that practice and conscience probably will not go hand-in-hand in the future, and that problems which exist may simply be eliminated through program cutbacks.

Definitive information was difficult to generate in the study of the athletic problems previously cited. It is true that almost everyone recognized that the outlook for nonrevenue sports in the Big Ten is less than promising. However, it seems that many do not consider the plight of these sports important enough for serious consideration. If this is the case, the situation can only deteriorate further. As stated earlier in the study, no one sport should be considered more important than another educationally. But because the present structure of intercollegiate athletics demands that we consider sports as revenue or nonrevenue producers, we are forced automatically to establish a hierarchy of importance for these sporting activities.

Implications for the Practicing Administrator

Seat-of-the-pants administration has been a way of life in our various institutions in past years, much to the detriment of the various organizations involved. Nowhere is that more obvious than in the administration of athletic programs throughout the country.

It has been typical for athletic administrators to look at problems as isolated entities and to develop problem-solving approaches that applied only to a very limited area of interest. This "fireman" approach has had the effect of compartmentalizing many of the situations in athletics, thereby preventing a look at total administration and the development of sound and lasting means of dealing with recurring problems.

Many problems that exist today are the very problems that developed when intercollegiate athletics became so important in our institutions of higher learning. It was probably inevitable that some of the problems would occur, and it was also probably inevitable that dealing with the problems was on an occurrence basis. Yet it need not have, nor must it happen today on this basis. Today's administrator has only to look back at the problems encountered and see that solutions are not difficult to come by as long as one is totally removed from the situation. In other words, it is simple to solve someone else's problems, particularly when one has years of history to use as input in arriving at decisions which affect no one. The problem arises when an administrator has to deal with a real situation with real consequences. Then it is not so easy to effect sound and fair decisions.

Years of experience have made good administrators out of many people, and yet in most cases, this experience has been of no assistance in developing sound administrative principles. It is true that there are few situations which require no improvisation or on-the-spot decision making; this is to be expected, but the best administrators have a great deal more to go on.

There have been few "universals" to go by in arriving at decisions which affect the operation of athletic departments. In past years this was of little consequence, partly because athletic plants were, in most cases, not as extensive as today's, partly because public exposure was somewhat more limited, and to a great extent because our inflationary economy has caused great problems in most large financial operations.

It seems critical then to determine whether or not intercollegiate athletics are or should be an integral part of our educational offering to students. If they are, steps should be taken to ensure athletic dynamism with an offering which does reflect the students' needs and interests. If they are not, then they should be eliminated entirely.

In either case, strong, functional administration is imperative, and for one who aspires to a career in athletic administration, a thorough understanding, not only of administration but of athletics, is of paramount importance.

From the study outlined, it has been shown that many of today's athletic programs are severely limited in what they are able to accomplish at this point in terms of a healthy, well-rounded outlook, and the trend is toward even greater limitations.

Assuming, from an administrative standpoint, that a program *is* desirable, where does one start to develop such a program? The decision has to be made as to what size program is desired and what can be funded. Unfortunately, funding is more of a determinant in program development than what is desired and educationally sound.

However, good programs can be developed, and athletic administrators are obligated to provide the very best programs that can be developed—with *equal emphasis* on each activity, not just on the revenue sports. The strength of such programs will depend almost entirely on sound administration.

The focus must be on the students' welfare, and not just on the dollar value of programs. However difficult it might be, priorities must be established that will reflect this thinking. There can be no other justification for even having an athletic program, and once the administrator loses this focus, a program can only deteriorate.

To a degree, this may be forced upon him, because there is a tendency to equate athletic programs with financial solvency; but nowhere else in higher education does this occur, and it should not occur in athletics.

The administration of college and university athletic programs is, at best, an extremely difficult function today, as is the administration of other areas in higher education; however, much of the criticism directed at athletics is justified when consideration is given to the fact that there has been little, if any, concentrated effort to promote changes of a lasting nature.

General Bibliography

Butler, Lyle, "After One-Hundred Years of American Football Nothing But Problems—Problems—Problems," *National Association of Collegiate Directors of Athletics Quarterly*, 4 (1970).

Cohn, Bob, and Steve Bull, "The High Cost of Winning," *National Association of Collegiate Directors of Athletics Quarterly*, 4 (1969).

Havel, Richard, "Intercollegiate Athletics: An Educational Dilemma," *National College Physical Education Association for Men—Proceedings*, 1962.

Krout, John, *Annals of American Sport*. New Haven: Yale University Press, 1929.

Mason, Robert T., "The Role of Intercollegiate Athletics in Higher Education as Perceived by College and University Presidents Throughout the United States." *Dissertation Abstracts*, 1969.

National Collegiate Athletic Association, *Proceedings of the Sixty-fourth Annual Convention*, 1970.

―――――, *Annual Report 1968-1969*. 1970.

"Pigskin Finance," *Literary Digest*, CXII (September, 1936), 41-43.

Savage, Howard J., *American College Athletics, Bulletin 23*. Boston: The Merrymount Press, 1929.

Williams, Dave, *How to Coach and Play Championship Golf*. Englewood Cliffs, N.J.: Prentice-Hall, Inc., 1962.

22

Physical Education Budgetary Processes in an Ontario School System

Terry R. Haggerty

Introduction

The primacy of goal attainment among the functions of a social system gives priority to those processes most directly involved with the success or failure of goal-orientated behavior. This means essentially the decision-making process which controls the utilization of the resources of the system as a whole in the interests of the goal (Parsons, 1956, p. 66).

Decision-making is one of the major functions that administrators perform; indeed, it is accepted by many as the *prime* function of administration. The following statements are but two examples that attest to this statement.

The central function of administration is directing and controlling the decision-making process. It is not only central in the sense that it is more important than the other functions, as some writers have indicated, but it is central in that all other functions of administration can best be interpreted in terms of the decision-making process (Griffiths, 1959, pp. 74-75).

Terry R. Haggerty is at Merritton High School in St. Catharines, Ontario.

Also, as Simon noted:

> The task of "deciding" pervades the entire administrative organization quite as much as the task of "doing." (1957, p. 1)

In education there are numerous areas that give rise to the need for administrative decision-making. There are problems that concern the scope of the educational programs offered, the quality and quantity of staff required, the pupil-to-teacher ratio, the provision of adequate facilities, the extent that extracurricular activities should be included in the school offerings, and alternate ways to meet stated objectives. The actual decision regarding many of these areas may be essentially a *budgetary* decision, particularly if financial resources are limited. In fact, a budget can be viewed as a set of goals with price tags attached—a simple outlook—but one that places crucial importance on the budgetary decision-making process. As a result of this importance, interest in educational budgeting has recently been greatly intensified.

Throughout the 1960s, almost any expenditure in the name of education was accepted. Now, there is a serious belief that a good bit of what had been spent was wasted, and that difficult financial decisions must now be made. This appears especially true in the case of physical education and athletics, because they are expensive, visible, and often labeled as a "fringe area" of education. The introduction of financial ceilings on school boards' ordinary expenditures in 1971 represented one attempt by the Ontario government to control the rate of increase in educational spending. Financial trends also fostered the Ontario Ministry of Education's positive attitude towards a Planning-Programming-Budgeting-Systems (PPBS) approach to the educational budgetary process. As a result, several Ontario school boards are currently engaged in various stages of PPBS (Hartley, 1972, p. 1). This shift from the traditional, *incremental* budgetary approach in effect in school budgeting to PPBS, a comprehensive approach, necessitates a major shift in one's focus of attention. The realization of the importance of an investigation of the *current* budgetary process, particularly when an innovation was imminent, resulted in the formulation of this investigation.

STATEMENT OF THE PROBLEM

The main problem of this study was to analyze the physical education supplies and capital budgetary decision-making processes of the secondary schools in an Ontario school system. Subproblems referred to the delineation of the *factors* that influenced the principals' and department heads' budgetary decisions, and the classification of the school physical education budgetary processes as essentially *incremental* or *comprehensive* in nature.

DEFINITION OF TERMS USED

Throughout this study some terms were used that are familiar, but require clarification. These terms are defined below to establish a common frame of reference.

Supplies—Refers to the account classification that includes instructional expenditures with a value of less than $50 and a life expectancy of less than three years. Typical items would include basketballs, athletic tape, badminton racquets, and so forth.

Capital—Represents the other major instructional expenditure classification investigated, and includes items with a value of $50 or more and a life expectancy of three years or more. Typical items would include a pommel horse, fiberglass vaulting pole, and a bicycle ergometer. Within this classification exist *new* capital and *replacement* capital. New capital items are *new* in the sense that they are not replacing worn-out equipment, but represent items not previously owned by the agent making the request.

Incremental budgeting—A budgetary approach that relies heavily on an historical base, with the result that the current year's budget amount often looks a great deal like the previous year's budget. Usually, programs are continued without serious examination regarding whether they are still useful, or whether a major or minor reallocation of resources among programs would lead to better results.

Comprehensive budgeting—This budgeting approach (also referred to as zero base) is essentially diametrically opposite to the incremental approach. A comprehensive approach calls for the detailed relative evaluation of each major budget item, as compared to every other, explicitly rejecting reliance on an historical base for allocation decisions. PPBS is a technique that embodies a comprehensive approach.

PPBS—This term, the abbreviated form for Planning-Programming-Budgeting-Systems, refers to a comprehensive budgetary process that attempts to:

1. define specific objectives,
2. delineate all programs that support these objectives,
3. "cost out" each program over several years,
4. select the most advantageous program on the basis of costs and perceived benefits,
5. operate the chosen program,
6. evaluate the effectiveness of the program against the criteria established for the program objectives, and
7. recycle the results to improve the process.

Other terms such as MERS (Management of Educational Resource System), ERAS (Educational Resource Allocation System), PABS (Programming and Budgeting System), and MBO (Management by Objectives) are essentially different labels for the same concept.

Background and Related Literature

AN OVERVIEW OF INCREMENTAL BUDGETING

Although budgetary decision-making is basically only an adjectival variety of decision-making, it does have inherent aspects that differentiate it from general discussions of decision-making. Wildavsky has indicated the unique complexity of the budgetary decision-making process as follows:

> Human nature is never more evident than when men are struggling to apportion resources they have to a myriad of claimants. Budgeting deals with the purposes of men.... Serving diverse purposes, a budget can be many things: a political act, a plan of work, a prediction, a source of enlightenment, a means of obfuscation, a mechanism of control, an escape from restrictions, a means to action, a break on progress, even a prayer that the powers that be will deal gently with the best aspirations of fallible men (1964, p. v).

How can administrators manage problems such as the decision regarding how to allocate scarce resources to numerous subunits? Several possibilities were apparent in the literature.

In "The Science of Muddling Through" (Lindblom, 1959, p. 79), the rational-comprehensive approach to making decisions was compared with the incremental method. In his analysis of the two methods, Lindblom rejected the rational-comprehensive approach to decision-making, stating that for complex problems, the rational-complex approach was unrealistic because it relied on information sources and intellectual capacities that men do not possess (Ibid., p. 80).

In 1940, Key stated that the problem basic to the expenditure aspect of budgeting was the decision, "on what basis shall it be decided to allocate X dollars to activity A instead of activity B?" (1940, p. 1138). In 1961, Wildavsky noted that "although several attempts have been made to meet this challenge [Key's basic economic question], not one has come close to succeeding" (1961, p. 183). One of the more noteworthy attempts was the "alternative budget system" in Lewis's "Toward a Theory of Budgeting" (1952, p. 42).

Methodological possibilities for investigating the budgetary decision-making process were advanced by Wildavsky (1961, pp. 187-88), and pursued in his in-depth analysis of the budgetary process surrounding the formulation of the United States federal budget (1964). His investigation, felt by some to be the definitive study in public budgeting, detailed the federal budgetary process by means of interviews with agency heads, budget officers, Budget Bureau staff, House Appropriations Committee staff, and congressmen.

Interviews revealed that particpants in the budgetary process dealt with their overwhelming burden by adopting "aids to calculation." He found that by far the most important aid to calculation was the *incremental method* (Davis et al., 1966, p. 529).

In summary, Wildavsky found that

> Budgeting turns out to be an incremental process, proceeding from a historical base, guided by accepted notions of fair shares, in which decisions are fragmented, made in sequences by specialized bodies, and coordinated through multiple feedback mechanisms. The role of the participants, and their perceptions of each other's powers and desires, fit together to provide a reasonable stable set of criteria on which to base calculations (1964, p. 62).

The attempt to formulate a theory of the public budgetary decision-making process was further advanced by Crecine's work with the municipal budgetary processes of Pittsburgh, Detroit, and Cleveland (1969). The formal municipal budgetary process was found to consist of three stages (1969, p. 4). First, the heads of the various city departments were asked to submit detailed requests for operating (supplies) funds to the mayor. Second, the mayor considered all detailed requests, modified them to reflect his policies, and included recommendations. Third, the city council reviewed the mayor's budget, made minimal modifications in the expenditure and revenue plans, and passed the appropriations bill. Crecine found that, in general, the municipal budget was largely under the control of the mayor because the department heads and council had only minimal meaningful input into the allocation decision. The similarity of these three municipal stages (and also the stages of the federal budget as revealed by Wildavsky) to those employed in the school budgetary process is exemplified by comparison with the school process stated in the following passage:

> The [school] budgeting process went something like this: teachers and department heads would strike a budget that they felt was needed in their areas. This would be submitted to the principal.... The department heads and principal would look over the combined school budgets and readjust any obvious overspending or inequalities. This would then be submitted to the board officials, who would look at each school's budget in comparison to the other schools in the system. A similar process would take place at that level, and so on (Legislature of Ontario Debates, May 26, 1972, p. 2868).

A further study that stemmed from the interest in the public budgetary process was Gerwin's budgetary analysis of an urban school district (1969). Gerwin investigated the budgetary process in terms of the decision inputs that impinged on the administrator when he prepared his budget, and the stable set of responses which he developed over time. In addition to providing a general understanding of the macro-supplies budgetary process in a school district, Gerwin's study was useful for his reference to capital budgeting, an area not mentioned in the literature surveyed. He noted that "there are two broad categories of materials requests [supplies and capital] which are not necessarily formulated in the same manner" (1969, p. 109).

The studies by Wildavsky, Crecine, Gerwin, and the article by Lindblom indicated that *precedent* was an integral aspect of nonmarket decision-making models, and that the incremental budgetary process was prominent in the supplies budgetary processes investigated. Although significant studies related to the capital budgetary process were not uncovered, Gerwin noted that the supplies and capital budgetary processes were not necessarily similar.

EMPIRICAL PHYSICAL EDUCATION BUDGET LITERATURE

There was a marked paucity of literature that related to the physical education budgetary process, particularly in Ontario. This was surprising in view of the fact that "of all the subject matter areas in elementary, secondary, or college and university systems, health and physical education require one of the largest outlay of funds" (Bucher, 1967, pp. 132-33). Bucher added that financial management was "one of the most important responsibilities that educators, and particularly administrators, have" (1967, p. 133).

The only empirical data uncovered in the literature that related to the physical education budgetary process was a cursory survey of selected school systems reported by Bucher (1967, p. 135).

PLANNING-PROGRAMMING-BUDGETING-SYSTEMS

The foregoing material presented budgeting as an historical, incremental process. Alternatives to the traditional, incremental approach to budgeting have been proposed in the literature. The most noteworthy alternative was Planning-Programming-Budgeting-Systems (PPBS), a comprehensive approach to the budgetary decision-making process. At present, the Ontario Ministry of Education favors a PPBS approach to the school budgetary process. The following material will briefly survey this approach to the budgetary decision-making process.

In 1960, Secretary McNamara invited the Rand Corporation, a systems group, to organize planning and budget procedures at the United States Department of Defense. At that time, the steps set down for a Planning-Programming-Budget-System were as follows: (1) specify program objectives, (2) devise procedures for obtaining these objectives, (3) set a time horizon, (4) cost it out from inception to terminal point, (5) examine and analyze alternatives, and (6) set up machinery for validation of the system (Umans, 1970, p. 45). On August 25, 1965, President Johnson's administration introduced a systems approach throughout the vast United States federal government (1970, p. 46). Since then, education in the United States has gradually moved toward the use of Planning-Programming-Budgeting-Systems.

One of the initial developments of PPBS in Ontario was undertaken in the Treasury Board Secretariat by the Program Analysis Branch. In April, 1968, the Program Review Branch was established in the new Programs and Estimates Division with its prime responsibility centering on the development and implementation of a PPB System (Treasury Board of Ontario, 1969, p. 62). The link between governmental commitment to PPBS and education in Ontario publically became apparent in a statement by the minister of education to the House of Commons in July 1971. He noted "what we are doing in government here, and what we hope that local school boards are doing; namely, getting into program budgeting" (Legislature of Ontario Debates, July 19, 1971, p. s-2324). More recently, in April 1972, a letter from the office of the Ontario minister of education revealed that

> most of the school boards recognize the necessity to develop some form of program budgeting to improve the management of their resources. Some have begun such a development. In general though, work in this area amongst boards is in a relatively early stage. . . .
>
> The Government of Ontario adopted the PPB System for its operations some years ago. All ministries are using the system, although still further development and refinement is necessary before it can be claimed to be fully effective. . . .
>
> From the foregoing it will be obvious that the Ministry wishes to encourage the school boards to develop such systems.

Just as the incremental process of budgeting had its critics, so too does the comprehensive (PPBS) process. Wildavsky noted that, "zero-base, comprehensive, non-incremental budgeting was infeasible in federal budgeting because it implies a completely defined system of values, a completely specified set of alternatives, and costs for achieving these alternatives" (1964, pp. 128-29).

An investigation of the attempt to introduce a comprehensive budgetary process into the United States Department of Agriculture indicated that participants found it impossible to calculate the relative benefits of programs within the department, let alone justify particular levels of programs (Wildavsky and Hammond, 1965, p. 34). Instead, it was found that the department, in effect, reverted to the previously employed incremental approach to arrive at its budget estimates.

In a presentation at the National Educational Association Committee on Education Finance, Furno stated that

> cost-effectiveness or cost-quality studies [such as PPBS] cannot be anything but shallow, and certainly no administrator should be so fool-hardy as to base management decisions upon such cost effectiveness studies. We know that cost is affected by many variables—social, psychological and political. We know that effectiveness is difficult to measure and subject to many different interpretations, both subjective and objective. Each analysis of cost-effectiveness in public education raises more questions than it does answer. (1969, pp. 141-42)

Physical educators have only recently begun to recognize PPBS. A recent article stated that "this writer urges those school administrators of physical education to jump on the PPBS bandwagon before it is federally and/or state mandated" (Avedisian, 1972, p. 39). Furthermore,

> Physical education's position in the nation's public school may well depend on fiscal matters, and the greatest hope for firmer support and acceptance may well lie in a new concept labelled PPBS—planning-programming-budgeting-systems. (1972, p. 37)

SUMMARY

It is hoped that the foregoing literature has assisted the reader in formulating a concept of the budgetary process, and has set the stage for an understanding of the findings and conclusions of this study. Initially, research related to the *incremental* budgetary approach was presented and followed by literature that dealt with the *comprehensive* PPBS process. These two budgetary approaches, *incremental* and *comprehensive*, represent the extremes on the budgetary continuum in the model in *Figure 1*.

Research Methodology and Techniques

To achieve the objectives of this descriptive study, a structured interview technique was employed to collect data from the school board's principals and male physical education department heads. On the basis of a literature review, a model of the budgetary decision-making process was formulated to assist in understanding the relationships of the factors that determine the budgetary process. (The model appears in *Figure 1*). Briefly, the model should be read as follows: If a budget decision-maker (for example, a principal) used, or was influenced by, factors associated with Box A in *Figure 1* rather than those in Box C, he would tend to formulate a decision, such as the amount to allocate to physical education, *incrementally*. That is, if the principal employed factors in

Box "A"
* previous budget experience
* historical budget data
  time limits
  line-item budget forms
* budget "guidelines"
* "expectation of base" concept
* "expectation of fair share" concept
  "costs" of innovation
  political expediency
* enrolment in department

Box "B"
* discretion available
  criteria of choice
  affective processes
* tendency to "pad" budget
* tendency to "cut" request
  focus of attention
  organizational 'slack'
  ceilings on expenditures
* amount of budget request
  tone of budget information

Box "C"
* program objectives
  needs of students
  needs of community
* program-oriented forms
* concept of P.P.B.S.
  evaluation of past decisions
* multi-year planning
* item justification
* scrutiny of budget

the above variables are some of the factors perceived to influence a budget decision-maker

Budget Decision-Maker

The perception of the decision-maker, and the actual importance of the various factors in effect, result in an approach to decision-making that can be positioned on the continuum below

Incremental approach .... continuum .... Comprehensive approach

the foregoing lead to a decision

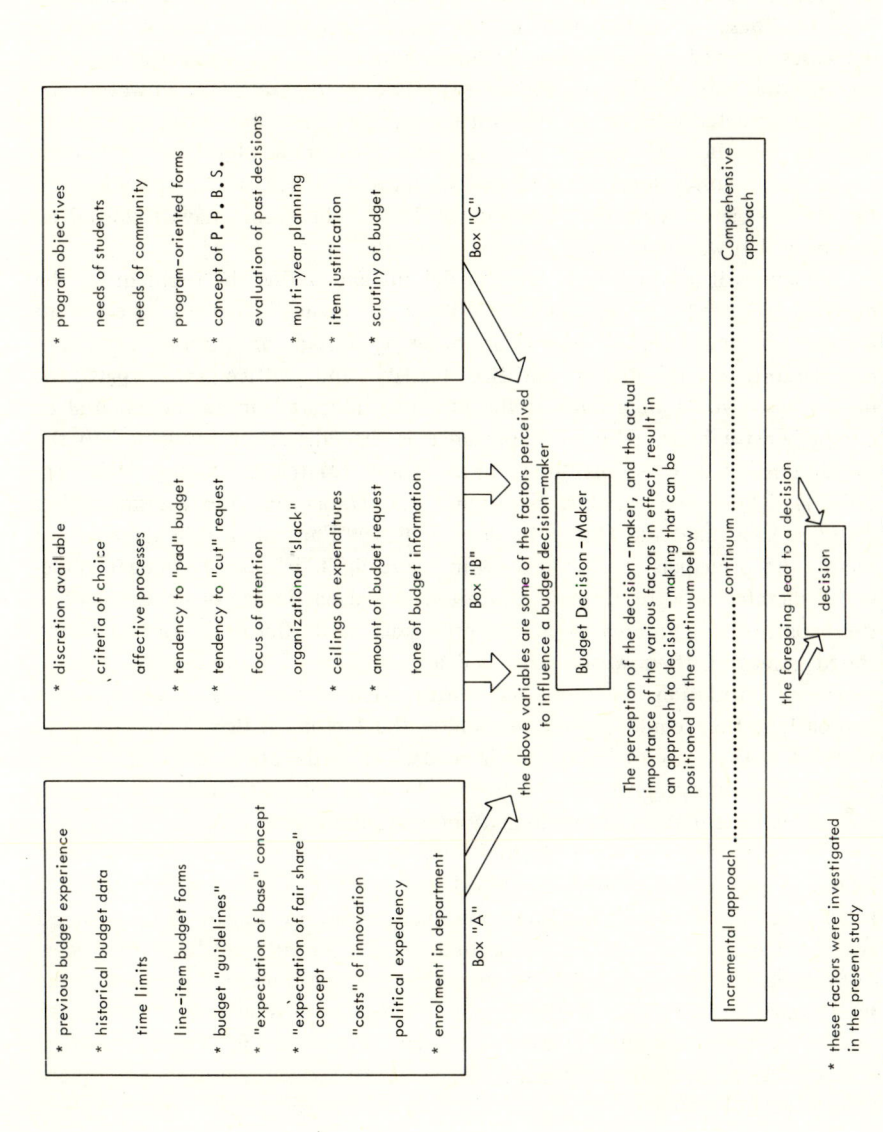

decision

* these factors were investigated in the present study

Figure 1. A Descriptive Model of the Budgetary Decision-Making Process.

Box A—for example, "line item budget forms," "historical data" such as the amount allocated in the previous year—or felt obligated to grant a department head his "base" allocation with a "fair share" percentage of any increases or decreases received by the school, he would have used factors associated with the incremental end of the continuum expressed in *Figure 1.* If, however, the principal rejected reliance on "historical data" and based his current allocation decision on Box C factors—for example, "program objective," "student needs"—and closely scrutinized all budget items requested, or perhaps employed factors associated with the "concept of PPBS," he would have followed an approach that was more comprehensive in nature.

Factors listed in Box B tend to delimit and define the problem for the decision-maker. Thus, the factor "criteria of choice"—that is, whether to consider a multitude of factors in order to obtain an optimal allocation distribution, or to merely satisfice (satisfy and suffice the department heads)—also would determine if the principal allocated on an incremental or comprehensive basis. Also of importance is the "discretion available" to the decision-maker and also his "focus of attention" (March and Simon, 1958, pp. 147-54). These two variables determine the factors that the decision-maker *could* consider and the factors he *must* consider. For instance, in some school boards the principals' budget discretions were limited because "budget guidelines" dictated straight formula allocations based on the factor "enrollment in the department." In such cases, the principals must allocate according to the stated guideline. If, however, they had a great deal of discretion and a broad focus of attention encompassing both incremental and comprehensive approaches, they could choose to employ the factors in Box A or Box B in *Figure 1* as they saw fit, to suit their needs. The model can be used, in a similar manner, to conceptualize the department head as a decision-maker in deciding how much to request in his preliminary budget submissions.

This model was used as the framework from which two structured interview questionnaires were developed. The principal's interview questionnaire focused on his decisions regarding how much money to allocate to the physical education supplies and to the capital budgets. The department head's interview questionnaire referred to his decisions concerning the amounts to request in the preliminary supplies and in the capital budget submissions. After a pretest, interviews were conducted with fourteen principals and twelve physical education department heads from fourteen of the sixteen schools in a Southern Ontario school system.

Findings and Conclusions

Selected findings of the study are listed in reference to the corresponding subproblems.

Subproblem—What factors influenced each major participant in the physical education budgetary decision-making processes?

PRINCIPALS' FINDINGS

1. The factor "amount of discretion" (freedom of judgment in suiting actions to circumstances) was of prime importance in determining the principals' supplies and capital budgetary decision-making processes. All fourteen principals surveyed indicated that they had freedom of judgment in deciding budgetary "means" and "ends." This discretion resulted in budgetary processes that were highly individualistic in each of the schools.

2. The department heads' supplies budget submissions were not factors considered by six of the fourteen principals. These six principals used their discretionary powers and did not request or make use of departmental submissions. Rather, they allocated amounts to the department head approximate to the previous year (department heads could obtain additional funds, if warranted).

3. Three principals were influenced by participatory decision-making arrangements. The considerable discretion of the principals fostered the formulation of three principals' administrative councils, which consisted of the principal, vice-principal, all department heads, and, in one case, a small rotating body of interested teachers. The council assisted the principal in decisions related to the majority of school concerns, including the supplies and capital departmental allocations.

4. Although all the principals indicated they had complete freedom in deciding physical education budgetary "means" and "ends," it was often noted that the area superintendents were relevant decision-makers in the capital budgets (in that they were able to veto any capital request).

5. The previous year's allocation was found to be an important factor in influencing the amount principals allocated to the current physical education supplies, but not the capital budgets. Although the data revealed that only four principals stated that supplies allocations were based solely on the amount allocated in the previous year, six of nine principals indicated that the previous year's allocation was "important" in determining their supplies allocation decisions. Moreover, ten of the fourteen principals felt that the previous year's supplies allocation was a "good indicator" for allocation decisions, unless something unusual occurred that necessitated funding.

6. In the capital budget, however, only two of nine principals considered the previous year's capital allocation as "important" in determining the current physical education capital allocation. In fact, ten of fourteen principals stated that capital allocations were based "solely on the needs" of the program, while the remaining four used a combination of stated needs and the previous year's allocation.

7. A comparison of actual amounts allocated to the 1971 and the 1972 physical education supplies and capital budgets revealed that the departmental supplies allocations were relatively stable, while the capital allocations fluctuated widely within each physical education department.

8. Planning-Programming-Budgeting-System (PPBS), a budgeting approach currently being introduced into various Ontario school boards, was not found to be a factor that influenced the principals' budgetary processes.

DEPARTMENT HEADS' FINDINGS

1. The factor "amount of discretion" (actually the lack of it) was found to be a central factor in influencing the budgetary decision-making processes that the department heads employed to formulate their supplies and capital budget requests. The budgetary processes used by the department heads were found to be dependent on the inputs required by their respective principals. As a result, six department heads had very limited discretion in deciding supplies budget amounts; they were not requested to submit a supplies budget request as an input into the physical education supplies budgetary decision-making process.

2. Only three of the twelve department heads were found to operate within what might be the "expected" supplies budgetary process, as referred to in the literature. Two of these three were in their first year as a department head. As mentioned earlier, six department heads did not even submit supplies budget requests, and three other department heads operated with participatory decision-making arrangements which also were distinct from the process described in the literature.

3. Eleven of twelve department heads formulated capital requests, including justification for need, as inputs into the "expected" budgetary process referred to above.

4. Factors central to the incremental and comprehensive processes, such as the reliance on the previous year's allocation and budget formulation based solely on need, were also investigated. The data revealed that four of the seven department heads who did submit supplies requests stated that the requested allocation was based solely on the needs of the program. The remaining three indicated that, in addition to the needs of the program, they also considered the allocation in the previous year.

5. In the capital budget, ten of the eleven department heads who submitted capital requests stated that the amounts asked for were based solely on the needs of the program, not the allocation in the previous year, an incremental factor.

Subproblem—Were the schools' physical education budgetary decision-making processes essentially incremental or comprehensive in nature?

Data from the principals' and department heads' interviews resulted in the classification of each school's supplies and capital processes on an incremental-comprehensive continuum. These processes are represented spatially in *Figure 2* and *Figure 3*.

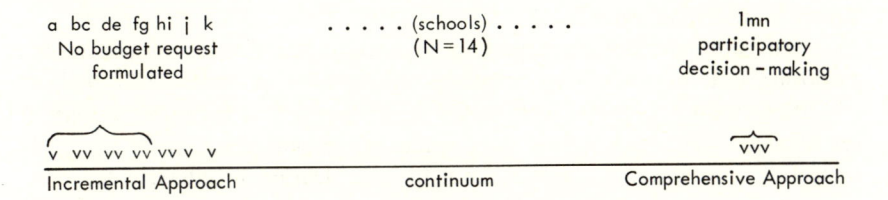

```
a bc de fg hi j k        . . . . . (schools) . . . . .        l mn
No budget request              (N = 14)                    participatory
formulated                                               decision - making

⌒
v  vv  vv  vv  vv  v  v                                        vvv
Incremental Approach          continuum              Comprehensive Approach
```

Figure 2. An approximate diagrammatic representation of the schools' physical education *capital* budgetary decision-making processes on a comprehensive-incremental continuum.

```
h e b                    . . . . . (schools) . . . . .        fgdja ck lmn
                               (N = 13)
v  v  v                                                        vvvvv vv vvv
Incremental Approach          continuum              Comprehensive Approach
```

Figure 3. An approximate diagrammatic representation of the schools' physical education *capital* budgetary decision-making processes on a comprehensive-incremental continuum.

A noteworthy aspect of this study was the supplies process employed by the schools at the extremes on the continuum presented in *Figure 2*. Three schools (n, m, and l) operated with a participatory decision-making arrangement (principal's administrative council) for budget decisions. These three budgetary processes tended to be *comprehensive* in nature. At the other extreme end of the continuum, several schools employed highly *incremental* approaches to their supplies budgetary processes. Briefly, the participatory, decision-making approach proceeded as follows: (1) the principal asked for summary budget requests from all the department heads, based on program needs; (2) on a master sheet, the principal listed each department head's total requested amount, also the total amount of money available for allocation, and the amount to reduce for a balanced budget; (3) this information was then sent to all department heads; (4) the principal later arranged and chaired a budget-reduction meeting which centered on "suggestive" questions from the members concerning possible areas where various department might reduce funds; and (5) a teamwork attitude usually resulted in a balanced budget in less than one hour.

At the other extreme end of the continuum, the supplies processes were fundamentally different. One principal did not ask for a departmental request but merely allocated on a per capita basis. Five other schools were clustered at the incremental end of the continuum and also did not ask for requests from the department heads; rather, the principals allocated funds as they saw fit. Generally, they employed the previous year's allocations as the prime determinants for current allocations.

An additional notable aspect of this study was the department heads' surprising lack of knowledge regarding the manner in which their budget allocations were determined. One would have thought that the recent emphasis on financial restrictions would have made department heads more aware of budgeting procedures. Why was this not the case? During the interview sessions, many department heads referred to revenue sources in addition to those funds received from the school board. The most common sources were gate receipts, athletic cards, soft-drink machines, and fund-raising drives by student athletic associations. Perhaps department heads were not well enough informed about the details of their principals' allocation processes because they were obtaining sufficient funds from these other sources. This aspect of physical education and athletic budgeting merits further study.

CONCLUSIONS

Within the limitations of this investigation, the following conclusions were drawn:

1. The schools' physical education *supplies* budgetary decision-making processes were essentially *incremental* in nature. The three schools that operated with participatory, decision-making approaches were important exceptions.

2. The schools' physical education *capital* budgetary decision-making processes were essentially *comprehensive* in nature.

3. The overriding factor that influenced the entire physical education supplies and capital budgetary decision-making process was the principals' extensive discretion in deciding both the approaches used to determine departmental allocations and the actual amount allocated. This discretion resulted in highly individualistic budgetary processes, several of which were different from the process that might be expected.

Implications for the Practicing Administrator

Based on the findings of this study and also the current status of Planning-Programming-Budgeting-Systems in education, it is suggested that the "practicing administrator" direct his attention to the following concerns:

Just as a good teacher strives for conscious and deliberate teaching behavior (Mosston, 1966, p. xiii), an administrator should strive for conscious and deliberate administrative behavior. He should be aware of the present budgetary process employed in his organization, whether it is incremental, comprehensive, or somewhere between these two extremes. This will likely necessitate time and effort interviewing financial officers and the like. It is hoped that *Figure 1* and the background literature will be useful in this regard. The administrator should also strive to understand the strengths and weaknesses of the current approach to budgeting employed, as well as those of alternative approaches (such as PPBS). Sensible decision depends as much upon knowing the present state of affairs as on knowing what *can* be and what *ought* to be.

In light of the current state of budgetary affairs, some mention should be made of the introduction of PPBS into schools, particularly at the subject-area level. The board that was surveyed did not dictate a common budgetary procedure for the departmental budget allocation process. As a result, each school adopted the budgetary techniques it favored (or that was passed on from previous years). Although the majority of approaches used were basically incremental, some interesting possibilities such as participatory, decision-making arrangements were found to be in existence, and merit further study. No school investigation relied on approaches similar to Planning-Programming-Budgeting-Systems. PPBS, however, is currently being introduced into various school boards in Ontario. Consider the following quote:

> To argue that an existing order is "imperfect" in comparison with an alternative order of affairs [such as PPBS] that turns out, upon careful inspection, to be unobtainable may not be different from arguing that the existing order is "perfect" (Buchanan, 1962, p. 19).

Obviously, "there is no special magic in the *status quo*. Inertia and ignorance as well as experience and wisdom may be responsible for the present state of affairs" (Wildavsky, 1964, p. 178). Nevertheless, education administrators should perhaps consider advocating a "better" incremental approach rather than a more comprehensive one such as PPBS.

Wildavsky noted that "human nature is never more evident than when men are struggling to apportion resources they have to a myriad of claimants" (1964, p. v). The "human nature" aspect of budgeting raises an interesting question. Can a rational model (such as PPBS) be effective in educational systems, particularly at the subject-level area, where sound economic thought must often give way to human nature, with its emotions, values, fixed obligations, and "satisficing" (satisfying and sufficing) rather than optimizing?

Wildavsky found that rather than attempt to be comprehensive, the men concerned with budgeting take short-cuts to deal with financial decisions (1964, pp. 146-47). Administrators, however, often find these "rules of thumb" embarrassing when brought to light. Wildavsky, however, was quick to point out that these aids to calculation were universally followed in dealing with complex problems (1964, p. 147). For example, he noted that business organizations use "share of the market" as an operational guide to simplify their calculations.

Citizens use party preference, a favorite columnist, or advice from a friend to cut their informational costs in making voting decisions. Will PPBS and the plethora of information that is necessary for its effective functioning eradicate the rules of thumb and aids to calculation that budgetary participants employ—or will it merely necessitate the development of more sophisticated aids? There are several additional questions to which physical education administrators should address themselves before jumping on the PPBS bandwagon. Briefly stated, these are as follows:

1. Is educational theory sufficiently advanced to provide significant, measurable objectives and also accurate and up-to-date evaluative techniques to determine the degree of attainment of these objectives? All are important criteria for an effective PPBS. Also, will PPBS overlook important intangible goals of physical education?

2. Will decisions made through PPBS yield classroom results and effect financial and human resource allocations that are much improved over, or even different from, those realized with the present processes?

3. What are the "costs" (financial, time, and morale) of rejecting the manner in which budget activities have been conducted for years in favor of an innovative process such as PPBS?

4. Will decisions made through PPBS effect the three-program structure (core program, intramurals, and athletics) that many Ontario schools currently operate with? Also, will the health program remain under the jurisdiction of the physical education department? Although a reordering of the present three-program structure might be in order, should the initiative arise from the financial concerns of the board or the careful analysis by physical education and other school departments?

5. Will physical education and athletics "suffer" mainly as a result of the physical education administrators' lack of expertise in PPBS and the current budgetary processes rather than possible limitations in the present concept of physical education and athletics in secondary schools? It is hoped that the bibliography at the end of this chapter will assist somewhat in alleviating this problem.

Callahan, in *Education and the Cult of Efficiency,* stated:

> It is hoped that the American people will see that the introduction into education of concepts and practices from fields such as business and industry can be a serious error. Efficiency and economy—important as they are—must be considered in the light of the quality of education that is being provided. (1962, p. 263)

One should realize that the foregoing "concerns" do not negate the possibility that PPBS might well be eventually beneficial to administrators. Education decision-makers should strive to utilize scientific techniques such as

PPBS in order to reduce irrational aspects of their decisions. They should, however, also strive to be critical, in a positive way, of such innovations. Callahan noted that in 1929, John Dewey warned educators that it was

> very easy for science to be regarded as a guarantee that goes with the sale of goods rather than as a light to the eyes and a lamp to the feet. It is prized for its prestige value rather than as an organ of personal illumination and liberation (1962, p. 247).

Administrators should realize that a concept such as PPBS is not a panacea; it can only at most *assist* in making better decisions, because decision-making is a uniquely human endeavor.

General Bibliography

Avedisian, Charles T., "Planning Programming Budgeting Systems," *Jopher*, 43, no. 8 (October 1972), 37-39.

Balls, H. G., "New Techniques in Government Budgeting 4: Planning, Programming and Budgeting in Canada," *Public Administration*, 48 (1970), 289-305.

Barnard, Chester I., *Functions of the Executive*. Cambridge, Mass.: Harvard University Press, 1938.

Buchanan, James M., "Politics, Policy, and the Pigovian Margins," *Economica*, 29 (February 1962), 17-28.

Bucher, Charles A., *Administration of School and College Health and Physical Education Programs*. Saint Louis: C. V. Mosby Co., 1967.

Callahan, Raymond E., *Education and the Cult of Efficiency: A Study of the Social Forces that Have Shaped the Administration of Public Schools*. Chicago: University of Chicago Press, 1962.

Crecine, John P., *Governmental Problem-Solving: A Computer Simulation of Municipal Budgeting*. Chicago: Rand McNally & Co., 1969.

Davis, Otto A., M. A. H. Dempster, and Aaron Wildavsky, "A Theory of the Budgetary Process," *American Political Science Review*, 60 (September 1966), 529-47.

Furno, Orlando F., "Planning-Programming-Budgeting Systems: Boon or Bane for Cost Effectiveness Studies?" in *Fiscal Planning for Schools in Transition*. NEA Committee on Educational Finance, *Proceedings of Twelfth National Conference on School Finance*. New Orleans, La., 1969.

Gerwin, Donald, *Budgeting Public Funds: The Decision Process in an Urban School District*. Madison, Wis.: University of Wisconsin Press, 1969.

Griffiths, Daniel E., *Administrative Theory*. New York: Appleton-Century-Crofts Inc., 1959.

Hamwood, John A., *Planning-Programming-Budgeting: Part II*, report prepared by the OTF Educational Finance Committee. Toronto: June 1971.

Hartley, Harry J., *Educational Planning-Programming-Budgeting: A Systems Approach*. Englewood Cliffs, N.J.: Prentice-Hall, Inc., 1968.

Ilavsky, John, "Planning Programming Budget System," *Bulletin*, 52, no. 3 (May 1972), 125-28.

Key, V. O., Jr., "The Lack of a Budgetary Theory," *American Political Science Review*, 34 (December 1940), 137-44.

Lewis, Verna B., "Toward a Theory of Budgeting," *Public Administration Review*, 12 (Winter 1952), 42-54.

Lindblom, Charles E., "The Science of Muddling Through," *Public Administration Review*, 19 (Spring 1959), 79-88.

March, James G., and Herbert A. Simon, *Organizations*. New York: John Wiley & Sons Inc., 1958.

Mosston, Muska, *Teaching Physical Education: From Command to Discovery*. Columbus, Ohio: Charles E. Merrill Publishing Co., 1966.

Parsons, Talcott, "Suggestions for a Sociological Approach to the Theory of Organizations," *Administrative Science Quarterly*, I (June 1956), pp. 63-85.

Penny, William J., "An Analysis of the Meanings Attached to Selected Concepts in Administrative Theory." Ph.D. diss., University of Illinois, 1968.

Perkins, Joseph A., Jr., "PPBS and MIS: Their Role in Managing Education," in *Fiscal Planning for Schools in Transition*. NEA Committee on Educational Finance, *Proceedings of Twelfth National Conference on School Finance*. New Orleans, La., 1969.

Simon, Herbert A., *Administrative Behavior: A Study of the Decision-Making Process in Administrative Organization*. New York: The Macmillan Co., 1957.

Treasury Board of Ontario, *Effective Management Through PPBS*, Imprint S22-a, October 1969.

Umans, Shelley, *The Management of Education: A Systematic Design for Educational Evolution*. Garden City, N.Y.: Doubleday Co., 1970.

Wildavsky, Aaron, *Politics of the Budgetary Process*. Boston: Little, Brown and Company, 1964.

―――, "Political Implications of Budgetary Reform," *Public Administration Review*, 21 (Autumn 1961), 183-90.

Wildavsky, Aaron, and Arthur Hammond, "Comprehensive Versus Incremental Budgeting in the Department of Agriculture," *Administrative Science Quarterly*, 10 (December 1965), 321-46.

IV

LOOKING INWARD, OUTWARD, AND TO THE FUTURE

23

The Employment of Philosophical Analysis to Supplement Administrative Theory and Research

Earle F. Zeigler

When a truly definitive inventory of administrative theory and research is developed, such knowledge can then serve as a foundation to be made available to all future administrative leaders in education. Such synthesis and integration of knowledge into concepts will inevitably have considerable practical value in providing the finest type of operational basis. The logic of this approach seems incontrovertible, but there appears to be one major flaw with such an assumption. Value-free, scientific investigation may in time tell us how to bring about such-and-such an effect, but it will *never* tell us whether it is desirable to function in a certain way in our own educational system. (The only possible exception to this statement seems to be in connection with the philosophy of pragmatism originally postulated by Peirce, James, and Dewey.) It is at this point that individual and group values come into the picture—a condition from which we can't, and perhaps shouldn't wish to, escape. Thus, now and in the future, each administrator has a responsibility to examine himself and to construct his own personal philosophy so that he may be an effective professional person.

At first glance an administrator may not see the need for such a disciplined approach. He may well argue that he hasn't time to be bothered with any sort of a detailed analysis, and that he is already practicing his profession quite effectively. His argument quite often is that he possesses a certain amount of common sense, and that this has proven quite satisfactory. This is a fairly difficult argument to overcome, especially if the individual has achieved considerable success. Such a person is operating on the basis of certain underlying opinion—a sort of "theoretical group bias." This *is* his philosophy of education and educational administration as a practitioner.

The Need to Construct a Consistent Personal Philosophy

But is this enough? The rebuttal to such an approach is that the common-sense system of planning and defining problems breaks down when long-range policy-making and planning become necessary. The premise being stated here is that a "common-sense" administrator may increase his influence and effectiveness markedly by the achievement of a unified philosophy—one that is as logical and consistent as possible in keeping with his background and experience. Certainly no one will argue that future planning is not important as we look ahead to the many persistent and recurring problems facing us in the final third of the twentieth century. We might through analogy liken the individual using the common-sense approach to an automobile moving along in second gear with the attendant stresses caused by continual progress in such a manner. In fact, a careful analysis of such "progress" might even indicate that the car is wandering all over the road. The question is, how can we get the car into high gear, or possibly into overdrive, *and follow a reasonably straight course?* At this point a basic hypothesis might be ventured that the field of educational administration needs a great many more people who are truly operating in high gear rather than in second or even, as often appears to be the case, in low.

Thus, the difference between a philosophical approach as compared to common-sense approach is one of degree. That the field has made progress in the past one hundred years or so is evident. But there are too many signs that many of the persistent problems are being handled in the same old way. If this assumption is true, the question then is how can we improve on common sense. The scientist improves on common sense by all kinds of experimentation. His task is to select a particular problem that can be defined narrowly and precisely. After precise problem definition has been accomplished, he begins his experimentation striving for as much reliability and objectivity as is possible under the circumstances. Conversely, the philosophic method of improving on common sense moves in a quite different direction. Instead of refining and delimiting, the "philosopher" uses an all-inclusive method by drawing from a wide variety of sources available in order to effect the best possible synthesis. In such a situation the plan is to bring common sense and tradition into alignment with the results of available scientific experimentation so that the philosophic process may be furthered as best possible.

The Reason for Philosophy of Education

When we consider the nature of existence from a metaphysical standpoint, there appear to be two major positions. Either we are confronted by a dynamic, changing world with evolving goals not yet fully realized, or we are part of a universe in which there are certain basic unchangeable aspects of reality which have emanated from a supernatural source or are simply present in the universe because of the nature of things—a question, in the latter case, of moral or natural law and order.

Looking at man himself, we again find two opposing positions. According to one viewpoint, man is regarded as an evolving organism in a changing world; any constancy that seems apparent in human nature is only relative. The other belief involves man as the possessor of a spiritual entity that somehow has a definite relationship to the Great Spirit or God. Human nature itself is unchanging, and man has freedom to choose between good and evil as he traverses this mortal sphere en route to possible immortality.

When it comes to the question of a theory of knowledge-acquisition, or epistemology—there appear to be three major theories. They all revolve about whether man can truly know reality through his intelligence. When we acquire knowledge through this means (the first belief) and find that it corresponds to actual reality, we have discovered truth and can then transmit knowledge through a prescribed curriculum. A second belief is that there are two worlds, so to speak. There is a world that can be known by man through his senses and another world the knowledge of which is forever unobtainable to man. A third view has gradually emerged which disregards the approach of the other two to the problem of knowledge-acquisition. This position involves the matter of environmental adaptation; if something works, then it is true and knowledge results.

The whole question seems here to resolve itself into whether there is one philosophy of education or whether many philosophies of education are possible. However you may view what often appears to be a hopeless impasse, a democratic setting of life allows the promulgation of many different philosophies of education. Facing such a situation, the task of the educational philosopher is actually quite complex. He can analyze and delineate the various positions to the best of his ability. Where possible, he may attempt a synthesis and try to resolve, or at least to reduce, the many philosophical discussions and arguments that are everywhere evident. Quite often his task seems to be almost hopeless, because he can't even get opposing factions to agree to a set of ground rules by which the game may be played.

Quite often we hear it said that science will eventually be employed to help us determine the facts in just about any given educational situation. If this becomes true, the task of the educational philosopher will then be one of assessing these findings and telling us whether these facts (or scientific data) seem to point in one educational direction or another. It will be impossible for him to be unbiased as he speculates about educational objectives (or values), but he will still be able to help us with normative and analytical investigation of the finest type.

The Possibility of an Educational Philosophy Spectrum or Continuum

Even if educational administrators are armed with value-free, tenable administrative theory and research, they will still need to prepare themselves more fully for the battlefield of ideas on the way toward the year 2000. The contention here is that an understanding of our society's philosophical foundations is necessary before sound and consistent value judgments can be made about the scientific evidence at hand. This approach is not going to be a panacea for all our ills, but such analysis of a philosophical nature will place us in a much better position to meet our recurring problems logically and consistently. In recent years the situation in education seems to have been more a case of a storm-tossed ship in the face of often almost uncontrollable winds of social force. How can an administrator exert educational leadership when he is merely reflecting social forces and handing down the cultural heritage?

To accomplish this goal we recommend that each concerned individual examine himself to the best of his ability and find his place on a somewhat loosely knit educational philosophy spectrum in accordance with some of the ideas expressed under the leading philosophical tendencies. In attempting to do this, keep in mind that experimentalism (or progressivism, if you will) is greatly concerned about such things as pupil freedom, individual differences, pupil interest, pupil growth, no fixed values, and the idea that education is life now. The essentialist (or traditionalist) believes that there are certain educational values by which the individual must be guided, that effort takes precedence over interest, and that this girds moral stamina, that the experience of the past has powerful jurisdiction over the present, and that the cultivation of the intellect is most important in education. These beliefs attributed to each broad position are, of course, only representative and not inclusive. There is reason to believe, however, that an administrator should at least be able to delineate his own position generally under one broad category or the other. With this in mind we shall now examine, albeit far too briefly, the implications for education from the leading philosophical tendencies of the Western World (as "translated" into particular educational philosophies). The following diagram is offered as a means of placing them approximately on an educational philosophy spectrum.

Philosophy of Education Spectrum

Note: The reader may wish to examine himself—his personal philosophy of education—based on this spectrum analysis.

Keep in mind that the *primary* criterion on which this is based is the concept of "individual freedom."

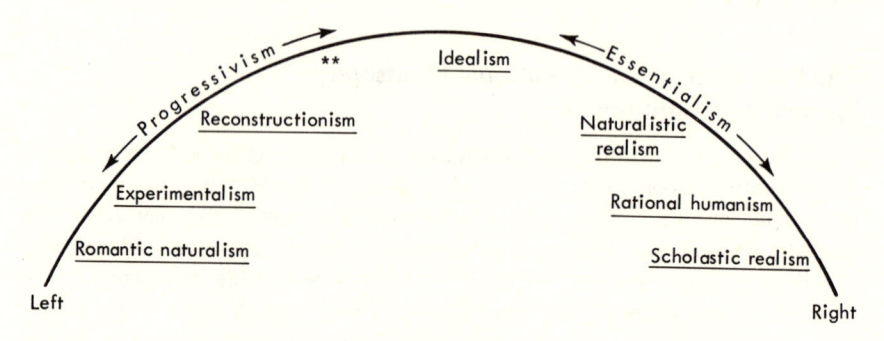

```
         Progressivism →           ← Essentialism
              **       Idealism
        Reconstructionism       Naturalistic
                                   realism
    Experimentalism              Rational humanism
  Romantic naturalism              Scholastic realism
Left                                              Right
```

Recent Trends

** Existentialism – a permeating influence; individualistic, with atheistic, agnostic, and Christian "branches."

Linguistic analysis – philosophy in "a new key"; the assumption here is that man's ordinary language has many defects that need to be corrected. Another objective here is the "rational reconstruction of the language of science" (Abraham Kaplan).

Language Analysis as Philosophy's Function

Language analysis has been a most interesting and important development that has gathered momentum in the past forty years or so. Despite the fact that men have engaged in philosophical thought for such a long time, there is still vigorous argument over the exact nature of philosophy. Developing scientific method has forced many of today's philosophers to ask themselves, "In what kind of activity am I engaging?" They wonder whether philosophical activity does result in knowledge after all. If true knowledge can come only from scientific experimentation, what is the justification for philosophy? What may be called "analytic philosophy" or "language philosophy" represents a type of logico-linguistic analysis—a departure from the world systems of the late nineteenth and early twentieth centuries. One of the basic assumptions here is that philosophers must learn to state their questions and answers just as clearly as we expect scientists to describe their research investigations. If this can be done, the philosopher may be able to make sufficient headway and come to some definite conclusions about his work upon which there could be fairly general agreement. Such an approach, it is argued, would put an end to what has actually been foolish disputation. Language is a phenomenon, the philosophers of language say, and it has "caught a disease." Thus, this new type of philosopher sees himself as the servant of science; his former role as purveyor of "nonsense knowledge" was indeed a masquerade. Philosophy will never be the "queen of sciences" again.

The Traditional Positions Have Been under Attack

Although it is most difficult to gain historical perspective on the philosophical trends and developments of the past one hundred years, it is obvious that language philosophy and existentialism have made great inroads on the so-called world systems. Prior to World War I, idealism had already lost some of the prestige which it had enjoyed in the late 1800s. Realism gradually became a sort of catchall for a variety of different shades of belief. Thus, the term must be qualified when it is used today. Pragmatism, which gathered much strength from naturalism, has continued to be influential, especially in the United States. Reconstructionism, currently a weak but utopian offshoot of the educational philosophy of experimentalism (pragmatism), is waning largely because of strong social forces leading the country toward increasing educational essentialism. Existentialism seems to be gathering momentum and has emerged as a significant force—at the very least a very strong permeating influence. This position affirms that man's task is to create his own ideals and values, inasmuch as science has shown that the transcendent ideals of the Church are nonsense. The substance of this approach is that man is "on his own" in a cold, cruel world. Man, quite often spelled with a capital "M," must give meaning and direction to a world lacking in these qualities. He must, that is, if he expects to have a future in this galaxy. Can he so direct his own existence that responsible social action will result? This is the fundamental, overriding question.

The Role of Educational Philosophy

Educational philosophy, really a subdivision of philosophy, devotes itself to an analysis of the implications from the various philosophical positions for three major areas: (1) the relationship among society, school, and the individual; (2) educational aims and objectives; and (3) the process of education. More specifically, questions have been asked (and partially answered) relating to standardization of instruction, administrative control, teacher control, the psychology of learning, the definition of subject matter, the role of measurement and evaluation, the aims of the process, the importance of interest in learning, the need for indoctrination and discipline, and many other related questions.

For some time we have been recommending that philosophy, and educational philosophy, can have true meaning for educators, if they would make a sincere effort to comprehend their philosophical foundations. In such a way the time-honored discipline of philosophy can and should be put to work. This approach won't provide answers to all of the many persistent and recurring

EDUCATIONAL PHILOSOPHIES	NATURE OF REALITY (METAPHYSICS)	EDUCATIONAL AIMS AND OBJECTIVES	EDUCATIONAL PROCESSES (EPISTEMOLOGY)
EXPERIMENTALISM*	Nature is an emergent evolution, and man's frame of reality is limited to nature as it functions. The world is characterized by activity and change. Rational man has developed through organic evolution, and the world is yet incomplete—a reality that is constantly undergoing change because of a theory of emergent novelty. Man enjoys freedom of will; freedom is achieved through continuous and developmental learning from experience.	The general aim of education is more education. "Education in the broadest sense can be nothing less than the changes made in human beings by their experience." Participation by students in the formation of aims and objectives is absolutely essential to generate the all-important desired interest. Social efficiency can well be considered the general aim of education. Pupil growth is a paramount goal, as the individual is placed at the center of the educational experience.	Knowledge is the result of a process of thought with a useful purpose. Truth is not only to be tested by its correspondence with reality, but also its practical results. Knowledge is earned through experience and is an instrument of verification. Mind has evolved in the natural order as a more flexible means whereby man adapts himself to his world. Learning takes place when interest and effort unite to produce the desired result. A psychological order (problem-solving as explained through scientific method) is more useful than a logical arrangement (from the simple fact to the complex conclusion). There is always a social context to learning, and the curriculum must be adapted to the society for which it is intended.

*Quoted material from George R. Geiger, "An Experimentalistic Approach to Education," *Modern Philosophies and Education.* Chicago: University of Chicago Press, 1955, Part I.

EDUCATIONAL PHILOSOPHIES	NATURE OF REALITY (METAPHYSICS)	EDUCATIONAL AIMS AND OBJECTIVES	EDUCATIONAL PROCESSES (EPISTEMOLOGY)
RECONSTRUCTIONISM**	Experience and nature "constitute both the form and content of the entire universe" (multiverse?). There is no such thing as a preestablished order of things in the world. Reality is evolving and humanity appears to be a most important manifestation of the natural process. The impact of cultural forces upon man are fundamental, and every effort must be made to understand them as we strive to build the best type of group-centered culture. In other words "the structure of cultural reality" should be our foremost concern. Cultural determinants have shaped the history of man, and he now has reached a crucial stage in the development of life on this planet. Our efforts should be focused on building of a world culture.	Social self-realization is the supreme value in education. The realization of this ideal is most important for the individual in his social setting—a world culture. Positive ideals must be molded toward the evolving democratic ideal by a general education which is group-centered and in which the majority determines the acceptable goals. Education by means of "hidden coercion" is to be avoided as much as possible. Learning is explained by the organismic principle of functional psychology. Social intelligence acquired teaches man to control and direct his urges as he concurs with or attempts to modify cultural purposes.	An organismic approach to the learning process is basic. Thought cannot be independent of certain aspects of the organism; it is related integrally with emotional and muscular functions. Man's mind enables him to cope with the problems of human life in a social environment. Social intelligence is closely related to scientific method. Certain operational concepts, inseparable from metaphysics and axiology (beliefs about reality and value) focus on the reflective thought, problem-solving, and social consensus necessary for the transformation of the culture.

**Quoted material from Theodore Brameld, *Toward a Reconstructed Philosophy of Education.* New York: The Dryden Press, Inc., 1956.

EDUCATIONAL PHILOSOPHIES	NATURE OF REALITY (METAPHYSICS)	EDUCATIONAL AIMS AND OBJECTIVES	EDUCATIONAL PROCESSES (EPISTEMOLOGY)
IDEALISM†	Mind as experienced by all men is basic and real. The entire universe is mind essentially. Man is more than just a body; he possesses a soul, and such possession makes him of a higher order than all other creatures on earth. "The order of the world is due to the manifestation in space and time of an eternal and spiritual reality." The individual is part of the whole, and it is man's task to learn as much about the Absolute as possible. There is divided opinion within this position regarding the problem of monism or pluralism. Man has freedom to determine which way he shall go in life; he can relate to moral law in the universe, or he can turn against it.	Through education the developing organism becomes what it latently is. All education may be said to have a religious significance, which means that there is a "moral imperative" en education. As man's mind strives to realize itself, there is the possibility of realization of the Absolute within the individual mind. Education should aid the child to adjust to the basic realities (the spiritual ideals of truth, beauty, and goodness) that the history of the race has furnished us. The basic values of human living are health, character, social justice, skill, art, love, knowledge, philosophy, and religion.	Understanding the nature of knowledge will clarify the nature of reality. Nature is the medium by which God communicates to us. Basically, knowledge comes only from the mind—a mind which must offer and receive ideas. Mind and matter are qualitatively different. A finite mind emanates through heredity from another finite mind. All finite minds are "materializations" of an infinite mind. Thought is the standard by which all else in the world is judged. An individual attains truth for himself by examining the wisdom of the past through his own mind. Reality, viewed in this way, is a system of logic and order that has been established by the Universal Mind. Experimental testing helps to determine what truth really is.

†Quoted material is from H. H. Horne, "An Idealistic Philosophy of Education," *Philosophies of Education.* Chicago: University of Chicago Press, 1942.

EDUCATIONAL PHILOSOPHIES	NATURE OF REALITY (METAPHYSICS)	EDUCATIONAL AIMS AND OBJECTIVES	EDUCATIONAL PROCESSES (EPISTEMOLOGY)
REALISM††	"The world exists in itself, apart from our desires and knowledges." There is only one reality; that which we perceive is it. "The universe is made up of real substantial entities, existing in themselves and ordered to one another by extramental relations.... To be is not the same as to be known...." Some feel that there is a basic unity present, while others believe in a nonunified cosmos with two or more substances or processes at work. Things don't just happen; they happen because many interrelated forces make them occur in a particular way.	"A philosophy holding that the aim of education is the acquisition of verified knowledge of the environment; recognizes the value of content as well as the activities involved in learning, and takes into account the external determinants of human behavior.... Education is the acquisition of the art of the utilization of knowledge." The primary task of education is to transmit knowledge, without which civilization cannot continue to flourish. Whatever man has discovered to be true because it conforms to reality must be handed down to future generations as the social or cultural tradition. Some holding this philosophy believe that the good life emanates from co-operation with God's grace and that development of Christian virtues is obviously of greater worth than learning or anything else.	There are two major epistemological theories of knowledge in this position. One states that the aim of knowledge "is to bring into awareness the object as it *really* is." The other emphasizes that objects are "represented" in man's consciousness, not "presented." Students should develop habits and skills involved with acquiring knowledge, with using knowledge practically to meet life's problems, and with realizing the enjoyment that life offers. A second variation of epistemological belief indicates that the child develops his intellect by employing reason to learn a subject. The principal educational aim here must be the same for all men at all times in all places. Others carry this further and state that education is the process by which man seeks to link himself ultimately with his Creator.

††Quoted material from John Wild, "Education and Human Society: A Realistic View," in *Modern Philosophies and Education*. Chicago: University of Chicago Press, 1955.

EDUCATIONAL PHILOSOPHIES	NATURE OF REALITY (METAPHYSICS)	EDUCATIONAL AIMS AND OBJECTIVES	EDUCATIONAL PROCESSES (EPISTEMOLOGY)
EXISTENTIALISM	The world of material objects extended in mathematical space with only quantitative and measurable properties is not the world we live in as human beings; our world is a human world–not a world of science. From the context of the human world all the abstractions of science derive their meaning ultimately. Man is first and foremost a concrete involvement within the world, and we distinguish the opposed poles of body and mind. Existence precedes essence; man decides his own fate. His self-transcendence distinguishes him from all other animals, and he cannot be understood in his totality by the natural sciences. Truth is expressed in art and religion as well as in science. Time and history are fundamental dimensions of human existence. The basic human task is for man to become an authentic individual in his own right. Life's present conditions can be transformed by man, an animal, who stands open	The existentialist is cognizant of the fact that the socialization of the child has become equally as important as his intellectual development as a key educational aim in this century. He is concerned, however, because the leading educational theories "see" the young as "things to be worked over in some fashion to bring them into alignment with a prior notion of what they *should* be." Even the Experimentalists seem to have failed in their effort to bring "the learner into a self-determining posture." Even if there is general agreement that a set of fundamental dispositions is to be formed, should the criterion used for the evaluation of the worth of individual dispositions be "public rather than a personal and private criterion?" "If education is to be truly human, it must somehow *awaken awareness* in the learner–existential awareness of himself as a single subjectivity in the world." Students should "constantly, freely, baselessly, and crea-	Childhood is viewed as a "pre-Existential phase of human life." About the time of puberty in the individual, there is an "Existential Moment" in the young person's subjective life. It is the time of the "onset of the self's awareness of its own existing." For the first time, the "individual sees himself as responsible for his own conduct." Then, and only then, "education must become an act of discovery." The learner's experience must be such that he gets "personally implicated in the subject-matter and in the situation around him." Knowledge must be "chosen, i.e., appropriated, before it can be true for that consciousness." It isn't something that is objective purely, nor is it merely purposeful in the person's life. Knowledge "becomes knowledge only when a subjectivity takes hold of it and puts it into his own life." It could be argued that "the Existentialist has little to offer in the way of a method of knowing,"

384

EDUCATIONAL PHILOSOPHIES (cont.)	NATURE OF REALITY (METAPHYSICS) (cont.)	EDUCATIONAL AIMS AND OBJECTIVES (cont.)	EDUCATIONAL PROCESSES (EPISTEMOLOGY) (cont.)
	to the future (paraphrased from William Barrett, *Irrational Man: A Study in Existential Philosophy.* New York: Doubleday and Company).	tively," choose their individual pattern of education." The subjectivity of the existentialistic learner should thrive in the arts (music, painting, poetry, and creative writing, etc.), but similar possibilities to study human motivation are available in the social sciences as well (quoted material from Van Cleve Morris, *Philosophy and the American School.* Boston: Houghton Mifflin Co., 1961).	Whether we are considering logic, scientific evidence, sense perception, intuition, or revelation, "it is the individual self which must make the ultimate decision as to what is, as a matter of fact, true." Perceptually and cognitively, the individual is aware of the objects of existence, but there is something more—an "internal, subjective awareness"—which enables him to know that he knows. Psychology seems to have given very few answers about this latter phase of the epistemological process to date.

problems overnight, but normative and analytical philosophical investigation could place the field in a much better position to meet its problems intelligently *when educators know where they stand.* Then conflicting philosophies could be discussed more logically and consistently than ever before.

Finding One's Place on the Educational Philosophy Spectrum

To accomplish this goal, in the absence of tenable administrative theory and research whether value-free or value-oriented, each professional educational administrator should examine himself to the best of his ability and find his place on a somewhat loosely knit educational philosophy spectrum or continuum in accordance with some of the ideas expressed under the leading philosophical tendencies. Distinguishing initially between progressivism and essentialism, and whether you lean toward one or the other, represents the beginning of an attempt to show consistency as you state your beliefs concerning the many persistent problems which you face almost daily. In attempting to do this, keep in mind that progressivism is greatly concerned about such things as pupil freedom, individual differences, pupil interest, pupil growth, no permanently fixed values, and that education is life now. The essentialist, conversely, believes typically that there are certain educational values by which the individual *must* be guided, that effort takes precedence over interest and that this girds moral stamina, that the experience of the past has powerful jurisdiction over the present, and that the cultivation of the intellect is most important in education.

Philosophical Analysis of Our Persistent Problems

We are now ready to apply these norms or "standards" to some of the more persistent problems facing education today. The philosophy of administration self-evaluation check list that follows distinguishes fairly broadly typically between progressivism and essentialism. Where possible, some finer distinctions have been drawn.

Administrative Self-Evaluation Check List for the Athletics Chairman*

BY EARLE F. ZEIGLER, Ph.D.

Directions: Make your responses directly on this questionnaire. Please select the *one* descriptive phrase under each item which best describes your own belief. *Circle* one letter from each question—the response that is closest to your present belief or "stance" in regard to the statement or question.

1. If you were to ask me how I view myself in regard to administrative outlook or philosophy, I would say that I am:
   a. Very essentialistic
   b. Essentialistic
   c. Eclectic (at times one way or the other; sometimes in the middle of the road)
   d. Progessivistic
   e. Very progressivistic
   f. Otherwise (don't see this approach—perhaps I'm existentialistic in orientation)

2. Insofar as my own personal philosophy is concerned, I subscribe generally to:
   a. A philosophy that the world exists in itself, apart from our desires and knowledges. There is only one reality; that which we perceive is it. The universe is made up of real substantial entities, existing in themselves and ordered to one another by extramental relations. . . . Man lives within this world of cause and effect, and he simply cannot make things happen independent of it.
   b. A philosophy stating that the order of the world is due to the manifestation in space and time of an eternal and spiritual reality. Mind as experienced by all men is basic and real; in fact, the entire universe is mind essentially. Man is more than just a body; he possesses a soul, and such possession makes him of a higher order than all other creatures on earth.
   c. A philosophy emphasizing that existence precedes essence, and that man decides his own fate. The world of material objects is not the world we live in as human beings. From the context of the human world all the abstractions of science

---

*This is a combined and updated version of several other similar check lists and has been prepared with the sports and athletics administrator in mind. It is based on the underlying assumption that there is a relationship between educational philosophy and administration. The advice of others—both colleagues and students—is appreciated.

derive their meaning ultimately. The basic human task is for man to become an authentic individual.
   d. A philosophy embodying the principle that nature is an emergent evolution, and that man's frame of reality is limited to nature as it functions. The structure of cultural reality should be our foremost concern. The world is characterized by activity and change.
   e. A position that finds speculation about the nature of reality quite futile. Some holding this position feel that man should be studied as a symbol-using animal. Then they ask what are the *universal* traits of the symbol-using species. Our problem, therefore, is to learn how to "analyze the structure" of statements made by man.
   f. Man's world is a human one, and it is from the context of this human world that all the abstractions of science derive their meaning ultimately. There is, of course, the world of material objects extended in mathematical space with only quantitative and measurable properties, but we humans are first and foremost concrete involvements *within* the world. Existence precedes essence, and it is up to man to decide his own fate—to transform life's present condition as a unique creature with a future that stands open.
3. My educational philosophy would include such statements as:
   a. The general aim of education is more education. Education in the broadest sense can be nothing else than the changes made in human beings by their experience. Social efficiency can well be considered the general aim of education. Some holding this position assert that the supreme value is social-self-realization in a world culture.
   b. The primary task of education is to transmit knowledge so that civilization will persist. True discoveries conforming to reality must be handed down to future generations as the cultural heritage. (Some holding this position believe that "the good life" emanates from cooperation with God's grace, and that the Christian virtues are of greatest importance in education.)
   c. Through education the developing organism becomes what it latently is. There is a moral imperative on education. Education should aid the child to adjust to the basic realities (the spiritual ideals of truth, beauty, and goodness) that the history of the race has furnished us. There is a possibility of the realization of the Absolute in the individual mind striving to realize itself.
   d. Granting that socialization of the child has become equally as important as his intellectual development, there is still the problem that many educational philosophies seem to assume the position that children are to be fashioned to conform to

a prior notion of what they *should* be. Even if there is general agreement on a set of fundamental dispositions to be formed, should the criterion employed for such an evaluation be publicly or privately determined? Education should seek to awaken awareness in the learner of himself as a single subjectivity in the world freely and creatively choosing his own educational pattern.
   e. Social self-realization is the supreme value in education. The realization of this ideal is most important for the individual in his social setting—a world culture. Positive ideals should be molded toward the evolving democratic ideal by a general education which is group-centered and in which the majority determines the acceptable goals. Education by means of "hidden coercion" is to be scrupulously avoided. Learning is explained by the organismic principle of functional psychology. Social intelligence acquired teaches man to control and direct his urges as he concurs with or attempts to modify cultural purposes.
4. Law and order is:
   a. Clearly necessary to maintain an organized society. The lack of respect for authority has led to many unfortunate incidents in the cities and on college campuses. The Supreme Court has gone too far in interpreting the constitutional rights of criminal offenders. We must generally strengthen our defenses against lawlessness.
   b. Now the emotional slogan of those groups and/or individuals who oppose desirable social change. Law and order without *justice* is characteristic of totalitarian societies. There should be no wire-tapping at all. Although rioting cannot be condoned, it usually occurs when there are underlying causes or reasons. It is essential that we attack these causes and not the symptoms of minority group unrest.
   c. Essential if America is to survive this period of turbulence and unrest. The Supreme Court has gone too far in protecting dangerous criminal offenders without regard to the safety of the American public. Wire-tapping by police in pursuit of their duty should be allowed. Rioting must be stopped; for example, students who rebel at universities should be removed by force. Further, they should be expelled when proven guilty, and public funds for their education should be cut off.
   d. The hypocritical slogan of a frightened and decadent society. The poor and minority groups are beginning to strike back at the absolute, but often concealed viciousness of an exploitive social order. "Law and order" means "keep the niggers and foreigners in their place, muzzle the communistic students, and protect the status quo."

e. The backbone of a free society. Absolutely no gains should be allowed as a result of rioting. This and other civil disturbances by communist-inspired Blacks and students should be suppressed ruthlessly. The Supreme Court has handcuffed our law-enforcement agencies by coddling criminals. You can't walk the streets anymore without fear of being molested or even killed.
f. Necessary to a democratic society, but the words as used by man have taken on an unpleasant overtone. Rising crime rates are a definite problem, but we must move positively, rather than negatively, to reach the causes. Prison rehabilitation programs should be strengthened. Crime rates will go down if better education and more jobs are provided.

5. I tend to view various types of administration and management in the following way:
   a. As an art. Many fine administrators have never had a course in administration, and I don't believe that any series of theoretical and practical courses would help them significantly. In general, I approve of the practice where a man or woman does well on the job; is gradually moved up the ladder; and eventually—if he has the knowledge, ability, and personality—is picked for a top administrative post. Such a person can learn to administer an enterprise most successfully while on the job.
   b. As a developing social science. The behavioral sciences are producing scientific evidence about human behavior—about man and his interrelationships—that is providing us with tenable theories and testable hypotheses for present and future use. This body of knowledge about human relations and the decision-making process can be presented to future administrators through problem-solving techniques as part of an internship experience. Such an individual should have a much better chance of becoming a more capable and successful administrator than he would have otherwise—all things being relatively equal, of course.

6. I believe that:
   a. There are valid principles of administration which should very rarely if ever be violated. Such principles provide many of the answers to administrative problems, and can be an indispensable help to the young administrator in search of an administrative pattern to follow.
   b. Practical rules or principles do not exist which can be applied generally in a fairly automatic fashion to many of the actual organizational problems that arise. Each new situation is unique, as are the people involved in it. Thus, the evidence is being gathered; theories are being formed; and the principles of administration "must themselves deal with the limitations

of both theory and theoreticians in an administrative environment."
7. My position about competitive sport is that:
   a. Intramural sports and voluntary physical recreational activities should be stressed, and this applies especially to team competition with particular emphasis on cooperation and the promotion of friendly competition. Extramural sport competition may be introduced when there is a need; striving for excellence is important, but it is urgent that materialistic influence be kept out of educational programs.
   b. We should help the authentically eccentric young person to feel at home in the program of competitive sport. Youth needs ways to commit itself to values and people. A person should be able to select a sport according to the personal and social values he or she wishes to derive from it. (Note: such selection is often difficult because of the extreme overemphasis on winning in this culture.)
   c. "Qualified approval" should be given to competitive sport and athletics at all educational levels, because they do help with the learning of sportsmanship and desirable social conduct if properly administered. Such activity helps with the development of physical vigor. All sports and recreational involvements are, however, definitely extracurricular and not part of the regular curriculum.
   d. Competitive sport helps youngsters of both sexes to develop "social intelligence" if educationally conducted. Those sports should be stressed which allow natural impulses to come into play. Intramural sport and regular physical education classes are more important to the large majority of students than interscholastic or intercollegiate sport and deserve priority if conflict arises over budgetary allotment, staff availability, and use of facilities. Full support can be given to team experiences in competitive sports, because they can be vital educational experiences under sound leadership.
   e. Competitive sport helps both education *of* the physical and education *through* the physical, so to speak. Also, the transfer of training theory can be activated to help with the development of desirable personality traits as well. Sports participation should always be strongly approached as a means to an end, however, and should not be stressed at the expense of one's academic subjects (and one's religious instruction when under certain auspices).
8. When considering the physical facilities, grounds, and equipment, I believe that:
   a. The physical situation isn't the important thing; what's important is the *human* situation, the quality of the coach

coaching. As an administrator, I am not going to worry too much about paint and grass seed if the coaches' salaries aren't as high as they should be.
  b. Facilities should be adaptable to allow for unexpected changes in program. My athletics program will be "undergoing continual change and revision. I don't want to have to build a whole new addition just to provide for it. I want movable bleachers, movable walls, modular construction, and, indeed, the whole concept of flexibility in the use of space."
  c. A "fixed interior pattern" will be just fine in my athletic facilities and grounds. Our program, by definition, does not need to change from year to year; it is always constant except for a few minor changes. Anyhow, buildings are not the most important thing about an athletics program; it's the people and the principles underlying the entire program.
  d. I want my facilities, grounds, and equipment to be functional and efficient. My program and institution should be an efficiently planned, systematized, and rational enterprise. You might say that I lean in the direction of the "factory" concept of architecture—perhaps something like a functional office building or municipal complex.
  e. We should have facilities and equipment, or grounds, where individual freedom, individual searching, and individual questioning can take place. Let's go back to the palaestra where Plato received instruction in wrestling as a youth, or to the olive grove and make like Socrates. For goodness sake, please liberate us from the rigidity of the present-day athletics architecture and the structured program that takes place within.
9. In regard to the athletic administrator's image of himself or herself and the whole question of staff relations, we find that those in charge of athletic programs take varying views of human relations and the decision-making process. In my opinion I see the person directing interscholastic or intercollegiate athletics as follows:
  a. The person in charge of that phase of the institution's program—one who is somewhat akin to the general of the army or the captain of a ship. Typically, this man or woman chairs meetings of athletic boards, receives advice informally on a person-to-person basis or in small group discussions, and issues directives to those working below on the table of organization. All work together in a line and staff relationship.
  b. The leader who is responsible for the athletic outcomes of the program—a program which has as its function the conservation and transmission of the established athletics

value pattern of the past (and present too!). This man has a respect for the athlete's personality, and he feels that the personality of the coach and other personnel are very important in guiding and molding the individual's personal development. Whether the athletic director is male or female, the position is that personal and social relations of a positive type are basic—if we want to get the best from people.
   c. An athletics chairperson who is interested in the process of administration. This person is really anxious to put democracy into action all the way up and down the line. All staff members find themselves drawn into policy formulation as a member of many committees. Deviation from precedent is fine, if this seems necessary to help some plan work out better. Flexibility and experimentation are the usual watchwords, and students are voting members of all committees.
   d. An athletics chairman who clearly works in the democratic tradition, although all decisions are not voted upon at all times, so to speak. Committees are employed to investigate problems of concern, and students are invited to serve in an advisory capacity whenever possible. Coaches are concerned with the individual, and decisions are made for the good of all only when necessary. The athletics chairman seeks advice often, quite often follows it, urges others to work democratically, and does his best to understand changing times and patterns of administration.
10. An administrator of athletics usually has an important part to play in the selection of coaches and other personnel, as well as in the development of general appointment policies. If I were making selections, I would:
   a. Be most concerned that the person I hire as a coach be sensitive in the area of human relations. Of course, I want this person to be competent and a student of the game, but I'm looking for an individual with some originality in his or her make-up. It's a changing world, and even the rate of change is increasing; thus, I want a coach who can and will adapt readily to needed change.
   b. Pay great attention to the personality of the candidate. The background and credentials are important, of course, but the individual's value system and whether he will come through to athletes as a person who is truly concerned about their growth and development as people are fundamental aspects of the entire selection process. The concept of "positive leadership" in the tradition of sport in the U.S. should shine through in this person who will assume such an important leadership role in the institution.
   c. Look for a coach who takes charge, but who isn't going to rock the boat too much in the rest of the organization. Such

a person understands clearly that there is a line-staff pattern or hierarchy in operation. This person is first and foremost a fine coach with a clear and logical mind—one who can get ideas across completely and thoroughly—a well-organized coach who wins a good share of his or her contests, and who stays within the letter and spirit of the rules to the greatest extent possible.

11. After a new coach is hired, the question often arises about some sort of evaluation or supervision. In fact, in many institutions such evaluation by superiors, peers, or students is often required for promotions and merit raises. As an administrator, I would be inclined to:
    a. Hire a competent individual, a self-starter who is certain to be a fine coach, and give him(her) his head, so to speak. I certainly wouldn't be running around checking up on this person and visiting practices regularly for purposes of evaluation or supervision. I've checked this coach out very carefully before I hired him(her); I'm reasonably certain that fine work will be done; and I don't wish to harass a coach by infringing on "academic freedom" by breathing down his or her neck while such a person is trying to do a job for me and the organization.
    b. Hire a competent individual, a self-starter who appears to have all of the qualities that a fine coach should have. But I believe that a new coach needs, and often wishes, to have supervision of his (her) teaching and/or coaching, especially at first. We need to improve our methods of determining whether learning through fine coaching is really taking place in the gymnasium and on the field. As new evidence becomes available from the behavioral sciences, this information and theory concerning how to be a more effective coach or teacher should be passed along to all—and especially the younger men and women involved.

12. The question of program development and the accompanying coaching method seems to be with us to stay (in some people's minds, anyhow). The administrator has responsibility in this area most certainly, and I would typically feel that:
    a. Any changes in the program and the accompanying coaching method ought to be made very slowly, carefully, and deliberately. Show me the facts and the evidence—perhaps a winning record—and I will then be willing to consider such a change. I am troubled when I see a proliferation of contrasting coaching methods and techniques offered, because I fear that the athletes may become confused and not receive the benefits that are to be derived from working with a coach in the old tradition of good hard work and discipline.

b. There should be regular meetings of coaches to discuss new methods and techniques. One's approach to coaching should never be static; it should be constantly evolving in the light of new needs that present themselves to coaches and administrators who are sensitive and alert. All those involved in the coaching enterprise should be interested in the progress of the institution as a whole. They should be willing to take a reasonable amount of time from their own personal area of interest to serve on committees concerned with the many problems of the total institution.

13. The twentieth century in North American education has been a perplexing affair. As Van Cleve Morris has stated, "whenever a vacuum appears in the community the school has been asked to fill it." As an administrator of athletics, my reaction to this is that:
    a. Many of the courses that have been added to the curriculum, such as home economics, sex education, driver and safety education, and a large variety of other subjects really are much like competitive sport in that they should not be considered as part of the school's basic offerings—the subjects that are offered during the regular school day, so to speak. It is difficult to teach the fundamental subjects well, and this cluttering-up of the curriculum inevitably results in a lowering of the educational quality of the school. Many of these experiences are important, but they should be made available by the home, the church, or some other community agency.
    b. The school and the community are working together as "partners" in every way, and this is not a simple matter to decide. Education should be conceived of as those changes which take place in an individual as a result of his or her experiences. You can't merely say on some artificial basis that some subjects are curricular and that others aren't. Sport and athletics are at the very least "cocurricular," if not fully "curricular" according to the definition above. The needs and interests of the child and young person must be met in the best possible way. If the schools are best equipped to undertake a particular task in this changing world, they should do it.

14. Determination of policies and procedures, especially the making of the important policy decisions, is most important in the educational world. In my particular area of competitive athletics, it is equally important that wise decisions be made. Typically, I would tend to:
    a. Involve as many members of the coaching staff as possible in the formation of policies. The assumption is, of course, that the resultant procedures established will be in keeping with

the principles basic to the policies themselves. If people are going to have to live with these policies, they have the right to be a part of the group that decides upon them. The same thing can be said for the making of important decisions which will inevitably affect the future of the program in which they are involved. A vote should be taken whenever possible.
b. Make decisions based on the best evidence and opinions available. I would talk the matter over carefully with the coaches and others most directly concerned, but the final decision and responsibility are mine. I would expect to have a good batting average insofar as my decisions are concerned, or else I might be replaced. I was hired as the administrator and manager of the competitive athletics program, and I don't want to waste the time of my coaches in endless meetings.
c. Seek advice from my colleagues, take "straw votes" on important policy formation and impending decisions, and even employ official balloting on long-range policy concepts upon which input seems necessary. But as the administrator I realize that many day-to-day decisions must be made by me and the assistant athletics director. This makes sense, because quite often I know more about the problem than anyone else—and the ultimate responsibility is mine.

Answers: Read only after *all* fourteen questions have been answered.

1. General Philosophy of Administration
   How did you view or categorize yourself? Please check this point carefully and look briefly at the diagram on p. 378. *Eclectics* could be thought of as middle-of-the-road, although their particular responses might veer sharply in either direction (toward essentialism or progressivism). Please note that there is an "otherwise" category as well. Such a person might be existentially oriented, or might see some type of language analysis as the role of educational philosophy.
   Now please check your answers for the next thirteen questions.
2. Personal Philosophy
   a. Essentialism (realism)—varying degrees
   b. Essentialism (idealism)—varying degrees
   c. Otherwise (existential philosophy; somewhat progressivistic)
   d. Progressivism (pragmatic naturalism)—varying degrees
   e. Otherwise (language analysis)
   f. Otherwise (the same as c. above—existential philosophy)
3. Educational Philosophy

Employment of Philosophical Analysis

   a. Progressivism (pragmatic naturalism and reconstructionism)
   b. Essentialism (includes naturalistic realism, rational humanism, and catholic moderate realism)
      (Note: the terms *scholastic realism* and *perennialism* have been used interchangeably with *catholic moderate realism* by many, whereas *experimentalism* has been often substituted for *pragmatic naturalism.*)
   c. Essentialism (idealism)—varying degrees
   d. Otherwise (existential philosophy; somewhat progressivistic)
   e. Progressivism (definitely reconstructionism)
4. Authority (Law and Order)
   a. Essentialism (moderately)
   b. Progressivism (definitely)
   c. Essentialism (definitely)
   d. Progressivism (extremely)
   e. Essentialism (extremely)
   f. Progressivism (moderately)
5. How Administration Is Viewed
   a. Essentialism—varying degrees
   b. Progressivism—varying degrees
6. Principles of Administration
   a. Essentialism—varying degrees
   b. Progressivism—varying degrees
7. Philosophy of Sport
   a. Progressivism (reconstructionism)
   b. Otherwise (existential philosophy; somewhat progressivistic)
   c. Essentialism (realism)
   d. Progressivism (pragmatic naturalism)
   e. Essentialism (idealism)
8. Facilities, Grounds, and Equipment
   a. Essentialism (idealism in orientation)
   b. Progressivism (pragmatic naturalism)
   c. Essentialism (strongly—possible catholic moderate realism)
   d. Essentialism (definitely—possibly naturalistic realism)
   e. Otherwise (existential orientation)
9. Leadership and Personnel Relations
   a. Essentialism (extremely or strongly so)
   b. Essentialism (definitely so; idealistic orientation)
   c. Progressivism (extremely or strongly so)
   d. Progressivism (moderately)
10. Staff Selection
    a. Progressivism (orientation is pragmatic naturalism)
    b. Essentialism (idealistic orientation)
    c. Essentialism (strongly so; naturalistic realism)
11. Supervision and Evaluation of Coaches

a. Essentialism—varying degrees
b. Progressivism—varying degrees
12. Program Development and Coaching Methods
    a. Essentialism—varying degrees
    b. Progressivism—varying degrees
13. The Role of the School or University
    a. Essentialism—varying degrees
    b. Progressivism—varying degrees
14. Policy Formulation and Decision-Making
    a. Progressivism (orientation is pragmatic naturalism)
    b. Essentialism (strongly so; realistic orientation)
    c. Essentialism (moderately so; idealistic orientation)

HOW DID YOU SCORE?

To compute your score or result, exclude but keep in mind the answer you gave to Question 1. Second, you should *declare yourself* wherever it says "varying degrees," or "moderately," or "strongly," etc. On this basis tally your answers to determine your position as well as possible according to the categories indicated in Question 1. A *majority* of your answers falling one way or the other would tend to classify you as "largely this" or "largely that." If your answers are half one way and about half the other, you can probably call yourself "eclectic" (which would seemingly call for greater self-examination). You may find that you are existentially oriented, which is probably at least somewhat progressivistic.

Second, in the light of your original answer to Question 1, would you now say that you were consistent and correct in your self-assessment?

Yes ( ) (Please mark "X" where
No ( )   appropriate)

Third, after tallying the answers as well as possible, keeping in mind the subjectivity of a check list such as this, did this quiz show you to be:

Strongly essentialistic ( )
Essentialistic ( )
Eclectic ( )
Progressivistic ( )
Strongly Progressivistic ( )
Otherwise (perhaps existentialistic) ( )

24

The Environments of the Administrator

Earle F. Zeigler

Consideration of the "environments" of the administrator involves an analysis of the social forces that impinge on the leader and his organization. Prior to any overview of the immediate and external environments, one cannot escape the thought that there are human beings at the very core of the administrative process whose purposeful behavior may bring about the goal realization of the entire organization. These individuals possess many and varied interests, and each person is inescapably unique. Furthermore, conflicts are almost inevitable as they function in a definite and specific environment. This phenomenon does appear to be true to a considerable degree because people's behavior is so often characterized by the lack of rationality of one type or another (Gross, 1964, chap. 14).

The structure of the organization in which human beings function is explained as a pattern or framework in which individuals and parts or units of the department, school, or company fulfill a variety of roles so that the purposes of the enterprise may possibly be achieved. In the process a number of hierarchical and polyarchical relationships are often established which function according to prevailing codes of behavior. It is vital to understand that there is typically a formal and an informal structure in every organization, both of which exert significant and influential amounts of power on specific occasions.

In this chapter there will be a discussion of the administrator's internal (immediate) and external (general) environments. The immediate environment includes the organizational clients, suppliers, controllers, advisers, controllers and controllees, adversaries, and publics with opinions.* The general environment is made up of the organization's resources, its social organization, the power structure, and a structure of values and norms. Further considerations are the need for the administrator to develop a working knowledge of social theory; to assist the larger community by assuming some direct responsibilities for society's welfare; to understand that the "world family of man" displays recurrent themes of rationality, activism, humanism, and concern with values; and to comprehend the concept that the rate of change in the world is increasing at a geometric ratio.

THE IMMEDIATE (INTERNAL) ENVIRONMENT

Departments of physical education and athletics are human organizations within larger human organizations. They are what can be designated as "open" systems, although there is undoubtedly great variation in the "openness" or "closure" of any such system. It is extremely difficult, if not impossible, to actually "close" any human organization.

Typically, four phenomena make organizational systems open to a greater or lesser degree. In the first place, there are usually entries into the department and exits from it. This means that outsiders become insiders and vice versa. Second, departmental members hold memberships in other organizations, which means that their loyalties may be divided. Third, a type of resource exchange typically exists: the larger community (general environment) sends students to the departments for both general and professional education. As a result, reciprocal influences take place, and students are graduated with various types of diplomas or degrees (depending upon the level of education under consideration). Finally, departmental members and "outsiders" (other faculty, administrators, alumni, other systems of education, legislators, and the public generally) become involved with mutual or reciprocal influence(s).

The "visibility" of the many people and/or organizations that interrelate with the department varies greatly for many reasons of both a formal and informal nature. In a sense they help to determine the "texture" of the department. The administrator and his associates typically develop and employ major and/or minor strategies of an offensive or defensive nature in their relationships with the people and/or organizations that "encircle" the organization known as the department of physical education and athletics.

The Clients. In the scope of the educational world, as opposed to the business world, for example, there are some differences but many similarities in

---

*Although a number of different references will be cited in this chapter, the writer leaned heavily on the work of Bertram Gross in regard to the components of both environments.

regard to the "clients," "customers," "consumers," or *students* (as is the case here). The clients form a network and are basically the receivers of the goods and services of the department. Thus, we might be talking about the graduates of the professional program, or about students in other areas taking courses within the department of physical education and athletics. Still further, we might be referring to those students who are taking part in the physical recreation and intramurals program *or* the program of intercollegiate athletics.

The "internal clients" of a department—to continue the analogy—are those people within the rest of the college or university who in some way come in contact with the "products or goods" of the department. They might be faculty and staff members who take part in the physical recreation program, or who have sons and/or daughters in some phase of the departmental program. Further, they might be faculty or staff members who attend athletic contests (either male or female), or perhaps even their children might have expressed needs or interests in physical education and athletics.

The "less visible clients" of physical education and athletics are a relatively large, amorphous, unorganized, and non-vocal group *typically,* but they can become very vocal on seemingly short notice. These are people in the community who have had good, bad, or so-so experiences with physical education and athletics in the past (taxpayers, merchants, professional people, legislators at all levels, etc.). We don't know how to reach these people—or at least we don't usually give much thought to the matter—until all of a sudden they begin "to come out of the woodwork" with attacks against us in times of crisis when problems of varying natures arise. For example, all educational institutions, and notably those at the college and university level, are encountering negative criticism of varying intensity from members of this group because of sharply rising costs and for other reasons.

The "number of clients" aspect of the immediate environment of the physical education and sport profession brings some highly interesting questions to mind. For years the profession has been working toward 100 percent involvement of all children and young people at all educational levels up through part of the university experience. This does make possible a great many opportunities for creativity and initiative, but it does also nevertheless place a tremendous burden upon the profession to care for *all* children and young people adequately according to their needs in health, physical education, recreation, and competitive sport. Now that the health and safety education group *and* the recreation and park administration profession are going their separate—but hopefully affiliated—ways, the profession of physical education and sport has fewer "masters" than before, and it is incumbent upon those involved to present the best possible professional image—admittedly a difficult task in a field where the body has been looked down upon, so to speak, in our cultural heritage.

In the past, businesses have been concerned with "the stability of client demand." In physical education and athletics the problem is similar but far from identical. The profession developed its position over the past hundred years, and has now reached the point where physical education, or some variation thereof, is included in the curriculum of the schools by legislation (to a greater or lesser extent from the standpoint of time involvement). The idea of a requirement at the college level has been meeting severe challenges, and it could well be that in time, as programs at the lower levels improve, the requirement will cease typically at the completion of grade ten (for example). As far as athletics is concerned, games and sports were tolerated at first by faculty and administration; then permitted to make great strides while flagrant abuses developed; and finally were brought under control to a degree—and have been generally considered as extracurricular ever since. So "client demand," of one type or another, with varying degrees of "quality and quantity," seems to be present; and it seems strongly probable that sport, dance, and exercise are "here to stay." The extent of the requirement in the schools will probably be lessened in the years immediately ahead.

The Suppliers. Departments of physical education and athletics do not operate in a vacuum; they need assistance in the form of resources, associates, and supporters in a similar way to that typically received by business organizations. In some ways their lot is not as difficult as is the case with private enterprise. For example, the taxpayers pay money into governmental coffers through different types of taxation, and through this source of supply the department receives funds that enable it to purchase the services of faculty and staff *and* the expendable, semi-expendable, and capital goods needed to carry out the department's various functions. On the other hand, this arrangement can cause severe handicaps to develop if, say, athletics are regarded as extracurricular or ancillary and thereby placed in a position whereby this phase of the program must sell itself to the public on the basis of a win-loss record. (One can't resist inquiring what would happen to many aspects of the so-called regular curriculum, including required physical education classes of a typical nature, if they were forced to function in such a profit-or-loss manner.)

One type of "associate" as mentioned above would be that individual or department within the school or university which gives help directly in the "processing of the product"—the male or female student moving up the educational ladder. Such an associate would be the educational counselor or a similar person in the office of the dean of students. Other examples of "associates" would be teachers of other subjects or members of the administrative staff (including those who maintain the buildings and grounds). "Supporters" considered as part of the category of suppliers would be alumni, legislators, "friends" of the school or university, etc. In a business organization they might be the investors or those who lend money to the enterprise.

The Advisers. All organizations have advisers, and physical education and athletics departments are no exception. In fact, they have probably had more advice given to them over the years than most other departments within the institution. This has been especially true in the area of interscholastic and intercollegiate athletics, but it is to be hoped that the need for such continuing advice will decrease in the future (at such time as a greater degree of sanity emerges within the programs). Those operating the gymnasium or classroom programs have received plenty of advice too. Often this has been from administrative and supervisory personnel who in a large number of cases had "graduated" from the physical education ranks into such positions.

Physical educators should not be ungrateful for the advice they have received in the past, or for that which they will continue to receive—perhaps to a somewhat lesser extent—in the future. It is inherently difficult for people to bring themselves to the point where they truly want to ask for advice from the "outside." Even if such advice is sought, quite often there is an immediate resistance to the counsel once it is given, unless it agrees quite completely with the plans which were submitted or presented to the adviser for review. There are various motives that underlie the employment of advisers, and one often has the feeling (when serving as an adviser) that he may be merely being used by administrators who wish him to echo their own thoughts and ideas, or who have been requested by their own superiors to seek such counsel. There is no doubt but that the presence of an outsider may tend to create an adversary relationship.

The above comments are not meant to imply for a moment, however, the idea that the various types of advice offered are usually worthless or never used if they don't conform to the predetermined plans of the administrators seeking such help. Such assistance can be of inestimable value as one seeks to weigh the alternative courses of action open to him and his associates. Sometimes it is simply a case of engaging someone to process information in a variety of ways, and it would be difficult for anyone to resent such information being made available to use in the decision-making process.

Often the question may arise as to the "detachment" or the "involvement" of the adviser. This is especially true if his advice proceeds beyond the stage of information provision and moves into the realm of the making of one or more recommendations for immediate or delayed action on the part of the department or program.

All things considered, the adviser should be viewed as a relatively senior person at least with a successful experience that would tend to lend credence to the "quiet wisdom" which he is transmitting in a variety of ways to those seeking his help. The adviser concerned needs to have the benefit of the confidence and friendliness of those from whom he is seeking information, and yet he should not be viewed either as a threat or an ally if he hopes to be in a position to offer detached and sound advice.

The Controllers. Departments or schools of physical education and athletics encounter regularly those who officially or unofficially exert a controlling function through their influence. The department head or director undoubtedly has an advisory committee or an executive committee. He will probably be guided or directed also by various boards of control or directorates, not to mention the dean, superintendent, academic vice-president, and others. These are the people or groups who fit at some point into the hierarchical pattern of the organization's formal structure; here it is more the intention to enumerate briefly those individuals, groups, agencies, or governmental units that exert a greater or lesser amount of control on different occasions and at different times.

An example of such a "controller" of physical education and athletics on the North American continent would be a state or provincial professional association whose members might agree on a recommended curriculum or type of program. This professional body would not have the power at the present time to actually enforce its recommendations upon any one high school, junior college, or university, but it could well cause embarrassment to the department of physical education of any one institution if that department didn't seem to be moving in the direction in which the professional association was presumably pointing its membership. This would be the case also at the national level, although the influence would typically be considerably less.

Accrediting agencies represent another example of a controller, only in this instance there is often no question as to the strength of the influence. Schools and universities will go to great lengths to avoid being put on probation or actually having their accreditation revoked until certain standards are met. Of course, on some occasions accrediting agencies are loathe to invoke restrictions or penalties on prestigious members because the prestige of the agency itself might be weakened. The field of physical education and athletics has had its share of such controllers over the decades, and the administrator resists or ignores them completely at his own peril. These controllers find representation either formally or informally "at the court" of physical education and athletics. This means that the wise administrator can display foresight by recognizing these influences (or potential influences), and by being ready to employ or deploy them to his department's best advantage.

The Adversaries. Administrators and their organizations are confronted by adversaries on a regular basis, although even in the area of interscholastic and intercollegiate athletics the competition is rarely so cutthroat as it might typically be in business where democratic capitalism prevails as a determining influence on the state of the economy. Those who compete with us for students at the college and university level are, of course, our adversaries, and this is especially true in those states or provinces where public universities are reimbursed by the government on a per capita basis. When enrollment projections do not hold up in these situations, university recruitment policies and procedures are stepped up sharply and begin to resemble the recruitment practices often attributed to representatives of university athletic programs.

Careful delineation of the specific meanings of such terms as recruitment, subsidization, and proselyting are needed to lessen the opprobrium of universities and colleges regarding each other strictly as adversaries in the strongest sense. This problem does not arise at the secondary school level in athletics except when occasionally parents are encouraged to move from one school district or city to another so that their child may play for such-and-such a school or coach—a practice which has been strictly regulated in recent years. Departments or schools of physical education rarely if ever have competed for students with high academic ability; in fact it is sad to relate that the idea of such competition—at least to a reasonable extent—tends to make one smile because the very idea is definitely anachronistic.

Gross attempts to distinguish among competitors, rivals, and opponents or enemies—all as subcategories under the main heading of "adversaries" (1964, pp. 427-29). Because they tend to overlap in their meanings, it is difficult to maintain the distinctions as explained. Competitors "produce the same or similar products." Rivals "produce entirely different products but compete for resources, assistance, or support," while opponents are "external individuals or organizations who, although not necessarily competitors or rivals, nevertheless impede the operation of an organization." Finally, "enemies are opponents whose opposition carries them into the more bitter forms of conflict."

Several analogies from physical education and athletics will help to place these adversaries in perspective. Another institution with whom you compete in a sport would be a *competitor* in this context, whereas a *rival* would be, say, the English department that wants to use an athlete for a dramatic performance during the basketball season—while at the same time requesting extra money for this operation from a limited school budget. An *opponent* would be the municipal recreation program with so many basketball leagues in operation that they are tending to encroach on the gymnasium time requested for the varsity, junior varsity, and freshman basketball teams. An *enemy*—to choose a perhaps "far-out" example—might be a community recreation director seeking to lure high school athletes into his basketball program because he wants to win an intercity league championship. It is obviously very difficult to employ these terms without simultaneous use of qualifying adjectives.

Publics with Opinions. Physical education and athletics, because of the high degree of visibility of its activities, encounters many different types of "publics with opinions." Of course, this has both good and bad implications for the success of the total program. If a star athlete breaks his wrist taking part in gymnastics in a required physical education program, all sorts of repercussions may develop based on the opinions and actions of people who don't fully understand the situation. Occasionally the instructor is deemed to be negligent, and this behavior reflects on both the individual concerned and on other personnel within the department and school. Basically all programs operate within the values and norms of the society or culture in which they function, and the instructor defies these strictures at his peril. Although times are changing, there are still many communities in which explicit sex instruction and discussion in a coeducational health education class would cause certain factions within the community to rapidly become a "public with negative opinions" about the school in general and the department of physical and health education in particular.

Obviously, there will always be diversity of opinion on any controversial subject in an evolving democracy where pluralistic philosophies of education are permitted to exist side by side. If problems develop, they will typically come from adverse opinions on the part of those within the immediate environment mentioned earlier in this chapter. The administrator cannot dismiss other quarters where possibilities for adverse opinions might surface at any given moment. These bad (or good) opinions might originate with organizations or individuals that might wish to engage physical education "services" in the future—or even might never wish to establish a connection and yet help to create a climate within the environment which would have a deleterious effect on the status of physical education and athletics. An example of this latter point might be when a community leader publicly deplores the poor leadership and behavior exhibited by a basketball or hockey coach over the course of a season's play. Such "adverse opinion" is almost intangible, but might well influence decision-makers in regard to the size of a future physical education and athletics budget.

The administrator should appreciate the complexity of obtaining an accurate measure of public opinion within the immediate environment. Descriptive research involving the sampling of opinion can be most helpful if carried out in a mature and sophisticated manner. In addition to discovering what "most people" think about the way things are going and discovering what they feel their future needs and interests may be, it is highly important further to keep in touch with what the *leaders* of the various groups and/or factions are thinking. Such analysis is difficult to carry out even for professionals. Thus, we often find that the obtaining of information is typically left to amateurs or chance within departments of physical education and athletics. Obviously, there is great room for improvement insofar as the development of true understanding about what the "public" thinks or feels concerning the many aspects of a total physical education and athletics program.

THE GENERAL (EXTERNAL) ENVIRONMENT

It is not always possible to state definitively where the immediate (internal) environment leaves off and the general (external) environment begins in a given society. All known societies are open systems, often involving a variety of sub-groups within their geographical boundaries. Careful definition of a particular society is a highly complex task, each one having certain unique qualities while undoubtedly possessing many similarities with other societies. The components of societies are usually described as subsystems (e.g., the economy, the polity, etc.). In a very real sense these subsystems have developed in order to "divide up the work," and it is with the interweaving of these systems that the following pages will be concerned. A society is, of course, infinitely more complex than any organization that exists within it, but it is true that many of the concepts and group roles can be transferred from one level to the other.

GENERAL ACTION SYSTEM HAS FOUR SUBSYSTEMS

Before considering a more general discussion of the external environment from the standpoint of resources, social organizations, the power structure, and the value structure, there will be a brief presentation of Parsonian "Action Theory"—a structural-functional theory which has been described by Johnson as being about "a type of empirical system."* Initially, to understand this complex social theory, the administrator should appreciate that the general action system is viewed as being composed of four subsystems: (1) culture, (2) the social system, (3) the personality, and (4) the behavioral organism. These four sub-systems together compose a hierarchy of control and conditioning.

The first of the subsystems is "culture," which according to Johnson "provides the figure in the carpet—the structure and, in a sense, the 'programming' for the action system as a whole." (1969, p. 46) The structure of this type of system is typically geared to the functional problems of that level which arise—and so on down the scale, respectively. It is the subsystem of culture which legitimates and also influences the level below it (the social system). Typically, there is a definite strain toward consistency. The influence works both upward and downward within the action system, thereby creating a hierarchy of influence or conditioning.

It is almost inevitable that strain will develop within the system. Johnson explains this as "dissatisfaction with the level of effectiveness on the functioning of the system in which strain is felt" (Ibid., p. 47). Such dissatisfaction may, for example, have to do with particular aspects of a social system as follows: (1) the level of effectiveness of resource procurement; (2) the success of goal attainment; (3) the justice or appropriateness of allocation of rewards or facilities; or (4) the degree to which units of the system are committed to realizing or maintaining the values of the system.

Strain may arise at the personality level, and the resultant pressure could actually change the structure of the system above (the social system). This is not an inevitable process, however, because such strain might well be resolved satisfactorily at its own level, so to speak. Usually the pattern consistency of the action system displays a reasonable degree of flexibility, and this is especially

---

*The writer owes a significant debt for this discussion to Professor Harry M. Johnson of the University of Illinois, Champaign-Urbana, who is a personal friend and a leading Parsonian theorist.

true at the lower levels. For example, strain might be expressed by deviant behavior or in other ways such as by reduced identification with the social system.

Thus, it is the hierarchy of control and conditioning which comes into play when the sources of change (e.g., new religious or scientific ideas) begin to cause strain in the larger social systems, whereas the smaller social systems tend to be "strained" by the change that often develops at the personality level. In addition, it is quite apparent that social systems are often influenced considerably by contact with other social systems.

Levels of Structure within the Social System. Just as there were four subsystems within the total action system defined by Parsons and others, there *appear* to be four levels within that subsystem which has been identified as the social system or structure. These levels, proceeding from "highest" to "lowest," are (1) values, (2) norms, (3) the structure of collectivities, and (4) the structure of roles. Typically the higher levels are more general than the lower ones, with the latter giving quite specific guidance to those segments or units of the particular system to which they apply. These "units" or "segments" are either collectivities or individuals in their capacity as role occupants.

Values represent the highest echelon of the social system level of the entire general action system. These values may be categorized into such "entities" as artistic values, scientific values, educational values, social values, etc. Of course, all types or categories of values must be values *of* personalities. The social values of a particular social system are those values that are conceived of as representative of the ideal general character that is desired by those who ultimately hold the power in the system being described. Most important social values in the United States are (1) the rule of law, (2) the social-structural facilitation of individual achievement, and (3) the equality of opportunity (Ibid., p. 48).

Norms are the shared, sanctioned rules which govern the second level of the social structure. The average person finds it difficult to separate in his mind the concepts of values and norms. Some examples of norms in the United States are (1) the institution of private property; (2) private enterprise; (3) the monogamous, conjugal family and (4) the separation of church and state.

Collectivities are interaction systems that may be distinguished by their goals, their composition, and their size. A collectivity is characterized by conforming acts and by deviant acts, which are both classes of members' action which relate to the structure of the system. Interestingly enough, each collectivity has a structure that consists of *four* levels also. In a pluralistic society one finds an extremely large variety of collectivities which are held together to a varying extent by an overlapping membership constituency. Thus, members of one collectivity can and do exert greater or lesser amounts of influence upon the members of the other collectivities to which they belong.

Roles refer to the behavioral organisms (humans) who interact within each collectivity (psychological system). Each role has a current normative structure specific to it, even though such a role may be gradually changing. For example, the role of the physical educator may be in a transitory state in that certain second level norms could be changing, and yet each *specific* physical educator still has definite normative obligations that are possible to delineate more specifically than the more generalized second-level norms. Finally, these four levels of social structure themselves also compose a hierarchy of control and conditioning. As Johnson explains (Ibid., p. 49), the higher levels "legitimate, guide, and control" the lower levels, and pressure of both a direct and indirect nature can be—and generally is—employed when the infraction or violation occurs and is known.

Functional Interchanges. A society is the most nearly self-subsistent type of social system and, interestingly enough, societies seem to have four basic types of functional problems. These four subsystems have been technically designated as *pattern-maintenance, integration, goal-attainment,* and *adaptation.* The economy of a society is its adaptive subsystem, while the society's form of government (polity) has become known as its goal-attainment subsystem. The integrative and pattern-maintenance subsystems, which do not have names that can be used in everyday speech, consist actually of a set or series of processes by which a society's production factors are related, combined, and transformed with *utility*—the value principle of the adaptive system—as the interim product. These products "packaged" as various forms of "utility" are employed in and by other functional subsystems of the society.

Thus, each subsystem exchanges factors and products, becomes involved as pairs, and engages in what has been called a "double interchange." It is theorized that each functional subsystem contributes one factor and one product to each of the other three functional subsystems. Considered from the standpoint of all the pairs possible to be involved in the interchange, there are six double-interchange systems. Factors and products are both involved in the transformational processes, each being functional for the larger social system. Factors are *general* and therefore more remote, while products are *specific* and therefore more directly functional. The performance of the functional requirements has been described as a "circular flow of interchanges," with the factors and products being continuously used up and continuously replaced.

To help in the achievement of an elementary understanding of interchange process, Johnson explains how one of the six interchange systems functions typically to create the political support system in a society. The reader should keep in mind that the functional problem of goal-attainment is resolved through the operation of the society's form of government (polity)—the interchange between the polity and the integrative subsystems. "The political process is the set of structured activities that result in choices of goals and the mobilization of societal resources for the attainment of these goals." (Ibid., p. 51) The integrative system contributes to political accomplishment by achieving a certain degree of consensus and "solidarity." The integrative system "registers" and "delivers" these qualities in the form of votes and interest demands. These are, in fact, forms of political support—that is, support from the integrative system *to* the polity. Conversely, in return, the government (polity) bolsters (integrative) solidarity through political leadership that, in turn, produces binding decisions. Thus, this leadership and the binding decisions can also be considered as "political support"—support *from* the polity (government) to the integrative system (one of the two systems that "produces utility"—i.e., implements one of the four values of which utility is one).

The Social Significance of Interchange Analysis. As can be readily seen, the interchange analysis has tremendous social significance. The interchange of factors and products identifies the *types* of processes that somehow *must* take place in any social system. This scheme specifies also their functional significance and also indicates relations between these processes that are broad but yet important. As was stated earlier, the functional subsystems compose a hierarchy of control and conditioning; thus, the processes involved are influenced, conditioned, and controlled. These same interchange processes must be going on in any functioning social system, but it should be understood that their specific forms vary greatly. The four levels of a particular social system (e.g., collectivities, etc.) provide the forms and channels by which any unique social system carries on its functionally necessary processes. Fundamental social *change* means that some basic transformation has taken, or is taking, place in one or more levels of the social system (structure). Obviously, basic change must inevitably affect the operation of the system in some distinct, measurable way.

The social change that may take place within a social system can be viewed as one of three types—i.e., there are three levels of analysis that may be distinguished as follows: (1) the analysis of "circular flow," which explains the pattern of interchange processes occurring within a stable social system; (2) the analysis of "growth patterns," which determines the growth or decline of particular attributes or products of the system (e.g., power or wealth); and (3) the analysis of structural change, which is the determination of whether a level or levels of the systems undergo any substantive change due to strong lower-level strain.

Critics of Parsonian theory seem to overlook the fact that it makes allowance for equilibrium and change; in fact, radical social change, with or without an actual revolution, does institute a *new* hierarchy of control and conditioning. This occurs, for example, when the strain at the three lower levels forces a *different* set of priorities in the value subsystem. These new values become resultantly the basic source of legitimation, guidance, and control for the levels below.

Parsons' general action system is then an "equilibrium model." Social systems may, or may not, be in a state of equilibrium, and change is certainly most possible within this theory's framework. This theory is a reasonable, theoretical explanation of how social change can and does take place. Social systems are conceived of as having a normative structure, which may or may not be stable. To understand how to achieve equilibrium within a social system, it is at least theoretically necessary to learn to distinguish between processes that will maintain or change a given social structure. Finally, it is important to understand that sometimes the higher levels of social structure may be maintained (if this is *desired* and *desirable*) by understanding how to change one or more of its lower levels. Quite obviously, this last point is most important to the administrator of any organization within a given social system.

Implications for the Administrator. The above extremely brief outline of some of the basic elements of developing Parsonian theory of action has necessarily for several reasons avoided the introduction of this information in great detail. For example, the concepts of economic theory involved in the adaptive subsystem of a society (money, utility, products, and factors of production) were not presented so that the reader would appreciate their close counterparts in the theory of the other three subsystems (e.g., goal-attainment, etc.). Nor has there been any discussion of the idea, presented by Parsons, that any analysis of the structure of complex societies demands careful differentiation of four levels of organization (*not* considered as an entity). These have been called the *technical, managerial, institutional,* and *societal* levels, and it is clear that these four primary-level outputs are closely related to the functional problems described above. Technical-level systems involving small groups of people using facilities and making decisions must be coordinated with the managerial level of organization—and so on up the scale through the regulation of institutionalized norms until the societal level is reached where the "single focus" of first-order values is brought to bear on the operation.

Still further, the symbolic media of society have not been introduced (*generalized commitments, influence, power, and money*) as fundamentally important, as they indeed are to the understanding and operation of the four basic types of subsystems with a social system as explained through the functional problems that have been technically identified as pattern-maintenance, integration, goal-attainment, and adaptation.

These omitted factors, and many others too numerous to mention, would need to be understood by the administrator before he truly understands what has been called the general or external environment. Obviously, an administrator cannot function on the basis of knowledge which he does not have, or which he understands but dimly. It is for this reason that it seemed wise to alert the reader to the great complexity of North American society, and also to cause him to understand how unwise it would be for him as an administrator to make any quick generalizations on this subject as a basis for administrative action at the so-called lower levels. (The writer feels that he has an adequate knowledge of what has been called the immediate or internal environment, for example, but he would "run, not walk" to the nearest consultant to make certain that he was not recommending specific action relative to his general environment based on fallacious, underlying social theory.)

Nevertheless, some applications of the above social theory have been made for the study of organizations, and several of these will be presented at this point.* Organizations, as a type of collectivity, do ascribe primacy to the matter of rather specific goal-attainment. They seek to exert environmental control through excellent performance so that certain desired goals will be realized in keeping with the organization's value system. The administrator should appreciate that his organization's value system is different, but ultimately derived from, the societal value system. Thus, a university, which has been characterized as a pattern-maintenance organization, would "tend to select only those goal-attainment, adaptive, and integrative alternatives which contribute to the maintenance of the pattern of its units" (Hills, 1968, p. 65).

As can be readily understood, different organizations within a society have different goals and are typically organized with this purpose in mind. Organizations accordingly may well have goals which are primarily adaptive, goal attainment-oriented, integrative, or pattern maintenance-oriented in nature. Whereas some organizations have goals related to economic production, others of a governmental nature work toward the achievement of group goals. A third type of organization is directed or oriented to the function of integration (e.g., legal services which assist in the resolution of conflicts or political parties which organize support for interest groups within the society). A fourth classification of organization correlates to the functional problem of pattern-maintenance and here, as mentioned above, the university may be categorized. Schools, churches, and even the family can be placed in this fourth category or classification.

As Hills makes clear (Ibid., p. 65), "any organization may be treated as a functionally differentiated subsystem of a society." The organization is a system directed toward the achievement of its goals. Its value system seeks primarily to continuously legitimate the organization's goals. These goals are typically functions which have a position of greater or lesser importance in aiding the larger social system to achieve its stated values. The system aims to produce and/or market some output that is used by some other viable system within the society. The organization is considered to be successful when the relationship between it and the other systems of the environment becomes a continuing one by virtue of the fact that the organization's processes of an internal nature are supported by the external environment.

Once the administrator understands that any organization has both *external* and *internal* functions, he is next confronted with the fact that the four

---

*Professor Johnson called to the attention of the writer a monograph by R. Jean Hills entitled *Toward a Science of Organization* in which Dr. Hills sought to apply the major elements of Parsonian theory connected with social behavior toward an analysis and understanding of organizations. This analysis has been most helpful and is employed extensively in the discussion that follows.

functional problems (e.g., goal-attainment) have both internal and external aspects. The reader will recall that "since organizations are defined by the primacy of a particular type of goal, the focus of their value systems must be the legitimation of that goal in terms of the functional significance of its attainment for the more inclusive system." (Ibid., p. 67) Viewed more specifically or precisely, if the primary function of the public schools is to socialize young people so that they can function successfully in their respective societal roles in the future, they need to develop (1) the competency to fulfill those *roles*; (2) the capacity to *behave interpersonally* in ways appropriate to their ascribed roles; (3) a commitment to live up to generally perceived and accepted *normative patterns*; and (4) an understanding and acceptance of the primary *values* of the society. Obviously, no organization can for long completely neglect other system problems with which any organization is confronted. What makes all of this so very complex is that "the various combinations of emphasis permit the identification of twenty-four organization types." (Ibid., p. 68).

The discussion of the implications of this social theory for the administrator has now come to the point where it is possible to list the four external problems of the organization in relation to the *general* environment. First, there is the problem of *legitimation,* which means simply that the primary goal of the organization must be validated, so to speak, as being consistent with the values of the society. Second, the *integration* problem presents itself, and it is here that the organization must ensure that its goals and program are acceptable to the community-at-large in which it functions. Third, there is the problem of *goal-attainment* for the organization involved, and this means that the end product must be so produced that the recipients of these services will seek out and accept the products. It is at this point, for example, that universities may eventually run into difficulty because of the "production" of very large numbers of male physical educators and coaches. Administrators should be asking themselves right now about the optimal relationship with the public school hiring authorities. Fourth, the *adaptation* or adaptive problem of the organization is fundamental, and this relates, of course, to procurement of the basic resources necessary for the production of the organization's end product. What is needed here is money through which the organization can bring to bear the necessary physical and human resources to achieve the organization's goal. At this stage of their development, administrators don't need to be reminded about the importance of this commodity.

It is perhaps time to return to a consideration of Gross' approach to the basic components of the external (general) environment in order to make a comparison with Johnson's and Hills' analysis of Parsons' action system in this regard. The similarities are immediately apparent, although the terminology employed is somewhat different. Initially, Gross refers to *resources* and subdivides his discussion of this topic into (1) output, (2) wealth, and (3) scarcity and abundance (1964, pp. 435-38). His next category is *social organization,* and he explains how administrators convert human and physical resources into the power to achieve significant results. The administrative revolution has brought with it "more organization, larger organizations, more bureaucracy, and more administrators" (Ibid., p. 439). Third, the *power structure* of the general environment is reviewed. The question of the distribution of power within the system is considered from the standpoint of who makes what decisions at what times. The power dispersion has resulted from the pluralism of interests within a given society, but the increasing size and complexity of societies seems to inevitably bring a variety of "power dispersion patterns." It is important for an organization—in the case of this text this would be a department or school of physical education and athletics—whether the administrator is attempting to function in a general environment where either a dictatorial or democratic pattern of power dispersion is in operation. How democratic a society is can be quite quickly determined by ascertaining "who participates how deeply in what" (Ibid., p. 451). Thus, in a society where the concept of "organizational democracy" is not very well developed in the sense that individual members of the organization don't have much to say about their own work and the direction in which their organization is moving, one of the mainstays of a so-called democratic society is lacking. Such a situation can be present in the *immediate* environment as well as in the *general* environment, and it holds great import for the administrator at either level.

Finally, Gross treats the *value structure* of the general environment, describing it as "a patterned set of general attitudes concerning what is desirable or undesirable" (Ibid., p. 457). At this level the administrator is alerted to the fact that the society in which his organization is functioning subscribes to certain basic human values, and he and his associates can ignore the needs and interests of the members of their organization to work toward the achievement of these values *at their own peril and to the detriment of the progress of their organization within that general environment.* The situation is that simple, and yet it is that complex! Assessment of the value structure of North American society has been attempted by many (e.g., see the values listed for the U.S.A. by Johnson on p. 591). One continually hears expressed such values as dignity for the individual, equality of opportunity, freedom, the rule of law, facilitation of personal achievement, etc. There do seem to be many contradictions, however, and it is with such discrepancies and inconsistencies that the administrator must deal both "internally" *and* "externally" as the "organization-environments confrontation" takes place continuously and continually. So that the administrator and his organization are understood insofar as their motives and output are concerned, they must be fully aware of both the values *and* the norms of their general environment. Obviously, developing the knowledge, competency, and skills necessary for successful administration requires understanding and practice in the art and science of verbal and nonverbal communication.

SOME FINAL CONSIDERATIONS

Several points need to be made as this relatively brief treatment of the "environments" of the administrator draws to a close. In the first place, an administrator should plan to assist the larger community (his *external* environment) by assuming some direct responsibility for society's welfare over and above his own immediate professional task. Second, keeping in mind that the *external* or *general* environment relates to the still broader social environment of the educational institution within the society typically, at present there are strong indications that this external environment has now become worldwide in scope. Finally, the concept of "future shock"—man's collision with the future, so to speak—is one which the administrator should make every effort to understand thoroughly through attempts at analysis of its various ramifications (see Toffler, 1970).

Community Responsibility. If organizations functioning in a society hope to prosper at the same time as the society itself is moving forward substantively and qualitatively, the administrator as a leader must assume some responsibility for the welfare of the external (general) environment. One should not expect that he, his associates, and those who sponsor the organization which he administers will reap the benefits of the society in which they operate and not offer something of themselves in return. Obviously, community service by any one individual can be overdone and truly negate his effectiveness on the job. On the other hand, society cannot hope to progress and to solve its pressing problems if organizational leaders and managers do not do more than just carry out their professional duties responsibly and pay taxes. Flory (1965, pp. 200-201) stresses three conditions that must be met by the mature member of a society in this regard. First, a man "must accept the fact of his existence in the world as it is at this time." Second, "the mature man has to accept the fact of individuality." By this he means that each member of the administrator's organization, including himself, is unique both physically and psychologically, and this means that he should appreciate, not denigrate, how and what unique individuals can contribute to the organization's growth and development—and that of the larger community as well. Third, "the mature man must recognize that no adult can be loved, or even liked, by every worthy citizen of his own community."

If an administrator or executive decides to accept some responsibility for the development of the community (the external environment) at the local, regional, national, or international levels, he must obviously make an effort to understand as fully as possible the structure and function of the larger society. The administrator should not assume this responsibility because he thinks that his organization will be more highly regarded or make more money. He should help the community to progress and solve its problems because such assistance is needed, because he sees a spot where he can be of help by virtue of some personal or professional qualifications, and because he wouldn't feel right about not helping out in some positive way.

Recurrent Themes in the "Family of Man." As mentioned above, it is really no longer sufficient for the administrator to think that his general environment is limited only to local and regional boundaries. Abraham Kaplan made a worldwide analysis of "the new world of philosophy," as he calls it. Most interesting in his approach is the identification of a number of themes which he has "identified as recurring elements in the various world philosophies" (1961, pp. 7-10). He explains that these various philosophical positions are far from identical, of course, but that they do show a strong "family resemblance." The themes he lists merit the consideration of administrators who would truly understand the ramifications of the extension of their general environment which is taking place:

1. A theme of *rationality*—the idea that the world is viewed as some sort of systematic unity, causal or historical, constituting a purely natural order or perhaps a moral order as well.
2. A theme of *activism*—the idea in this second theme is that it is not enough to understand only—that understanding should serve as a guide to positive action. Knowledge provides us only with "a map by which to find our way."
3. A theme of *humanism*—the position here is that man is usually central in the philosophy itself, if not in the world that is being philosophized about. There is a continuity of man and nature in both the East and the West. A "theory of human nature . . . is either the starting point or the culmination of the whole movement of thought."
4. A preoccupation with *values*—the view that the life of man should be related strongly to values, especially moral and spiritual. Although it is interpreted in a variety of ways, there is great emphasis on the question of freedom. In other words, man fulfills his highest aspirations by the realization of values in his life, and not by the mere accumulation of goods and in other ways.

As administrators explain and compare their programs of physical education and athletics, they should not expect that these programs would ever become identical. The need for preservation of indigenous games and activities can certainly be appreciated. Yet there is no reason not to expect that "family resemblances" will *not* be found, because these recurring themes do run through the basic value systems and philosophies—and hence through societies including their educational systems and sports and games. The administrator should realize that these activities, and the emphases that are placed on different aspects of them, will vary according to the value structures of the societies in which they are performed. In their work with colleagues abroad, administrators can seek to share, explain, and—most of all—understand. Internationalism in physical education and athletics is truly one of the highest of goals for which administrators should strive.

The Environments and Future Shock. In this chapter up to now, a case has been made for the position that, to the best of his ability and comprehension, the administrator should seek to understand both his internal and external environments. And, according to Cowley, each of these environmental subdivisions has breakdowns which may be considered "natural" and "cultural," so to speak (in Jones and Westervelt, 1963, pp. 46-47). The natural environment of an organization has to do with such aspects as geographic locale including climate and physical resources—all factors which can influence greatly the operation or malfunction of an organization. The opposite of this influence—cultural environment—applies to "the whole complex of artifacts and ways of behaving developed by man and, further, the subjective knowledge and attitudes associated with them" (Ibid.).

After all of this, therefore—the discussions of the internal (immediate) environment, the external (general) environment, and such other aspects as implications for the administrator—it is necessary to leave a firm reminder with the reader about the "administrative revolution" which is taking place and about threats to mankind which Gross describes as (1) the dehumanization of man, (2) the sickness of society, and (3) the possibility of self-destruction (1964, chap. 4). In addition to this, administrators must be well aware of the implications of the term "future shock" in their attempts to lead others toward the achievement of organizational goals. There is no doubt but that many intelligent people were quite aware of the great amount of change that was taking place, and also there was some awareness that the *rate* of change was increasing, but somehow it remained for Toffler to alert literally millions of people to the stern reality of a "roaring current of change, a current so powerful today that it overturns institutions, shifts our values and shrivels our roots" (Toffler, 1970, p. 3).

And so, it is with this parting note that the discussion of the administrator's environments, both internal and external, concludes. How can the profession of physical education and sport prepare its administrators of the present and of the years immediately ahead for this "abrupt collision with the future"? Facile answers abound, but this writer contends that the profession sees the problem but dimly, and may well now be reaping the fruits of past and present unpreparedness for this enormous task. Unless young people are prepared for purposeful human motor performance in sport, exercise, play, and dance as a vital component of their lives, the profession will not be worthy of the name, and other more vital organizations will be created to meet the demand of the onrushing future.

Selected Bibliography

Cowley, W. H., in *Behavior Science and Guidance: Proposals and Perspectives*, ed. E. L. Jones and E. M. Westervelt. New York: Bureau of Publications, Teachers College, Columbia University, 1963.

Flory, Charles D., ed., *Managers for Tomorrow*. New York: New American Library, Inc., 1965.

Gross, Bertram M., *The Managing of Organizations*, 2 vols. New York: The Free Press of Glencoe, 1964.

Hills, R. Jean, *Toward a Science of Organization*. Eugene, Oregon: Center for the Advanced Study of Educational Administration, 1968.

Johnson, Harry M., "The Relevance of the Theory of Action to Historians," *Social Science Quarterly* (June 1969), pp. 46-58.

Kaplan, Abraham, *The New World of Philosophy*. New York: Random House, 1961.

Toffler, Alvin, *Future Shock*. New York: Random House, 1970.

25

Looking into the Future: Theoretical Approaches to Administrative Action

Earle F. Zeigler

Despite the fact that the task of administrators is becoming steadily more complex, and that it is becoming very difficult to retain the services of administrators for a variety of reasons, in the field of physical education and athletics there are many people with at least average qualifications willing to assume administrative responsibilities. One can speculate as to why this is so, although it is impossible to claim absolutely correct knowledge on the subject.

No matter what the reasons may be—higher pay, more responsibility, the nature of the field, unwillingness or inability to make a scholarly contribution, more prestige, greater power, a lesser amount of teaching and coaching, etc.—it is the deep and sincere belief of the editors and others involved that almost all prospective and beginning administrators have only a vague understanding of the many aspects and ramifications of the positions to which they may be aspiring. Further, although it soon becomes obvious to the new administrator that some sort of a managerial revolution is, and has been, taking place, he still would typically be unaware of the development of administrative theory and research in the behavioral sciences and related fields. Certainly any examination of the professional literature in physical education and athletics prior to, say, 1965 would reveal practically nothing relative to administrative theory that would be especially helpful.

Thus, this text is the first of its type in physical education and athletics to explore this matter as fully as is possible at the present time. The editors, authors, and investigators herein believe that it is vitally important to prepare men and women professionally as administrators, even though such people may well be "dually" prepared in that they will have a background as well in some subdisciplinary aspect of the field such as sport psychology. Or they may wish to combine administrative *theory* with administrative *practice*.

Interestingly enough, there has been a proliferation of administration and/or organization courses in physical education and athletics over the years at both the undergraduate and graduate levels. One must comment both sadly and wryly, however, that the addition of these new courses could hardly be substantiated by the development of a body of knowledge within this aspect of the field—the usual reason why additional courses in a subject matter are added to most curricula. It is true that there have been many master's and doctoral studies in physical education that could be called "administrative" in nature, but neither these investigations nor the various texts and monographs that have appeared have gone beyond the listing of prescriptive policies and procedures. Further, the identification and establishment of utilitarian principles in this way have provided practicing professionals with material that often has dubious application to actual life situations and very little if any predictive strength.

This volume has for the first time, therefore, sought to provide physical education and athletics with at least the beginnings of the means whereby a social-scientific foundation may be built for the use of the endeavors of its many administrators. A corollary to this is that those guiding the field's professional preparation schematic should build upon this foundation and incorporate the tenable knowledge into their curriculum plans at the first possible moment.

No effort will be made in this concluding chapter to summarize fully and completely the findings and conclusions that have been presented in each of the previous chapters based on earlier investigations. There will be two sections basically that will be entitled (1) Summary and Conclusions, and (2) Recommendations. In the first section the editor will be selective in what he includes; the second section will have a "freewheeling" nature most certainly not characteristic of the rest of the volume.

SUMMARY AND CONCLUSIONS

The reader will recall that the text was divided into four parts, the first of which sought to introduce him to the background and development of this new dimension in the administration of physical education and athletics. In Part II the reader was presented with a succinct review of eleven studies which investigated the so-called *broad* and *specific* administrative processes of administration. Each included the scope, background literature, research methodology, findings and conclusions, and implications for the administrator of that particular investigation. Six studies of what have been designated as *technical* administrative concerns made up Part III of the book, while in Part IV the student of administrative theory and practice was encouraged to "look inward, outward, and to the future."

What can be said, therefore, about that which has been included in this volume? What is the essence of *some* of the findings and conclusions of the various investigators? In the next several pages the reader will find what may be considered a "representative enumeration" of that which has been reported.

The field of physical education and athletics still has an opportunity to relate to the developing social science of administration, although most professionals in the field are only dimly aware that in the twentieth century there has been an emergence of a rapidly growing scientific foundation for the profession of administration. This step should, and perhaps must, be taken by physical education and athletic administrators because organized efforts in the profession have resulted in a vast enterprise which demands wise and skillful management. At this very moment there is an urgent need for qualified professional administrators in the field (even though such a need is not generally recognized).

Despite the fact that such an urgent need exists, there has been, until the mid 1960s at least, an almost total lack of theoretical orientation in the design of research and the interpretation of the findings in administrative research in physical education and athletics. This means that in this area physical educators can only be regarded as parasites—this despite the fact that literally hundreds of studies of an administrative nature have been undertaken each year for decades! There is no valid reason why a good proportion of these investigations in the future can't be of a programmatic nature. If this were to become a reality, those individuals struggling with the problems of administrative leadership would relatively soon have a reasonably definitive inventory of administrative theory and research with special application to physical education and athletics.

The prevailing situation has had a truly significant effect on the *quality*—not the *quantity*—of administration courses in the field. Only in a few instances are reasonably substantive sections of administrative theory included. The courses are largely directed toward the practical and/or technical concerns of the job. One important concern is the need to devise ways and means of upgrading the formal preparation of those who are selected to teach administration at both the undergraduate and graduate levels. In the process it will be necessary for physical education and athletic administrators to attach highly similar meanings to the various concepts typically employed in administrative theory and research in the behavioral sciences. As matters now stand, physical education and athletic administrators are not "talking the same language" as those who are teaching educational administration, and the same statement can be made to a lesser extent in regard to those physical educators teaching graduate administration courses in physical education and athletics.

The results of the investigations included in this volume exhibit a wide variety of findings about leadership, group cohesion, organizational climate, job satisfaction, influence of economic factors, reasons for crowd violence in sport, role expectations, communication, environmental characteristics, human relations, planning and construction of facilities, organizational structure, employment practices, sport status, and budgetary processes. In each of these areas of investigation, the researcher involved would be the first to admit that a lifetime of research endeavor remains for interested scholars. In almost every case, the investigator was just "getting the first olive out of the bottle" from the standpoint of making any application to the field of physical education and athletics.

The writer must at this point ask rhetorically, "Who is going to carry on with the recommendations for future study which immediately come to mind upon the conclusion of an investigation—and which thesis advisers typically request should be included at that point?" Obviously, the whole idea of a Ph.D. specialization in administrative theory and practice in physical education and athletics is that those following this endeavor will continue to spend at least a portion of their time in the future carrying out further studies along this line, tending in the direction of tenable theory at some not-too-distant point in time. It must be immediately apparent to the reader, however, that much more help is needed in order to reach the desired goal—and that *he* or *she* is being invited to "jump in because the water feels fine."

Two other aspects of the administrative process—one individual and one social—bear repetition at this point in the final chapter. The first has to do with the editor's position over the years that an administrator ought to employ a type of philosophical analysis to supplement the body of knowledge that has been generated by administrative theory and research. This recommendation does not for a moment imply that such analysis is meant to supplant or supersede any definitive inventory of administrative theory and research that may be developed. Such knowledge, to the extent that it may prove to be tenable, can and must serve as a foundation to be made available as part of an internship experience based on a problem-solving approach to all future administrators. The assumption here is that any such synthesis and integration of knowledge into concepts will inevitably also have considerable practical value in providing administrators with the finest type of operational basis. We can never forget, however, that value-free, scientific investigation may in time tell us how to bring about a particular effect, but in all probability it will *never* tell whether it is desirable from an individual or social standpoint to function in a certain way within any phase of societal functioning. For this reason it is urged that each administrator examine himself in an effort to construct a personal philosophy that may assist him to be a more effective professional person.

In addition to recommending that the administrator "look inward" in an effort to develop a personal philosophy, it also appears to be absolutely imperative that the administrator "look outward" at both his immediate and general environments in an attempt to analyze the social forces that impinge daily on the leader and his organization. Of course, it it not always possible to state exactly where the immediate (internal) environment leaves off and the general (external) environment begins in a given society. All known societies are open systems, often involving a variety of subgroups within their geographical boundaries. A society is, of course, infinitely more complex than any organization that exists within it, but it is true that many of the concepts and group roles can be transferred from one level to another. So that the administrator and his organization are understood insofar as their motives and output are concerned, they must be fully aware of *both* the values and the norms of their general environment. Obviously, developing the knowledge, competencies, and skills necessary for successful administration requires understanding and practice in the art and science of verbal and nonverbal communication.

RECOMMENDATIONS (FOR THE FUTURE)

In this last section of the final chapter, the editor has reserved the right to "freewheel" a bit, to display what might be considered prejudices (or prejudgments) by some, and to sound off to a certain extent. None of the opinions, suggestions, or recommendations that follow will be out of phase or discordant in relationship to this entire volume (at least in the editor's opinion).

The Temporary Society. Physical education and athletic administrators need to be aware of the fact that bureaucratic forms of organizations may not be able to withstand the varieties of organizational upheaval that are taking place. "New shapes, patterns, and models are emerging which promise drastic changes in the conduct of corporation and of managerial practices in general" (Bennis, 1965, p. 31). A new ad-hocracy is being predicted that will be consistent with the rise of the temporary organization as a general "collapsing of hierarchy" takes place. We are told that "it is this combined demand for *more* information at *faster* speeds that is now undermining the great vertical hierarchies so typical of bureaucracy" (Toffler, 1970, p. 125). What will this sort of development—or at least the beginnings of it—mean to the administration of physical education and athletics? If superindustrial man operates within temporary systems, how will that influence the administrative task? Physical education and athletics has been used to "organizational man" who is typically "subservient to the organization," "immobilized by concern for economic security," and who is "fearful of risk," for example. Will the field be ready to cope with "associative man" who is "insouciant to" the organization, who "increasingly takes" economic security "for granted," and who "welcomes risk" because in a rapidly changing society even "failure is transient" (Ibid., p. 134)?

The Concept of Freedom. Within the type of society described above, the concept of individual freedom should be discussed more and understood better within the framework of evolving democracy. To what extent, for example, does the individual choose his goals in life and then have the opportunity and means to attain them to a reasonable degree? Is freedom crucial to "the good life" of the future, or will there be a social system that leads man to look "beyond freedom and dignity à la Skinner? How much freedom can man expect to have in the near future in a bureau-technocratic society which is described as "a pattern of social management wherein the hierarchized, pyramidal, depersonalized model of human organization (bureaucracy) is linked with standardized, rationalized means (technology) with the overall aim of achieving control, flexibility, and efficiency in reaching some commercial or social objective" (Tesconi and Morris, 1972, p. 7)? The fear is that such a developing situation is working against the best interests of man and woman in our society (*The Anti-Man Culture*). Quite obviously, administrators of physical education and athletics—a group not typically noted for their so-called progressive administrative and educational philosophies—should remind themselves of the "pragmatic realities" of the life style that is coming to pass. The ability to cope with "future shock" must be fostered for survival's sake, not on the basis of whether one is "liberal" or "conservative."

Determination of Organization's Objectives. Perhaps one of the administrator's most neglected areas of concern is the determination of the organization's objectives. Everyone gives lip service to the need for "managing by objectives" as espoused by Drucker in 1954, but the moment one tries to pin down a practicing administrator in this regard one is almost inevitably doomed to the recital of words and phrases that display "the lack of a well-developed language of organizational purposefulness" (Gross, 1965, p. 195). One of the best responses to such a deficiency would seem to be a plan based on systems analysis that can enable an organization to develop a workable general-systems model. Basic to such an analysis is the fashioning of a performance-structure model which explains the operation of the input-output concept within the particular organization under consideration. The organization chooses the means whereby it can seek to attain the chosen objectives while at the same time observing internal and external codes (rules, principles, laws, etc.). Resources are acquired, some of which are invested in the future. Efficient use is made of the necessary inputs in order to achieve the output production objectives that will ultimately satisfy the interests of the clientele (Tesconi and Morris, pp. 196-208). At the same time the administrator must show dedicated concern for so-called structure objectives. Here the organization operates within the values and norms of the social system, keeping in mind the fundamental importance of people and the absolute necessity of so-called nonhuman resources. The administrator must be able to determine and guide the various subsystems that have been created within the organization on the basis of sound internal relations and wise external relations as well. Finally, the quality of the "guidance subsystem"—the means whereby the management process is executed—will determine the ultimate effectiveness of the organization in the society in which it functions. (Ibid., pp. 208-11).

Positive Approach to Administration. Administrators (prospective ones included too) are encouraged to think of their assumed responsibility positively and to seek to make the position a creative one. There is far too great a tendency on the part of the educator, for example, at all levels to assume the burden of administration reluctantly. The idea seems to be that he will take the post even though it will obviously keep him from his primary task of scholarship and teaching. This may well be true, but it is a negative way to view the situation. There is no escaping the fact that the administrative revolution is with us, and as Gross states, "it provides the people of this planet with their first opportunity of discovering their vast potentials for self-development" (1964, p. 807). Viewed in this light, administration is a social skill that will have to be employed wisely to help the inhabitants of this earth work their way out of the predicament into which they have gotten themselves. Transferred to the educational setting, who will not admit that an inadequate administrator of physical education and athletics can soon bring a department or school down to a level where the program is barely subsisting? Thus, considering the importance of the role of administrator and the steadily increasing complexities of the organizational management task, young men and women in the field should be encouraged to prepare themselves for the vital task of administrative leadership. Further, the assumption of this challenge does not mean that the individual involved must automatically put scholarship and research aside. He should be equipped to promote the idea of administration as an emerging social science, and should insist upon arranging his schedule regularly or at least periodically so that he can personally make a contribution to the developing body of knowledge upon which the future of his profession rests. As a matter of fact, it is indeed possible to view administration as *both* a tangential profession *and* an all-encompassing profession depending upon the administrator's interests and choices based on his life goals.

Need for Action-Theory Marriage. Some substantiation for the above point has been provided by Gross in his discussion of the emergence of administrative science. Many say that administrative thought is too practical, while others avow that it is usually too theoretical. This may seem to be true, but it may be said more accurately that really practical administrative thought will have to be based on far more tenable knowledge and theory than is yet available. It may not be recognized by some, but Gross believes strongly that "administrative thought cannot attain a truly academic level until it comes closer to grips with the observable facts of real-life administration" (1964, p. 843). Quite obviously, the administrator is not faced with a theory, but with a real-life situation which he may possibly resolve by means of a *tenable* theory. A research strategy is evidently needed, and it should be characterized by the restoration of a "proper theory-research balance"; the establishment of a better balance between pure and applied research; the introduction of comparative and international research in the area; an increase in interdisciplinary approaches to persistent administrative problems; and the addition of multidimensional aspects to empirical studies of organizations employing a much larger number of research techniques and tools than used in the past (Ibid., pp. 844-56).

The Current Theory Debate. The mushrooming of the behavioral sciences has made it literally impossible for a scholar to keep up with the vast quantities of literature being produced all over the world in many languages. As a result those preparing for the profession of administration have found themselves facing the impossible task of keeping up with an information overload as well as retrieving a great deal of knowledge that forms a human behavior inventory. Very puzzling, however, are the conflicting approaches that compete for the attention of the administrator in the many books, monographs, and journals. These have been conveniently defined by Gordon as (1) the traditional, (2) the behavioral, (3) the decisional, and (4) the ecological. Adherents of the *traditional* view see the task of administration as "rationalizing and engineering an efficient means to ends relationship" (Gordon, 1966, p. 9). The *behavioral* approach analyzes organizations basically as social systems in which people act, interact, compete, cooperate, and perceive others, to name a few, and the role of the administrators is to somehow harmonize the many relationships so that cooperative behavior will result with subsequent goal accomplishment. The theory that *decision-making* deserves centrality in organizational operation is more recent, and is heralded by some as a "new science." Here the administrator is faced with problem-solving under often highly competitive conditions and provided with information, objectives, plans, and probable consequences, etc. The basic task then is to so employ his intelligence, imagination, and courage through the use of management science techniques that his primary objectives are largely achieved. The fourth current theory competing for the attention of the prospective administrator is the most recent and has been named the *ecological* approach. It is concerned with the relationships that develop and are fostered among individuals in organizations within their internal and external environments. This tends to be a future-oriented outlook in that the administrator and his associates are held responsible for developing the "cope-ability" of the organization as environmental conditions change. The theory has appeal because of its eclectic, "borrowing" nature and because of its cultural and cross-cultural orientation.

The lure of each of these theories or approaches is strong, and one can become thoroughly confused when he gets beyond the superficial analytic stage in each view. Gordon worries that an administrator or executive may well be trapped by the "special perspective" of each of these approaches and lose sight of the advantages of the other three if he tries to adopt one view of administration exclusively. He believes that a flexible framework should be employed as a synthesis of the four approaches is attempted. Such a synthesis will tend to give a much fuller perspective, and it will enable the student of administrative theory and research to build a conceptual framework for administration that includes a variety of variables that may be manipulated while engaging in both qualitative and quantitative analysis. Such a framework must make room for the inclusion of personal and social values. The remaining building blocks of a conceptual framework is the selection of a unifying or "process" concept that can serve in the conceptualization of the total administrative process within one conceptual framework. Finally, it seems necessary to identify a basic position or point of view that will give a focus or direction to the conceptual framework or "working model" of the administrative process that is being postulated as a provisional working theory of administration (Gross, 1964, p. 6 ff.).

Human Problems Confronting Organizations. Keeping in mind what has been said previously in this section regarding societal changes and how these might affect the individual, and also how a managerial revolution had taken place accompanied by a concurrent development in the so-called behavioral sciences, it seems logical that many of the problems typically confronting leaders in organizational management may have to be viewed somewhat differently than has been the case in the past. Administrative science may in time provide the evidence upon which future approaches to leadership will be determined. In the meantime Bennis and Slater have enumerated the main problems or tasks of leadership in contemporary organizations as occasioned by recent twentieth-century conditions (1968, pp. 101-13). The first of these has been identified as the *integration* of individual needs and organizational goals. This had not really been seen as a serious problem earlier, but in recent years North American society has shown greater concern for the rights and aspirations of individuals.

The second of six human problems is *social influence,* or the "distributing power and sources of power and authority" (Ibid., p. 68). The bureaucratic solution to this human problem was the placing of final authority in the hands of the man at the top of the pyramid. Today executive power is being distributed to a team of leaders or administrators who see things similarly and who are able to work together cooperatively to bring about the realization of the organization's objectives. Closely related to social influence is the third problem of *collaboration,* or "producing mechanisms for the control of conflict" within an organization. The hierarchical system often seemed to operate on a "keep them sullen but not mutinous" basis and that adequate financial rewards were sufficient to "keep the ship on course." More recent conditions have seemingly warranted the building of a collaborative climate by the creation of a structure that is flexible in which "members of the unit should have a high degree of autonomy and a high degree of participation making key decisions" (Ibid., p. 105). Other human problems in organizations which require further investigation because of constantly changing conditions are listed as *adaptation, identity,* and *revitalization.*

New Concepts for Leadership. In this newer type of changing organizational environment (both internal and external), the interpersonal skills of the leader(s) will also need examination and further study. Certainly the leader must know himself and know those with whom he associates directly and indirectly. In order to accomplish this reasonably effectively, the executive needs to create a climate in which his associates will collect information about a problem accurately, bring this data back to the decision-making group, and then take part in the planning and execution of future actions (Bennis and Slater, 1968, pp. 114-23).

Generalizations and/or Constants. From this point on in this final chapter the emphases will be even more specific in regard to recommendations for administrators to consider as they look to the future. Quite obviously, organizational management is being faced with a relatively fast-moving social system—one that seems to be changing its course from time to time but that gives no absolutely certain guidance as to its ultimate destination. Such a condition as is outlined above is seemingly taking place within the field of physical education and athletics (perhaps to a somewhat lesser degree than in many other segments of the society). It is nevertheless true, however, that administrators of physical education and athletics at all levels should feel that they have been put on notice about the fluid nature of their environments, and that they should avail themselves of every opportunity to prepare themselves to keep ahead of their associates intellectually so that they will be ready to meet change head-on and make the necessary changes that will ensure growth (if desired) and eventual survival.

The above momentary digression is not meant to imply for an instant that there are not a great many generalizations or constants which carry over from yesterday to today and thence to tomorrow which help to maintain the structure and vitality of physical education and athletics. This means, for example, that much of what is known about human nature today will be quite similar or identical. It forewarns the administrator that he shouldn't throw the baby out with the bath water just because so many changes seem to be taking place all around him. The great problem seems to be the urgent need to strengthen the body of knowledge available to the administration profession so that the astounding development in the area of technology is reasonably approximated by the understanding and knowledge available about appropriate and efficient administrative behavior. While this balance is being established, the tried-and-true generalizations or constants from the past should be used daily and only discarded or modified when there is ample scientific evidence available to warrant any change.

Increase Own Knowledge. In addition to relying upon the wisdom of the past, the executive should make it a habit over the years to increase both his theoretical and practical knowledge. This is especially true if at any point he should detect an area of weakness in his managerial knowledge, competencies, or skills. It is perhaps a sad fact that the "knowledge explosion" has been so great that it is a physical impossibility for any one person to digest all of the literature made available even in his own area of specialization. This leaves no doubt but that the successful manager must read widely and occasionally "deeply," and that he must choose in-service learning experience selectively. Inquiring as to what administrators should learn, Gross classifies his answer into three categories as follows: knowledge, abilities, and interests. He implies that it is one thing to obtain a sound general education and a high level of technical knowledge which includes a substantial understanding of administrative theory and practice, but that it is also vital to understand the requirements of his position and the nature of the organization in which he works. Last, but certainly not least, the administrator should seek to gain knowledge about himself so that he may possibly retain some objectivity when he makes judgments about the behavior of others (1964, pp. 874-80).

Improving One's Communication. Generally speaking, it is quite reasonable to assume that people will work more enthusiastically with an administrator who communicates with them in terms that they can readily understand. All would readily pay lip-service to this premise, but they don't truly understand the penalty that must be paid for the miscommunication that takes place every hour of the day all over the world. Part of the difficulty is that there are many different definitions of the word "communication," and the term must first be defined most carefully and specifically before any meaningful investigation can take place. Obviously, there is a long history to the subject starting perhaps with the gesture of primitive man.

In recent years there has developed what might be called a science of communication. Basic to this is the understanding of communication as a social process between at least two organizations (peoples or groups) which occurs through the medium of some type of symbolic behavior. In organizations there are both formal and informal networks of communication and, by and large, it is quite safe to say that very little research has been carried out in physical education and athletics on the subject. This situation must change, and it is for this reason that the editors were so pleased to include two of the first studies of this type in the field within this text. It is highly interesting to note, and undoubtedly most important to the administrator, that the informal communication structure is quite selective when it comes to transmitting information, but that the speed of such transmission by the "grapevine" or informal structure is faster than that of the formal structure typically. Most important also is the fact that in order to promote communication within the organization the administrator must make a special effort to provide an atmosphere where inter-work unit communication can take place.

Investing Oneself in the Environment. A most interesting question to consider is the possible responsibility that an administrator has to the community—to the internal and external environments to which he is related.

The position always taken by the editor has always been what might be called by some an intermediate one. In essence, this implies that the executive does have a definite community responsibility, and that he should be prepared to "invest himself" at least *to a reasonable degree*. The rationale here is that the educator is actually in a strongly service profession to begin with, and so the administrator of physical education and athletics—if he invests himself in the larger educational community in which he is practicing his profession (i.e., serves on college, senate, and all-university committees)—will not find himself with very much time left to "invest" in the so-called outside community.

In university situations, for example, there always seem to be people who assume, or who are asked to assume, many responsible committee posts. Some of these people also turn up in important leadership roles in the outside community. Such people are very rarely physical educator/coaches, however, and there are a number of possible reasons why this is the case. In the first place, of course, one wonders how and/or if active individuals like this ever spend enough time in preparation for teaching and to what extent they are productive in scholarly and research endeavor. It is important to remember too that coaches put in many hours, especially during their sport's season (and it should be noted that these hours are spent at exactly the time when many committees meet because others are relatively free).

Whatever the case may be, the argument presented here for executives in this field is that they, just as all others, have a responsibility to accept regularly some of the burdens and obligations of a free and complex system in which they expect to profit from the benefits and rewards. The administrator is presumably a mature person who sets an example for others teaching and coaching in his program. Democracy thrives when people work together freely to solve their problems at all levels.

Anticipating Inevitable Change. First it was death, then taxes, and now the inevitability of change has been added to the certainties of life. To the administrator of physical education and athletics this semi-humorous statement means that he and his associates are going to have to be ready to improvise, adapt, adjust, and innovate in order to solve the many problems that will present themselves because "the times they are a-changin'." In this field the fact that the *rate* of change in the environment is increasing at a geometric ratio spells impending disaster or at least decline because of the rather traditional nature of the physical education and athletics profession.

Such a condition does not need to prevail forever, however, because the native intelligence and adaptability—and often his "survival instinct"—are usually well above average. In order to survive, the field must be ever ready to adapt and/or change. Adaptation and change mean that all concerned with the program will be faced with a greater or lesser amount of psychological stress. Question: What human behavior, knowledge, competencies, and skills will the executive need to have to keep his associates so stimulated that they will continue to be highly effective faculty and staff members? In the past it may have been possible to answer this with a recommendation that the administrator improve his human relations. Now and in the future it appears that managers will need to be "practical behavioral scientists" in order "to obtain human acceptance and support for innovation" (Flory, 1965, pp. 276, 279). There are basic human needs which have often been neglected in traditional management procedures; "improved management stems only from improved men" (Ibid.).

The Strengthening of Organizational Democracy. There are many today who long for "the good old days" when affairs were not so complex and when "the boss was boss." The simplicity of former times will hardly return, but so-called strong and directive leadership could return either through erosion of personal freedom or revolution. It hardly seems possible to slow down or stop the administrative revolution that has been taking place for decades now, but in keeping with the value system of the evolving democratic culture, the "new frontier" as envisioned by Gross is most definitely what he terms as "organizational democracy" (1964, pp. 812-22). He foresees "a rebirth of individualism in the administered society of the future"—thus "organizational individualism" (p. 814). With this type of development in which people have even more mobility, the opportunity for continuous learning, and yet a security base, a new type of leadership will gradually emerge: "the strong leader, therefore, is he who strengthens organizational democracy by promoting individual participation, self-development, rights, and responsibilities" (Ibid., p. 822).

Improvement of the Profession of Administration. The question might well be asked if administration is a profession with a disciplinary base. Certainly an examination of the literature would seem to indicate that such is becoming the case, but is perhaps not yet truly so. The term "profession" usually implies that someone is "professing" something on behalf of others in the society. It used to mean that such service would not necessarily be viewed in the light of pecuniary reward. People usually follow a profession for their entire lives—or at least until what is considered "retirement age" arrives. A profession is based on an inventory of scientific knowledge. In addition, a profession is typically promoted and supported by one or more professional associations that develop codes of ethics for professional practitioners.

It is immediately obvious that the field of administration possesses some of these qualities or qualifications, but others have not been achieved yet—and possibly may never be. For example, a profession like physical education and sport (a "holding pattern" title for the field) may have performers, teachers and coaches, teachers of teachers, and scholars and researchers in its midst. Some of these professional people may assume the responsibility of administration for a period of time, and then they may return to practice their profession in one of the previously mentioned ways. On the other hand, some people get involved with the administration of physical education and athletics early in their careers and eventually retire, never having relinquished such an "involvement." What does this mean? It seems to imply that administration is a new and perhaps different kind of profession that presently may be viewed as either a tangential or all-encompassing vocation. At this moment it is not possible to predict with unerring accuracy how it will be viewed in the year 2050. Time will tell, and it is to be hoped that the field of physical education and athletics will be "blessed" with a high quality of administrative leadership.

The Improvement of Administrative Education. One thing is certain: physical education and athletics will not be blessed with a high quality of administrative leadership in the future unless definite and positive steps are taken soon to expand and improve the quality of the administrative education that is currently being offered. At the present time, with notable exceptions, administration courses in physical education and athletics are taught usually by harried administrators who are themselves too busy to give adequate time to class preparation. These courses are not taught in such a way that problem-solving, laboratory experiences are the rule, and the texts and readings are quite often routine and pedestrian. Administrators and teachers of administration (if not the same person) do not seem to be aware of the tremendous development that has taken place in the behavioral sciences. If they are aware of this inventory of knowledge, they either do not have the time to master it or do not feel that it is important enough to include in their courses. Quite obviously, the field of physical education and athletics is presently highly vulnerable in this important aspect of professional programs, and the situation *must* improve markedly and soon.

Education in the Future. The entire educational structure of North America has been challenged as never before in the writer's memory. Is it as bad as some people say it is? It can't be! If it were that bad, the students who want to tear the walls down brick by brick are right. Can the educational structure be revitalized by "evolution" rather than "revolution?" Do we really want, for example, "schools without walls"? What are educators going to do—if anything—about dropouts and stopouts?

Certainly much of the administrative hierarchy of education does give every evidence of foundering. Fortunately (or unfortunately), students in physical education and athletics, instead of being sullen and mutinous as in some disciplines, have been relatively happy and satisfied. This is no reason for complacency, however; this field should be sponsoring "committees on the future" in each and every educational establishment. If the prime educational objective is to "increase the individual's 'cope-ability' " within the social system (Toffler, 1970, p. 357), it is quite apparent that many physical education curricula need to be seriously revolutionized and pointed toward the future. This means that the organizational structure needs quite radical reorganization. Does the phrase "teaching yesterday's curriculum today" apply to this field? The cope-ability of students can be developed by preparing them "in certain common skills needed for human communication and social integration" (Ibid., p. 366). One last thought—as administrators of physical education and athletics, will it be possible to organize and administer programs in this field so that students will truly acquire the three skills of learning, relating, and choosing (Ibid, p. 367) that may help them to lead full, rewarding, and creative lives in a world characterized by peace and good will? This should be our goal.

General Bibliography

Bennis, Warren, "Beyond Bureaucracy," *Trans-Action* (July-August 1965), pp. 31-35.

Bennis, Warren, and Philip E. Slater, *The Temporary Society*. New York: Harper & Row, Publishers, 1968.

Drucker, Peter F., *The Practice of Management*. New York: Harper & Row, Publishers, 1954.

Flory, Charles D., *Managers for Tomorrow*. New York: The New American Library, 1965.

Gordon, Paul J., "Transcend the Current Debate on Administrative Theory," *Hospital Administration,* 11, no. 2 (Spring 1966), 6-23.

Gross, Bertram M., *The Managing of Organizations*. New York: The Free Press of Glencoe (Macmillan), 1964.

———, "What Are Your Organization's Objectives?" *Human Relations,* 18, no. 3 (1965), 195-215.

Tesconi, Charles A., Jr., and Van Cleve Morris, *The Anti-Man Culture*. Urbana: University of Illinois Press, 1972.

Toffler, Alvin, *Future Shock*. New York: Random House, 1970.

APPENDIX

A Selected Bibliography of Completed Research on Administrative Theory and Practice in Physical Education and Athletics[*]

Earle F. Zeigler / Marcia J. Spaeth

1. Aitken, Margaret H., "A Study of Physical Education Facilities for College Women with Implications for Western Washington College of Education." Ph.D. diss., Teachers College, Columbia University, 1958.
2. Alderson, Curtis J., "Analysis of Legal Background, Status, and Principles with Special Reference to Physical Education; A Report of a Type C. Project." Ph.D. diss., Teachers College, Columbia University, 1949.
3. Allen, Patricia, "An Investigation of Administrative Leadership and Group Interaction in Departments of Physical Education for Women of Selected Colleges and Universities," Ed.D. diss., University of Oregon, 1971.
4. Allsen, Philip E., "An Evaluation of the Physical Education Program for Men in Selected Junior Colleges." Ph.D. diss., University of Utah, 1965.

[*]This selected bibliography has been updated over the years (up to 1972) and is by no means all-inclusive. The studies included relate to both theory and practice. Most studies covering different aspects of "professional preparation" were excluded, and there are many in this area of investigation. Some "hard" decisions were made about what to include and what to exclude, and we apologize for possibly pertinent studies that were excluded or inadvertently omitted. The compilers would appreciate learning about other studies that "ought" to be included (and because of what emphasis).

Grateful appreciation is expressed to Miss Sue Cook, Research Assistant to Professor Zeigler, for some very recent help, and we acknowledge also the assistance of Mrs. Greta Jones, Secretary, The University of Western Ontario.

5. American Association for Health, Physical Education, and Recreation, Division of Girls and Women's Sports, "Statement of Policies and Procedures for Competition in Girls, and Women's Sports," *Journal of Health, Physical Education, Recreation,* 28 (September 1957), 57-58.
6. Anderson, George F., "A Study of Certain Aspects of Physical Education in New York State." Ph.D. diss., Syracuse University, 1950.
7. Appenzeller, Herbert T., "An Analysis of Court Cases Pertaining to Tort Liability for Injuries Sustained in a Public School Program of Physical Education." Ed.D. diss., Duke University, 1966.
8. Arce, William B., "Planning Boys' Gymnasium Facilities for Secondary Schools." Ph.D. diss., Stanford University, 1956.
9. Bagley, Martha C., "Situational Leadership in Graduate Departments of Physical Education." Ph.D. diss., University of Illinois, 1972.
10. Baker, Clyde C., "A Study of the Duties and Functions of the Supervisor of Physical Education in the Public Schools in Western Washington." Master's thesis, Washington State University, 1962.
11. Baker, Gertrude M., "A Survey of Administrative Relationships of Departments of Physical Education in Colleges and Universities," *Research Quarterly,* 13 (May 1942), 217-28.
12. _____, "Survey of the Administration of Physical Education in Public Schools in the United States," *Research Quarterly,* 33 (December 1962), 632-36.
13. Baker, Gertrude M., Elsie Annis, and Jean Bontz, "Supervision of Physical Education in the Elementary School; Part I. The Supervisor's Viewpoint," *Research Quarterly,* 23 (December 1952), 379-90; "Part II. The Classroom Teacher's Viewpoint." 25 (December 1954), 378-86.
14. Baker, Robert E., "The Implications of School Liability for Teachers of Health (Physical) Education in New York City." Ph.D. diss., Teachers College, Columbia University, 1956.
15. Barnes, Samuel E., "Criteria for Evaluating the Administration of Intercollegiate Athletics." Ph.D. diss., Ohio State University, 1956.
16. Barrett, V. F., "Liability in Athletics in Oregon," *Research Quarterly,* 10 (March 1939), 99.
17 Barrow, Lloyd, "An Analysis of Insurance Principles and Practices with Implications for Physical Education." Ph.D. diss., Columbia University, 1953.
18. Bartelma, David D., "Study of the Practices and Policies of State Departments of Education in the Administration and Supervision of Health, Physical Education, Recreation and Safety." Ph.D. diss., University of Colorado, 1948.
19. Batchelder, Robert W., and James R. Hall, "Principles for the Administration of Athletics for Member Institutions of the National Collegiate Athletic Association," vols. I, II, Research Study no. 1. Ph.D. diss., Colorado State College, 1965.

20. Bedelle, Fred, Jr., "Identification and Analysis of Selected Administrative Problems Confronting Public School Physical Education Directors." Ph.D. diss., The University of Tennessee, 1962.
21. Beeman, Harris Frank, "Analysis of Human Relations in the Administration of Intramural Sports Programs of the Western Conference." Ph.D. diss., University of Michigan, 1960.
22. Bell, Lacey Dell, "A Study of the Policies Governing Interscholastic Athletic Programs for Girls in American Public Secondary Schools." Ph.D. diss., New York University, 1959.
23. Berridge, Harold L., "A Study in the Field of Accreditation of Professional Physical Education." Ed.D. diss., University of Texas, 1948.
24. Billett, Ralph E., "A Survey of Health and Physical Education Programs in the Public Elementary Schools of Ohio by Means of the Laporte Score Card." Ph.D. diss., The University of Michigan, 1956.
25. Bierhaus, Frederick W., "The Organization and Administration of Intramural Sports for Men in Selected Colleges and Universities." Ph.D. diss., University of Colorado, 1956.
26. Blamer, William C., "A Study of Physical Education in the Public, Junior, and Community Colleges of the Continental United States." Ed.D. diss., Michigan State University, 1967.
27. Bloom, Martin, "Types of Actions Used in Resolving Intergroup Problems in Physical Education Experiences of the Springfield College Physical Education Faculty Members." Master's thesis, Springfield College, 1947.
28. Bole, Ronald E., "An Economic Analysis of the Factors Influencing Football Attendance at the University of Illinois, 1926-1968." Ph.D. diss., University of Illinois, 1970.
29. Borcher, William J., "An Analysis of Public Opinion in Regard to Physical Education in Public Schools." Ph.D. diss., University of Oregon, 1964.
30. Bowers, James H., "A Study of Spaces for Physical Education." Ed.D. diss., University of Tennessee, 1967.
31. Boyd, Scott, "A Survey of Safety Practices in the Physical Education Program for Boys of Secondary Schools in North Carolina." Ph.D. diss., Indiana University, 1955.
32. Boydston, Donald N., "The Duties and Responsibilities of State Directors of Health and Physical Education with Special Reference to Oklahoma." Ph.D. diss., Columbia University, 1949.
33. Bridgeman, Donald F., "A Study of the Job Competencies Utilized by Directors of Health, Physical Education and Recreation." Ph.D. diss., Springfield College, 1959.
34. Bronzan, Robert T., "Attitudes of University Publics toward the Contributions of the Intercollegiate Football Program to General Education." Ed.D. diss., Stanford University, 1965.
35. Broom, Eric, "A Comparative Analysis of the Central Administrative

Agencies of Amateur Sport and Physical Recreation in England and Canada." Ph.D. diss., University of Illinois, 1971.
36. Burkhart, Roy W., "Contrasting Role Expectations of College Directors of Physical Education and Athletics." Ph.D. diss., Wayne State University, 1965.
37. Calisch, Richard, "Spectator Problems in Secondary School Athletics," *Research Quarterly*, 25 (1954), 261-68.
38. Campbell, Laurie E., "The Administration of the Physical Education Activity Area in Professional Physical Education." Ph.D. diss., New York University, 1943.
39. Carlson, Gordon, "The Finances of Interscholastic Athletics in Selected High Schools of California." Ph.D. diss., the University of California (Berkeley), 1955.
40. Case, Robert, "An Analysis of the Communication Structure of a University Administrative and Instructional Unit." Ph.D. diss., University of Illinois, 1969.
41. Clark, Dana E., "Relationship of Certain Factors to the Quality of Administrative Provisions for Physical Education in New York State." Ed.D. diss., Syracuse University, 1953.
42. Clarke, H. Harrison, "Administrative Problems in Required Physical Education for Men in Universities," *Research Quarterly*, 3 (May 1932), 218.
43. Clements, W. S., "The Administration of School Playgrounds in the Educational System of Chicago," *Research Quarterly*, 8 (December 1937), 55.
44. Colgate, Thomas, P., "An Evaluation of the Public Relations Programs of Physical Education Departments in Selected Colleges and Universities in the State of Iowa." Ph.D. diss., University of Iowa, 1967.
45. Coma, Anthony S., "The Characteristics of Male Disciplinary Offenders and the Male Disciplinary Problem at a Large Urban High School." Ed.D. diss., Temple University, 1964.
46. Cooper, Samuel M., "The Control of Interscholastic Athletics." Ed.D. diss., Western Reserve University, 1955.
47. Cordts, Harold John, "Status of the Physical Education Required or Instructional Programs for Men and Women in the Four-Year Colleges and Universities of the United States." Ed.D. diss., Syracuse University, 1958.
48. Cutter, Alexander R., "Objectives, Policies, and Administrative Procedures for Junior High School Intramural Athletic Programs for Boys." Ed.D. diss., University of California (Berkeley), 1964.
49. Daly, John A., "An Analysis of Some Philosophic Beliefs Held by Australian Physical Educators with Implications for Administration." Master's thesis, University of Illinois, 1970.
50. Daniel, Juri V., "Differentiated Roles and Faculty Job Satisfaction within Departments of Physical Education and Athletics in Ontario Universities." Ph.D. diss., University of Illinois, 1971.

51. Dannehl, Wayne, "The Organizational Climate of Physical Education Administration Units in Selected Mid-Western Universities." Ph.D. diss., University of Illinois, 1970.
52. Daves, M. Marise, "A Study of Practices Used by Women's Athletic Associations in Illinois Colleges to Conduct Extramural Sports Programs." Ph.D. diss., New York University, 1964.
53. Davis, Charles C., "An Analysis of the Duties Performed by the Administrative Head of Health, Physical Education, and Recreation in State-Supported Colleges and Universities in the United States." Ph.D. diss., Ohio State University, 1972.
54. Davis, Michael G., "Role Perceptions and Expectations of College Physical Education Chairmen's Responsibility Priorities by Faculty Chairman." P.E.D. diss., Indiana University, 1972.
55. Dayries, John L., Jr., "An Analysis of Selected Functions of State Departments of Education in the Area of Health and Physical Education." Ph.D. diss., University of Oklahoma, 1966.
56. DeGroat, H. S., "A Study Pertaining to the Athletic Directorship of Intercollegiate Athletics," *Research Quarterly,* 7 (October 1936), 14-35.
57. DeLuca, Eugene T., "A Study of Physical Education Facilities in the Public High Schools of the State of Rhode Island." Ed.D. diss., Columbia University, Teachers College, 1967.
58. DeShaw, Charles G., "An Evaluation of the Established Regulations Employed by the States to Ensure the Health and Safety of Varsity Competitors in Secondary Schools." Ph.D. diss., New York University, 1948.
59. DeVazier, James A., "Opinions Expressed by Members of Selected Civic Organizations in Arkansas Regarding Health, Physical Education, and Recreation." Ed.D. diss., University of Arkansas, 1967.
60. Dimock, Hedley S., "Supervisor's Group—New Slants in Supervision," *Research Quarterly,* 5 (December 1934), 58-59. (Not a Physical Education study).
61. Dingman, Raleigh E., "Policies and Practices in Intramural and Interscholastic Athletics in Junior High Schools in North Carolina." Ph.D. diss., The University of North Carolina, 1961.
62. Dittus, Loren K., "The Role of the Physical Education Director." Ed.D. diss., Colorado State College, 1966.
63. Dornbos, S., "A Survey of Intramural Athletics for High School Boys in Metropolitan Grand Rapids, Michigan." Master's thesis, University of Michigan, 1962.
64. Doscher, Nathan, and Nelson Walke, "The Status of Liability for School Physical Education Accidents and Its Relationship to the Health Program," *Research Quarterly,* 23 (October 1952), 280-94.

65. Douglas, John William, "An Analysis of Administrative Leadership in Physical Education Departments." Ph.D. diss., Ohio State University, 1969.
66. Durand, Earl S., "Analytical Study of Policies and Practices Relating to Physical Education Expenditures in Fifteen Representative Public School Systems in Eastern Cities." Ph.D. diss., Columbia University (T.C.), 1953.
67. Earthman, Glen I., "A Critical Study of Research in Administrative Theory Done at Colorado State College for the Period 1959 to 1964." Ph.D. diss., Colorado State College, 1964.
68. Ecker, Charles I., "Analysis of Criteria for the Maximum Utilization of Indoor Physical Education Facilities in Terms of a Functional Program in Selected Senior High Schools of Maryland." Ph.D. diss., University of North Carolina at Chapel Hill, 1964.
69. Eick, William F., "Institutional Policies and Procedures of Personnel Administration with Implications for Departments of Physical Education for Men in Colleges and Universities." Ed.D. diss., Columbia University, Teachers College, 1954.
70. Elliott, Allan R., "Space and Facilities for Physical Education and Community Use in Public Schools." Ph.D. diss., Stanford University, 1953.
71. Enos, V. Rodney, "An Analysis of the Training, Experience, and Responsibilities of Athletic Directors in Junior Colleges of the United States." Ph.D. diss., Washington State University (Pullman, Washington), 1964.
72. Erickson, Hal A., "A Proposed Plan for Supervision of Health Education and Physical Education in the Public Schools of Utah." Master's thesis, University of Utah, 1959.
73. Evans, Ruth, and Robert Berry, "Report of a Study of Administration and Finance of High School Athletics for Boys," *Research Quarterly*, 17 (October 1946), 204-7.
74. Ezersky, Eugene M., "Planning Physical Education Facilities for Boys in the Proposed New York City High Schools." Ed.D. diss., New York University, 1968.
75. Falgren, Lloyd H., "An Analysis of Physical Education Legislation Applying to Public Schools of the Forty-Eight States." Ph.D. diss., University of Oregon, 1950.
76. Fant, Helen E., "An Investigation of Certain Aspects of Physical Education in Selected Universities in the United States." Ph.D. diss., Louisiana State University, 1964.
77. Fauver, Edwin, "The Relation of the Department of Student Health to the Department of Physical Education," *Research Quarterly*, 2 (March 1931), 44-50.
78. Finger, Bernice, "An Administrative Guide for the Program of Physical Education for College Women." Ph.D. diss., Columbia University (T.C.), 1957.

79. Flanigan, Thomas, "An Assessment of Specified Environmental Characteristics of the College of Physical Education at the University of Illinois." Ph.D. diss., University of Illinois, 1973.
80. Fox, John Willis, "Practices and Trends in Physical Education Programs for Boys in Selected Oregon Schools." Ph.D. diss., University of Oregon, 1960.
81. Fritz, Harry G., "An Evaluation of the Boys' Health and Physical Education Program in Selected White Secondary Schools of Missouri." P.E.D. diss., Indiana University, 1954.
82. Gillanders, Dorothy F., "Attitudes of Arizona Citizens toward Physical Education in Public Schools." Ed.D. diss., University of Southern California, 1956.
83. Gillett, Arley F., "A Study of Boys' Interschool Athletics in Selected Elementary Schools of Illinois." P.Ed. diss., Indiana University, 1954.
84. Gingerich, Roman L., "An Evaluation of the Physical Education Service Programs for Men in the Church-Related Senior Colleges and Universities of Indiana." P.E.D. diss., Indiana University, 1958.
85. Gonella, Adolph Floyd, "An Examination of Physical Education Programs." Ed. D. diss., University of California, Berkely 1968.
86. Grambeau, Rodney James, "A Survey of the Administration of Intramural Sports Programs for Men in Selected Colleges and Universities in North and South America." Ed.D. diss., University of Michigan, 1959.
87. Graybeal, Elizabeth, "A Consideration of Qualities Used by Administrators in Judging Effective Teachers of Physical Education in Minnesota," *Research Quarterly,* 12 (December 1941), 741.
88. Greenberg, Alan, "An Analysis of the Problems Faced by Personnel Relating to Physical Education in an Inner City and in a Suburban Area." Ph.D. diss., University of Illinois, 1970.
89. Greenberg, Jerrold S., "The Relationship between the Frequency and the Effectiveness of Selected Supervisory Behaviors as Perceived by Physical Education Teachers and Their Supervisors in Selected Secondary Schools in New York State." Ed.D. diss., Syracuse University, 1969.
90. Groves, Quentin D., "A Guide for the Evaluation of Programs in Physical Education." Ed.D. diss., The University of Kansas, 1962.
91. Guenther, Donald, "National Status of Physical Education and Sports Insurance Plans," *Research Quarterly,* 21 (1950), 20-23.
92. Guerrea, Joseph, "A Survey of Physical Education Facilities," *Scholastic Coach,* 22 (January 1953).
93. Guley, Marc, "The Legal Aspect of Injuries in Physical Education and Athletics." Ed.D. diss., Syracuse University, 1952.
94. Gagnier, E., "A Survey of Gymnastics Equipment Sold by Selected Companies in the United States." Master's thesis, University of Michigan, 1959.

95. Haag, Jessie Helen, "An Analysis of Certification Requirements for Health and Physical Education in the U.S." Ed.D. diss., Temple University, 1950.
96. Hallbert, Edmond C., "A Cost Analysis of Physical Education in Terms of Utilization of Facilities." Ed.D. diss., Stanford University, 1960.
97. Haniford, George W., "The Utilization of the 'Recreational Gymnasium' by Purdue University Undergraduate Students." Ph.D. diss., Indiana State University, 1962.
98. Harristhal, Joann W., "A Student Reaction Inventory for Rating Teachers in the College Women's Physical Education Service Program." Ph.D. diss., University of Oregon, 1962.
99. Hart, James E., "Administration of Athletic Scholarships at the University of Missouri." Ph.D. diss., The University of Missouri, 1956.
100. Havel, Richard C., "The Professional Status of Head Coaches of Athletics in Colleges and Universities," *Research Quarterly,* 24 (March 1953), 8-17.
101. Hawkes, Arthur E., "A Set of Operational Principles for County-Level Supervision of Physical Education in California." Ph.D. diss., University of Southern California, 1965.
102. Healey, William A., "An Analysis of the Administrative Practices in Competitive Athletics in Selected Colleges of the Midwest." Ph.D. diss., Indiana University, 1952.
103. _____, "National Survey: Extra Pay for Coaching," *Scholastic Coach,* 30 (October 1960), 44, 46, 68-69.
104. Hendricks, E. Troy, "The Organization and Administrative Operation of Physical Education Service Programs in Land-Grant Colleges and Universities." Ph.D. diss., University of Missouri, 1951.
105. Hickes, Roy M., "An Evaluation of the Discretionary Administrative Practices in the Interscholastic Athletic Program of the Member Schools of the Pennsylvania Interscholastic Athletic Association." Ph.D. diss., University of Pittsburgh, 1952.
106. Hill, Leo, "A Manual for the Organization, Administration, and Conduct of Senior High School Programs of Physical Education for Boys in Washington, D.C." Ph.D. diss., New York University, 1958.
107. Hinman, Strong, "The Organization and Administration of Health and Physical Education in Large Cities," *Research Quarterly,* 11 (December 1940), 97-108.
108. Hoffer, Joe R., "An Activity Analysis of the Duties of Recreation and Informal Education Leaders and Supervisors," *Research Quarterly,* 15 (March 1944), 50-59.
109. Hollingsworth, Lloyd E., "Development of a Manual for Physical Education and Related Recreational Facilities for the State of Minnesota." Ph.D. diss., New York University, 1958.
110. Hoy, Joseph T., "Current Practices in the Control of Intercollegiate Athletics in Selected Conferences." Ph.D. diss., Indiana University, 1966.

111. Hughes, James Marshall, "Standards for Facilities for Physical Education in Senior High Schools." Ph.D. diss., University of Texas, 1960.
112. Hughes, William L., "A More Unified Administration of Health, Physical Education and Athletics," *The Journal of Health and Physical Education*, 4 (February 1933), 7.
113. _____ , "The Administration of Health and Physical Education for Men in Colleges and Universities." Published Ph.D. diss., Columbia University, Teachers College, 1932.
114. _____ , "Round Table Discussion on the Administration of Intercollegiate Athletics," *Research Quarterly*, 3 (May 1932), 70.
115. _____ , "Problems of Intercollegiate Athletic Administration in a Modern Program of Physical Education," *Research Quarterly*, 2 (March 1931), 51.
116. Humphrey, James H., "A Job Analysis of Selected Public School Physical Education Directors." Ed.D. diss., Boston University, 1951.
117. Hunter, James E., "An Analysis of the Meanings Attached to Selected Concepts in Administrative Theory by Athletic Administrators of the Big Ten Conference and Central Intercollegiate Athletic Association." Master's thesis, University of Illinois, 1971.
118. Hunter, Milton Dial, "A Dictionary For Physical Education," Ph.D. diss. (*Abstracts*, 27:941a), Indiana University, 1966.
119. Husman, Burris F., Warren R. Johnson, and Arthur D. Strom, "A Nationwide Survey Analysis of Major Administrative Problems in Required College Physical Education Programs," *Research Quarterly*, 24 (March 1953), 67.
120. Hutter, David M., "A Study of the Attitudes Affecting the Behavior of the Administration of Intercollegiate Athletics." Ph.D. diss., Ohio State University, 1970.
121. Irace, Sebastian C., "Case Studies in the Administration of Intercollegiate Athletics for Men with Reference to the Member Institutions of the College of the City of New York." Ed.D. diss., Teachers College, Columbia University, 1958.
122. Irwin, Leslie W., and Ross Stephens, "A Survey of Safety Conditions of Buildings and Grounds in Secondary Schools," *Research Quarterly*, 12 (December 1941), 726-38.
123. Irwin, Leslie W., and William C. Reavis, "Practices Pertaining to Health and Physical Education in Secondary Schools," *Research Quarterly*, 11 (October 1940), 93-109.
124. Jenny, John H., "A Study of Selection, Orientation, and Screening Practices Carried On by Departments of Health and Physical Education in Accredited Colleges in the United States." Ph.D. diss., Temple University, 1953.
125. Johnson, Georgia B., *Organization of the Required Physical Education for*

Women in State Universities. Teachers College Contribution to Education, no. 253, Bureau of Publications, Teachers College, Columbia University, 1927.

126. Jones, Annie L., "A Fiscal Study of Physical Education at the School District Level in Wisconsin." Master's thesis, University of Wisconsin, 1965.

127. Jorgensen, LaVernia, "A Survey of Recruitment and Selected Practices and Procedures of Women Physical Educators in Colleges and Universities." Ph.D. diss., Indiana University, 1959.

128. Kelliher, Mayville S., "A Job Analysis of the Duties of Selected Athletic Directors in Colleges and Universities." Ph.D. diss., The University of Oregon, 1956.

129. Kimball, Edwin R., "Current Practices in the Control of Intercollegiate Athletics." Ph.D. diss., University of Oregon, 1955.

130. Kleinman, Seymour, "A Study to Determine the Factors that Influence the Behavior of Sports Crowds." Ph.D. diss., The Ohio State University, 1960.

131. Koehler, Robert W., "A Study of Legal Liability in Education with Emphasis on Physical Education in Selected States from 1955 to 1965." Ed.D. diss., University of Utah, 1967.

132. Koldus, John J., III, "An Appraisal of the Secondary School Physical Education Programs in Arkansas." Ph.D. diss., University of Arkansas, 1964.

133. Koss, Rosabel Steinhauer, "Guidelines for the Improvement of Physical Education in Selected Public Elementary Schools of New Jersey," *Research Quarterly*, 36 (October 1965), 282-88.

134. Krablin, George H., "Selected Principles for the Administration of the Secondary School Winter Sports Programs." Ph.D. diss., Syracuse University, 1956.

135. Kruse, William Lewis, "Administrative Policies and Practices of Intercollegiate Athletics in Illinois Two-Year Institutions." P.E.D. diss., University of Indiana, 1972.

136. Lacy, Dan Edgar, "Teacher Liability in Physical Education in California." Ph.D. diss., Stanford University, 1960.

137. Lehsten, Nelson, G., "An Organization and Appraisal of Methods Utilized in the Conduct of Physical Education Activities for Boys in the Secondary School." Ph.D. diss., Indiana University, 1953.

138. Leidy, Rita O., "A Guide for Effective Organization and Conduct of Girls' Athletic Associations." Ph.D. diss., Teachers College, Columbia University, 1958.

139. Leslie, David K., "A Study of the Factors which Facilitate or Inhibit Adoption of Innovative Practices in Boys' Physical Education in Secondary Schools." Ph.D. diss., University of Iowa, 1970.

140. Locke, Lawrence F., "The Performance of Administration-Oriented Physical Educators on Selected Psychological Tests." Ph.D. diss., Stanford University, 1961.

141. Long, James W., "A Guide for Planning Indoor Physical Education Facilities in Southern Colleges and Universities." Ph.D. diss., University of North Carolina, 1953.

142. Loveless, James C., "An Analysis of the Duties of the State Directors of Health and Physical Education in the United States." P.E.D. diss., Indiana State University, 1952.

143. Luce, Richard H., "A Survey of the Nature, Circumstances, Frequency, and Severity of Accidents in the Intercollegiate Athletic Programs of the New York State Teachers Colleges," P.E.D. diss., Indiana State University, 1956.

144. Luck, Emory F., "An Analysis of Employment Theory and Practice in Physical Education in Big Ten Universities." Ph.D. diss., University of Illinois, 1971.

145. Lux, Lloyd N., "The Application of Guides for the Development of Intramural Activities for College Men." Ph.D. diss., Teachers College, Columbia University, 1950.

146. MacKenzie, Marlin M., "Public Relations in College Physical Education." Ph.D. diss., Teachers College, Columbia University, 1951.

147. Mackey, Ann, "A National Study of Women's Intramural Sports in Teachers Colleges and Schools of Education." Ph.D. diss., Boston University, 1957.

148. Mackey, Helen T., "Job Analysis of Women Supervisors of Physical Education in United States Public Schools." Ph.D. diss., Boston University, 1954.

149. _____, "Job Analysis of Women Supervisors of Physical Education in United States Public Schools," *Research Quarterly,* 27 (1956), 32.

150. Madden, John E., "Safeguarding College Students from Financial Loss Due to Physical Education Incurred Injuries with Particular Reference to Medical Reimbursement Insurance." Ph.D. diss., Teachers College, Columbia University, 1954.

151. Mand, Charles L., "A Study of Physical Education in Selected Elementary and Secondary Schools of Ohio." Ph.D. diss., Ohio State University, 1955.

152. Marks, Walter E., "A Study of Existing State High School and Other Selected Athletic Benefit Plans." Ph.D. diss., Indiana University, 1948.

153. Marley, Jack E, "A Case Analysis of Operating Interscholastic Athletics in Pennsylvania." Ph.D. diss., Pennsylvania State University, 1953.

154. Matthews, David O., "Programs of Intramural Sports in Selected Ohio Schools." Ph.D. diss., Western Reserve University, 1958.

155. McBride, Jack E., "The History and Development of Faculty Controls of Intercollegiate Athletics at Oklahoma University." Ph.D. diss., University of Oklahoma, 1965.

Bibliography of Completed Research

156. McCristal, King J., "A Study of the Relationship between Certain Undergraduate Success Factors at Michigan State College and the Vocational Competence of Male Physical Education Graduates." Ph.D. diss., Teachers College, Columbia University, 1953.
157. McIlroy, Jane S., "An Evaluation of the Physical Education Program for Women in Selected Institutions of Higher Learning in Three Northwest States." Ph.D. diss., Indiana State University, 1961.
158. McQuarrie, Agnes M., "Community Use of Selected Public Elementary Schools in the State of Washington." Ph.D. diss., Indiana State University, 1963.
159. Meinhardt, Thomas, "An Evaluation of the Male Student–Teaching Experience in Athletic Coaching in Illinois Public Higher Education." Ph.D. diss., University of Illinois, 1970.
160. Miller, Henry, "Selection Procedures for Physical Education Personnel in State Teachers Colleges." Ph.D. diss., University of Southern California, 1959.
161. Miller, James O., Jr., "Coeducational College Recreation—the Present Status of Its Organization and Administration." Ph.D. diss., Indiana State University, 1950.
162. Mitchell, Elmer D., "The Administration of Intramural Athletics in a Large University," *Thirty-Seventh Annual Proceedings,* The College Physical Education Association. Houston, Texas: The Association, 1933.
163. Moench, Francis J., "The Formulation of Standards for the Functional Planning of Physical Education Facilities for Secondary Schools as Applied to New York State." Ph.D. diss., New York University, 1949.
164. Montebello, Robert A., "Situational Case Studies of Selected Colleges and Universities in which the Required Program of Physical Education has been Challenged." Ph.D. diss., Teachers College, Columbia University, 1958.
165. Moriarty, Richard J., "The Organizational History of the Canadian Intercollegiate Athletic Union, Central (CIAUC) 1906-1955." Ph.D. diss., Ohio State University, 1971.
166. Mott, Robert A., "Athletic Control in Member Institutions of the Pacific Coast Intercollegiate Athletic Conference." Ph.D. diss., Stanford University, 1953.
167. Mublin, Daniel T., "The Expressed Judgment of College and University Presidents Concerning Preferred and Minimal Qualifications for the Chief Executive Officers of Physical Education Compared to the Qualifications Possessed by Sub-Chief Administration Officers." Ph.D. diss., University of Maryland, 1964.
168. Murdock, Robert L., Jr., "A Study and Evaluation of the Intramural Sports Programs for Men at the White Four-Year Colleges Supported by the Louisiana State Board of Education." Ph.D. diss., George Peabody College for Teachers, 1961.
169. Nash, Jay B., "Governmental Powers and Responsibilities in the Organiza-

tion and Administration of Playground and Recreational Activities." Ph.D. diss., New York University, 1929.
170. ———, "Report of the Committee on High School Administrative Standards for the Department of Physical Education," *Research Quarterly* (May 1932).
171. Nash, John C., "An Analysis of the Relationship Between the Physical Education and Athletic Departments in Selected Canadian Universities." Master's thesis, University of Illinois, 1966.
172. National Education Association, Educational Policies Commission, "School Athletics, Problems and Policies." Washington, D.C.: National Education Association, 1954.
173. *National Survey of Health and Physical Education in High Schools.* Bloomington: Bureau of Service and Research, School of Health, Physical Education and Recreation, Indiana State University, 1954.
174. New York State AAPHER Study, *Administration: Evolving Principles, Formulating Policies, Suggesting Procedure.* Albany, N.Y.: 1955.
175. Nitardy, Walter John, "A Study of Intercollegiate Athletic Programs in the Colleges of Education of the State University of New York, with Particular Implications for the College at Oswego." Ph.D. diss., Teachers College, Columbia University, 1961.
176. Nixon, John E., "A Study of the Organization of Physical Education in American Colleges and Universities." Ph.D. diss., University of Southern California, Los Angeles, 1949.
177. Nordly, Carl L., "The Administration of Intramural Athletics for Men in Colleges and Universities." Ed.D. diss., Teachers College, Columbia University, 1937.
178. Nyikos, Michael S., "A History of the Relationship between Athletic Administration and Faculty Governance at the University of Michigan, 1945-1968." Ph.D. diss., University of Michigan, 1970.
179. Olafson, Gordon A., "Leadership Behavior of Junior College and University Physical Education Administrators." Ph.D. diss., University of Illinois, 1969.
180. Owen, James S., "A Study of Certain System-wide Administrative Practices Concerning Physical Education in the Public White Schools of Alabama." Ph.D. diss., Alabama Polytechnical Institute, 1956.
181. Palmer, Lawrence Lee, "A Study of Athletic Insurance Plans." Master's thesis, University of Utah, 1955.
182. Pash, Ladd, "An Assessment of Non-Gate Receipt Sports in Big Ten Universities." Ph.D. diss., University of Illinois, 1971.
183. Paton, Garth A., "An Analysis of Administrative Theory in Selected Graduate Administration Courses in Physical Education." Ph.D. diss., University of Illinois, 1970.
184. Patterson, Norris A., "A Guide for Long-Range Planning with Special

Bibliography of Completed Research 449

Reference for Physical Education Facilities at William Jewel College." Ph.D. diss., Teachers College, Columbia University, 1958.
185. Peace, James S., "A Manual of the Organization and Conduct of an Intramural Recreational Program for Colleges and Universities." Ph.D. diss., New York University, 1943.
186. Pechar, Stanley F., "A Study of the Nature, Frequency, and Related Personal and Administrative Factors of Physical Education Accidents among Boys in the Junior and Senior High Schools of New York State." Ph.D. diss., New York University, 1961.
187. Peck, Robert R., "An Analysis of Practices in the Administration of Intercollegiate Athletics in Selected Colleges." Ph.D. diss., Teachers College, Columbia University, 1958.
188. Penny, William J., "An Analysis of the Meanings Attached to Selected Concepts in Administrative Theory." Ph.D. diss., University of Illinois, 1968.
189. Perry, Richard H., "Policies Pertaining to Hiring and Teaching Assignments of Coaches of Interscholastic Athletic Teams in Southern California Secondary Schools." Ph.D. diss., University of Southern California, 1968.
190. Peterson, James A., "A Case Analysis of the Process Involved in the Planning and Construction of Intramural-Physical Education which Were Financed Primarily through Student Fee Revenues." Ph.D. diss., University of Illinois, 1971.
191. Pierce, Douglas Richard, "An Analysis of Contemporary Theories of Organization and Administration." Diss. Abstracts, 1963.
192. Pierce, Juanita G., "The Organization and Administration of Health, Physical Education, and Recreation in the Atlanta University Center." Ph.D. diss., New York University, 1945.
193. Powell, John T., "The Development and Influence of Faculty Representation in the Control of Intercollegiate Sport Within the Intercollegiate Conference of Faculty Representatives from Its Inception in January 1895 to July 1963." Ph.D. diss., University of Illinois, 1964.
194. Reno, John Eugene, "An Evaluation of the Duties of Athletic Directors in Small Colleges in Selected States of the Midwest." P.E.D. diss., Indiana University, 1963.
195. Rice, James Joseph, "Status in Health and Physical Education Score Card; Number II Standards Compared with Selected Outcomes in Physical Education." P.E.D. diss., Indiana State University, 1957.
196. Rice, Sidney W., "A Job Analysis of Selected Directors of College Physical Education." Ph.D. diss., Boston University, 1955.
197. Richards, James W., "Analysis of Duties and Responsibilities of Physical Education Supervisors in the First Class Districts of Washington, University of Washington, 1964-65." Master's thesis, University of Washington, 1965.
198. Richey, Burton L., "A Survey of the Responsibilities and Qualifications of

Athletic Directors in Selected Colleges." Ph.D. diss., University of Colorado, 1963.

199. Ridinger, William H., "Principles and Policies for the Organization and Administration of School-Community Recreation." Ph.D. diss., New York University, 1963.

200. Rodin, William R., "An Analytical Survey of Health and Physical Education Programs for Boys in Selected Arkansas High Schools," P.E.D. diss., Indiana University, 1956.

201. Rolloff, Bruce D., "The Organization and Administration of a Program in Public Relations for Physical Education (Research Study No. 1)." Ph.D. diss., Colorado State College, 1965.

202. Rosenthal, William, "An Evaluation of Current Practices in Financing Interscholastic Athletics in the New York City High Schools." Ph.D. diss., New York University, 1956.

203. Salario, Isadore, "An Analysis of Administrative Policies and Practices Governing the Interscholastic Athletic Program in Selected Public High Schools in Chicago." Ph.D. diss., University of Wisconsin, 1962.

204. Sanford, John D., "A Study of Existing and Desired Practices in the Conduct of Intercollegiate Athletics in Selected North Carolina Colleges and Universities." Ph.D. diss., University of North Carolina, 1961.

205. Savage, Howard J., et al., *American College Athletics.* New York: Carnegie Foundation for Advancement of Teaching, 1929.

206. Schieffer, Joseph H., "Community Attitudes toward Interscholastic Athletics in a Selected School District." Ph.D. diss., University of Arizona, 1965.

207. Schooler, Virgil E., "Standards for Facilities for Athletics, Health, Physical Education, and Recreation for Secondary School Boys." Ph.D. diss., Indiana University, 1950.

208. Schroeder, Louis C., "A Selected Bibliography on the Planning and Construction of Facilities for Physical Fitness Activities, 1929-1944," *Research Quarterly,* 16 (October 1945), 221-30.

209. Scott, Elmer B., Jr. "An Evaluation of Intramural Sports Programs for Men in Selected Liberal Arts Colleges in Terms of Selected Criteria," P.E.D. diss., Indiana University, 1954.

210. Scott, Harry A., Personnel Study of Directors of Physical Education for Men in Colleges and Universities (Teachers College Contributions to Education, no. 339). New York: Teachers College, Columbia University, 1929. (Published doctoral dissertation.)

211. Sells, James L., "Analysis of Functions Performed and Competencies Needed to Administer Programs of Intercollegiate Athletics." Ph.D. diss., Columbia University, 1958.

212. Shea, Edward J., "A Critical Evaluation of the Policies Governing American Intercollegiate Athletics with the Establishment of Principles to

Bibliography of Completed Research 451

Guide the Formation of Policies for American Intercollegiate Athletics." Ph.D. diss., New York University, 1954.
213. Small, Ella, M., "Staff Relationships in College and University Physical Education Departments." Ph.D. diss., University of California, Los Angeles, 1955.
214. Smith, Glenn M., "The History of the Society of State Directors of Health and Physical Education." Ph.D. diss., Columbia University, 1953.
215. Smith, Willis Edward, "Organizational Approaches for the Development of a Service Program of Physical Education in a College Program of General Education." Ph.D. diss., University of Florida, 1953.
216. Spaeth, Marcia J., "An Analysis of Administrative Research in Physical Education and Athletics in Relation to a Research Paradigm." Ph.D. diss., University of Illinois, 1967.
217. Sponberg, Adryn L., "The Evolution of Athlete Subsidization in the Intercollegiate Conference of Faculty Representatives (Big Ten)." Ph.D. diss., University of Michigan, 1969.
218. Stafford, George T., "Guidance in Required Physical Education," *Research Quarterly,* 12 (May 1941), 278.
219. Stagg, Paul, "The Development of the National Collegiate Athletic Association in Relationship to Intercollegiate Athletics in the U.S." Ph.D. diss., New York University, 1947.
220. Stansbury, E. E., "The Status of State Directors of Health and Physical Education," *Research Quarterly,* 12 (March 1941a), 98-114.
221. Steele, Thomas W., "An Analysis of Communication Patterns within a School of Health, Physical Education and Recreation." Ph.D. diss., Ohio State University, 1971.
222. Struck, Raymond F., "A Study of the Administrative Procedures, Opinions, and Preferences which Affect the Status of High School Athletic Coaches in Indiana," P.E.D. diss., Indiana University, 1956.
223. Swenson, Reed K., "Intercollegiate Athletics in the Junior Colleges of the United States." Ph.D. diss., University of Utah, 1951.
224. Swisher, Ivan Wesley, "Selected Criteria for the Evaluations of the Administration of College Physical Education." Ph.D. diss., University of California, Los Angeles, 1959.
225. Thompson, Howard E., "A Guide for Administrators in Planning Functional Secondary School Gymnasia." Ph.D. diss., George Washington University, 1952.
226. Tinkle, Maybelle, "A Survey of Health and Physical Education Programs in the Public Secondary Schools of Texas by Means of the LaPorte Score Card." Ph.D. diss., University of Michigan, 1955.
227. Trethaway, Edwin H., "The Relationship between Research in Physical Education, Interschool Athletics, and School Recreation, and the Major

Developments in these Fields (1895-1940)." Ph.D. diss., New York University, 1953.
228. Trotter, Betty J., "A Study of Interscholastic Athletics for High School Girls in the State of Texas." Ph.D. diss., Columbia University, Teachers College, 1962.
229. Truex, Wayne O., "A Survey of the Attitudes of College and University Deans of Instruction, Faculties, Students and Chairmen of Physical Education Departments for Men in the State of Illinois Regarding Physical Education Activities." Ed.D. diss., University of Utah, 1966.
230. Unrah, Daniel W., "An Analysis of the Community Uses of Facilities of Selected Public Elementary Schools in Municipalities of Indiana." P.E.D. diss., Indiana State University, 1955.
231. Van Ryswyk, Ronald L., "A Study of Extra Duty Compensation for Teachers in Certain Small, Medium, and Large Public Senior High Schools in the Eastern District of the American Association for Health, Physical Education and Recreation." Ed.D. diss., Syracuse University, 1960.
232. Van Vliet, Maurice L., "A Guide to Administrative Policies for Physical Education in Canadian Public Schools, Grades One through Nine." Ph.D. diss., University of California, Los Angeles, 1949.
233. Vaughan, Andrew T., "A Personnel Study of Men Physical Educators in Selected Colleges and Universities." Ed.D. diss., Teachers College, Columbia University, 1958.
234. Wagner, Edward P., "Present Status of Required Physical Education Programs in Colleges and Universities Enrolling More Than 5000 Students." Ed.D. diss., Pennsylvania State College, 1950.
235. Wallis, Earl L., "Factors Related to the Recruitment of Young Men for Physical Education Teaching." Ed.D. diss., University of Southern California, 1957.
236. Walmsley, Harry A., "A Comparative Survey of Selected Duties and Responsibilities of Collegiate Chairmen in Physical Education Departments in Selected Institutions in the United States." Ed.D. diss., University of Utah, 1970.
237. Warren, Ned L., "A Study of Conditions Affecting the Health and Physical Education Programs in the Public Secondary Schools of Tennessee." Ed.D. diss., George Peabody College for Teachers, 1952.
238. Wesener, Arthur A., "Job Analysis of Supervisors of Elementary School Physical Education in Wisconsin." Master's thesis, University of Wisconsin, 1963.
239. Whited, Clark V., "An Investigation of the State Contract Method of Purchasing Physical Education Supplies for the New York State Public Schools." P.E.D. diss., Indiana University, 1967.
240. Wiley, Mary S., "The Evaluation of Policies for the Organization and Administration of Extra-Curricular Recreational Programs in the State Colleges of California." Ed.D. diss., New York University, 1954.

Bibliography of Completed Research

241. Wood, Helen Anne, "An Evaluation of Principles for Supervision on the Basis of Expressed Rural Teacher Needs in the Supervision of Physical Education." Ph.D. diss., New York University, 1953.
242. Wood, Shirley J., "Reciprocal Role Expectations of Women Physical Education Teachers and Chairmen." Ph.D. diss., University of Illinois, 1971.
243. Woodbury, Darwin S., "The Administrative Relationships between Athletics and Physical Education in Selected American Universities." Ed.D. diss., University of Utah, 1966.
244. Yeager, Beatrice V., "An Analysis of Interpersonal Communication Patterns Utilized by a Selected Small Group." Ph.D. diss., University of Illinois, 1971.
245. Yinger, Harold L., "Evaluation of Criteria for Selection and the Determination of Success of Male Physical Education Teachers by Selected Missouri Superintendents." P.E.D. diss., Indiana University, 1962.
246. Yost, Charles P., "An Analysis of Graduate Theses in School Safety in the United States from 1925 to 1950." Ph.D. diss., University of Pittsburgh, 1956.
247. Youngberg, Richard S., "A Comparative Analysis of the Qualifications Suggested for a Successful Intercollegiate Athletic Director." P.E.D. diss., Indiana State University, 1971.
248. Zaleski, Joseph F., "An Evaluation of the Administration of Interscholastic Athletics in High Schools of the Western Pennsylvania Interscholastic Athletic League." Ed.D. diss., University of Florida, 1957.

Index

AAUP Bulletin, 335
Absenteeism, group cohesion and, 118-19
Academic Marketplace, The, 90
"Action Theory," Parsonian, 407-11
Action-theory balance, 425-26
Activism, in general environment of administrator, 416
Adaptation, in general environment of administrator, 413
Administrative Behavior (Simon), 71
Administrative Behavior in Education (Campbell and Gregg), 69
Administrative Center for Sport and Recreation, Ottawa, 329
Administrative Science Quarterly, The, 70
Adversaries, of administrators, 404-5
Advisers, of administrators, 402-3
Aloofness, leadership and, 136, 137, 144-49
Amateur Athletic Union, 318
American Association for Health, Physical Education, and Recreation (AAHPER), 9, 103, 183, 195, 281
American Association of School Administrators, 6, 7-8, 23, 24, 49, 69
American Association of University Professors, 335, 337, 340

Architect, selection of, 298-99, 307-8
Authority, control of communication and, 232-33
Automation, 57-58
Autonomous organizational climate, 139
Awareness, faculty and student perception of, 270, 272, 273, 274

Bagley, Martha, 98-112
Beeman, Frank, 280-93
Behavior in Education (Campbell and Gregg), 71
Berlo model of communicative act, 253
Big Ten Body of Knowledge Project in Physical Education, 24
Blue Book of Junior College Athletics, 90
Bole, Ronald, 176-88
Bond acts, 250
British Columbia Sports Federation, 320, 321, 325-28
Broom, Eric F., 316-31
Budgetary processes, in Ontario school system, 355-72
    conclusions, 368
    findings, 364-68
    implications, 368-71

Index

Budgetary processes (*continued*)
    literature on, 358-62
    methodology, 362-64

Canadian Amateur Athletic Union, 318
Case, Robert Lewis, 228-46
Case problem technique, 281
Central administrative agencies, comparison of, 316-31
    conclusions, 329
    findings, 320-28
    implications, 330
    literature on, 317-19
    methodology, 319-20
Central Council of Physical Recreation (CCPR), England, 320-30
Chance to Share, The: Cooperation in the Provision of Facilities for Educational Establishments and the Community, 325
Clients, of administrators, 400-402
Closed organizational climate, 139-40
Collectivities, in general action system, 408
College and University Environment Scales, 2nd ed (CUES II), 267, 270-75
College Characteristics Analysis (CCA), 267
College Characteristics Index (CCI), 143
College Classification Index (CCI), 267
College Physical Education Association, 282
Communication:
    defined, 248-49
    improvement of, 429
Communication patterns, interpersonal, 247-64
    conclusions, 259-60
    historical review of, 251-52
    literature on, 251-53
    methodology, 253-59
    models of communicative acts, 253-56
    recommendations, 260-62
    research, 252-53
Communication structure, 228-46
    conclusions, 240-41
    findings, 239-40
    formal, 232-35
    implications, 242-44
    informal, 234-35
    methodology, 235-39
    overview of, 231-35
Community, faculty and student perception of, 270, 272, 273
Community responsibility, environments of administrator and, 415-16
Comprehensive budget, 356, 357, 362-64, 367-69

Concept identification, 66-77
    findings and conclusions, 72-74
    implications, 74-76
    literature on, 68-70
    methodology, 70-72
Consideration, leadership and, 136, 138, 144-49
Construction contracts, 301-3, 311-12
Contact acts, 249
Controlled organizational climate, 139
Controllers, of administrators, 403-4
Cooperative Program in Educational Administration (CPEA), 8, 69, 140
Critical incident technique, 281, 283-84
Culture, in general action system, 407

Daniel, Juri V., 152-75
Dannehl, Wayne E., 135-51
Decision-making, 426
    analysis of theory, graduate administration courses and, 57-58, 62
    budgetary, 355-71
Department of Education and Science Report, 190
Departmental Dimensions Questionnaire, 90, 91, 93-94
Descriptive research method, 39
Design, of recreation facilities, 297-99, 307-9
Directory of Professional Preparation Institutions, 51, 103
Discipline, control of communication and, 232-33
Disengagement, organization climate and, 136, 138, 144-49

Economics of athletics, 176-88
    conclusions, 186
    elasticity of demand, 178
    findings, 184-86
    implications, 186-87
    literature on, 179-83
    methodology, 183-84
    substitution effect, 178-79
Education of American Teachers, The (Conant), 9
Educational Administration Quarterly, The, 70
Effectiveness contingency model, leadership, 98-112
    conclusions, 107-9
    definition of terms, 99-100
    findings, 107-9
    implications, 109-11
    literature on, 100-103
    methodology, 103-6

Employment theory and practice, 332-43
  conclusions, 338-39
  findings, 337-38
  implications, 339-42
  literature on, 334-35
  methodology, 335-37
Encyclopedia of Educational Research, 37, 38, 45
Environmental characteristics, in physical education unit, 265-78 (*see also* Organizational climate)
  findings and conclusion, 272-75
  implications, 275-76
  literature on, 267-70
  methodology, 270-72
Environments of administrators, 399-418, 423, 429-30
  general (external), 406-16
  immediate (internal), 400-406
  implications, 411-14
  Parsonian "Action Theory," 407-11
Evaluative research method, 39-40
Existentialism, concept of, 379, 384-85
Expectation agreement, 215, 221-25
Expectation perception, 216, 222, 224-26
Experimentalism, concept of, 379, 380

Fabun model of communicative act, 253
Facilities, planning and construction of, 294-315
  administrative approval for, 296-97, 305-7
  conclusions, 312-13
  design, 297-99, 307-9
  financing, 299-301, 309-11
  findings, 305-12
  implications, 313-14
  literature on, 296-303
  methodology, 303-5
  planning input, 301-3, 311-12
Familiar organizational climate, 139
Fiedler, Fred E., 82, 98-111
Financing, of recreational facilities, 299-301, 309-11
Fitness and Amateur Sport Directorate (FASD), Canada, 319, 320, 322, 325-28, 330
Flanigan, Thomas E., 265-78
Football attendance, economic factors of, 176-86
Freedom, concept of, 423-24
Functions of the Executive, The (Barnard), 71, 140

Galton, Sir Francis, 283
General action system, 407-11
Goal-attainment, in general environment of

Goal attainment (*continued*)
  administrator, 413
Graduate administration courses, analysis of, 49-65
  conclusions, 63
  findings, 53-54
  generalizations based upon, 54-63
  implications, 54-63
  literature analysis, 52-53, 54
  methodology, 51-53
Group atmosphere measure (leader-member relations), 104
Group cohesion, 113-34
  absenteeism and, 118-19
  conditions that facilitate, 116-17, 124-25
  consequences of, 118-19, 126-28
  defined, 113-16, 121-24
  findings, 120-28
  implications, 128-29
  methodology, 119-20
  productivity level and, 118-19, 126-28
  tension and, 118-19, 126
Group Dimensions Description Questionnaire, 143

Haggerty, Terry R., 355-72
Harvard University Business School, 280-81, 284
Higher Education for Business (Gordon and Howell), 52
Hulett model of communicative act, 254, 255
Human Behavior (Berelson and Steiner), 11
Human relations (*see also* Intramural sports and recreative services, human relations and):
  in graduate administration courses, 53, 55-57
Humanism, in general environment of administrator, 416

Idealism, concept of, 379, 382
Incongruency phenomenon, job satisfaction and, 157-58
Incremental budgeting, 356, 357, 358-60, 362-64, 367-69
Integration, in general environment of administrator, 413
Integrative reserach method, 39
Interchange analysis, 409-10
Intercollegiate Conference Faculty Representatives, 346
Intimacy, organizational climate and, 137, 138, 144-49
Intramural Sports, 285

Index

Intramural sports and recreative services, human relations and, 280-93
    findings and conclusions, 287-88
    implications, 289-93
    literature on, 283-85
    methodology, 285-86

Job Descriptive Index *(JDI)*, 161, 162-63, 166, 171-75
Job satisfaction, 152-75
    analysis of theory, graduate administration courses, 55-56
    concept of, 158-59
    conclusions, 166-67
    factors affecting, 159
    findings, 163-66
    implications, 167-69
    incongruency phenomenon, 157-58
    literature on, 157-61
    measurement of, 160-61
    methodology, 161-63
    morale and, 158
    role differentiation and, 160
Journal of Educational Administration, The, 70

Kellogg Foundation, 8, 69
Kruskal-Wallis one-way analysis of variance, 221

Language analysis, as function of philosophy, 378-79
Laws of Nature, The (Peierls), 11
Leader Behavior Description Questionnaire (LBDQ), 84, 85, 86, 88-94
Leadership:
    administrators, junior college and university, 80-97
    aloofness and, 136, 137, 144-49
    analysis of theory, graduate administrative courses, 56-57
    consideration and, 136, 138, 144-49
    dimensions of, 138-39
    effectiveness contingency model, 98-112
    new concepts for, 428
    production emphasis and, 136, 137, 144-49
    thrust and, 136, 137, 144-49
Least-preferred coworker measure (LPC), 101-4, 107-8
Legitimation, in general environment of administrator, 413
Link acts, 249-50

Mann-Whitney U test, 221
Marketing Problems (Copeland), 284
Mass communications, 29
Measurement of Meaning (Osgood et al), 70
Mikalachki, A., 113-34
Minnesota Daily, 176
Mobile Professors, The (Brown), 336
Morale:
    faculty and student perception of, 270, 272, 273, 275
    job satisfaction and, 158
    organizational climate and, 138, 141, 144-49

National Advisory Council (NAC), Canada, 319, 320, 324-25
National Association for Physical Education of College Women, 282
National College Physical Education Association for Men (NCPEAM) Convention, 347
National Collegiate Athletic Association Convention Annual Report, 348
National Conference on Graduate Study, 9
National Conference on Intramural Sports for College Men and Women, 280, 285
National Conference of Professors of Educational Administration (NCPEA), 8, 36, 68-69, 140
Negro Family, The: A Case for National Action (Moynihan), 201-2
Nongate receipt sports, assessment of, 344-54
    findings and conclusions, 351-52
    implications, 352
    literature on, 346-49
    methodology, 349-50
Norms, in general action system, 408

Objective indices, organizational climate and, 142
Ohio State Bureau of Business Research, 88
Olafson, Gordon A., 80-97
Ontario school system, budgetary processes in, 355-72
Open organizational climate, 139
Organization Man, The, 90
Organization theory:
    in graduate administration courses, 52, 58-61
    propositions, 28
Organizational Analysis Audit, 143
Organizational climate, 135-51 (*see also*

Organizational climate, *(continued)*
   Environmental characteristics, in physical education unit)
      conclusions, 147
      findings, 145-47
      implications, 147-50
      literature on, 140-43
      methodology, 143-45
      methods of studying, 140-43
      statement of problem, 136-40
Organizational Climate Description Questionnaire (OCDQ), 88, 136-50
Organizational democracy, 431
Organizations (March and Simon), 71
Organizations in Action (Thompson), 71
Organizations, determination of objectives of, 414-25
Osgood Semantic Differential Instrument, 25

Parsonian "Action Theory," 407-11
Pash, K. Ladd, 344-54
Paton, Garth A., 49-65
Penny, William J., 66-77
Personality, in general action system, 407-8
Peterson, James A., 294-315
Philosophy:
      analysis, 386-98
      educational, 374-98, 422
      language analysis as function of, 378-79
      need to construct, 375
      role of, 379, 386
      spectrum, 386
Physical recreation facilities (*see* Facilities, planning and construction of)
Planning-Programming-Budgeting-Systems (PPBS), 356, 357-58, 360-62, 370-71
Position, role expectation and, 218
Position-power measure, 105
Power structure, of general environment of administrator, 414
Practicality, faculty and student perception of, 270, 272, 273
President's Council on Youth Fitness, 281
Principal Behavior Description Questionnaire (PBDQ), 88
Production emphasis, leadership and, 136, 137, 144-49
Productivity level, and group cohesion, 118-19, 126-28
Profile of a School (Likert), 103
Promotion, job satisfaction and, 164
Propriety, faculty and student perception of, 270, 272, 273, 274-75

Provision of Facilities for Sport, 325
Provision for Sport, 325

Rationality, in general environment of administrator, 416
Realism, concept of, 379, 383
Reconstructionism, concept of, 379, 381
Recreation Canada, 319
Remuneration, job satisfaction and, 164
Report of the Task Force on Sport for Canadians, 316
Research:
      in administration of physical education, 2-21, 35-48
      applied, 29-30
      communication, 242-53
      conclusions, 43-44
      findings, 42-43
      implications, 44-46
      literature on, 36-38
      methodology, 39-41
      need for, 9-11
      propositions, 28
      recommendations, 12-19
      small-group, 28
Research Quarterly, 38
Resources, in general environment of administrator, 413
Responsibility, Authority, and Delegation Scales (RAD Scales), 88
Review of Educational Research, 37, 45
Role differentiation, job satisfaction and, 160
Role expectations, 214-27
      background, 216-19
      conclusions, 223-24
      consequences of disparities, 216
      expectation agreement, 215, 221-25
      expectation perception, 216, 222, 224-26
      findings, 221-23
      implications, 224-27
      methodology, 219-21
      position and, 218
      role, role behavior and role attributes, 218-19
      sanctions and, 219
Roles, in general action system, 408-9

Sanctions, role expectations and, 219
Scholarship, faculty and student perception of, 270, 272, 273, 275
Shannon model of communicative act, 253
Sixteen Personality Factor Questionnaire, 236-41
Social organization, of general environment

Index

Social organization *(continued)*
    of administrator, 414
Social system, in general action system, 407-11
Southern States Cooperative Program in Educational Administration, 27
Space survey, 297
Sport Canada, 317, 319
Sport and the Community, 319
Sport and Recreation, 328
Sports Council (England), 320-22, 324-25
Sports Development Bulletin, 330
Sports Federation of Canada, 319, 322, 325, 326
SRA Employee Inventory, 160
Substantive Information on Respondent, 90-91
Supervision, job satisfaction and, 165
Suppliers, of administrators, 402
Symbolic interactionist models, 254, 255, 256, 259-60

Task Force on Sport for Canadians, 319
Task structure measure, 104-5
Task studies, administrative research, 42
Tension, group cohesion and, 118-19, 126
Theory in Physical Education (Brown and Cassidy), 37
Theory and Research in Administration (Halpin), 71
Theory-research balance, 425-26
Thompson model of communicative act, 253

Thrust, leadership and, 136, 137, 144-49
University Council for Educational Administration (UCEA), 8, 37, 69, 140
University of Illinois:
    College of Physical Education, communication structure at, 229-44
    economic factors influencing athletics at, 177-86
    Group Effectiveness Research Laboratory, 100

Value structure, of general environment of administrator, 414
Values:
    in general action system, 408
    in general environment of administrator, 416
Violence, in spectator sports, 189-213
    findings and conclusions, 200-208
    implications, 208-11
    literature on, 191-95
    methodology, 195-200

Western Conference Intramural Administration, 282, 285-93
Western Conference Physical Education Meetings, 9
Who Shall Survive? (Moreno), 237
Wood, Shirley J., 214-27

Yeager, Beatrice V., 247-64